Writing the English Republic

POETRY, RHETORIC AND POLITICS, 1627–1660

The English republic of the mid-seventeenth century is traditionally viewed as an aberration in political and literary history. In this magisterial history of republican political culture, David Norbrook argues that the English republican imagination had deep roots in humanist literary culture, and that the 'triumph of Augustanism' after 1660 marked a sharp reaction against powerful anti-Augustan trends. Key texts by Marvell and Milton, including *Paradise Lost*, are set in the context of previously neglected writings by Edmund Waller, George Wither, Thomas May and many others, showing how writers re-imagined English political and literary culture without kingship. The book draws on extensive archival research, bringing to light exciting and neglected manuscript and printed sources. Offering a bold new narrative of the whole period, and a timely reminder that England has a republican as well as royalist heritage, *Writing the English Republic* will be of compelling interest to historians as well as literary scholars.

David Norbrook's publications include *Poetry and Politics in the English Renaissance* (1984) and *The Penguin Book of Renaissance Verse* (1992), as well as numerous articles and reviews in literary and historical journals. He has held a British Academy Research Readership and visiting fellowships in the United States, and has made a lecture tour of Australia supported by the British Council. Fellow and Tutor in English at Magdalen College, Oxford since 1978, he was appointed in 1998 to a Professorship at the University of Maryland, College Park.

Writing the English Republic

POETRY, RHETORIC AND POLITICS, 1627–1660

DAVID NORBROOK

CAMBRIDGE
UNIVERSITY PRESS

PUBLISHED BY THE PRESS SYNDICATE OF THE UNIVERSITY OF CAMBRIDGE
The Pitt Building, Trumpington Street, Cambridge CB2 1RP, United Kingdom

CAMBRIDGE UNIVERSITY PRESS
The Edinburgh Building, Cambridge CB2 2RU, UK   http://www.cup.cam.ac.uk
40 West 20th Street, New York, NY 10011-4211, USA   http://www.cup.org
10 Stamford Road, Oakleigh, Melbourne 3166, Australia

First published 1999
First paperback edition 2000

Printed in the United Kingdom at the University Press, Cambridge

Typeface Adobe Minion 10/12.5pt   *System* QuarkXPress® [SE]

A catalogue record for this book is available from the British Library

Library of Congress cataloguing in publication data
Norbrook, David, 1950–
Writing the English Republic: poetry, rhetoric, and politics, 1627–1660 / David Norbrook.
p.   cm.
Includes bibliographical references and index.
ISBN 0 521 63275 7 (hardback)
1. English poetry – Early modern, 1500–1700 – History and criticism.
2. Great Britain – History – Civil War, 1642–1649 – Literature and the war.
3. Rhetoric – Political aspects – Great Britain – History – 17th century.
4. Politics and literature – Great Britain – History – 17th century.
5. Milton, John, 1608–1674 – Political and social views.
6. Republicanism – Great Britain – History – 17th century.
7. Political poetry, English – History and criticism. 8. Great Britain –
Politics and government – 1625–1649. 9. Great Britain – Politics and government –
1649–1660. 10. English poetry – Roman influences. 11. Republicans in literature.
I. Title.
PR545.H5N67   1998
821'.409358 – dc21   98-3856 CIP

ISBN 0 521 63275 7 hardback
ISBN 0 521 78569 3 paperback

Contents

❦

Illustrations

Acknowledgements

As this book goes to press, it becomes a valediction, and an opportunity to express my gratitude, to Magdalen College and to the Oxford University English Faculty. They greatly facilitated this project in many general ways and in particular by granting terms of leave and by financial assistance. I have been very fortunate to be able to call on the services of Joad Raymond and Frank Romany for teaching in my absence. Teaching is, of course, an essential stimulus to thinking about what really matters in research and several generations of undergraduate and graduate students have helped me here. Early parts of the book were rehearsed in classes on 'Literature and the English Revolution' with my colleague Nigel Smith, to whose book on the 1640s and 1650s the present study is in so many ways complementary, and who has generously shared much work in progress. Involvement in the Oxford BA in Modern History and English has been invaluable in exploring the problems and possibilities of interdisciplinary work. I have benefited greatly from teaching for the Classics and English BA with my colleague Oliver Taplin and from discussions with Matthew Leigh, Andrew Laird, Ingrid de Smet, and Ben Tipping, who have generously helped out in difficulties with Latin texts. My Magdalen colleague John Fuller has always been a pleasure to work with. Magdalen College Library has been an invaluable resource over the years and I am grateful to Christine Ferdinand and Sally Speirs for much help. The bulk of the research was done in the Bodleian Library, which has made it particularly pleasant to be able to write of the Bodleian's honourable dealings with that notorious republican Milton; the Library's staff have been unfailingly helpful. I have also benefited (on this side of the Atlantic) from the co-operation of the staff of the Cambridge, Leeds and Newcastle University Libraries, the Oxford University English and History Faculty Libraries, the Hartlib Papers Project, the University of Sheffield, the Public Record Office, the Nottinghamshire Archives, the National Library of Scotland, and above all of the British Library. The book was finished while I was the fortunate recipient of a British Academy Research Readership for a complementary project on Lucy Hutchinson.

I began work on this book at the Folger Shakespeare Library, Washington DC. I am very grateful to the English-Speaking Union for the award of a

Fellowship, and to the Library for providing a British scholar with such a welcoming introduction to a wider republic of letters. Some of the material for the book was tried out in a graduate seminar at the City University of New York, which provided another stimulating environment. At a concluding stage, material from the book was presented in a series of seminars at the Newberry Library, funded by the National Endowment for the Humanities. I am very grateful to Mary Beth Rose, then Director of The Center for Renaissance Studies, for her help in making this possible, and to all the participants for such challenging debate. On various visits to the United States, I have also benefited from using the libraries of the University of Chicago, Columbia University, Harvard University, the University of Illinois at Urbana-Champaign, Princeton University, and the New York Public Library. The length of the book's gestation makes it impossible to thank all those who have provided thoughtful responses to the presentation of early versions in Britain, Italy, the USA and Australia.

Material has been incorporated from the following articles, in some of which fuller documentation of some points may be found, and to whose publishers I am grateful for permissions:

Chapter 1: 'Lucan, Thomas May, and the Creation of a Republican Literary Culture', in Kevin Sharpe and Peter Lake (eds.), *Culture and Politics in Early Stuart England* (Macmillan, 1994), pp. 45–66.

Chapter 3: 'Milton's *Areopagitica*, Censorship, and the Early Modern Public Sphere', in Richard Burt (ed.), *The Administration of Aesthetics: Censorship, Political Criticism and the Public Sphere* (University of Minnesota Press, 1994), pp. 3–33; copyright 1994 by the Regents of the University of Minnesota.

Chapters 2 and 4: 'Levelling Poetry: George Wither and the English Revolution, 1642–1649', *English Literary Renaissance* 21 (1991), 217–56; reprinted with permission of the editors.

Chapter 6: 'Marvell's "Horatian Ode" and the Politics of Genre', in Thomas Healy and Jonathan Sawday (eds.), *Literature and the English Civil War* (Cambridge University Press, 1990), pp. 147–69, and 'Is Marvell's "Horatian Ode" a Horatian Ode?', in William Lamont (ed.), *Religion, Renaissance and Civil War, Proceedings of the Folger Institute Center for the History of British Political Thought*, vol. 3 (Washington, DC, 1990), pp. 221–58.

Chapter 7: David Norbrook, 'Lucy Hutchinson versus Edmund Waller: An Unpublished Reply to Waller's *A Panegyrick to my Lord Protector*', *The Seventeenth Century* 11 (1996), 61–86.

Chapters 8 and 9: ' "Safest in Storms": George Wither in the 1650s', in David Margolies and Maroula Joannou (eds.), *Heart of the Heartless World: Essays in Cultural Resistance in Memory of Margot Heinemann* (Pluto Press, 1995), pp. 19–32.

This book attempts to show the importance of setting individual writers in a larger process of agency, and can claim no exception for itself. When it was begun, republicanism was wholly outside the mainstream of British politics. Writing the book has been stimulated by a process of change which has seen the re-emergence of constitutional reform as a significant agenda, and Henry Marten's being honoured not only by a plaque in Oxford but by giving his name to a musical group. This book could not have been undertaken without the magnificent contributions of J. G. A. Pocock, Quentin Skinner and Blair Worden to the history of republicanism, and without Christopher Hill's reminders of a world larger than that of republicanism. I am of course much indebted to a large quantity of literary criticism, full acknowledgement of which would have swollen the book to monstrous proportions. I have tried to point readers towards a good selection of the most significant recent work, while also paying tribute to earlier work in a field which has not always seen linear progress.

Some more specific thanks remain. Sandra Sherman stimulated a rethinking of a lot more than Milton. Margaret Williamson helped me to think about the wider aims of academic writing and to keep on course in some difficult times. I warmly thank the following, who commented on some or all of the typescript or whose ideas have contributed particularly to its shaping: Sarah Barber, Peter Davidson, Jim Holstun (whose correspondence over the years has been an inspiration), Lorna Hutson, Nicholas von Maltzahn, Annabel Patterson, whose intellectual example and personal support have done much to make this book possible, Tom Paulin, Joad Raymond, John Safford and Erica Sheen. To my wife, Sharon Achinstein, I am grateful, amongst very many things, for struggling with an unconscionable number of 'final' drafts. The three readers for Cambridge University Press made enormously helpful reports, and David Loewenstein and Jonathan Scott, in yielding up their anonymity, have enabled me to thank them personally. Margaret Hanbury gave valuable advice over publication. Josie Dixon has brought the book over the pre-publication hurdles with impressive speed and efficiency. I also thank my copy-editor, Clare Richards. Katherine Lambert saved the book from many infelicities at a late stage. Whatever the multiplicity of agencies, I am happy to take sole responsibility for remaining errors.

Writing the English Republic is dedicated to two friends and colleagues whom it has been one of the great good fortunes of my life to know. They have been spared any direct involvement in the book, but their sustaining friendship over many years helped to make it possible.

Note on references and abbreviations

The aim of the references is to make it as easy as possible to understand texts in their historical moment. Where practicable, citations follow the original spelling, though the forms of transliteration vary slightly in drawing on such a range of texts and editions. Except in some cases where there is a modern edition providing contextual material, I have given identifying numbers: British Library pressmarks (those beginning with E or 669) for books included in George Thomason's collection from the years 1641–61 (though I have not always used the Thomason copy), and *STC* (numerical) and Wing (alphanumerical) numbers for non-Thomason books up to 1640 and 1641 respectively. All three collections are available on microfilm.

Place of publication is London where not otherwise indicated. Dates are given Old Style, save that the year is taken to begin on 1 January. Quotations in Greek have been transliterated.

ABL	John Aubrey, *'Brief Lives', Chiefly of his Contemporaries*, ed. Andrew Clark, 2 vols. (Oxford, 1898)
Beal	Peter Beal, *Index of Literary Manuscripts, Volume II: 1625–1700, Part 2: Lee-Wycherley* (1993)
BL	British Library
CJ	*The Journals of the House of Commons*
CL	*The Letters of Sir Cheney Culpeper, 1641–1657*, ed. M. J. Braddick and Mark Greengrass, in *Seventeenth-Century Political and Financial Papers*, Camden 5th Series VII (1996)
Corns, *UV*	Thomas N. Corns, *Uncloistered Virtue: English Political Literature, 1640–1660* (Oxford, 1992)
CSPD	Calendar of State Papers, Domestic Series
Hill, *WR*	*The Collected Essays of Christopher Hill, vol. I: Writing and Revolution in Seventeenth-Century England* (Brighton, 1985)
HMC	Historical Manuscripts Commission Reports
HP	Sheffield University Library, Hartlib Papers. With the exception of *CL*, above, I have used the reproductions prepared by the Hartlib Papers Project, *The Hartlib Papers on CD-ROM* (Ann Arbor and Godstone, 1995), with occasional silent omissions of repeated words.
HPW	*The Political Works of James Harrington*, ed. J. G. A. Pocock (Cambridge, 1977)
Hutchinson	Lucy Hutchinson, *Memoirs of the Life of Colonel Hutchinson*, ed. James Sutherland (Oxford, 1973)

JMLR	*The Life Records of John Milton*, ed. J. Milton French, 5 vols. (New Brunswick, 1949–58)
May	*Lucan's Pharsalia*, second edition, trans. Thomas May (1631; *STC* 16888)
ML	Brotherton Library, University of Leeds, Marten-Loder Papers
MPL	*The Poems and Letters of Andrew Marvell*, ed. H. M. Margoliouth, third edition, revised by Pierre Legouis with the collaboration of E. E. Duncan-Jones, 2 vols. (Oxford, 1971)
MPW	*The Complete Prose Works of John Milton*, ed. Don M. Wolfe *et al.*, 8 vols. in 10 (New Haven and London, 1953–82)
MQ	*Milton Quarterly*
MR	David Armitage, Armand Himy and Quentin Skinner (eds.), *Milton and Republicanism* (Cambridge, 1995)
Norbrook, PP	David Norbrook, *Poetry and Politics in the English Renaissance* (1984)
OED	*Oxford English Dictionary*
PRO SP	Public Record Office, State Papers
RLCS	David Wootton (ed.), *Republicanism, Liberty and Commercial Society, 1649–1776* (Stanford, 1994)
Smith, LR	Nigel Smith, *Literature and Revolution in England 1640–1660* (New Haven and London, 1994)
SR	*A Transcript of the Registers of the Worshipful Company of Stationers; from 1640–1708 A.D.*, ed. G. E. Briscoe Eyre, 3 vols. (1913–14)
STC	A. W. Pollard and G. R. Redgrave, *A Short-Title Catalogue of Books Printed in England, Scotland, and Ireland: And of English Books Printed Abroad 1475–1640*, second edition, 3 vols. (1976–91)
TSP	*A Collection of the State Papers of John Thurloe*, ed. Thomas Birch, 7 vols. (1742)
Tuck	Richard Tuck, *Philosophy and Government 1572–1651* (Cambridge, 1993)
Williams, 'Marten'	C. M. Williams, 'The Political Career of Henry Marten with special reference to the origins of republicanism in the Long Parliament', unpublished D. Phil. thesis, Oxford University, 1954
Wing	Donald Wing, *Short-Title Catalogue of Books Printed in England, Scotland, Ireland, Wales, and British America and of English Books printed in Other Countries 1641–1700*, second edition, 3 vols. (New York, 1972–94).
WMW	*Miscellaneous Works of George Wither*, 6 vols. (Manchester, 1872–78; rptd New York, 1967). Page references are to individual works within each volume.
WP	*The Poems of Edmund Waller*, ed. G. Thorn Drury (London and New York, 1893; references are to the two-volume reprint, 1905)

Introduction: acts of oblivion and republican speech-acts

When Samuel Pepys was a fifteen-year-old schoolboy, he was present at the execution of Charles I on 30 January 1649. Being 'a great roundhead', he applauded the act, exclaiming to a friend that if he had the chance of preaching a sermon, his text would be 'The memory of the wicked shall rot' (Proverbs x.7). Eleven years later, in November 1660, Pepys found himself placed at dinner close to another schoolfriend. 'I was much afeared', he confided to his diary, 'he would have remembered the words that I said the day that the King was beheaded . . . but I found afterward that he did go away from schoole before that time.'[1] Pepys was desperate that his youthful desire to obliterate the king's memory should itself be forgotten.

Fortunately, he had not only chance but the law on his side. Forgetting was officially sanctioned: the Act of Indemnity and Oblivion banned 'any name or names, or other words of reproach tending to revive the memory of the late differences or the occasions thereof'.[2] This book is one attempt to counter that process of erasure, which has had long-term effects on English literary history and, arguably, on wider aspects of political identity. In the short term, the Act of Indemnity and Oblivion can be seen as an enlightened piece of legislation. Twenty years of bitter contention between and within families and social and religious groups needed oblivion to heal them. In the longer term, however, such forgetting has had its costs. Suppressing the republican element in English cultural history entails simplifying a complex but intellectually and artistically challenging past into a sanitized and impoverished Royal Heritage. The period from 1649 to 1660 has become a blank space, an 'Interregnum' standing wholly outside the nation's temporal process. The derogatory label 'the Rump', attached to the republic's Parliament by its enemies in 1660, has moved without any sense of strain from royalist propaganda into the notionally value-free technical terms of academia. The republic's political

---

1 *The Diary of Samuel Pepys*, ed. Robert Latham and William Matthews (1970–83), I, 280.
2 Cited by Smith, *LR*, p. 1.

1

institutions 'continue to languish in a historiographical blind spot'; much the same applies to its artistic culture.[3]

At a simple documentary level, the process of oblivion creates problems for the literary history of the mid-century. Milton is and always has been at the centre of the spotlight: magnificent scholarship has helped to set his work in its political context. There is a singular exception, T. S. Eliot's attempt to 'dislodge' him. Interestingly, Eliot regarded as the 'most important fact' about Milton the prime topic of seventeenth-century royalist propaganda: his blindness. While for republicans this might symbolize sublimity, for royalists it marked a divine punishment for his republicanism. As one who had urged the rehabilitation of the absolutist Sir Robert Filmer, Eliot may have slily enjoyed this oblique restaging of old controversies. He did not push his assault far, however – perhaps in part because he realized that the strongly ideological nature of his own royalism was as likely to stir up as to bury radical memories.[4]

As soon as one leaves Milton for his republican contemporaries, however, the shadows start to descend. Several of the figures discussed in this book – Fisher, Hall, Marten, May, Wither – have received hardly any attention in print. Their memory has been kept at bay by a *cordon sanitaire* of defensive ridicule. Though none of them equals Milton as a writer, they deserve something better. What most readers of seventeenth-century literature remember about George Wither is that during the Civil War he was captured and condemned to be hanged. He was reprieved by Sir John Denham, who declared that 'whilest G. W. lived, he [Denham] should not be the worst Poet in England'.[5] In fact, Wither was never captured and during the campaign in question it was Denham who surrendered. Another much-cited anecdote links Wither to the republican Henry Marten, whose image has never recovered from his presentation in royalist newsbooks as a buffoonish libertine. Marten allegedly raided the jewel-house at Westminster and dressed Wither clownishly in the royal robes. Though Marten and Wither were involved in the fate of the jewels at different periods, there is no evidence for this story.[6] Thomas May is best known from Marvell's satire, which presents the debauched poet's republicanism as a mask for frustrated ambition.

3 Sean Kelsey, *Inventing a Republic: The Political Culture of the English Commonwealth 1649–1653* (Manchester, 1997), p. 226.

4 T. S. Eliot, 'Milton I', in *On Poetry and Poets* (1957), pp. 138–45 (139). On Eliot's anomalous monarchism see Tom Nairn, *The Enchanted Glass: Britain and its Monarchy* (1988), pp. 345–9, and David Bradshaw, 'Lonely Royalists: T. S. Eliot and Sir Robert Filmer', *Review of English Studies* 46 (1995), 375–9.

5 Bodleian MS Aubrey 6, fol. 105v, *ABL*, I, 221.

6 On these anecdotes see David Norbrook, 'Levelling Poetry: George Wither and the English Revolution, 1642–1649', *English Literary Renaissance* 21 (1991), 217–56 (217–19).

As recycled uncritically by generations of literary historians, such anecdotes have succeeded in burying republican history in snobbish laughter. That was the purpose with which the antiquarian Anthony Wood put many of them in print, often citing selectively the more sympathetic account in one of his main sources for the republicans, the compilations of John Aubrey. To pursue the facts a little further is often to make the humour less evident. 'Tom May's Death' declares that the poet's body will be expelled from Westminster Abbey; this prophecy was fulfilled in a grisly way when in 1661 his body was disinterred in a mass exhumation that extended to many republicans and Cromwellians. The violence of such acts betrayed unease about the efficacy of the Act of Oblivion: forgetting would not happen of its own accord, the evidence must be actively erased. Wood was writing at a period of renewed Tory alarm over a renewal of the republican spirit, when some of Milton's political works were publicly burned in Oxford.[7]

The more violent the erasure, however, the more it can be seen that there was something to hide. In 1662 Sir George Downing, the English Resident in the Netherlands, captured three of the men who had signed Charles I's death warrant. The Dutch government had not been particularly enthusiastic about the extradition of men condemned to agonizing death, but Downing insisted, and the exiles were shipped home to be hanged, drawn and quartered. The king rewarded him with the strategic piece of land in Westminster that has now become Downing Street. That particular part of England's royal heritage is now little remembered; but it may stand for many lesser episodes where anti-republican violence was used to compensate for a past which itself lacked monarchist purity. Only three years earlier, indeed, Downing had been a faithful servant of the Protectorate, a colleague of Andrew Marvell, and had been vigorously harassing not republican but royalist exiles in the Netherlands. A poem for his marriage had been written by Payne Fisher, who had been effectively Cromwell's poet laureate. None of this, it is true, made Downing a republican: he was a fierce defender of Cromwell's semi-monarchical regime against its republican critics. For some republicans, Cromwell's coup of 1653 was at least as crucial a historical moment as the regicide. The blurring of any distinction between the Commonwealth and the Protectorate in the national memory is perhaps the most striking example of the elision of a republican perspective. Repellent as it may have been to some republicans, however, it is true that Cromwell's regime, with its written constitution and attempts to separate executive from legislature, was itself an anomaly in English history.[8]

---

7 Nicholas von Maltzahn, 'Wood, Allam, and the Oxford Milton', *Milton Studies* 31 (1994), 155–77.

8 John Beresford, *The Godfather of Downing Street: Sir George Downing 1623–1684* (1925), pp. 83ff, 69, 60; Ralph C. H. Catterall, 'Sir George Downing and the Regicides', *American Historical Review* 17 (1911–12), 268–89.

The ferocity of the anti-republican crackdown in 1660 was arguably out of all proportion to the political danger. It was fuelled by a minority of extreme reactionaries and often checked by more moderate counsels. But the fact that it was considered necessary at all is itself one kind of tribute to the republicans' achievement. If Charles's return was greeted by celebratory bonfires, we need to remember that some frantic burning of incriminating papers probably went on that year. Only recently have architectural historians begun to recognize that many interesting buildings conventionally given a post-1660 date in fact date from the 1650s.[9] Our knowledge of the portraiture of the republican period remains extremely shadowy in comparison with the attention that has been paid to court culture. One point this book tries to emphasize is that what has been referred to as the Augustan era of English poetry, initiated in 1660 and brought to perfection with Dryden's *Aeneid* (1697), was a reactive phenomenon. Strong anti-Augustanism preceded, and continued to engage with, courtly poetry. With the passing of time, however, the desperation with which England worked to eliminate compromising republican traces from its culture has been widely forgotten, and a bland monarchist surface has been substituted.

Yet in fact the process of erasure has been a continuing and active one. When Queen Elizabeth II gave an address in Westminster Hall in 1988 to celebrate the tercentenary of the Glorious Revolution, a plaque marking the execution of Charles I was discreetly covered with a curtain.[10] The celebrations in France the following year for the bicentenary of the French Revolution called up a wave of self-congratulation in England over the contrast between foreign regicide and Britain's peaceful evolution.[11] This involved a strategic silence about the regicidal revolution of 1649, which had been taken as one point of reference by the French revolutionaries. Milton's *Defence of the English People* was published in translation in 1789 and again in 1792, as part of a campaign for the trial of Louis XVI, and works by Marchamont Nedham, James Harrington and Edward Sexby were involved in French debates.[12] Some English republicans had indeed taken as much pride in exporting their revolution as the French were to do a century and a half later, and encouraged the dissemination of the Levellers' ideal written constitution in rebellious areas of south-west France. In a remarkable

---

9 Timothy Mowl and Brian Earnshaw, *Architecture without Kings: The Rise of Puritan Classicism under Cromwell* (Manchester and New York, 1995).

10 Christopher Hitchens, *The Monarchy* (1990), p. 12.

11 A point noted by Jonathan Scott, *Algernon Sidney and the Restoration Crisis, 1677–1683* (Cambridge, 1991), p. 108 n. 13.

12 Tony Davies, 'Borrowed Language: Milton, Jefferson, Mirabeau', *MR*, pp. 254–71 (269); Olivier Lutaud, *Des Révolutions d'Angleterre à la Révolution Française: le tyrannicide et 'Killing No Murder' (Cromwell, Athalie, Bonaparte)* (The Hague, 1973).

anticipation of French slogans, a title-page of 1652 carried the slogan 'Vive la Re Publick'.[13] Title-pages, as in revolutionary France, were sometimes dated according to the year of liberty.[14] England produced a poetics of sublimity that has parallels in revolutionary France.[15] The American Revolution can more easily be seen as continuing aspects of English republicanism, but Americans can still find it hard to understand how little those links are acknowledged in the founding fathers' Old World. At the basic level of imagining a political and literary culture divested of monarchy and its attendant trappings, however, the mid-seventeenth century can make modern Britain look archaic. The reform group Charter 88 is making demands that were voiced by the Levellers in the 1640s.

Where did this energetic republican culture come from? Did it spring from nowhere, only to disappear from sight within a few years? One might draw that conclusion from much recent historiography. A 'revisionist' movement has contested liberal and Marxist readings that traced the seventeenth-century revolution back to long-standing constitutional or social conflicts, reaffirming instead the profound social and intellectual conservatism of early Stuart England. On that analysis, republicanism was largely a response to, rather than the cause of, the execution of Charles I; before the 1640s republicanism was effectively unthinkable.[16] Some of the most exciting and innovative work on the history of political thought has accepted parts of the revisionist analysis. J. G. A. Pocock, Blair Worden and other scholars, in some important studies, have begun to explore a vigorous and energetic republican culture; but they have tended to side with the revisionists, insofar as they see that culture as a response to, rather than a significant influence on, the revolution of 1649. Before then, writes Pocock, English republicanism was ' a language, not a programme'. [17] Certainly there was a lack before then of the kind of obsessively detailed

---

13 Walter Blith, *The English Improver Improved* (1652; E666.4); Andrew McRae, *God Speed the Plough: The Representation of Agrarian England, 1500–1660* (Cambridge, 1996), p. 227.

14 For example Payne Fisher's volume of neo-Latin panegyrics to the republic's leaders, *Irenodia Gratulatoria* (1652; E796.30), is dated in the 'Aera' both 'Salutis Humanae MDCLII' and 'Libertatis Angliae IIII'.

15 Compare Ronald Paulson, *Representations of Revolution 1789–1820* (New Haven and London, 1983), pp. 57ff, and Yves Abrioux, *Ian Hamilton Finlay: A Visual Primer*, second edition (London, 1992), pp. 250–5.

16 For a strong statement of this view see Kevin Sharpe, 'A Commonwealth of Meanings: Languages, Analogues, Ideas and Politics', in *Politics and Ideas in Early Stuart England: Essays and Studies* (London and New York, 1989), pp. 3–71, and for a counter-view, David Norbrook, 'Rhetoric, Ideology, and the Elizabethan World Picture', in Peter Mack (ed.), *Renaissance Rhetoric* (1994), pp. 140–64.

17 HPW, p. 15. Pocock's *magnum opus*, *The Machiavellian Moment: Florentine Political Thought and the Atlantic Republican Tradition* (Princeton, 1975), ch. 10, offers a superb conspectus of pre-Civil War political discourses.

constitutional programme provided by James Harrington, who for Pocock is the paradigmatic republican; but the present study will try to show that republican language was a more powerful presence than has been recognized. Worden, who has written with great insight of such vigorously enthusiastic republicans as Marchamont Nedham, nonetheless emphasizes the fact that most of those who 'cut off King Charles' head' then 'wondered what to do next'. And what they did next, in his view, fell short of anything one can legitimately term a republic. After 1653, when Cromwell dissolved the Long Parliament, republicans 'retreated into nostalgia'.[18] Republicanism did not exist before 1649, was not put into effect then, and quickly became an object of distant nostalgia: such a fleeting phenomenon hardly disturbs a general model of English culture as overwhelmingly monarchist.

This analysis of the dominance of conservative monarchism has united commentators with widely differing political views. In literary studies, the paradigm offered by Michel Foucault, who projects a massive shift in signifying systems precisely at the mid-seventeenth century, has been attractive to writers on English cultural history, where the execution of Charles I provides an obligingly neat watershed.[19] On Perry Anderson's influential neo-Marxist analysis, the persistent strength of monarchism is a symptom of the nation's backwardness, its retention of a culture of deference that has discouraged political modernization and thus contributed to economic decline. Over the last few years there has been a gradual thawing of the strict taboo on criticism of the royal family, but the new generation of British republicans seems often to have little sense of occupying a space in cultural history that is not wholly new. Tom Nairn, in the most powerful modern critique of monarchism, has reinforced that verdict, considering the term 'bourgeois revolution' to be 'over-flattering' to the deeply conservative republicans of the mid-seventeenth century.[20] The republican John Streater was saying something rather similar on the eve of the Restoration in a retort to those who claimed that kingship was natural to England:

> the long Continuation of Kingly Government in this Nation . . . created so
> many corrupt Props and Pillars to support its Dignity, that were like so many

18 Blair Worden, 'Milton's Republicanism and the Tyranny of Heaven', in Gisela Bock, Quentin Skinner and Maurizio Viroli (eds.), *Machiavelli and Republicanism* (Cambridge, 1990), pp. 225–45 (226); 'Classical Republicanism and the Puritan Revolution', in *History and Imagination: Essays in Honour of H. R. Trevor-Roper*, ed. Hugh Lloyd-Jones, Valerie Pearl and Blair Worden (1981), pp. 182–200 (199).

19 See David Norbrook, 'Life and Death of Renaissance Man', *Raritan* 8:4 (Spring 1989), 89–110, and James Holstun, 'Ranting at the New Historicism', *English Literary Renaissance* 19 (1989), 189–225.

20 Nairn, *The Enchanted Glass*, pp. 151ff. For a stimulating riposte, see Ellen Meiksins Wood, *The Pristine Culture of Capitalism: An Historical Essay on Old Regimes and Modern States* (London and New York, 1991).

Sores and Phistula's to the Nation: the taking away of which on a suddain, would be something against Nature; though it was a burden to Nature, and a Disease[.][21]

It is true that even at the high tide of the 1650s the proportion of committed republicans in the population was a very small one, and the quasi-republican regime that was toppled by the monarchy was probably the most despised government in English history. This book is very far from offering a representative cross-section of political opinion. Yet neither republicanism nor monarchism was a single coherent entity. Under the Protectorate, England had experimented with a compromise form of government. The republican Parliament had the double misfortune of being hated both by high-flying monarchists and by republicans for whom it had not gone nearly far enough. The Restoration of 1660 did not exactly mark the return of an unquestioningly monarchist people to a natural order; it was to inaugurate further experiments and instabilities. The emotive cult of Charles the martyr-king was at least as much a post-regicide phenomenon as its opposing ideology; it was subscribed to by people who had not been exceptionally vigorous in preventing his demise. Though there was an eclipse for much of the eighteenth century, republicanism underwent another major revival between the 1790s and the 1840s.[22] The nineteenth-century reinvention of the English as a people particularly devoted to royal ceremony was as much a reaction to new forms of radicalism as a residual legacy of the nation's archaism.[23]

This book aims to trace the early development of English republicanism not through the texts of 'high' political theory but through literary culture, and more specifically through poetry. Contemporary republican poets like Tony Harrison and Tom Paulin have had to do a certain amount of excavating to establish their tradition, for literary history in the twentieth century has often had a strongly monarchist bias.[24] A modest hope for this study is to help to open up different traditions. Many of the writers here dealt with were much more current two centuries ago than they are today. In 1802 Wordsworth could still write, with an air of familiarity:

21 J. S[treater]., *A Shield Against the Parthian Dart* (1659; E988.11), pp. 17–18.
22 Peter J. Kitson, "'Sages and patriots that being dead do yet speak to us": Readings of the English Revolution in the Late Eighteenth Century', in James Holstun (ed.), *Pamphlet Wars: Prose in the English Revolution* (1992), pp. 205–30.
23 D. A. Cannadine, 'The Context, Performance and Meaning of Ritual: The British Monarchy and the "Invention of Tradition", *c.* 1820–1977', in Eric Hobsbawm and Terence Ranger (eds.), *The Invention of Tradition* (Cambridge, 1983), pp. 34–73.
24 T. W. Harrison, 'English Virgil: The *Aeneid* in the XVIII Century', *Philologica Pragensia* 10 (1967), 1–11, 80–91, shows an awareness unusual at the time of the Whiggish and republican cult of Lucan, Milton and Marvell (I owe this reference to Oliver Taplin); Tom Paulin, *The Faber Book of Political Verse* (London and Boston, 1986).

Great men have been among us; hands that penned
And tongues that uttered wisdom – better none:
The later Sidney, Marvel, Harrington,
Young Vane, and others who called Milton friend.[25]

'O that I might have such an action to remember on my Death-bed!' wrote Coleridge of the regicide.[26] At this time Thomas May still retained a certain stature, his history of the Long Parliament vying with Clarendon's royalist version down to the mid-nineteenth century, when the last 'modern' edition appeared. Southey and other poets contributed to a cult of Henry Marten; Coleridge and Lamb rehabilitated Wither; while Walter Savage Landor – who was delighted that his birthday coincided with the anniversary of the regicide – maintained a poetic cult of the republicans.[27] As for William Blake, the motto for his 'Republican Art' was:

The Strongest Poison ever known
Came From Caesar's Laurel Crown[.][28]

Wordsworth, it should be noted, includes in his canon a mixture of poets and prose writers. He himself, however, was also involved in a process that contributed greatly to the later eclipse of literary republicanism: the split between rhetoric and poetry, between the public world and a 'literature' defined in increasingly narrow terms as concerned with a private, intimate sphere. Writing of the Romantic reaction against rhetoric, Martin Thom observes: 'After the Terror . . . a line would be drawn between the space of the heart and the space of the agora'.[29] If not exactly new, such a line certainly became much more emphatic. And it has to some extent become embodied in academic institutions. Of the writers mentioned in Wordsworth's list, Milton and Marvell have become canonized as poets, and their prose, especially the latter's, has until relatively recently been placed in a separate compartment. Harrington, on the other hand, has become a key figure in the study of republican thought, but the fact that he wrote poetry, and wrote prose with a keen eye to poetic allusion, has received hardly any attention. The history of political thought has made great strides in recent years, but its practitioners have paid more attention to generalized patterns of meaning than to the texture of

25 *The Poetical Works of William Wordsworth*, ed. Ernest de Selincourt and Helen Darbishire, 5 vols. (Oxford, 1940–9), III, 116.

26 *The Collected Works of Samuel Taylor Coleridge, 12: Marginalia*, part 2, ed. George Whalley (London and Princeton, 1984), p. 970.

27 One of Landor's last works was 'Andrew Marvel [sic] and Henry Marten', in John Forster, *Walter Savage Landor: A Biography*, 2 vols. (1869), II, 584–6.

28 From 'Auguries of Innocence', in G. E. Bentley, Jr. (ed.), *William Blake's Writings*, 2 vols. (Oxford, 1978), II, 1314.

29 Martin Thom, *Republics, Nations and Tribes* (London and New York, 1995), p. 46.

the writings, so that readers might not recognize amidst the high seriousness just how witty many of these texts could be. The role of poetry like Lucan's in giving a powerful emotional colouring to the abstract categories of political theory has yet to be fully recognized. In any case, the mid-seventeenth century was a period when conventional boundaries between prose and verse were especially permeable, whether in Wither's versified tracts or Milton's image-dense prose. In approaching the period, we do well to set aside a narrow model of what counts as literary and to be open to experimentation that linked poetry with popular newsbooks and classical oratory.

In line with other recent studies, the present book removes canonical writers like Milton and Marvell from their timeless pantheon and looks at the poems as they were first composed or circulated, setting them in the political flux along with many much less well-known contemporaries. When Marvell placed May in a sordid, resentful republican Grub Street, he was uneasily aware that others might locate him in the same venue, and a reading of his poetry can only gain from a consciousness of such tensions. I have tried to allow other voices – from Puritan saints to deft opportunists – to speak at some length without reducing them to a mere background to the familiar literary history. The republican crisis generated a lot of powerful writing that is often difficult of access.

Broadening the scope of literary history in this way makes it evident how a narrower model of the literary has often served to obscure the origins of republican culture. An idealized and ultimately conservative literary Culture has been pitted against republican Anarchy, or at least philistinism. If political historians often see 1649 as a watershed that suddenly ushers in republicanism, for some literary scholars the execution of Charles I has been a key moment in a shift from a poetic monarchical order to a republican or Whiggish world of prose. The poetic imagination, on this reading, was stimulated by traditional rituals which established intricate analogies between the individual and the natural and social orders. T. S. Eliot's idea of a 'dissociation of sensibility' in the mid-seventeenth century was reinforced by E. M. W. Tillyard's claim that up to that point a universally held 'Elizabethan World Picture' made monarchy the natural centre of the cosmos, with any other form of government effectively unimaginable.

Recent 'new historicist' and 'cultural materialist' criticism has moved beyond these paradigms, offering a wider model of the text and of culture to cover a broad range of signs and representations.[30] The present study shares these critics' concern to view literary texts in the context of social rhetoric, and

---

30 H. Aram Veeser (ed.), *The New Historicism* (New York and London, 1989); Jonathan
  Dollimore, *Radical Tragedy: Religion, Ideology and Power in the Drama of Shakespeare
  and his Contemporaries*, second edition (New York and London, 1989).

to explore parallels between artistic and political representation: republican politics produced a republican poetics. Some developments in recent literary and cultural theory, however, have had the effect of overemphasizing the influence of monarchy from a different direction. 'Anti-humanist' theorists have presented language and ideology as all-pervasive and ultimately unconscious structuring influences on the individual 'subject'. Such theories produce a passive model of the relation between ideology and political culture: whether the form of government is republican or monarchical, the history produced is one of subjects, not citizens. A more dynamic view of the relations between language and political change needs to be found. In common with many historians of political thought, therefore, the present study draws on the 'speech-act theory' or 'pragmatics' derived from J. L. Austin. As the name implies, this approach is concerned with the links between language and action, with the kinds of public intervention that speech, and writing, can make. To understand a text by Sidney or Hobbes, Quentin Skinner argues, we need to analyse not only its cognitive content, considered as timeless truths, but the kinds of 'illocutionary act' the author was performing in publishing it: i.e. which positions he or she was attacking, how he or she was intervening in a contemporary context of debate.[31] The history of political thought is thus reconceived as one part of the history of political action. It is also part of the history of reading: the study of the recovery of classical republican texts is also the study of their deployment in contemporary debates.

This is not the place to explore the technicalities, and the possible limitations, of speech-act theory.[32] While it has spawned a large, and highly technical, theoretical literature, its value as a heuristic device in cultural history emerges best in practice – indeed it is in some ways a rationalization of the practice of good historians. No use will be made below of its panoply of technical terms beyond the simple, and yet easily overlooked, distinction between the overt content of a text and the illocutionary act or acts involved in composing or circulating it. The locutionary force of much of Milton's *Readie and Easie Way* is that the English people have turned irredeemably to monarchy and are beyond hope; the illocutionary force of publishing two editions in concert with other republicans is a significant shade less despairing. The same applies, I shall try to show, to the political connotations of *Paradise Lost*.

31 See the essays collected in James Tully (ed.), *Meaning and Context: Quentin Skinner and his Critics* (Princeton, 1988), pp. 29–132.

32 While the use of 'speech' to cover written texts is a broad one, the present study's focus on rhetoric is a reminder that oral and written discourses were still being considered in closely similar terms. Sandy Petrey, *Speech Acts and Literary Theory* (New York and London, 1990), offers the best discussion of the theoretical issues as they are relevant to literature, and engages with the deconstructionist critique of the concept of 'speech' in a way that is not possible here.

When Tom Paulin cites some gloomy lines from Book XII and then declares: 'It is time to build the English Republic', we seem to be faced with a complete *non sequitur*[33]; I shall try to show that Milton is more likely to have applauded Paulin's sentiment than is allowed by critics who read the poem as designed to undermine any faith in human action. An approach through speech-acts points us away from closed systems of thought into dialogue, into the constant invention of arguments and counter-arguments. Rather than reading monarchist texts as expressions of a unified symbolic order, we are directed to asking what texts they were answering, why it was felt necessary to defend monarchy in these particular terms. We can then better approach a culture like early modern England, where monarchy was being reinvented in response to recurrent challenges. The aim is to read poems not as timeless monuments or as part of a generalized and uniform culture but as engagements with other texts, involved in an ongoing process.

It is no accident that speech-act theory should have appealed to historians of republicanism, for it can be seen as a reinvention of rhetoric, that central art of civic humanism. 'Humanism' in this context does not mean placing man at the centre of the universe but, more technically, the movement to give the arts of language a central place in the academic curriculum. From the sixteenth century this was the major intellectual driving force behind the English educational system. Rhetoric, which was given renewed prominence at the expense of scholastic logic, emphasized the public implications of all speech, whether in verse or prose, whether of the heart or the agora. There was a terrible irony in the fact that the injunction 'Scribere est agere', 'to write is to act', should have been used to condemn Algernon Sidney to death for writing his *Discourses*: in different circumstances he would have agreed.[34] Humanist education placed a premium on adapting language to particular and unpredictable contexts: skill in persuasion depended on quickly anticipating counter-arguments. The exercise of arguing *in utramque partem*, on both sides of a question, was central to humanist education.

The Renaissance revival of rhetoric easily took on political implications. The 'civic humanism' that originated in Italian city states, and became widely diffused in northern Europe, aimed to revive the classical arts of government as well as of language. The strong emphasis on the *vita activa*, on public service, went with a contempt for regimes which stifled political debate and subordinated the public good to that of a private dynasty. Again and again students were confronted with texts and orations whose central premise was that monarchy was a backward and barbaric form of government: killing a

33 Tom Paulin, 'Milton – One of Us', in Anthony Barnett (ed.), *Power and the Throne: The Monarchy Debate* (1994), p. 181.
34 Scott, *Algernon Sidney and the Restoration Crisis*, p. 329.

tyrant was one of the noblest deeds that anyone could perform. Students would be encouraged to compose speeches in which Brutus justified the assassination of Caesar to save the republic. As Milton put it in the *Second Defence*, 'we kill [Virgil's tyrant] Mezentius over and over again in stale anti-theta' (*Pro Se Defensio, MPW*, IV:2, 795). From Tacitus and other classical writers, many Renaissance humanists inherited the view that rhetoric had declined under the Roman emperors. The spirit of free and open speech amongst equals that had been enjoyed by the political elite under the republic gave way to one-sided praise.

The shift from deliberative to demonstrative rhetoric, from argument to praise, could be claimed to have its positive side. Since poetry was often classed as part of demonstrative rhetoric, courts could lay claim to an alliance with that art. Nevertheless, in many early modern poets we can find a chafing at the constraints of courtly panegyric. More's *Utopia* is torn between the practical demands of royal service and a playful revival of the classical city state. Sir Philip Sidney, who was uneasy with his status as a courtier, included a republican faction in his imagined Arcadia. He certainly did not endorse the republicans' views, but nor did he present them as some strange aberration: republicanism emerges rather as an easy academic indulgence, appealing only to 'the discoursing sort of men', 'a matter more in imagination than practice'.[35] For humanists who lived under a well-established monarchy, republicanism was indeed a matter of imagination. Like the More of the *Utopia*, Sidney was led by his own humanist principles to prefer active service of the state as currently constituted over utopian contemplation. And after all, the Elizabethan state was a long way from the decadence of the Roman Empire. It possessed institutions ready to challenge royal power and had traditions of political resistance. Patrick Collinson has gone so far as to describe Elizabethan England as a 'monarchical republic', with active citizens contained within the shell of subjecthood.[36] Civic humanism could provide an ideological rationale and a classical precedent for everyday political practice.

It was still a long way from Elizabethan London to republican Rome, but Elizabethan and Jacobean writers encouraged a degree of openness to alternative forms of political order. Shakespeare and Jonson vividly realized past republican cultures for a popular audience. Historians of political thought have remarked on the absence of explicit republican theory in England before the 1650s; they have paid less attention to the many situations in which republican political practice was actively imagined. In a famous letter, Machiavelli described his evening's reading of classical writers as a kind of personal

---

35 Sir Philip Sidney, *The Countess of Pembroke's Arcadia (The Old Arcadia)*, ed. Jean Robertson (Oxford, 1973), p. 321.

36 Patrick Collinson, 'De Republica Anglorum' and 'The Monarchical Republic of Queen Elizabeth I', in *Elizabethan Essays* (London and Rio Grande, 1994), pp. 1–29, 31–58.

dialogue with them.[37] Most of the writers to be studied below engaged in that kind of dialogue; in that sense, classical writers belonged as much to the seventeenth century as the panegyrists of courts and monarchs. This kind of passionate involvement with the past emerges especially vividly in the title-page to May's continuation of Lucan (figure 10 below): the ghosts of past writers could drink the blood of the present. Nor was this passion confined to a narrow elite. Classical histories as well as studies of foreign republican constitutions were widely published in early modern England and addressed a readership far beyond the court.[38]

With the collapse of censorship in the 1640s, the political debates that were at first conducted obliquely through the dramatization and publication of the classics became much more urgent and direct. This period arguably saw the first appearance of what Jürgen Habermas has termed the 'bourgeois public sphere'. This he defines as a space for the critical discussion of public issues independent of the traditional monopolies of discourse held by the church, the court, and the professions. This was 'bourgeois' in the Marxist sense of belonging to an emergent middle class; but Habermas is concerned with the bourgeois not merely as *homo economicus* but as citizen, as exercising positive public responsibility as well as a negative freedom from old economic and social ties. Habermas's model has been criticized as idealizing and schematic, and certainly the present study will take issue with his chronology. He passes over the mid-century revolution, which arguably anticipated the developments he consigns to a later period, and even went beyond them – for a time the public sphere was far wider than merely 'bourgeois'.[39] Yet his model is helpful, not least because of the congruence between its own terms and those of seventeenth-century republicans. Habermas's development of speech-act theory can be seen as one more attempt at recovering the spirit of the classical forum and adapting it to modern conditions.

Republicanism before the 1640s may not have had the practical option of being a programme rather than a language; but a distinctively republican emphasis on language could become a programme. In two of the very last

---

37 Machiavelli to Vettori, 10 December 1513, Familiar Letter no. 137, in J. R. Hale (ed.), *The Literary Works of Machiavelli* (London, New York and Toronto, 1961), p. 139.
38 A point demonstrated in detail by Markku Peltonen, *Classical Humanism and Republicanism in English Political Thought 1570–1640* (Cambridge, 1995).
39 Jürgen Habermas, *The Structural Transformation of the Public Sphere: An Inquiry into a Category of Bourgeois Society*, trans. Thomas Burger with Frederick Lawrence (Cambridge, Mass., 1989). David Zaret points out the gap in 'Religion, Science, and Printing in the Public Spheres in Seventeenth-Century England', in Craig Calhoun (ed.), *Habermas and the Public Sphere* (Cambridge, Mass., and London, 1992), pp. 212–35. See also Sharon Achinstein, *Milton and the Revolutionary Reader* (Princeton, 1994) and Dagmar Freist, *Governed by Opinion: Politics, Religion and the Dynamics of Communication in Stuart London 1637–45* (London and New York, 1997), pp. 13ff.

republican tracts to appear before the Restoration, republicans were rallied under the banner of *Plain English*, and Milton celebrated 'the language of the good old cause' (*The Readie and Easie Way*, MPW, VII, 387). Radical Protestantism insisted that the printed Word should be available to all believers, and linked open reading and interpreting with power structures in the church: an intolerant state church had a vested interest in blocking interpretation. To be able to use a language that was open to the divine purpose and that also spoke for the public interest, it was necessary to diminish the power of religious and civil monopolies of discourse. As long as it seemed possible that the monarchy might co-operate in this process, it did not seem inimical to a regime in which the *res publica* was fulfilled. During the 1630s and 1640s, however, the monarchy emerged ever more strongly as the central bulwark of those monopolies, and it was abolished. The execution of Charles I, sometimes held to mark the end of the Renaissance, could be legitimately taken as its fulfilment. Some of the regime's most prominent defenders took it as a badge of political pride to be able to write in the Latin of the republican era, and failure to consider these writings has distorted our picture of the period. The republican culture of the 1650s was at once excitingly new and as familiar as a dog-eared school-book.

The wager of this book is that it is possible to construct a coherent narrative of the emergence of republican prose and poetry. Rather than hitting some invisible barrier at the year 1649, with a completely different world-view suddenly emerging, it is possible to demonstrate a fundamental continuity between the post-1649 writings of poets sympathetic to the republic and their earlier works. Readers who already know that this is impossible are of course at liberty to tear the book in two and begin with chapter 5, but I hope that they will start from chapter 1. Not all the writers I focus on were consistent or committed republicans, but they were open to republican influences and from a variety of motives they played a part in contributing to the political cultures of the Commonwealth and Protectorate. The book's framing chapters juxtapose May's translation of Lucan's *Pharsalia* with Milton's *Paradise Lost*. The latter work is often interpreted as the product of the author's despair at the collapse of republican hopes. In trying to show close structural parallels between the two epics, I argue for a very different model of the fortunes of republican literary culture. The vogue for Lucan in the 1620s helps us to see the royalist poetry of the 1630s, as represented by Edmund Waller, not as part of a natural order to be rudely shattered in 1649 but as an attempt to ward off radical challenges. I try to show the degree of overlap between court poetry and republicanism by giving a prominent role in this story to Waller, a figure who occupied an awkward position at their margins and thus incurred the wrath of both sides. If *Writing the English Republic* concentrates on writers from the elite, it is not to claim that the classics were the only source of republican ideas, but rather to trace republican elements not just on the extreme margins of pre-1649 literary culture but close to its centre. These 'middle of the road' republicans may not have caught the modern imagination as much as the Levellers, Diggers and radical prophets, but they deserve attention. I am far from claiming that poetry caused the English Revolution; there have been decades of debate over the economic, social and ideological causes. In recent years, however, there has been a tendency for revisionists to deny that there was a revolution at all; insofar as the literary evidence itself calls such claims in question, it may have a galvanizing role in the wider debate.

In current cultural history, grand narratives of the kind here attempted are often dismissed as Whiggish or teleological. The present narrative does unashamedly aim at a long view, at conveying the sharply shifting rhythms of the mid-century's crises, the recurrent blockages, sudden accelerations, and drifts back to some form of stasis. But the narrative is not teleological in any simple sense. It will emerge clearly enough that republican culture, while less marginal than conventionally assumed, was always in a precarious situation; this is a story of discontinuity as well as continuity. In some respects, after all, English constitutional debates of 1659 were more 'modern', less deferential towards the monarchy and the House of Lords, than those of the late-twentieth century. In dividing the book into sections of a few years, I have tried to place the reader in the uncertain position of contemporaries for whom the political horizon was bafflingly open and the meanings of new political formations were constantly uncertain. The tempo is deliberately slowed at such crucial points as the periods leading up first to the regicide and then to the Restoration, to show how far from inevitable these events seemed to contemporaries. For all these mutations, however, republicans were able to find long-term continuities which had helped to give meaning to their lives. George Wither wrote shortly after the king's execution that he had been struggling consistently against the same enemies for thirty-six years. He was aware that he had markedly changed the terms in which he spoke of the monarchy, and yet it is important to understand how he could nonetheless have experienced a continuity of belief and writing.[40]

Comments like Wither's are exasperating to scholars in search of more precise definitions. 'Republicanism' presents as many problems for today's historians as 'socialism' will for the future. In their concern to distinguish true republicans from others, historians can sound rather like Oliver Cromwell in 1658, exhorting his republican critics to explain

---

40 George Wither, *Carmen Ternarium Semi-Cynicum* ([1649]; W 3150), in J. Milton French, 'Four Scarce Poems of George Wither', *Huntington Library Bulletin* 2 (1931), 91–121 (104).

what they meant by the good old cause? and bid them instance but in one
perticuler, wherein he had departed from it, stateinge to them what he understood by the good old cause in perticuler. But they kept themselves in generall
termes. . . .[41]

Cromwell's frustration is understandable: the officers' unassailable confidence in the justice of their cause seemed hard to square with their inability to
say what it was. The phrase 'the good old cause' was itself not very old, and
had emerged to paper over the cracks in a fragile coalition of very different
forces. And yet it aroused passionate emotions.

'The good old cause', or 'the common cause', are vague terms; yet they are
also in effect translations of 'res publica', in the broader Latin sense that was
rendered in English as 'common weal'. That elusive word 'res' could refer to a
specific institution, the state, or a cause, an ideal, and 'res publica' fluctuated
in Latin usage between a specific political form and the state or society in
general.[42] The Romans managed to fight a civil war over a republican
constitution even though they lacked a specific word for 'republican'. It is then
not so surprising that the word should have emerged relatively late in
England. Before the Civil War, 'republic' and 'common weal' still tended to be
relatively broad and bland terms, needing a modifying 'free' to suggest
unequivocally a popular form of government.[43] Caution is in order, however,
in generalizing about what meanings a word could not have had before a
certain date; we need to look at the speech-acts it performed. Wither used the
word 'Republikes' in 1648 to refer to a party calling for the abolition of monarchy (see below, chapter 4), and this sense is not recorded in the *OED*. One
historian implies that the word 'common weal' never connoted non-
monarchical government before the civil war.[44] It does seem to have been
sometimes perceived as a blander word than 'republic'.[45] But the prominent
poet Samuel Daniel commented in 1613 that the freedom to write a true
history is 'a liberty proper onely to Common-wealths, and neuer permitted to
Kingdomes, but vnder good Princes'.[46] When in 1636 John Dury wrote from
Sweden that changes of government would 'tend to a Republican forme of
State'[47] (predating any of the *OED*'s usages by more than fifty years), he was
referring to a strictly limited monarchy rather than a non-monarchical
government; but the sense that excessive royal power would threaten 'republican' common good could easily facilitate a move towards more radically anti-

41 Thurloe to Henry Cromwell, 16 February 1658, *TSP*, VI, 806.
42 *Oxford Latin Dictionary*, 'respublica', 3–4.
43 Thomas N. Corns, 'Milton and the Characteristics of a Free Commonwealth', *MR*,
    pp. 25–42 (p. 27 n. 4) surveys the *OED* evidence.
44 Sharpe, 'A Commonwealth of Meanings', pp. 65–8.   45 See chapter 6, n. 78 below.
46 Samuel Daniel, *The First Part of the Historie of England* (1613; 6247), sig. A4r.
47 Dury to Hartlib, July 1636, *HP*, 9/1/30A.

monarchical sentiment in times of crisis. In 1642 the poet Francis Quarles could write at one point of 'a *Prince*, or a *Republique*' as alternatives, and a few pages later use 'Republique' for any form of government: the political context would determine the word's precise meaning.[48]

Linguistic change and political change went hand in hand: as the possibility that monarchy could ever realize the values of a 'commonwealth' came to seem more remote, so 'commonwealth' or 'republic' became more and more firmly identified with non-monarchical government. There was a continuum between advocacy of a limited monarchy and advocacy of a republic, such that adherence to the Commonwealth did not necessarily represent a cataclysmic break with earlier views. Support for a distinction between the king's person and the public interest could be found in the common-law tradition which defined the king as possessing both a natural body and a 'body politic' which would become effectively identified with the public interest. Though royalists used the emotive imagery of the body to stress the mystical marriage between king and kingdom, it was possible to stress the distinction instead.[49] Independently of the English common law, classical and biblical authorities made it easy to conceive of a public interest as inherently opposed to kingship. The simplest sense of 'republican', as advanced by Zera S. Fink in a pioneering study, is a supporter of 'a state which was not headed by a king and in which the hereditary principle did not prevail in whole or in part in determining the headship'.[50]

Advocacy of rule without a king did not in itself imply major reform of government. A few leaders of the Commons in 1649 showed an almost mystical conviction that once the king as the central symbol of private interest had been removed, the public interest would establish itself with little further change. Generally, however, dislike of monarchy implied the need for a more systematic overhaul of institutions to permit the public interest to be better accommodated. Emphasis on the public interest implied that power resided in 'the people' in some form, but just how that power was to be manifested aroused great disagreement. It was in principle possible to believe, as the Levellers did at some points, that a constitutional monarchy could represent the public interest better than an oligarchical republic. Republicans preferred

---

48 Francis Quarles, *Observations Concerning Princes and States, Upon Peace and Warre* (1642; E116.36), p. 10.
49 Ernst H. Kantorowicz, *The King's Two Bodies: A Study in Mediaeval Political Theology* (Princeton, 1957), ch. 1. The reception of this work in recent criticism has, however, tended to strengthen court-centred readings: see David Norbrook, 'The Emperor's New Body? *Richard II*, Ernst Kantorowicz, and the Politics of Shakespeare Criticism', *Textual Practice* 10 (1996), 329–57.
50 Zera S. Fink, *The Classical Republicans: An Essay in the Recovery of a Pattern of Thought in Seventeenth Century England* (Evanston, 1945), p. X.

a clean sweep at the top. Some of them, notably James Harrington, strongly believed in beginning a new state from scratch: only a precise constitutional blueprint set out for all time could consolidate their values. Others, such as Milton, were more concerned with the virtue of those in power than with the precise model, and were ready to place high hopes in Cromwell's semi-regal government. Insofar as Cromwell's rule was monarchical, some of the central figures in this study were not republicans in a strict sense; but I shall try to show in chapter 8 that their representation of Cromwell retained something of the imaginative appeal of more radical republicanism. In religious terms, most republicans were strongly opposed to the established church, which they saw as an illegitimate buttress of absolutism, but beyond that point there was a huge divergence between near-freethinkers like Marten and Chaloner and Puritans for whom the heavenly kingdom in the end mattered more than secular freedom. 'Republicanism', then, was not a fixed entity. Nor, for that matter, was 'royalism', and these labels need always to be used in relation to particular political circumstances.

Despite these differences, republicans did share common factors. They were ready to criticize customary hierarchies in the state and the church, to see the state as a political artifact rather than a mystical body handed down in a virtually natural order. They could unite in seeing monarchy as a central obstacle to a society of open speaking and just behaviour, and in trying to offer 'the people', defined with various degrees of narrowness, freedom from old political, religious and, perhaps, economic monopolies. Just how the details were to be worked out provoked so many divisions that the republican experiment collapsed. For royalists, and many subsequent literary historians, the upshot was mere chaos, an uproarious Babel. It takes more attunement to the republican ethos to hear potential creativity in that chaos, and the voice of Babel instead in the panegyrics that greeted the king on his return. The process of discovery, of learning the full nature of liberty in the course of working for it, had an excitement that cannot be contained within the precise categories of the history of political thought. Or of religious denominations: in both secular and religious terms, the mid-century was a period of experiment, of constantly moving on to a place that could not have been foreseen from the starting-point. The letters of Sir Cheney Culpeper in the 1640s (see chapter 3 below) give a vivid sense of living in a time of sudden acceleration, when changes he might have hoped to see in the distant future suddenly seemed plausible; but they also show his own sense of living ahead of his time, of planning ahead for future generations. Milton too sometimes thought of himself as writing not for his own time but for the future.

It is no accident that this period should have seen the emergence of a poetics of the sublime, of what lies just beyond the available means of understanding.[51] It is well known that a later theorist of the sublime, Edmund Burke, paralleled courtly culture with the beautiful and republican violence with the sublime; it has not been properly recognized that in engaging with the French Revolution controversy he was also recapitulating seventeenth-century debates.[52] This is not so surprising given that Burke based much of his theory of the sublime on *Paradise Lost*, and was himself in an ambivalent relationship with the Whig tradition that had at once inherited and contained the republican legacy. The very act of situating this period historically, then, also entails bringing out its utopian dimension. A text like *Paradise Lost* engages with its time but also looks beyond it. Habermas's analysis of the 'bourgeois public sphere' recognized this dimension. For him, indeed, all communication has a built-in momentum towards an openness of dialogue that can escape the distortions of social and political inequities.[53] Once openness of communication is privileged over traditional hierarchies and mysteries of state, there are always grounds for a further critique of exclusions from the public realm.

To speak of the utopian and the universal in relation to mid-seventeenth century republicanism, however, has its difficulties. Many republicans prided themselves on a hard-nosed political 'realism' and pragmatism. Their writings often have a harsh, sardonic edge that resists an easy assimilation to contemporary political agendas. Early modern republicanism differed from modern liberalism in being concerned with civic virtue and responsibility more than with individual rights, and this emphasis made it possible to dismiss the political participation of those deemed unworthy – Milton's doubts about the English people's worthiness are a recurrent theme of this book. It can be argued that republicanism as an ideology served to justify, rather than to question, the inequalities that distort communication. Modern cultural theory is

51 As a primarily historical study, this book does not attempt to disentangle the intricacies of the sublime in contemporary literary theory. It can be said, however, that this early modern sublime needs to be distinguished from the version in postmodern theory, which involves a critique of Enlightenment models of representation, both in politics and in language: see, for example, Jean-François Lyotard, *The Postmodern Condition: A Report on Knowledge*, trans. Geoff Bennington and Brian Massumi (Minneapolis, 1984), pp. 77–9. I shall try to show how a poetics of sublimity and a politics of representation could to some extent work together in this period – though there were also tensions. See also Annabel Patterson, *Reading Between the Lines* (Madison, 1993), pp. 256–72.

52 Tom Furniss, *Edmund Burke's Aesthetic Ideology: Language, Gender, and Political Economy in Revolution* (Cambridge, 1993), pp. 19–34, argues that Burke found it very difficult to maintain a distinction between the acceptable, non-revolutionary sublime of English culture and the subversive sublime of the French Revolution; I would argue that the difficulty was inherent in the Whig relationship to English republicanism.

53 Jürgen Habermas, 'What is Universal Pragmatics?', in *Communication and the Evolution of Society* (1976; trans. Thomas McCarthy, 1991), pp. 1–68.

alert to the repressive potential of the characteristic republican language of enlightenment. Classical and early modern republicans stigmatized royalist culture as blind and barbaric, and this ideology of cultural superiority could easily be mobilized for purposes of external aggression.[54]

The English republic ran true to form in the vigour with which it opposed its allegedly unenlightened enemies. Since the days of the Athenian republic, it has been clear that a political form which is democratic and empowering for those given citizenship can be combined with harsh measures against its external and internal enemies. One of the classical republicans' major arguments for the superiority of republican government was its fitness for expansion at the expense of its neighbours. English republicanism emerged in part as a vehicle for English nationalism. Britishness emerged as an identity based on dynastic rather than constitutional factors, and it crumbled rather rapidly in the mid-century.[55] The republican regime's fierce measures against the Scots and the Irish helped to generate a royalist backlash that identified the Stuarts more firmly than ever before with the interests of those peoples.

The ideology of monarchist backwardness could also work against women's political and cultural agency. The abolition of the court closed down significant avenues for political influence and cultural practice which had been open to many women under Charles I. The speech situation of the republic was far from ideal for them. The Machiavellian ideal of *virtù* was firmly masculine and militaristic, asserting a masculine sublimity against a merely decorative beauty. The court offered a kind of public sphere for women which had no direct equivalent in the public political spaces opened up during the 1640s. Classical republics offered no franchise to women, and in reading modern historians of republicanism, one could be forgiven for gaining the impression that women were invented some time in the nineteenth century. Historians of women's writing, by contrast, have tended to emphasize the strongly royalist identities of figures like Katherine Philips, Margaret Cavendish and Aphra Behn.[56]

This study will try to take account of such critiques. It would distort early modern republicanism to turn it into a genially ecumenical movement. Yet the aspiration to a politics of open speech and dialogue was always potentially in conflict with more rigid forms of social exclusion. And it bears emphasizing how many modern critiques of republicanism are still coloured by a

---

54 The classic statement is Theodor W. Adorno and Max Horkheimer, *Dialectic of Enlightenment* (1944; trans. John Cumming, 1973). Habermas's work on the public sphere marked a qualification of this model.
55 Derek Hirst, 'The English Republic and the Meaning of Britain', *Journal of Modern History* 66 (1994), 451–86.
56 See especially Catherine Gallagher, 'Embracing the Absolute: The Politics of the Female Subject in Seventeenth-Century England', *Genders* 1 (1988), 24–39.

fusion of modern attacks on the Enlightenment with the stock themes of older royalist propaganda. Antagonistic though Ireland and Scotland seemed to the republic's leaders, they had themselves not been entirely unreceptive to republican discourse. After all, for much of the 1640s their own assemblies took decisions for themselves and they were *de facto* republics. When the English Parliament triumphed in its own civil war, however, the balance of power shifted and Scotland and Ireland rallied behind the Stuart dynasty, which became associated with their national independence. Yet it was the most outspoken of all the English republicans, Henry Marten, who pleaded for Irish independence and toleration of Catholics; and the most eminent of Scots poets, George Buchanan, who helped to inspire the English literary revolution. The republican vanguard's proposal for a national union with the Dutch is a reminder that ideological affiliations could cut across national ones. To them, an engrafting of Dutch republican culture was as necessary for England as English republican culture was for Ireland. One of the major republican criticisms of Cromwell's Protectorate was his expansionist foreign policy in the West Indies.

As for the question of communication for women in a republican order, it is certainly helpful to avoid a simple narrative in which political progressivism runs on all fronts. The role of women in literary culture has been highly uneven at different periods, rather than a continuous progress. The same, of course, is true of republicanism, and the mechanisms of exclusion from the national memory have been not dissimilar. Where both forms of exclusion operate, the picture may become especially distorted. One of the leading women writers of the mid-seventeenth century was Lucy Hutchinson, who has attracted far less interest in recent years than her royalist contemporaries, and whose life history, beyond the light cast by her own writings, remains in the shadows of so much republican culture. Hutchinson would have played a larger part in this book as originally conceived, but the bulk of material will demand a separate book. Given the obscurity in which so many male republicans still languish, we can expect further evidence of the agency of female republicans to come to light. Women, after all, played a particularly active role in the radical sects which were most sympathetic to republicanism. Similar complaints to those which had been heard in the 1630s, against the huge influence of the wives of courtiers, were levelled in the 1650s against the religious and political enthusiasm of the wives of such figures as Oliver St John and Robert Overton. The analysis of *Paradise Lost* in the final chapter will try to show that the questions of speech and inequality trouble the entire text, in a way that is not always apparent in studies more specifically focussed on Milton and gender.

Much remains to be discovered about mid-century republicanism; I hope that the present study will help to stimulate new areas of inquiry. In 1650

Marchamont Nedham tried to win over his readers to the Commonwealth by appealing to their sense of adventure: 'One, two, or three yeers setlement would yield an infallible experiment'.[57] The Commonwealth itself fell far short of the aspirations of the more radical republicans, and did not achieve even the three continued years that Nedham called for. Yet that spirit of experiment informed some of the best prose and verse of the mid-century, and has left traces that are open to recovery despite repeated acts of oblivion.

57 *Mercurius Politicus* no. 1, 6–13 June 1650, E603.6, p. 10.

Lucan and the poetry of civil war

Politics and poetry in the *Pharsalia*

In July 1642, England stood on the brink of civil war. The king had withdrawn from London and there had been a long war of 'paper bullets', opposing political manifestoes, with each side accusing the other of subverting the constitution. One of the leading Parliamentarians, Bulstrode Whitelocke, rose in the House of Commons to warn of the dangers ahead. He quoted from the beginning of Lucan's *Pharsalia*:

> Bella per Emathios plus quam civilia campos,
> Iusque datum sceleri canimus, populumque potentem
> In sua victrici conversum viscera dextra[.]
> Warres more then civill on Æmathian plaines
> We sing: rage licens'd; where great Rome distaines
> In her owne bowels her victorious swords[.] (May, sig. A1r)[1]

This was one of the most celebrated passages of classical poetry. The first book of Lucan's epic of the Roman civil wars offered a gory flashback to the carnage and savagery of the civil tumults in Rome under Marius and Sulla, only to prepare the way for a narrative of an even more gory conflict. Whitelocke's quotation could, then, be taken as a bid for peace and reconciliation. Undoubtedly it served as a warning. The dangers of civil war had been a recurrent theme of Elizabethan and Jacobean literature, and continued in the 1630s to preoccupy court poetry, which contrasted England's peace with the devastation of the Thirty Years' War on the Continent.

Whitelocke's quotation, however, was double-edged. He went on to

---

1 [Bulstrode Whitelocke], *Memorials of the English Affairs* (1682; w1986), p. 58, citing Lucan, *Pharsalia*, i.2–3. Citations unless otherwise stated are from the Loeb edition of *Lucan*, trans. J. D. Duff (Cambridge, Mass., and London, 1928), and from *Lucan's Pharsalia*, second edition, trans. Thomas May (1631; 16888); this 'corrected' edition, however, introduces some errors, and I read 'distaines' (sheathes) from the 1627 edition, 16887. May's translation is given as the version best known to seventeenth-century readers, but in its attempts at literal fidelity it fails to do justice to Lucan's flair and wit. Of several recent translations, I would particularly recommend that by Jane Wilson Joyce (Ithaca and London, 1993).

declare that he did not support a tame resignation of their lives and liberties into the hands of their adversaries. While keeping the possibility of peace open, they must prepare for a just and necessary defence. Early in the war, Lucan was invoked in a similar context in a treatise dedicated to a leading Parliamentarian nobleman, the earl of Northumberland. The author urged the king to remedy evils by returning to Parliament and 'sheathing your sword in the scabbard ordeined for it, not in the Bowels of your owne deare People'. And he protested that 'this Bellum plusquam ciuile wch your party wageth is another Weight wch lieth heavy on all vertuous, & religious Soules'. As in Lucan, blame for the civil war was laid on high-flying monarchists who ruthlessly overrode constitutional precedent.[2] Around the same time, Sir William Waller wrote in a much-cited letter to his royalist adversary, Sir Ralph Hopton: 'That great God which is the searcher of my heart, knowes, with what a sad sence I goe upon this service, and with what a perfect hatred I detest this warr without an Enemie'.[3] Up to a point, this letter bears out the point made by so many revisionist historians, that the protagonists in the Civil War took up arms only with extreme reluctance. What has not been noticed by modern readers is that Waller is here quoting from the first book of the *Pharsalia*, where a panicking woman prophesies disaster and denounces 'bellum . . . sine hoste', a war without an enemy (i.682). As with the Whitelocke reference, one might expect the implication to be the need for a peaceful settlement. But in fact the context is one in which Waller refuses further negotiation; his sentence continues: 'but I looke upon it as Opus Domini, which is enough to silence all passion in mee. . . Wee are both upon the stage, and must act those parts, that are assigned us in this Tragedy.'[4]

If we are to understand the mentality of those who took up arms in the Parliamentary cause, some of whom were to become committed republicans, it is important to pay attention to texts which placed immediate political actions in a longer historical and imaginative perspective. Lucan was the central poet of the republican imagination, and his traces can be found again and again amongst leading Parliamentarians. Yet he has disappeared from sight in much modern literary history. We are constantly told of the importance for early modern poetry of the classical heritage as embodied in the poetry of Horace

2 'Regicola, Publicola', Alnwick Castle MS 538 22/3, unpaginated; cited by permission of His Grace the Duke of Northumberland.

3 Waller to Sir Ralph Hopton, 16 June 1643, facsimile reproduced in Mary Coate, *Cornwall in the Great Civil War and Interregnum 1642–1660* (1933; second edition, Truro, 1963), facing p. 77. The quotation (unattributed) gives its title to Richard Ollard's *This War Without an Enemy: A History of the English Civil Wars* (1976).

4 Waller believed that the English excelled all other nations, and notably the French, in writing tragedy, and there may have been a political dimension in his celebrating this truth-telling quality: Hartlib's 'Ephemerides', 1640, *HP*, 30/4/40A.

and Virgil, both of whom, with whatever subtle qualifications and sub-texts, ultimately celebrated the reign of Augustus. The dust jacket of the current Loeb edition still feels it necessary to apologize: Lucan's 'weighty verse, powerful rhetoric, sour satire, pungent sayings, and belief in a Cause have led readers from the middle ages to quite modern times to over-estimate him'. Reprehensible as such qualities may appear to a certain form of philological purism, they were calculated to fire the early modern period with enthusiasm. Lucan's reception was indeed more troubled than Virgil's precisely because his poetry was a frontal challenge to the norms of courtly writing; but he had his admirers, especially those who had other reasons for disaffection with the court. Samuel Hartlib, a friend of Sir William Waller and of many leading Parliamentarians, recorded in 1640 the opinion of a member of his circle that 'Lucan herin [i.e. in eloquence] hase shewen a Master-peece and should not bee thus slighted as hee is by ordinary Criticks'.[5] A reading of the *Pharsalia* can help us to understand why for Whitelocke and his allies, a civil war was a great evil but failure to fight in a civil war would be even worse. A poem charged with paradox, the *Pharsalia* at once denounces civil war and incites it.

Let us return to the passage cited by Whitelocke. Lucan's epic is sometimes entitled *De Bello Civili*, *The Civil War*, but already in his first line Lucan characteristically pushes beyond conventional expectations: these wars will be more than civil. The simplest meaning is that they also break family loyalties, Pompey and Caesar being kinsmen; and there is a characteristic pun on the sense of 'civil' as 'civilized, well-ordered'. The 'plus quam' also takes on wider connotations. The poet sings not just of a single civil war but of wars. He looks back to earlier conflicts, and forward to an ongoing struggle between the forces of liberty and empire, a struggle in which the writing, and reading, of his poem is involved. War is the traditional subject-matter of epic – Virgil's 'arma virumque', arms and the man – and poetry legitimizes the imperial victor. Here the 'man' is split into rival factions, and civil war is vividly imaged as a suicide. Physical breakdown is mirrored by linguistic breakdown. 'Iusque datum sceleri' is a reminder that the meaning of words like 'justice' can be controlled by physical force. This is not because language is naturally monarchical: on the contrary, political values and meanings established by some form of consent have given way to an anarchic competition of warlords until one of them, Caesar, has enough power to arrest the process. Anarchy and monarchy are different, equally arbitrary faces of the same phenomenon. The poem will constantly remind us that now that Caesar's party has triumphed, the victor has been able to rewrite history and redefine its words. What name, asks Lucan, will be given to the crime of murdering Pompey by those for whom the murder of Caesar was a sin (viii.609–10)? The question reveals his

5 *HP*, 30/4/44B.

awareness that by and large it is the emperors who control the names and their meanings.[6]

The narrator goes on to lament the squandering of energies that should have been devoted to defeating Rome's enemies, and gives a haunting image of the devastation that has been wrought on the Italian landscape:

> But now that walles of halfe fall'n houses so
> Hang in Italian Townes, vast stones we see
> Of ruin'd walles, whole houses empty be,
> And ancient Townes are not inhabited;
> That vntill'd Italy's with weedes orespread,
> And the neglected Plowes want labouring hands . . .
> (i.24–9; May, sig. A1v)

This passage inverts the panegyrics of imperial peace to be found in Augustan court poets like Virgil and Horace, for whom the Empire marked a renewal of the landscape. Lucan returns to this subversion of imperial imagery just before the climactic battle at Pharsalia:

> One towne receiues vs all, and bondmen till
> Th'Italian lands, old houses stand alone
> Rotten, and want a man to fall vpon:
> And wanting her old Citizens there slaine,
> Rome with the dreggs of men is fill'd againe.
> This slaughter makes that Rome hereafter free
> From civill war for many yeeres shall be. (vii.402–7; May, sig. M4v)

The final sentence is heavily ironic: the nation is so degraded that it lacks the spirit needed for civil war.

Having thus inverted the conventions of Augustan poetry, the poem now makes a sudden, startling reversal. All these evils, we are told, are more than compensated for by the fact that Nero is now the ruler:

> Let dire *Pharsalia* grone with armed Hoasts,
> And glut with blood the Carthaginian Ghosts . . .
> Yet much owes Rome to civill enmity
> For making thee our Prince[.] (i.38–9, 44–5; May, sig. A2r).

In a passage modelled on Virgil's praise of Augustus in the *Georgics*, Lucan looks forward to Nero's apotheosis in heaven, and cautions him not to sit anywhere other than the centre of the celestial sphere or his weight will bring it crashing down. In fact, the poet proclaims, to him Nero is divine already: no need to invoke Apollo or Bacchus as his Muse, the emperor himself is Muse

---

6 For a stimulating reading along these lines see John Henderson, 'Lucan/The Word at War', *Ramus* 16 (1987), 122–64.

enough. This passage disappointed some republican readers. The Leveller John
Lilburne wrote that 'I should have doted on the *Roman Poet* of the *Civil Wars*,
had I not found him blessing his Fates for bringing forth a *Nero* through those
bitter Pangs and Throws.'[7] Lilburne was not, however, notably sensitive to
irony, and most seventeenth-century commentators took it that this passage
was 'meere Ironicall flattery'[8], a wicked parody of the ceremonial language of
court poetry, with imperial and divine *gravitas* or weightiness being ludi-
crously literalized in the image of Nero's divine bulk ruining the cosmos. On
that reading, Lucan's audacity is the more to be admired: it was very difficult for
the Emperor to take offence without making himself look ludicrous.

If the panegyric of Nero is comparably ironic, in Lucan irony often mingles
with tragedy. The image of cosmic dissolution is immediately taken up in the
poet's analysis of the causes of the civil war. Rome, he declares, collapsed of its
own weight; it had become too huge to stand any longer. Rome's fall conjures
up images of the cosmos's reversion to chaos at the end of time. Lucan argues
that the attempt by Pompey, Crassus and Caesar to divide the Roman world
between them was doomed to failure, for as long as the sun goes round in its
endless course, those who try to share power will end up trying to seize it. The
cosmic analogies here are characteristically disorienting. First the narrator
has imagined the cosmos collapsing under Nero's weight, then he uses its final
collapse to image Rome's instability, then he contrasts its permanence with
the instability of the republic. Within a few hundred lines we will be told that
the sun hid its face and the earth stopped on its axis when Caesar advanced on
Rome (i.543–53). Where imperial poetry aimed to assert a natural harmony
between the state and the cosmos, here tenor and vehicle are dizzyingly unstable. There follows another striking oxymoron for the unstable union between
the rival warlords Pompey, Caesar and Crassus: 'concordia discors' (i.98,
'iarring concord'; May, sig. A2v).[9] Although Lucan is at this point describing
the breakdown of the republican system, he observes that such discord went
back to the very founding of Rome, when Romulus killed Remus. For Lucan,
then, there is no easy harmony between social order and cosmic order. The
state is the product of human agency, and if its original design is flawed, the
long-term consequences may be disastrous. Rome's central flaw is top-heavi-
ness, with power being concentrated first in the triumvirate and then in the
single figure of the emperor; the greater the weight at the top, the more precarious the building.

It thus becomes clear that this poem will not have an unambiguous hero; it

---

7 John Lilburne, *The Afflicted Mans Out-Cry* (1653; E711.7*), p. 5 (I owe this reference to
  Nigel Smith).   8 *Lucans Pharsalia*, trans. Sir Arthur Gorges (1614; 16884), p. 4.
9 The phrase had been used by the Augustan Horace in a more straightforward sense:
  Horace, *Epistles* 1.12.19.

is at once fiercely partisan and critically detached. The partisanship emerges in a celebrated line: 'Victrix causa deis placuit, sed victa Catoni' (i.128), 'heaven approoues/The conquering cause; the conquerde *Cato* loues' (May, sig. A3r). The obtrusive alliteration gives an impression of judicious balance, yet this only intensifies the audacity of valuing a human against the gods. For as the poem will make clear, the gods chose the less just side, and Lucan's narrator repeatedly denounces Caesar's party and champions Pompey's. It is also clear from the start, however, that this is only the lesser of two evils. The famous character-sketches of Caesar and Pompey which now follow (i.129–57) complicate our sympathies. Pompey's military ambitions were suspect, but he has now abandoned them for the sake of easy popularity: 'plausuque sui gaudere theatri', 'his Theaters loud shout/Was his delight' (i.133; May, sig. A3r). Besides alluding to the theatre that Pompey had constructed, the phrase conveys an image of Pompey as a being of surfaces, acting out his own fantasies, and this impression is reinforced by the words: 'Stat magni nominis umbra', 'And stood the shadow of a glorious name' (i.135; May, sig. A3r). This is a characteristic play on words: Lucan consistently describes Pompey by the title he had been awarded by the bloody dictator Sulla, 'Magnus'. As the poem continues, our sense of just what greatness consists in will become complicated; at this point Pompey has lost his older greatness without finding a new, inner greatness in the service of liberty. He is compared to an old oak whose roots have rotted to instability: again, an image from the natural world which might be expected to connote stability conveys the reverse. Meanwhile, Caesar, while lacking a traditional 'nomen' (i.144), has the 'virtus' or violent energy required to rush into the Roman power vacuum; Lucan compares him to lightning, a mysterious force which is never contained in a single place. The image makes him merely destructive, and there can be no question of favouring his cause as just, but Lucan has made his Pompey more of an anti-hero than a conventional epic hero. Cato himself joins in the war mainly to prevent Pompey from becoming as bad a tyrant as Caesar, and is aware that historical conditions make possible the recovery of no more than the shadow of freedom (ii.303). The narrator proceeds to denounce even Cato as motivated by an excessive desire for civil war (ii.325).

Lucan was indeed so disrespectful to epic convention that he was often criticized for being more of a historian than a poet. Behind that charge, however, lay an unease with the poem's politics.[10] If Lucan champions history, it is because of his violent resistance to the myths in which Augustan poets had clothed the triumph of the imperial dynasty. Lucan's is a sharply demystifying poetry, and after his sketch of his protagonists he proceeds to set their

---

10 Gerald M. MacLean, *Time's Witness: Historical Representation in English Poetry, 1603–1660* (Madison and London, 1990), pp. 26ff, 34.

qualities in a larger social context, analyzing the breakdown of civic virtue in Rome (i.158–82). He lays heavy blame on the quest for excessive wealth, including the enlargement of agrarian estates and their sale to foreign owners (i.160–70). The 'greatness' of Pompey and Caesar is thus a reflection of a nation's moral degeneration. The first book continues with a shameful chronicle of defeatism. Caesar's advance over the Rubicon and towards Rome is greeted by panic and despair; Pompey flees the city; and the book ends with a series of grim prophetic visions of the defeat of the republican cause. The scholar Figulus warns that:

> it bootes vs not to craue
> A peace: with peace a master [domino] we shall haue.
> Draw out the series of thy misery,
> O Rome, to longer yeares, now onely free
> From [i.e. because of, during] civill warre. (i.669–73; May, sig. B3r)

'Dominus' is for Lucan a loathsome word, signifying the decline from citizenship to subjection, to being subordinate to the will of a single person. Peace, the normal hoped-for outcome of an epic poem, is here ironically revealed as even worse than the civil war that preceded it.

Civil war, then, emerges from the poem as a disaster, and yet again and again these terrors are invoked only in order to make the point that the imperial peace is even worse. Terrible as the war was, the narrator reproaches the republicans for having failed to fight it better, and thus blighted the lives of posterity. He looks back disconsolately to a moment when Pompey's scruples made him hold back from victory: had he won, Rome might have been 'libera regum', 'free of kings' (vi.301; perhaps from political caution, May, K7r, omits 'of kings'). After the defeat at Pharsalia, the narrator laments:

> These swords subdue all ages that shall serue.
> Alas what could posterity deserue
> To be in thraldome borne? fought we with feare?
> Spar'd we our throates? the punishment we beare
> Of others flight. To vs, that since doe liue,
> Fates should giue war, if they a tyrant giue. (vii.641–6; May, sigs. M8r–v)

But his generation are denied an opportunity to fight the old battles anew. Liberty has withdrawn beyond the Rhine, never to return (vii.433).

Lucan projects this sense of an irreversibly lost historical opportunity back on to Pompey's contemporaries: they lament that they were not born in the age of real heroism, of the Punic Wars (ii.45–6). The poem has a recessive structure, with the real liberty for which it mourns receding into the past. Cato, the most unequivocally virtuous hero of the poem, has no illusions about Pompey. There may be a tinge of impatient irony in Lucan's exaggerated presentation of Cato's own virtues. He belongs to a generation for whom the values of the old republic are so remote that however much they might hate the present, it was hard to think of recovering the past without a certain nervous embarrassment.[11] The more devastating the picture of the calamitous effects of the loss of liberty, the harder it was to believe that a single individual could somehow transcend that process, could recover a pure republican language from the debased language of transactions at the imperial court.

One of the poem's crucial moments – often recalled during the English Civil War – is Caesar's raid on the state treasury, a classic instance of the subordination of the common good to personal will: 'Rome then first then *Caesar* poorer was' (iii.168; May, sig. D6v). When the tribune Metellus tries to take a stand, a colleague counsels against resistance on the paradoxical ground that liberty can only be preserved by losing it; even the shadow is better than nothing:

> The freedome of men subjugated dyes,
> By freedomes selfe (quoth he) whose shadow thou
> Shalt keepe, if all his proud commands thou doo. (iii.145–7; May, sig. D6v)

Lucan is writing at the end of a long series of such compromises, trading in the substance of liberty for residual shadows. The Roman republic is the last vestige of republicanism throughout the ancient world, so that in extinguishing it Caesar is suppressing 'The worlds last liberty' (vii.579–81; May, sig. M7v). Opposition slowly becomes stifled into silence (v.31); kings have even stopped the mouths of the gods by closing down oracles (v.114). The grisly scene in which the witch Erictho tries to prophesy the future by briefly reanimating a recently dead corpse (vi.750ff) glances at Lucan's own scepticism about the possibility of recovering past voices. However much he may dream of reviving the rhetorical world of Cicero and Brutus, republican rhetoric in his own day seems destined to remain impotent.

In fact, while the poem makes the conventional epic claims for its own immortality, it is shot through with anxiety that true republican voices will be drowned out by the pompous mechanisms of imperial praise. In reciting lines from his own poem while he was dying – a moment illustrated on the title-page of May's translation (figure 2) – Lucan enacted the process by which republican poetry was suppressed by imperial power. The gesture's self-consciousness is indicated by the ways in which it is anticipated in the poem. The most poignant moment is the burial of Pompey's headless corpse on a bleak shore, with fire borrowed from a neighbouring pyre, and a four-word epitaph scrawled with a charred stick, his name inscribed so low that strangers have to stoop to read it (viii.793). The name is inscribed by Cremutius Cordus, an echo of the Cordus

---

11 On this point see W. R. Johnson, *Momentary Monsters: Lucan and his Heroes* (Ithaca and London, 1987), pp. 96ff.

whose history of the Roman civil wars had been burned on Tiberius's orders (an incident dramatized for the early modern period in Jonson's *Sejanus*).[12] Lucan may have drawn on now-lost books from Livy's history of Rome, a work which Augustus had tolerated even though its cult of liberty had republican implications; but it was no longer possible to undertake such a project in Lucan's day. He contrasts Cordus's fate with the temple built to the cruel tyrant Caesar in Rome (viii.835) and the magnificent pyramids of which the Egyptian kings are unworthy (viii.695). Pompey's son threatens to exhume the kings from their pyramids and send them down the Nile (ix.155). Though Cato restrains this political vandalism, the narrator himself later imagines an alternative future in which liberty has been recovered, and the tomb of that madman Alexander the Great, the image of monarchical futility, is preserved only for people to mock him (x.20).

Yet even that alternative future is mere wishful thinking, expressed in a past conditional tense ('libertas . . . si redderet', x.25). For the dynasties have in fact won out. Pompey's true refuge must be in the hearts of the virtuous republicans Cato and Brutus (ix.17–18). The poem enacts a gradual process of sublimation, in which the spirit of liberty becomes dissociated from physical embodiments. The meeting of the senators who have fled Rome is truer to the spirit of the republic than the coerced assembly held by Caesar in Rome (v.17ff). Caesar malevolently refuses to bury the republican dead, but the narrator declares that his spite is ultimately in vain, for their spirits will ascend to the heavens and Caesar will soar no higher. Though the dead may be denied a pyre, in the end all things will be consumed by fire. And those who lack a funeral urn are covered by the sky ('caelo tegitur, qui non habet urnam', vii. 819). Pompey's burial-place is in one sense universal, reaching as far as the Roman name (viii.795ff). It is in fact only in his death that his full greatness is released. Although the senate insist that they are not Pompey's party (v.13), as long as the battle is one between two great warlords, private interests will inevitably corrupt the public good. It is only when Pompey leaves the battlefield at Pharsalia that the cause fully transcends his own interests:

> The battels greatest part fought not for thee:
> Nor shall the honour'd name of *Pompey* be
> Wars quarrell now; the foes that still [i.e. always] will be
> 'Mongst vs, are *Caesar*, and Romes liberty:
> And twill appeare more plaine after thy flight
> Thy dying Senate for themselues did fight. (vii.693–7; May, sig. N1r)

After Pompey's death, the whole party is the party of freedom (ix.29–30), their goal being never to let any Caesar reign in peace (ix.90). Cato rebukes

---

12 Blair Worden, 'Ben Jonson among the Historians', in Kevin Sharpe and Peter Lake (eds.), *Culture and Politics in Early Stuart England* (1994), pp. 67–90.

the troops who want to give up now that Pompey is dead: if they were fighting only for Pompey, not for the cause, they were really defending tyranny (ix.257).

As the poem becomes more concerned with the cause in its purest form, its focus shifts towards Cato as the last great representative of the pure republican tradition. Where Virgil describes Aeneas as 'pius', alluding to his respect for tradition, Cato's 'virtus' is more rational and impersonal, implying a transcendence of the merely local.[13] He is given a powerful speech in which he declares that God is not to be found in particular shrines; all men partake of the divine (ix.573ff). In contrast, imperial architecture is shown as growing steadily more fixed and monumental. The reception given for Caesar by Cleopatra demonstrates a kind of oriental luxury which is not yet known at Rome – but will be introduced by the emperors (x.111–2).

These counterpointed themes of imperial monumentality and republican sublimity are concentrated in the remarkable passage where Caesar visits the ruins of Troy. The buildings are a reminder that no regal monument, however magnificent, will endure for ever; if no stone in this place is without a name (ix.973) it is because of Homer's poetic gifts. Caesar himself is only partially aware of this. He walks over the body of Hector without realizing it, and the guide has to rebuke him for his insensitivity. He proceeds to invoke the spirit of Aeneas, and offers to rebuild Troy. The man who has devoted himself to destroying Rome's liberties can identify himself with its founder. It is at this charged moment, which recalls Virgil's praise of Caesar, that the narrator himself directly addresses him:

> Oh great, and sacred worke of Poesy,
> That freest from fate, and giv'st eternity
> To mortall wights; but, *Caesar*, envy not
> Their living names, if Roman muses ought
> May promise thee, while *Homer's* honoured,
> By future times shall thou, and I be read;
> No age shall vs with darke oblivion staine,
> But our Pharsalia ever shall remaine. (ix.980–6; May, sig. R4v)

Normally a poet's claim of immortality is a promise, but in the light of Lucan's savage attacks on Caesar, here it is a threat. That 'nostra', 'our', gives poet and emperor a very ironic kind of equality: if Lucan does gain his poetic fame it will be because he has had the opportunity of narrating the eclipse of the political values he holds most dear.

---

13 Frederick M. Ahl, *Lucan: An Introduction* (Ithaca and London, 1976), pp. 276–7. We may contrast the 'militiae pietas' of Caesar's devotees, which is specifically directed to the service of an individual usurping the common cause: 'virtus' is a great crime in a civil war (iv.499, vi.147–8, Ahl, *Lucan*, pp. 118–19).

The *Pharsalia*, then, is a dark poem, offering the stark alternatives of dehumanizing civil war or tyrannical peace. It is an anti-epic, vandalizing the conventions of Augustan imperial art. And yet its overall effect is much more than negative. As has been seen, the experience of reading the poem is a destabilizing one, as the poet constantly disrupts our expectations; and the poem displays a manic delight in its own iconoclastic creativity, its radical generic revisions. It is, after all, a young man's epic: Lucan was only twenty-six at his death. This perhaps helps to account for his relentless over-insistence; but the relentlessness does have a certain exuberance. For all the gloom expressed in the poem, Lucan himself, the early modern period believed, had not himself renounced hope of some form of political action: he committed suicide after the discovery of his involvement in an attempt to overthrow the emperor. Even if hopes of practical resistance were limited – as Lucan's failed conspiracy confirmed – the poet could damage the icons of imperial rule. His subject-matter, the civil wars from Caesar's crossing the Rubicon down to his arrival in Egypt, parallels Caesar's own account in his own *De Bello Civili*, but systematically undermines Caesar's claims to moral authority. In blackening the founder of the Augustan dynasty, the epic also of course systematically undermines Virgil.

Where Virgil and Horace liked to sing of concord, Lucan describes both the Roman state and the cosmos as a 'discors/Machina' (i.79–80), an unstable, discordant mechanism, epitomized in the 'concordia discors' (i.98) of the triumvirate. His own poem enacts that kind of discord, distrustful of verbal music and rhetorical symmetry which his own tortured, elliptical style implicitly indicts as specious and dishonest. He has found a way of emulating Virgil without bowing to his authority, and there is a kind of grim vitality in the midst of the poem's darkness.[14] Even if the imperial monuments appear to be lasting and the republican legacy is reduced to a scrawled message in charcoal, Lucan's constantly shifting, irreverent, unmonumental poem may be able to scribble an alternative in the very margins of the imperial culture on which it depends. Thus Lucan can say to the defeated party at Pharsalia:

> Greatest of men, whose fates through the earth extend,
> Whom all the gods haue leasure to attend;
> These acts of yours to all posterity
> Whether their owne great fame shall signifie,
> Or that these lines of mine haue profited
> Your mighty names; these wars, when they are read,
> Shall stir th'affections of the readers minde,
> Making his wishes, and vaine feares inclin'd

---

14 For a good characterization see Colin Burrow, *Epic Romance: Homer to Virgil* (Oxford, 1993), p. 183.

As to a thing to come, not past, and guide
The hearts of all to favour *Pompey's* side.(vii.207–13; May, sig. M1v)

A sense of irrecoverable loss, a shift from hope in political action to an inter-nalization of virtue, moments of intensely partisan narratorial intrusion – these are characteristics of *Paradise Lost* as well as the *Pharsalia*. In Milton's case, they have been ascribed to his despair at the collapse of his cause after 1660. That, I shall try to show later, is only partially true. Behind such claims there seems to be an unexamined assumption: poetry that is politically radical will be positive and optimistic. That assumption will survive only a brief acquaintance with the poetry, say, of Shelley – a great admirer of Lucan. For those committed to political change, much of past history will be perceived as tragic; without such a perception, there would be little motivation for change. The almost mechanical repetition of injustice may at the same time give history an aspect of gruesome, black comedy – which can again be seen both in Lucan and in the characteristic wit of Milton and other republicans. As will emerge in a study of the reading of Lucan in the seventeenth century, such humour as the times seemed to offer was often decidedly black. English admirers of the Roman republic were never particularly sanguine about the political future.

Trojan horses: Lucan, May, and the emergence of republican literary culture, 1614–1629

'A pretty conceit of the Authors for those that shall read his booke'. Thus did Sir Arthur Gorges gloss Lucan's address to Pompey's side in his 1614 transla-tion of the *Pharsalia*.[15] His marginal note presents the book as a space in which seventeenth-century readers can become involved in a universal strug-gle between absolutist and republican values. And that is how some readers responded. John Aubrey believed that May's 'translation of *Lucans* excellent Poeme made him in love wth ye Republique – wch Tang [*Odorem*] stuck by him'.[16] The reception of the *Pharsalia* is a classic example of a phenomenon repeatedly denounced by Thomas Hobbes. There was 'never any thing so deerly bought,' he complained, 'as these Western parts have bought the learn-ing of the Greek and Latine tongues . . . the *Universities* have been to this nation, as the wooden horse was to the Trojans'.[17] He argued that:

as to Rebellion in particular against Monarchy; one of the most frequent causes of it, is the Reading of the books of Policy, and Histories of the antient Greeks, and

15 *Lucans Pharsalia*, trans. Gorges, p. 270.   16 Bodleian MS Aubrey 8, fol. 27r; *ABL*, II, 56.
17 Thomas Hobbes, *Leviathan*, II.21; ed. C. B. Macpherson (Harmondsworth, 1968), p. 268;
   Behemoth, or The Long Parliament, ed. Ferdinand Tönnies (1889; reprint, ed. Stephen
   Holmes, Chicago and London, 1990), p. 40.

Romans; from which, young men, and all others that are unprovided of the Antidote of solid Reason, receiving a strong, and delightfull impression, of the great exploits of warre, atchieved by the Conductors of their Armies, receive withall a pleasing Idea, of all they have done besides; and imagine their great prosperity, not to have proceeded from the æmulation of particular men, but from the vertue of their popular forme of government.[18]

Hobbes is ready to allow that one may derive exemplary moral lessons from classical texts: they provide patterns of individual heroism – as, for example, did Lucan's Cato for that strong monarchist Dante. Where the rebels go wrong is in moving from the moral to the political: they assume that the virtues they admire will mostly be found under particular kinds of political structure. This makes them prefer rhetorical partiality to disinterested impartiality. Lucan was a prime offender in this respect: '*Lucan* shews himself openly in the *Pompeyan* Faction, inveighing against *Caesar* throughout his Poem, like *Cicero* against *Cataline* [*sic*] or *Marc Antony*, and is therefore justly reckon'd by *Quintilian* as a Rhetorician rather than a Poet'.[19] Hobbes went so far as to declare that ''tis a very great fault in a Poet to speak evil of any man in their Writings Historical'; Tacitus and other writers were wrong to censure the Roman emperors who had no chance of answering their charges (II, 71).

Hobbes clearly responded to Lucan's iconoclastic imagination, but it was in terms of the deepest alarm. He acknowledged that 'fancy' was an important element in poetry, and that Lucan excelled in it; but his discussion of fancy was heavily informed by a sense of its political dangers. It is associated for Hobbes with 'Sublimity . . . that Poetical Fury which the Readers for the most part call for', and this leads them to 'give to it alone the name of Wit' and to disdain reason and judgement (II, 70). Lucan's fancy, Hobbes argues, calls attention to the poet at the expense of his subject-matter; it 'is fitter for a Rhetorician than a Poet, and rebelleth often against Discretion' (II, 72). Here again Hobbes's suspicion of rhetoric reveals its political charge. It is interesting that his example of this rebellious wit is the celebrated 'Victrix causa deis placuit, sed victa Catoni' (i.128). Hobbes is appalled both by the line's political partiality and by its religious irreverence. Though himself hardly orthodox in his religious outlook, he found political implications in speaking 'disgracefully to the Depression of the Gods', in contrast with Homer who always made Jupiter impartial (II, 73). Though Hobbes was writing long after the Restoration, when the monarchist cause had triumphed, he was still anxious about the power of a poem like Lucan's to resist such triumphs, to unsettle the regime's ideological stability and unleash a heterodox imagination.

18 Hobbes, *Leviathan*, II, 29, Macpherson, p. 369.
19 Hobbes, preface to *Homer's Odysseys* (1675; H2556), in J. E. Spingarn (ed.), *Critical Essays of the Seventeenth Century*, 3 vols. (Oxford, 1908), II, 73.

An admiration for Lucan did not in itself imply republican sympathies. His more orthodox and humourless readers could persuade themselves that the invocation to Nero was the expression of a genuine monarchism. And it was found possible to do with Lucan what Hobbes felt to be almost imposs- ible: to treat his characters in apolitical terms without relating their virtues to specific institutions. The tendency of humanist literary scholarship, however, was to set literary texts in sharply specific political contexts, and it became ever harder to ignore Lucan's hostility to monarchical rule. Whereas Virgil's imperial epic centres on one central figure, Aeneas, who functions as a type of Augustus, Lucan's republican epic is suspicious of locating political salvation in an individual. As in *Paradise Lost*, the most obvious hero is also the villain. Caesar is a single-minded and unified figure because he subordinates the interest of the state to his own private interest (iii.108, 168). There is undoubt- edly an ambivalent fascination with Caesar's heroic energy, but the poem questions the nature of true heroism: its repeated gory invocations of blood- shed lead to doubts about whether the war was worth fighting. Pompey, his chief opponent, is almost an anti-hero, liable to disastrous lapses of judge- ment such as his proposal after the defeat at Pharsalia to ally with the Parthians (viii.262ff). Here again an ideological point is at issue. Pompey is less dramatic as a character precisely to the degree that he is more of a republi- can: the Parthian debate is presented partly to show Pompey allowing himself to be outvoted (viii.455). Lucan brings the tension between individual heroism and collective decisions to its height by demonstrating that each may be flawed, especially in these final days of the republic. In fact in agreeing to go to Egypt instead of enlisting the Parthians, Pompey goes to his death. Before the battle that gives the poem its traditional name, Pompey suggests that a less bloody way of proceeding could be found, but he is urged on by Cicero, the voice of republican integrity. In a double irony, Pompey proves himself as a hero in a republican mould by obeying the will of the Senate rather than fol- lowing his personal impulses, but in doing so unleashes horrifying bloodshed and dooms himself. As has been seen, Lucan emphasizes after Pompey's death the distinction between a struggle for Pompey and a struggle for liberty.[20] His analysis, contrary to Hobbes's, is that the loss of a 'popular forme of govern- ment' doomed Rome, whatever might have been expected from 'the æmula- tion of particular men'.

Lucan's poem, then, encouraged its readers to relate individual charac- ters to broader social and political processes. The first book of the *Pharsalia* was in fact much cited by two of the leading seventeenth-century theorists

20 Lucan thus combats a Roman mode of historical revisionism, inaugurated by Augustus himself, which cast the Empire's enemies as 'Pompeiani', motivated by personal rather than ideological factors: Ahl, *Lucan*, p. 56.

of republicanism, James Harrington and Algernon Sidney.[21] In Harrington's case, his allusions to Lucan can be linked with his explicit rejection of Hobbes's anti-republican mode of reading: for Harrington, it was indeed institutions rather than men that created virtue. As will be seen in more detail in chapter 8, Harrington could find support in Lucan's anti-Augustanism for a republican theory of history. Virgil's eclogues allegorized the agrarian problems of the late Roman republic which the Empire, unable to solve, only made worse. Once the aristocracy began to consolidate their power by military means, they became more and more dependent on armed defenders. Under the Empire this became a hereditary caste and increasingly unreliable; the emperors instead sought aid from the Goths, who eventually took over power themselves.[22] Though Lucan had not given an extensive analysis of Roman social and economic structures, his poem, as summarised by May, certainly showed that Rome 'could neither retaine her freedom without great troubles, nor fall into a *Monarchy* but most heavy and distastfull' (sig. A4v). For Harrington, the central error was the degree of structural inequality in the state. Rome had taken a wrong turning at an early stage; and its effects had gradually become more and more destructive. Harrington dated the period narrated by Lucan, Caesar's rise to supreme power, as a crucial turning-point in world history. The first period ended

> with the liberty of *Rome*, which was the course or *Empire*, as I may call it, of *antient prudence*, first discovered unto mankind by God himself, in the fabrick of the *Common-wealth* of *Israel*, and afterward picked out of his footsteps in nature, and unanimously followed by the *Greeks* and *Romans*. The other beginning with the Arms of *Caesar*; which extinguishing liberty were the Transition of *ancient* into *modern prudence*, introduced by those inundations of *Huns, Goths, Vandalls, Lombards, Saxons*, which breaking the *Roman Empire*, deformed the whole face of the world, with those ill features of Government, which at this time are become far worse in these Western parts...[23]

The long-term effects of the Roman civil wars, then, had been incalculably great, leaving their mark on every level, from landholdings to language. The pattern of the subordination of public to private had been perpetuated by the monarchies that succeeded after the barbarian invasions. Citizens became subjects, forced to revere their king as a father rather than debating with him

---

21 Algernon Sidney, *Discourses Concerning Government*, ed. Thomas G. West (Indianapolis, 1990), *passim*. Not all the citations given as such in the index are in fact from Lucan; but the powerful denunciation of absolutist peace (II, 26, p. 260) seems to echo *Pharsalia*, i.24ff.

22 'A Note upon the Foregoing Eclogues', *HPW*, pp. 579–81.

23 *James Harrington's 'Oceana'*, ed. S. B. Liljegren (Lund and Heidelberg, 1924), p. 12; *HPW*, p. 161.

as an equal. The shift from ancient to modern prudence 'overwhelmed *ancient Languages, Learning, Prudence, Manners, Cities, changing* the Names of Rivers, Countries, Seas, Mountains and Men; *Camillus, Caesar and Pompey*, being come to *Edmund, Richard, and Geoffrey*'.[24] Humanists were ruefully aware that their mother tongues were products of the 'barbarism' they deplored. With a strong sense of building up to a climax, Milton wrote that the fall of the Empire led to the decay of 'Learning, Valour, Eloquence, History, Civility, and eev'n Language it self' (*History of Britain, MPW*, V.1.127). In their early phases those languages might at least have had a pristine simplicity; but they had steadily absorbed the vainglorious titles of the imperial and ecclesiastical hierarchies, in a process parallel to the Roman decline charted by Lucan. He records Caesar's manipulation of traditional political offices until they become empty names:

> For all those words then their beginning had,
> With which ere since our Emperours we claw.(v.385; May, sig. H6v)

May glosses: 'Then beganne all those names of flattery, which they afterward vsed to their Emperours, as *Diuus*, Ever *Augustus*, Father of his countrey, Founder of peace, Lord, and the like' (sig. I6r). This restriction of the good of the whole to the private interest of an individual or a few families was for Harrington characteristic of modern prudence; it was an empire of men and not of laws, while ancient prudence placed the public above the private, laws above men.

For Harrington, modern prudence had disastrous effects on religion as well as on civil life: Tiberius murdered Roman liberty at the same time as Pilate murdered Christ. The values of early Christianity had been congenial to those of the Roman regional cities which still retained some degree of political autonomy. The Christians had borrowed the word *ecclesia* from civic assemblies to describe their own democratic meetings. As the Empire grew in power, however, its hierarchical structure both corrupted and was corrupted by the organization of the church, which became a monarchy under the Pope.[25] State and church vied with each other for monopolies of religious life; when the papacy took control of the church from the Emperors, public revenues were siphoned into an unaccountable religious bureaucracy, and the public preaching of the word was confined to a mystical elite. Harrington and other republicans and radical Puritans went beyond what had become the orthodox Protestant analysis of church-state relations. On that analysis,

---

24 Harrington, *Oceana*, ed. Liljgren, p. 42; *HPW*, p. 190.
25 Mark Goldie, 'The Civil Religion of James Harrington', in Anthony Pagden (ed.),
   The Languages of Political Theory in Early-Modern Europe (Cambridge, 1987),
   pp. 197–222.

the Emperors had been the proper guardians of the church; their authority had been usurped by the Papacy, but in the sixteenth century Protestant monarchs were able to reclaim their legitimate position as heads of the church. In Foxe's immensely influential *Acts and Monuments*, and in such literary allegorizations as Spenser's *Faerie Queene*, the monarch is aligned with the true church, in the struggle against the Pope who is identified with the Antichrist of the book of Revelation. Protestantism could thus become a powerful legitimation for monarchy, and it remained so for many on both sides of the English Civil War.

But even within the Foxean paradigm there were some problems for monarchists. If kings had for so many centuries allowed themselves to become willing dupes of the papacy, and if the quest for a vainglorious monopoly of power was the governing force behind papal rule, could monarchy ever really transcend the corruptions to which it was always liable? In the mid-seventeenth century there emerged new readings of Revelation which placed the thousand-year rule of Christ on Earth in the future, rather than identifying it with the uncorrupt phase of the Empire. Kings who opposed religious reform came to be identified themselves with the Antichrist, who opposed the advent of Christ as the one true king. The ecstatic millennial republicanism which came to a climax in the 1650s seems a long way indeed from Harrington's secular voice, but it was possible to forge an alliance between millennial and Harringtonian republicanism, between religious and civil liberty. Humanist practices of reading, when applied to biblical texts, would produce a highly politicized analysis. Religious radicals looked back to an early stage of Christianity before communication had been distorted by the monopoly interests of the church. Republicans could link that ideal with their nostalgia for the classical agora. English republicanism spanned a broad range of religious opinions, from extreme Puritanism to the scepticism of May and Chaloner, but anticlericalism was a common factor.

The emergence of secular and religious republicanisms can be traced in the reception of Lucan. Indeed a prominent example of the word 'républicain' in its modern sense comes in the preface to one of the most important early modern poems to be composed in Lucan's shadow, Agrippa d'Aubigné's *Les Tragiques* (published in 1616). The preface to this work records d'Aubigné's fears that its publication would gain him 'le nom de turbulent, de republicain'. It is clear from the context that the word here implies someone who 'affectoit plus le Gouvernement Aristocraticque que Monarchique'. D'Aubigné insists that unlike these republicans he opposes only tyranny, not monarchy itself. His answer to such doubts, however, is less reassuring to monarchists than it first appears: he declares that the French monarchy in its founding principles is the best government in the world, and that after it he prefers the Polish system.[26] The Polish monarchy was elected by the aristocracy, and it was widely argued that this had also been the case with the early French monarchy.[27] For d'Aubigné, then, to be a 'républicain' is to desire a state without any kind of monarchy, while his own non-republican position involves a strictly limited, elective monarchy. It was certainly not inconsistent with taking up arms against the monarch. In the year *Les Tragiques* appeared he was involved in an aristocratic rebellion, and in an earlier poem he had contrasted himself explicitly with Lucan as one who was prepared to take up arms rather than suffering martyrdom.[28]

If we use the term 'republican' in the sense to which d'Aubigné here assigns it, we can say that there were very few republican readers of Lucan in pre-Civil-War England. But the poem did become identified with a particular kind of political grouping that, while not specifically anti-monarchical, had distinct hankerings after a severely limited monarchy which, as far as some absolutist theorists were concerned, would be in practice little better than a republic. Protestants nurtured on the Foxean tradition were ready to believe that throughout Europe the Habsburg monarchies, working in tandem with the militant Counter-Reformation, were engaged in a conspiracy to suppress political and religious liberty. It seemed that the terrible history Lucan told might repeat itself, unless the champions of liberty were better organized this time round. And there was a strong consciousness of the need for concerted international action. The favoured strategy of the absolutists, it was held, was to pick nations off one by one by undermining the king, courtiers and church-men. Lucan's English readers were alert to this danger.

D'Aubigné's *Les Tragiques* demonstrated the ways in which Lucan could be linked with a Protestant world-view. It is saturated with allusions to Lucan: the poet had in fact composed a Latin poem on the French wars made out of extracts from the *Pharsalia*, directly linking the Roman civil wars with those of his own country. At the start of *Les Tragiques* d'Aubigné boldly outdoes Lucan by identifying his Muse with Caesar at the Rubicon. Since Rome is now the centre of political as well as religious corruption, a civil war that strikes at Roman power is to be celebrated. Like Lucan, d'Aubigné mingles poetry with history, lamenting the fate of the Huguenots at the hands of their adversaries. He later composed a prose account of his times in the polemical *Histoire Universelle*, which was condemned at Paris on its publication in 1620. Where

---

26 Agrippa d'Aubigné, *Les Tragiques*, ed. Jean-Raymond Fanlo, 2 vols. (Paris, 1995), I, 5, 16 (Fanlo, unlike previous editors, takes the late manuscripts as representing the author's final revisions). Jean Céard, '"République" et "Républicain" en France au XVIᵉ siècle', in Jacques Viard (ed.), *L'Esprit républicain* (Paris, 1972), pp. 97–105, concludes that in general the term was 'vide de tout contenu positif' (p. 105).

27 David Quint, *Epic and Empire: Politics and Generic Form from Virgil to Milton* (Princeton, 1993), pp. 200–1.   28 Quint, *Epic and Empire*, p. 192.

Lucan generalizes the struggle at Pharsalia into a universal struggle between Caesarism and liberty, d'Aubigné gives the opposition a Protestant apocalyptic colouring, linking the cause of liberty with that of the persecuted truth, the wandering woman in the wilderness of the Book of Revelation. His epic therefore addresses not just French history but the universal Protestant cause. Amongst his cast of martyrs are the Englishwomen Anne Askew, Lady Jane Grey, and Queen Elizabeth I.

This international concern marked the first English translators of the *Pharsalia*. Christopher Marlowe, whose version of the first book was posthumously published, had also written a play on the French civil wars, *The Massacre at Paris*, in which the Catholic leader Guise was patterned on Lucan's Caesar.[29] The first full English version, by Sir Arthur Gorges, appeared in 1614, at a time when there were growing fears that King James I was abandoning Elizabethan policies of hostility to Catholic Spain. Spanish influence lay behind the imprisonment of Gorges's friend Sir Walter Ralegh; and in 1614 Ralegh's *History of the World*, which appeared from the same publisher[30], was called in for irreverence towards monarchy. This act of censorship recalled Lucan's chronicle of the ways in which imperial authority stifled free speaking, and in a commendatory sonnet to Gorges's translation Ralegh presented Lucan and his translator as martyrs to the cause of truth. Throughout the poem, Gorges invokes the spirit of Elizabethan militancy. Lucan was unusual amongst ancient poets in describing naval as well as land warfare, and like Ralegh in his *History*, Gorges drew frequent parallels between ancient warfare and the exploits of the English.[31] He recalls English participation in the siege of Antwerp (p. 77, see note to ii.676–7): Elizabeth had supported the young Dutch state in its struggle against the Spanish monarchy, but James was much more wary about this alignment. The Antwerp allusion would have been pleasing to the Dutch statesman and republican theorist Hugo Grotius, who visited England in the year Gorges's translation appeared, and brought out his own edition of the *Pharsalia* in the same year. He was a great admirer of Lucan, and is said always to have travelled with a copy of the *Pharsalia* in his pocket. Lucan, he declared, was a freedom-loving, aristocratic, and tyrant-hating poet; let the Dutch read it so that the more they loved the Spanish bard (he had been born at Cordoba), the more implacably they would hate

---

29 William Blissett, 'Lucan's Caesar and the Elizabethan Villain', *Studies in Philology* 53 (1956), 553–75 (565).   30 I owe this point to Anna Beer.

31 On the reading of classical texts as storehouses of military wisdom, see Lisa Jardine and Anthony Grafton, '"Studied for Action": How Gabriel Harvey Read His Livy', *Past and Present* no. 129 (1990), 30–78 (69ff); and on Lucan's reputation as a military poet see Walter Fischli, *Studien zum Fortleben der Pharsalia des M. Annaeus Lucanus* (Luzern, n. d.), pp. 47, 49.

the Spanish king.[32] Grotius exercised a great influence on English political thought, and his championship of Lucan strengthened the poem's republican colouring. We do not have to read Gorges's translation as a specifically republican gesture[33]; but it did serve as a kind of rallying cry for a common cause in a general European struggle to safeguard religious and civil liberties.

Gorges's Lucan would have found an attentive audience in the MPs who assembled in 1614 for a particularly contentious Parliament. When one MP was imprisoned for a seditious speech, the diplomat Sir Henry Wotton dismissed him as 'a young gentleman fresh from the school, who having gathered together divers Latin sentences against kings, bound them up in a long speech, and interlarded them with certain Ciceronian exclamations'. Hobbes's Trojan horse was having its effect. Wotton observed that such comments were more appropriate in 'a Senate of Venice, where the treaters are perpetual princes, than where those that speak so irreverently are so soon to return (which they should remember) to the natural capacity of subjects'.[34] Like the imagined readers of Gorges's Lucan, the MP had transported himself out of monarchical language.

The next English Lucan appeared at a time of heightened political polarization. In 1619 King James's son-in-law, Frederick V of the Palatinate, was elected King of Bohemia. The election, which shifted the European balance of power in a Protestant direction, was repudiated by the Habsburg powers. A contemporary pamphlet used extracts from the *Pharsalia* to illustrate the transformation of fortunes by which Frederick began as a militant Caesar and ended as a defeated Pompey, driven with his wife Elizabeth into life-long exile.[35] The Habsburg regime stripped the Bohemian nobility of their traditional liberties and suppressed the region's strong Protestant traditions. For Bohemia, with its traditions of limited monarchy, these events had long-term consequences as great as Pompey's defeat for Rome. Frederick's son and heir Charles Louis was so fond of the poem that he ordered his tutor to translate it.[36] There was strong pressure for James and then Charles to

---

32 Letter to Daniel Heinsius, 20 April 1614, in *Briefwisseling van Hugo Grotius*, I, ed. P. C. Molhuysen (The Hague, 1928), 307. For Grotius's influence on English republicanism, see Tuck, *passim*.

33 Burrow, *Epic Romance*, pp. 188–9, writes that in a passage where Gorges greatly expands on Lucan (pp. 332–7, cf. viii.480), he outlines an orthodox theory of good council; but the warning that '*Rome* doth Monarchie disdaine' and may therefore expel kings, glossed 'Rome euer an enemy to Monarchy' (p. 335), goes well beyond what would have been prudent at the court of James I.

34 *Life and Letters of Sir Henry Wotton*, ed. Logan Pearsall Smith, 2 vols. (Oxford, 1907), II, 37–9.

35 *Violenti imperii imago* (n. pl., 1621), pp. 12–16. The volume begins with quotations from Seneca.   36 Fischli, *Studien zum Fortleben der Pharsalia*, p. 57.

intervene in what many hoped would be a decisive apocalyptic struggle against the forces of Antichrist and of political absolutism. While religion was a decisive factor in the war propaganda, there was also in some cases a strong infusion of one of the main themes of classical republican discourse: the need for great states to allow their citizens enough independence to be able to fight for their country.[37] The agitation for a shift away from James's pacific foreign policy put pressure on existing constraints on public discussion of mysteries of state, with an escalating circulation of manuscript reports of the debates of increasingly turbulent Parliaments.

The war party got some of what they wanted – at the start of his reign Charles did declare war first against Spain and then France. The expedition to relieve French Protestants at the Ile de Rhé fulfilled a long-standing demand from militant Protestants for more decisive aid to their co-religionists on the Continent. The ageing d'Aubigné took a great interest in this development: seeing England as the only major power capable of resisting Counter-Reformation forces in the Thirty Years' War, he considered moving there, and sent to London for safe keeping a copy of his revision of the *Tragiques*.[38] At home, however, the government's intentions appeared more ambiguous. Money for the expedition was raised by a controversial forced loan, which aroused fears that Charles was using war to aggrandize his powers. And the campaigns were under the supervision of his favourite the duke of Buckingham, who was widely loathed and a poor leader.

It was into this highly charged scene that the poet and dramatist Thomas May (1595–1650) introduced his translation of Lucan in 1627. The dedications indicate that just as much as Gorges's 1614 translation, the publication of this volume was a gesture of support for an international anti-absolutist alliance. May conspicuously omitted Buckingham, whose antipathy to Lucan's disciples had been registered by one of his flatterers in 1619: 'Let *Lucan* . . . with all his lunaticke Companions go shake their eares'.[39] Instead he addressed a group of leading 'patriot' peers who had been long-term supporters of military intervention on the Continent. Book III is addressed to Edmund Sheffield, earl of Mulgrave, recalling his naval victories in 'blest *Elizaes* ne'r forgotten reigne'. Book IV is dedicated to the third earl of Essex, who had a long-standing history of alternating between Parliamentary and military service while remaining aloof from the court. Book V is addressed to Robert, earl of Lindsey, who was about to set sail with the Ile de Rhé fleet. May had to

37 Markku Peltonen, *Classical Humanism and Republicanism in English Political Thought 1570–1640* (Cambridge, 1995), pp. 225ff, 249ff, noting particularly the presence of republican language in the writings of the Puritan controversialist Thomas Scott.

38 Fanlo (ed.), *Les Tragiques*, II, 753–5.

39 A. D. B., *The Court of . . . James, the First* (1619; 1022), dedication to Buckingham and sig. A3r.

strain here to reconcile a compliment to naval prowess with this book's sardonic treatment of Caesar's scorn for the waves – though one could regard his alignment of Lindsey with Caesar as prophetic, for Lindsey alone of his dedicatees was to side with the king in the Civil War. May was on clearer ground in the dedication of Book VII, dealing with the climactic battle at Pharsalia at which

> Great *Pompey's* fortune, and the better cause
> Were all enforc'd to yeild to *Caesar's* fate[.]

This dedication goes to Sir Horatio Vere, a veteran of conflict with Spain who had fought to defend the Palatinate; his eventual failure was blamed on Buckingham's hostility. May recalls his role in the Dutch battle against the Spanish at Nieuwpoort in 1600, thus evoking a common Protestant cause against Spanish absolutism. Book VIII, which chronicles the death of Pompey, is addressed to Theophilus Clinton, earl of Lincoln, with the declaration that these

>   life-giuing lines by times to come
> Shall make that little, and vnworthy Tombe,
> That kept great *Pompey's* dust, more honor'd far
> Then the proud Temples of the Conquerer.

Book IX was dedicated to Robert Rich, earl of Warwick, who was about to depart on a privately financed raid against the Spanish treasure fleet. His vice-admiral, Sir Francis Stuart, had been the dedicatee of Farnaby's 1618 edition. If dedicatees read their books, England's Parliament and harbours were crammed with admirers of the republican poet.

The military emphasis of these dedications accorded to some degree with the royal campaign for war in 1627. But the choice of dedicatees encountered political tensions that cut across nationalistic concerns.[40] Four of the men May addressed – Lincoln, Warwick, Essex, and the earl of Devonshire, the dedicatee of the volume as a whole – had recently refused to pay the forced loan. Devonshire had a keen interest in Venetian republicanism – though his opposition to the crown on this occasion did not last long, and he was soon employing Thomas Hobbes to make collections.[41] As a measure of his alienation from royal policy, Essex turned down an invitation to lead a regiment in the Rhé expedition; in June his resistance to the forced loan led to his being deprived of the Lord Lieutenancy of his home

---

40 The Puritan Walter Yonge, who took a keen interest in political writing at this time, was scrutinizing dedications as an index of godliness: *Diary of Walter Yonge*, ed. George Roberts (1848), p. 118.

41 Tuck, p. 281; Quentin Skinner, *Reason and Rhetoric in the Philosophy of Hobbes* (Cambridge, 1996), p. 224.

county.[42] Mulgrave had strongly opposed Buckingham in the 1626 Parliament.[43] Lincoln, the most determined of all the campaigners, was in political trouble at the time the poem was entered in the Stationers' Register on 12 March 1627 for circulating a pamphlet which accused Charles of seeking to 'suppresse Parliaments' and called on the people to take action without being daunted by fear of imprisonment.[44] In giving Lincoln pride of place as the patron of Book VIII, thus making him the custodian of Pompey's spirit, May's dedication was venturing on very sensitive ground. Warwick, who is identified by May with Cato, Lucan's other surviving representative of the republican spirit (figure 1), was encountering the opposition of Buckingham who tried to prevent his naval expedition. Warwick was also a key figure in resistance to the high church party through his patronage of the Puritan preacher Hugh Peters, who was forced to leave the country later in the year. These last four peers were all to side with Parliament in the Civil War.

The language of May's introductory address to Virgil echoed the terms of his dedications:

> Thou gott'st *Augustus* loue, he *Nero's* hate;
> But twas an act more great, and high to moue
> A Princes envy, then a Princes loue.[45]

This point was brought home by an engraving of Lucan's suicide (figure 2).[46] May added a few lines to tie up the narrative that Lucan had not lived to finish, imitating the celebrated contrast between the gods' justice and Cato's:

> *But he* [Caesar] *must liue vntill his fall may prooue*
> Brutus *and* Cassius *were more iust then* Ioue. (sig. T1v)

Soon after the volume was published, the dedications were cut out, sometimes with signs of great haste and damage to other pages. Even May's presentation copy to Ben Jonson, who had contributed commendatory

42 On resistance by Essex and other peers see Richard Cust, *The Forced Loan and English Politics 1626–1628* (Oxford, 1987), pp. 102ff, 170–75, 229ff.

43 Roger Lockyer, *Buckingham: The Life and Political Career of George Villiers, First Duke of Buckingham 1592–1628* (London and New York, 1981), p. 304.

44 The pamphlet, which was circulated in manuscript, anticipated central themes of the Parliamentarian literature of 1640–42 (Cust, *The Forced Loan and English Politics*, p. 174).   45 May, *Lucan's Pharsalia*, facing frontispiece.

46 The engraving was by Frederick van Hulsen, whose other work was devoted to anti-Catholic and anti-Arminian works by George Carleton, Daniel Featley, Christopher Lever, and Michael Sparke: Margery Corbett and Michael Norton (eds.), *Engraving in England in the Sixteenth and Seventeenth Centuries, Part III: The Reign of Charles I* (Cambridge, 1964), pp. 213–15. The poet displays a certain resemblance to the earl of Essex.

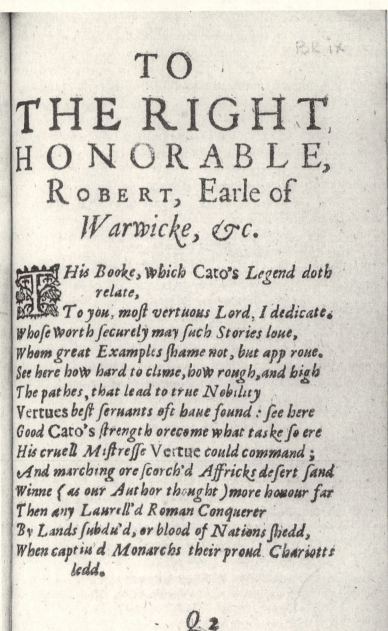

TO
THE RIGHT
HONORABLE,
ROBERT, Earle of
Warwicke, &c.

His Booke, which Cato's *Legend doth
relate,
To you, most vertuous Lord, I dedicate.
Whose worth securely may such Stories loue,
Whom great Examples shame not, but app roue.
See here how hard to clime, how rough, and high
The pathes, that lead to true Nobility
Vertues best seruants oft haue found : see here
Good* Cato's *strength orecome what taske so ere
His cruell Mistresse* Vertue *could command ;
And marching ore scorch'd Affricks desert sand
Winne (as our Author thought)more honour far
Then any Laurell'd Roman Conquerer
By Lands subdu'd, or blood of Nations shedd,
When captiu'd Monarchs their proud Chariotts
ledd.*

Q2

1 *Lucan's Pharsalia*, trans. Thomas May, 1627, sig. Q2r.

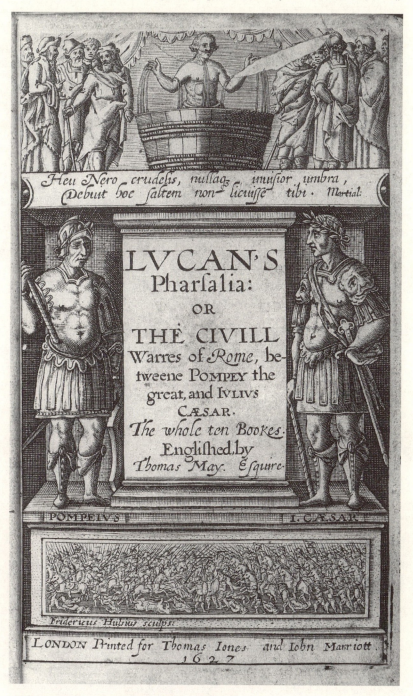

2 Title-page to Thomas May (trans.), *Lucan's Pharsalia*.

verses, was mutilated.[47] The reasons for the excisions are uncertain, but political caution on the part of the author or his dedicatees may have been involved. The year 1627 was a high point of political influence for those who were deeply suspicious of 'popularity' and dissension in the realm. The Dutch scholar Daniel Heinsius, from whom May quoted in his preface, called for his name to be deleted from a published letter that criticized William Laud's ally Richard Montague: he had so much power that caution was needed.[48] Another Dutch classicist, Isaac Dorislaus, the nominee of Sidney's old friend Fulke Greville for the first chair of history at Cambridge, found himself in trouble when he chose Tacitus as his topic. The series was discontinued after the second lecture, in which he declared that the Roman emperors had had no legitimate authority and that power had still rested with the Roman people.[49] After his dismissal, Dorislaus turned to chronicling the battle of Nieuwpoort, which May had mentioned in his dedication to Vere. The study of history was far from an antiquarian pursuit; it was a very short step from studying Tacitus to analyzing the tactics of contemporary warfare.[50] Dorislaus's scholarship was the kind of 'Trojan horse' that Hobbes warned against. In a sermon addressed to Parliament on its opening in March 1628, Laud declared triumphantly that he was speaking on the anniversary of the defeat of the last republican forces by Julius Caesar at Munda. For Laud as for Lucan's admirers, the battles of the Roman civil war were still being fought; his sermon publicly and provocatively aligned the Anglican church with the goal of crushing republican liberty.[51] One royalist

---

47 Library of Congress copy. In the score or so of copies I have been able to examine, there is no clear pattern either in the number of dedications removed or in which ones were chosen. It is possible that these excisions were caused by an embarrassing misprint: the printer had rendered the recently ennobled Mulgrave's name as Mowbray, whose conflict with Bolingbroke had initiated the overthrow of Richard III. Perhaps it was deemed impossible to excise one dedication without excising them all: F. B. Williams, Jr, *Index of Dedications and Commendatory Verses in English Books Before 1641* (1962), p. 241. But political factors cannot be ruled out. I am grateful to Professors D. F. McKenzie and Katherine Pantzer for help on this matter.

48 Paul R. Sellin, *Daniel Heinsius and Stuart England* (Leiden and London, 1968), pp. 91–2.

49 P. Alessandra Maccioni and Marco Mostert, 'Isaac Dorislaus (1595–1649): The Career of a Dutch Scholar in England', *Transactions of the Cambridge Bibliographical Society* 8 (1981–4), 419–70 (425). See also Kevin Sharpe, 'The Foundation of the Chairs of History at Oxford and Cambridge: an Episode in Jacobean Politics', in *Politics and Ideas in Early Stuart England: Essays and Studies* (London and New York 1989), pp. 207–30 (pp. 221–2). On royal suspicion of Tacitus see Alan T. Bradford, 'Stuart Absolutism and the "Utility" of Tacitus', *Huntington Library Quarterly* 46 (1983), 127–55.

50 Isaac Dorislaus, *Praelium Nuportanum* (1640; 7060; heavily based on the commentaries of Sir Horatio Vere's brother Francis); Maccioni and Mostert, 'Isaac Dorislaus', 432.

51 William Laud, *A Sermon . . . at Westminster* (1628; 15305), p. 42 (I owe this reference to Meiling Hazelton).

reader of May's version wrote opposite the narrator's attack on Caesar's refusal to bury the republicans: 'Lucans railinges will not make Caesar run'.[52] Gloatingly confident though it was, the annotation testified to the poem's power to provoke royalists in May's time as in Lucan's.

May's speech-act in his publication of his Lucan, then, evoked Lucan's own actions, while signalling the hope that he might be able to achieve greater distance from the court than the Roman poet. Lucan had 'published', by reading aloud, three books, including a flattering dedication to Nero, before the poem was suppressed by imperial jealousy. In what seems rather like a conscious parallel, May published the first three books of his translation in 1626, but without any dedication. When he brought out the complete version the following year, he dedicated it neither to the king nor to his favourite but to a group of aristocrats who were known for firm independence of courtly pressure. Their histories also drew attention to a characteristically Lucanian contrast between different modes of heroism. Just as Pompey was scrupulous to gain glory not just for his private interest but in consultation with the public good, so these noblemen had proved themselves in conflict but were equally reluctant to rush into battle unless it was clear that Parliament's and the nation's interests were being consulted. The issue was not just one of war versus peace but of the kind of war that was in question. In his poem to Lincoln, May contrasted the immoral glory of Caesar with Pompey's virtue:

> the good (though fall'n) doe ly
> Great in their ruines[.]

Cato, May told Warwick, gained far more honour than 'any Laurell'd Roman Conquerer'. And just as Lucan had hinted that Pompey's own struggle was corrupted by personal aims, so May praised the earl of Pembroke as one who like Brutus and Cato could stand above private interests:

> these fauour'd neither side,
> Nor fought for *Caesars* reigne, nor *Pompey's* pride,
> Nor came engaged by a priuate cause.
> For *Rome*, her state, her freedome, and her lawes
> Their loyall virtue stood.

Pembroke was 'free from faction . . . a noble Patriot'. The clear implication of that freedom from faction, however, was that it entailed the defence of liberties against pressure from monarchical power. The 1627 dedications then counterbalanced Lucan's pessimism with the hope that England was still able to produce true rather than shadow-heroism. In dedicating the poem to a

52 Copy of the 1627 edition in the University of Chicago Library, sig. N7r; reproduced by permission of the Department of Special Collections, University of Chicago Library.

group of leading figures rather than to a single ruler, and in committing it to the wider public of the printed book, May was setting up an implicit contrast with the narrowly personal world of court patronage.

Nevertheless, May had not lost hope in the possibility of a union between king and patriots. In June 1627 he praised Charles in a poem in honour of his visit to the fleet at Portsmouth before it departed for France. May invoked a straightforward nationalism in appealing to the spirit of Edward III.[53] Such hopes were dashed, however, by the fiasco at the Ile de Rhé. May composed an elegy on one of those slain, Colonel Charles Rich. He here showed his interest in the long-term fortunes of the Protestant cause: Rich had served in the Netherlands and the Palatinate.[54] In letters to Essex, his patron, Rich had expressed his forebodings about an expedition dominated by courtiers as opposed to experienced military men: 'I must both seeke to them that I do not care for, and must do nothing that I haue a minde to'.[55] May's elegy takes up the theme of his Lucan dedications, of the danger that heroism will disappear from the cultural memory. Here the added twist is that the Rhé campaign is so shameful that he would wish it to be forgotten but for the consequent forgetting of men like Rich:

> How fayne would we forgette this fatall war,
> and blott from out our mourning Kalender
> a day so blacke, but that we dare not take
> comfort from such Ingratitude, or make
> th'oblivion of those Worthyes y[t] then dyde
> our Owne? no, rather let our griefe abide.
> Thou there wer't slayne, renowned Rich, & we,
> rather then lose the memory of thee,
> will court our sorrow ...

May does not go into political detail, however, and the poem ends with a generalized appeal to monarchical nationalism, reverting to the praise of Edward III in his court poem.[56]

Many elegists were less restrained, and there began an outpouring of attacks on Buckingham – whose title provided a useful opportunity for ribald

---

53 May, 'Neptune to King *Charles*', PRO SP 16/68/74, calendared under June 1627.
　　Buckingham is known to have staged a masque for the king in his own and his fleet's
　　defence on 15 May 1627, and the speech perhaps had some relation with that masque; but
　　May never praised the favourite in print.

54 Rich was at first reported as only wounded in a coranto report that tried to maintain a
　　brave face, *The Continuation of our Weekely Newes* no. 25 (1 August 1627), sig. B1r.

55 BL Add. MS 46,188, fol. 98r, 21 March 1627. Cf. the letter of 8 January, fol. 95r: 'We haue
　　no newes heere, nor thinke of any thinge but of masks and playes'.

56 Thomas May, 'An Elegy on Sir Charles Rich slayne at th'Ile of Rez', BL Add. MS 33,998,
　　fol. 88.

rhymes.[57] Often these satires inverted the conventions of public poetry. It was becoming increasingly common for the universities to issue collective volumes in honour of royal occasions, and Prince Charles's return from Spain in 1623 had been greeted by a huge number of poems in the classical genre of the *prosphonetikon*, the poem greeting a hero's return. Satirists greeted Buckingham's return from the Rhé expedition with sardonic variants on this form, reminding the reader of the kind of ceremonial volume that was conspicuously absent on this occasion. One poem savagely declared that bonfires should be lit – to burn the duke.[58] 'And art thou returned?' asked another, mourning

> those Heroes lamentable fall:
> Rich, Best and Cornwall, w[ith] the rest; whose bones
> Want euen a monument of pible stones.[59]

More explicitly than May in his Rich elegy, this poet contrasted the ceremonial surrounding Buckingham with the fate of the fallen heroes who had suffered a lack of recognition comparable to Pompey's.

In the most comprehensive poetic indictment of the military mission, John Russell resolved to erect an 'everlasting *Pyramis* of prayse' to '*Brave Rich*' to compensate for the disaster in which

> the flow're of all the land
> Haue perish'd vnder *Buckinghams* command.[60]

Things would have gone differently if 'noble *Essex*', Warwick, or Vere 'whom *Newport* sounds' – three of May's dedicatees – had been in charge (sig. E3r). For Russell, there could be no question of peace with honour: England was always already at war:

> An endles bloudy war, that never yet
> Cessation, truce, or peace did once admit
> From the worlds Cradle, [to] it's hoary age
> Hath still beene wag'd, with vnappeased rage,
> By cursed *Sathan*, and his damned bands
> Of reprobates, against Christs church . . .
> Nor will it end but with the latest man
> Time shall produce. (sig. A3r)

Like d'Aubigné, Russell offered a spiritualized version of Lucan's conflict between Caesar and Pompey. He lamented England's betrayal of Princess

---

57 '*He* loves well *Fuckingham*': BL Add. MS 5,832, fol. 206v, omitted with other ribald matter from the edition of F. W. Fairholt, *Poems and Songs relating to George Villiers, Duke of Buckingham* (1850; hereafter *PS*), pp. 1–2.

58 BL Sloane MS 826, fol. 170v; *PS*, p. 18.　59 BL Sloane MS 826, fol. 33r; *PS*, p. 23.

60 I[ohn]. R[ussell?]., *The Spye Discovering the Danger of Arminian Heresie and Spanish Trecherie* (Strasbourg, 1628; 20577), sigs. E2v, E4r.

Elizabeth and the Palatinate (sigs. D3r–v). There was nothing intrinsically antimonarchical about this opposition: a godly prince might play a leading role in the struggle against Antichrist. But Russell presented James and Charles as weakly duped by their enemies; he invoked Ralegh as seeing more deeply into events than either king (sig. D2r) and blamed his execution on Spanish influence in England (sig. D2v). The Spanish wanted to turn England into an English province, and they were using the Anglican clergy as their fifth column (sigs. D2r, B4r). The role of Parliament was being undermined:

> Affaires, of such great consequence, of old
> (When great ones did not scorne to be controll'd)
> Were wont to be concluded by consent
> Of the states body in a *Parliament*,
> And not by factious spirits, made alone
> Of plying mettle, to be wrought vpon . . . (sigs. E3v–4r)

Russell did not share May's optimism that the current aristocracy were living up to their role of defending liberty. Titles were being offered to buy off opposition: 'Earles would be *Dukes*: and *Dukes* would faine be Kings' (sig. E4v). Looking back to the second earl of Essex and other figures of Elizabeth's reign, Russell asked

> Where are such fearelesse, peerelesse *Peeres* become?
> All silenc'd? (sig. A1v).

Silencing was a recurrent theme of Russell's poem:

> what soe're they be
> In presse, or pulpit, dare of speech be free
> In truth's behalfe; and vent their grieved minde
> In phrase more serious, or some graver kinde

were condemned as seditious (sig. A1r). It should be emphasized that he did not favour universal freedom of speech. On the contrary, books propagating the 'Arminian' revision of Calvinist predestination that was fashionable at court should be banned (sigs. C3vff). Russell's viewpoint was not that of a liberal but of one certain of an evangelical truth, which it was a divine as well as civil obligation to broadcast. He declared that he had intended to publish the poem at the opening of the last Parliament but 'the supercilious lookes of over-awing greatnesse had so danted these degenerous times, that none durst adventure, to giue wings to their desire' (sig. †2r). Political criticism was being driven into a private realm, or suppressed even there:

> Councels, of old, encourag'd such men still
> (Till those made Councellours did curbe their will)
> Who boldly would, for publiq; safety, vtter

What, now, the best, in private, dare not mutter
Vnder the *Fleetes* [i. e. prison's] damnation[.] (sig. A1r)

What appeared to May to be Pembroke's moderation was viewed by Russell in darker terms:

Then zealous in Gods cause, and ours wert thou
Earle *Pembroke*, but the case is alter'd now[.] (sig. F3v)

Where Parliamentarian leaders faltered, it was up to the poet to become an orator and try to sway a wider public. Russell apologized for addressing such serious themes in verse at all, even in his uncourtly 'naked raptures': it would be more appropriate to model himself on the great orators of the ancient republics, Demosthenes and Cicero (sig. A1r), quotations from whom fill his margins. For Russell, Puritan zeal and enthusiasm for secular republican rhetoric are inseparable.

Russell's poem belongs to what has been called the underground poetry of the 1620s, with deliberately rough language and anti-courtly sentiments offering a counterpoint to the idealized terms of masques and panegyrics.[61] This poetry reached its high point in responses to Buckingham's assassination in August 1628. The assassin, John Felton, a discharged naval officer, saw himself as embodying a national movement of opposition, and owned a copy of Parliament's remonstrance against Buckingham. Parliament's action in printing this remonstrance had been a momentous step in bringing mysteries of state into a wider sphere; the assassination seemed to vindicate those who feared that it had been a very dangerous move. Court spokesmen denounced Felton's crime as stemming from personal motives; but many poets who commented on the act viewed it instead within a classical republican discourse of justified tyrannicide.

Not all the defences of Felton, it is true, can be attributed to republican or even particularly radical sentiments. Buckingham had alienated the old nobility by encouraging the sale of titles of honour, so that his demise could paradoxically be read as reaffirming social stability. A republicanizing rhetoric was adopted by some poets with strong court connections and even with close links with Buckingham's own circle.[62] Jonson himself, a frequent

---

61 On the general theme see Thomas Cogswell, 'Underground Verse and the Transformation of Early Stuart Political Culture', in Susan D. Amussen and Mark A. Kishlansky (eds.), P *olitical Culture and Cultural Politics in Early Modern Europe* (Manchester and New York, 1995), pp. 277–300, and Alastair Bellany, '"Raylinge Rymes and Vaunting Verse": Libellous Politics in Early Stuart England, 1603–1628', in Sharpe and Lake (eds.), *Culture and Politics in Early Stuart England*, pp. 285–310.

62 Thus one panegyric of Felton was written by James Smith, a member of a circle of strongly royalist wits: see Timothy Raylor, *Cavaliers, Clubs, and Literary Culture: Sir John Mennes, James Smith, and the Order of the Fancy* (Newark, London and Toronto, 1994), pp. 55–6.

defender of the court, was accused of writing a panegyric of Felton.[63] Yet even
if the speech-act of writing such poems was not one of sedition, the fact that
poets found it so easy to turn to classical models in this context was itself significant. One poet drew attention to the contrast between Roman and
modern views of tyrannicide:

> His valor great did proue a Roman spirit,
> And by their Lawes a thousand heavens meritt.[64]

The poet and essayist Owen Feltham explored that contrast more subtly,
making explicit the split consciousness of readers torn between opposing ideologies. He expresses pity for the Duke, but continues:

> yett should I speake the vulgare I should boast
> Thy bould Assasinate and wyshe all moste
> hee weare noe Christian, that I vpp might stand
> To prayse the Intente, of his Misguyded hand
> And sure when all the Patriotts in the shade
> Shall ranke, and their full Musters ther bee made
> Hee shall sitt, next, to Brutus, and Receiue
> Such Bayes as Heathenish Ignorance can giue
> But then the Christian Checking that, shall say
> Though hee did good hee did ytt the wrong way
> And oft thay fall into the worste of Ills
> That Acte the Peoples wish, w^{th}out thayr wills.

From a classical republican point of view, Felton's deed is heroic and ranks
him amongst the 'patriots'; but as a modern Christian Feltham must censure
him. The terms in which he does so, however, are curiously ambivalent. Even
the Christians acknowledge that he did 'good'. The final line seems to indicate
a paradox rather like that of Lucan's Pompey: it is not enough to act out the
people's 'wish' on an individual basis, one must follow their legally established 'wills'. Yet the verbal echo suggests how will and wish may inter-
penetrate even as it tries to make the distinction.[65] Moreover, Feltham's poem
suppresses an obvious fact, that Felton was motivated not so much by classical

---

63 The authorities could have drawn sinister conclusions from his signature in a copy of
   Russell's *The Spye* (Bodleian shelfmark Malone 824).
64 BL Sloane MS 826, fol. 196v; *PS*, p. 77.
65 'On the murder of the Duke of Buck:', Bodleian MS Ashmole 38, p. 20 [with the very
   heavy, and apparently later, punctuation silently modified]; also in BL Sloane MS 826,
   fol. 197r; *PS*, pp. 54–5. For differing interpretations, see Gerald Hammond, *Fleeting
   Things: English Poets and Poems 1616–1660* (Cambridge, Mass., and London, 1990),
   pp. 62–3, and James Holstun, '"God bless thee, little David!": John Felton and His Allies',
   Journal of English Literary History 59 (1992), 513–52 (533–4). Holstun speaks of 'a mode
   of tyrannicidal dialectical thinking'; both critics compare Marvell's 'Horatian Ode'.

emulation as by a strongly Puritan belief in a divine command to work justice. The opposition between classical and Christian on the question of tyrannicide is itself unstable.

Protestant themes indeed predominate in the many elegies and epitaphs for Felton; but Lucan's spirit is invoked in the finest of all the epitaphs, which alludes to the fact that Charles would not allow Felton's body to be buried but had it hung in chains. The poet turns this grisly fate into a moral victory:

> his bodye, Is Intombd, In Ayre:
> Archt ouer wth heauen and A thowsand fayre,
> And glorious Diomond starrs; A Sepulcher,
> That tyme, shall neuer Ruinatte; and whear
> The Impartiall worme [which] is nott bribed to sparr,
> Princes Corruptt In Marble; shall not share
> his flesh: wch yf the Charritable skyes
> Imbalme wth Teares, doing Those obsequies
> Belonge to men; shall live tell pittiing foule
> Contend to reach his bodye to his soule[.]

'Archt over with heaven' alludes to Lucan's 'caelo tegitur, qui non habet urnam', a point made explicitly in some manuscripts. Felton's fate recalls not only those left unburied after Pharsalia but also Pompey's humble memorial. As Lucan so often does, the poem polemically contrasts this purer, more sublimated form of immortality with the vainglorious physicality of princes' tombs, here caught in the oxymoronic 'Corruptt In Marble' and the contemptuous reference to the worms as the only courtly creatures immune to bribery. The stars are the true diamonds.[66]

The Lucan allusion works in a more specific and pointed way. It shifts attention from Felton and Buckingham to the king himself. In denying Felton due burial, Charles recalls the tyrannical Caesar. Felton's action, by contrast, had aligned him with Brutus. The movement from Buckingham to his living defenders has ominous implications: Charles himself may one day meet his Brutus. None of the poems takes such a view explicitly. They all follow the orthodox assumption that the king himself is virtuous and has simply been led astray by evil counsellors. But there are signs of a more critical analysis of the basic structures of monarchical power: if similar figures kept recurring under monarchical government, might the fault lie not in individuals but in the system itself, in the degree of freedom given to the king's private will in

66 'Jo Feltons Epitaph', Bodleian Library, MS Ashmole 38, p.20 (see previous note); also in BL Sloane MS 826, fol. 197r; *PS*, p. 78; reprinted in *The Penguin Book of Renaissance Verse*, selected and introduced by David Norbrook, edited by H. R. Woudhuysen (Harmondsworth, 1992), pp. 148–9. The attribution of this poem in one manuscript to John Donne, though implausible, indicates the admiration it aroused.

choosing those who held the highest positions? In one anti-Buckingham satire the duke attacks his critics with the claim that

> Coblers their latchetts ought not to transcend.
> Meddle w[i]th com[m]on matters, com[m]on Wrongs,
> To th' howse of Com[m]ons com[m]on things belongs,
> Th'are *Extra Sphæram* that you treate of now . . .
> Leaue . . . State to him that best the State doth knowe.[67]

The duke uses 'common' in a social sense, as contrasting with noble blood; but in the early modern period that word was becoming revalued into a more positive sense of the public and universal.[68] The contending senses crystallize the dispute over the relative weightings of public and private in 'ancient' and 'modern' prudence. The duke's disdain for the 'common' involves taking a private, personal interest as if it were the public good. How far could the king himself be immune from responsibility for placing his own private will before the public in elevating the duke so high? Was monarchy inimical to the common cause, the commonwealth?

None of the poems openly blames Charles. The assassination of Buckingham is held to have delivered the realm of its ills – as one rather Lucanian line put it, 'Thou stabe'st o[u]r Desolation w[i]th a stroke'.[69] But it was hard entirely to separate the favourite from the man who had kept him in power. One poet has Felton push the conventional language of courtly deference to its limits

> Syr, I y[ou]r servant, (who haue sett you free,
> *Christs* freeman am, y[ou]r Prisoner though I bee)
> Haue one good boone to begg of o[u]r good King:
> Not libertie, nor life, nor noe such thing:
> But that you would Gods *Mercie* magnifie,
> ffor that salvation hee hath wrought by mee.
> ffor know (great *Charles*) how high thou honour'd art
> To bee but King of *Mee*, of soe stout heart.[70]

Felton confers liberty and honour on the king, not the other way round; he is a citizen, not a subject. He goes on to list celebrated tyrannicides from Scripture. Another poem warns that 'Gods *Siccle* spares not either King or Crowne'.[71] The anxiety voiced in the poems goes beyond a particular favourite's domination to a general sense that openness and honesty of speech are being stifled at every level of society. Judges are 'tongue-ty'd'.[72] One poem

67 BL Sloane MS 826, fol. 158v; *PS*, pp. 30–1.
68 Jürgen Habermas, *The Structural Transformation of the Public Sphere: An Inquiry into a Category of Bourgeois Society*, trans. Thomas Burger with Frederick Lawrence (Cambridge, Mass., 1989), p. 6.   69 BL Sloane MS 826, fol. 191r; *PS*, p. 69.
70 Sloane MS 826, fol. 195v; *PS*, pp. 72–3.   71 Sloane MS 826, fol. 190r; *PS*, p. 54.
72 Sloane MS 826, fol. 194v; *PS*, p. 71.

praised the Remonstrance which had inspired Felton to his deed. It singled out the way in which the Parliamentarian leaders – Eliot, Selden and Coke – had summoned up the courage to name Buckingham rather than merely offering a generalized list of grievances; and the terms of its praise were significant:

'Tis due you to the world bee vnderstood
More then *Romes Cato*, hee who durst bee good
When *Caesar* durst bee badd: ffor that great *Duke*
ffeares noething more then y[ou]r severe rebuke . . .[73]

The reference to the contending parties in the Roman civil wars daringly opens up the possibility of Charles's own complicity, which is then quelled by the identification of Caesar with Buckingham; but as in the Feltham poem, there is an element of verbal hesitation.

Moreover, many of the poems are concerned less with Buckingham than with the way Felton is treated after his death. As has been seen, one epitaph implicitly paralleled Charles with the vindictive Caesar. James Smith similarly took the instruments of punishment and sublimated them into spiritual ornaments:

Thy ffetters (ransom'd England) and thy ffeares,
Triumphant, Trophie-like, stout ffelton weares
On him like seemely Ornam[en]ts, They deck
His Armes and Wrists, and hang about his Neck
Like gingling Braceletts, And as rich as they bee;
So much the cause can alter Miserie.[74]

'Why is o[u]r Age turn'd coward,' exclaimed another poet,

 that noe Penn
dares weeping mourne thy glorie? are all Men
doom'd to dull Earth at once, that thy great Name
Must suffer in their silence, and thy ffame
Pante to flie higher then their endles hate
Who toyle to kill thy memory, and bate
The glorie of thy Act?[75]

That striking idea of the courtiers as killing Felton's memory is very much in the spirit of Lucan's portrayal of regal control of political memory.

The poems, then, participate in the process they celebrate. They are written with a sense of exhilaration at breaking out of mental and verbal chains that have confined their authors as surely as Felton's physical chains bind him. Coke's boldness in naming Buckingham is an act worthy of the

---

73 Sloane MS 826, fol. 154v; *PS*, p. 24.   74 Sloane MS 826, fol. 194v; *PS*, p. 71.
75 Sloane MS 826, fol. 190r; *PS*, p. 67.

classical orators; it must be the poet's aim to emulate that kind of courage. 'Naught but illusion were wee,' wrote a poet who attacked the flattering, mythological art in vogue at court; these poems steer clear of mythology as determinedly as Lucan.[76] They demand the right to speak out on public issues which courtiers may regard as secret mysteries of state. As Holstun observes,

> they are private men insisting on a public voice . . . They handle the *arcana imperii* with a rough familiarity bordering on contempt. The effect is finally that of a repressed republican *conversazione civile*, in which the anonymous space of English poetic manuscript culture takes the place of the Florentine piazza.(532)

Felton is made to declare that while his grief is private, his joy is public; he sets a pattern for his poets. But this conversation was indeed repressed: the poems were far too outspoken to be printed. The public language of the king and his poets remained deferential to Buckingham. From some satirists' point of view, things were the wrong way round: the king's private friendship thus controlled public discourse, while poetry written with a stronger sense of the common, public interest had to remain private, in the sense of lacking a printed outlet. Manuscript culture, with its strictly selective circulation amongst the elite, could provide a certain kind of outspokenness at that time impossible in the public press without risking political disorder; but there are signs here of a demand for something more like a full public sphere, and of an awareness that monarchs were unlikely to share this demand.[77] In a significant sense, these poems have remained private. Though some of the Felton poems were eventually printed and a substantial group were reprinted in the nineteenth century, literary history has tended to pass them by. Their boldness, even savagery, does not accord with the model of English society as a harmonious organic community, or with the taste for 'cavalier' poetry as evoking a lost world of polite refinement. They would have appealed, however, to those encouraged by Lucan's admirers to demand a more discordantly truthful form of verse. And there is evidence that manuscript celebrations of Felton spread to social levels well beyond the gentry (see below, chapter 3).

The political climate indicated by these poems greatly alarmed the king, and in 1629 he dissolved Parliament and ruled without it for the ensuing decade. Hobbes would have agreed with this move. In the same year he published a translation of Thucydides which made a very different intervention from May's Lucan in the debate over classical republicanism. Hobbes had begun work some years earlier, and the translation can be seen as his considered response to the whole troubled decade of the 1620s. He had encountered

---

76 Sloane MS 826, fol. 192r; *PS*, p. 70.
77 Harold Love, *Scribal Publication in Seventeenth-Century England* (Oxford, 1993), p. 184.

turbulence both in the political and literary spheres. Hobbes told Aubrey that he devoted two whole years to reading romances and plays, time which he later regretted but which, Aubrey argued, may after all have furnished him with 'copie of words', with heightened articulacy.[78] It would also have alerted him to the rising temperature of political debate in the drama, which was engaging with sensitive political issues. He was helped with the introductory material by Ben Jonson, who was fighting a rearguard action against the fashion for news and subversive politics in works like *The Staple of News*.[79] Hobbes's Thucydides was dedicated to the son of May's dedicatee, the late earl of Devonshire; Hobbes, however, presented classical republicanism in a significantly different light. His aim in the translation, clearly signalled in his editorial comments, was to contain the excesses of the current cult of classical liberty by presenting a sceptical, conservative perspective on democracy.[80]

Thucydides was a prestigious writer, yet he did not have the inflammatory quality Hobbes found in some kinds of classical writing. His preface emphasized that though Thucydides presented major events through the form of '*Deliberatiue Orations*' (sig. (a)3r), his style was very different from that of spoken oratory, 'rather to be read, then heard' (sig. (b)1r), precisely because he aimed at a detached and rational scrutiny of events which only the learned elite would fully understand. He also differed from the majority of historians, to whose reading most men came

> with an affection much like that of the *People*, in *Rome*, who came to the spectacle of the *Gladiators*, with more delight to behold their bloud, then their Skill in Fencing. For they be farre more in number, that loue to read of great Armies, bloudy Battels, and many thousands slaine at once, then that minde the *Art*, by which, the Affaires, both of Armies, and Cities, be conducted to their ends[.] (sig. A4r)

It is possible to read in this comment a particular hit at the cult of Lucan, whose stylized descriptions of battles may indeed have been influenced by gladiatorial combats.[81] And while the *Pharsalia* was serving to legitimize a cult of war, Hobbes offered Thucydides's history as showing a city ruined when demagogues whipped up war fever. Where Lucan was presented as a martyr to the evil ways of courts, Thucydides prudently avoided becoming a victim of democracy. He deliberately abandoned the active for the contemplative life, rhetoric for truth: he saw that 'such men onely swayed the Assemblies, and were esteemed wise and good Common-wealths men, as did

---

78 Bodleian MS Aubrey 9, fol. 42v; *ABL*, I, 361.   79 *ABL*, I, 25–6.
80 Thucydides, *Eight Bookes of the Peloponnesian Warre*, trans. Thomas Hobbes (1629; 24058). See also Skinner, *Reason and Rhetoric in the Philosophy of Hobbes*, pp. 244–9, and Jonathan Scott, 'The Peace of Silence: Thucydides and the English Civil War', in Miles Fairburn and Bill Oliver (eds.), *The Certainty of Doubt: Tributes to Peter Munz* (Wellington, 1996), pp. 90–116.   81 Ahl, *Lucan*, pp. 86ff.

put them vpon the most dangerous and desperate enterprizes' (sig. (a)1v). He had been taught rhetoric by Antiphon, who was 'feared by the *People*, for his eloquence' because he was one of the few articulate opponents of democracy, and eventually 'contriued the deposing of the *People*, and the setting vp of the gouernment of the 400' (sig.(a)1v). For this enterprise Antiphon was put to death when the people returned to power; more prudently, rather than vainly trying to seek 'the acclamations of Popular Auditories' (sig. (a)2v), Thucydides turned from rhetoric to history.

Hobbes himself had not entirely repudiated rhetoric – he instructed the young earl of Devonshire in the art – but he was always very wary of its political ramifications. The title-page of his translation (figure 3) portrayed on the left hand a view of Sparta, the Spartan king Archidamos, and a calm scene of deliberation in a council headed by a crowned king with a sceptre; on the right hand was a view of Athens, a picture of Pericles, and an orator in a pulpit inflaming 'hoi polloi', the masses. The contrast expressed a preference. One of Thucydides's best-known passages was Pericles's funeral oration with its paean to Athenian democracy (2.35–46). Pericles idealized the Athenians' intellectual power and open-mindedness, and their tolerance of each other's differing customs. Hobbes however gives a somewhat disenchanted perspective in his marginal note: 'He glanceth againe at the *Lacedaemonians*, because they euer looked sowrely on soft and loose behauiour . . . This is spoken with enuie towards the *Lacedaemonians*' (p. 102). When Pericles declares that his citizens have 'a care, both of their owne, and of the publique affaires, and a sufficient knowledge of State matters, euen in those that labour with their hands', Hobbes adds an acerbic note: 'In *Athens* no man so poore but was a Statesman. So *S. Luke, Act.17.21*. All the Athenians spend their time in nothing but hearing and telling of newes. The true Character of polititians without employment' (p. 103). Insofar as Hobbes expresses admiration for Pericles, it is because he is in his view virtually a king: Thucydides's admiration for him in fact showed that he 'best approued of the *Regall Gouernment*. . . it is manifest that he least of all liked the *Democracy*' (sigs. (a) 2r, 1v). As Hobbes put it much later, Thucydides

> says Democracy's a Foolish Thing,
> Than a Republick Wiser is one King.[82]

The Thucydides translation signalled a model for the citizen, and more particularly the intellectual, very different from May's idealization of activist Parliamentarian aristocrats: retirement from the turbulence of political rhetoric, to gain a detached philosophical scrutiny. That was the role Hobbes

---

82 Hobbes, *The Verse Life*, in J. C. A. Gaskin (ed.), *The Elements of Law . . . with Three Lives* (Oxford and New York, 1994), p. 256.

3 Title-page to Thucydides, *Eight Bookes of the Peloponnesian Warre*, trans. Thomas Hobbes, 1629.

followed up to 1640, acting as what the Spanish termed a *privado*, an adviser to aristocratic patrons who might wield considerable influence but kept discreetly in the background. And yet what is striking about the book is not just that Hobbes should have felt it necessary in the 1620s to mount a sustained argument against republican democracy, but that he should have done so from within the discourse of classical republicanism.[83] Though he draws very different political conclusions from republican readers, he shares with them a belief that history should offer not just moral examples but an analysis of how specific virtues are made possible within specific political structures. Though Hobbes expresses a clear preference for Sparta over Athens, the Spartan monarchy was limited and the Spartan constitution was often viewed as a model aristocratic republic. The Spartan scene on Hobbes's title-page seems to depict a fairly animated debate offering multiple opinions, not a transcendent monarch laying down the law from above: many hands are being raised to make a point. By contrast, the Athenian scene seems to illustrate Hobbes's later comment that a democracy was an aristocracy of orators sometimes interrupted by the temporary monarchy of one orator.[84] And however conservative Thucydides may have been, he retained a patriotic admiration for Athens. In fact Edward Hyde indignantly retorted to Hobbes's later attacks on classical studies that he himself had translated a work which contained 'more of the Science of Mutiny and Sedition, and teaches more of that Oratory that contributes thereunto, then all that *Aristotle* and *Cicero* have publish'd in all their Writings'.[85] The Leveller William Walwyn later declared himself 'much delighted' with Thucydides, whom he must have read in translation.[86] To counteract the effects of the republican Trojan horse, Hobbes himself had found it necessary to climb inside.

---

83 On Hobbes's debt to humanist republicanism see Tuck, pp. 311ff. Three essays in the volume *Horae Subsecivae* (1620; 3957) recently attributed to Hobbes show the strong influence of Tacitism, though already inclining towards admiration for Augustus's skill in defusing republican opposition. See Noel B. Reynolds and Arlene W. Saxonhouse (eds.), *Thomas Hobbes: Three Discourses* (Chicago and London, 1995).

84 Hobbes, *De Corpore Politico*, ch. 21, in Gaskin (ed.), *The Elements of Law*, p. 120.

85 Edward Hyde, earl of Clarendon, *A Brief View and Survey of . . . Mr Hobbes's Book, Entitled 'Leviathan'* (Oxford, 1676; C4420), p. 85.

86 *Walwyns Just Defence*, in *The Writings of William Walwyn*, ed. Jack R. McMichael and Barbara Taft (Athens and London, 1989), p. 403. Hobbes's Thucydides was reprinted in 1648.

2

The king's peace and the people's war, 1630–1643

Discord and concord: public poetry under the personal rule

In 1630 Thomas May dedicated to Charles I a continuation of the *Pharsalia*. This new poem significantly diluted Lucan's anti-Caesarism. The last book in particular, which takes the story up to the sensitive ground of Caesar's assassination, is hedged with reservations about the republican cause: the civil wars proved 'What horrid dangers follow'd libertie'.[1] The Romans had already lost

> that vnsafe prerogatiue
> Their libertie, and gladly would adore
> A safe and peacefull Scepter.[2]

This milder tone made it hard for May to treat the assassination of Caesar, with which the poem ended, in Lucan's spirit. The attempt to regain liberty, he concluded, had merely resulted in further bloodshed. Though space is given for the republicans' views, Caesar is finally more of a martyr than a villain, and the imperial succession which for Lucan is tragic becomes providential for May. Lucan's obtrusively unsatisfactory ending is softened into a more conventional narrative pattern. May writes that Augustus's accession was to be welcomed, not least because it favoured poetry:

> the Muse before lack'd power to clime,
> Or else disdain'd her highest notes to raise,
> Till such a Monarch liu'd to giue the Bayes.[3]

In 1628 he had published a translation of Virgil's *Georgics*, a founding text in the Augustan mythology of the emergent empire bringing peace and concord to the realm.

---

1 Thomas May, *A Continuation of Lucan's Historicall Poem till the Death of Ivlivs Caesar* (1630; 17711), sig. H6r.   2 Ibid., sig. J5r.
3 Ibid., sig. H6v. Howard Erskine-Hill, *The Augustan Idea in English Literature* (1983), pp. 184–5, notes the Augustan tone of the *Continuation*.

Taking these hints, Charles commissioned two historical poems from May. These narratives of the reigns of Henry II and Edward III proclaimed on their title-pages that they were written by royal command, and demonstrated the evil results when aristocrats escaped the control of the monarchy.[4] In the Henry II poem, May presented a figure of Sedition who pretended to defend 'religion, law, or liberty' but was really 'a foe To peace and lawfull power'; he was associated with the Spartan Ephors, the Roman tribunes, and the agrarian reforms of the Gracchi.[5] Edward III had been on May's mind in the political crises of the 1620s, and the king became for him a means of steering away from crisis. His preface pointed out that his historical poem ended when that king's fortunes started to decline, which was matter more suitable for a historian than a poet.[6] He thus reaffirmed precisely the kind of distinction that Lucan's historical poem had challenged, and obtrusively steered clear of a period that was constitutionally very sensitive – precedents for annual Parliaments went back to Edward's reign. He composed effusive verses for the Queen's birthday.[7] He became so closely associated with the court that it was later alleged that he sided with Parliament in the Civil War only because he was aggrieved at not having been made poet laureate. The king himself called May 'his Poet' and personally intervened when the Lord Chamberlain attacked him at a court masque, believing him an intruder.[8] The bitterness of attacks on May's inconstancy perhaps reflected a memory that he had already changed his tune on an earlier occasion.

One possible explanation of May's greater political caution is that he had taken fright at the political tumults of the 1620s, in which his own writings had played their part. He seems to have been disconcerted by the depth of popular fury unleashed by Buckingham's assassination. Writing when he had nothing to gain by doing so, he declared that Buckingham's death had provoked 'such expressions, as indeed were not thought fit nor decent by wise men, upon so tragicall and sad an accident', and cited lines from Seneca on the need for sacrilegious hands to forbear from desecrating the tomb.

4 R. Malcolm Smuts, *Court Culture and the Origins of a Royalist Tradition in Early Stuart England* (Philadelphia, 1987), p. 272.

5 Thomas May, *The Reigne of King Henry the Second* (1633; 17715), sigs. C3r-v. This figure was however to some degree balanced by the figures of Luxury and of Ambition, whose entourage included Lucan's greatest targets, Alexander and Caesar (sig. C2v); and it should be recalled that Lucan's aristocratic republicanism itself condemned the democratic tendencies of the Gracchi (*Pharsalia*, vi.796). I am grateful to Professor J. G. A. Pocock for showing me a draft of an essay which discusses the historical poems.

6 Thomas May, *The Victorious Reigne of King Edward the Third* (1635; 17719), sig. A3v.

7 Thomas May, 'A new yeares gift to her maiestye', Bodleian MS Rawl. poet. 116, fol. 48v.

8 *The Earl of Strafforde's Letters and Dispatches*, ed. William Knowler, 2 vols. (1739), I, 207, George Garrard to Strafford, 27 February 1634.

May suggested that the personal rule of Charles might have been a divine punishment for the excesses of popular joy.[9] At the time, however, he seems to have been one of many courtiers who hoped that with Buckingham removed the king might follow better counsels. The tumults in Parliament may have accelerated the death of his kinsman Sir Humphrey May, who had desperately tried to reach some kind of accommodation between the king for whom he was a spokesman and his critics. In an epitaph, the poet praised Sir Humphrey as

> A Councellor that kept State pollicye
> W[th]in those bounds w:[ch] antient vertue sett;
> W[ch] first made kingdomes good & good men Great;
> ffrom w:[ch] in no adulterate Path he swerued[.][10]

During the tumults of the previous decades, perhaps both sides had gone beyond their 'bounds'; for the moment May was ready to accept the status quo as an appropriate balance.

May's discourse was thus moving towards that of his close friend Sir Richard Fanshawe (1608–66), with whom he had shared chambers in the Inns of Court. In 1630 Fanshawe wrote an ode modelled on Horace's celebrations of the Augustan peace. Charles had issued a proclamation commanding the gentry to return to their traditional obligations of tending their estates. In the aftermath of the breakdown of Parliament in 1629, there was a political significance in the poem's idealization of the peace of the country as opposed to the turbulence of London. Fanshawe suggested that the Golden Age, exiled from the rest of the world, had been tied to this one 'blest Isle' with a 'golden chaine' – he evoked here Homer's description of a chain linking heaven to earth, an image of cosmic rule and cosmic order. Charles had now made peace with France and Spain, and Fanshawe contrasted England's peace with the evils of the wars raging on the Continent. He recalled Virgil's description of England in his first eclogue as an island cut off from the world: such isolation was a virtue. Here Fanshawe celebrated Charles's turn away from involvement in European conflict during the years of the personal rule: lacking funds from Parliament, he could not afford large-scale warfare. If this peace continues, writes Fanshawe, the land may breed a new Virgil who will praise

9 Thomas May, *The History of the Parliament of England: which began November the third, M.DC.XL.* (1647; M1410; hereafter *History*), I, 12.

10 Thomas May, 'An Epitath [*sic*] on sir Humphry May', University of Nottingham Library, Portland Collection, MS PW V 305; reproduced by permission of the Department of Manuscripts, University of Nottingham. Garrard believed that the Lord Chamberlain was 'the more indulgent' to May after the incident at the masque 'for his Names sake' (Strafford, *Letters and Dispatches*, I, 207).

'Th'*Augustus* of our world'.[11] The contrast here could not be sharper with Lucan's polemical anti-Augustanism. The new Virgil will grow organically from the countryside: poetry is cut off from the political debate of the city and made an emanation of a spontaneous monarchism.

The years of the personal rule saw a strong emphasis on an Augustan poetics. Not only was Roman imperial poetry given great emphasis, but newer forms of poetic praise were developed as the Stuart masque reached its apogee. After Buckingham's assassination, Charles's wife became his central emotional focus, and he played a part in devising the masques that celebrated his marriage as an image of universal concord. As in Fanshawe's poem, the masques presented the monarch as the ultimate source both of political and of artistic order and harmony. Similar imagery of cosmic concord abounded in increasingly frequent volumes of poetry issued by the universities to commemorate royal occasions.[12] Lucan's 'concordia discors' gave way to an apparently easier kind of harmony. As Markku Peltonen notes, this devaluation of the active life reflects 'a sense of frustration with politics' and a 'partial decline of the classical humanist tradition'.[13]

This shift can be exaggerated, however. Literary critics have tended to pay more attention to courtly verse than to the continuing traditions of more militant public poetry. About 1630 the dramatist Philip Massinger attacked Thomas Carew and fellow cavalier-poets for writing 'seruile Encomions' and pandering to great men's licentiousness. By writing 'In corners' rather than offering their compositions to 'indure the publique test', they were betraying the poet's public responsibilities.[14] Massinger implied a strong imperative for poets to enter the public sphere. Carew indignantly rejected Massinger's criticisms, but other poets did continue the patterns of the 1620s. Gustavus Adolphus of Sweden had become the great champion of the Protestant cause in the Continental war, and his death in battle in 1632 was greeted with great alarm in England. In 1634 John Russell ventured into print again with an elegiac volume which consciously challenged Carew and his friends. One of the commendatory poems moved more directly to the present in attacking critics 'That th'Empire claim of *Poetrie* and *Prose*' – an apparent retort to

11 *The Poems and Translations of Sir Richard Fanshawe*, vol. I, ed. Peter Davidson (Oxford, 1997), pp. 55–9. On this poem see Annabel Patterson, *Pastoral and Ideology: Virgil to Valéry* (Berkeley and Los Angeles, 1987), pp. 148–50; Gerald M. MacLean, *Time's Witness: Historical Representation in English Poetry, 1603–1660* (Madison and London, 1990), pp. 87ff; and James Loxley, *Royalism and Poetry in the English Civil Wars: The Drawn Sword* (London and New York, 1997), pp. 46–8.

12 Loxley, *Royalism and Poetry*, ch. 1.

13 Markku Peltonen, *Classical Humanism and Republicanism in English Political Thought 1570–1640* (Cambridge, 1995), pp. 287, 289.

14 Peter Beal, 'Massinger at Bay: Unpublished Verses in a War of the Theatres', *Yearbook of English Studies* 10 (1980), 190–203.

Carew's praise of Donne as aspiring to the universal monarchy of wit.[15] John Saltmarsh, who was to be championed by the republican Henry Marten for suggesting that the king might be deposed, elaborated a vigorously martial poetics:

> Let those soft *Poets*, who have dipt their brains
> In am'rous humours, thaw to looser strains ...
> *Mars* is thy theme; thy *Muse* hath learn'd to talk
> The *Cannon-language* of the Warre, and walk
> A loftie March; while thy faint readers dread
> And tremble at each syllable they reade.
> Leade on, Stout Poet, in thy Martiall state;
> And let these *Pages* on *GUSTAVUS* wait,
> Armed with verse of proof. (¶¶3v)

In a figure with which we have become familiar, Saltmarsh contrasts courtly modes of immortalization with those of independent, patriotic poetry, and associates the chain of being with an ideological rather than social elite:

> Then rest GUSTAVUS: do not change thy room
> Within this Book, for any marble tombe.
> Each line's a golden chain to hoise thee farre
> 'Bove *Fate*[.]

Russell himself declared that his lines' martial sounds would displease English ears grown tender and effeminate; but

> the more *Discords* that my verses show,
> The better *Harmonie* from thence will flow. (p. 33)

In a manner that is again familiar in the reception and imitation of Lucan, Russell contrasts his poetics with the courtly poetics of easy harmony: it is only by confronting discord and difficulty that a stronger kind of poetry can emerge. Readers of pacific poems like Fanshawe's would have been well aware that there were alternative ways of representing political life. In the Lucanian tradition, monarchical peace might be at least as suspect as the war to which it was counterposed.

This volume also raised the issue of censorship. One contributor claimed that the poem could not possibly displease the censors:

> And if the People prove
> Thy hand hath rudely op't a publick wound
> Newly clos'd up; the *Magistrate's* not bound
> (As *Athens* mulcted *Phrenicus*) to be
> Their *Censor*, and to fine thy *Historie*. (sig. ¶¶2r)[16]

---

15 John Russell, *The Two Famous Pitcht Battels of Lypsich, and Lutzen* (Cambridge, 1634; 21460), sig. ¶¶1r.   16 For discussion see MacLean, *Time's Witness*, pp. 52ff.

The reference here was provocative. The Athenian dramatist Phrynichus had staged a protest play against the Persian invaders at a time when the conservative ruling oligarchy favoured peace, and the play had been suppressed.

The comment is a reminder that censorship was an issue for poets of the 1630s. There has been much debate about its significance.[17] Certainly it was by no means consistent, for it was delegated amongst conflicting authorities which were always liable to pressure and evasion. A merely quantitative account of censored texts, however, misses the subjective dimension, the ways in which contemporaries read the experience. Poets alert to the oppositional tradition of Lucan would always be on the look-out for signs of a courtly suppression of political memory. And such signs were visible. May wrote of the celebrations for Prince Charles's return from Spain in 1623, which inspired several volumes of verses: 'the like consent, without any interposing authority, hath not been often knowne'.[18] The implication is that authority did often interpose to produce the required consent. In 1632 May published a poem in praise of Alexander Gil, a neo-Latin poet – and friend of Milton – who had been sentenced to have his ears cut off for bitter attacks on Charles and Buckingham, and had spent two years in prison.[19] Like many educational institutions, Westminster School regularly produced collections of ceremonial verse on royal occasions. In 1633 the young Abraham Cowley likened Charles to Caesar at Pharsalia.[20] The following year the school failed to produce a collection, and this was to be one of the pieces of evidence later used to convict the headmaster, Lambert Osbaldeston, of sedition. He was fined £5,000 and ordered to have each ear in turn nailed to a pillory in the presence of his pupils. Though he managed to escape, such incidents will have made comparisons between Charles and Lucan's Caesar somewhat uncomfortable.[21]

Yet external censorship seems an inadequate explanation for the fact that oppositional and satirical voices did dwindle substantially in the 1630s. Historians have found it hard to locate evidence of openly expressed dissent in the earlier 1630s. Many later writers located a moral flaw in the writers of the period, a failure to speak out boldly when occasion arose. With the hindsight of the Civil War period, May argued that the apparent beauty and

---

17 Christopher Hill, 'Censorship and English Literature', *WR*, pp. 32–71, countered by Blair Worden, 'Literature and Political Censorship in Early Modern England', in A. C. Duke and C. A. Tamse, eds., *Too Mighty to be Free: Censorship and the Press in Britain and the Netherlands* (Zutphen, 1987), pp. 45–62, and by Professor D. F. McKenzie in his unpublished Lyell Lectures.   18 May, *History*, I, 7.

19 May's verses to Alexander Gil, *Parerga* (1632; 11877), are cited by Leo Miller, 'Milton's *Patriciis Cicutis*', *Notes and Queries* 226 (1981), 41–2. Like Fanshawe, Gil had been a pupil of Thomas Farnaby (*Parerga*, pp. 18–19).   20 BL Royal MS 12A58, fol. 3r.

21 Arthur H. Nethercot, *Abraham Cowley: The Muses' Hannibal* (1931), pp. 26ff.

harmony of the court's culture had been specious. A traveller from abroad 'would verily believe, a Kingdom that looked so cheerefully in the face, could not be sick in any part'.[22] Many lords and gentlemen, he wrote, looked no further than their present prosperity, finding that England was better off than Continental countries: in effect they pleaded for their own servitude. The republican John Hall wrote that courtiers had known how to lull the people asleep 'with some small continuance of peace (be it never so unjust, unsound, or dangerous) as if the body politick could not languish of an internall disease, whilst its complexion is fresh and chearfull'.[23] The poet-prophet George Wither agreed that the age's beauty, though impressive, was but skin-deep:

Justice and *piety*, wore in that day,
The fairest *out side*; and, were trim'd about
With many *Ornaments*, now, nigh worn out;
And *goodnes*, had a very glorious *shell*,
Although the *kernels* therein prov'd not well.[24]

That kind of analysis, however, risks seeming facile. Why should we blame the Caroline poets for not foreseeing the Civil War? The accusations against court culture are all the more problematic when they come from poets who had participated in it. May, as has been seen, had radically revised his own view of Roman republican history. Wither (1588–1667), a veteran who had been publishing anti-court satires since the early Jacobean period, brought the sequence to a temporary end when the publication of his *Britain's Remembrancer* (1628) met with political difficulties and turned to a largely apolitical emblem-book. And yet, within a few years, the political and literary culture of the Caroline court was coming in for fierce retrospective denunciation. This double vision was graphically expressed by George, Lord Digby in 1641:

Take into your view Gentlemen, a State in a state of the greatest quiet and security that can be fancyed, not only injoying the calmest peace it selfe, but to improve and secure its happy condition, all the rest of the world at the same time in Tempest, in Combustions, in uncomposable Warres . . . A King that had in his own time given all the Rights and Liberties of his Subjects a more cleare and ample confirmation freely and gratiously, then any of his Predecessors (when the people had them at advantage) extortedly, I mean in the *Petition of Right*.

This is one Mappe of *England*, Mr *Speaker*, A man Sir, that should present unto you now, a Kingdome, groaning under that supreme Law, which *Salus*

22 May, *History*, I, 17–18, 21.
23 J[ohn]. H[all]., *The Grounds & Reasons of Monarchy Considered* (1651; H348), p. 7.
24 George Wither, *Westrow Revived* (1653; E1479.4; *WMW*, III), 68. For evidence that Wither had difficulties with the Caroline censors see *HMC Rutland*, I, 520.

populi periclitata [the endangered safety of the people] would enact. The liberty, the property of the Subject fundamentally subverted, ravisht away by the violence of a pretended necessity; a triple Crown shaking with distempers; men of the best Conscience ready to fly into the wildernesse for Religion. Would not one sweare that this were the Antipodes to the other; and yet let me tell you *Mr. Speaker*, this is a Mappe of *England* too, and both at the same time true.[25]

It could be argued that subsequent historians have simply continued this juxtaposition of opposed images. Those sympathetic to Parliament, from May onward, have stressed the difficulties underlying the elegant façade; those more hostile to Parliament, from Clarendon onward, have stressed the fundamental stability of Caroline culture and located the causes of the Civil War in more short-term factors.

By beginning with May in the 1620s, the present study has already indicated its preferences. However, to ask which image of the 1630s is the correct one is perhaps to pose the wrong question. As Digby suggested, both may have been correct. Harrington was to offer a very striking image of the Janus-faced nature of seventeenth-century political culture:

He was wont to find fault, with the constitution of our Goverment, that it was *by jumps*, and told a story of a Cavaliero he sawe at ye Carnival in Italie, who rode on an excellent managed horse, that with a touch of his toe would jumpe quite round: One side of his habit was Spanish, the other French. wch sudden alteration of the same person pleasantly surprized ye spectators. just so, s^d he, 'tis with us, when no Parliament, then absolute Monarchie; when a Parliament, then it runnes to Commonwealth [i.e. republic].[26]

Discourse is never entirely free-floating: to be articulated at all it requires public genres and media. Sessions of Parliament were powerful stimuli towards the production of political debate and satire, whose authors knew that they had the opportunity of swaying the opinion of members and thus influencing policy. In the absence of such occasions during the personal rule, the public framework for such writing was lacking. Some of Charles's fiercest critics of the 1630s seem to have decided that a cooling-off period would help to temper the king's more extreme reactions; and they may have shared May's ambivalence towards the dangers of turbulence to which the pressures for an expanding public sphere were leading. The moment Parliament resumed in 1640, however, there was a sudden renewal of the discourses of the 1620s. Harrington's 'jumps' reflected the massively uneven development of the public sphere and of a Parliamentary culture which the monarchy could not entirely dispense with but which seemed increasingly threatening to its autonomy.

25 *The Speeches of the Lord Digby* (1641; E196.6), pp. 14–15.
26 Bodleian MS Aubrey 6, fol. 98v; *ABL*, I, 291–2.

Waller and Denham: court poetry
and the containment of the public sphere

Harrington's analysis of a profoundly fissured political culture can be sub-stantiated even in the writings of the court poet who became best known for perfecting a new kind of poetic and political harmony. Edmund Waller (1606–87) has today fallen dramatically from the status he enjoyed amongst his contemporaries, and through the eighteenth century. S. R. Gardiner could barely overcome the distaste of one reared in Romantic literary, and liberal political, traditions when he spoke of Waller's combining a 'dissolute' life with an artificial formality. Yet Gardiner did recognize that 'it is difficult to find a more instructive personage in the whole course of the century . . . Waller was floating on a tide which ran with a greater sweep than could be accounted for by the peculiarities of his individual character'.[27] If it is hard today to understand why his blandness seemed so appealing, it is partly because we are no longer sensitive to the immense difficulty Waller had in imposing such apparently easy concord. His artifice effaced itself so consum-mately that it obscured the tensions that motivated it. He became celebrated as a co-founder, with Sir John Denham (1615–69), of a new form of Augustan poetry, celebrating political concord in predominantly closed couplets where the accent was placed on balance and antithesis. Choice of the heroic couplet did not in itself indicate political allegiance: it was becoming the more or less inescapable form whatever one's affiliations.[28] A distinction can be made, however, between the workman-like medium of an everyday plain style and the sophisticated courtly ease aimed at by Denham and more par-ticularly by Waller.[29] Waller's career showed how difficult it was to sustain such ease.

---

27 S. R. Gardiner, *History of the Great Civil War 1642–1649*, 4 vols. (1893; rptd, 1987), I, 8.
28 For analogies between Denham's couplets and the 'Puritan minimalism' of mid-century architecture see Timothy Mowl and Brian Earnshaw, *Architecture without Kings: The Rise of Puritan Classicism under Cromwell* (Manchester and New York, 1995), pp. 2–3.
29 A. W. Allison, *Toward an Augustan Poetic: Edmund Waller's "Reform" of English Poetry* ([Lexington], 1962), pp. 89–91, analyses Waller's distinctive preference for a medial caesura dividing the line into two equal five-syllable sections. On political implications see also Paul J. Korshin, *From Concord to Dissent: Major Themes in English Poetic Theory 1640–1700* (Menston, 1973), pp. 53–63. Waller has not received the attention that his prominence in his own time deserves; Dr John Safford is working on a biography. In the meantime, biographical information can be found in Warren L. Chernaik, *The Poetry of Limitation: A Study of Edmund Waller* (New Haven and London, 1968), and in two unpublished Ph.D. dissertations: Margaret C. Deas (Mrs Cohen), 'A Study of the Life and Poetry of Edmund Waller', University of Cambridge, 1931, and James Arthur Steele, 'A Biography of Edmund Waller', University of London, 1965.

Waller enjoyed favour at court, and dedicated a manuscript of his poems to Queen Henrietta Maria with a gallant reminder of how many poets were pre-occupied with her praise:

> And though the court and universities have no other mater of theer song, yet if your Ma[tie] please to listen what Echo the country returnes to so loud a praise, Wee shall likwayes teach the woods to sound your royall name ...[30]

If Waller here established himself as a 'country' poet, it was to echo the courtly allegory of Virgil's eclogues. For all his courtly manners, however, Waller did belong to the 'country' in the emergent sense of a political opposition.[31] The queen had become a focus for patronage partly independent of the king, and attracted some support from those calling for a more militant foreign policy and a new Parliament.[32] With these circles, Waller had close connections. As Clarendon put it, he 'had been even nursed in Parliaments'.[33] He had family links with Hampden and Cromwell, and he had sat in the Parliaments of 1624 and 1628–29. He had aligned himself with the strong political as well as poetic traditions of the Sidney dynasty through a poeticized courtship of Dorothy Sidney ('Sacharissa'), daughter of the earl of Leicester. In political terms, the Sidney circle were associated with 'Elizabethan' values in literature and in politics: with support for a vigorous foreign policy and a strongly Protestant ecclesiastical order at home. The Sidneys' relations with the monarchy had often been strained. As Blair Worden has shown, both the first and second earls were well versed in Roman republican texts and deeply suspicious of the ways of courts.[34] Philip Sidney had criticized the dangers to which monarchical government is liable in his portrait of the weak ruler Basilius. By the 1620s, parallels between Basilius and King James, retreating from public responsibilities to private indulgences, seemed very close.[35]

---

30 *WP*, I, v, echoing Virgil, *Eclogues*, i.4–5.

31 For classic statements which have been contested but remain important see Perez Zagorin, *The Court and the Country: The Beginning of the English Revolution* (1969), pp. 33–9, and P. W. Thomas, 'Two Cultures? Court and Country under Charles I', in Conrad Russell (ed.), *The Origins of the English Civil War* (London and Basingstoke, 1973), pp. 168–96.

32 R. M. Smuts, 'The Puritan Followers of Henrietta Maria in the 1630s', *English Historical Review* 93 (1978), 24–45.

33 *The Life of Edward Earl of Clarendon* (Oxford, 1759), p.25.

34 Blair Worden, 'Classical Republicanism and the Puritan Revolution', in *History and Imagination: Essays in Honour of H. R. Trevor-Roper*, ed. Hugh Lloyd-Jones, Valerie Pearl and Blair Worden (1981), pp. 182–200 (185ff). In *The Sound of Virtue: Philip Sidney's 'Arcadia' and Elizabethan Politics* (New Haven and London, 1996), Worden gives a detailed reading of the earlier Sidney's critical, though not republican, take on monarchical institutions.

35 William Hunt, 'Civic Chivalry and the English Civil War', in Anthony Grafton and Ann Blair (eds.), *The Transmission of Culture in Early Modern Europe* (Philadelphia, 1990), pp. 204–37 (p. 221).

Those political traditions had been reinforced by the marriage in 1616 of Dorothy's father to a daughter of Henry Percy, ninth earl of Northumberland. The Northumberland dynasty had a proud tradition of independence from, and if necessary overt resistance to, monarchical power. The brother of 'Sacharissa', Algernon Sidney, was to become a leading republican theorist. His father, the tenth earl, if not a republican was at least in favour of a strongly limited monarchy. Many leading members of the aristocracy were looking back to the medieval period when they had been able to exercise greater control over the king.[36]

That nostalgia for greater aristocratic authority was not confined to an English context; it could fuse with an admiration for the Roman republic. In 1631 Northumberland made some notes on the Roman emperors which took a somewhat disenchanted view of their line. Thus we are told that Claudius succeeded 'Notwithstanding the purpose of the Senate to extirpate the race of the Caesars and to restore Rome to her ancient libertie'. Nero 'put to death the famous poet Lucan'; the tyrant's death was 'pleasing to the people', who 'congratulated with bonetts on theire heads in signe of libertie'. Northumberland often emphasizes the Senate's role in choosing the emperor and in controlling historical memory: 'much ioyed' at the death of Domitian, it caused 'all memorialls of him to be defaced' and 'elected Nerua'.[37] Northumberland's circle included at least one political writer who was to draw heavily on Cicero, Lucan and other republican voices to urge the king to make sweeping concessions before he provoked popular revolution.[38] Northumberland had been associated with the opposition to Buckingham in the 1620s, and though during the 1630s he received royal honours culminating in being created Lord High Admiral, he took an independent line.

Waller's poetry of the 1630s seeks to remain true to these political attachments, but it also celebrates royal authority in a way that suggests a sharper unease than May's at the political tumults of the 1620s. He wrote a poem on the king's response to Buckingham's death which praised his combination of compassion and composure. Waller thus distanced himself both from the joy of Felton's admirers and from the violent vituperation of some of Buckingham's champions.[39] In a poem possibly written in 1623 and revised in the 1630s, Waller confronted the political storms of the 1620s by describing Prince Charles's struggle with a storm on his return from the aborted Spanish

---

36 J. S. A. Adamson, 'The Baronial Context of the English Civil War', *Transactions of the Royal Historical Society* 5th series 40 (1990), 93–120.

37 Alnwick Castle MS 104, pp. 4, 5, 6, 9.

38 'Regicola Publicola', Alnwick Castle MS 538 22/3, alludes to Cicero's *De Officiis* to urge that relations between king and subjects must be reciprocal, and warns that the 'very name of a free Commonwealth sounds sweetly in the eares of the Mulitude' [*sic*].

39 *WP*, I, 11–12.

marriage negotiations, on an occasion when his boat was nearly shipwrecked. (There was a precedent for linking rebellion with storms at sea, and its calming with oratory, in the *Aeneid*, i.148–50). Since his mission had been a reckless personal initiative, his death would have crystallized the irresponsibility of the whole exercise, and he was accused by his critics of having behaved thoughtlessly during the storm. One of those critics was the Puritan Sir Simonds D'Ewes, whose career was to intersect critically with Waller's at a number of points.[40] As so often in his poetry, Waller responds to attacks on the court by reworking hostile imagery into positive form. Charles's braving the elements might recall Caesar's challenging the storm in Book V of the *Pharsalia*. Lucan had reworked the *Aeneid*'s storm-rebellion imagery in that episode; Waller characteristically returns to Virgil, comparing Charles to the pious Aeneas, with the Infanta as his Dido whom duty must reject. For all the poem's confident predictions of dynastic continuity, however, the ending retains an element of unease:

> O see the then sole hope, and in designe
> Of heaven our ioy supported by a line,
> Which for that instant was heavens care above
> The chaine that's fixed to the throne of *Jove*,
> On which the fabrick of our world depends;
> One linke dissolv'd the whole creation ends.[41]

The golden chain which Fanshawe invoked as symbol of a secure cosmic hierarchy has become a storm-soaked rope, to which the prince's boat has to reach out precariously to remain afloat. Though Waller's couplets often replicate the idea of a chain of being in their smoothly-joined chains of rhymed lines, here the final line disrupts the closing couplet with its assertion of fragility. The sense of the precariousness of the cosmic machine recalls the opening of the *Pharsalia*.

Waller again opposed the harmony of his poetry to the tumults of the public sphere in a poem about Charles's restoration of St Paul's Cathedral, with a new façade by Inigo Jones begun in 1635 (figure 4).[42] The cathedral and its surroundings had become the heart of London's transitional public sphere. It

---

40 Norbrook, *PP*, p. 226.
41 'Of the danger His Majestie (being Prince) escaped at the rode at St *Andere*', *Poems...
written by Mr. Ed. Waller* (1645), p. 10; *WP*, I, 7. Quotations are from the third of the 1645 editions (w513, hereafter *Poems*). All work on Waller must be provisional until the new edition currently in progress is completed; Beal, 547–619, reveals how widely his poetry circulated in manuscript. There is a facsimile of the second 1645 edition (w512) by the Scolar Press (Menston, 1971), but the readings of w513, which claims to be 'Printed by a Copy of his own hand-writing', often seem preferable and are closer to later editions (cf. Chernaik, *The Poetry of Limitation*, p. 137 n. 42).
42 Waller, 'Vpon his Majesties repairing of Pauls', *Poems*, pp. 15–19; *WP*, I, 16–18. The poem is also available in Brendan O Hehir, *Expans'd Hieroglyphicks: A Critical Edition of Sir John Denham's 'Coopers Hill'* (Berkeley and Los Angeles, 1969), pp. 276–83.

4 Engraving of Inigo Jones's additions to St Paul's Cathedral, from William Dugdale, *The History of Saint Pauls Cathedral*, 1658.

was the centre of the oral diffusion of political opinion from which manuscript culture fed. News was exchanged in the aisles, and sermons – which in the 1620s had often been inflammatory – were preached from the outdoor pulpit. Access to this oral culture was often limited by personal relations of intimacy and dependence, and in this sense it was not fully 'public'; but Paul's Churchyard was also the home of the booksellers whose wares could be disseminated with no restriction other than price.[43] In the 1630s, under Laud's influence, theological controversy in print was banned, the sermons were restricted, and the newsgatherers were banished to a portico overlooked by royal statues.

Waller's Paul's poem has much in common with the idealizing idiom of the court masques of the 1630s. Waller contributed to at least one masque[44], and the imagery of his poem is strikingly close to Sir William Davenant's

43 Harold Love, *Scribal Publication in Seventeenth-Century England* (Oxford, 1993), pp. 194–5, suggests that a public sphere in the Habermasian sense requires written circulation. See also Richard Cust, 'News and Politics in Early Seventeenth-Century England', *Past and Present* no. 112 (1986), 60–90.

44 See 'The Misers speech in a Mask', *Poems*, p. 68; *WP*, I, 111.

Britannia Triumphans, performed in January 1638, which opened with a backdrop of a view of London looking towards St Paul's Cathedral, presented a chorus of loyal poets, and culminated in a vision of the royal fleet.[45] In Waller's poem, which ends with a tribute to Charles's naval power, the king is a source of harmony:

> He like *Amphion* makes those quarries leape
> Into faire figures from a confus'd heape:
> For in his art of regiment is found
> A power like that of harmony in sound. (lines 11–14)

Waller here introduces a figure that was to haunt political poetry for the next two decades: that of the artist-legislator who founds a new state and imposes a new kind of beauty.[46] Waller's immediate concern here is with the church, but in considering Charles in his role as head of the state church, he brings together religious and secular issues. This figure was consistently problematic. According to received accounts of the constitutional position, the structure of king, lords and commons had been passed down from time immemorial and the monarch's role was to preserve rather than transform it: 'innovation' of all kinds was dangerous. The state was more a natural than an artificial phenomenon.[47] Yet both absolutist and republican theorists were sympathetic to more radical changes that would permit a sounder basis for the state, betraying fears that the old constitution was not going to last.

The Paul's poem tries to harmonize differing representations of the artist-ruler. There are absolutist implications in Waller's insistence that power is handed down from above; the poem is full of instances of downward motion. The subjects' hearts are strings to be played; that they give 'Consent of motion' (line 18) may seem, beyond its musical sense, to have faint overtones of manipulating a Parliament.[48] As so often in Waller, however, poetic and

---

45 Sir William Davenant, *Britannia Triumphans*, in Stephen Orgel and Roy Strong, *Inigo Jones: The Theatre of the Stuart Court* (London, Berkeley and Los Angeles, 1973), II, 662–7; Kevin Sharpe, *Criticism and Compliment: The Politics of Literature in the England of Charles I* (Cambridge, 1987), pp. 247–51.

46 Ruth Nevo, *The Dial of Virtue: A Study of Poems on Affairs of State in the Seventeenth Century* (Princeton, 1963), p. 25, takes the Paul's poem as marking a shift towards increasing emphasis in royalist poetry on the king's dominant role in shaping the entire social order.

47 Kevin Sharpe goes so far as to claim that the idea of 'the state as an artifice which needs to be justified' was 'essentially alien to early Stuart political thinking': 'A Commonwealth of Meanings: Languages, Analogues, Ideas and Politics', in *Politics and Ideas in Early Stuart England: Essays and Studies* (London and New York, 1989), pp. 3–71 (10). Waller's poem, insofar as it bears on state as well as church, is one of many counter-examples; see also Sharpe's own examples on p. 44.

48 On Waller's fondness for 'consent' see Allison, *Toward an Augustan Poetic*, p. 28.

political concord prove problematic. It turns out that Charles is not quite like Amphion. Rather than starting from a *tabula rasa*, from mere heaps of stones, he is confronted with a building that already exists, and which he wants to preserve:

> Two distant vertues in one act we finde,
> The modesty and greatnesse of his minde.
> Which not content to bee above the rage
> And iniury of all impayring age;
> In its owne worth secure, doth higher clime,
> And things halfe swallow'd from the jawes of time,
> Reduce[;] an earnest of his grand designe,
> To frame no new Church, but the old refine[.][49] (lines 29–36)

The normally closed couplets open to register the gulf of time and Charles's heroic effort to overleap it at 'Reduce'. Waller uses 'reduce' in its Latinate sense of 'bring back, restore'. The poetic strategy is then to make this restoration appear at one and the same time an Amphion-like dynamic creation and a conscientious return to the past, accepting the restraint of regular forms: renovation without innovation. Charles's heroic breaking of the chains of the couplet is also a return to traditional forms. Anxieties about Laudian 'innovations' are thus contested: in referring to the cathedral as Paul's rather than St Paul's, Waller reassures Puritan readers.[50]

Waller offers a reassuringly organic analogy for the remodelling of the district:

> So ioyes the aged oak when wee divide
> The creeping Ivy from his injur'd side. (lines 25–6)

In thus defending Caroline harmony, however, Waller has to acknowledge that there has been resistance. The inhabitants of the houses that clustered round Paul's had opposed the changes, which they saw as an exploitation of royal power to override traditional liberties of the city.[51] Waller's poem is uncompromising in its attitude to these people: the king must 'deface' the houses of these vipers; they are a chain that would imprison the king unless he broke it. In general terms the poem celebrates unity, but in practice it enacts division: those who do not give their consent, who are not taken by the beauty of the king's power, must be broken, defaced, cast out. To assert the royal grace it is necessary to 'conspire' (line 19); the Latinate sense of 'breathe together' perhaps does not quite cancel a stronger meaning.

---

49 One of the early manuscript versions of this poem signals the significance of this line by breaking off at this point: Bodleian MS Malone 21, fol. 20v.

50 I owe this point to John Safford.

51 Per Palme, *Triumph of Peace: A Study of the Whitehall Banqueting House* (1957), p. 314.

Waller's Paul's poem, then, has to work hard to gain its concord at the cost of strong resistance to opposing elements, but it is able to combine the figures of monarch and artist in ways that reflect favourably both on Charles and on his poets. Within a few years of its composition, that synthesis was looking precarious, as can be seen in a tribute by Waller's co-founder of the new poetics of concord. Sir John Denham's *Coopers Hill*, first published in 1642, is best known as a celebration of harmony in the landscape, with the smooth flow of the Thames symbolizing the smoothness he aims at in verse. When first composed, however, the poem took a darker view of the possibilities of such concord. Denham addresses

> Pauls' the late theame of such a Muse whose flight
> Hath bravely reacht & soar'd above thy height,
> Now shalt thou stand, though time or sword or fire
> Or zeale more feirce then they thy fall conspire,
> Secure, while thee the best of Poetts sings
> Preserv'd from ruine by the best of Kings. (lines 15–20)[52]

In a significant shift of emphasis, the transcendence of Waller's poetic architecture serves to accentuate the fragility of the actual church. Denham transfers to Waller the achievement that Waller had ascribed to Charles: of loftily redeeming the cathedral from the enmity of time. Charles's rule, meanwhile, is under threat from a menacing cloud which evokes not only the smoke pollution that was already gaining notoriety for London but also the indeterminacy, the breakdown of traditional boundaries, of an emergent political crisis. The poem's affirmation of balance cannot erase an awareness of the centrifugal forces that are liable to erode it. Lucan's *concordia discors* has not been entirely banished.[53]

The end of the poem presents a dark view of the possibility of establishing a balance between king and people, recounting a series of tussles in which first one side and then the other was on top. If Parliament pushes its demands too far, there will be chaos. Husbandmen can erect banks to stop a storm-swollen river overflowing, but if they try to force it into a new or narrower course,

> Stronger & feircer by restraint he roares
> And knowes noe bounds, but makes his power his shores. (lines 327–8)

---

52 From the second draft, which O Hehir dates to early 1642, *Expans'd Hieroglyphicks*, pp. 93–4; on links with Waller see O Hehir, *Harmony From Discords: A Life of Sir John Denham* (Berkeley and Los Angeles, 1968), pp. 20ff. Denham's tribute indicates that the Paul's poem had acquired celebrity even while circulating only in manuscript; Denham's publisher, Thomas Walkeley, was to bring out Waller's poems in 1645, and Denham's reference formed a kind of advance publicity. Denham echoed the Paul's poem in 'On the Earl of Strafford's Tryal and Death', Bodleian MS Locke e.17, cited by O Hehir, *Harmony from Discords*, p. 37.

53 See O Hehir, *Expans'd Hieroglyphicks*, *passim*, and the title of his *Harmony From Discords*. O Hehir does not mention Lucan's version of the concept.

A similar figure had been used by Machiavelli, a translation of whose *Prince* had appeared in 1640. He compares Fortune to a river whose destructiveness in stormy weather can be contained by 'banks and fences', and politically well-ordered states to a plain with careful river-works.[54] Denham adopts a more negative view of political agency, and in particular of popular agency: the prince is in the end a natural force whose ways the people may not restrain beyond a certain point.

May and the Parliamentary cause

The political crisis which turned Waller's optimism into Denham's darker note had been precipitated by Laud's and Charles's remoulding of the church. In 1637, attempts to impose on the Scots a prayer-book which was regarded as superstitious provoked riots, and in 1639 a Scots army moved against England. Many English leaders, including Northumberland, were very uneasy about fighting against their co-religionists. May later dated a wide-spread revulsion against royal policies from the time of the Scots war.[55] After an inconclusive treaty was signed, in early 1640 Thomas Wentworth, Lord Deputy of Ireland, returned to England to help the king suppress his enemies more thoroughly. Wentworth, now created earl of Strafford, had been a leader of the 'patriots' in the 1620s, but he had become more uncompromisingly monarchist: Northumberland found him 'Spanish' in his ways.[56] May likened Strafford's defection to the king to Curio's defection to Caesar in Lucan (iv.814–9).[57] The political nation was about to make another of Harrington's 'jumps'. Strafford proposed that a Parliament should be called to raise funds for a renewed Scottish war the following year; he and Charles were convinced that such a peaceful and contented people would easily support their aims. From a very early stage, however, the leading Parliamentarians refused the royal agenda, harking back instead to the constitutional impropriety of the dissolution in 1629. Memories of the 1628 Parliament were soon revived by the publication of a record of its proceedings.[58] Under the energetic leadership of John Pym, who was in close contact with 'patriot' peers in the Lords, the Commons outlined a comprehensive programme of reforms designed to eliminate the abuses of the personal rule: ship money, arbitrary arrests, defences of monopolies, the repressiveness of the Laudian clergy, the timorous foreign policy.

54 *Nicholas Machiavel's Prince*, trans. E[dward]. D[acres]. (1640; 17168), ch. 25, p. 203.
55 May, *History*, I, 29.
56 Northumberland to the earl of Leicester, 5 December 1639, in *Letters and Memorials of State*, ed. Arthur Collins, 2 vols. (1746), II, 621.   57 May, *History*, I, 20.
58 *The Diurnall Occurrences of Every Dayes Proceedings in Parliament* (1641; E178.12).

Charles's initial response was to dissolve the 'Short' Parliament and turn again to absolutist strategies, seeking financial aid from the Spanish in exchange for defending their treasure-fleet against the Dutch. However, there was strong domestic resistance to his strategies for extra-Parliamentary means of raising money for the Scots campaign. Charles was forced to summon a new Parliament, which assembled in November 1640 and was to become known as the 'Long Parliament'. This time, the leaders of the Commons were not content with merely going back to the days before the personal rule. Their resolve was heightened when news came of a rebellion in Ireland, which was believed or alleged to form part of a Catholic conspiracy in which at least the queen and possibly the king were involved. Pym and his allies embarked on a series of unprecedented constitutional measures. Their ends may not have been significantly different from before, but they now believed that far more drastic means were called for. A key measure was the Triennial Act, which required the king to summon Parliament at least every three years and forbade him to dissolve the present Parliament without its consent. In May 1641 Strafford was executed.

The king's hands were now more firmly tied; but Parliament's position was far short of republicanism. Its official statements constantly proclaimed its loyalty to the king as opposed to his unworthy counsellors. Yet many defences of the Parliamentarian cause betray a lack of confidence in the traditional political system that implied the need for more radical measures. The crises of the early Stuart period could be located not in the moral failings of individual rulers but in much deeper, more systemic problems. This can be seen in the writings of Thomas May, who in the 1640s performed his notorious shift from court poet to official historian to the Long Parliament. Royalist charges that this change was motivated by personal grievance do not stand up to the evidence of his writings. It is possible to trace a certain distancing from monarchism in his project of the later 1630s, a Latin translation of his *Continuation* of the *Pharsalia*. The process of addressing the international humanist republic of letters seems to have made him more critical again of the defects of monarchy. He pared away his earlier extenuations of Caesar's conduct, bringing the poem's political standpoint closer to Lucan's own.[59] The volume certainly retained the monarchist panoply of the English version, with a fulsome dedication to Charles. Several of the commendatory poems praised the king for allowing the Roman liberty that had been stifled under Nero to be re-enacted under his rule.[60] Yet the quotation on the title-page was politically ambivalent: May applied to his own poem Lucan's 'Venturi me teque legent'

59 R. T. Bruère, 'The Latin and English Versions of Thomas May's *Supplementum Lucani*', *Classical Philology* 44 (1949), 145–63.
60 Thomas May, *Supplementum Lucani* (Leiden, 1640), sigs. *4, *5v.

(ix.985), his claim after the description of Troy that future generations will read his own account of the civil wars as well as Caesar's.[61] As courtier, May submits himself to Charles; as heir to Lucan, he proclaims his independence of monarchs.

Amongst those who contributed commendatory verses to May's *Supplementum* was Sir Richard Fanshawe. By the summer of 1642, however, the two friends had parted company. Despairing of being able to influence Parliament, Charles had left for Oxford. After what May termed 'long and tedious Paper-conflicts', he raised his standard against Parliament in August.[62] It was around this time, according to Aubrey, that Fanshawe had a long political discussion with May.[63] It is not unlikely that their thoughts turned to Lucan. As has been seen, that poet's message would have been ambiguous. Despite portraying the horrific consequences of war, he also warned that a point would come when it was too late to resist tyranny, and that the consequences would be terrible not only for one's own but for future generations. Charles's setting up his standard could be felt to resemble Caesar's crossing the Rubicon. For Puritan readers, the poem was a reminder that an apocalyptic struggle was already taking place, and that neutrality was to side with Satan. But the Roman poet's chronicle of epic carnage could, rather more simply, be taken as a warning to side with the king to save the realm from further disorder.[64] Fanshawe evidently took this line, for he left for Oxford.

It is perhaps possible to reconstruct something of the two friends' conversations from a *Discourse* which May published in July 1642. Here he reveals a profound scepticism about the possibility of reconciling royal and Parliamentarian demands. He was moving towards Harrington's idea of an inherent instability, a series of 'jumps', which might perhaps become as precarious as the Roman constitution analysed by Lucan. Though Parliament may be the 'Basis' of the constitution, it is the nature of monarchy that princes are invested with so much majesty that it would seem a mockery if no considerable power were entrusted to them. The more power the king has, the more likely it is that if he is weak or bad he will abuse it. So necessary it is, declares May, for all human ordinances to leave something to chance; in the end there must always be recourse to God's providence. Put in rather less sanguine terms, what May implies is that only divine intervention can save monarchical

---

61 May presented a copy of his Latin poem to the Dutch scholar Daniel Heinsius, who disliked Laud's meddling with freedom of scholarly expression: Sotheby's sale, 19 July 1990 (I owe this information to Peter Beal); Paul R. Sellin, *Daniel Heinsius and Stuart England* (Leiden and London, 1968), pp. 82ff.   62 May, *History*, II, 96.

63 *ABL*, II, 55.

64 The absolutist Sir Robert Filmer cited Lucan (iii.145–6) in the royalist cause: *The Anarchy of a Limited or Mixed Monarchy*, in *Patriarcha and Other Writings*, ed. Johann P. Sommerville (Cambridge, 1991), p. 131.

government from structural instability. For the consequence of monarchs' desire to vindicate their power is that their 'soules' are not 'large', nor their 'affections . . . publike'. Their interest is in the end a private one, which may work at variance with the public interest. They are always vulnerable to the flattery of courtiers, who make them 'afraid to look their faces in so true a glasse as a Parliament'. The more the affairs of the state need Parliaments, the more reluctant princes become to call them, knowing they and their favourites will be called to account.[65]

And the blurring of private and public interests inherent in monarchical government has a further deleterious effect. The people, who are used to judging their rulers in purely personal terms, will be reluctant to believe that the realm is in a bad state as long as they see that their monarch is virtuous. In a paradox that was to become a central republican theme in the 1650s, May argues that good princes may actually have a worse effect on the commonwealth than bad ones. Henry III, Edward II, Richard II – and, implicitly, Charles – had undermined liberty even though their moral character was not intrinsically evil. They were manipulated by favourites who diverted their attention from the public interest to private gratification. Even the removal of a favourite from power, May later argued, might be counter-productive: looking on Buckingham as the only hindrance to the kingdom's happiness, the people had been too indulgent to Charles after his death.[66]

The worse things become, the more need there is of a 'long Parliament' to remedy them (p. 8); but the longer a Parliament lasts, the more danger there is that both prince and people will become disillusioned at the inevitably slow course of major reform. Parliamentarians may find it difficult to restore a true sense of their rights, and the people will often forget them altogether, remaining content with the prince's personal virtues. Their 'inconstancie' to their liberties 'seemes to be grounded upon loyaltie to the King'. Often, after a long Parliament, the people have turned against the reformers and championed the 'Delinquents' who had oppressed them. While the people may be to blame for this, there is also a structural reason: 'in the *Interim* betweene Parliaments, the People are too scattered and confused a body, to appeare in vindication of their proper interests'. They need a 'Representative Body'; but all too often they fail to recognize that need (pp. 9, 2).

This analysis of the political situation on the eve of the Civil War does not square with the received image of May as an ingrate who seethed with resentment at Charles for failing to grant him favour. In fact he implicitly aligns Charles with those princes who are personally virtuous; his reservations are not so much about Charles's character as about the institution of monarchy

---

65 [Thomas May], *A Discourse Concerning the Successe of Former Parliaments* (1642; E154.51), p. 6.   66 May, *History*, I, 12.

in itself. On the other hand, he is pessimistic about the possibility of reform: the dice seem to be so loaded against the process that it may well collapse as so many previous reforming Parliaments have done. His tract certainly does not call for a republic. It ends by saying that great princes should no more find it an indignity to be guided by Parliaments than do steersmen to be guided by a compass. That sanguine conclusion, however, is not really borne out by the body of the work, whose mode of analysis, with its emphasis on the conflict between public and private interests, is close to that of early modern republicanism. In making similar points in the *History of the Parliament* a few years later, May was to quote from Machiavelli.[67] But we know that May already had an intimate acquaintance with one form of republican discourse from his translation of Lucan. The strong emphasis on the theme of memory in the *Discourse* echoes Lucan's gloomy view of the means by which the memory of freedom gradually dwindles. The prince will delay a Parliament 'till the People tired with expectation of it, have by degrees forgot the sharpnesse of those diseases, which before required it' (*Discourse*, p. 10). While May's poetic account of Edward III's reign had steered clear of sensitive constitutional issues, the revived demand for regular Parliaments, which could be traced back to his reign, now made him reflect on the fickleness of cultural memory. Those things 'which by constitution of the Government, the people may challenge as due from the Prince, having been long forborne, become at last to be esteemed such Acts of extraordinary grace, as that the Prince is highly thanked for granting of them'.[68] It had taken a major crisis for the Long Parliament to be able to convert those graces back into rights. If Parliament did make any compromise with the king, it would have to be wary.

English Lucans: Cowley, Wither, May, and the outbreak of the Civil War

Although May's reading of Lucan hardened his hostility to the royalists, other readings were possible in this uncertain period. When Fanshawe said farewell to May and moved to the exiled court at Oxford, he would have encountered the precocious poet Abraham Cowley. Soon after the paper conflict had turned into physical warfare, Cowley began work on an epic whose title, *The Civill Warre*, inevitably aroused associations with Lucan.[69] His poem, however, amounts to a sustained subversion of the tradition of reading Lucan as it had developed amongst Parliamentarians like May; Cowley creates a politically more orthodox poem which then founders on intractable realities. He had contributed to the poetic cult of the king's peace, and the opening of

67 May, *History*, I, 54.   68 May, *History*, I, 100–1.
69 Abraham Cowley, *The Civil War*, ed. Allan Pritchard (Toronto and Buffalo, 1973).

the poem is shot through with nostalgia for that firmly monarchical order. Though Cowley also set himself in the manner of Lucan to base his poem on historical fact, and indeed drew heavily on newsbook reports, his mythologizing, celebratory impulse grew increasingly at odds both with Lucan's poetics and with the course of events. Cowley lacks any of Lucan's sense of the tensions and disharmonies within political orders:

> Then Sixteene Yeeres we endur'd our Happinesse:
> Till in a Moment from the *North* we find
> A *Tempest* conjur'd up without a *Wind*. (i.92–4)

The paradise of the 1630s is destroyed in a moment by outside forces, the rebellious Scots who cross the new Rubicon, the Tweed (i.97ff). Cowley is supremely confident, however, that base-born rebels will always be defeated by socially superior monarchists. And the first year of the war permitted some confidence. Royal forces succeeded in hemming in the mainly urban-based Parliamentarians within their city walls.

What proved to be a crucial turning-point came when after a desperate mobilization in London, Essex led an army to relieve Gloucester, and on his return fought off the king's forces at Newbury. These events were also a turning-point in Cowley's poem. It is at the point where he comes to the relief of Gloucester that he abandons a basically historical narration and turns to myth. The setback is explained by the eruption from the underworld of Rebellion, who foments Satanic energy amongst the Londoners and thus raises the siege. Cowley's Hell is a kind of political unconscious of royalist panegyric: all those aspects of history which do not square with a simply monarchical patriotism are banished to this realm of darkness, from which, however, they then return. Cowley draws on the vision of the underworld in Lucan's sixth book; and Lucan's aristocratic republicanism would have shared some of Cowley's disdain for popular rebels – one element his portrait of Rebellion shares with May's Sedition. But there is no nostalgia for feudal aristocratic independence in Cowley's poem; he brutally destroys the Parliamentarians' constitutionalist idols:

> There thowsand stubborne Barons fetterd ly,
> And curse their old vaine noyse of Liberty. (ii.457–8)

No nation, he laments, has produced more rebels than England (ii.456). He hits at Warwick the King-maker (ii.487–8), having already dismissed the current earl as 'the Publick *Pyrat*' (ii.307). Of other figures praised in May's Lucan, Lindsey is celebrated for fighting in the royalist cause (i.281) but Essex is ridiculed for lacking eloquence (iii.329ff).

Immediately after chronicling the battle of Newbury, Cowley broke off. The turn of the tide in the war had undermined his original narrative direction. It was, however, already clear that his own poem's ideological rigidity would prevent its emulating Lucan's tragic portrayal of civil conflict. His Charles lacks Pompey's complexity because he is under no constitutional obligations, he feels no tension between military and political imperatives. In ideological terms, Cowley's Charles as living embodiment of the state has something in common with Lucan's Caesar. Conversely, it is the Parliamentarians who are more politically complex; even more than in the *Pharsalia*, this is a narrative where the constitutionalist party cannot have a single hero. Cowley tries to create an equivalent of Caesar's restless energy in his personification of Rebellion; but the personification then splits into end-lessly sub-dividing sects and schisms. In a parody of the epic catalogue, Cowley goes through all London's sects from the Presbyterians to 'Hemerobaptists, and Sebaptists too . . .' (iii.180). The sheer multiplicity of such names goes beyond Cowley's rigidly hierarchical sense of poetic decorum:

> What should I here their Great ones Names rehearse?
> Low, wretched Names, unfit for noble Verse? (iii.383–4)
> But with them let their Names forever dy;
> Too vile, and base for well-writ Infamy. (iii.453–4)

Cowley sports with the crude monosyllabic names of the citizens killed at Newbury. Though there is some striking grotesque humour, there is a cheap-ness about these passages that is hard to reconcile with Cowley's attempts to defend Charles's regal dignity.[70]

Yet in the manic energy he gives to Rebellion, Cowley is acknowledging that he has to deal with a new phenomenon, one that eludes traditional poetic values. For this is a war in which military nobility alone will not prevail: it is a war of ideas. And where in Lucan republican principles motivate only the elite, Cowley is describing a society where ideas are being made widely access-ible through the printing press. The king's side claims to be the true champion of liberty against mob rule:

> Is't *liberty*? what are those threates we heare
> From the base rout? can *liberty* be there? (i.549–50)

In Cowley's world, the answer is self-evidently in the negative. Ideas them-selves become villains. The serpent in the Eden of the 1630s is the book:

> Then onely'in *Bookes* the *learn'd* could mis'ery see,
> And the *unlearn'd* ne're heard of Miserie. (i.85–6)

---

70 For a burlesque equivalent of Cowley's poem, which frequently satirizes Lucan and pos-sibly also May's translation, see Timothy Raylor, *Cavaliers, Clubs, and Literary Culture: Sir John Mennes, James Smith, and the Order of the Fancy* (Newark, London and Toronto, 1994), pp. 181–5.

The analysis recalls Hobbes on the baleful effects of humanism. The people would be most happy if they remained in blissful ignorance of the mysteries of state; it is the restless intellectuals who sully monarchical peace. For Cowley, the Parliamentarian leader John Hampden is 'curst by *too good a Wit!*' (i.392). Rebellion's 'Words were Bullets' (ii.417) and the preachers cast 'mouth-Granadoes' (ii.598).

This intellectual restlessness is particularly destructive to the church, and Cowley sees its destruction as the rebels' main aim. But his poem also reveals the way of thinking that was to forge an oppositional alliance between republicans and Puritans. In his oration before the Battle of Newbury, the king makes his own order of priorities very clear: the church is 'The thing more deare then Crowne or Libertie' (iii.324). The church, then, is quite separate from liberty: this church is one in which independent thought gives way to obedience and reverence. The king is in fact using the church's mystifications to buttress his authority even as he claims to be defending it for its own sake. It is only at the end of the poem that Cowley strikes a more complex note, in an intense elegy for Lucius Cary, Viscount Falkland. Falkland had been a leading figure in the intellectual life of the 1630s, an independent thinker on religious and political questions whose eventual siding with the king brought prestige to the royalist cause. Falkland himself, however, had responded to the war with an anguished division far more complex than anything in Cowley's poem, and his death at Newbury is sometimes seen as a kind of suicide. Perhaps Cowley came to see that in exclaiming 'would my Verse were nobler for your sake!' (iii.462) he was condemning his own poem.

Failure though it may be, *The Civill Warre* is a fascinating experiment in the possibilities and the limits of representing a modern ideological conflict through the medium of classical epic. Cowley was too much out of sympathy with the values of Lucan and his admirers to be able to make that model work under these circumstances. That did not as yet prove that it could not be done; but it is true that a poetry of civil war was slow to develop on the Parliamentarian side. Some of the reasons emerge if we compare *The Civill Warre* with a poem written in the same year by George Wither, who had fought at Gloucester and Newbury. Wither was now in his mid-fifties.[71] His prophetic voice had been subdued during the 1630s, but as soon as war broke out he was quick to take up arms for Parliament.[72] He clashed with

---

71 Charles S. Hensley, *The Later Career of George Wither* (The Hague and Paris, 1969), gives biographical data, though it is not always reliable on political contexts.

72 He did not finance a troop of his own, as is normally stated, but was commissioned for a Surrey troop: John Gurney, 'George Wither and Surrey Politics 1642–1649', *Southern History* 19 (1997), 74–98(75); for a fuller discussion of his political role see also Gurney, 'The County of Surrey and the English Revolution', unpublished PhD thesis, University of Sussex, 1991, pp. 141ff. I am grateful to Dr. Gurney for his help with Wither.

royalist poetic as well as military forces when Denham plundered his house; from then on Wither pursued a personal feud against Denham that also involved hostility to the balanced, urbane couplets popularized by *Coopers Hill.*

Wither had always represented himself as a 'country' poet. Thirty years before the outbreak of the Civil War he had belonged to a group of pastoral poets for whom the celebration of England had become increasingly a matter of national rather than specifically dynastic loyalty.[73] Still more than Michael Drayton and William Browne, he had turned from idealized nymphs and shepherds to the actualities of political life. In his first major satire he had taken pride in having resisted London fashions with his 'ancient-vsed *Hampshire Dialect*'.[74] Richard Baxter wrote that 'Honest *George Withers*, though a Rustick Poet, hath been very acceptable as to some for his Prophecies, so to others for his plain Country-honesty: The Vulgar were the more pleased with him for being so little Courtly . . .'[75]

Wither's first publication during the war lived up to this image. In the one issue of the newsbook *Mercurius Rusticus* he claimed (with a touch of irony) that there was a rural public sphere, the 'Countrey-Exchanges' such as the ale-house and the barber's shop. In his rural persona, Wither attacked courtly culture:

> the Queen will not have so many Masks at Christmas and Shrovetide this yeare as she was wont to have other yeeres heretofore; because *Inigo Iones* cannot conveniently make such Heavens and Paradises at *Oxford* as he did at *White-hall*: & because the Poets are dead, beggered, or run away, who were wont in their Masks to make Gods and Goddesses of them, and shamefully to flatter them with Attributes neither fitting to be ascribed or accepted of.

Though he concentrated his attack on the queen and evil counsellors, and claimed that the king was still redeemable, his comment that the king was supported by 'a wandring Prince or two' was not calculated to deepen reverence for monarchy.[76] And the newsbook signalled his firm commitment to militancy. Himself an outsider from Surrey where he had taken up his command, he wanted the county's troops to be a roving offensive force, rather than the defensive force called for by the more cautious localists.[77] His 'country' persona was a political artifice rather than a direct reflection of local opinion.

73 Richard Helgerson, *Forms of Nationhood: The Elizabethan Writing of England* (Chicago and London, 1992), pp. 105–47.

74 Wither, *Abuses Stript and Whipt*, in *Juvenilia* (1622; 25911; rptd. Manchester, 1871), I, 9.

75 Richard Baxter, *Poetical Fragments* (1681; B1349), sig. A6v.

76 [George Wither], *Mercurius Rusticus* (n. pl., 1643; E73.2), pp. 1, 10, 15; he strongly supported the creation of a new Great Seal (p. 9; see below, p. 94).

77 Gurney, 'The County of Surrey and the English Revolution', pp. 141ff.

During late 1643, Wither turned from the sword to the pen: he would '*by this Engine more strengthen your* Army *then a full Regiment of horse*'.[78] Characteristically immodest though this claim may have been, it did indicate something important about the war, something that Cowley had been forced to confront. This was such a heavily ideological conflict that military morale was crucially dependent on intellectual conviction. A Parliamentarian chronicler of the siege of Gloucester declared that:

> The Action of these times transcends the Barons Warres, and those tedious discords betweene the houses of *Yorke* and *Lancaster,* in as much as it is undertaken upon higher Principles, and carried on to a nobler end, and effects more universall.[79]

This statement runs counter to the commonly-voiced idea that civil wars are worse than other kinds. For John Corbet, this civil war is different from aristocratic struggles for personal influence because it involves fighting for clear principles, for a common cause.

A lot then depended on making those principles matter. Wither's account of his military exploits in *Campo-Musae* says next to nothing about what actually happened in battle, apart from one striking vignette:

> In Meadowes, where our sports were wont to be,
> (And, where we playing wantonly have laine)
> Men sprawling in their blood, we now doe see;
> Grim postures, of the dying, and the slaine ... (p. 16)

Wither immediately draws back from specific experience to general issues:

> But, what are private Losses, while we view
> Three famous *Kingdomes,* wofully expos'd
> To miserable Ruine, and so few,
> Lament that plague, wherewith we are inclos'd?
> My selfe, and my estate, I shall contemne,
> Till we, in freedome, sing our *Syon-Songs* ... (p. 16)

That last comment will be read with some amusement by those who have encountered Wither's endless complaints over the next twenty years about the way the war had damaged his estate. He was not always able to maintain the philosophical detachment with which he here recalled Lucan's invocation of the temple of the heavens:

> My *Quarter* was the *Field:* my *Tent* and Bed,
> A well-made *Barley-cocke:* the Canopie

---

78 George Wither, *Campo-Musae: or the field-musings of Captain George Wither* (1643; E1144.4; *WMW,* I), sig. A3r.

79 John Corbet, *An Historicall Relation of the Military Government of Gloucester* (1645; E306.8), sig. A2v; cited by Smith, *LR,* p. 51.

And Curtains, which, to cover me, were spread,
No meaner then the starre-bespangled skie. (p. 72)

Nonetheless, the poem does show a commitment to setting personal experience in a wider political context. Wither makes it clear that his resolution in the fight depended on his being able to think and argue through the issues to his satisfaction, without glossing over difficulties. His equivalent of Cowley's Sedition is the figure of '*Deluding-Reason*' with her 'paper pellets' (pp. 27, 30). The striking difference is that Wither gives her a speech of two and a half pages in which she voices royalist arguments, before offering a point-by-point refutation. Wither's arguments are extremely tortuous in their attempts to square his earlier praise of Charles and condemnation of resistance with his willingness now to take arms against him; but the way he makes the military conflict blur into an allegorical war of ideas illustrates how important it is for him to link the two, in sharp contrast with Cowley's suspicion of political and religious debate.

It is only once the issues are settled to his satisfaction that Wither turns to celebrating the heroes on his side. And here again there is a striking contrast with Cowley in his rejection of traditional ideas of honour:

Let them, that shall hereafter counted be
Most honourable persons, never more
Be they, who shew the longest Pedigree,
From Kings, and Conquerors, as heretofore ... (p. 71)

Where Cowley contemptuously declared the Parliamentarian masses unworthy of his fine writing, Wither expresses regret at not being able to 'remember' thousands more. And in a later edition of the poem he highlighted his preference for active virtue over birth by downgrading the dedication to Essex, whose zeal for the cause seemed by then to be flagging.

Campo-Musae does not fit into any conventional poetic category. It is not in any obvious sense a war poem, and bears out Nigel Smith's claim that epic in the Civil War period tended towards interiority.[80] The poem's stance is intensely subjective, such that it is never very clear where the action is taking place. Subjectivity may not be quite the right term, however, for the poem presents an inner dialogue more than a monologue. It sets up a space in which the 'paper bullets' of the rival sides' arguments can be weighed against each other so that the writer can re-emerge into the world of action: 'Place to the *Sword*, my *Pen*, againe, must yeeld' (p. 73). That emergence is only provisional. Wither has reached a resolution for the time, but by referring back extensively to *Britain's Remembrancer* and looking forward to a forthcoming poem, he draws attention to the partial nature of one's understanding at any

---

80 Smith, *LR*, pp. 218ff.

time, to the possibility of further revelations and insights. Metrically, Wither reinforces this sense of a resolution that is only provisional by casting the poem as a long sequence of Shakespearean sonnets, where the clinching couplets did not always fully resolve the discrete quatrains.

There was a certain provisionality even in his frequently reiterated claims to prophetic powers. Aubrey thought that though he was 'an easie Rymer, & no good Poet, he was a good Vates [prophet]: he had a strange sagacity, & and foresight into mundane affaires'.[81] But prophecy for Wither involved 'rationally pre-conjecturing the most probable *events*': it could never lay claim to absolute certainty because 'the *intentions* and *actions* of men were no infallible grounds of hopes or fear'.[82] Though he draws inspiration from the prophecies of the Book of Revelation, which ultimately provide his greatest authority for resistance, he concedes that they are as yet not fully understood. At this stage, Wither represents himself as following the official Parliamentary line and defending the king against his evil advisers. He makes it clear, however, that this is not because he believes in subordinating himself to traditional institutions but because he has thought the position through himself. This is very overtly the poetry of a citizen, not of a subject.

Campo-Musae was something of a bestseller, going through three English editions and one in Scotland in two years. Wither's sense of provisional commitment clearly spoke to many on his side. It was not easy to reconcile with a more conventional epic standpoint, even one as ironically distanced as Lucan's. So it is perhaps not surprising that the poet who would have been the obvious candidate for the Lucan of the English Civil War, Thomas May, failed to provide an epic. Not, at any rate, in verse. He was commissioned by Parliament to write the official history of its cause, which appeared in 1647. His *History*, though today eclipsed, became for many years a standard point of reference, and it did set out to place immediately contemporary events in a long-term context and thus invest them with a certain epic grandeur. Though it is unlikely that May would have known Cowley's *Civill Warre*, which remained in manuscript, the two works offer revealing parallels and contrasts in responding to the same events. May's prose is coloured by a poetics of liberty which carries with it a certain suspicion of the mythologizing and demonizing flights characteristic of Cowley's royalist poetics. May begins with an explicit echo of Lucan's 'bella ... plus quam civilia', and announces his intention of following Lucan in tracing the underlying causes of the war. As an official historian, of course, May does not have Lucan's licence for wild and satirical wit; his sober tone can make for dull reading. Even the sobriety, however, has a certain polemical force. May is concerned to show that his is

---

81 Bodleian MS Aubrey 8, fol. 50v; *ABL*, II, 306.
82 George Wither, *Furor-Poeticus (i.e.) Propheticus* (1660; E1818.2; *WMW*, V), sig. A2r.

the broader and more comprehensive cause, that an openness to opposing points of view is built into it. He avoids turning Charles into a melodramatic villain: as in his *Discourse*, he tends to read political issues in structural rather than merely ethical terms. He was to be criticized by Lucy Hutchinson for being too lenient toward Charles.[83] Like Cowley, May ends his story with the battle of Newbury, but he regrets that he does not have an account from the royalist side. May is consistently interested in the difference made by the new public sphere to the conduct of warfare, in demonstrating that this is a war of ideas as well as of battles.

May's treatment of events is socially as well as intellectually more open than Cowley's. He is ready to idealize the aristocratic leadership in chivalric terms. Some of the patrons he had addressed in 1627 as embodying Lucan's virtues were now putting them into practice on the English stage. Essex is given great prominence in Book III, and Warwick receives high praise.[84] Thus far he is able to imitate Lucan's aristocratic tone, and to counter the propaganda of those like Cowley for whom rebels against their king must necessarily be base-born. May is also, however, well aware that the social basis of the struggle for liberty has undergone profound changes in seventeenth-century England; the party of liberty has broadened from the Roman elite to a much wider social grouping. Thus the Scottish covenanters, whose movement had a strong popular element, can be compared to Lucan's Cato.[85]

May remains socially cautious: he continues to pay respect to the earl of Essex at a time when radicals were calling for the war to be transformed into a direct popular rising. He is, however, open to a certain degree of populism. In discussing the battle of Edgehill, he draws on classical sources which give a less socially elevated basis to the republican cause than Lucan. Brutus and Cassius, he writes, lost their war in part because the bulk of their support came from the people, from those with only limited resources; they were fighting to defend their liberty but not huge amounts of property. Caesar was able to consolidate his position by appealing to the propertied and by bribing those less well off. In the *History* May frequently emphasizes that the common people were the most vehement in their support for the cause of freedom, that many of the gentry and aristocracy cared more for wealth than for liberty.[86] He thus directly challenges the social prejudice of Cowley and his allies, with their rigid criterion of decorum in church, state and poetry; he tries to give heroic dignity to a broad cross-section of the people. Where Cowley had structured his third book towards an inevitable triumph of his side, and thus foundered when literary decorum failed to coincide with reality, May angled his action very differently, emphasizing the frailty of the Parliamentary

83 Hutchinson, p. 53.   84 May, *History*, III, 6, II, 104.   85 May, *History*, I, 29.
86 May, *History*, I, 64, II, 108, 112, III, 30.

forces, showing how close they came to defeat, and how they avoided defeat by an ideological solidarity that cut across social differences. He pays special attention to the efforts made by Londoners to throw up new defences:

> nor could they, if their Enemies, then Masters of the field, had come upon them, have opposed any Walls, but such as old SPARTA used for their guard, the hearts of couragious Citizens...[Walls were begun, with] all Professions, Trades, and Occupations, taking their turnes; and not onely inferiour Tradesmen, but Gentlemen of the best quality, Knights, and Ladies themselves, for the incouragement of others, resorted daily to the Workes, not as spectators but assistors in it[.][87]

Cowley saw the Parliamentarians' energy as Satanic rather than creative. For May, however, the risk of defeat was releasing new kinds of creative energy, a recovery of the achievements of the ancient Greeks: the energy that Milton was to celebrate, and embody, in *Areopagitica*.

87 May, *History*, III, 91.

Rhetoric, republicanism and the public sphere: Marten, Waller and Milton, 1641–1644

Marten's republicanism

So far we have been concerned with republicanism not as a practical project but as an imaginative colouring for a poetry of patriotic independence. The civil war which May recounted was not a war against kingship. Wither and May both remained within the framework of official Parliamentary propaganda, which proclaimed loyalty to the institution of monarchy and even punctiliously observed celebrations for royal birthdays. Wither's banner read 'Pro Rege, Lege, Grege' – for king, law, and people. The king, it was maintained, had been kidnapped by a cabal of religious and political extremists; once he was rescued from their clutches, the traditional balance of the constitution would be maintained.

Parliament's solicitude for the king, of course, had distinct limits: 'or otherwise,' as Edmund Ludlow later put it, 'the Earle of Essex would not have judged himselfe at liberty to have fyered the great gun that was on the left wing of his army against the right of the King's, where it was thought the King in person then was'.[1] By the winter of 1642–3, even publications with official Parliamentarian sanction were exploring the possibility of deposing the king. David Wootton has pointed out that the Huguenot resistance tract *Vindiciae Contra Tyrannos* was recycled in an officially sanctioned compilation by William Prynne. But if we look to the poets we can push such arguments earlier. For May had quoted extensively from the *Vindiciae* in the summer of 1642.[2] And in February 1643 there appeared an officially commissioned translation of the neo-Latin drama *Baptistes* by George Buchanan, the Scottish poet best known as a fierce propagandist in favour of the deposition of

---

1 Edmund Ludlow, *A Voyce from the Watch Tower. Part Five: 1660–1662*, ed. A. B. Worden (1978), p. 140.
2 David Wootton, 'From Rebellion to Revolution: the Crisis of the Winter of 1642/3 and the Origins of Civil War Radicalism', *English Historical Review* 105 (1990), 654–9 (660–1); [Thomas May], *A Discourse Concerning the Successe of Former Parliaments* (1642; E154.51), pp. 2–3.

Charles's grandmother, Mary Queen of Scots. Though there is no evidence that this translation was by Milton, as has sometimes been argued, it should be remembered that Buchanan was a towering figure in British, if not specifically English, literary history. As will be seen, his *History of Scotland*, with its chronicle of the regular deposition of tyrants was to become a favourite republican text. Parliamentarians did not need to turn to Continental resistance theory to support deposition. Even Prynne, who remained squarely within the Foxean apocalyptic tradition and was concerned to rescue the king from papistical advisers, was nonetheless ready at this stage of the conflict to provide numerous precedents for Parliamentary deposition of kings.[3]

Justification of resistance to tyrants still fell short of overt preference for a republic. By this point in the story, however, we encounter at last an acknowledged and committed republican activist. In August 1643, the radical MP Henry Marten (1602–80) was expelled from the Commons for declaring that the death of the royal family would be a lesser damage to the kingdom than wholesale destruction.[4] To sustain Parliament's official claim of loyalty to the king's office was, in Marten's view, to 'cant'.[5] And from the start of the war he tried to erode the royal mystique. When an occasion presented itself to break into the room in Westminster Abbey where the regalia were stored, Marten overrode strong opposition to do so. A royalist newspaper reported that his real aim was to present the king himself as an outmoded relic; and some such symbolism did attach itself to the act. He was similarly in the vanguard of a raid on the queen's chapel, a building designed by Inigo Jones with elaborate machinery to give its religious images a realistic effect.[6] This was a frontal assault on Caroline aesthetics and Caroline politics: he demystified courtly poetics in the name of republican rhetoric. Later in the decade, Marten and his friend Thomas Chaloner scandalized royalists by satirical allusions to courtly plays staged at Oxford.[7] Marten was in the forefront of those who called for Parliament to make its own Great Seal. Even though this seal still bore Charles's head, its authorization in November 1643 was widely seen as a first step towards ruling without the king. It was one of the episodes that were to move May to declare: 'things

3 William Prynne, *The Soveraigne Power of Parliaments and Kingdomes* (1643; P4087A), Part I, pp. 38, 43, 45, 80.

4 As Tuck points out, p. 250, this was a much more extreme statement than merely advocating a republic, and he suggests that 'Marten's general republicanism may not have been as unusual even in 1643 as has often been thought'.

5 [Henry Marten], *A Word to Mr Wil. Prynn Esq.* (1649; E 537.16), p. 9.

6 R. Malcolm Smuts, *Court Culture and the Origins of a Royalist Tradition in Early Stuart England* (Philadelphia, 1987), pp. 228–9.

7 For details see David Norbrook, 'Levelling Poetry: George Wither and the English Revolution, 1642–1649', *English Literary Renaissance* 21 (1991), 217–56 (219, 250).

were growne beyond any president of former ages, and the very foundations of Government were shaken'.[8]

Marten has played an odd role in the historiography of English republicanism. He was a favourite butt of royalist newsbooks, his radicalism together with his alleged loose living making him an image of the anarchy that would ensue without monarchical government. Their portrayal of Marten is double-edged: while vilifying him they also ascribe to him the kind of festive energy associated with traditional carnivalesque forms of popular culture. He was seen as a character of massive, anarchic sexual potency.[9] Modern historians have often taken over the royalist stereotypes, and finding no other equivalents to this lurid and aberrant figure, have declared that he was the unique representative of republican views in the House. Conrad Russell warns against the assumption that 'inside every Parliamentarian there was a Henry Marten struggling to get out'; but we are still left to inquire how there could have been a Henry Marten inside Henry Marten.[10]

Marten sometimes seems to be a figure out of the Enlightenment rather than the mid-seventeenth century; and yet it is partly because of a distorted, royalist-centred view of the period that he seems so anomalous. He was not a unique sport of nature, living in a completely different mental world from his colleagues. His father had been a prominent statesman, and he knew Hyde and Waller well. The fact is that as a member of the gentry with a conventional education, he had ample access to a republican view of the world. Though it can be argued that his republicanism emerged from political practice as much as classical theory, he could write Latin poetry which testified to his knowledge of republican discourse (see below, chapters 6–7). He had a particular fondness for Epictetus, one of the few writers of the classical world who had been a slave and thus brought with him a sceptical view of social distinctions.[11] At least by the later 1640s he was a close friend and drinking companion of Thomas May. And there was not such a huge gulf from the views the relatively cautious May was expressing by the start of the war to Marten's own analysis.

8 Thomas May, *The History of the Parliament of England: which began November the third, M.DC.XL.* (1647; M1410), III, 47.

9 Susan Wiseman, '"Adam, the Father of all Flesh": Porno-Political Rhetoric and Political Theory in and after the English Civil War', in James Holstun (ed.), *Pamphlet Wars: Prose in the English Revolution* (London and Portland, 1992), pp. 134–57.

10 Conrad Russell, *The Causes of the English Civil War* (Oxford, 1990), p. 136. Until the publication of a forthcoming study by Sarah Barber, see Williams, 'Marten'; C. M. Williams, 'The Anatomy of a Radical Gentleman: Henry Marten,' in D. H. Pennington and K. Thomas (eds.), *Puritans and Revolutionaries: Essays in Seventeenth-Century History Presented to Christopher Hill* (Oxford, 1978), pp. 118–38.

11 Williams, 'The Anatomy of a Radical Gentleman', p. 127. Epictetus was later translated by John Hall's friend John Davies (1670). On possible debts to Montaigne's humanism see Tuck, p. 250.

Edward Hyde later recorded his horror when in the summer of 1641 he ran into Marten, whom he knew to be at odds with Pym, and asked what his aims were. The reply was: 'I do not thinke one man wise enough to gouerne all us'.[12] At that stage Hyde was still closely involved with Parliamentarians, but suddenly the scales seemed to fall from his eyes and he saw deep republican designs lurking behind the lip-service sometimes paid to monarchical orthodoxy.

But Marten's comment in the end was a possible, if extreme, extrapolation from modes of political analysis that were circulating even amongst royalists. In the summer of 1641, some of the king's spokesmen presented themselves as defending a mixed or balanced polity where monarchical, aristocratic and popular elements were carefully co-ordinated. Many conservatives, Hyde included, regarded this move as a dangerous hostage to fortune: what was here abandoned was an older discourse of the three estates – clergy, nobility and people – presided over by the king. That paradigm presented political liberties as handed down from above, with the monarch transcending the political world. The state could be presented in mystical, sacramental language as a unified body which it would be sacrilege to tamper with. The mixed-constitution paradigm both abandoned the church, traditionally viewed as a buttress of social order, and brought the monarch down to the level of the other contenders in the political forum. The state became an artefact whose different components needed to be kept in balance by a form of secular political calculation. The role of the monarch in that balance became open to question. The more one insisted on the need for all parts of society to participate in government, the more anomalous the lofty eminence of a single person became.[13] Though the paradigm had been more widely diffused before 1640 than is often assumed[14], invoking it under current conditions involved a much more dangerous speech-act. Marten's comment to Hyde was developing a logic that May's *Discourse* of the following year still stated more cautiously: that moral virtues had to be considered in the context of political structures, and that there were structural reasons why monarchy might be unacceptable regardless of the qualities of the individual ruler.

When Marten had the opportunity of designing the Great Seal for the republic of 1649, he took as the inscription: 'In the First Yeare of Freedome by God's Blessing Restored'. The notion that abolishing the monarchy could be a restoration of tradition may seem bizarre, but it was a possible development

---

12 Bodleian MS Clarendon 123, p. 123; *The Life of Edward Earl of Clarendon* (Oxford, 1759), p. 41.

13 Corinne C. Weston, 'Co-ordination – a Radicalising Principle in Stuart Politics', in Margaret Jacob and James Jacob (eds.), *The Origins of Anglo-American Radicalism* (1984), pp. 85–104.

14 Markku Peltonen, *Classical Humanism and Republicanism in English Political Thought 1570–1640* (Cambridge, 1995), p. 309 and *passim*.

of the mixed-constitution paradigm. To Marten, the monarchy as it had developed under the Stuarts had become so massively disproportionate to its traditional role that it had gained a private interest of its own that was structurally irreconcilable with the public interest. Only its abolition would restore ancient liberties, in the sense which Marten later glossed as to 'co[n]stitute and restore a Com[m]onwealth'.[15]

'Restoration' was a term with a potentially wide appeal on the Parliamentarian side because it permitted radical measures to acquire a conservative gloss. The language was, however, in origin a republican one. Machiavelli had declared in his *Discourses* that: 'For the maintenance of a Religion or Commonwealth long in being, it is necessary oftentimes to reduce them to their first grounds'.[16] Machiavelli's examples included the French Parlement, which had repeatedly renovated the state by contesting their princes' judgements. Amongst ancient instances he cited Lucius Junius Brutus's calling for the death sentence on his own sons to be executed when they resisted the republican government. Such exemplary acts of justice, Machiavelli argued, were the best way of discouraging corruption and restoring states to their first principles; and because the popular memory was so short, they should be renewed at least every ten years. Machiavelli, less committed to a static balance than some republican theorists, believed that a certain degree of instability was necessary to achieve political dynamism, and such regular 'reduction' had the effect of at once permitting and controlling the process of change.

The language of restoration was current during the 1640s far beyond any circle that can be termed specifically republican. Despite its radical implications, this process of reduction could be presented by its supporters as a matter of ultimately defending rather than overthrowing the traditional constitution. In religious terms the campaign for 'restoration' was more radical, with some MPs determined not just to go back to the situation before Laud's rise to power but to abolish episcopacy altogether; but others sought a compromise in what became known as 'reduced' episcopacy. One poet compared the process to recasting a cathedral bell so that its 'discord' would turn to 'good Musick, & lesse noyse': the basic material would remain the same even though it was deployed differently.[17] The drastic limitations of royal powers were given a traditional gloss by the revival of medieval

15 ML93/39–40, fol. 4r, cited by Williams, 'Marten', p. 541.

16 *Machiavels Discourses upon the First Decade of T. Livius*, trans. E[dward]. D[acres]. (1636; 17160), p. 433; *Discourses*, III, 1. I am much indebted to Victoria Kahn, 'Reduction and the Praise of Disunion in Machiavelli's *Discourses*', *Journal of Medieval and Renaissance Studies* 18 (1988), 1–19.

17 Anon., 'Vpon Arch-bishop Laud, Prisoner in yᵉ Tower. 1641', Bodleian MS Rawl. poet. 26, fol. 131.

offices of state.[18] It was on such grounds that Northumberland was encouraged to move from his grudging support of the king to endorsing the Parliamentarians' reforms.

An interesting usage of this idiom in a 1641 Commons speech by William Drake illustrates its potential for both conservative and more radical interpretations. Drake justified the Triennial Act on the grounds that one of the most powerful and effectual means to preserve all governments is 'often to reduce and recompose them to the rules of their first institution'.[19] In one sense the act was a return to the past, and a moderate one: precedents for annual Parliaments had been traced back to the reign of Edward III, so that triennial Parliaments constituted a concession. The fact remained that what was being restored in the Triennial Act went back not a handful of years but several centuries. To secure such restoration it was necessary to innovate, to counter the inherent tendency of the constitution otherwise to drift back towards the monarch's private interest.[20] The process carried within it a potential dynamic for ongoing radical change. Drake would have seen the execution of Strafford as the kind of exemplary image that Machiavelli had urged on Parliaments to provide; before many years the king would be forced to play the same role.

An important consequence of the Triennial Act was a significant expansion of the public sphere. Here going back to the past involved important change: for regular Parliaments in the Middle Ages had not been accompanied by a lively press, a phenomenon that now transformed the situation. Traditionally, the pitch of political excitement had subsided in the long

---

18 J. S. A. Adamson, 'The Baronial Context of the English Civil War', *Transactions of the Royal Historical Society* 5th series 40 (1990), 93–120; see also Brian Manning, 'The Aristocracy and the Downfall of Charles I', in Manning (ed.), *Politics, Religion and the English Civil War* (1973), pp. 36–80.

19 Michael Mendle, 'A Machiavellian in the Long Parliament Before the Civil War', *Parliamentary History* 8 (1989), 116–24 (119). Drake had been taught by George Morley, with whom Waller read the classical authors; on his papers see Stuart Clark, 'Wisdom Literature of the Seventeenth Century: A Guide to the Contents of the "Bacon-Tottel" Commonplace Books', *Transactions of the Cambridge Bibliographical Society* 6 (1972–6), 291–305, 7 (1977–80), 46–73. Drake had attended one of Heinsius's lectures on Tacitus in 1634 (48).

20 George Wither later commented that God had shown mercy

> To move the *King*, a *Parliament* to call,
> That should be made destructive unto all
> His own *Designes*; permitting, that he should
> Maugre, his *Fine-Devices*, be so fool'd,
> As to restore, (of that *Just-power* it had)
> So much, as that, It could not be *un-made*,
> Without it [*sic*] own *Assent*;

(George Wither, *The British Appeals* (1649; W3143), p. 35).

intervals between Parliaments, but now it was to be maintained at a regular level. Parliament's proceedings had been a jealously kept secret, though in practice speeches had circulated widely in manuscript. From the beginning of the Long Parliament, however, printed speeches began to appear, sometimes in collections, even with a portrait of the speaker, as if in a collection of poems.[21] Parliament began to print its own official documents.[22]

A further momentous shift towards the opening of political discourse came in November 1641 when reports of Parliamentary debates began to be printed in weekly newsbooks. The very first newsbook was self-conscious about its own speech-act, reporting the debate over whether Parliament's 'Grand Remonstrance', a comprehensive denunciation of the realm's evils since Charles's accession, should be printed. Opponents of its printing objected to allowing such outspoken attacks on royal policy being circulated amongst the common people – Felton had been carrying an earlier remonstrance when he killed Buckingham. But the advocates of printing were ready to take the risk of such an expansion of the public sphere. This was not necessarily because they had an idealistic commitment to freedom of expression; but opening up in this way could be seen as a 'reduction', a radical counterbalance to a preceding excess in the direction of exclusivity and mystery in government. Readers of the first newsbook were thus made aware that they were participating in a new political process: medium and message were both innovative. The editor of the best of the Parliamentarian journals, Marchamont Nedham (1620–78), was to become a leading figure in popularizing republican theory.[23] May probably contributed to newsbooks and Wither, as has been seen, experimented with one of his own.

This democratizing process was partly generated by unusual pressures on Parliament from below. The limited constitutional revolution in Parliament was being matched and outgone by a revolution in the government of London.[24] In the early 1640s the political and economic monopolies of the mainly pro-royalist City oligarchy were challenged by a previously excluded group of merchants who were to form a central element of the republican regime in 1649. These 'new merchants' needed a broader power-base and

21 See *A Collection of Speeches made by Sir Edward Dering* (1642; E197.1).

22 Sheila Lambert, *Printing for Parliament, 1641–1700*, List and Index Society Special Series, 20 (1984).

23 On the social and political impact of the newsbook see Joad Raymond, *Making the News: An Anthology of the Newsbooks of Revolutionary England 1641–1660* (Moreton-in-Marsh, 1993), and *The Invention of the Newspaper: English Newsbooks 1641–1649* (Oxford, 1996).

24 Valerie Pearl, *London and the Outbreak of the Puritan Revolution: City Government and National Politics 1625–1643* (Oxford, 1961); Robert Brenner, *Merchants and Revolution: Commercial Change, Political Conflict, and London's Overseas Traders, 1550–1653* (Cambridge, 1993), pp. 316ff.

allied themselves with more radical religious and political groupings that were emerging in the breakdown of the old central authorities. This disruption of the traditional structures of power and communication undermined civil as well as religious authority. Studies of republicanism have concentrated on its appeal to a political elite, but much wider sections of the community were imagining a state without a king. While official Parliamentarian propaganda claimed to be defending the monarchy against a king misled by evil advisers, the 'verbal graffiti' of many men and women of the middling and lower sorts had no time for such sanitized language. Idolization of Felton extended far beyond the verse satires circulating amongst the gentry.[25] Parliament's leaders might be horrified at such radicalism, but they depended on financial aid from the City, whose new leaders traded such support for political concessions, and showed their strength by massive petitions and popular demonstrations. New forms of political oratory emerged, with the private citizens who presented the petitions presuming to expound on them with long political harangues – a presumption without any precedent.[26] Amongst those involved in this radical politicization were John Lilburne, Richard Overton and William Walwyn, the future leaders of the Leveller movement. The combination of relative financial independence, more open elections, and the breakdown of censorship made London the basis of a strong public sphere, with something of the flavour of a mini-republic.

Against this background, Marten begins to look less anomalous; he was a crucial figure in mediating between the House of Commons and more radical groups in the City. His celebrated wit crackled with the political energies that were being newly released. He welcomed any move to open up the mysteries of state to a wider public. For him, returning to first principles meant checking the excessive power of the aristocracy. He early began a campaign against the House of Lords, moving a remonstrance which declared that the Commons alone were 'the Representative Body of the whole Kingdom, and their Lordships being but as particular Persons, and coming to Parliament in a Particular capacity'.[27] In a characteristic classical republican way, Marten insists on the priority of a common, public interest. His republicanism had a strongly democratic, or at least populist, cast, contrasting with the decorous aristocratic constitutionalism favoured by figures like Northumberland. Thus, when on a delegation to the Lords, he refused to raise his hat, a key symbol of the deference that was insisted on at every level of society. When he

---

25 Dagmar Freist, *Governed by Opinion: Politics, Religion and the Dynamics of Communication in Stuart London 1637–45* (London and New York, 1997), pp. 183ff (assuming the 'Felon' on p. 186 to be Felton).

26 Pearl, *London and the Outbreak of the Puritan Revolution*, p. 230.

27 *CJ*, II, 330, cited by C. M. Williams, 'Extremist Tactics in the Long Parliament, 1642–1643', *Historical Studies* 57 (1971), 136–50 (144).

aroused Northumberland's anger by opening a personal letter on the suspicion that he was intriguing with the king, the earl publicly assaulted him. The act was characteristic of Marten's eye for symbolism, contrasting an aristocratic world of closed, secret communication serving private interests with the public world of the common interest.[28] In 1649 the House of Lords as well as the monarchy was to fall victim of Marten's programme of 'restoration'.

Waller: from poetry to rhetoric, 1640–1643

Marten was the fulfilment of Hobbes's worst nightmare: the republican Trojan horse had entered the city. Hobbes himself very quickly decided that his fears of a drift to democracy would be realized. Though selected for a seat in the Short Parliament, he had held back from the public fray, and at the beginning of the Long Parliament he fled the country, fearful that his recently completed *Elements of Law* and *De Cive* might be considered subversive. In these works he had returned more vehemently to the doubts about popular assemblies he had expressed in his preface to Thucydides. Rhetoric appealed to the passions, not to reason, and could stir people into irrational activities like rebellion or tyrannicide.[29] His reaction against republican ideas was not complete: he still spoke with favour of the stability of aristocratic regimes. But he had no time for the turbulence of the Athenian or Roman republics with their large assemblies. He sharpened the criticisms of the cult of Pericles that he had expressed in 1629, and declared that the tongue of man was 'a trumpet of warre, and sedition'.[30] The title of *De Cive* was pointedly ironic, for his repeated burden was that participation in public life was to be reserved for a very few, and he almost always translated the Latin word 'ciuis' as 'subject'.[31]

Yet the cult of ancient eloquence had a sway even over some who shared Hobbes's anxieties about democracy. Edmund Waller's response to the political crisis is an especially striking instance. The struggle against the Trojan horse was for him, as to some extent it had been for Hobbes, an internal struggle. Rather than something totally alien, republican discourse was one strand in his cultural and political experience which he tried to integrate with others,

28 In 1645 Marten and May collaborated in the publication of some of the kings' secret correspondence as *The Kings Cabinet Opened* (E292.27). On the importance of secrecy in royalist discourse see Lois Potter, *Secret Rites and Secret Writing: Royalist Literature, 1641–1660* (Cambridge, 1989).

29 J. C. A. Gaskin (ed.), *The Elements of Law ... with Three Lives* (Oxford and New York, 1994), p. 120.

30 Thomas Hobbes, *De Cive: The English Version*, ed. Howard Warrender (Oxford, 1983), p. 88.

31 Quentin Skinner, *Reason and Rhetoric in the Philosophy of Hobbes* (Cambridge, 1996), pp. 284ff.

before abandoning the attempt. Like Northumberland, Waller had no desire for radical constitutional and religious reforms, but he was also uneasy about many aspects of the personal rule, and initially supported aspects of the reformers' programme. He was a friend of Digby, whose sharply divided retrospective view of the 1630s he shared. His county of Buckinghamshire had been a centre of opposition to ship money, and he was related to its prominent MP John Hampden as well as to Oliver Cromwell. In the Short Parliament he resumed the seat for his native town of Amersham which he had held in 1628, and offered the House his memories of that Parliament, the legality of whose dissolution in 1629 was still hotly contested.[32] William Drake, one of those who early used the rhetoric of 'restoration' in Parliament, was a neighbour and fellow-MP for Amersham. In the Long Parliament Waller was returned for St Ives, which had connections with the Sidney-Northumberland circle – it had previously been held by Viscount Lisle, brother of 'Sacharissa' and Algernon Sidney.[33]

Waller's return to Parliament at a time of burgeoning public debate offered to him the opportunity of a new role: as an orator reviving the best of classical political rhetoric, to complement his previous role as coterie poet circulating his verses in manuscript. The classical analogies of which he was fond took on a new resonance with the nation becoming an animated political forum. Waller's speeches circulated widely, not only in manuscript but in print. Just as a few generations earlier there had been a tension between poets' desire to enter a literary public sphere and a traditional prejudice against placing one's writing in the market-place, so members of Parliament began to publish their speeches even while at first denying their own involvement.[34] Waller seems to have been willing to encourage the process. His speech against ship money was entered in the Stationers' Register, making it an address to the general public rather than merely to MPs; while it seems hardly likely that 20,000 copies were sold, as legend has it, he certainly reached a very wide audience. David Hume later speculated:

> Had such a cultivated genius for oratory, as WALLER's for poetry, arisen, during the civil wars, when liberty began to be fully established, and popular assemblies to enter into all the most material points of government; I am persuaded so

32 *The Short Parliament (1640) Diary of Sir Thomas Aston*, ed. Judith D. Maltby (1988), p. 16.

33 According to Mary Frear Keeler, *The Long Parliament 1640–1641* (Philadelphia,1954), p. 376, Waller may have owed his seat to his friendship with the poet Sidney Godolphin, whose family had prominent local connections. Like Waller, Godolphin had links with the earl of Northumberland and also wrote a poem on his wife's death: David Norbrook, 'An Unpublished Poem by Sidney Godolphin', *Review of English Studies*, 48 (1997), 498–500.

34 A. D. T. Cromartie, 'The Printing of Parliamentary Speeches November 1640–July 1642', *Historical Journal* 33 (1990), 23–44.

illustrious an example would have given a quite different turn to BRITISH eloquence, and made us reach the perfection of the ancient model.[35]

Waller was in fact aiming at, and looked for a time on the way to achieving,
such eminence in oratory as well as poetry.

He found it increasingly difficult, however, to adjust to the conditions of
the tumultuous public sphere of the 1640s. He could use an elevated, semi-
republicanizing rhetoric of patriotism and the public interest, but did not
want such language to inflame democratic passions. He was ready, like Drake,
to call for 'restoration'. In one speech he recalled an episode in the early republic, recounted by Livy, when the tyrannical *decemviri* were forced to summon
the Senate after a long interval and the people, regaining their courage,
deposed them.[36] The return of Parliament was a comparable return to first
principles. Another speech called for the clock to be set back to the time
before the personal rule: 'let us . . . restore this Nation to the fundamentall and
vitall liberties, the propriety of our goods and freedome of our persons'.
Waller's 'restoration' was a cautious one, however: he refused to put any
blame on the king. The error had been that of the divines, 'who would per-
swade us that a Monarch can be absolute, and that the King may doe all things
ad libidinem'. Even if this form of government which had lasted five hundred
years were not convenient – an 'if' Waller clearly anticipated his hearers
would reject out of hand – 'we all know *how dangerous Innovations are, though
to the better*'. Waller had thus shifted his ground somewhat from his Paul's
poem. There Charles had been at one with the Laudian clergy in 'reducing',
restoring, ancient traditions rather than innovating. Now it turned out that
the Laudians had been innovators, and what really had to be restored was the
state of the realm before their ascendancy. Once that had been done, however,
all would be concord. Waller presented himself as the moderating speaker
who would bring beauty and harmony to the House's turbulence: the MPs
were like the Spartans whose 'forward valours required some [softer]
Musique to allay and quiet their spirits, too much moved with the sound of
Martiall Instruments'.[37] Waller's ethos was that of a poet-orator who was
familiar with the language of classical republicanism but also reassuringly
confident that its values could be reconciled with loyalty to the king, in a
restored balance that would be both constitutional and linguistic.

Waller found to his alarm, however, that it was ever more difficult to use a
republicanizing language without performing republicanizing speech-acts.[38]

---

35 David Hume, 'Of Eloquence', in *Essays and Treatises on Several Subjects*, 2 vols. (1788), I,
   98.   36 *Mr Wallers Speech in Parliament* (1641; E198.37), pp. 10–11.
37 Edmund Waller, *A Worthy Speech* (1641; E198.11), pp. 4, 5, 2 (reading 'softer' for 'faster').
38 On the anxiety about popular politics shown by Waller, Digby and others, see Brian
   Manning, *The English People and the English Revolution*, second edition (1991), ch. 3.

Like Hyde, he became increasingly concerned that figures like Marten represented not just a lunatic fringe but a potent new political force which must be resisted before it grew out of control. Even while cultivating a reputation as a patriotic Parliamentary rhetorician, he worked to restrict new forms of popular politicization. In February 1641 he clashed with the radical London MP Isaac Pennington, who took issue with his abusive references to the multitude. Waller was afraid that poetry was coming under threat: the anti-episcopal 'Root and Branch Petition' had attacked amatory verse. His friend George Digby, in a speech attacking Parliament's subjection to 'irregular, and tumultuous assemblies of people', retorted: 'Did ever any body think, that the gaites of *Ovid*, or *Tom. Caryes* muse, should by 15000. have beene presented to a Parliament, as a motive for the extirpation of Bishops?'[39] Waller was to become associated with the courtly enemy when his poem on Northumberland's sickness and recovery was published as Carew's in the 1642 edition of his poems. He also spoke up for an ally of another royalist poet, Richard Lovelace.[40] When his opposition to Strafford's execution became known, he escaped the wrath of an irate crowd only by disguising himself as the staunch Parliamentarian, and future republican, Sir Arthur Haselrig. He strongly opposed the publication of the Grand Remonstrance.[41] In December, when royalist militia under the earl of Dorset opened fire on a demonstration, Waller 'much inveighed against the Londoners in comming downe after soe tumultuous a manner', and justified the action by necessity – an argument he had attacked when deployed in defence of ship-money.[42] He warned against stronger links with the Scots, quoting from Buchanan's *History* to demonstrate their 'tumultuous government'.[43]

Waller expressed his fear of the social consequences of this new public sphere most forcefully in a speech on the church printed in July 1641. We had now pared the bishops' claws, he said, 'and may if we see cause, yet reduce it [episcopacy] into narrower bounds'. But the reduction should not go beyond a certain point:

> I look upon Episcopacy, as a Counter-scar[p], or outwork, which if it be taken by this assault of the people, and withall this Mysterie once revealed, that we must deny them nothing when they aske it thus in troopes, we may in the next place, have as hard a taske to defend our propriety, as we have lately had to recover it

39 *The Third Speech of the Lord George Digby* (1641; E196.30), pp. 8–9.
40 *The Private Journals of the Long Parliament, 2 June to 17 September 1642*, ed. Vernon F. Snow and Anne Steele Young (New Haven and London, 1992), p. 93.
41 *Verney Papers*, ed. John Bruce (1845), p. 124.
42 *The Journal of Sir Simonds D'Ewes from the First Recess of the Long Parliament to the Withdrawal of Charles from London*, ed. Willson Havelock Coates (New Haven and London, 1942), p. 225; *Mr Wallers Speech in Parliament*, p. 4.
43 BL Sloane MS 3,317, fol. 22r.

from the prerogative. If by multiplying hands, and petitions, they prevail for an equality in things Ecclesiasticall, this next demand perhaps may be *Le[x A]graria*, the like equality in things Temporall.

The *Roman* Story tels us, that when the people began to flock about the Senate, and were more curious to direct and know what was done, then to obey, that Common-wealth soon came to ruine. Their *Legem rogare* [asking for a law] grew quickly to be a *legem ferre* [making a law], and after, when their Legions had found that they could make a Dictator, they never suffered the Senate to have a voyce any more in such Election . . . when ever an equall division of Lands and Goods shall be desired, there will be as many places in Scripture found out, which seem to favour that, as there are now alleadged against the Prelacy or preferment in the Church.

For every man who had been abused by the bishops there were a thousand who had received hard measure from their landlords.[44] Here Waller returns to the architectural imagery of his Paul's poem, again bringing to religious issues a language of political artifice and innovation. Now, however, though he is still willing to 'reduce' the old institutions to some degree, he insists that there is a point beyond which it is very dangerous to go. Waller's allusion to the marginalization of the Senate is a warning to those Parliamentarians who envisaged some kind of aristocratic republic or at least a very limited monarchy. Once the episcopacy, which was closely bound up with the monarchy, was gone, there would be no secure barriers against democracy or anarchy. In warning against demands for a *lex agraria*, Waller was inverting Machiavelli's interpretation of Roman history, in which the republic fell precisely because the aristocracy were too selfish to grant agrarian reform, and the discontented masses became a ready prey for imperial manipulation. Waller's speech was in many ways prophetic. Within a decade biblical precedents would indeed be found for regicide, and Harrington and the Diggers in their very different ways would be calling for more equitable distribution of land.

The following month Waller elaborated on his disquiet at events. Sir Henry Vane the younger roundly declared that

the whole Fabrick of this building [the church] is so rotten and corrupt, from the very foundation of it to the top, that if we pull it not down now, it will fall about the eares of all those that endevour it, within a very few yeares.[45]

Waller responded by taking up the imagery of the end of Denham's *Coopers Hill*:

it was not the best way to take downe yᵉ wodden causey, before it was secconded by another of earth or stone, else the waters would overflow all the grounds, &

---

44 *A Speech Made by Master Waller Esquire . . .. Concerning Episcopacie* (1641; E198.30), pp. 4–6 (reading 'Counter-scarp' for 'Counter-scarf' and '*Lex Agraria*' for 'Leæ graria'.
45 *Sir Henry Vane his Speech in the House of Commons* (1641; E198.20), pp. 3–4.

hinder even y^t better proiect, so would now all kinds of sects so overspread this church, y^t it was to be feared y^t ye would hardly find where to lay new foundations for another discipline[.][46]

Here it is the people rather than the prince who are represented by chaotic water, and Waller shows rather more confidence than Denham in the possibility of successful political architecture; his language is in some ways closer to Machiavelli's in chapter 25 of *The Prince*.[47] But the fear of boundlessness is very strong.

Waller's analysis of the political situation was beginning to move closer to Hobbes's. When the Commons was discussing Strafford's betrayal of the fundamental laws of the realm, Waller had caused outrage by asking what those laws were, and was told that he was not worthy to sit in the House if he did not know.[48] Waller may have been hinting at a Hobbesian scepticism about the status of laws when the traditional political framework had broken down; Hobbes was to ridicule the appeal to any law more fundamental than that which subjects people to the sovereign for their own safety.[49] Waller was one of a small band of MPs who maintained a rear-guard action in the Commons against every new escalation of the campaign against the king. He consistently warned that such escalation would lead to civil war, and Parliamentarian militants, still committed in public to peaceful courses, censured him for being provocative.[50] Clashing with Marten in July 1642 over the appointment of the earl of Essex as commander of Parliament's forces, he invoked Roman imperial history, recalling the ways in which Otho and Vitellius had battled for power.[51]

When Hyde, Falkland and others had gone over to the king, however, Waller stayed on in London, probably in order to mediate some kind of negotiated peace. Clarendon suggests that if Waller was allowed to speak with

---

46 Speech of 11 June 1641, BL Sloane MS 1,467, fol. 101r. Brendan O Hehir, *Harmony From Discords: A Life of Sir John Denham* (Berkeley and Los Angeles, 1968), p. 32, dates the first draft of *Coopers Hill* up to mid-1641.

47 Waller's copy of *Il Principe* was bound in with the *Vindiciae*: Beal 563. Waller presented a petition on behalf of Denham's wife to Parliament on 11 May 1643, BL Harleian MS 164, ff. 388v–9r; *CJ*, III, 80 (I owe this reference to John Gurney).

48 But the question may have been less pointed, cf. J. G. A. Pocock, *The Ancient Constitution and the Feudal Law: A Study of English Historical Thought in the Seventeenth Century*, second edition (Cambridge, 1987), p. 48 n. 3; contrast his praise of 'the fundamentall and vitall liberties', *A Worthy Speech*, p. 2.

49 Thomas Hobbes, *Behemoth, or The Long Parliament*, ed. Ferdinand Tönnies (1889; rptd, ed. Stephen Holmes, Chicago and London, 1990), pp. 67–8.

50 Speech of 8 June, Snow and Steele (eds.), *The Private Journals of the Long Parliament*, p. 44.

51 Speech of 15 July, Snow and Steele (eds.), *The Private Journals of the Long Parliament*, p. 217.

greater sharpness and freedom, it was because it was clear that he would never sway enough members to win a vote.[52] His eloquence thus took on an emptily ceremonial character. Nonetheless, it seems to have been powerful enough to disturb May. Waller is surely one of the people he has in mind when in the *History* he writes of those who defected to the king: they were often praised as men of good parts and eloquence, but these were not the same as wisdom, and wit and eloquence were a kind of 'witchery' that could often disguise false-hood.[53] If rhetoric came under suspicion from Hobbes as opening the way to democracy, for May it was associated with florid, courtly language which reflected the political problems from which Parliament was trying to dis-entangle the realm.

Though Waller's polished rhetoric may have been at odds with the mood of many in Parliament, his hopes of rallying enough support to bring about a peaceful settlement had some foundation. Marten flung himself enthusiasti-cally into the war effort, but there were many on both sides who were still very reluctant to push the nation's divisions any further and who found the con-flicts of loyalties very difficult to resolve. Though Hyde, Falkland and others of the former Great Tew group had joined the king, Selden remained with Parliament, sceptical of the legality of the king's raising troops against his subjects.[54] In the autumn of 1642 he presented Waller with one of his books.[55] There were enough conflicting tugs on Waller's loyalty to leave him irresolute. Finally, however, in the spring of 1643, he became implicated in a plot involv-ing some of the more conservative London citizens who had been ousted by the radicals, and royalists including Northumberland's brother.[56] The details of this conspiracy – if it was one – remain obscure, but its discovery became an occasion for the militants to strengthen their control, forcing all MPs to take an oath strengthening their commitment to the cause.

Waller was liable to the death penalty. And here he encountered the severity of republican discourse head on. The advocate of the army, who tried two of his co-conspirators and secured their execution, was Isaac Dorislaus, the Tacitist lecturer whose voice had been silenced in 1629 – and who was to be enlisted for the prosecution in the trial of Charles I.[57] Waller fought desperately to evade

52 Edward, earl of Clarendon, *The History of the Rebellion and Civil Wars in England*, ed. W. Dunn Macray, 6 vols. (Oxford, 1888), III, 38–9.   53 May, *History*, II, 62.

54 Richard Tuck, ' "The Ancient Law of Freedom": John Selden and the Civil War', in John Morrill (ed.), *Reactions to the English Civil War 1642–1649* (1982), pp. 137–61.

55 Eutychius, *Ecclesiae suae . . . origines* (1642; Wing E 3440), British Library pressmark 200.a.21.

56 Pearl, *London and the Outbreak of the Puritan Revolution*, pp. 136 n. 117, 148 n. 161, 265, indicates the role of conservative Londoners in Waller's plot.

57 P. Alessandra Maccioni and Marco Mostert, 'Isaac Dorislaus (1595–1649): The Career of a Dutch Scholar in England', *Transactions of the Cambridge Bibliographical Society* 8 (1981–4), 419–70 (433).

martial law, and attracted widespread condemnation by his abject behaviour. He tried to implicate Northumberland, apparently without any foundation. He distributed bribes to MPs and appeared before them to beg for mercy, 'all clothed in mourning as if he had been going to execution'.[58] He appealed to his family ties with Hampden, and reminded members that 'my education ... hath been almost from my child-hood in this House'.[59] He adopted a fervently Puritan discourse, acknowledging his carnal ways and determining to repent. Clarendon bitterly commented that 'he does as much owe the keepinge his head to that oration, as Catyline did the loss of his, to those of Tully'. It was with heavy irony that he observed that Waller 'by what he spoke, and in the manner of speaking it, exceedingly captivated the good-will and beneuolence of his hearers, which is the highest parte of an Orator'.[60] In fact many members despised his speech, since his pious rhetoric was so palpably a stratagem. Earlier he had had to disguise himself as Sir Arthur Haselrig to escape from a crowd; now he was disguising himself rhetorically. Yet Waller was proud enough of the speech to have it printed, and it was to appear as the last item in a collection of his *Poems* that appeared in 1645.

In that position it cast an ironic light on his career. He had moved from courtly poetry to Parliamentarian rhetoric, seeking in each a temperate balance; but his final speech displayed him as being trapped within a discourse with which he was palpably ill at ease. He wrote a desperate appeal to Henry Marten, who may have played a leading role in gaining his reprieve as he was to do for other royalist wits.[61] Waller's poetry and oratory had aimed over twenty years at establishing an ideal balance and harmony between subjecthood and citizenship; he had not been able to find a space in which he could make that balance real. One sentence stands out from his parting speech: 'Necessity has of late forced you into untrodden paths; and in such a case as this where you have no president of your own, you may not do amisse to looke abroad upon other States and Senates, which exercises [*sic*] the Supreame Power, as you now doe here'.[62] Waller proceeded to offer a Roman analogy, acknowledging that events had gone decisively beyond any simple attempt to 'restore' an ancient English constitution. Since sovereignty now lay decisively with Parliament, he was implying, England was effectively a republic. After going into exile, he wrote to Hobbes and offered to translate *De Cive* into English.[63]

---

58 From D'Ewes's account, BL Harleian MS 165, fol. 144r.
59 *Mr Wallers Speech in the House of Commons* (1643; E60.11), p. 4.
60 Bodleian MS Clarendon 112, p. 365; Clarendon, *History of the Rebellion*, III, 52.
61 ML, box 78, fols. 56–7, Williams, 'Marten', pp. 194, 567–8.
62 *Mr Wallers Speech in the House of Commons*, p. 2.
63 *ABL*, II, 277; *Thomas Hobbes: The Correspondence*, ed. Noel Malcolm, I (Oxford, 1994), 124, letter to Waller, 29 July 1645.

Milton's early pamphlets and the rhetoric of liberty: church and household

Waller's career in the 1640s throws light on Milton's, by parallel and still more by contrast. Milton fully embraced the republicanizing public sphere from which Waller had ultimately shrunk, and tried to synthesize the poetic modes of the 1630s with the demands of the new decade. It is often said that Milton's earlier pamphlets steered clear of political issues; not until 1649 did he turn to political theory.[64] In his own retrospective survey in 1650, however, he set out a rationale for his writings that gave them a clear political logic (*Second Defence, MPW*, IV:1, 621ff); and however coloured by hindsight, the outline points to real interconnections. He began, Milton says, with religious liberty, which was an essential precondition for civil liberty. Finding that the government was dealing well with liberty in the state, he turned to domestic liberty, in which he included marriage, education, and freedom of speech. This is a very broad category; but one of Milton's aims is to span conventional distinctions between the political and the religious, the public and the private, authorship and citizenship. Milton often approached the political issues of the time from a somewhat oblique angle, from his concerns as a poet with the relationship between language and politics. His succeeding pamphlets both discuss and embody those relationships in a period of revolutionary change. And the classical republics form a consistent point of reference.

It is very difficult to isolate one point in Milton's career when he became a republican. His poetry of the 1630s often followed courtly modes, but as I have argued elsewhere, he set himself to undermine easier forms of poetic harmony, so that his verse can be connected with more directly oppositional poetry.[65] An early sign of interest in republicanism comes in his commonplace book from around 1637–38, where he notes that the historian Sulpicius Severus says that the name of kings has always been hateful to free peoples, and he condemns the action of the Hebrews in choosing to exchange their freedom for servitude (*MPW*, I, 440). Severus was discussing the passage in the Book of Samuel (I Samuel VIII) where the people of Israel ask Samuel for a king, and he retorts with a catalogue of the evils that will befall them: they would be insane to abandon their freedom. This was to be a central passage for republicans because it could link civil and religious liberties. The Hebrew polity, Harrington later argued, had been a republican one, and once monarchs gained power, both civil and ecclesiastical corruption intensified. The edition Milton was reading had appeared in the Dutch republic, where links between biblical paradigms and the current constitution could be made.

---

64 Corns, *UV*, p. 12; but see Annabel Patterson, *Reading Between the Lines* (Madison, 1993), pp. 225ff.   65 Norbrook, *PP*, ch. 10; on the 1645 *Poems* see also chapter 4 below.

Milton later wrote that he had returned from his Continental tour in 1639 because of the political crisis. His actions on his return stopped some way short of direct engagement: he set up a school. This pursuit did, however, give him the prized opportunity to continue independent study, to resist the pressures inherent in becoming a churchman or a courtier. He maintained the public posture of a retired student who intervened only with reluctance in the hurly-burly of public affairs. To some extent, however, this was a matter of rhetorical ethos, for Milton showed every interest in stirring up political commotion. There can be no doubt of his determination that Parliament should win the war. There is evidence that he contributed to plans for a war-engine, a kind of rudimentary tank, developed by John Felton's brother.[66] And in the pamphlet wars of the 1640s, he consistently came down on the side that opened up the public sphere.

The series of five tracts against the bishops that erupted from Milton between the summer of 1641 and the spring of 1642 have often dismayed his commentators by the savagery and vehemence with which he calls down curses on the Anglican hierarchy. Certainly his feelings were passionately engaged; but it is always worth bearing in mind that he was also committed to the classical arts of rhetoric, of persuasive speech very carefully targeted to a particular occasion. If we look at the speech-acts these tracts were performing, they emerge as protagonists in a political as well as a religious conflict. As has been seen, it was in the summer of 1641 that Waller was rallying support for the church as a last bastion of political order; and it was in defence of the church as part of a traditional body politic that a new party of constitutional royalists began to emerge. For their part, many of Parliament's leaders were uneasy about the extent to which they depended on popular support, and in mid-1641 schemes were being floated for a compromise that would retain episcopacy under a 'reduced' form. Such schemes might appeal to figures like Waller, but Milton's pamphlets were calculated to wreck them.

Milton's tracts are far more concerned with destroying episcopacy than with the details of the order that will replace it. He aligns himself with the Presbyterians who wanted to restructure the national church with an elective clergy, and claims with them that such an order is spelt out in Scripture. This is a much more rigid position than he was later to accept; within a few years he was strongly opposed to any nationally imposed church order, and already in the later anti-episcopal tracts he is more sympathetic to sects than the Presbyterian mainstream. His emphasis is mainly on the evils of the system he wants to destroy, on a hierarchy in which power is handed down from above. In religious matters, authority must be reclaimed from this monopoly. This calls for a full and clinical surgery to be performed on the body politic. In a

66   Timothy Raylor, 'New Light on Milton and Hartlib', *MQ* 27 (1993), 19–31.

drastic revision of the traditional image of the body, he compares the church to a huge wen which has to be chopped off (*Of Reformation, MPW*, I, 583–4). He twice takes issue with a speech by Waller's associate Digby, who had spoken of 'the Connection and Interweaving of the Church-Government with the Common Law': 'In *Gods* name let it weave out againe . . . Tis not the common Law, nor the civil, but piety, and justice, that are our foundresses' (I, 605 and n. 129; see also I, 803 n. 21). Milton satirizes the secular architectural language used by the bishops' defenders, 'as if the heavenly City could not support it selfe without the props and buttresses of secular Authoritie' (I, 554). It is the bishops who are 'mining, and sapping the out-works, and redoubts of *Monarchy*' (I, 592); the 'towring, and stedfast heighth' of regal dignity does not need the 'painted Battlements . . . of Prelatrie' (I, 582–3). Milton rejects with particular force the idea of the clergy as one of the three estates of the realm. In his view, they have been waging 'a hereditary, and perpetuall civill warre' in England (I, 593).[67] Like some of Lucan's seventeenth-century readers, Milton counters fears of civil war by arguing that the existing polity, rather than a model of balance, is inherently unstable and at war with itself, calling for drastic remedies.

In presenting the bishops as the real underminers, Milton tries to outflank their defenders' political arguments and to situate himself as a defender of royal authority. To this extent he remains within the Foxean tradition which sees the monarchy as reclaiming a lost balance between civil and ecclesiastical power; but for Milton the balance is by now very problematic. In his private studies he had worked his way through the histories of Greece and Rome and was shocked when he moved on to the reign of Constantine, the first Christian emperor, to find a marked and steady process of decline in civility (*An Apology against a Pamphlet, MPW*, I, 943–4). The ferocity of Milton's attack on Constantine would have shocked many Puritans, and marked a decisive break with the Foxean tradition. Milton shares with Harrington a dark view of the relations between monarchy and papacy. If the clergy extolled Constantine, it was because he extolled them, and this sharply calls his judgement in question. Emperor and church become a corrupt mutual admiration society (*Of Reformation, MPW*, I, 554), and this is because of structural connections between political inequality and corruptions of discourse. It is not just that monarchs are led astray by the corrupt blandishments of the clergy: if that were the case, once monarchs regained control of the church a proper balance would return. Milton's starting point is that even after the Reformation, with the monarchy notionally in charge of the church, corruption had continued. He does, it is true, insist that Presbyterian religion is perfectly consistent with civil obedience, but the examples he gives are the

---

67 For church history as 'intestine quarrell', cf. Hutchinson, p. 281.

Dutch and Swiss republics, and the French Huguenots who had been urged in the 1620s to take up arms against their king (I, 609–10). Milton urges the merits of close alliance with the Dutch republic as a counter to the prelate-supported pro-Spanish foreign policy (I, 586).

Milton's dark view of history since the rise of the bishops contrasts with his recurrent references to the virtue and civility of classical republics. The ancient heroes were willing to return to the people after they had served them; the modern clergy aspired to raise themselves above the people. The primitive church had been democratic, or at least aristocratic. Its officers were elected, as in parliamentary elections, so that the 'voyce of the people' was heard (I, 544). Milton says that if God gave the people episcopacy 'he did it in his wrath, as he gave the Israelites a King' (*The Reason of Church-Government, MPW*, I, 781). Here he refers back to the incident which had led Sulpicius Severus, a frequent point of reference in the anti-episcopal tracts, to describe the people as insane in wanting a king; and though Milton omits to draw the parallel, the allusion links ecclesiastical and courtly systems. In an ingenious reworking of traditional architectural imagery, Milton praises the apostles because

> like those heroick patricians of Rome (if we may use such comparison) hasting to lay downe their dictatorship, they rejoys't to call themselves and to be as fellow Elders among their brethren. Knowing that their high office was but as the scaffolding of the Church yet unbuilt, and would be but a troublesome disfigurement, so soone as the building was finisht

(I, 791). This is a much more radical architectural image of reduction than anything Waller had offered. Fabritius and Curius are other models of this kind of self-abnegation (I, 855), and Milton invokes the still more extreme case of Curtius who leapt into a chasm for the sake of his country (I, 792). If Brutus was 'forc't to be as it were a King' for a short time after he had heroically expelled the kings from Rome, eventually 'matters were set in order, as in a free Commonwealth' (*Of Prelatical Episcopacy, MPW*, I, 640). The Greek republics, and especially democratic Athens, are also frequent points of appeal. Milton contrasts the bishops with Pericles, 'a powerfull and eloquent man in a Democratie, [who] had no more at any time then a Temporary, and elective sway, which was in the will of the people when to abrogate' (1, 640). And he traces a parallel between the decline in political virtue from the ancient republics and the decline of language: the bishops' appeals to Parliament are like a pitiful, low-spirited imitation of Pericles's funeral oration satirized by Lucian (*Animadversions, MPW*, I, 701). Where Hobbes had defended Sparta and ridiculed Pericles's oration, Milton attacked the bishops for trying to establish a 'prelatical Sparta' (*Reason of Church-Government, MPW*, I, 855).

What was then needed was a return to that lost civic virtue and purity of language. Milton uses the common language of 'reducement' to first princi- ples: the Presbyterian system is '*Episcopacy* reduc't to what it should be' (*Of Reformation, MPW*, I, 606). The church, if she would 'reform her self rightly by the Scriptures, must undresse them of all their guilded vanities, and reduce them as they were at first, to the lowly and equall order of Presbyters' (*Reason of Church-Government*, I, 853). Up to a point, as has been seen, that language of reduction was compatible with a reformed monarchism; and several times Milton declares himself content with that solution. Yet his monarchism, which early and decisively rejects the old three-estates model for a balanced- polity model, already has a republicanizing inflection[68]:

> And because things simply pure are inconsistent in the masse of nature, nor are the elements or humors in Mans Body exactly *homogeneall*, and hence the best founded Common-wealths, and least barbarous have aym'd at a certaine mixture and temperament, partaking the severall vertues of each other State, that each part drawing to it selfe may keep up a steddy, and eev'n uprightnesse in common.
>
> There is no Civill *Goverment* that hath beene known, no not the *Spartan*, not the *Roman*, though both for this respect so much prais'd by the wise *Polybius*, more divinely and harmoniously tun'd, more equally ballanc'd as it were by the hand and scale of Justice, then is the Common-Wealth of *England*: where under a free, and untutor'd *Monarch*, the noblest, worthiest, and most prudent men, with full approbation, and suffrage of the People have in their power the supreame, and finall determination of highest Affaires. (*Of Reformation, MPW*, I, 599)

Here Milton appeals to Polybius, the stock point of reference for classical republican theories of mixed government. He sees the state not as a descend- ing hierarchy but as a dynamic interaction of component parts which share a common interest. This is a *common*wealth in which all the parts are sub- ordinated to the whole rather than the body's being subordinated to the monarchical head. The parts are seen in terms of functions rather than indi- viduals. As with May and still more Marten, there seems no reason why the monarchical function as head of state should not be taken by a committee. If it is Parliament that has 'highest Affaires' in its power, it is not entirely clear in what sense it is 'under' the monarch, whose role seems to be syntactically sec- ondary; and it appears that Parliament's control in turn depends on the 'suffrage' of the people. An ascending, democratic model of power and authority lurks behind the apparently traditional language of hierarchy. If monarchy is made up of two parts, the liberty of subject and the supremacy of the king, it is the former that is the 'root' (I, 592).

68 For fuller discussion see Janel Mueller, 'Contextualizing Milton's Nascent Republicanism', in P. G. Stanwood (ed.), *Of Poetry and Politics: New Essays on Milton and his World* (Binghamton, 1995), pp. 263–82.

Here as so often in his verse and prose, Milton's syntactical complexities enact a more complex kind of political as well as stylistic balance than could be found in Waller. At this stage monarchy still has a role to play in maintaining the balance; but already there are signs of the unease that were to make Milton move further than the Presbyterians from a model of monarchical balance.[69] The domination of a corrupt clergy may be contrary to the interests of a virtuous king, but it may also suit the interests of a tyrant. The clergy 'lift up their eyes to the hils of the Court, from whence only comes their help' (*Reason of Church-Government, MPW*, I, 853): this audaciously irreverent jibe (cf. Psalm cxxi.1) is notionally directed at the clergy but also rebounds against the traditions of monarchy. If Milton targets the clergy in the first instance, it is because they offer a tyranny worse than anything known in classical times, one over 'the inward persuasion' (*An Apology against a Pamphlet, MPW*, I, 925). Liberation from this tyranny would thus surpass in civic virtue anything achieved by the ancients. But Milton again and again emphasizes the interdependency of religious and civil corruptions: tyranny is 'an ambiguous monster, and to be slaine in two shapes'. Where Waller had been alarmed by Strafford's execution, Milton acclaims it as a notable victory opening the way to the defeat of religious tyranny, with one stroke 'winning againe our lost liberties and Charters, which our forefathers after so many battels could scarce maintaine'. Tyranny had been laid 'groveling upon the fatall block' (I, 924): though here Milton claims that tyranny can be defeated without regicide, the metaphor is ominous. If the processes of recovering civil and religious liberty were indeed deeply interconnected, further civil changes might yet be needed.

Milton's next two pamphlet wars also had political implications. By 1643 the Anglican church had been eclipsed and the new religious settlement was in the balance. Milton now feared that the Presbyterian system he had previously championed might reproduce the old structures of authority, and in attacking the divorce laws and the licensing of printing he was challenging the more conservative Puritans. Once again, he was hitting political nerves that went beyond the immediate subject-matter. Milton's defence of divorce caused great scandal, especially because an attack on marriage seemed to threaten state as well as church. The relations between king and subject were often figured as a marriage; if marriage were some kind of contract, the implication would be that the same applied to the state.[70] Though Milton's engagement with the divorce question may have had direct personal causes, it shared characteristic general emphases of the republican mentality.

---

69 On Presbyterians and balance, see Tuck, pp. 233ff.
70 Susan Dwyer Amussen, *An Ordered Society: Gender and Class in Early Modern England* (Oxford, 1988), ch. 2.

Milton's marriage in July 1642 raised political questions. His wife came from a royalist background and when she fled her new home, she may have felt trapped not only in an unloving marriage but also in a city that from Oxford was being presented as a wild tumult of anarchic violence. When war broke out, the lines between royalists and Parliamentarians ran also through Milton's marriage. At a later stage he generalized the situation:

> in vain does he prattle about liberty in assembly and market-place who at home endures the slavery most unworthy of man, slavery to an inferior . . . I published several books, at the very time when man and wife were often bitter foes, he dwelling at home with their children, she, the mother of the family, in the camp of the enemy, threatening her husband with death and disaster. (*Second Defence, MPW*, IV:1, 625)

This scenario does not coincide precisely with Milton's situation; but it serves to politicize the issue of marriage. It does so in terms that seem to confirm the patriarchal character of his republicanism. Mary Nyquist writes that this is 'Milton's most sustained commentary on women's participation in the revolutionary activity of the 1640s'.[71] Milton takes it for granted here, as in *Paradise Lost*, that the female is inferior, though he was prepared to concede at one point that she might in some cases be entitled to initiate divorce (*The Judgement of Martin Bucer, MPW*, II, 448). Overwhelmingly, however, Milton assumes a situation where the female is at once unequal and ideologically antagonistic. For Milton there are close links between the two. Royalism subordinates public rationality to private desire, and women are especially liable to this error both from their nature, as Milton construes it, and from their situation as denizens of a mainly private household world. The republican male must be fit for the public sphere, and ideological antagonism in marriage disrupts that fitness.

There was a wider context for this emphasis on household subordination. As has been seen, a general preoccupation of republican thought was the need to reclaim a public sphere from the private monopolies of church and state. In the classical world there had been a sharp distinction between state and household, between *polis* and *oikos*. In the medieval world, with rule in the hands of a personal lord, public and private realms became inextricably mingled. The *polis* came under the hegemony of a super-*oikos*, the household of the emperor or monarch. Sir Robert Filmer's *Patriarcha*, probably written in the 1630s, was a classic instance of the way in which absolutist thought collapsed distinctions between state and family: for Filmer subjection to the

---

71 Mary Nyquist, '"Profuse, Proud Cleopatra": "Barbarism" and Female Rule in Early Modern English Republicanism', *Women's Studies* 24 (1994), 85–130 (95). See further Diane Purkiss, *Broken Men: Masculinity and the Irrational in the English Civil War* (Cambridge, forthcoming).

monarch was as natural as subjection to a father.[72] Some republicans went so far as to be uneasy about the assumption that subjection to fathers was entirely natural – Algernon Sidney, a second son, rejected the principle of primogeniture in the family. The description of monarchical government as natural was more widely challenged. Under monarchical rule, the king's personal household became equated with the nation. Parliamentarians were particularly scandalized by the way in which Charles had allegedly allowed himself to be swayed by his Catholic wife: this was to allow private marital relations to undermine public accountability. When some letters between Charles and Henrietta Maria were captured, they were published as *The Kings Cabinet Opened*, a title which drew attention to the question of public and private. Courtiers had reduced politics to personal intrigue, whereas Parliament was publishing its own goals and proceedings.

Milton would have drawn such unease about female influence in politics from his literary reading. In the Greek drama he would have encountered portrayals of an earlier, monarchical stage of Athenian history, a stage when the *polis* was subordinated to the royal household, and when in consequence women could exercise sway in the public world; and the plays represent the consequences as being disastrous. In democratic Athens, by contrast, women were normally denied access to the public sphere and confined to the household.[73] Milton saw Charles I's court as a reversion to barbarous pre-political values: 'Court ladies, not the best of Women . . . when they grow to that insolence as to appeare active in State affaires, are the certain sign of a dissolut, degenerat, and pusillanimous Common-wealth' (*Eikonoklastes*, III, 370). Such were the ladies who had taken part in Caroline masques, whom Waller complimented in his poems – and some of whom were allegedly involved in his plot.

Yet in the domestic as in the religious sphere, Milton was not simply advocating a return to classical practice. The classical household was a site of economic production as well as the rearing of children; with the emergence of a market economy the productive and familial sides of the *oikos* moved further apart, and the household came to offer an idealized spiritual centre. Puritan ideology laid special emphasis on the household as an instrument of godly

---

72 For dating see *Patriarcha and Other Writings*, ed. Johann P. Sommerville (Cambridge, 1991), pp. xxxiii–iv.

73 This generalization, made by Hannah Arendt and accepted by Jürgen Habermas, *The Structural Transformation of the Public Sphere: An Inquiry into a Category of Bourgeois Society*, trans. Thomas Burger with Frederick Lawrence (Cambridge, Mass., 1989), p. 52, is increasingly coming under challenge. One area in which women did have a public identity was in certain religious rituals, forming an interesting parallel with seventeenth-century women's quest for a voice through prophecy: Margaret Williamson, *Sappho's Immortal Daughters* (Cambridge, Mass., and London, 1995), pp. 102ff.

reformation which could do its work even when the public world was corrupt. A sharp public-private split was thus broken down: if under 'modern prudence' the state became a household, there were counter-tendencies towards making the household a *polis*.[74] Some precedent for this model could after all be found in antiquity. Whatever the overall pattern, there were records of women who pursued some form of intellectual independence. Lucan portrayed a culture in which divorce was taken for granted and women such as the formidable Marcia and Cornelia, the wives of Cato and Pompey, placed political goals above familial sentiment. Algernon Sidney cited the relations between Pericles and his mistress Aspasia as evidence that women were fitted for government.[75] Republican ideology did not necessarily demand women's exclusion from the public sphere. Newsbooks would often report the presentation of petitions by women sympathetically.[76] Both royalists and Parliamentarians tended to condemn female participation in the public sphere if the females in question were antagonistic on political grounds, but to be far more pragmatic in other circumstances. Milton praised the 'wisdome' of a Parliament which could admit petitions from 'the meanest artizans and labourers, at other times also women' (*An Apology*, I, 926). He himself was liable to the same kinds of attack as the royalists were levelling at the sexual libertinism of the sects. He was perfectly well aware that the radical religious groups whose cause he consistently championed down to 1659–60 offered women a degree of participation which conservatives considered outrageous.[77] Nowhere in his tracts did he speak against that development.

It remains true that Milton was more defensive than some republicans on the question of female participation, just as he was over political democracy. But he does not make the female sphere an entirely private one, even in the domestic space. Rational communication rather than natural generation is for him the prime purpose of marriage, in his quest for 'an intimate and speaking help . . . a fit conversing soul' as opposed to 'a mute and spiritles mate' (*Doctrine and Discipline of Divorce, MPW*, II, 251). This emphasis on conversation – a word from which he sublimated its older sexual element – led an opponent to claim that 'you count no woman to due conversation

74 Habermas, *Structural Transformation of the Public Sphere*, pp. 43ff; cf. Christopher Hill, 'The Spiritualization of the Household', in *Society and Puritanism in Pre-Revolutionary England* (1964; corrected edn., Harmondsworth, 1986), pp. 429–66.

75 Algernon Sidney, 'Of Love', in Sir Walter Scott (ed.), *A Collection of Scarce and Valuable Tracts*, 13 vols. (1812), VIII, 612–19 (618).

76 Sharon Achinstein, 'Women on Top in the Pamphlet Literature of the English Revolution', *Women's Studies* 24 (1994), 131–63.

77 Freist, *Governed by Opinion*, gives detailed examples of female participation in debate during the 1640s.

accessible . . . except she can speak Hebrew, Greek, Latine, & French, and dispute against the Canon law as well as you'.[78] The recurrent depreciation of physical sexuality in the divorce tracts is often read biographically, but such readings risk underplaying its rhetorical significance as a radical and polemical revaluation of the household sphere. Sexuality is presented in terms of meeting a bodily need, identified with the realm of necessity, so that the role of conversation as nurturing freedom can be brought out by contrast; the *oikos* becomes a little *polis*. If a bad marriage to a royalist woman produced a vicious circle, a good marriage could potentially produce an enabling relationship for the male citizen between the household and the private sphere. Lucy Hutchinson's *Memoirs* present a working model of such a household: Hutchinson was quite ready to read theological disputes and win her husband over to what she considered the correct view.[79]

Yet Milton's divorce tracts are riven with contradictions. As in his relations with democracy, a certain opening in the direction of wider communication creates an abrasive effect when it is then sharply limited. He expected wives to converse, but the ideal curriculum he set out in *Of Education*, soon after the divorce tracts, made no mention of women. His friend Cyriack Skinner wrote in the terminology of Harringtonian republicanism that the divorce tracts were 'the mending of a decay in the Superstructure', whereas *Of Education* was 'laying a Foundation also of Public Weale': there is a clear order of priorities here.[80] Milton insists that the head of the household should have a pre-political, God-given authority, and presents marital conversation as a relief, 'delightfull intermissions' (*Tetrachordon, MPW,* II, 597). The woman's role is at once to provide dialogue and to listen to a monologue; she must become a vehicle for agency without herself achieving it. This comes close to what Habermas describes as 'systematically distorted communication'. As James Turner puts it, we are faced with 'an oxymoron: only the woman is obliged to be mutual'.[81] Milton was to return to these questions in *Paradise Lost*, placing them at the heart of his epic.

Liberty, the public sphere and the sublime: *Areopagitica*

It was this concern with broken communication in the private sphere that precipitated Milton's major contribution towards the celebration of the

78 Anon., *An Answer to a Book, Intituled, The Doctrine and Discipline of Divorce* (1644; E17.12), p. 16, reprinted in William Riley Parker, *Milton's Contemporary Reputation* (Columbus, 1940).   79 Hutchinson, p. 169.
80 Helen Darbishire, *The Early Lives of Milton* (1932), p. 24.
81 James Grantham Turner, *One Flesh: Paradisal Marriage and Sexual Relations in the Age of Milton* (Oxford, 1987), p. 221.

public sphere, *Areopagitica*. The anti-episcopal tracts had had the effect of undermining compromise and pushing towards a more radical political position. *Areopagitica* had a comparable aim. When it appeared, in November 1644, Parliament's war effort was in disarray, hampered not only by poor supplies but by constant bickering between the commanders. In November Essex and Sir William Waller attacked the earl of Manchester in Parliament for his poor leadership. Manchester was one of many people on Parliament's side who had little stomach for the war, which was allowing an ever-increasing proliferation of sects and thus seemed to be fulfilling Edmund Waller's darkest convictions. Ironically enough, the poet himself was funding the war effort, having recently been granted a pardon in exchange for a fine of £10,000.

Milton's pamphlets of 1644 are informed by a sense of great urgency about the war. In *Of Education* he constantly compares his ideal students to groups of soldiers, and urges that they be given instruction in military discipline:

> They would not then, if they were trusted with fair and hopefull armies, suffer them for want of just and wise discipline to shed away from about them like sick feathers, though they be never so oft suppli'd[.] (*MPW*, II, 412)

This hit indicates his concern about the current conduct of the war; and it is possible that the month after *Areopagitica* appeared he was offered the post of adjutant in Waller's army, which would have given him the opportunity of putting classical precepts of military strategy before his commander.[82] There was a direct connection between the limitations of Parliament's military campaign and its anxiety about becoming beholden to religious radicals. *Areopagitica* makes those connections and draws very different conclusions. Throughout the treatise, Milton compares the quest for truth with military victory, as in the rousing picture of London at war (*MPW*, II, 553–4), or the famous emendation of 'wayfaring Christian' to 'warfaring Christian' (*MPW*, II, 515). Milton sees the divisions of his side as a virtue because they heighten military effectiveness. The royalists will see their opponents' 'small divided maniples [parts of a legion] cutting through at every angle of his ill united and unweildy brigade' (II, 556; cf. 562, 567). The terminology of classical rhetoric often involved military metaphors, the 'ornaments' of figurative language referring to armour; Milton brings these half-buried analogies to the surface. A key motif of Caroline poetry had been the closing of the gates of Janus's temple, an image of peace under a wise monarch. Milton provocatively inverts that image: 'The Temple of *Janus* with his two *controversal* faces might now not unsignificantly be set open' (II, 561). The closed gates signify closed

82 Robert Thomas Fallon, *Captain or Colonel: The Soldier in Milton's Life and Art* (Columbia, 1984), p. 60.

minds, a premature harmony, a false balance which stands in the way of deeper knowledge.

This militant aspect has often been forgotten as *Areopagitica* has become celebrated as a universal plea for free expression, leading to puzzlement when it is recognized that Milton nowhere calls for universal freedom.[83] At the beginning he acknowledges that books need to be controlled since they can 'spring up armed men' (II, 492), and he warns that 'the wet sheets' of 'that continu'd Court-libell' *Mercurius Aulicus* are circulating from secret presses (II, 528). Notoriously, Milton refuses 'tolerated Popery, and open superstition' (II, 565) because 'it extirpats all religions and civill supremacies'. The argument here is basically a political one, 'Popery' being an institutional monopoly which threatens civil society; it is coloured by the suspicion that the king's side had strong support from the international Counter-Reformation.

Milton then does not object to the suppression of royalist opinions in a time of war. Drastic measures had in fact been taken in June 1643 to limit the spread of royalist propaganda after the failure of Waller's plot, and Milton probably supported them. His objection is partly to the means of censorship and partly to its current targets. The system according to which publishers had to license a book with an authorized official before it could be printed had lapsed with the breakdown of royal power, but Parliament had reaffirmed it in 1643. It did so with the strong support of the Stationers' Company, which had a financial interest in a licensing system that maintained a monopoly for its members. Wither had long campaigned against that monopoly, which he blamed for suppressing his prophetic voice.[84] Milton does not object to Parliament's exercising control over printing – far better that it should be in the public hands than dominated by the private interests of court and church – but he does object to this collusion with a monopoly. He particularly objects to pre-publication licensing because it parallels the domination exercised by the clergy, a control over the mind. Licensing confines what ought to be a public space to a particular interest, that of the Presbyterian 'at home in his privat chair' (II, 540). *Areopagitica*, Milton insisted, was not 'the disburdning of a particular fancie' but was voicing a 'common grievance', the 'generall murmur' (II, 539). Writing ought to be a collaborative process – a writer 'likely consults and conferrs with his judicious friends'. This process is one reason why good texts are seldom fixed and finished: a writer who is 'copious of fancie' will want to keep revising his text (II, 532).

Milton objects not only to the general effects of licensing but to its particular targets: the views being suppressed, he argues, are not retrograde

83 On traditions of interpretation see William Kolbrener, *Milton's Warring Angels: A Study of Critical Engagements* (Cambridge, 1997), ch. 1.
84 See Wither's *The Schollers Purgatory* (1624?; *WMW*, I; 25919).

royalisms but the emergent radical Protestantism of the sects. At this time it was the sects who were protesting against licensing because it seemed to be being mainly used to restrict their ideas. Many military leaders were proving half-hearted in their pursuit of the war because it was allowing sects to proliferate; but for Milton that was precisely a reason for winning. The wars of truth were directly parallel to the war against royalism. He was rather late in joining his voice to the sects' protests; but he had had time to reflect and to broaden the issues. His account of the development of licensing is factually very dubious: he lays the chief blame on Laud and religious reactionaries, but the mechanism had a much longer history. Milton is still steering clear of direct confrontation with the English monarchy, which had a better claim than the Papacy to have pioneered the censorship of printed books. But the alarm he raises about Catholic influence in England was calculated to stiffen resistance to the king's party and to those in London who were moving towards it.

Milton's historical analysis places licensing in a larger political framework, as another instance of the decline in civility from the ancient world which did not regulate texts in this way. Livy's *History* had not been censored even though its sympathies were clearly republican. What had gone wrong was the monopolization of power, with 'the Popes of *Rome* engrossing what they pleas'd of Politicall rule into their owne hands' (II, 501) and public revenues being siphoned into an unaccountable religious bureaucracy.[85] In *Animadversions* Milton had argued that the clergy presented more of a challenge than any of the adversaries of ancient civic virtue because they tyrannized over the mind, and he now develops this idea. At the beginning of *Areopagitica* he celebrates the victories gained so far:

> wee are already in good part arriv'd [at civil liberty], and yet from such a steepe disadvantage of tyranny and superstition grounded into our principles as was beyond the manhood of a *Roman* recovery[.] (II, 487)

The people are now trying 'to reassume the ill deputed care of their Religion into their own hands again' (II, 554). But there is more to be done; Milton's warning is that if Parliament loses its zeal for reform and settles with the king, England will lapse into the intellectual stagnation of countries under Habsburg dominance.

Milton offers a compressed sketch of the shift from ancient to modern political life in his satirical description of Italian title-pages: 'Sometimes 5 *Imprimaturs* are seen together dialogue-wise in the Piatza of one Title page,

---

85 On the language of 'engrossing' in anti-monopoly discourse, see Sandra Sherman, 'Printing the Mind: The Economics of Authorship in *Areopagitica*', *Journal of English Literary History* 60 (1993), 323–47, and Michael Wilding, 'Milton's *Areopagitica*: Liberty for the Sects', *Prose Studies* 9 (1986), 7–38.

complementing and ducking each to other with their shav'n reverences' (II, 504). The piazza looks back to the Roman forum, the scene of political debate under the republic, and recalls also the revival of republican culture in the early Renaissance. In most of Italy, however, that culture had indeed been suppressed, and Milton's image of the new Italy is of a claustrophobic elaboration of empty form over spiritual content. The imprimaturs act 'dia-logue-*wise*' (emphasis added) because the genuine dialogue of republican culture has been reduced to empty stage-dialogue. Elsewhere Milton com-pares the imprimatur to the Papal prison, the 'castle St *Angelo*' (II, 537). Milton warns that such values have been transferred to England: licences are obtained from 'the West end of *Pauls*' (II, 504).

In attacking monopolies of discourse, Milton drew on the anti-monopoly language current amongst the opponents of the old City oligarchy. He also had a more specific involvement with the circle of Samuel Hartlib, who were formulating projects for reorganizing the economics of intellectual culture with the collapse of the old court system.[86] Hartlib had welcomed the Parliamentary reforms of the 1640s as an opportunity for establishing international communications in news and in theological and scientific knowledge, and made elaborate plans for an 'Office of Address for Communi-cations', which was to carry through Bacon's plans for advancing learning and Comenius's plans for the reform of education. A new mechanism of patron-age had to be created which would allow intellectuals to pursue their interests independently of royal patronage which, it was held, had tended to limit the imagination and keep it within narrow bounds. This mechanism, unlike the court system, would be accountable to the public; despite their anti-monop-oly rhetoric, most Hartlibians advocated not uncontrolled *laissez-faire* but a modified system of state regulation.[87] Milton wrote *Of Education* on Hartlib's suggestion; he claims to have been 'loaded . . . with entreaties and perswa-sions' (II, 539) to write *Areopagitica*, and the Hartlib circle would be a source for such persuasions. Milton's much-quoted claim that 'a good Booke is the pretious life-blood of a master spirit, imbalm'd and treasur'd up on purpose to a life beyond life' (II, 493) has troubled modern critics for its uncharacter-istic ritualism. It would, however, have been recognized by the Hartlib circle as intensifying Bacon's already ritualistic praise in *The Advancement of Learning* of libraries as 'the Shrynes, where all the Reliques of the ancient

86 Barbara K. Lewalski, 'Milton and the Hartlib Circle: Educational Projects and Epic *Paideia*', in Diana Treviño Benet and Michael Lieb (eds.), *Literary Milton: Text, Pretext, Context* (Pittsburgh, 1994), pp. 202–19.

87 Kevin Dunn, 'Milton among the Monopolists: *Areopagitica*, Intellectual Property and the Hartlib Circle', in Mark Greengrass, Michael Leslie and Timothy Raylor (eds.), *Samuel Hartlib and Universal Reformation: Studies in Intellectual Communication* (Cambridge, 1994), pp. 177–92.

Saints, full of true vertue, and that without delusion or imposture, are pre-
serued, and reposed'.[88]

There is evidence both for the popularity of *Areopagitica* in that circle, and
for its radical political implications, in the correspondence of the Kentish
lawyer Sir Cheney Culpeper (1611–63), a friend of Hartlib's. In Culpeper's
letters of the early 1640s we find the Machiavellian idea of reduction or
restoration being pushed ever further, and fused with an apocalyptic
Protestantism. He sees the reforms that Parliament has begun as an ongoing
process with no clear limit. 'Restoration' for Culpeper begins with an assault
on episcopacy, whose veto in Parliament must be removed:

> there will be noe right regulatinge of these negatiues, thes corner stones of
> Babylon, but by takinge them away & restoringe the People to theire primitiue
> liberty of disposinge of themselues by theire representatiue w*i*thout askinge leaue
> of a 100: selfe interessed men[.]

Annual Parliaments are similarly part of the process of restoration. Elections
to Parliament should be 'reduced to be annuall . . . when our representatiue
hathe done its woorke . . . it selfe wowlde be allsoe soe farre reduced as to be
able to doe all thinges but not make it selfe perpetuall'.[89] Culpeper was aware
that he was pushing beyond the limits of accepted political discourse. He early
championed the abolition of the House of Lords as part of the process of
reduction:

> as for this reason the [Parl*iament*] wowlde be restored againste the [K*ing's*] pre-
> tences, soe will it (in time) deserue a seconde consideration of resstoringe (that
> firste Parente of all Gouernement) the howse of Commons to its vigour againste
> the L*or*ds . . .

He added in a note to Hartlib: 'My paper is done; when you haue read it I pray
burne it as that which (thowgh it muste & will be done) better fitts to the nexte
age, & (whensoeuer) better done then written'.[90] Culpeper was not at this
stage a republican, yet his conception of monarchy was so limited that in
January 1644 he could easily entertain the idea of deposing Charles in favour
of the Elector Palatine.[91] By the following year he was still more confident that
Charles would build up the war until he was ruined and

> the democraticall growinge spirite (for the presente not soe stronge) haue taken
> such roote in this Nation as (vpon the same reason & grownde) to question the
> Lord & Presbiter as [thems*elves*] haue firste done the [K*ing*] & Bish*ops* & thus will

---

88 *The Twoo Bookes of Francis Bacon: Of the Proficiencie and Aduancement of Learning*
   (1605; 1164), Book II, fol. 2v (II.5 in modern editions). The phrase 'and that without delusion or imposture' was cut from Latin editions to avoid offending Catholics; Milton is
   bold by comparison.   89 Culpeper to Hartlib, February 1644?, *CL*, pp. 197–98.
90 Culpeper to Hartlib, 16 May 1644, *CL*, pp. 201–2.
91 Culpeper to Hartlib, 9 January 1644, *CL*, p. 192.

euery generation thruste out the other; & as wee come neerer the center of Spirituall & Ciuill truthe soe will the motion be quicker & the stay (in any one place or kinde of gouernemente) will be shorter.[92]

Culpeper saw the Office of Address and attendant projects for the reform of communication as part of a wider, apocalyptic process of bringing down monopolies: after the 'monopoly of Power which the [King] claimes' there would fall 'the monopoly of trade', the 'monopoly of Equity ... the monopoly of matters of conscience & scripture ... all these & many more wee shall haue in chace & what one hownde misses another will happen in the sente of & thus will Babilon tumble, tumble, tumble.'[93] Culpeper's language is at points so close to Milton's as to suggest that he had read *Areopagitica*. In a letter of 20 November, a few days before Thomason received his copy, he wrote the following:

> thowgh this present age haue soe muche reuerence to our owne or ancestors wisdome as euery thinge (in churche or state or any other kinde) yf newe to vs (thowgh not in itselfe or the principles of scripture or reason) findes as yet a difficulte passage in mens thowghts; yet from the three yeeres liberty which men haue taken of ransackinge & touzinge those starched vp & vnjointed postures wherein our ancestors lefte vs like soe many images without motion but from without) I cannot but conceiue wee shall by degrees (hauinge firste freede ourselues from a slauishe reuerence of some fewe men or bookes) try euery spirit & that as well in rationall as spirituall thinges[.][94]

A few weeks later he urged men to 'rowze themselues out of the muddines of custome & conformity'.[95] The wording recalls Milton's 'sicken into a muddy pool of conformity and tradition', 'what a fine conformity would it starch us all into?' (II, 545), and the description of man without freedom as 'a meer artificiall *Adam*, such an *Adam* as he is in the motions' (II, 527).

Areopagitica, then, could be viewed by contemporary readers as an instrument in a very wide process of reform. There is evidence that the Hartlib circle considered issuing a German translation. Milton's Latin defences of the Commonwealth were to prove very popular amongst republicans in Germany, and this would have been an early address to that audience. Admittedly, one of Hartlib's German correspondents complained that *Areopagitica* was 'rather too satyrical throughout ... and because of his all too highflown style in many places quite obscure'.[96] And Culpeper himself had reservations about Milton:

---

92 Culpeper to Hartlib, 11 March 1646, *CL*, p. 271.
93 Culpeper to Hartlib, 4 March 1646, *CL*, pp. 269–70.
94 Culpeper to Hartlib, 20 November 1644, *CL*, p. 204.
95 Culpeper to Hartlib, 21 January 1645, *CL*, p. 209.
96 Anonymous document, 25 April 1647, *HP*, 59/9/8B; Leo Miller, 'A German Critique of Milton's *Areopagitica* in 1647', *Notes and Queries* 234 (1989), 29–30. *Areopagitica* is not named in the letter, but Miller suggests that it is the only plausible candidate; it is just possible, however, that the reference could be to one of the divorce tracts.

he praised *Of Education* but nonetheless complained that it did not descend enough into particulars.[97] Milton's high style did not appeal to a circle whose view of language and communication was mainly utilitarian, and *Areopagitica* would have been still less accessible to the artisans who were enthusiastically entering political debate. It speaks for, rather than to, them; the community it speaks to is that of intellectuals deeply versed in literary culture.

Milton had some success in appealing to young Parliamentarians; but he was probably also targeting waverers who might have gone over to the royalist cause but could still be shamed into changing their minds. Waller had argued that the new radical London would destroy learning; Milton retorts with one of the most erudite and allusive political pamphlets ever composed. He had anticipated this strategy in a sonnet written in the autumn of 1642, when the royalists were launching their major assault on London and the city was starting to build its new defences. There Milton had compared the effects of his poem in warding off violence with Euripides's recital of his verses during the Spartan assault on Athens. He both compliments his antagonists on their learning and manoeuvres them into a position where they are classed as either tyrants or philistines. The newly-rising walls of the beleaguered London are linked with those of Athens.[98] The allusions were calculated to strike home to members of the former Great Tew circle, who had only recently gone over to the king, or to Waller, who was still wavering.

Milton alluded to Euripides in very similar terms on the title-page of *Areopagitica* (figure 5). In the body of the pamphlet he compares censored title-pages to Counter-Reformation piazzas; he makes his own resemble rather the Athenian assembly by including some lines from Euripides's *The Suppliant Women*:

> This is true Liberty when free born men
> Having to advise the public may speak free,
> Which he who can, and will, deserv's high praise,
> Who neither can nor will, may hold his peace;
> What can be juster in a State then this?[99]

Here again an ideological opposition is set up between Athens and Sparta. In the play, a herald arrives from Thebes, a despotism which was often associated

---

97 Culpeper to Hartlib, 12 November 1645, *CL*, pp. 249–50.

98 Milton, 'Captain or Colonel, or Knight in Arms' (Sonnet 8). For republican implications of Milton's sonnets, and of *Areopagitica*, see also Howard Erskine-Hill, *Poetry and the Realm of Politics: Shakespeare to Dryden* (Oxford, 1996), pp. 152ff.

99 See Annabel Patterson, *Censorship and Interpretation: The Conditions of Writing and Reading in Early Modern England* (Madison, 1984), p. 115; David Davies and Paul Dowling, '"Shrewd Books, with Dangerous Frontispices": *Areopagitica*'s Motto', *MQ* 20 (1986), 33–7.

5 Title-page to John Milton, *Areopagitica*, 1644.

by the Athenians with Sparta – it had been a Theban who was calling for the city's destruction when it was saved by Euripides's verse.[100] He asks who is king (*tyrannos*) in this city. Theseus immediately retorts that Athens is a free

100 On Thebes as the Other of Athens, see Froma I. Zeitlin, 'Thebes: Theater of Self and Society in Athenian Drama', in J. Peter Euben (ed.), *Greek Tragedy and Political Theory* (Berkeley, Los Angeles, and London, 1986), pp. 101–41, especially pp. 116ff.

republic in which all have an equal stake. The herald then plunges into a denunciation of democracy very similar in theme to the Hobbesian diatribes that were flowing from Oxford towards London: the people are not capable of judging public affairs and will be manipulated by demagogues. Theseus retorts with a spirited defence of the Athenians' right of participation and of free speech as the only just political order – so spirited that some sixteenth-century editors felt obliged to insert condemnations of democratic turbulence in their editions, though others were less inhibited (figure 6).[101] Whether Euripides himself endorsed these opinions is another matter. When the modern radical journalist I. F. Stone described him as the Walt Whitman of Athens, he was perhaps overstating the case.[102] Yet Milton was later to cite this same speech in a defence of the English republic. Theseus's willingness to submit to the people could be seen as a form of 'reduction' parallel to what Milton had praised in Brutus. Euripides's plays epitomized the spirit of bold thinking and speaking which the title-page quotation at once alluded to and embodied (for comparable allusions to Greek tragedy cf. I, 803, 905). His most celebrated sixteenth-century translators, Erasmus and George Buchanan, were celebrated both for intellectual independence and for scepticism about the divine right of kings.[103] When Parliament had commissioned a translation of Buchanan's *Baptistes*, it could be seen as reviving that spirit, and Milton launches his appeal in that hope.[104]

The title-page quotation, then, broadens the specific issue of licensing into a more general consideration of the relations between language and political structure. The edition Milton used glossed the quotation by a reference to the Greek concept of *parrhesia* or open, bold speech.[105] The right to speak out boldly on any issue was effectively identical with the civic identity of free Athenians. They had at least four different words for freedom of speech, of which perhaps the strongest was *parrhesia*, a favourite word in Euripides; it occurs twice in the *Electra*, the play with which Milton in 'Captain, or colonel' imagined charming the royalists. The word's fortunes had declined with the decline of Greek democracy. The more conservative Romans had often

---

101 *Euripidis tragoediae*, ed. Gulielmus Xylandrus (Basel, 1558), pp. 424–5, glossing the herald's speech as a vituperation of democracy, while Theseus's reply, from which Milton quotes, is a vituperation of tyranny and praise of democracy.

102 I. F. Stone, *The Trial of Socrates* (1988), p. 221.

103 See F. L. Lucas, *Euripides and his Influence* (1924).

104 Milton cited the transgressive voice of Euripides's *Medea* on the title-page of *Tetrachordon*; for evidence of Milton's close attention to title-pages see his satire of an antagonist's 'sitting in the chaire of his Title page upon his poore cast adversaries both as a Judge and Party, and that before the jury of Readers can be impannell'd' (*An Apology against a Pamphlet, MPW*, I, 876–7).

105 *Euripidis tragoediae*, ed. Paulus Stephanus, 2 vols. (Geneva, 1602, Bodleian don.d.27–8), II, sig. Piiv.

SVPPLICES.   425

Vbi primùm non sunt leges   "Tyranni-
Communes: unus imperat, & habet legem   "dis uitupe
Ipse pro se, & alteri nihil relinquetur.   "claus Demo
Scriptis autem legibus, imbecillis   "cratie.
Et diues habent æquum ius: "
Et licet imbecillibus accusare   "Legum uis.
Potentem, quando malè audit   "
Et uincit minor potentem, habens iustam causam. "
Illud etiam est liberum, si quis uult urbi   "
Proponere in medium bonum consilium,   "
Et uolenti hoc est splendidum: qui non uult,   "
Tacet: quid est æquabilius ciuitati quàm hæc?   "
Et quidem ubi populus princeps est terræ,   "
Delectatur præsentibus ciuibus fortibus.   "
At rex putat hoc sibi inimicum,   "
Et præstantissimos quos putat sapere,   "
Interficit metuens de regno.   "
Quomodo ciuitas potest esse firma,   "
Quando aliquis, sicut ex prato uernospicam,   "
Aufert audaces ciues, & demetit iuuenes?   "
Quid opus est liberis comparare opes,   "
Vbi quis parat maiorem partē facultatū tyrāno? "
Item honestè educari filias,   "
Futuras uoluptati tyranno quando uult,   "
Et lachrymis parentibus? Ne uiuam amplius,   "
Si mei liberi nubant ui coacti.
Et hæc respondi tibi adhæc.

            D   5   Quid

6 'Vituperation of tyranny and praise of democracy; the power of laws'. *Euripidis tragoediae*, ed. Gulielmus Xylandrus, Basel, 1558.

translated *parrhesia* more pejoratively as *licentia* or *contumacia*, and a negative view of *parrhesia* was retained in Renaissance rhetorical treatises:
rhetoric had moved from the open forum to the princely court where indirec-
tion was essential.[106] In recovering the spirit of the Greek word, Milton was
also implicitly calling for a recovery of the political potential of Greek democracy.

That recovery could not, however, involve direct imitation. The rhetorical
culture of a city-state was impossible to reproduce in a modern nation-state.
Milton signals the difference by terming his pamphlet a *Speech*. That, of
course, is precisely what it was not; in a Parliamentary system, speaking was
for a minority. In the conditions of the 1640s, however, with the printing of
Parliamentary speeches for reading by the general public and, conversely,
addresses to Parliament by those presenting petitions, that distinction was
not so sharply maintained. The Levellers in their campaign for a more
accountable Parliament were able to turn a pamphlet into a 'demonstration
on the page'.[107] Milton never went so far as the Levellers in attacking
Parliament in public, nor was he sympathetic to theories of democratic representation. His 'speech' retains a respectful distance from Parliament. All the
same, it lays claim to boldness of speech, and one of the things Milton praises
about Parliament is its readiness to listen to 'the voice of reason from what
quarter soever it be heard speaking' (*Aeropagitica*, *MPW*, II, 490). This is the
product of 'the magnanimity of a trienniall Parlament' (II, 488): here Milton
makes a direct link between the moral qualities he praises and the political
structure that makes them possible, the Triennial Act which has both guaranteed Parliament's constitutional status and expanded a public sphere that can
scrutinize its acts.[108] The printed press has made possible an equivalent of the
classical forum, and Parliament has to take that forum into account.

The preliminaries of *Areopagitica*, then, hint that London has become a
new Athens in the political as well as cultural sense. As in the 'Captain or
colonel' sonnet, readers with a humanist education are urged to choose this
Athens against a royalist Oxford – which provocatively functions in this
analogy as Sparta. The celebrated passage where he acclaims Londoners'

---

106 Stone, *The Trial of Socrates*, pp. 221ff; a forthcoming study by David Colclough will
    explore the term's history in detail.
107 Smith, *LR*, p. 139. Smith's discussion of the Levellers and print culture is very illumi-
    nating.
108 Compare Nedham's scoffing comment in *Mercurius Britanicus* no. 67, 20–27 January
    1645, E26.6, p. 528: the royalist *Mercurius Aulicus* is 'out of love with the word *Trienniall*
    ever since it was joyned to *Parliament*', and Milton's later comment on Presbyterians
    who objected to Parliament's being named a 'representative' 'and were perhaps of that
    Classis, who heretofore were as much staggerd at *Trienniall*' (*Eikonoklastes*, *MPW*, III,
    328).

intellectual creativity even in times of war (*MPW*, II, 553–4) is an imitation of Pericles's funeral oration, as well as of Theseus's speech in Euripides, and is thus a pointed counter to Hobbes's doubts about Athens in his Thucydides. Milton praises '*Athens* where Books and Wits were ever busier then in any other part of *Greece*' (II, 494) and derides the 'muselesse and unbookish' Spartans whose 'surlinesse' minded 'nought but the feats of Warre' (II, 496). Readers like Hobbes and Waller would undoubtedly have picked up the allusions. Hobbes had translated a Euripides tragedy when young; Waller owned a copy of Euripides and his fellow-MP William Drake had taken detailed notes from the dramatist.[109]

Yet Milton was sending out a complex message to such readers. They would also have picked up a tension on his title-page between the democratic implications of the Theseus speech and his idiosyncratic title, *Areopagitica* (things concerning the Areopagus). For the Areopagus was a vestigial element of an older, aristocratic constitution, a body which censored morals and served as a counterweight to the democratic Assembly. Milton's title alludes to an oration by Isocrates which advocated greater powers for the Areopagus; he belonged to the conservative, aristocratic group in Athens which greatly feared the turbulence of democracy. Since Milton is calling for the relaxation instead of the tightening of social controls, his title may carry some degree of irony; but it also serves as a reassurance that this new polity need not lapse into complete chaos, that it possesses controls on pure democracy. Throughout the treatise Milton is careful to address 'Lords and Commons', implying a parallel between the dual authorities of Athens and London and, as has been seen, he did not join the Levellers in their demands for better representation. In *Of Reformation* he had gone along with those who admired the Spartan constitution as especially well balanced.

Though Milton's republicanism always had a conservative element, his position in *Areopagitica* remains critically distant from traditional English institutions. It has to be recalled that Marten had been expelled the previous year for hinting that the king should be deposed. Milton is a lot more oblique, but he is still pushing official discourse to its limits. The English monarchy dwindles to a dead voice from the tomb of Henry VII (II, 567), just as the figure of the king is conspicuously absent from Milton's reworking of the story of Solomon's temple (II, 555). For all the respect with which he treats Parliament, he contemptuously dismisses the traditional reverence for its antiquity and tries to direct it towards classical republican models: 'how much better I find ye esteem it to imitate the old and elegant humanity of Greece, then the barbarick pride of a *Hunnish* and *Norwegian* statelines' (II, 489). Parliament functions for Milton as an energetic vanguard of institutional change. He

109 Clark, 'Wisdom Literature of the Seventeenth Century', p. 49.

describes the people's intellectual achievements as 'the issue of your owne vertu propagated in us' (II, 559): Parliament instils a *virtù* in the people that is at once moral and Machiavellian. *Areopagitica* displays far greater trust in the broad masses of the people than his later writings, but he was consistently wary of the conservatism of much popular culture, and believed that a radical process of re-education was necessary to overcome it; this would be the new aristocracy of his mixed polity. In 1644 he still envisaged the Lords as embodying this aristocratic element, and indeed there was a small but highly energetic group of reforming peers. *Of Education* offers a programme for the ruling elite, but unlike a courtly finishing school his academy will insist on civic virtue, on martial and rhetorical discipline, fitting a man 'to perform justly, skilfully and magnanimously all the offices both private and publike of peace and war' (*MPW*, II, 378–9). Their studies will be like 'the last embattelling of a Romane legion' (II, 407). They will thus differ from the current generation of backsliding politicians who are of 'a tottering conscience' (II, 398) – Waller may have been in his mind.[110]

Milton's Athenian allusions have a similar radical edge. The Areopagus had multiple associations. St Paul had addressed it, trying to convert the Athenians from the common ground between pagans and Christians and quoting Greek poetry in the process (Acts XVII.19–34). Harrington later cited the Athenian openness to other ideas as a precedent for religious tolerance: for him the *ecclesia* of the classical assembly was virtually identical with the church as a gathering of independent-minded Christians.[111] Though Milton does not make this association explicit, his title assimilates Christian prophecy to classical rhetoric in a spirit of intellectual tolerance. In constitutional terms, the Areopagus might have been a conservative institution, but it was firmly associated with republican forms of government. The Greek dramatists had been ready to claim the Areopagus as part of their democratic heritage. Aeschylus had presented an idealized version of the Areopagus at the climax of the *Oresteia*, where the emphasis is laid on the role of the people, in however mediated a form, in taking major decisions. In *Eikonoklastes* Milton noted that the Areopagus had tried and executed Orestes, though 'by succession King of *Argos*'.[112]

Antiquarian evidence was growing for a republican reading of Greek history. In 1624 the Dutch scholar Jan Meurs – also the author of a treatise on Greek tragedy – had dedicated a book on the Areopagus to the Venetian

---

110 Martin Dzelzainis, 'Milton's Classical Republicanism', *MR*, pp. 3–24 (10–15), discusses the republican implications of *Of Education*.

111 James Harrington, *A Letter unto Mr Stubs* (E1017.13), p. 2; *HPW*, p. 892; Joseph Anthony Wittreich, Jr, 'Milton's *Areopagitica*: Its Isocratic and Ironic Contexts', *Milton Studies* 4 (1972), 101–15.

112 *MPW*, III, 589.

republic, drawing parallels between Athens and Venice.[113] Similar parallels had been made in a treatise of 1637 by Francis Rous, son of a leading Parliamentarian.[114] Milton's Italian journey would have made him well aware of the links between Athens and Venice, a city which prided itself on its tradition of intellectual openness including freedom of the press.[115] Later Milton and other republicans were to seek other institutional embodiments for the aristocratic element, and such prominent republicans as Marchamont Nedham, John Hall, James Harrington, and Algernon Sidney all looked back to the Areopagus.[116] Another republican, Nathaniel Bacon, went so far as to suggest that the Anglo-Saxons might have been descended from the Greeks because of the parallels between their forms of government. He emphasized the checks on democratic elements in their constitution, seeing it as a mixture of Athens and Sparta.[117] There was a humanist tradition of claiming that the English vernacular was particularly close to Greek.[118] Sparta was also an important republican frame of reference – though Hobbes's Thucydides had stressed its monarchical aspects, these were very limited.[119] Waller and May had both compared the London of the 1640s to Sparta; it was Milton's preference for Athens that was exceptional, and indicated a distinctive emphasis in cultural politics.

Milton's praise of Athens, then, was calculated to split royalist support, suggesting that humanists who went over to the royal party had betrayed the deeper spirit of their own learning which could only be fulfilled by returning to London. It is interesting that at a time when communication between London and royalist Oxford was difficult, *Areopagitica* was one of a handful of London books bought by the Bodleian Library.[120] It was even calculated to

---

113 *Ioannis Meursi Areopagus, sive, De Senatu Areopagitico* (Leiden, 1624); Meurs uses Isocrates's Areopagitic Oration as one of his sources, p. 27. On this and the following note see Tuck, pp. 230–1, 254, 258.

114 Francis Rous, *Archaeologiae Atticae Libri Tres* (Oxford, 1637; 21350). Rous was not himself sympathetic to popular democracy, declaring, p. 30, that Pericles brought in an ochlocracy by weakening the power of the Areopagus.

115 Peter Lindenbaum, 'John Milton and the Republican Mode of Literary Production', *Yearbook of English Studies* 21 (1991), 121–36.

116 See chapter 5, below, and Algernon Sidney, *Discourses Concerning Government*, ed. Thomas G. West (Indianapolis, 1990), p. 169.

117 Nathaniel Bacon, *The Continuation of an Historicall Discourse* (1651; E624.1), p. 15, cited by Tuck, p. 237.

118 J. B. Trapp, 'The Conformity of Greek and the Vernacular', in R. R. Bolgar (ed.), *Classical Influences on European Culture, A.D. 500–1500* (Cambridge, 1971), pp. 239–44.

119 Elizabeth Rawson, *The Spartan Tradition in European Thought* (Oxford, 1969), ch. 11–13.

120 Gwen Hampshire, 'An Unusual Bodleian Purchase in 1645', *Bodleian Library Record* 10 (1979–82), 339–48. The victory at Naseby opened up communications between London and Oxford for a time.

appeal to some of the licensers. Parliament had appointed three licensers for books of philosophy, history, poetry, morality and the arts: Sir Nathaniel Brent, John Langley and Thomas Farnaby. Closest to Parliament in ideological terms was Langley, who had succeeded Milton's close friend Alexander Gil as headmaster of St Paul's School, and had just published a rhetorical manual.[121] He licensed educational works including Comenius's celebrated *Ianua Linguarum* as well as Wither's *Campo-Musae*, May's *History* and John Hall's *Poems*. Perhaps less expected is that another of the licensers should have been the man who had had Langley suspended as 'puritanicall'.[122] However, though Brent had served under Laud to correct ecclesiastical abuses, he later joined Langley in attacking him. He had wide literary interests; he had been the dedicatee of Rous's *Archaeologicae Atticae*, and had translated the *History of the Council of Trent* of the Venetian intellectual Paolo Sarpi, on which Milton drew heavily in *Areopagitica*. Whatever he thought of Milton's assault on licensing, Brent was to license his 1645 *Poems*. The choice of Farnaby was most surprising in political terms. He was an eminent classicist, whose edition of Lucan had been dedicated to Selden and who had also written extensively on rhetoric. But his skills as a licenser were never called on, for only four months after he was nominated he was being questioned by the Commons on charges of involvement in a royalist uprising, and he was still in confinement two years later.[123] That Parliament should have entrusted scrutiny of books to these malignant hands brought home the conservative political implications of the system; yet Milton may also have considered Farnaby a significant enough classicist to be worth trying to shame into rethinking his ideas. He breaks off for a moment from his denunciation of licensing to express a moment of sympathy for the licensers, who are being worn out by importunate authors. Yet if they resign, their successors will be 'either ignorant, imperious, and remisse, or basely pecuniary' (*MPW*, II, 530).

Against the conservatives' betrayals of the classical spirit, Milton appeals to the excitement of recovering lost political and cultural achievements. He alludes to Livy's story of the heroic struggles of the young Roman republic, with the royalists cast in the role of the barbaric Carthaginians (II, 557). And the architectural imagery that runs through the treatise reinforces this sense of founding a new order. Waller had feared that the collapse of the state church would lead to 'a flat and levell in lear[n]ing too'[124], and compared the church to a fortress defending social stability. Milton attacks those who

---

121 [John Langley], *Totius Rhetoricae Adumbratio* (1644; L404A).

122 J. T. Cliffe, *The Puritan Gentry: The Great Puritan Families of Early Stuart England* (London, Boston, Melbourne and Henley, 1984), p. 81.

123 *CJ*, III, 181, IV, 280; on Farnaby's role in the rising see Alan Everitt, *The Community of Kent and the Great Rebellion 1640–1660* (Leicester, 1966), pp. 190–200.

124 Waller, *A Speech . . . Concerning Episcopacie*, p. 5.

denounce the common people as 'giddy, vitious, and ungrounded' (II, 536), and sees such attacks as deriving from a narrow, philistine defensiveness. He parodies the fears of the rigid Presbyterian:

> if his rear and flanks be not impal'd, if his back dore be not secur'd by the rigid licencer, but that a bold book may now and then issue forth, and give the assault to some of his old collections in their trenches, it will concern him then to keep waking, to stand in watch, to set good guards and sentinells about his receiv'd opinions . . . (II, 547)

While criticizing such metaphorical defence-works, Milton at the same time appeals to Londoners' experience of building fortifications. His emphasis is on the constructive, rather than defensive, aspect of architecture. Waller, a poet who was celebrated for the balance of his elegant closed couplets, had been disturbed by the unrepresentable chaos, the floods of new discourse that disrupt the foundations of the church. Milton calls for a more complex kind of balance, closer to the tense dynamic found by Machiavelli in the Roman republic, where the discord between aristocratic and democratic elements produced greater energy than the sterile unity of monarchical order. Such a polity would always be vulnerable to the instability that Lucan found in the Roman republic, but Milton is confident that a *concordia discors* can form a strong state. He praises God for shaking kingdoms with 'strong and healthfull commotions to a generall reforming' (II, 566). The striking oxymoron of 'healthfull commotions' would have startled conservative readers, but for Milton such turbulence was far preferable to 'a grosse conforming stupidity' (II, 564).

Milton incorporates his ideal of a tense, complex balance of the polity in his use of language:

> Yet these are the men cry'd out against for schismaticks and sectaries; as if, while the Temple of the Lord was building, some cutting, some squaring the marble, others hewing the cedars, there should be a sort of irrationall men who could not consider there must be many schisms and many dissections made in the quarry and in the timber, ere the house of God can be built. And when every stone is laid artfully together, it cannot be united into a continuity, it can but be contiguous in this world; neither can every peece of the building be of one form; nay rather the perfection consists in this, that out of many moderat varieties and brotherly dissimilitudes that are not vastly disproportionall arises the goodly and the gracefull symmetry that commends the whole pile and structure. (II, 555)

Small-scale formal balances are here set against large-scale conceptual and syntactic asymmetries: 'continuity' and 'contiguous' insist on their difference through their similarity of sound. The 'goodly and the graceful symmetry' arises with its verb out of a long sentence with many divisions and subordinate clauses, and while it forms a climax it is itself displaced by the concluding subordinate clause 'that commends the whole pile and structure'. Throughout the text, present participles – 'building', 'cutting', 'squaring', 'hewing' – are given predominance over past participles with their possible overtones of premature completion – note how long it is in the first sentence above before 'building' becomes 'built'. Where Waller's couplets had tried to contain opposition at the cost of narrowness, Milton's sinuous syntax dramatizes the difficulty of accommodating differing views, in order to give the impression of a structure that is ultimately all the more solid for the work it has done, a more complex kind of symmetry which accepts that contiguity and continuity do not quite balance each other out. A lot here depends on the sleight of hand on 'arises', which converts Waller's uncontrolled multiplying into a triumphant process of construction.

We have moved from politics to style, but as has been clear throughout, for Milton these are closely related. The open-mindedness and magnanimity of his discourse is itself a part of the spirit of free inquiry for whose expansion it calls. Milton is offering in this tract not only an implicitly republican politics but also an implicitly republican poetics. At the very beginning of the tract, Milton draws attention to his own speech-act, speaking of himself as having changed the character of his introduction through 'the very attempt of this addresse thus made'; he aims to manifest the degree of liberty which the nation has already achieved 'by the very sound of this which I shall utter' (II, 487). He constantly presents the truth he is uttering as breaking out of the constraints of the tract's formal structures: 'See the ingenuity of Truth, who when she gets a free and willing hand, opens her self faster, then the pace of method and discours can overtake her' (II, 521). Milton finds a historical precedent for this openness that is now being recovered in a free nation: '*Julius Agricola* . . . preferr'd the naturall wits of Britain, before the labour'd studies of the French' (II, 552). In the eighteenth century, *Areopagitica*'s cult of British freedom in the arts was to become a cornerstone of Whig-republican poetics, giving inspiration to Shaftesbury's concept of the 'public voice' and to the romanticization of British bards.[125] A more recent republican poet, Tom Paulin, has compared Milton's prose in *Areopagitica* to Whitman's free verse.[126]

If this is a poetics, it is almost an anti-poetics, pushing conventional forms to the limit. Humanists had often seen the decline of classical rhetoric as running parallel to the decline of political liberty, with the emergence of ornate courtly poetry as the sign of a limited political awareness. *Areopagitica* is the culmination of a process in which Milton experimented more and more

---

125 See Michael Meehan, *Liberty and Poetics in Eighteenth Century England* (1986), pp. 25ff.
126 Tom Paulin, *Minotaur: Poetry and the Nation State* (London and Boston, 1992), pp. 30–1.

boldly with the possibilities of discursive prose, with recovering the fullness of classical rhetoric. It is true that in several of the prose tracts he presents himself as turning with reluctance to public controversy from his projects for a heroic poem, or from his private meditations; the cool element of prose employs only his left hand. In *The Reason of Church-Government* he writes that 'it were a folly to commit any thing elaborately compos'd to the carelesse and interrupted listening of these tumultuous times' (*MPW*, I, 807). Poetry does often need the kind of distancing from everyday language offered by quiet and privacy, and that desire need not in any case be interpreted as apolitical. But Milton's caveats about his prose should not be taken fully at face value.[127] The man who composed eleven pamphlets in three years and had a bound collection presented to the Bodleian Library was no reluctant controversialist. Soon after declaring that he regrets leaving his 'calme and pleasing solitarynes . . . to imbark in a troubl'd sea of noises and hoars disputes' (*MPW*, I, 821), he is launching into an assault on the bishops with immense polemical vigour.

Milton dramatizes his own process of self-education as he becomes aware of his civic duties in turning his linguistic gifts to the public service: 'ease and leasure was given thee for thy retired thoughts out of the sweat of other men', and those privileges must be repaid (*MPW*, I, 804). Yet this reluctance, while springing from genuine concerns, also has an element of rhetorical performance. If the divorce tracts are seen as a distraction from his poetry, before long he will be seeing the invitation to write *Of Education* as a distraction from the divorce tracts (*MPW*, II, 363). Though he still spoke at this time of working on an epic of early English history, no material survives from this project. Given how careful Milton was to preserve his early verse, one may be sceptical about how far he had got or was likely to get; his imagination was engaged elsewhere. The excitement that informs the prose works belies the claim of being forced into them out of duty. They are bursting with linguistic energy, with constant shifts between vernacular vituperation and self-consciously poetical flights which then career to earth as a blast of invective takes over. One does not normally think of a political tract as being in prose, one takes it for granted. In drawing attention to the fact that he is choosing prose, Milton makes his reader think about the medium as well as the message, about the social contexts of language. It is fitting that these experiments should culminate in *Areopagitica* with a tract which is precisely concerned with the social contexts of the production of texts.

One of Milton's most remarkable flights of prose-poetry comes where he

---

127 James Grantham Turner, 'The Poetics of Engagement', in David Loewenstein and James Grantham Turner (eds.), *Politics, Poetics and Hermeneutics in Milton's Prose* (Cambridge, 1990), pp. 257–75.

reworks the traditional figure of the body politic (*MPW*, II, 557–87). Conservatives saw the ferment of new debate as a feverish, unhealthy over-heating of the body politic. Milton takes this as a sign of health, and points out that the healthy body is always in a process of change, casting off the wrinkled skin, and proceeds to push the analogy to breaking-point. The body may not be able to grow younger, but a culture can, if it restores lost energies in the way Milton is restoring classical eloquence. He registers this process of change in his own shifts of imagery, as the body becomes identified both with that of Samson and of a female personification, and then becomes an eagle bold enough to risk staring straight at the sun, a traditional image of regal author-ity. The passage pushes at the limits of representation and embodies the process it celebrates, the exploration of the 'solidest and sublimest points of controversie, and new invention'.

The word 'sublime' here points towards another literary point of reference for the prose tracts.[128] Hobbes was to object to Lucan's aiming at sublimity, which he identified with soaring fancifully above due limits. The Latin 'sub-limis' literally means simply 'high, elevated', but the term was taking on more specific meanings as interest emerged in Longinus's treatise *Peri Hypsous, On the Sublime*. Interest in Longinus was found in royalist as well as Parliamentarian circles, but Milton and his followers gave the sublime a dis-tinctively republican accent.[129] Longinus's sublimity is consistently opposed to easy, specious harmony. Language that is too neatly patterned leads to pre-mature closure, so that the hearers 'foreseeing their periods join with them in the *close*, and as in a *consort anticipate* the *conclusion*'.[130] Longinus quotes as an example of trivial elegance a line about a storm: 'A *little* timber keeps *them out of* hell' (p. 23, ch. 8). He could almost be referring to the last line of Waller's poem on Charles's escape from drowning, which, as has been seen, tries however precariously to find an order in the chaos of the 1620s. Waller's prose style is liable to the charges Longinus raises against Isocrates: that he tries to make his language so smooth that he diminishes the emotional effect.

Longinus's description of the opposite pole to such writing, the sublime, could apply in almost every respect to Milton's prose in *Areopagitica*. Milton

---

128 On 'sublime' as used by Henry Parker, and its role in the 'generation of a republican vocabulary in the 1640s', see Nigel Smith, '*Areopagitica*: Voicing Contexts, 1643–5', in Loewenstein and Turner (eds.), *Politics, Poetics, and Hermeneutics in Milton's Prose*, pp. 103–22 (109). The word 'sublimat' (*MPW*, II, 507) is mainly alchemical. See also Smith, *LR*, pp. 123–7, 189, 215.

129 See T. J. B. Spencer, 'Longinus in English Criticism: Influences Before Milton', *Review of English Studies* 8 (1957), 137–43.

130 J[ohn]. H[all]., *Peri Hypsous, or Dionysius Longinus of the Height of Eloquence* (1652; E1294.2), p. 74, ch. 41 (for ease of reference I give the chapter-numbers of modern edi-tions rather than of Hall's). He declared that the translation had been made 'some yeares past' (sig. B6r), and that he had originally intended to include a commentary.

had placed Longinus on his ideal syllabus in *Of Education*, and praised poetry as 'that sublime art' (*MPW*, II, 404); it was appropriate that the first English translation of Longinus should have been composed by his young disciple, John Hall. In *Areopagitica* Milton takes Isocrates as his generic model; yet his prose style is in fact very different from Isocrates's, pushing beyond balance into a precarious asymmetry. The Isocratic allusion can, however, be seen as indicating an aristocratic element that is in tension with a more sublimely democratic rhetoric. And it is not harmony in itself that Longinus rejects but its premature, specious approximation; the sublime is indeed harmonious and unified, but only just – 'things . . . widely *different* are here by a strange *artifice* brought *together*' (p. 22, ch. 8). He has high praise for Euripides and other tragic dramatists because they refuse easy resolutions. Against Isocrates, the orator of smooth language and also of conciliation with Philip of Macedon, Longinus counterposes Demosthenes, the orator of resistance, whose 'very *order* seems to be *disorderly* and his *disorders* are *rang'd* into a certain kind of *order*' (p. 43, ch. 20). He will pile up striking images so that we are 'drawn from the *Argumentative* part to a *smiting phantasie*, whereby the other is both *hid* and *enlightned*' (p. 36, ch. 15); he 'casts the Auditour into a *fear* least the whole Oration *fall* to *pieces*' (p. 46, ch. 22). These could be descriptions of Milton's dazzling, almost surreal clusters of images and his asymmetrical periods in *Areopagitica*.

Longinus's resistance to easy harmony is linked with a hostility to external wealth and honour: the sublime spirit goes beyond such things. That independent stance takes on political connotations at the end of the treatise, where a speaker gives a classic formulation of the thesis that

> a *Democracie* is the best *Nurse* of *high* Spirits . . . just liberty *feeds* and *nourishes* the thoughts with great *notions*, and *draws* them forward, and encreases their *emulations* and the *strong* desires they have to obtain the *priority* of honour, and that by the rewards propos'd to them in such *Republicks* . . . 'tis impossible for a *servile man* to be a true *Oratour*, for presently his *Liberty* and his *boldnesse decayes* and *consumes*, and being as it were by custome used to *buffeting* we dare never speake *out* but onely *mutter*. (pp. 78–9)[131]

Longinus does not directly endorse this view, but he has earlier declared that '*Wealth, Honour, Repute, Empire*, and all those other things that to the *outward* appearance seem most *majestick*' are inimical to the sublime (p. 11, ch. 7). Hall translated the work in an explicitly republican spirit. The 'corruption of time', he wrote, 'hath diseas'd most Governments into *Monarchies*', eloquence being confined to 'the hearing of one voice' (sigs. A8r–v). Like Milton, Hall recognized that eloquence could never revive the conditions of a

---

131 Patterson, *Reading Between the Lines*, pp. 258ff, discusses political aspects of Hall's translation.

classical republic where 'the same men acted both parts' [i.e. speaker and audience] (sig. A7v); but the implication of his translation was that eloquence could revive under modern forms of liberty if the narrowness of courts could be transcended. The cult of sublimity could also link with a distaste for religious ritual and set forms: the sublime was 'somewhat *Ethereall*, somewhat above man' (sig. B4r). In Waller's career, Milton had seen the different identities of poet, rhetorician, and Protestant breaking apart under political pressure; Milton had fused them until they became one. He had set a lead which others were to follow.

4

Uncivil peace: politics and literary culture, 1645–1649

Wither and the democratic sublime

Areopagitica, for all its openness to religious radicalism, retained an aristocratic caution. It was George Wither who democratized the sublime. In the 1640s his was in many ways a more important public voice than Milton's; his poetry reached the artisanal and military audience which Milton spoke for rather than to.[1] One of the few major critics to have taken him seriously, Samuel Taylor Coleridge, praised an address to Parliament from the sequel to *Campo-Musae, Vox Pacifica*, which appeared in 1645:

> But, let them know, [when they were elected] 'twas for another thing,
> Which they but *represent*; and, which, ere long,
> Them, to a strict account, will, doubtlesse, bring,
> If any way, they do it wilfull wrong:
>   For that, indeed, is, really, the *Face*,
> Whereof, they are the *shadow*, in the glasse . . .[2]

Wither, wrote Coleridge, had caught one of those rare moments in national history when the voice of the people was the voice of God. His 'writings, with all their barren flats and dribbling commonplace, contain nobler principles, profounder truths, and more that is properly and peculiarly *poetic*' than the works of Pope. It is significant, however, that in order to make Wither noble and profound, Coleridge has had to rephrase him. Where Wither writes that Parliament's majesty merely represented 'another thing' – the people – Coleridge has it representing 'a deeper life'.[3] Coleridge is working with a model of the sublime, the unrepresentable, that opposes the authentic inner life to the inauthentic public world, the world of civic representation. That

---

1 For parallels see Christopher Hill, 'George Wither (1588–1667) and John Milton (1608–74)', *WR*, pp. 133–56.

2 George Wither, *Vox Pacifica* (1645; E1242; *WMW*, II), p. 199.

3 Samuel Taylor Coleridge, *On the Constitution of the Church and State*, in *The Collected Works of Samuel Taylor Coleridge*, vol. 10, ed. John Colmer (London and Princeton, 1976), p. 101.

opposition was becoming much sharper in Coleridge's time, and can be traced down to postmodern theorists for whom representation, whether in politics or in art, is reductive and simplifying. But Wither is writing at a historical moment where a democratic concept of representation is excitingly new, offering the properties of imaginative exploration which for later generations it has been felt to lack. The difficulties faced by conventional political and linguistic forms in representing the turbulence of the revolution were not a mere lapse into Babel but promised better and juster forms of representation in the future.

In political terms, Wither pushes that desire for fuller representation further than Milton. Milton had celebrated the classical *polis* as a realm where modern divisions between public and private, between individual and state, were overcome (for the free male, at least) in the forum. Beyond declaring an enthusiasm for ongoing political progress, however, he does not specify the constitutional mechanisms for overcoming that split. Isolated individual readers may be able to create a collective identity, but they will remain outside the Houses of Parliament, trying to persuade these bodies to act as they wish. Milton never formulated a clear concept of political representation. Wither, by contrast, was in the vanguard of an important shift in political vocabulary in the mid-1640s, when the modern concept of Parliamentary representation was first formulated. (He uses the word 'represent' far more than any contemporary poet.[4])

Earlier constitutionalist writers might have claimed in general terms that sovereignty lay in the people, but the idea of counting voters in elections was considered rather demeaning. Elections normally amounted to discreet soundings amongst the nation's 'natural rulers', with varying degrees of participation from those lower down the social hierarchy. The voice of the people was a kind of collective voice; allowing it to fragment into individual voices conjured up traditional fears of the many-headed monster. During the crisis of the 1620s, however, rival candidates in fiercely contested elections might each consider it worth appealing to a broader section of voters. It has been estimated that by 1640 from 27 per cent to 40 per cent of adult males were eligible to vote.[5] That is an average: in London and some other urban constituencies, where radical

---

4 According to the Chadwyck-Healey *English Poetry Full-Text Database*, 'represent' occurs 39 times in Wither's authenticated works, more than four times as often as in any other poet in the period 1600–1660 (though admittedly he was one of the period's most verbose poets in general).

5 Derek Hirst, *The Representative of the People? Voters and Voting in England Under the Early Stuarts* (Cambridge, 1975), p. 105; see also Richard Cust, 'Politics and the Electorate in the 1620s', in Richard Cust and Ann Hughes (eds.), *Conflict in Early Stuart England: Studies in Religion and Politics 1603–1642* (London and New York, 1989), pp. 134–67.

movements flourished, the suffrage could be still broader. This historical experience of democratic participation meant that by the 1640s it was possible to present a very wide suffrage of male householders not as a radical innovation but as part of the Englishman's birthright, a restoration.

The war greatly strengthened this demand for participation. The Parliamentary leaders of the struggle against Charles I were no democrats. They were anxious to secure their rights and privileges against assault from above, but did not desire to yield them to pressure from below. As royalists were quick to argue, this placed them in an inconsistent position. Their propaganda presented them as defenders and representers of the people's liberties against assault from absolutist courtiers and clerics, but their concept of representation remained vague. Power had been transferred from the people to Parliament in the distant past, but Parliament had no obligation to be a transparent mirror of the present popular will. When May used the figure of the mirror in 1642, it was to describe Parliament as a glass for the king's face, not the people's (above, p. 82). Both royalists, motivated by tactical mischief, and some radicals began to press on the concept of representation, arguing that Parliament was unrepresentative in terms that implied a criterion of full legal accountability, with representation 'deriving not from an original act of submission, but from recent elections'.[6] Parliament's more zealous soldiers saw themselves as a citizen army fighting for liberty rather than as neutral instruments of the state. If they had risked their lives for their liberties, they were the readier to insist on the right to civil representation; and as Parliament's victory became more and more likely, their fear was that the leaders might simply throw away what they had fought for by restoring the king without proper safeguards. The growing public sphere at once facilitated and helped to cause the pressure towards representation, as citizens who were becoming accustomed to wide public debate found that they were still treated as subjects by Parliamentary oligarchs.

Religious radicalism could reinforce and interact with the pressure for new constitutional forms. Many Parliamentarian soldiers had thought of themselves as above all resisting the encroachments of the papal Antichrist with whom Charles had formed an unholy alliance. This general Puritan crusade united English and Scots, Presbyterians and Independents; but it was only in England that it received a particular constitutional colouring. The breakdown of the old church had permitted the rapid growth of congregations which came together on a voluntary basis and insisted on their right to elect their church officers. There was no necessary link between elective forms in church and state, and tensions between religious and secular priorities were

6 David Wootton, *Divine Right and Democracy: An Anthology of Political Writing in Stuart England* (Harmondsworth, 1986), p. 47.

to bedevil what became known as the 'Good Old Cause' throughout its history. The separated congregations were a self-proclaimed elite who denied participation for backsliders: this was a model appropriate to a radical vanguard but not for a settled democracy. However, the Puritan emphasis on spiritual experiment, on pushing beyond traditional forms, was a powerful reinforcement for political change. To be represented politically was analogous to the exhilarating process of spiritual self-discovery once the external forms of the old religion had dropped away.[7] The voice of the people, not yet quantified and fragmented by opinion polls, assumed the elusive power of God's hidden voice.

Wither's writings of the mid-1640s were popular with soldiers and reformers because they dramatized that process in all its turbulence and contradiction. The four cantos of *Vox Pacifica* draw attention to their experimental nature. Written in successive bursts of inspiration, they dramatize the fortunes of Parliament's cause from the dark days of military uncertainty in the winter of 1644 through to the aftermath of the great victory of the New Model Army at Naseby in June 1645. At one stage Wither planned a further two cantos: as a prophet his role was to offer himself to the cross-currents of the historical process and follow his inspiration. He describes his inspiration as an inward voice, which emerges from the sublime inner depth of his heart:

> (*looking inwardly*) I saw distensions
> So boundlesse, in their *Width*, their *Depth*, and *Height*,

that they reminded him of the depths glimpsed from the top of a mountain or cliff. It was

> a *Place* (if *Place* we call it may)
> Within the Concave of whose wondrous *Orb*,
> The Eye of *Contemplation* may survay
> Sights, which no *Bounds*, or *Shaddowes*, do disturb. (p. 13)

Although this inner world exhilaratingly escapes the bounds of representation, it also animates a demand for representation in the public world. The inner voice is a call to peace, and Wither at first excitedly seizes on the possibilities of the peace negotiations in progress at Oxford. He comes to realize, however, that the peace there promised was premature, offering superficial concord and harmony before the nation has undergone the deeper moral and spiritual changes that are essential for the foundation of a more stable order. In the title-page quotation (Hebrews IV.7), Paul had warned that God had hardened the Hebrews' hearts before they could reach their place of rest. The poem tries to melt English hearts so that the journey can resume. The 'voice of peace' in the sense of rumour and public opinion must be held at

7 A. S. P. Woodhouse, 'Introduction', *Puritanism and Liberty* (1938).

bay while Wither seeks that inner voice, and yet to listen then entails campaigning for further public action.

Wither charts in the course of his poem a progression from the broad con-
sensual Puritanism of his earlier writings. In the earlier parts of the poem he is
still fairly sympathetic to the Presbyterians and even to episcopacy: a compromise can be found that will allow a stable settlement and keep anarchy at bay.
Wither seems to echo the language of Waller's defences of the established
church when he warns against allowing

> every man, at pleasure, to deface
> Those *Out-works*, which (though faultie) were a stay
> Not uselesse, till some better came in place.
> For, he that would prevent an inundation
> (By false-built *Sea-banks*) lets not every one
> Teare down the Piles, and breake the old *Foundation*[.] (p. 72)

Here, however, the defence-works are tactically rather than strategically necessary, and will eventually be taken down. Though he cautions against the
extremes of the sects, later in the poem he also urges toleration of diversity,
and he does so in language close to Milton's reworking of Waller's imagery in
Areopagitica:

> as within a pallace,
> There may be more conveniency, more state,
> More beautie, and more pleasure for the solace
> Of him that builds it, when there are, in that,
> Some equall *Structures*; higher some, some lower,
> Some pyramids, some flats, some rounds, some squares,
> With here a single, there a double tower,
> And such like, as in Princely *Piles* appears;
>   So, in the Church, true *comlinesse*, may be,
>   And *Vnion*, without uniformitie.
> Nay *discords*, do not generally marre
> Essentiall *unity*[.] (p. 131)

Wither certainly had in mind the architecture praised in Waller's Paul's poem,
for he warned Charles that his soul could not be saved

> at the cost
> Of trimming up the Western end of PAVLS,
> By Fines, extracted from afflicted Soules. (p. 186)

And he attacked the

> artificiall-heav'n,
> Which flatring *Poets*, and his *Painters* made[.] (p. 189)

He thus contrasts the open, experimental architecture of his own poem with
Caroline monumentalism.

That openness cuts across conventional boundaries between poetry and prose even more radically than *Areopagitica*. The royalist John Taylor parodied Wither's distinctive manner:

> In the mean space, thou Pigmey Impe of Warr,
> Rodomontado, champion for *Par-*
> *Lament*.[8]

The enjambement that violently breaks the heroic couplet's bounds is linked here with Wither's support for Parliament – and enables Taylor punningly to prophesy doom for its supporters. Taylor seizes on the way in which Wither is pushing at older boundaries of poetic and of political representation. *Vox Pacifica* is certainly the first English poem to have served as an election manifesto and a treatise on political representation. In fact Wither refers the reader to one of his prose works on the subject which had attracted a lot of attention (p. 135). Since the summer of 1644, while Wither's inner voice was prompting further self-examination, he had been energetically involved in public campaigning. In July 1644 he published a reforming speech which he claimed to have delivered at a mass meeting outside Parliament.[9] Wither hinted at the need to purge Parliament to make it more accountable to the popular voice (pp. 6, 14). His tone was harsh and uncompromising towards the royalists, whom it was a holy duty to hate (p. 14), and especially to the 'barbarous Irish' (p. 7). He also struck a note of social radicalism. Delinquents should be stripped of their lands and titles: 'What unreasonablenesse can there be in making them Peasants (a degree, to which honest men are borne, and too good for these) some of them being made Lords and Knights for attempting to enslave Free-men?' (p. 5). The new landed elite would hold their land from conquests in a righteous cause, not foreign adventures motivated by covetousness (pp. 4–5): civil war here becomes a greater cause than foreign war. Wither emphasized that 'our greatest deliverances have bin by the meanest persons and places' (p. 13). He called for soldiers to be given medallions which would bind them to the public cause as had been done in the early days of Rome (p. 6).

Like Milton in *Areopagitica*, Wither presented himself as a citizen with a right to address Parliament. He adopted a fairly respectful tone towards that body. But by entitling his pamphlet *The Speech Without Doore*, emphasizing the large crowds who attended, and pointing out that the speech was in fact delivered 'in the absence of the SPEAKER', to whom it was addressed, he was

---

8 John Taylor, *Aqua-Musae* (1645; E269.22), p. 12.
9 [George Wither], *The Speech Without Doore* (1644; E4.30). John Gurney, 'George Wither and Surrey Politics 1642–1649', *Southern History* 19 (1997), 74–98, demonstrates the link of Wither's wider national campaign in print with campaigns by radicals in Surrey.

highlighting the growing gap between the closed world of an unrepresentative Parliament and the widening public sphere in which Wither exercised considerable influence. By November (the month of *Areopagitica*) his
tone had become much sharper. In *Letters of Advice: Touching the Choice of
Knights and Burgesses* he attacked Parliamentarians who put 'such an
immeasurable distance, betwixt themselves and others, of that Body whom
they represent, and out of which they were chosen, as if they had forgotten
what they were'.[10] At a time when radicals were deeply impatient at what they
considered the lukewarm leadership of aristocratic commanders like Essex,
there was a marked anti-aristocratic emphasis in Wither's list of those who
should not be chosen in the coming 'recruiter' elections. The 'conspiracies
and apostacies of *Waller*' – who had just bought his pardon when the pamphlet was written – were roundly condemned (p. 14).[11] No countenance
should be given to men addicted to hunting and hawking and any dependents
of peers: 'though some *Lords* have honourably persisted faithfull to the Republike, both now and in all times of Triall; yet, the greatest part prefer their
will and *pleasure* before the just liberties and priviledges of the Commons' (p.
5). 'Re-publike' here presumably has the general sense of the public good or
the state; but the more emphasis was placed on representation, the harder it
was to justify particular interests, whether peers or monarchs, who had no
claim to representativeness. As the radical journalist John Harris complained
a few years later,

> the Commons, representing all *England*, at a Conference with the Lords, who
> represent only their simple selves and their dogs, must stand with their hats in
> their hands, whilest they sit with their hats on like Demi-Gods.[12]

In his desire to broaden public participation, Wither called on those who
bought his pamphlet to read it aloud to 'those illiterate persons, whose Voices
are, usually, given by an implicit Faith': the public voice must become an
informed public opinion (p. 2). His proposals went beyond by-elections: he
called for the principle of election to be extended throughout society to
public offices and to the universities, which badly needed purging (p. 10).

This pamphlet was very much in the vanguard: it was the first response in
print to the discussions in Parliament of 'recruiter' elections to fill the places
left by defectors to the Parliament in Oxford. This was a momentous step

10 George Wither, *Letters of Advice: Touching the Choice of Knights and Burgesses* (1644;
   E15.9; *WMW*, I), p. 4.
11 Waller's seat at St Ives went to John Fielder, an associate of Denham's whom Wither later
   accused of defrauding him: Hubert Berry, 'Sir John Denham at Law', *Modern Philology*
   71 (1973–4), 266–76 (273).
12 *Mercurius Militaris* no. 5, 14–21 November, 1648; E473.8, p. 35.

since it put an end to the hopes of mediating figures like Waller for a reunion of the opposing sides. It was a further step towards claiming Parliamentary sovereignty. The step was taken with extreme caution, and writs were not issued until the following August. Wither was a candidate in Guildford, challenging a political ally of a leading conservative grandee, and issued a second edition of the *Letters*. His campaign was part of a long-term programme to give 'men of *midling-Fortunes*' more influence against the traditional county elite.[13] His own election, however, was an ignominious fiasco: he was forced to write an embarrassing letter of apology for attacks he had made on his rival, and he withdrew from the poll.[14] His experience was a common one for radicals. Though Henry Marten returned to Parliament with the reinforcement of a few allies, a war-weary electorate generally repudiated inflammatory rhetoric.

Wither's claim to be the people's voice might have been compromised, but his voice did inspire other radicals. The writings of 'honest Major *George Withers*'[15] were important to the reform movement that became known as the Levellers. The lines on representation that so struck Coleridge were quoted at the end of *Englands Miserie and Remedie*, a pamphlet of September 1645 which has been singled out as the first text overtly to assert the total accountability of Parliament to the people as a whole.[16] The author may have been Edward Sexby, to be encountered later in the vanguard of republican opposition to Cromwell. He made a sharp distinction between the 'two Bodies of the people, the representative and the represented', the shadow and the substance, which 'together make up the body of the Common-wealth' (p. 1). Members of Parliament were merely agents and servants of those who had sent them there. This pamphlet is particularly interesting because it links the new language of representation with republican language. As has been seen, these were not exactly the same thing. One could advocate an end to monarchy without advocating wider political representation – hence the split that was to open between regicides and Levellers in 1649; and in principle a king could be regarded as a legitimate representative of the people. What the new concept of representation did accomplish was to undermine mystical conceptions of monarchy. Briskly dismissing the sacramental language of the body

---

13 Wither, *Justitiarius Justificatus* ([1646]; E506.30; *WMW*, III), p. 7.
14 Anon., *A Letter Sent to George Wither, Poetica Licentia* (1646; E365.24), p. 7; letter from Wither to the Mayor and Burgesses of Guildford, 28 November 1645, Guildford Muniment Room BR/OC/5, no. 21.
15 *Perfect Passages of Each Dayes Proceedings in Parliament* no. 49, 24 September–1 October 1645, E303.28, p. 391.
16 *England's Miserie and Remedie* (1645; E302.5), p. 8. The tract has variously been attributed to Lilburne, Overton, and Wildman; Wootton, *Divine Right and Democracy*, pp. 52–3, 273, makes a case for Sexby.

politic, Wither had written that if the head, the king, failed in his duty, the people had the right 'To take one off, and set another on'. Though he had expressed the hope that Charles might be brought to repentance, he left no doubt that Parliament had every right to depose him and '*advance an other in his place*'.[17] The author of *Englands Miserie and Remedie* goes further than Wither in invoking the Roman republic. He repeatedly quotes from Livy, and praises the office of tribune: 'the Common-wealth of *Rome* (which remaineth a patterne and example to all ages both for civill and Military government) ... did allow of this last refuge or appeale to the People' at the time of its 'best perfection' (that is, the earlier republic) (p. 4). The logic of his case for representation is linked with his case against absolutism: if it is blasphemous for mere mortals to be 'immitators of the power of God' (p. 3), then Parliament should not claim a comparable superiority, or it will risk the fate of the fallen angels. As in Culpeper's letters, democracy is on the side of the angels.

Englands Miserie and Remedie was a defence of John Lilburne, the most charismatic Leveller, who himself praised Wither in his own manifesto, *Englands Birth-Right Justified* (October 1645). Amidst general proposals for political and economic reforms he included a call for annual elections and urged his readers to consult 'that Gallant man, Major *George Withers* advice ... in his late Book'. He used the same kind of visual language as Wither: 'who wonders then to see a crooked representation of a crooked Commonwealth it is no true glasse that casts not a shadow as crooked and deformed as the substance'.[18] He also cited the warning against electing too many lawyers in *Vox Pacifica*. The reforming lawyer John Cook, who was to be charged with the prosecution of Charles I, saluted 'ingenious Mr. *Withers*'; another of his friends was John Bradshaw, who was to preside over the trial, and acted for Lilburne.[19] Wither came to be regarded as Lilburne's poet.[20] When in 1646 the Presbyterians grew in influence in Parliament, Wither suffered imprisonment at the same time as Lilburne and Overton. He was penalized for radicalizing the public sphere, for publishing a pamphlet which impugned the more cautious Parliamentarians of Surrey on behalf of campaigners for radical measures. The debate on his case in Parliament divided along partisan lines, with the leading Independents Haselrig and Cromwell supporting him.[21]

---

17 Wither, *Vox Pacifica*, pp. 138, 149.
18 [John Lilburne], *Englands Birth-right Justified* (1645; E304.17); in William Haller (ed.), *Tracts on Liberty in the Puritan Revolution 1638–1647*, 3 vols. (New York, 1933), III, 291–2, quoting from Wither, *Letters of Advice*, p. 20, and *Vox Pacifica* (p. 183).
19 John Cook, *The Vindication of the Professors and Profession of the Law* (1646; E320.17), p. 77.
20 [Samuel Sheppard], *Animadversions upon Iohn Lilburnes Two Last Books* (1646; E362.24), p. 7; Anon., *The Reformados Righted* (1647; E406.13), p. 3.
21 Wither, *Justitiarius Justificatus*; Gurney, 'George Wither and Surrey Politics 1642–1649', 187.

We can perhaps see Wither's influence also in the language used by another Leveller, Richard Overton: the representers of free men

> must be substantial and reall *Actors* for *freedome* and *liberty*, for such as is the represented, such and no other must the figure or representation be, such as is the proportion, countenance and favour of the man, such and so must be the picture of the man, or else it cannot be the picture of that man, but of some other, or of something else, as the picture of a grim, meager, frowning face is, not the picture of an amiable, friendly smiling countenance; so tyranny neither is nor can possibly be the Representor of Freedome[.][22]

Wither's attempt to stand for Parliament disrupted his activities as a prophetic poet. In two versified pamphlets issued in 1646 he set out to explain why he had not produced the promised continuation of *Vox Pacifica*. In *What Peace to the Wicked?* he argues that even if the king were brought back to London, there would be no prospects for lasting peace unless he had explicitly sung a '*Palinode*'.[23] In the promised continuation, *Opobalsamum Anglicanum*, Wither maintained this aggressive tone. *Vox Pacifica* had been interrupted because Fairfax's triumphs in battle had not been followed up (as Milton was to say to Cromwell, peace had her victories as well as war). The pamphlet takes the form of imaginary speeches by the 'Well-affected' at the '*Senate-doore*'. As in *The Speech Without Doore*, Wither pushes at the margins of political discourse: though his crowd declare their respect for Parliament, they nevertheless firmly assert their right to pass judgement on the MPs.[24] He calls for a 'purge' (pp. 1, 15). He returns to the attack on Waller, alleging that he got off so lightly for his treason only because of secret allies who were still sitting in the House (p. 7). Appealing to Machiavelli and to natural law, he insists on the need to return the nation's liberties to 'the first *Foundation*', removing

> *Superstructures*, which pervert
> The works of *Nature*, by the Quirks of *Art*.

The Commons declare their resolution

> To keep unchanged, GOD'S and *Natures* Lawes,
> And, change all other things, as there is cause. (p. 3)

Those 'other things' could clearly include the monarchy. Wither's 'well-affected' speakers imply that it would be quite legal, though at present inexpedient, to change the form of government (p. 16) and raise the possibility that Charles has angered God until He

22 Richard Overton, *An Appeale from the Degenerate Representative Body* (1647; E398.28); in Don M. Wolfe (ed.), *Leveller Manifestoes of the Puritan Revolution* (1944; rptd New York, 1967), p. 169.
23 George Wither, *What Peace to the Wicked?* (1646; E510.11; *WMW*, I), p. 1.
24 George Wither, *Opobalsamum Anglicanum* (1646; E513.6; *WMW*, V), p. 10.

peradventure, hath decreed,
To cast both him and His, down from the *Throne* (p. 17).

Wither extended this hint in *Amygdala Britannica* (May 1647), where he
denounced abuses in a riddling manner, and declared that the realm could be
made stronger

if you could add
To strengthen and adorn the same,
Some parts of the *Venetian Frame*.[25]

The way to peace was not an immediate deal with the king but permanent
constitutional change that would bring the realm closer to the Venetian
republic. Wither does not explicitly call for a republic; but the implication of
his writings is that the king's powers would not be much greater than those of
the Venetian Doge.[26]

In the mid-1640s it was still dangerous for Parliament's supporters to
express even limited admiration for republics. In early 1646 Nedham's
editorials in *Mercurius Britanicus* became increasingly hostile to Charles,
appealing to Buchanan to demonstrate the perfidy of monarchs to the extent
of undermining any distinction between tyranny and monarchy. The newsbook was suppressed.[27] Once Charles had been defeated and taken refuge
with the Scots in May 1646, a powerful bloc in Parliament, with strong
support in the City, began pressing for his return in a settlement that would
call a halt to further political and religious change. The radical Independents
who had gained control of the City had been displaced by a predominantly
Presbyterian grouping which saw the king as by now the lesser of two evils.[28]
The Presbyterians used their dominance to imprison Lilburne, Wither and
other critics, though 1646–47 nonetheless saw a growing campaign against
the king by Marten, Nedham and others whose republicanism was very thinly
veiled. One tract, *Vox Plebis*, made censorship an issue on its title-page:
'printed 1646, in the sitting of Parliament; during which time the Presse

25 George Wither, *Amygdala Britannica* (1647; E516.2; *WMW*, I), p. 9.

26 For appeals to Venice at this time see Zera S. Fink, *The Classical Republicans: An Essay in
the Recovery of a Pattern of Thought in Seventeenth Century England* (Evanston, 1945),
pp. 46ff.

27 *Mercurius Britanicus* no. 130, 11–18 May 1646, E337.24, p. 1111; Blair Worden, '"Wit in a
Roundhead": the Dilemma of Marchamont Nedham', in Susan D. Amussen and Mark
Kishlansky (eds.), *Political Culture and Cultural Politics in Early Modern England*
(Manchester and New York, 1995), pp. 301–337 (315–6).

28 'Presbyterian' and 'Independent', as historians have reminded us, are problematic
terms, and the use of a capital letter should not imply the existence of clearly defined
entities. In contemporary polemic the terms referred both to positions on church order
and to relative degrees of hostility to the king, and to various compounds of religious
and political positions. It is hoped that the context will make it clear which sense is predominant in a particular case (as, here, the political sense).

ought to be free and open, as the Parliament declared to the Bishops at the beginning thereof'. Parliament was urged to 'lay the foundation of a new State, or Soveraignty', with its role directly comparable to that of the tribunes under the Roman republic. Livy and Machiavelli were invoked, and the pamphlet ended with a ringing call for God to 'raise up some noble English Romane Spirit' like Caius Flaminius, who despite his noble birth fully aligned himself with the people and acknowledged power to reside in them.[29] More explicitly than Wither, this pamphlet makes the people's voice militantly anti-aristocratic: Caius Flaminius was hated by the aristocracy for challenging their privileges (Livy, *History*, 21.63). The pamphlet lends support to the hypothesis that some Levellers were modelling their own political behaviour in part on reading histories of the Roman plebeians.[30] In *Vox Plebis* the Leveller call for Parliament to become more representative is fused with an appeal to a Roman return to first principles, an exemplary self-sacrifice on the part of the rulers. If there is no explicit call for a republic here, the implications are clear.

While republicans and other radicals felt their position to be precarious, the Presbyterian grip on power was insecure. The army remained resistant to Parliamentary control. Many of the rank and file considered that their long fight for liberty obliged them to maintain a political role. In May troops seized the king, fearing that he was to be exploited in a renewed Scots invasion. After a tense series of stand-offs, the army marched into London in August 1647 and lent its protection to a purge of the Presbyterian leaders – a purge of the kind Wither had long called for, and an anticipation of Pride's Purge the following year. Wither welcomed this move. In *Carmen Expostulatorium*, published immediately after the army's arrival, Wither addressed the approaching army, declaring that thousands of them were his friends. They were justified, he said, in having exceeded normal constitutional channels, for necessity made the law.[31] At the climax of the poem Wither broke off dramatically:

> whil'st this *line* is writing, I am told,
> Our *Line* is enter'd, and our *Southerne-Hold*.
> And, therefore, here I pawse —————
>   These words are vain; and, all that we can do,
> Except, GOD adds his blessing thereunto. (sig. c4v)

29 Anon., *Vox Plebis* (1646; E362.20), pp. 60, 62, 68. Worden, 'Wit in a Roundhead', pp. 320–1, attributes this pamphlet's republican sections to Nedham (though they lack Nedham's characteristic wit), and suggests that Nedham's later links with the Marten circle go back to this period.

30 Samuel Dennis Glover, 'The Classical Plebeians: Radical Republicanism and the Origins of Leveller Thought', unpublished Ph.D. thesis, University of Cambridge, 1994, opens up this area.

31 George Wither, *Carmen Expostulatorium* (1647; E401.10; *WMW*, I), sig. c3v; on *salus populi* as 'the summe of all the Charters in the world', cf. *Letters of Advice*, p. 13.

By the break in his syntax the poet equates his lines with the lines of London's defences, constructing the illusion that the New Model Army has decisively and irreversibly entered not only London but also his text. Wither was opening the way for the sublimity of revolution.

The balance of power had changed: Wither, Overton and Lilburne were able before long to go free. The press was now controlled by the army, which made publication harder for Presbyterians but enabled Wither at length to bring out *Prosopopoeia Britannica*, the long-promised continuation of *Vox Pacifica*. He had begun this poem before the army's intervention, but, as he retorted to an imagined critic,

> *Truth* gets *License* hardly; and, the *Presse*
> Was, then, at your disposure, not at his.[32]

The work finally appeared the following May. Wither's tone has now hardened, whether because his views have changed or because the change in censorship control allows him to speak more openly. He still calls for national unity, and he falls short of Leveller demands for Parliament to dissolve and a completely new 'Representative' to be created. But he shows little confidence in either king or Parliament. Parliament, which should speak for the nation, has become inured to calls for justice, 'dreaming on/In *private projects*' at the expense of '*Publike-Safety*' (p. 59). It can be forgiven only insofar as such corruption is the product not just of individuals but of institutions:

> The *Fathers* of your *being*, in this *Nation*,
> Were an unsound, corrupted *Generation*;
> And, did begin a *Representative*,
> As like themselves, as ever, man alive
> Begot a child: with *members*, crooked, lame,
> Blind, deaf, and dumb, into the world you came[.] (p. 66)

Elections have been corrupted by nepotism: seats in Parliament should not be treated as hereditary possessions, and electoral reform is essential (p. 61). National renewal will be possible only

> When you have purg'd your *House* (until which day
> All will be spoke in vain, that I shall say)[.] (p. 45)

If representation is corrupt, this reflects a more general corruption of language and communication. Though Wither belongs to the godly party, he is aware that godly rhetoric can be abused. '*Holy Flatt'rers*' are glorifying their patrons in Parliament, while the apocalyptic rhetoric becoming increasingly frenzied in the army is equally suspect:

> others, make the *Army*, at the least,
> S. *Michael*, and his *Angells*[.] (p. 71)

---

32 George Wither, *Prosopopoeia Britannica* (1648; E1149.2; *WMW*, IV), sig. A2v.

The Putney Debates in the autumn of 1647, at which army radicals put their case to the grandees, were almost as preoccupied with the apocalypse as with political representation, and the implications were ominous to Charles. Wither had used apocalyptic language in the Foxean tradition to vindicate Charles against his evil counsellors, but the king was starting to be identified with one of the ten horns of the Satanic beast of the Book of Revelation, whose destruction would pave the way for the return of Christ to reign on earth.[33] Wither worried about the political presumption of such easy biblical identifications, which were indeed to lead the army to become a law unto itself. Nor did he have much faith in the sottish '*Common rabble*' (p. 48). Like May, he is concerned about the people's forgetfulness: their concern with short-term issues makes them forget long-term injustices, undermining their loyalty to Parliament and leaving them vulnerable to a sentimental cult of pity for the king (pp. 15, 74ff). They

> fear to practise, what agrees with reason,
> Because it hath been falsly called *Treason*,
> By *Parasites*, and *Priests*; who, that a *King*
> Might make them *something*, made him *any thing*,
> Which he desir'd to be[.]

The people gain an illusion of importance by identifying themselves with the king: rather than a realm in which their interests are properly represented, they thus gain a stage-play realm which trades substance for shadows, for '*Court-Idolatries*' (p. 48). The result has been that

> men first grew afraid
> To think (untill of late) what may be said,
> And must be resolutely done, before
> GOD, will, these *Isles*, to their lost *Peace* restore.

Timidity of action leads to narrowness of speech which causes boldness of thought itself to dwindle. In fearing to call the king to account, the people are like children fearing scarecrows they set up themselves (p. 48).

If the people and Parliament are found wanting, it is for the king that Wither reserves his bitterest attacks. The poem opens by calling on him to repent and warning him against flatterers who tempt him Narcissus-like with '*pictures of himselfe*' (p. 10). Wither is afraid that Charles may be so bewitched by these flatterers that he will be unable to show penitence. The tone of royalist literature was indeed becoming more and more high-flying, moving towards that very self-conscious piece of image-making, *Eikon Basilike*, the king's personal testament. Wither is concerned that the people will be

---

33 Noel Henning Mayfield, *Puritans and Regicide: Presbyterian-Independent Differences over the Trial and Execution of Charles (I) Stuart* (Lanham, MD and London, 1988).

betrayed into forgetting their past wrongs in the immediate bewitchment of royal authority, allowing kingly beauty to overlay the sublime possibilities of further reformation. To counter that response, he offers a long catalogue of the king's crimes, going back to the early years of his reign (pp. 28–31).

This fear is in strong tension with his desire for a moderate political compromise, which would depend on maintaining some faith that the king, and the institution of monarchy, are capable of regeneration. Wither tries to defend that faith against the republicans, who, he claims, are mad enough to hope that Charles will not reform so that there is sanction for abolishing the monarchy. It would be absurd, he claims, to knock out one's brains to cure a headache (p. 52). And yet he has himself constantly drawn attention to Charles's obstinate refusal to listen to the voice of Parliamentary reason. He cites an old prophecy:

> *A Man, a Child, a Furious-One;*
> *A Maid, a Fox, a Lion, None.* (p. 25)

This seems to have come to fruition, for in a sense Charles has already left the throne:

> now there's *none,*
> Who either weares the *Crowne,* or fills the *Throne*[.] (p. 25)

Wither also turns to biblical prophecies of the fates of tyrants: if Charles does not repent, he will undergo Belshazzar's fate. Wither recalls God's warning against kingship in I Samuel VIII (p. 34). He states quite clearly that if a king pursues his private interests he may be deposed (p. 46) and the most he can offer Charles is

> that *Kingly-Liberty,* which will
> Confine him, from all power of *doing ill*[.] (p. 51)

It is not the king but the '*Body Representative*' that is 'the *soule* of *Government*' (p. 78). It is then not surprising that Wither feels it necessary to call on his readers to

> Excuse me, if ('twixt what concernes the *King,*
> And these *Republikes*) with some staggering,
> I seem to Counsell you . . . (pp. 52–3)

By now, the word 'Republike' for 'republican' was clearly current in a sense that was specifically antithetical to monarchy. In a rather evasive strategy, Wither goes on to compare himself to King David who wept over the rebellious Absalom: if the king were put to death, Wither would grieve in the same way (p. 53). This analogy allows Wither to indulge in some of the sentimental pathos of monarchism he has condemned in the masses, but only by himself stepping into the kingly role, and in a kind of anticipatorily posthumous mode that is combined with acknowledging the possible need for revolutionary judgement:

> But, if he still persist, as he begun,
> Then, do, as GOD shall move you; I, *have done.* (p. 53)

Exactly what should be done remains obscure, however. At the end of the poem he offers a cloudy prophecy that was to become celebrated and frequently reprinted.[34] Society will break down into anarchy, which will bring forth '*A* Creature, *which you have no* name *for, yet*'; this will beget first an aristocracy and then a democracy. The crisis will be resolved only when the different constituents '*into [t]heir first* elements *returne*' until a '*true* Supreme, *acknowledged by all*' emerges (p. 99). The language is that of a Machiavellian reduction to first principles, in which each part of society abandons the quest for private interests that have obscured common communication:

> A King, *shall willingly himself unking;*
> And, *thereby grow far greater then before.*
> . . . A Parliament, *it selfe shall overthrow;*
> And thereby, *shall a better being gaine;*
> The Peers, *by setting of themselves below,*
> A more innobling honour shall obtaine:
> The people *for a time shall be inslav'd;*
> And, *that shall make them for the future free.*
> By private *losse, the* publike *shall be sav'd;*
> An Army *shall by yeelding* Victor *bee.*
>   The Cities *wealth her poverty shall cause:*
>   The Lawes corruption, shall reform the *Lawes*[.] (p. 100)

Wither later wrote that the poem's aim had been 'to reduce the late *King*, to make use of that means which would have effected his *restoration*'; restoration and reduction are here identified.[35] Wither's prophetic language is obscure about constitutional specifics, but he seems, like Culpeper, to want the Lords to be 'reduced' into the Commons and the Commons to be thoroughly purged, and to envisage the emergence of a new sovereign authority to replace the traditional status of the monarchy. Throughout the poem he disparages tradition: he is appealing not to 'worme-eaten' Acts of Parliament but to nature and common practice (p. 98), and above all to 'necessity' and 'the *Publike-safety*' (p. 79).

Does this imply the creation of a republic? Just as he has done earlier in the poem, Wither draws back from this conclusion. The king may yet repent of his sins. But if he does not, God will certainly cast him from his throne. Monarchy was after all not the most sublime possible theme in poetry or politics:

---

34 The prophecy was reprinted in 1659 (see below, chapter 9 n. 102), 1688, 1691, and 1714.
35 George Wither, *The Dark Lantern* (1653; E1432.3; *WMW*, III), sigs. A1r–v.

> at this present, upon him depends
> The Fortune of his *House*: And, therewithall
> Shall many other, either stand or fall . . .
> Yea, thereupon, dependeth greater things,
> Then are the *Risings*, and the *Falls* of *Kings*. (p. 8)

The iconoclastic rhyming of 'king' with 'thing' was to become a favourite verbal tic of republicans like Nedham. It equated monarchy with jingling, obvious rhyme as opposed to republican sublimity – though Wither's own tendency to just such rhymes blunted the effect.[36]

Wither wrote the last part of the poem after the Vote of No Addresses of January 1648, when radicals in Parliament broke off further negotiations. Wither is characteristically divided in his response to this measure. He regrets that it makes it impossible for him to bring the king into his poem's dialogue: it represents a final breakdown in the distorted communication that Wither has been trying to repair. Marten had followed through the republican logic of calls for open communication and representation:

> no treaty can indeed be altogether equal betwixt the King, and the peoples Parliament, for he deals but for himself and perhaps for some of his own Family or Posterity; they for two whole Nations.[37]

Wither cannot quite give up on negotiation. The poem's fiction is that its voice is not directly that of Wither but of his persona, Britain's Genius, who as angel or messenger of the nation declares himself able to bring his speech to Charles despite the Vote of No Addresses (p. 103). If Charles can be brought to write down a full confession of the wrongs he has done the realm, the whole nation will be seized by that

> *spirit of Communication,*
> Whereby, most secret actions, are made knowne, (p. 104)

and the nation will rejoice at finding again its long lost king.

Wither thus offers two alternative modes of resolution for his prophetic poem: a more conventional mode in which the king's return is enough to renew the realm, and a more radical solution which re-makes the nation's institutions and constitutes a wholly new, possibly republican, supreme power. Even the first solution is not really conventional, however. Charles's return is predicated on strict limitations of his power. He must become part of a structure of government that is fully representative of the people. And, with what Charles would have regarded as outrageous audacity, Wither presumes to lecture the greatly erring king on his duties, with the confidence of being himself a kind of representative of the people, via his fictitious 'Prosopopoeia'

---

36 See further chapter 10, n. 112.
37 Henry Marten, *The Parliaments Proceedings Justified* (1648; E426.2), p. 10.

of the nation's genius. That representation is presented as being itself accountable to the people, though in a more complex way than the corrupt structures of power and flattery normally allow. The poem's late appearance due to its failure to obtain a licence becomes a mark of its integrity, of its refusal to compromise with unjust authority.

The main part of the poem ends by juxtaposing two voices which offer rival accounts of Wither's role as prophetic poet. A '*feare*' warns him that it is futile to cast his pearls before swine, that many will misunderstand his poem. He has struggled for years to recover his lost fortunes and risks hazarding them by alienating the kind of foe who '*to the* publike *faithfulnesse pretends*' (p. 107). Wither is referring here to his long struggle to gain repayment of a loan on the '*Publick Faith*'.[38] Wither's 'feare' tells him to give up the struggle, to

> *Provide for thine owne safety and thine ease:*
> *As others do, write those things that may please:* (p. 108)

This is, however, the voice of the poet's 'owne corruptions'; another voice reassures him that God will provide for him and his family, and insists that '*thousands favour what thy Muse intends*'. Many inside and outside Parliament will be glad that there was in these times an Englishman who did not fear to speak of what he thought essential for the public safety (p. 109). Let him then not fear to be undone,

> *For, by* undoing, *thou shalt be* new-made;
> *By thy* destruction, *safety shall be had* [.] (p. 110)

Having signed himself as 'Terrae Filius', the name of a licensed fool at academic revels, Wither proceeds to address Parliament in his own name, explaining that he chose anonymity because he feared his views might not otherwise be taken seriously. Wither thus dramatizes his own participation in the process of reduction he is calling for. He has exposed himself to public ridicule by laying aside the conventional beauties of poetry and making himself accessible even to children (p. 98), thus making his poetry a force for wide and unrestricted communication.

Wither does not quite end here: he tags on a final two pages of improvised verse in which he outlines what he would say to the king if the Vote of No Addresses did not prevent him (pp. 112–3). Let the king honestly repent and if he is a friend to himself he will find that Wither too is a good friend, who will show solidarity even in the depths of his adversity. Wither would rather be crucified with a penitent thief than save his life like Barabbas with public acclamation. Like the earlier David–Absalom reference, this analogy is a remarkable combination of humility and presumption. Royalist propagandists were more and more comparing Charles to Christ, whether the

38 George Wither, *Ecchoes from the Sixth Trumpet* (1666; w3155; *WMW*, VI), p. 125.

crucifixion was seen in metaphorical terms as the contention between Presbyterians and Independents for his soul and body, or more literally in fearful anticipation that he would be executed. For Wither it is the prophetic poet who is the Christ figure, his 'reduction' in abandoning conventional literary prestige parallelling Christ's humility. Wither is ready to accept the king as an equal to the poet only if he shows a comparable degree of humility. It is not surprising that his poem provoked outrage from a royalist journalist:

> Proud foole, *dost thinke within thy* coxco[m]bes pate
> T'incircle reason, *lay rules for a* State[.][39]

Wither's answer was yes.

Forward youths: Milton, Marvell, Hall, and the politics of post-war culture

Prosopopoeia Britannica presents a nation in crisis, with a republic as one possible remedy. But the gloomy tone of this prophecy was not the only voice of Parliamentary poetry at this time. Alongside Milton's and Wither's prophetic sublime, there was a revival of semi-courtly beauty. Having crushed the Presbyterian counter-revolution, the army's leaders wanted space for negotiation and rejected radicals' calls for the king to be immediately tried. He was useful as a bargaining counter, and as giving a reassuring air of social stability. Though he was not allowed to return to London, Charles was installed at Hampton Court, seeming, as May put it, 'not at all a restrained man, but a Prince living in the splendor of a Court'.[40] Meanwhile, protracted negotiations went on, with Presbyterians and Independents putting forward different settlements while the king dallied with both. Cromwell and the grandees made some concessions to the Levellers, who were suspicious of any further deals with the king. The Independent constitutional schemes would have been not far from an aristocratic republic – resembling the ideal implied by *Areopagitica* – in which concessions to radical groups would be counterbalanced by the political influence of aristocratic magnates.[41] The king would remain as a symbol of continuity and social order, but the more radical proposals would have reduced his powers so strictly that there would be little to offend republicans. In keeping with the spirit of this period,

---

39 *Mercurius Publicus* no. 3, 22–9 May 1648, E445.19, pp. 23–4.
40 Thomas May, *A Breviary of the History of the Parliament* (1650; E1317.1), p. 168.
41 J. S. A. Adamson, 'The English Nobility and the Projected Settlement of 1647', *Historical Journal* 30 (1987), 567–602.

Northumberland, who had been given custody of the king's son, the duke of York, commissioned from Lely a celebrated portrait of father and son. At the same time as this gesture paid tribute to the king, it revealed the cultural authority of Northumberland himself, who at this time was 'Lord Protector in all but name'.[42] The effect of the Independents' settlement was virtually to transform the king into a work of art, a piece of impressive but impotent furnishing like the Titians and Rubenses that adorned Northumberland's house. A poem by Richard Lovelace on the Lely portrait explored this ambiguous status[43], which was more baldly indicated by Wither's reference to

> those high *Courts,* by whom the *Pow'r-supreme,*
> Is exercised in the *name* of *him*
> Who now is laid aside[.][44]

Charles had no desire to be laid aside, but it was to be some time before the Independents fully understood this.

The cultural life of the period from the summer of 1647 to the king's execution in January 1649 had an eerie quality. There was a muted revival of royalist writing. Poets went to court to pay tribute to the returned king. The scholar-poet Thomas Stanley founded a society whose members wore a black ribbon, apparently to express their grief at the royalists' defeat. Amongst his associates were several celebrated 'cavalier' poets, including Lovelace, Robert Herrick, and James Shirley. They were poised uneasily between hopes of restoration of the old court culture and fears of further disasters. The royalist publisher Humphrey Moseley continued to print a series of volumes of poetry which evoked the world of the 1630s. His edition of the plays of Beaumont and Fletcher, which appeared early in 1647, had been prefaced by a huge collection of poems which amounted to a manifestation of royalist support.

Thomas May's *History of the Parliament*, with its frequent evocations of Lucan, appeared in 1647, and this seems to have been one provocation for his old friend Sir Richard Fanshawe to prepare for publication – by Moseley – a defence of poetic and political Augustanism. Though he reprinted his poem in praise of May's continuation of Lucan, he also printed his Horatian ode of 1630 in praise of the Caroline peace, and added 'Two Odes out of *Horace,* relating unto the Civill Warres of *Rome*'.[45] Horace reappears in the prose work

---

42 J. S. A. Adamson, 'The Baronial Context of the English Civil War', *Transactions of the Royal Historical Society* 5th series 40 (1990), 93–120 (113).

43 James Loxley, *Royalism and Poetry in the English Civil Wars: The Drawn Sword* (London and New York, 1997), pp. 155–68.   44 Wither, *Prosopopoeia Britannica*, p. 43.

45 *The Poems and Translations of Sir Richard Fanshawe*, vol. I, ed. Peter Davidson (Oxford, 1997), 55–9, 131–42. These were the sixteenth epode and the twenty-fourth ode of the third book, both of them fiercely moral pieces in which Horace denounces the people's vices.

that concludes the volume, 'A Summary Discourse of the Civill Warres of *Rome*', which like the volume as a whole was dedicated to Prince Charles. Fanshawe recounts the civil disorders that beset the republic, including the popular tumults caused by the Gracchi and Curio in their calls for agrarian reform – a reference that would have had topical force for those alarmed by Leveller activities. He praises Horace for overcoming the political despair that had led him to think of emigrating, and deciding that in the end it was better to accept monarchical rule as a source of order than to fight any further for his republican principles. Fanshawe ended with a translation from the prophecy of Rome's imperial mission in Book VI of the *Aeneid*.

In this uncertain cultural space, writers with differing allegiances could share common ground. At the very top of the social hierarchy, amongst those who waited on the king at Hampton Court was James Harrington (1611–77), a young wit who had returned from his grand tour with a passion for republican constitutions, his imagination particularly caught by the aristocratic splendour of the Venetian republic. According to Aubrey, they often disputed about government, but Charles 'would not endure to hear of a Co[m]monwealth'.[46] Nothing catches the strange flavour of this period better than the idea of the irrepressible Harrington, appointed by the Parliament as a combination of deferential attendant and spy, trying to instil an unlikely enthusiasm for republican government in this king for whom any communication between king and subjects must be completely unequal. Harrington made his debut as a poet in 1648, providing complimentary verses for Lawes's *Choice Psalmes*, a volume prefaced by a portrait of Charles and a lament for his brother's death 'in the Service and Defence of the King his Master'. Immediately below his verses was a sonnet by Milton (figure 7).[47]

It is striking, but not altogether surprising for this time, to find these two admirers of republics sharing space in a strongly royalist volume. Milton had clearly been giving a lot of thought to the cultural politics that would emerge after the war was over. His poem to Lawes had been written in February 1646, when the royalist cause was collapsing, and thus constituted a kind of gesture of reconciliation with the musician who had set his Ludlow masque. As one would expect with Milton, however, there was still a sting in the tail. Milton compared Lawes to the musician Casella, who had set some of Dante's songs: when Dante encountered him in Purgatory, he reached out to embrace him but met only empty air. The image strikingly expresses Milton's tense attitude towards his former royalist friends: the gesture of friendship is there, but so

---

46 Bodleian MS Aubrey 6, fol. 98v, *ABL*, I, 288. Pocock, *HPW*, pp. 41–2, points out the relevance of *Oceana* to the debates of 1647.

47 Henry and William Lawes, *Choice Psalmes* (1648; L640), 'To the Reader', sig. a1v, cited in Willa McClung Evans, *Henry Lawes: Musician and Friend of Poets* (New York, 1941), p. 178.

To his Friend Mr. *Henry Lawes,* upon his Compositions.

TO chaine wilde Winds, calme raging Seas, recall
From profound Hell, and raise to Heav'n, are all
Of Harmony no fables, but true story;
Man has within a storme, a paine, a glory:
And these in me struck by that art divine,
Submit to Musique, above all to thine.

F. Harington.

To my Friend Mr. *Henry Lawes.*

H*Arry,* whose tunefull and well measur'd song
First taught our English Music how to span
Words with just note and accent, not to scan
With *Midas* eares, committing short and long,
Thy worth and skill exempts thee from the throng,
With praise enough for Envie to look wan:
To after age thou shalt be writ the man
That with smooth Aire couldst humour best our tongue.
Thou honour'st Verse, and Verse must lend her wing
To honour thee, the Priest of *Phœbus* Quire,
That tun'st their happiest Lines in hymne or * story.
* The story Dant è shall give Fame leave to set thee higher
of Ariadne set by him in Then his *Casella,* whom he woo'd to sing,
Music. Met in the milder shades of Purgatory.

F. Milton.

7 Henry and William Lawes, *Choice Psalmes*, 1648, sig. a1v: poems by Milton and Harrington.

too is the acknowledgement of a huge ideological gulf, compared to the gulf between the living and the dead.[48]

Yet Milton's determination to find ways of bridging that gulf emerged also in the publication of his 1645 *Poems*, which had just appeared when he wrote the sonnet (was it sent with a presentation copy?). His publisher was Humphrey Moseley, who declared that it was readers' 'clear and courteous entertainment of Mr. *Wallers* late choice peeces' that had encouraged him to bring out this new collection. The title-pages of the two volumes of *Poems* were indeed almost identical; both were dated 1645, both emphasized that some of the verse had been set by Henry Lawes of the king's chapel. Moseley's collections of poems were looking back nostalgically to the courtly culture of the 1630s from the turbulence of the 1640s when 'the slightest Pamphlet is . . . more vendible then the Works of learnedest men'.[49] We seem to be facing another of the 'jumps' so familiar in the period: the Milton who had thrown himself eagerly into the new possibilities of the public sphere now cast himself as an heir to the harmony of the King's Peace. One critic speaks of him as having been 'virtually kidnapped . . . and transformed against his will into a royalist'.[50] It is indeed uncertain how much of a say Milton had in the presentation of the edition, but he had enough advance warning to be able to add satirical verses to his poorly drawn portrait.

The speech-act performed by the 1645 volume was, however, a complex and ambiguous one. Moseley may indeed have been concerned to claim this promising poet for royalism. Milton, still known mostly as a notorious libertine and enemy of the family, may have wanted to establish for himself a more elevated profile.[51] But more was at issue than a retreat from the open spaces of the public sphere into a closed poetic world. The comparison with Waller in itself raised complicated issues. Waller's 1645 *Poems* had been published after he made his ignominious retreat from the public sphere. Bound in with many copies were two of his most famous Parliamentary speeches and his speech of recantation to the Commons. The speech in defence of episcopacy was not included. The image projected was then of a poet who had begun with many contacts with the court, had moved into the public sphere as an orator, had wavered but had seen the error of his ways.

48 On the sonnets' political ethos see John H. Finley, Jr., 'Milton and Horace: A Study of Milton's Sonnets', *Harvard Studies in Classical Philology* 48 (1937), 29–73.

49 'The Stationer to the Reader', John Milton, *Poems* (1645; E1126), sig. A3r.

50 Warren Chernaik, 'Books as Monuments: The Politics of Consolation', *Yearbook of English Studies* 21 (1991), 207–17 (210); see also Peter Lindenbaum, 'The Poet in the Marketplace: Milton and Samuel Simmons', in P. G. Stanwood (ed.), *Of Poetry and Politics: New Essays on Milton and his World* (Binghamton, 1995), pp. 249–62.

51 See Thomas N. Corns, 'Milton's Quest for Respectability', *Modern Language Review* 77 (1982), 769–79, and 'Ideology in the *Poemata* (1645)', *Milton Studies* 19 (1984), 195–203.

This was a comparison from which Milton could benefit.[52] Milton had produced so much polemic in the 1640s that it would have been difficult to bind in his prose writings with his poems. The volume of pamphlets he presented the following year to the Bodleian Library was a fat one. He had not wavered from commitment to the cause of reform. His *Poems* are given a strongly retrospective cast. The engraving on the title-page, which places him against a calm pastoral landscape, depicts him at the age of twenty-one, and several times a note calls attention to the author's youth. The effect is to distance the engaged writer of the 1640s from the more conservative figure who emerges in some of the earlier poems.[53] The fact is that the 'jumps' between the 1620s and the 1640s meant that very few Parliamentarian poets could present an entirely consistent profile. Wither was teased in 1641 by the reprinting of some passages of his earlier *Britain's Remembrancer* which celebrated King Charles and warned of the dangers of sects. May was to become notorious as a turncoat. Milton's 1645 volume openly acknowledges points where he has changed his views. At the same time, it reveals underlying consistencies: he combines Waller-like polish with a fidelity to a 'Spenserian' tradition of political protest.[54]

The contrast with Waller emerges in the separate title-page to the volume's Latin poems. Though this once again emphasizes how long ago some of the poems were composed – and several of them have an eroticism and political conservatism at odds with the prose works – it also describes the author as 'Londinensis'. Waller's encounter with the radical politics of the city had been a bruising one; Milton proudly bears the title of a Londoner. The Latin poems were prefaced by poems from Italian friends, one of which, by Carlo Dati, was addressed specifically to John Milton the Londoner and compared him to Ulysses, the many-troped wanderer, who moved easily between different cultures. Milton described the 1645 volume as a twin-leaved book, and if one face pointed back to the 1630s, another looked to the international republic of letters in which Milton was anxious to establish a reputation.[55]

The 1645 *Poems*, then, is not entirely different in its cultural politics from *Areopagitica*. In *The Reason of Church-Government* he had said that he would

52 See Raymond B. Waddington, 'Milton among the Carolines', in C. A. Patrides and Raymond B. Waddington (eds.), *The Age of Milton: Backgrounds to Seventeenth-Century Literature* (Manchester and Totowa, 1980), pp. 338–64.

53 Richard M. Johnson, 'The Politics of Publication: Misrepresentation in Milton's 1645 *Poems*', *Criticism* 36 (1994–5), 45–71, suggests that the title-page may have been designed as an oblique satire of Milton to which he riposted.

54 For further links between the early poems, the Spenserian tradition, and the prose, see Norbrook, *PP*, ch. 10.

55 On Milton's bringing courtly discourse into the public sphere, see Anne Baynes Coiro, 'Milton and Class Identity: The Publication of *Areopagitica* and the 1645 *Poems*', *Journal of Medieval and Renaissance Studies* 22 (1992), 261–89.

'covnant with any knowing reader, that for some few yeers yet I may go on trust with him toward the payment of what I am now indebted' – that is, the poetry which has been interrupted by polemic (*MPW*, I, 820). *Poems* represents a preliminary 'payment'. In *Areopagitica*, Milton had shown that the traditionally despised pamphlet could aspire to the complex allusiveness of poetry; his poetry, for its part, had developed a tradition of political criticism without compromising formal discipline. As in *Areopagitica*, the 1645 volume counters royalist charges that London has lapsed into unlettered chaos by demonstrating that he can not only meet the royalist culture of the 1630s on its own terms, but also has the potential to go further.

Milton sent a copy of the *Poems* to the Bodleian Library along with his prose tracts, but the book was lost in transit. In sending a new copy early in 1647, Milton composed his longest poem of the 1640s, the Latin ode, 'Ad Joannem Rousium', addressed to Bodley's Librarian.[56] The poem indicates how much thought he gave to the speech-acts of publishing and disseminating his poems. In some ways it follows from the Lawes poem, as an address to a figure with political sympathies different from Milton's own. As the Parliamentary authorities engaged in a post-war purge of Oxford, Rous's position in his college was to come under threat because he had not clearly distanced himself from the royalist cause – indeed Hartlib was proposed as a more reliable candidate to replace Rous.[57] Yet he had maintained political independence from either faction, and Milton's interest in Oxford libraries did not signal a retreat from a sense of the writer's public engagements.

Milton's ode, while sensitive to the appeal of the contemplative life, has a strongly public face. At the beginning, its tone recalls the wit and playfulness of the Roman elegiac poets, whom Milton had imitated in his earlier Latin poems. The second part, however, marks an elevation of tone, as Milton echoes Pindar's second Olympian ode and the second ode of Horace's first book in calling for some god or hero to save the nation. Horace's candidate for the divine hero had of course been the Emperor Augustus, and his odes had been much imitated in the volumes of panegyrics issued for royal occasions during the 1630s and earlier 1640s. Milton conspicuously refuses that solution, however: there is no reference to a royal settlement. And whereas many of Horace's odes celebrated the leisure, the *otium*, that returns to the nation after war, Milton retains something of *Areopagitica*'s tense balance between war and peace. Though he laments the war's disastrous effects on poetry – as he did also in a letter to his old friend Dati in April 1647 (*MPW*, II, 763–5) – he

---

56 On Rous see Sir Edmund Craster, 'John Rous, Bodley's Librarian', *Bodleian Library Record* 5 (1954–6), 130–46. See also Stella P. Revard, '*Ad Joannem Rousium*: Elegiac Wit and Pindaric Mode', *Milton Studies* 19 (1984), 205–26.
57 G. H. Turnbull, *Hartlib, Dury and Comenius: Gleanings from Hartlib's Papers* (1947), pp. 30, 256.

also says that it should end only if the nation has done enough penance for its former luxury and 'degener otium', enervating idleness. He thus qualifies any idealization of the period before the war, and warns against a return to a leisure that will sacrifice liberty. It is for his books rather than himself that he wishes peace and rest, and when he speaks of the evil tongues of the multitude who condemn them, he is probably thinking of the attacks he had come under from the Presbyterians. He looks forward to the poems' being properly understood in future generations; he had voiced similar hopes in the inscription to his prose tracts. Milton enacted his desire for strenuous independence in his poem's metre, which imitated the relatively irregular forms of the Pindaric ode but pushed them further than any previous neo-Latin poetry in the direction of metrical irregularity. Beginning in informality, the ode achieves its own version of the sublime.

The ode remained in manuscript, but the 1645 *Poems* made an important impact. Milton was able to span the different groups the Independents were courting – while passionately supporting the sects, he could also speak the language of courtly culture. He offered a different response to the settlement of the late 1640s than a simple desire to turn the clock back. His example can be measured in the careers of two younger writers, Andrew Marvell and John Hall.

Marvell's poetry is conventionally, and not unjustly, celebrated for a particular quality of detachment, an oblique and impersonal approach to his subject-matter. The causes advanced for that detachment, however, have often been obfuscatory. Down to 1921, when his tercentenary was celebrated, Marvell had a joint reputation as lyric poet and as a political controversialist aligned with the Dissenting Whig tradition. T. S. Eliot's essay of that year decisively shifted the terms of praise. Some of the men who supported the republic, he somewhat patronizingly observed, were 'men of education and culture, even of travel', so that 'some of them were exposed to that spirit of the age which was coming to be the French spirit of the age' and was 'quite opposed to the tendencies latent or the forces active in Puritanism'.[58] The Marvell who fiercely opposed Charles II's intrigues with Louis XIV would have been startled by this praise. Eliot claims that Marvell's wit is 'Latin', which in this context means French; but Latinate wit was a distinctive feature of English republicans. For the critical tradition established by Eliot, Marvell's ability to praise both Charles and Cromwell derived from his roots in an old world-view whose complexity was undermined by the simplifications of republican radicalism. His lyrics are seen virtually as sacramental spaces, embodying a traditional unified sensibility which was lost in the descent into modernity.

58 T. S. Eliot, 'Andrew Marvell', in *Selected Essays* (1951), p. 294.

To that view, William Empson made an effective reply:

> Marvell, when he came to live in London as MP for Hull, so far from marking the end of an old line of virtue, was inventing a new type of Londoner who has since then almost always been present; the next well-known example was Defoe. The type is a generally left-wing politician, considered rather shifty, with strong literary interests kept on the leash, keen to have a finger in any important pie but preferring to stay in the background.[59]

His post-Restoration detachment may have reflected not traditionalism but a double heterodoxy, as a republican with a past to hide and a homosexual.[60] When Marvell came to London as a younger man around 1647, his career was less fixed, and the evidence does suggest that he did not align himself unambiguously with one grouping. From what has already been seen of the political world he was entering, however, it becomes clear that this detachment was far from unique, and that it reflected the post-war period's complicated cultural politics.

Marvell was certainly able to speak the language of the royalists at the Fleece Tavern. He had contributed to one of those pre-war volumes of ceremonial verse whose memory was being revived, imitating the second ode of Horace's first book, the one on which Milton drew for his Rous ode, and heightening its element of idealizing myth. The royalism of this poem does not seem to have run particularly deep, however. Marvell supported neither side in the Civil War. Many years later, he declared that 'the Cause was too good to have been fought for'.[61] This teasing paradox has given rise to many different commentaries, and should perhaps not be abstracted too much from its immediate polemical context, but it does indicate that in 1642 he had no particular enthusiasm about taking up arms for Parliament. As Christopher Hill observes, however, it also indicates that the cause was too good to be fought against as Charles did.[62] Marvell had ample opportunity to contemplate the issues, for one of the fiercest paper wars preceding the outbreak of hostilities centred on his native Hull. The governor, Sir John Hotham, refused to hand over to the king the contents of its armoury. The following year, however, he thought better of his stand and intrigued to admit the king's forces; his plot was discovered and he was executed. These events would certainly serve to discourage active participation in the war by those who had doubts. In early 1642

---

59 William Empson, *Argufying: Essays on Literature and Culture*, ed. John Haffenden (1988), pp. 365–6.

60 Paul Hammond, 'Marvell's Sexuality', *The Seventeenth Century* 11 (1996), 87–123.

61 Andrew Marvell, *The Rehearsal Transpros'd and The Rehearsal Transpros'd: The Second Part*, ed. D. I. B. Smith (Oxford, 1971), p. 135.

62 Christopher Hill, 'John Milton (1608–74) and Andrew Marvell (1621–78)', *WR*, pp. 157–87 (172).

we find Marvell in London witnessing a transfer of documents involving the Yorkshire nobleman Thomas Lord Savile, who was at this time close to the court, though his political commitments constantly wavered.[63] We do not know whether this was a significant connection beyond an indication of patronage from a fellow-Yorkshireman, but Savile's response to the outbreak of war was not unlike Marvell's much later comment: 'For as much as I love the king, I should not be glad he beate the p[ar]liam[t] though they were in the wrong'.[64] Fear that the king's raising his banner was a Caesarian crossing of the Rubicon could be found amongst many who were far from radical. Waller's attempts to find some kind of neutral space had failed and driven him into a Continental exile; Marvell opted to avoid the conflict altogether by setting out for the Continent, possibly as tutor to a nobleman's son.

Our only extended glimpse of Marvell's Continental years indicates that whatever his uncertainty about the Civil War he was decided enough in certain issues. In the spring of 1646 he was in Rome and became involved in a 'Poetical Academy' presided over by a young émigré, George Villiers, duke of Buckingham, the son of Charles I's murdered favourite.[65] Marvell may have known him at Cambridge; his brothers had attended Marvell's college, Trinity, and had contributed along with Marvell to the 1637 volume of panegyrics. Villiers and his brother Francis had interrupted their studies to take up arms for the king. Their estates had been sequestered but rather than being further punished they were placed under the care of the earl of Northumberland, who was also guardian to the duke of York.[66] Northumberland saved the late duke's picture collection and sent his sons on a grand tour not unlike the one Marvell was undertaking. Marvell's poem was probably motivated in part by desire for patronage. Though Villiers's personal position at this time was fragile, he was a link with Independent grandees like Northumberland.[67]

Buckingham was, then, a figure with complex political associations. His circle in Rome would have included high-flying cavalier exiles. It also included Catholic aesthetes such as the priest-poet Richard Flecknoe.[68] Marvell's poem, however, conspicuously distances him from such figures. If the young Marvell had been susceptible to the lure of the baroque art of the Counter-Reformation, by the time of his visit to Rome he seems to have been

63 Pauline Burdon, 'Marvell after Cambridge', *British Library Journal* 4 (1978), pp. 42–8.
64 *Papers Relating to the Delinquency of Lord Savile*, ed. James J. Cartwright, Camden Miscellany VIII (1883), p. 7.
65 See Richard Flecknoe, *Epigrams of All Sorts* (1671; F1219), p. 66. Flecknoe's admiration for Fulke Greville, mentioned by Marvell, l. 4, appears in an epigram on p. 10.
66 Hester W. Chapman, *Great Villiers: A Study of George Villiers Second Duke of Buckingham 1628–1687* (1949), p. 38.
67 Adamson, 'The Baronial Context of the English Civil War', 113.
68 Edward Chaney, *The Grand Tour and the Great Rebellion: Richard Lassels and 'The Voyage of Italy' in the Seventeenth Century* (Geneva, 1985), pp. 347–50.

more detached. 'Flecknoe' consistently profanes Catholic sacramental language; and it images that profanity in its own structure. Marvell presents himself listening to Flecknoe's terrible poetry as undergoing the torments of a martyr in a baroque painting, and he ends up by declaring that he will hang his account in St Peter's as a votive offering. In his black, spuriously traditional cloak covering a chameleon-like ability to reflect any colour, Flecknoe images the epistemological trickiness of the Roman church itself. There is a similar tension between the claustrophobic narrowness of his room, which is described in terms consistently recalling the confined space of the sacrament, and the specious flow of his poetic stanzas. The poem implies a preference for more open spaces to these closed, semi-private spaces. And it is interesting that the poet borrows a phrase from the Miltonic sublime of *Lycidas*. He longs to have a witness to his martyrdom at Flecknoe's hands, an ambition he describes as the 'last distemper of the sober Brain' (line 28, cf. *Lycidas*, line 71). 'Flecknoe' is light-hearted enough, and in concentrating on literary rather than directly religious issues it avoids the kind of direct denunciation of Catholicism one might have expected from a militantly Puritan poet. But then, Milton himself had paid lavish compliments to Italian Catholics in their role as his hosts. In its self-mocking way, however, Marvell's poem does offer Villiers a warning about the kinds of company he should avoid keeping.

Buckingham was back in England the following year, Northumberland having managed to get his estates back for him. By the autumn of the same year Marvell was back in Hull and began to frequent literary circles in London. If Marvell was struck at this time by the image of the king, he seems to have responded to it in the peculiarly distanced, aestheticized manner that was newly possible in this period. He was a friend of Lovelace's and would have known his poem to Lely, and Buckingham could have given him entrée to Northumberland's circle. There are intriguing affinities between the detached, aesthetic presentation of Charles in Lovelace's poem and Marvell's 'The Unfortunate Lover', which has sometimes been seen as a direct allegory on King Charles's fate. That poem seems, however, rather to be using some contemporary political metaphors to catch an elusive amatory state than the other way round, much as Marvell is able to refer casually to the dispersal of the king's picture collection as an analogy in 'The Gallery'. If a political reading is involved, the poem seems to mingle sympathy with detachment in a portrait of the king's attempt to present himself in mystical images.[69]

69 For political readings see Annabel M. Patterson, *Marvell and the Civic Crown* (Princeton, 1978), pp. 20–5; Margarita Stocker, *Apocalyptic Marvell: The Second Coming in Seventeenth Century Poetry* (Brighton, 1986), pp. 257–305, who brings out the scepticism; P. R. K. Davidson and A. K. Jones, 'New Light on Marvell's "The Unfortunate Lover"?', *Notes and Queries* 230 (1985), 170–2.

That kind of detachment would have been reinforced by different influences that were working on Marvell. Marvell and Lovelace may be regarded as the target audience for a pamphlet published shortly after the army entered London, John Hall's *A True Account and Character of the Times*. Hall is a significant figure in trying to put into practice an Independent cultural politics which would bring together former royalists and quasi-republicans.[70] Hall (1627–56) was something of an *enfant terrible*, a youthful admirer of Bacon who had begun corresponding with Hartlib and proposing to join in his schemes of intellectual reform even before he studied at Cambridge. His writings show the clear influence of *Areopagitica* and *Of Education*, and he had a strong, though at this stage apparently unreciprocated, desire to meet Milton. Hall was full of enthusiasm for the possibility of a great renewal in learning, which he expressed both in his prose and in the little of his poetry that survives as a sublime and utopian breaking of boundaries.[71] He praised More's and Campanella's utopias.[72] His immediate concerns were with literary and educational reform, but his writings indicate the need for a political basis for any lasting reform. Though he was not at this stage opposed to monarchy,[73] his letters are full of scorn for the old monopolies of patronage and learning, and he again and again praises Parliament for placing these monopolies in public hands. He repeatedly proclaimed his determination to be 'subservient to ye Com[m]onwealth of l[ette]rs'.[74] In the spirit of Milton's critique in *Areopagitica* of a 'fugitive and cloister'd virtue' (*MPW*, II, 515), and Culpeper's attack on scholars who were 'suffered to liue a monkishe life to the prejudice of the publike',[75] Hall wrote that they must be 'forct from y^t solitude wherein they wold be imersed'.[76]

This emphasis on the public life placed him in disagreement with Stanley

---

70 On Hall see John Davies, 'An Account of the Author', in John Hall (trans.), *Hierocles upon the Golden Verses of Pythagoras* (1657; E1651.1); John W. Pendleton, 'The Prose Works of John Hall of Durham', University of Oxford B. Litt. thesis, 1934; John Burnham Shaw, 'The Life and Works of John Hall of Durham', Johns Hopkins University Ph.D. thesis, 1952, whose account of the canon, pp. 204ff, I follow; Joad Raymond, 'John Hall's *A Method of History*: A Book Lost and Found', *English Literary Renaissance*, forthcoming.

71 For example John Hall, *Poems* (1646; E1166.1*), pp. 38–9; also in *Minor Poets of the Caroline Period*, ed. George Saintsbury, 3 vols. (Oxford, 1906), II, 175–225 (203). Davies reports that Hall wrote at least twice as many poems again as appear in his only published volume: *Hierocles upon the Golden Verses of Pythagoras*, sig. b6v.

72 John Hall, *Horae Vacivae* (1646; E1191), p. 196.

73 J[ohn]. H[all]., 'A Method of History', Bodleian MS Rawl. D152, sig. 4v.

74 Hall to Hartlib, 8 February ?1647, *HP*, 60/14/20A. Extracts from the correspondence have been published by G. H. Turnbull, 'John Hall's Letters to Samuel Hartlib', *Review of English Studies* N.S. 4 (1953), 221–33.

75 Culpeper to Hartlib, 28 January 1645, *CL*, p. 216.

76 Hall to Hartlib, 2 January 1646, *HP*, 9/10/1B.

and other royalists. It was to Stanley that Hall had dedicated his volume of poems in 1646. Hall described him in a letter as 'a Gent: (vnder whose shade I enioy my studious leisure)'; here he made a familiar allusion to Virgil's first eclogue with its idealization of leisured contemplation as a retreat from the horrors of war.[77] Yet Hall did not support Stanley when he proposed to found a literary academy: 'I was euer of the opinion that it was far too slight, to advance any way ye Publique being rather a private Conglobation'.[78] Although Hall modestly lamented his 'back-wardness to the Publick service'[79], his recurrent theme was that the intellectual must be forward in appearing in public, that with the emergence of apocalyptic upheavals in the 'Politique or literary Republickes'[80] it was impossible to go back to the old order in which learning had been the prerogative of semi-private interests and monopolies. Hall could not be content with a narrowly literary public sphere. On Hartlib's advocacy, Hall translated two works by the utopian writer Andreae about a society of scientists, which showed 'what the results of associated labours are, in comparison of sequestred'.[81] Hall would have fully endorsed the comment of another member of the circle in 1648: 'that Cursed Privatum-Publicum, hath Banished all thoughts of entertaining Any thing, that is truely Publicke'.[82] Culpeper was already tending to the view that monarchy embodied a structural confusion of the public and the private which could only be resolved under a republic, and Hall was certainly speculating about different political forms. He set himself to 'express an Idea of a Commonwealth & Colledge in a Romance'.[83] A friend later wrote that his time at Cambridge had sharpened his antipathy to monarchy. The number of idle people at college, in his view, epitomized the luxury and waste of the aristocratic ethos.[84]

In 1647, however, Hall was still ready to look for political compromise. All wits must be brought together in reshaping a more satisfactory cultural and political order, and the severely limited monarchy envisaged by the Independents was compatible with such an order. His *True Account* was cast as a letter to a royalist whose estates had suffered in the war – he could have had Lovelace in mind – and Hall declared that 'the flower of the Gentry' had fought for the royalists.[85] He called for an end of the term 'malignant' (p. 8), and attacked the sequestrators of royal property as 'vermine' (p. 2). He was

77 Hall to Hartlib, 29 [March?] 1647, *HP*, 9/10/5A.
78 Hall to Hartlib, 20 April 1647, *HP*, 60/14/32A.
79 Hall to Hartlib, 2 January 1646, *HP*, 9/10/1A.
80 Hall to Hartlib, 13 April 1647, *HP*, 60/14/31A.
81 Johann Valentin Andreae, *A Modell of a Christian Society*, trans. John Hall (Cambridge, 1647; H74B), sig. A3r.   82 Joshua Rawlin to Hartlib, 25 April 1648, *HP*, 10/10/3A.
83 Hall to Hartlib, ?late March 1647, *HP*, 60/14/39B.
84 Davies (ed.), *Hierocles upon the Golden Verses of Pythagoras*, sigs. a8v ff.
85 [John Hall], *A True Account and Character of the Times* (1647; E401.13), p. 2.

thus appealing to a widespread body of gentry opinion – not all royalist – which disliked the arbitrary aspects of some of Parliament's exercise of its power.[86] In its ecclesiastical policy the nation was like the man who pulled down his house to repair it before he had another one to put his head in (p. 3); Hall felt that most of the nation favoured a 'moderate Episcopacy' (p. 7), but expressed general suspicion of clerical ambitions. Hall was very soon to use a similar architectural analogy in a more radical sense[87], but here his call is for reformation, not revolution. In a somewhat patrician tone, he attacks the London merchants for trying to meddle in political affairs they did not understand. The Presbyterians are branded as the party of ungentlemanly subversives, and though the army is criticized, its intervention is seen as offering possibilities for restoring a proper balance. Hall finds common cause between gentleman royalists and religious radicals in an onslaught on Presbyterian culture. On the one hand, he renews the themes of Milton's critique of licensing, seizing on a case where the Presbyterians tried to stop the licensing of books challenging their opinions, and attacking the 'detestable' Thomas Edwards, scourge of the heretics in general and Milton in particular (pp. 4, 7). His arguments here were pragmatic: 'It is no great policy to give heterodox opinions life by opposition' (pp. 6–7). On the other hand, he takes up what had become a grievance for many royalist poets, the closing of the theatres, and calls for their re-opening, though he gives this policy a utilitarian, Hartlibian gloss by stressing their educational role (p. 8).

Hall's pamphlet thus has a conservative side, declaring that 'the government of one comming into the hands of many, who are unskilfull Pilots, is to be wished againe, though accompanied with some inconveniences' (p. 6), and criticizing Fairfax for not doing enough to this end (p. 7). That is not, however, a particularly ringing endorsement of the king, and there are distinct limits to his conservatism. In content and tone Hall's pamphlet is very close to a recent work by Marchamont Nedham, *The Case of the Kingdom Stated*. Nedham had drawn on Machiavelli and on Rohan's theory of political interest to offer a pseudo-scientific analysis; the Independents formed a balancing power between the bishops and the Presbyterians and therefore should form an alliance with the monarchy – precisely the solution Hall too advocated.[88] The contending factions, Hall lamented, had tried to take the realm to pieces like a watch and now found it was hard to put it together again (p. 2). The process of reintegrating the nation then was a mechanical rather

---

86 On the political context see Robert Ashton, *Counter-Revolution: The Second Civil War and its Origins, 1646–8* (New Haven and London, 1994).

87 John Hall, *An Humble Motion to the Parliament of England Concerning the Advancement of Learning* (1649; H350; ed. A. K. Croston, Liverpool, 1953), p. 20; see below, chapter 5, n. 57.   88 Worden, '"Wit in a Roundhead"', p. 317.

than organic one, involving a careful balance of opposing interests. Eventually the names of parties would become irrelevant. Yet differing interests had to be acknowledged; there would be far more room for divergent opinions than in the pre-war world for which some royalist poets were expressing nostalgia. One interest that must never be neglected was that of the people – one of his first maxims is that *'people are never so forward, nor so daring, as to preserve or regaine their Liberties'* (p. 2). Hall is remarkably optimistic about the king's willingness to co-operate in such a settlement. He had high hopes from John Dury's being appointed to educate the royal children, with the chance of turning them into prodigies of concern for the public interest. Dury considered that the best poet for children to read was the fiercely anti-monarchical George Buchanan.[89]

Hall's programme was calculated to appeal to writers like Lovelace and Marvell, and there is some evidence that Marvell responded.[90] He and Hall both wrote commendatory verses for Lovelace's collection *Lucasta*. Dating the poems creates problems, for while the volume was licensed in February 1648 it did not appear until May 1649.[91] In its cultural politics, however, Marvell's poem (*MPL*, I, 2–4) seems to reflect the immediate post-war era when Lovelace was planning publication. Hall's poem to Lovelace makes the same kind of conciliatory gesture towards former royalists as the *True Account*. He addresses him as 'Colonel' and emphasizes Lovelace's greatness both as writer and as soldier.[92] Marvell's poem, which has many points of contact with Hall's *True Account*, is in some ways more detached than Hall's from the royalist soldiery.[93] His Lovelace is 'Mr' and his only reference to the

89 John Dury to Smart, 28 May 1647, *HP*, 68/4/2B.

90 On this and on many other aspects of Marvell's career I am indebted to Denise Cuthbert, 'A Re-Examination of Andrew Marvell: A Study of the Poems of the Cromwell Era', unpublished Ph.D. thesis, University of Sydney, 1987.

91 Arguments for a dating in 1647–8 can be supported by the poem's giving the impression that trouble about licensing lies in the future: *MPL*, I, 239; Nicholas Guild, 'The Politics of Marvell's Early "Royalist" Poems', *Studies in English Literature* 20 (1980), 125–36 (128). Hilton Kelliher, 'Some Notes on Andrew Marvell', *British Library Journal* 4 (1978), 122–44 (122–4), argues that the reference to Kent's first petition must date the poem after the celebrated petition of May 1648, and points out that one contributor referred to seven years' wars. On the other hand, there were several Kentish petitions in 1642, and Alan Everitt, *The Community of Kent and the Great Rebellion 1640–1660* (Leicester, 1966), p. 107, speaks of the 'battle of petitions'. Corns, *UV*, p. 225, also favours a late date. On the Lovelace poem see also Cuthbert, 'A Re-Examination of Andrew Marvell', pp. 22ff.

92 'To Colonel RICHARD LOVELACE, on the publishing of his ingenious Poems', in *The Poems of Richard Lovelace*, ed. C. H. Wilkinson (Oxford, 1953), pp. 9–10.

93 'To his Noble Friend Mr. *Richard Lovelace*, upon his Poems', *MPL*, I, 2–4. James Loxley, 'Prepar'd at Last to Strike in with the Tyde? Andrew Marvell and Royalist Verse', *The Seventeenth Century* 10 (1995), 39–62 (48–50), notes the lack of direct political polemic.

Civil War is strikingly detached: 'Our Civill Wars have lost the Civicke crowne'. The Roman civic crown was awarded for saving a fellow-citizen's life. Hall used the phrase rather loosely in his poem, declaring that Lovelace's temples bore 'Both th'*Delphick* Wreath and *Civic* Coronet'. Marvell's line juxtaposes 'civil' and 'civic' in a half-punning way reminiscent of Lucan's first line, refusing to romanticize the war and calling attention to the tragic destruction of public life (line 12). He begins by lamenting 'Our times', possibly recalling the title of Hall's pamphlet. He contrasts them, like so many poems of the later 1640s, with the pre-war world; but unlike many, he makes no reference to the king. Marvell looks back not to the court but to the 'Towne', a literary public sphere where writers were candid and ingenious, advancing worthy men by honest praise.

What is restricting this public sphere is the power of the 'barbed Censurers', who are compared to the 'reforming eye' of the 'yong Presbytery' (lines 21–4). After the army's entry to London licensing was entrusted to military authorities, but Marvell emphasizes the Presbyterian ethos, and thus offers common ground with royalists. Like Milton and Hall, Marvell does not echo the laments of conservatives like Edwards at the proliferation of books as a threat, rather he presents it in terms of growth and fruitfulness. It is the censors who try to arrest the process who are the menacing forces, the caterpillars and – a striking coinage – 'Word-peckers'. It is they who 'rise in arms'; Marvell thus deflects imputations of political subversiveness against Lovelace, and suggests that any attempt to restrict the book because of Lovelace's royalist activities back in 1642 would be an absurd piece of over-politicization. He turns this point into comedy by having Lovelace's supporters, the ladies, assume that he himself is in league with the 'reforming eye' of the Puritan censors so that they 'Mine eyes invaded' (line 43). As in the Flecknoe poem, Marvell presents himself as an outsider in the circles he describes; though he then declares that he would be ready to die in their defence or in Lovelace's cause. How we are to read that phrase depends on the poem's date. If it was written after Lovelace was imprisoned in October 1648, it has a directly political connotation. If it was earlier, however, it belongs to the world of post-war reconciliation, parallelling the gesture of solidarity across party lines that Milton made in his sonnet to Lawes. The censorship, at least insofar as it was dominated by Presbyterians, was a common bone of contention to opponents of the Presbyterians on the right and on the left. It formed a central target for Nedham when in the summer of 1647 he went over to the royalists.[94] All the same, the Marvell of the poem is somewhat on the outside of Lovelace's circle, liable to suspicion by its members.

The relatively conciliatory atmosphere expressed by these writings of

94 *Mercurius Pragmaticus* no. 1, 14–21 September 1647, E407.39, p. 2.

Marvell, Hall and Lovelace was difficult to sustain. In the spring of 1648 the London royalists who had been cowed the previous August were again showing their strength. There was a resurgence of the royalist underground press. Local protests and petitions throughout the country seemed on the way to fusing into an outbreak of civil war. The effect of these risings was to break down the uneasy attempts at compromise of the previous year and renew older polarizations. Lovelace's role in presenting a Kentish petition back in 1642 became relevant again now that Kent was up in arms. And his old friend John Hall found himself breaking from Lovelace's circle.

We have a revealing record of Hall's motivation from his friend John Davies:

> the affections of the City were extreamly retrograde, absolutely alienated from an adored Parliament to a persecuted King, whose cause was devolved from Arms to Pens. The wits of the ruin'd party had their secret *Clubs*, these hatched *Mercuries*, *Satyres*, and *Pasquinado's*, that travelled up and down the streets with so much impunity, that the poor weekly *Hackneyes*, durst hardly communicate the ordinary Intelligence. This was the true state of affairs when Mr. *Hall* made that appearance for the State, not disconsonant to his former principles, even in the University, which were sufficiently anti-monarchicall, and subservient to the interest of a Common-wealth.[95]

Davies was writing after Hall's death when his republican convictions were clear, but the link between appearing for the State and serving a general interest, as against the particular interest of the monarchy, is indeed characteristic of the way in which Hall's thought was tending. One of Hall's opponents alleged that he was sponsored by the astrologer William Lilly, whose prophecies of Charles I's impending doom were becoming increasingly vigorous.[96]

Hall's title – *Mercurius Britanicus* – was a bold one. He had usurped Nedham's title, down to its idiosyncratic spelling. In the most spectacular conversion in English journalistic history, the previous year Nedham had offered his services to Charles and begun a new newsbook, *Mercurius Pragmaticus*, which bitterly attacked Parliament and especially the Presbyterians. He had left a space in the public sphere which Hall was ready to fill. In fact Hall did not nearly live up to Nedham's precedent, lacking the will or means to build up Nedham's superb intelligence network. His newsbooks were devoted mainly to extended retorts to royalist counterparts, often following the stock patterns of the Renaissance academic controversy. And yet his appearance was calculated to strike a nerve. For there was a certain tension

95 Davies (ed.), *Hierocles upon the Golden Verses*, sig. b3v.
96 On Lilly's politics see Ann Geneva, *Astrology and the Seventeenth Century Mind: William Lilly and the Language of the Stars* (Manchester and New York, 1995). Joad Raymond, *The Invention of the Newspaper: English Newsbooks 1641–1649* (Oxford, 1996), p. 63, is dubious about Lilly's participation.

between the role of the newsbook and allegiance to the royal cause. Nedham had specialized in detailed and particular military and political analysis, bringing into the public sphere matters that had previously been discussed within a small elite. His main royalist adversary, *Mercurius Aulicus*, had shown no interest in stirring up such debate, concentrating on abuse of Parliament and on generalized panegyrics of the king and his supporters. This strategy continued to apply to most of the new wave of royalist newsbooks that emerged in 1647–48: for example, *Mercurius Publicus*, whose attack on Wither was quoted above, was 'public' only in a limited sense, presenting the return of Charles as a sufficient political objective without wishing to get involved in constitutional discussions. Nedham's *Mercurius Pragmaticus* stood out in this company as the only royalist newsbook to offer detailed analysis of different power blocs and interests. As its name indicated, its approach was practical and particular, though its pragmatism was informed by interest theory. To that degree, Nedham's break with his former principles was not as sharp as it might appear. Though like other royalist newsbooks, *Mercurius Pragmaticus* published panegyrics of the injured Charles, the speech-act involved was more complex. Nedham implied the need for an extensive public to assess different social and political interests, and to see how support for the king was essential as a counterweight to the twin tyrannies of the army and the Presbyterians.[97]

Hall's newsbook, as has been said, did not operate quite at this level, yet it did have significant elements in common with the Nedham of *Mercurius Pragmaticus* as well as of *Mercurius Britanicus*. Hall aims to show that those who share Nedham's values have no business siding with the royalists, that they have made a disastrous tactical and intellectual error which can only be redeemed by abandoning support for the royalist rebels. And in doing so he invokes the spirit not only of the earlier Nedham but of Milton, who was a clear inspiration for his venturing into the public sphere. When royalists attacked the anti-royalist bias of the courts, Hall compared them to the Areopagus.[98] He also echoed the condemnation in *Areopagitica* of the Presbyterians' '*Atlantick* and *Eutopian* polities' (*MPW*, II, 526) in aiming at total control of discourse: they would

> let nener [*sic*] an honest man speak for himselfe, but muzzle all mens mouths, that we may silently run back into *Babel*, and relapse to the former causes of our Civill Warre, which might by this meanes end more unhappily then ever it begun; for were this *New-Atlanticall*, *Vtopian* advise once followed, no sooner should an honest man open his mouth and speake, but he should be hit in the teeth and be forced to be quiet.[99]

97 Worden, 'Wit in a Roundhead', pp. 322–3.
98 *Mercurius Britanicus* [*sic*] no. 2, 16–25 May 1648, E444.7, p. 14.
99 *Mercurius Britannicus* [*sic*] no. 10, 18 July 1648, E453.10, p. 77.

Like Milton, Hall is not advocating unlimited freedom of speech for all factions; on the contrary, just as Milton was alarmed at the circulation of royalist newsbooks in London in wartime, Davies points to Hall's dislike of the new wave of royalist newsbooks. Nevertheless, his rhetoric assumes that if the Independents triumph the result will be the opening up of new modes of thought and expression, whereas in a long humanist tradition he associates the royalists with rigid, inflexible duncery. He hopes that the Welsh will no longer listen to 'the dull orations, of their *Sir Johns* and the *Cavaliers*.'[100] He attacks royalist dons at Cambridge who can turn even the innovative medium of the newsbook into a tired, repetitive ritual: 'that can with an huge deal of delight and extasie con a *Pragmaticus* seven times over, and that with as much pleasure as an old papist would say *Avie-maries* for a wager, or the Fellow at Westminster run over the Catalogue of Tombes when he is paid aforehand'.[101] Given that the royalists had now allied with the Presbyterians, their triumph would stifle the nation's growth in political and religious maturity by forcing it back into the mould of an ecclesiastical structure even more rigid than the old Anglican church. Like Milton, Hall associates the nation's breaking out of set forms with a classical sublimity. The actions of the Parliamentary forces would 'hereafter seem *poeticall*',[102] and the poetry in question would be sublime. Hall had recently been working on his Longinus translation, and some of his phrasing, like Milton's, could apply both to rhetorical and military power: Fairfax's force 'like an impetuous *torrent*, carries down all before it, and hath broken down greater *banks*, then you are likely to make', just as sublimity 'bears down all before it like a whirlwind'.[103]

Like *Areopagitica*, and *Prosopopoeia Britannica*, *Mercurius Britanicus* never openly declares that this kind of sublimity of speech is incompatible with monarchical government, yet Hall's language resonates more and more with distinctively republican associations. He waxes satirical about conventional injunctions to political obedience: 'These that tell you dreadfull thing, [*sic*] of Rebellion and disobedience, and makes the thirteenth to the Romanes a generall common place against all breach of Allegiance' are busiest spreading libels.[104] He attacks '*Majesty* or *Prerogative* or any *specious* name of *Tyranny* whatsoever'.[105] He presents the Army's exploits in terms of an exalted civic virtue. The common soldiers are 'framed to ciuilty',[106] and they are led by men like Skippon 'whose forward activenesse in the common Cause, can

100 *Mercurius Britanicus* no. 10, p. 74.   101 *Mercurius Britanicus* no. 1, 16 May 1648; E442.19, sig. A2r.   102 *Mercurius Britanicus* no. 11, 25 July 1648, E454.7, p. 82.

103 *Mercurius Britanicus* no. 4, 8 June 1648, E446.22, p. 28; J[ohn].H[all]., *Peri Hypsous, or Dionysius Longinus of the Height of Eloquence* (1652; E1294.2), p. 3.

104 *Mercurius Britanicus* no. 1, sig. A1v.

105 *Mercurius Censorius* no. 2, 1–8 June 1648, E446.20, p. 14.

106 *Mercurius Britanicus* no. 3, 25–30 May 1648, E445.14, p. 22.

never be enough commended',[107] Lambert, a 'gallant man (being by the forward affections of the people, encreased many hundreds)',[108] and Haselrig, a man likewise distinguished by his 'forwardnesse'.[109] Hall repeatedly compares the Parliamentary leaders to the heroes of ancient Rome. Selden is praised for his '*Roman* magnanimity'.[110] Hall invokes Machiavelli in comparing Fairfax to a Caesar or Alexander.[111] Henry Marten is praised as 'our English *Brutus*, that durst in the beginning of these Times speak more then others could wish.'[112] Hall here defends the forthrightness that had led to Marten's expulsion from Parliament in 1643 for his republican declarations. Marten aroused especial controversy during the Second Civil War by raising a military force of his own without consulting Parliament and was allegedly calling for the king's death.[113]

Mercurius Britanicus, then, carries on the radicalizing impulses of *Areopagitica*. Yet like that work, and some of Milton's more recent writings, the newsbook also leaves open the way for a common cause between Independents and royalists against the Presbyterians. Hall insists, however lukewarmly, that the Independents are serving the king's interests: despite his 'backwardnes' in coming to a settlement, eventually 'more *publicke* and mercifull *thoughts* might have had some sway'.[114] Here, characteristically, Hall implies that the monarchy tends to the pursuit of private interests but expresses the hope that it may be brought to more public concerns. His aim is not so much to provide information as to win the battle for cultural politics, inspiring other young intellectuals to 'appear' for the Parliamentary cause, and he keeps up a close dialogue with royalist waverers: 'There are some that wish the Cavaleers better then *Elencticus* [a royalist newsbook], and would give them better counsell, if they would hearken to it'.[115] They are like men under enchantment who will come to see reason. As in the *True Account*, Hall appeals to a common hostility to the Presbyterians' restrictiveness; he repeatedly compares them to caterpillars, Marvell's term for the enemies of wit in his Lovelace poem.[116] Hall also tries to shame the cavaliers by presenting them

---

107 *Mercurius Britannicus* no. 12, 1 August 1648, E456.12, p. 95.
108 *Mercurius Britannicus* no. 8, 4 July 1648, E451.1, p. [58].
109 *Mercurius Britanicus* no. 13, 16 August 1648, E459.6, p. 103.
110 *Mercurius Britannicus* no. 5, 13 June 1648, E447.9, p. 34.
111 *Mercurius Britanicus* no. 4, p. 28.
112 *Mercurius Britannicus* no. 5, p. 35.
113 *Mercurius Pragmaticus* no. 11, 6–13 June 1648, E447.5, sig. L4r.
114 *Mercurius Britannicus* no. 6, 21 June 1648, E449.5, p. 47.
115 *Mercurius Censorius* no. 2, p. [16].
116 *Mercurius Britanicus* no. 3, p. 21, no. 10, p. 75. The caterpillar analogy was commonplace, but it is interesting that it was used with reference to censorship by Marchamont Nedham about this time, *Mercurius Pragmaticus* no. 3, 28 Sept.–6 Oct. 1647, E410.4, p. 18.

as representatives of drunkenness rather than civility, and adopts a satirically conciliatory tone, urging them to save themselves by abandoning the campaign:

> Were it not better for you to eschew all these inconveniencies and timely contain your selves at your Clubs, and there under the *Rose* vent all your set forms of execrations against the Parliament and Army . . . This were the fittest employment for your Degeneracies, and if you want any Rulers, sixe beer-glasses of Sacke brings the King and all his Progeny unto you; and the glasses inverted in a *Grecian* health represents you with those lovely Idaeas of your Mistresses and Whores[.]

And indeed some royalists did hold back from involvement in the rising, amongst them Richard Lovelace; there is no evidence that he took up arms, and though he was to be arrested on suspicion of involvement in royalist activities, this was not until October 1648.[117]

If Hall intended to shame the royalists into following him into the Parliamentarian camp, he was not entirely successful. His targets were quickly recognized as including his own former drinking companions at the Fleece. A rival journalist, George Wharton, retaliated in *Mercurius Elencticus*:

> Art thou a fit *Associate* for such *Ingenious* and candid *soules* as Col. *Lovelace*, *Captaine Sherburne*, Mr. *Shirley*, or Mr. *Stanley*? they shall kick thee out of their *acquaintance* and tel thee thou art no *legitimate* Son of the *Muses*, but a *Traytor* to *Ingenuity*, a meere *excrementitious scabb* of *Learning*.[118]

The tone of Wharton's attacks, however, was relatively mild: just as Hall urged the royalists to join his group, so the royalists treated him as an errant who might return to the fold. Sir John Berkenhead, who had been a leading writer for *Mercurius Aulicus*, the royalist newsbook that had been the main target of Nedham's *Mercurius Britanicus*, expressed sorrow rather than anger that '*Jack Hall* of *Cambridge* (whom because I know him to bee a man of parts sufficient, I will not divulge him) should so farre lose himselfe, as to justifie the Rebels in a weekly *Gazet*'.[119] Berkenhead doubtless felt that if Nedham had changed sides, so might Hall. And Lovelace himself was a few years later to respond graciously to Hall's death, recalling Hall's commendatory verses to *Lucasta*.[120] The bonds formed in those immediate post-war years were not easily broken.

This meant that Hall took a markedly more conciliatory line than some of the other newsbooks on military matters. One of the most controversial events was the killing of Lord Francis Villiers, brother to the duke of

117 *Mercurius Britanicus* no. 1, sig. A3r; Wilkinson (ed.), *The Poems of Richard Lovelace*, p. 345.
118 *Mercurius Elencticus* no. 27, 24–31 May 1648, E445.23, p. 206.
119 *Mercurius Bellicus* no. 19, 30 May–6 June 1648, E446.2, p. 7.
120 'To the Genius of Mr. *John Hall*', Lovelace, *Poems*, p. 190.

Buckingham. Several reports of Villiers's death adopted a gloating and militantly anti-aristocratic tone, and his death went down amongst the army as an image of the rightful end of a feckless and licentious cavalier.[121] On the other side, a royalist asked: 'Why should such Noble blood by such a hand/Be shed?', compared him to Caesar, and saw his death as opening the floodgates to the 'Sacrilegious *Levellers*'.[122] Hall gave a more complicated analysis, devoting much of an issue to the social connotations of the event. Like other newsbook – writers he scorned the courtly affectations of Holland and Buckingham: such conduct, he wrote, might almost make us wish the doctrine of John of Leiden revived, that all men were equal. True nobility, after all, lay in the mind.[123] On the other hand, Hall was careful to point out that there were noblemen amongst the Parliamentary leadership: they were distinguished by showing 'active vigilance' for the Commonwealth – he would have been thinking of men like Northumberland – as opposed to Buckingham and his friends who were led astray into pursuing childish romantic fantasies. But Hall, unlike the other newsbook-writers, does show a certain admiration for Villiers: 'the *Lord Francis Villers*, a fine yong Gentleman *expiated* part of the folly of his companions, and dyed by a many wounds, which had been brave enough, had they been received in another cause'.[124] Another leader, the earl of Holland, was redeemable: he might

> have leisure to repent his juvenile folly, and dresse himself; and when he has bemoaned and cryed *peccavi*, perhaps be admitted to *London*, to make cringes and shew himself before the Ladies, who may be as glad of the recovery of this old *Otho*, as they were lately sorrowfull for the death of the young *Adonis*.[125]

The Adonis of course was Lord Francis Villiers. Newsbooks reported that pleas were being made for mercy to Buckingham – Northumberland played a leading role here, as he did in the arrangements for his brother's burial – and Hall contributes to such pleas by presenting the rebellion as a childish prank as much as a serious political engagement. He thus continues to make possible bridges between his cavalier drinking partners and the Parliamentarian cause. For their part, they saw his appearance for Parliament as a youthful folly. Hall presents men like Buckingham as forward youths whose energy

121 *Perfect Occurrences of Every Daies Journall in Parliament* no. 80, 7–14 July 1648, E525.5, p. 387; *The Memoirs of Edmund Ludlow*, ed. C. H. Firth, 2 vols. (Oxford, 1894), I, 198.

122 *An Elegie and Epitapth [sic], upon the Right Honourable the Lord FRANCIS VILLARS* (1649; 669f12.99); see also *Elegie on the Untimely Death of . . . FRANCIS, Lord VILLIERS* (1649; 669f12.74). Elegies for Villiers were collected in a compilation of royalist verse published after the regicide, *Vaticinium Votivum* ([1649]; E1217.2), pp. 61–7. For rejection of spurious attributions of this book to Wither, see David Norbrook, 'Some Notes on the Canon of George Wither', *Notes and Queries* 241 (1996), 276–81 (279).

123 *Mercurius Britannicus* no. 9, 11 July 1648, E452.3, pp. 68–9.

124 *Mercurius Britannicus* no. 9, p. 70   125 *Mercurius Britannicus* no. 10, p. 75.

must be reclaimed if possible for the public interest; Francis Villiers's death is then a source of tragedy rather than gloating. And it could be pointed out that the Holland–Villiers group had issued a manifesto that was relatively conciliatory, the only one of the royalist manifestoes of 1648 that stressed Parliament's role. Holland had only recently defected from Parliament, and the king's advisers put pressure on Buckingham to accept his leadership, even though he was of lower social rank, in order to stress the breadth of the coalition.[126]

Moderation was, however, absent from the longest and perhaps the goriest of the elegies for Villiers, which has been attributed to Hall's friend Marvell.[127] The attribution has been much disputed; many critics would be happy to exclude from the canon a poem that praises Villiers for erecting a whole pyramid of vulgar bodies. The only attribution is from an informed but very late source. Even if Marvell did not write it, analogies with other poems suggest that he had read it, and it offers a glimpse of the range of cultural influences to which he was exposed. Unlike the other elegies for Villiers, this poem lays claim to intimate personal acquaintance: the author has seen him engaging in military exercises, defends his affair with the married Mary Kirke, and appears himself very responsive to his physical charms. If it is Marvell's, the poem could be seen as maintaining the contacts with the Villiers family he had already established, and taking out an insurance policy in the ultimate event of a royalist victory. As Harold Love points out, Marvell's whole career 'is one of exercising the maximum amount of influence with the minimum amount of visibility'.[128]

126 Ashton, *Counter Revolution*, pp. 408, 450.

127 'An Elegy upon the Death of my Lord Francis Villers' (1648; M870), *MPL*, I, 429–32. The only surviving copy was ascribed to Marvell by the eighteenth-century antiquarian George Clarke. Warren Chernaik, *The Poet's Time: Politics and Religion in the Work of Andrew Marvell* (Cambridge, 1983), pp. 236–7, rejects Clarke's attribution on the grounds that it was made many years after Marvell's death, and that the author claims to have been a member of the royalist army; but the only direct claim made by the author is to have seen him engaging in military exercises. John M. Wallace, *Destiny His Choice: The Loyalism of Andrew Marvell* (Cambridge, 1968), p. 30, sees the elegy as signalling Marvell's opposition to the army and support of moves for peace, but does not argue strongly for Marvell's authorship. Michael Craze, *The Life and Lyrics of Andrew Marvell* (1979), pp. 54ff, firmly attributes the elegy to Marvell, noting the echo of *Lycidas*, a poem by which Marvell was heavily influenced. Guild, 'The Politics of Marvell's Early "Royalist" Poems', 129ff, argues for the attribution but queries its royalism. John Rogers, *The Matter of Revolution: Science, Poetry, and Politics in the Age of Milton* (Ithaca and London, 1996), p. 91, notes an apparent echo of the Villiers elegy, lines 81–2, in 'Upon Appleton House', lines 355–6.

128 Harold Love, *Scribal Publication in Seventeenth-Century England* (Oxford, 1993), p. 63; Love considers that doubts about Marvell's authorship 'display a naïve attitude towards the politics of patronage as they affected the scribal medium'.

The poem opens with an address to Fame, evoking the world of the rival newsbooks which constantly printed rumours of the deaths of enemies; Fame would rather have told of the deaths of Cromwell or Fairfax. Having begun by rebuking her, however, the poem holds back with an echo of *Lycidas*:

Yet what couldst thou have done? 'tis alwayes late
To struggle with inevitable fate. (lines 11–12)

The Miltonic echo reads as if a passage from *Mercurius Elencticus* has suddenly been interrupted by an intrusion from Hall's *Mercurius Britanicus*. After this moment of resignation, the poet goes on to call for revenge, but much of the rest of the poem turns from public to private matters. Villiers's death is compared to the assassination of his father, who is discreetly unmentioned in other elegies, but the king himself is nowhere directly mentioned. Remarkably in an elegy, hardly anything is said of Villiers's moral virtues; what is celebrated is his beauty and his role in the 'Monarchy of Love' (line 60). He is presented as part of a private, aesthetic and semi-sacramental space; the kind of space that became claustrophobic in 'Flecknoe'. He is like a coin so perfectly minted that it bears its stamp without any distortion, or clay buried in the earth to form crystal for a royal feast. Marvell was later to use this china analogy pejoratively to attack the brittle sterility of monarchs.[129] Villiers is described as being 'of purpose made' (line 49), like a decorative ornament: he 'scarcely seems begotten but bequeathd' (line 38). Buckingham had sold off the collection of pictures Northumberland had saved for him to fund the rising, and it is almost as if his brother is himself one of these artefacts. The poet draws analogies from nature as well as art. Villiers and his mistress are placed in a libertine paradise where they 'restore man unto his first estate' contrary to 'honours tyrannous respect' (lines 78–9). Villiers is compared to Adonis, and his death is eroticized, with Venus hurrying him to the 'immortall shade' of her garden (line 114). It is interesting that the poem shares the Adonis analogy with Hall's newsbook. If Marvell did write the poem, he was taking further the sympathy he had shown in the Lovelace poem for cavalier eroticism, a sympathy which Hall to some degree shared. Hall had, however, come to criticize the cavalier discourse of love and war for separating private aristocratic concerns from the public interest. There is perhaps a note of strain in the way the elegy so determinedly abstracts Villiers's beauty from the public world, and then in its closing lines turns back savagely to warfare:

And we hereafter to his honour will
Not write so many, but so many kill.
Till the whole Army by just vengeance come
To be at once his Trophee and his Tombe. (lines 125–8)

---

129 See *The First Anniversary*, lines 19–22.

The motivation for fighting is a personal vengeance; in closing its concerns so firmly within a private dynastic space, the poem resists the sublime. The idea with which it ends, that fighting is superior to writing, was to open Marvell's 'Horatian Ode' two years later. If Marvell did write the Villiers poem, he had certainly undergone political changes. But the foregoing analysis has shown that there could have been continuities as well.

'Dissention more then Civil': Milton, May and the aftermath of the Second Civil War, 1648–1649

The Villiers elegist's call to arms rang hollow. If there had been a unified and coherent royalist cause, perhaps the formidable military obstacle of the New Model Army could have been overcome. But in fact the different risings failed to coalesce. The national divisions which Wither had lamented could work against the king as well as Parliament. The government managed to make enough concessions to London Presbyterians to keep them loyal, and the deep divisions in Scotland meant that military aid from the north arrived too late. Fairfax and Cromwell mopped up the remaining resistance.

By August 1648 the nation had come once more to an uneasy peace. Once again, as in the Rous ode of 1647, Milton chose that situation to write a poem in the Horatian manner which aimed to crystallize the situation, turning from martial to civic affairs:

> Fairfax, whose name in armes through Europe rings
>   Filling each mouth with envy, or with praise,
>   And all her jealous monarchs with amaze,
>   And rumors loud, that daunt remotest kings,
>
> Thy firm unshak'n vertue ever brings
>   Victory home, though new rebellions raise
>   Thir Hydra heads, & the fals North displaies
>   her brok'n league, to impe their serpent wings,
>
> O yet a nobler task awaites thy hand;
>   For what can Warr, but endless war still breed,
>   Till Truth, & Right from Violence be freed,
>
> And Public Faith cleard from the shamefull brand
>   Of Public Fraud. In vain doth Valour bleed
>   While Avarice, & Rapine share the land.[130]

---

130 Milton, 'On the Lord Gen. *Fairfax* at the siege of Colchester' (Sonnet 15), from the Trinity MS, as transcribed in the Scolar Press facsimile, *John Milton: Poems* (Menston, 1972), p. 47.

This is the first of Milton's poems fully to deserve the title of 'heroic sonnet', following sixteenth-century Italian poets who had used variations in diction and word order to give an elevated, Horatian timbre to a verse-form often associated with bland panegyric. The sonnet on public themes in fact went back to Petrarch, and Milton may have known that Fairfax himself had translated one of Petrarch's celebrated denunciations of the Roman church.[131] He may also have heard of the political sonnets of the man whom he was to succeed as Secretary for Foreign Tongues, the German exile Georg Rudolf Weckherlin. Enjoying a substantial reputation as a poet in his native country, Weckherlin had addressed heroic sonnets to pillars of the Protestant cause. One of his odes was addressed in vigorously anti-courtly terms to Sir Oliver Fleming, who was to become Master of Ceremonies to the Commonwealth.[132] Milton's sonnet, however, differs in tone from Petrarch and Weckherlin, its idiom being more secular and Roman than apocalyptic. And it is Roman in a distinctively republican sense.

The Horatian analogy only goes so far: as in the Rous poem, there is no question of looking to the monarch to restore the nation. Unlike the Villiers elegy and many other royalist poems, but like Hall's celebrations of Parliamentary leaders, the sonnet places Fairfax's actions very firmly in a public context. His 'vertue' has the Latinate sense of military courage, but the latter part of the sonnet implies that it also has a more specifically republican, or Machiavellian, sense of civic activism.[133] The positioning first of 'each mouth' and then of 'jealous monarchs' as the object of 'Filling' brings home the effect of Fairfax's name as being crammed into unwilling monarchical mouths, of Parliamentary language overcoming regal discourse. This language is then passed on as 'rumors loud', and the first line's already hyperbolical 'through Europe' is surpassed by the vision of the army's victories passing ever further to daunt 'remotest kings'. The poem is very clear about the ideological nature of fame. If its opening is calculated to bring a blush to the cheek

---

131 'A Carracter of the Romish Church by Francisco Petrarca', printed from Bodleian MS Fairfax 40, pp. 604–5, in *The Poems of Thomas Third Lord Fairfax*, ed. Edward Bliss Reed, *Transactions of the Connecticut Academy of Arts and Sciences* 14 (1909), 237–90 (282–3).

132 There is evidence that Weckherlin knew Milton's Italian sonnets: Leo Miller, 'Milton and Weckherlin', *Milton Quarterly* 16 (1982), 1–3. Weckherlin was a significant figure in seventeenth-century German literature, and a comparative study would be revealing. On his political views see Leonard Forster, *Georg Rudolf Weckherlin: Zur Kenntnis seines Lebens in England* (Basel, 1944), pp. 166ff, and for a survey in English, Norbrook, *PP*, pp. 216, 228, 276, 281; for the heroic sonnets see *Georg Rudolf Weckherlins Gedichte*, ed. Hermann Fischer, 3 vols. (Tübingen, 1894–1907), I, 423ff, II, 309, 329ff, and for the poem to Fleming, II, 250–6.

133 When Edward Phillips published the poem in 1694, 'vertue' had become 'valour': a discreet toning down?

of the celebratedly modest Fairfax[134], the praise is then given a slight edge. His name is in every mouth, but not always in positive terms, and more attention is given to the hostility of his enemies than to his allies' praise. His actions do indeed arouse wonder, as is appropriate for the sublime struggle for liberty, and the praise is all the higher because it comes from his enemies. But we never forget that his fame is not static and monumental but has a militant effect. Milton sees English events in a European perspective; he is already anticipating the *Defences* in revelling in the impact England's victories against its king will have on the Continent. Milton links the hostile hydra with the proliferating rebellions of 1648.[135] The reference to the rebels' 'serpent' wings evokes the Latin sense of 'creeping', offering a strong oxymoron to bring home the contrast between the sublimity and elevation of the Parliamentary forces and the dubious, indeed Satanic, aspirations of the rebels, a kind of parody of the sublime.

Though the poem's octave celebrates military victory, this elevation risks collapse in the final lines, which establish a sharp contrast between the ills defeated in war and the comparable hydra-like proliferation of civil evils that have yet to be confronted. Some of the abstractions would have been given force by the political context. The vigorous alliterative juxtaposition of 'Public Faith' and 'Public Fraud' draws attention to Parliament's betrayal of those who had given it financial support – as has been seen, this was also a concern of Wither's, voiced again in a petition that August.[136] Milton's conversion of 'faith' into 'fraud' violently undermines a catchphrase of his own party.

But how far can the very general advice for the defence of truth and right be translated into a specific programme? In the late summer of 1648, Fairfax was coming under a lot of pressure for some very definite action. At about the time Milton probably wrote the sonnet, just after the fall of Colchester, the committed republican MP Edmund Ludlow went to Colchester to warn Fairfax that the cause was being betrayed. Presbyterian strength in Parliament had been rallying, and a number of leading Independents, alarmed at the groundswell of political discontent even amongst those who had avoided rising openly for the king, and anxious to hold their coalition together, had made political concessions. The Vote of No Addresses had been suspended, and negotiations began at Newport for a new peace treaty. To Ludlow it seemed that everything that had been fought for was in danger of being thrown away. He urged Fairfax to purge Parliament – a demand which, as has

---

134 Though a triumph was held to greet Fairfax's entry to London in November 1646, con-
    temporary accounts claim that he listened very modestly: Joshua Sprigge, *Anglia
    Rediviva* (1647; S5070), pp. 315, 317.
135 Cf. Wither, *Prosopopoeia Britannica*, p. 3: 'SEE, SEE! how MISCHIEF, like the *Lernean
    Snake*, Renewes her heads, and still new life doth take!'
136 George Wither, *A Si Quis*, in *Ecchoes from the Sixth Trumpet*, pp. 119–25.

been seen, Wither strongly supported. Fairfax blandly 'declared himself resolved to use the power he had, to maintain the cause of the publick, upon a clear and evident call'; Ludlow concluded 'by such a general answer that he was irresolute'.[137] Irresolute Fairfax may have been – he was far less confident on civilian than military matters – but as head of the armed forces he was at least nominally in charge of the ongoing negotiations between radicals in the army and in Parliament. He was eventually involved, however distantly, in the purge of Parliament by Colonel Pride that December.[138] The republican ethos of Milton's octave suggests that the task awaiting Fairfax's hand may have been just such a purge. Radicals were calling more and more vehemently for the king to be tried for treason: might one of the hydra-heads the Herculean Fairfax was to chop off be the king's?

Against such a conclusion, of course, there stands the poem's strong resistance to military solutions: 'what can Warr, but endless warr still breed' (or 'Acts of War' in the 1694 text). In that question lay what was already emerging as the central dilemma of English republicanism. As Marvell tersely phrased the idea:

> The same *Arts* that did *gain*
> A *Pow'r* must it *maintain*.
>   ('Horatian Ode', lines 119–20)

In *Prosopopoeia Britannica* Wither had analysed a nation in systemic crisis, but had expressed the hope that somehow the king might be persuaded to patch it up; in envisaging a more radical transition to a new form of supremacy, he had given no idea of the specific means. If the nation was indeed in such crisis, it seemed that only an external force could reform its institutions. The New Model Army indignantly denied that it was 'external': it held itself to be no mere mercenary army but the expression of a general public interest. The fact remained that for many citizens it was illegitimately meddling in affairs in which it had no concern. In the political situation of late 1648, however, there was no other force to which those who had abandoned hope in Charles could turn. It seemed that the effect of all the renewed bloodshed of the Second Civil War was to be a return to the kinds of long-drawn-out deals with the king that would gradually erode everything so far gained in halting his encroachments. The only option was to depose the king and either elect another or found a republic. A republic on a classic pattern would have to be established from above, without a strong basis in popular support, if it were to be established at all. Why, after all, address a sonnet to Fairfax on his

---

137 *Memoirs of Edmund Ludlow*, I, 203–04.
138 David Underdown, *Pride's Purge: Politics in the Puritan Revolution* (Oxford, 1971), pp. 135, 189ff.

civil obligations unless it was expected that he would make a decisive intervention? Yet that conclusion brought Milton back in a circle: if the aim was to move from military to civil virtues, it was deeply ironic for the means to be military ones.

The previous year, Joshua Sprigge had ended a book in praise of the New Model Army with an account of Fairfax's ceremonial reception in November 1646 which drew a parallel with a celebrated episode in Lucan:

> never had *Julius Caesar* the honor in those *Civil wars* when he came to *Rome* as a *Conquerour*; one poor *Metellus* confronts him and gives check to his Victory, sweld spirit, breaking up the Doors of *Saturnes Temple*: Indeed there is a manifest cause of difference; *Caesar* did not plead the *Senates* cause did not fight for the *Roman* Liberties. The *Senate* fled when *Caesar* drew neare, but his Excellencies Warre was the Parliments *Peace*; by his *Motion* they sat *still*.[139]

At the beginning Sprigge had adapted the speech of Lucan's Pompey to rally the republicans:

> blood has already dy'de
> *Caesars* polluted swords: (ii. 536; May, sig. C6r)

to show that the Parliamentary cause was merely defensive:

> Blood had already dy'de
> The King's stain'd sword, and God did well provide
> That there the mischief should begin, and we
> First suffer wrong. —- Let no man call our Arms
> Offensive wars; but for received harms
> Our Countries just revenging ire.[140]

And after recounting the battle of Naseby he offered a '*counter-prospective*' of what would have happened had Parliament lost, and quoted, again in May's version, from Lucan's account of Caesar's advance on Rome.[141] Sprigge felt it necessary to go to some length to show that Fairfax was not a Caesar, as if many people thought otherwise. And yet a Fairfax who was an indecisive Pompey might also be a threat to liberty. The republicans were to be impaled on the horns of this dilemma for many years to come.

May himself, as Parliament's official historian, would have read Sprigge's recycling of his own lines attentively. Though the first instalment of his history, published in mid-1647, had ended on the upbeat note of the relief of Gloucester, its continuation, published after the regicide as the *Breviary*, was much darker in tone. As a close friend and drinking companion of the militant republicans Henry Marten and Thomas Chaloner, May might have been expected to present the establishment of the republic as part of a steady,

---

139 Sprigge, *Anglia Rediviva*, pp. 315–16. 140 Sprigge, *Anglia Rediviva*, p. 4.
141 Sprigge, *Anglia Rediviva*, p. 41.

inevitable historical evolution. Instead, his account has a somewhat Lucanian gloom about the forces remorselessly pushing towards tyranny. He introduces the peace following the First Civil War with an adaptation of Lucan's opening: 'the Civil War being ended, a dissention more then Civil arose among the Conquerors'. He also compares the foreign armies Charles tries to enlist to Marius's and introduces the Second Civil War with a simile from Lucan.[142] May laments that London had repudiated its own principles so far that Parliament could meet there only under military protection. He emphasizes Charles's endless propensity for intrigue and dissimulation, so that the readiness of the Presbyterians to negotiate with him emerges as an astonishing blindness. He presents the debate on the Vote of No Addresses as recognizing that England was a *de facto* republic: nothing remained in January 1649 but to settle the Commonwealth without the king. The trouble was that the people's unquiet minds could not be appeased by rational argument; force alone could prevent conspiracies. By the spring of 1648, Parliament, though victorious, was never in more danger (p. 185), and the king was more formidable that summer than ever before, since the 'pity of the Vulgar gave a greater Majesty to his Person' (p. 186). May emphasizes Fairfax's military skill and courage in dealing with each 'new head of this *Hydra*' (p. 195 – cf. Milton's sonnet). Amazingly, however, the Presbyterians failed to praise Fairfax and Cromwell but instead led the way in re-opening negotiations with the discredited king (p. 210). When he comes to narrating the events leading up to the regicide, May abandons any attempt at a causal sequence: 'another strange alteration happened; which threw the King from the heighth of honor into the lowest condition' (p. 212).

This evasiveness about agency possibly reflects some unease on May's part about the regicide. The book ends lamely with the claim that 'because the full search and enarration of so great a business would make an History by it self, it cannot well be brought into this Breviary, which having passed over so long a time, shall here conclude' (p. 215). The army, having been celebrated as the main agency in preventing a return to tyranny, suddenly drops out of the picture, and a series of passive verbs presents the king's trial and execution as a kind of accident. It is as if May's model of political analysis is so habitually dark that he finds it hard to come to terms with success. Royalists were appealing to Virgilian and Horatian analogues in hoping for a *deus ex machina* in the case of a royal restoration; a *deus ex machina* in the shape of the absence of a king was harder to envisage. Perhaps, however, he still finds a darkness in the fact that the republic had to be imposed by force on a people who were obstinately immune to the kinds of argument he considers rational.

At the time he wrote the Fairfax sonnet, Milton seems to have been at least

---

142 May, *Breviary*, pp. 156, 101 (citing ii. 96–8) and 185 (citing v.565–7).

as dark about the English people's readiness for a republic. He had probably begun work on his *History of Britain*, a work which quickly confounds any expectation that it would be an epideictic nationalistic work.[143] On the contrary, it presents the island's history as a series of opportunities for enlightened liberty each of which was lost not only because of foreign invasion but because of the lack of civility and moral discipline. When he comes to the fall of the Roman Empire, he shows how the Britons lamentably failed to take this opportunity for civility without tyranny. And it is in beginning to narrate this period that Milton draws an explicit parallel with the present moment, which he terms 'this intereign' (V:1, 129). He expanded on the parallels in an extensive 'Digression'. There has been much scholarly controversy over the date of the 'Digression'; 1647, 1648, 1649 – in the period between the regicide and the settlement of the form of government – and 1660 are all candidates.[144] It seems impossible to settle the argument decisively; but the claim that it is too pessimistic to have been written in the late 1640s fails to do justice to the gloom at this period of so many Parliamentarians with republican leanings. Nurtured in Lucan and other chroniclers of the decline of liberty, they were well aware that the arrest of tendencies towards tyranny was an enormously difficult enterprise. The Rous ode of 1647 and the letter to Dati of that year indicate Milton's low expectations for political renewal. As has been seen, Wither was undergoing violent oscillations between hopes of national reconciliation and the belief that there was no real hope of recovery from a superstitiously monarchical people, an irredeemably corrupt Parliament and a narcissistic and self-willed king. May likewise regarded Britain in the years 1647–49 as set on a course towards tyranny that would have been inexorable had military force not intervened. Milton's 'this intereign' could refer to that whole period. His comment that the people 'had bin kept warme a while by the affected zele of thir pulpits' (V:1, 449) recalls Wither's strictures on the abuse of the language of godliness. Both in the 'Digression' and in the Fairfax sonnet he joined Wither in attacking the abuse of the 'public faith', and his long account of the anguish involved in following financial affairs through

143 Milton himself declared that he began the history in 1649, but Hartlib reported in June or July 1648 that he was working on a history; for differing datings of the work's inception, see *MPW* V:1, xxxvii–xl, and Nicholas von Maltzahn, *Milton's 'History of Britain': Republican Historiography in the English Revolution* (Oxford, 1991), p. 28 n. 20.

144 For 1647 see *MPW*, V:1, 433; Austin Woolrych argues for 1660, von Maltzahn for 1649; and further debate in Austin Woolrych, 'Dating Milton's *History of Britain*', *Historical Journal* 36 (1993), 929–43 and Nicholas von Maltzahn, 'Dating the Digression in Milton's *History of Britain*', *Historical Journal* 36 (1993), 945–56. Worden, 'Marchamont Nedham and the Beginnings of English Republicanism', *RLCS*, 45–81 (p. 417 n. 27), favours 1649 but gives 1648 as his second choice. Janel Mueller, 'The Mastery of Decorum: Politics as Poetry in Milton's Sonnets', *Critical Inquiry* 13 (1986–7), 475–508 (492ff) persuasively links Milton's sonnets with the digression.

Parliamentary committees is very close to Wither's. Like Wither, he found a near-universal devotion to private ends as opposed to the public interest. Milton in the 'Digression' differs from Wither mainly in the all-embracing dismissal of the potential of the English people. However despairing Wither may become, he is ready to be reassured that there may still be good men in Parliament.

If Milton offers much less in the way of hope, it is partly because he is a less humane writer, but also because of his greater constitutional radicalism. Though Wither has republican leanings, he is ready to accept a compromise with monarchy. Milton is not; but he feels himself very acutely in a minority. The only way fully to secure the public interest is to institutionalize it in the form of the state, as a republic. But here, he believes, he faces the lack of a specifically republican culture in England. There is a vicious circle: republican culture is impossible without republican institutions of education and politics, but those institutions depend on the culture. Military force may be able to break out of the circle, but at the potentially fatal cost of undermining the values of civility. Whenever he wrote it, his analysis of the Britons' loss of their 'occasion' reveals an acerbity that always underlay his moments of political optimism:

> For libertie hath a sharp and double edge fitt onelie to be handl'd by just and vertuous men, to bad and dissolute it become[s] a mischief unwieldie in thir own hands . . . the heroic wisdo[m] which is requir'd surmounted far the principle[s] of narrow politicians: what wonder then if the[y] sunke as those unfortunate Britans before them[,] entangl'd and oppress'd with things too hard and generous above thir straine and temper. For Britain (to speake a truth not oft spok'n) as it is a land fruitful enough of men stout and couragious in warr, so is it naturallie not over fertil of men able to govern justlie & prudently in peace; trusting onelie on thir Mother-witt, as most doo, & consider not that civilitie, prudence, love of the public more then of money or vaine honour are to this soile in a manner outlandish; grow not here but in minds well implanted with solid & elaborate breeding; too impolitic els and too crude, if not headstrong and intractable to the industrie and vertue either of executing or understanding true civil government: Valiant indeed and prosperous to winn a field, but to know the end and reason of winning, unjudicious and unwise, in good or bad success alike unteachable. For the sunn, which wee want ripens witts as well as fruits; and as wine and oyle are imported to us from abroad, so must ripe understanding and many civil vertues bee imported into our minds from forren writings & examples of best ages: wee shall else miscarry still and com short in the attempt of any great enterprise. Hence did thir victories prove as fruitless as thir losses dangerous, and left them still conquering under the same grievances that men suffer conquerd[.] (v:1, 449–51)

The conclusion of this passage strikingly resembles that of the Fairfax sonnet; in each case the central theme is the distinction between martial and civic virtue. The establishment of a republic would be a sublime act, and Milton presents its failure as an entanglement in narrow, constricting bonds. The people are 'unteachable'.

That is indeed an extraordinary remark to come from the author of the soaring panegyrics of the English people in *Areopagitica*. And even if we date the 'Digression' to a later period, the early books of the *History* in themselves reveal a striking loss of faith. They do scant justice to the determination with which the Levellers were fighting for their cause: for all his partial openness to democratic tendencies, Milton remained in some ways rigidly insensitive to their virtues. He might address a sonnet to Fairfax, but he did not publish it in a newsbook to bring it into the public sphere. He never joined the Leveller poets who later in the year mourned one of their leaders, Colonel Thomas Rainsborough:

> that precious flame,
> Whose heat divine once beautifi'd his frame,
> Lives 'bove your rage, and in our thoughts we find,
> The fair re-publique built in his brave mind[.][145]

That tribute, however, shows how uncertain the Levellers too were about the future. The less willing they were to compromise with the grandees, the less likely it was that a republic would ever exist save in the mind, but to compromise was to sacrifice a republic's aims. To that extent, their perception of events was not so different from Milton's disillusion.

To describe a political analysis in terms of a psychological state can be misleading, however. Milton's writing even at its most personal is always focussed on rhetorical and ideological factors. Concurrently with the *History*, he was to launch into hyperbolical praise of the English vindication of liberty in the *Defences*. When writing with an immediate polemical aim he was always ready to idealize the people; the *History*, however, aims at a detached, long-term analysis of power relations, and here it is essential to focus on weaknesses if they are ever to be overcome in the future. In the Roman sections we can see Milton's narrative voice straining to achieve some kind of Archimedean point outside both British and Roman self-interest. As is shown by the currency of the *Pharsalia*, the republican tradition incorporated not so much a disillusioned as a tragic view of history, aware of the extreme difficulty of overcoming structural tendencies towards private interest and tyranny. Whether or not we accept that *Samson Agonistes* may have been drafted in this period, Milton was much concerned with Greek tragedy, and most admired the disturbing, questioning generic instability of Euripides.[146] Milton

---

145 *Mercurius Militaris* no. 5, p. [38].
146 Smith, *LR*, p. 375 n. 83. For the argument that the quotations from Euripides in *De Doctrina Christiana* support Milton's authorship, see David Norbrook, 'Euripides, Milton, and *Christian Doctrine*', *MQ* 29 (1995), 37–41.

proposed the *History of Britain* as a possible source for poets, but whereas early legend was often used for heroic and ultimately optimistic subjects, his own drafts for works on British themes concentrated on tragedy – not just the tragedy of individuals, but social and political tragedies.

Yet tragedy for Milton did not imply the quietistic acceptance of an unchanging natural order, just as Lucan's half-acceptance that the gods had ordained Caesarism's triumph did not prevent his urging that their will should be resisted. What tragedy did imply was the extreme precariousness of political and ethical triumph, the ease with which it could collapse altogether; that awareness could serve as an incentive to action rather than as an existential despair. Milton cannot have meant his claim that the English were 'unteachable' quite literally, for he was proposing a programme of republican education which he clearly believed could bear fruit if there were only time. On the other hand, when he described the Irish as 'indocible' (III, 304), he was making the claim that they were so lacking in the potential for civility that they were beyond redemption. The *History* and still more the 'Digression' testify to how precariously he believed the English themselves were evading that fate. Yet the Fairfax sonnet indicated a conviction that decisive action might turn potential tragedy into republican triumph. It did; at a predictable price.

5

Defending the Commonwealth, 1649–1653

Regicide as restoration: Milton in the vanguard

On 6 December 1648, the republican moment of which Milton had started to despair suddenly opened up. Troops descended on the House of Commons and Colonel Pride prevented Members who had been identified as 'malignant' from taking their seats. Negotiations with the king were broken off; instead, preparations were made to put him on trial for treason in a specially convened court. The king refused to answer any of the charges because he would not recognize the court. Some of the organizers of the trial had expected that it would lead to his deposition and the substitution of another candidate for the throne. Charles made any such compromise impossible, and he was executed on 30 January 1649.

The regicide provoked angry and anguished reactions throughout Britain and Europe. Charles's death was compared to the Crucifixion; again and again the regicide was presented as a complete break with the old order, a betrayal of all the values in which Englishmen had believed. These views were crystallized by the appearance of the king's pietistic testament, the *Eikon Basilike*, which became an unprecedented best-seller. It went through sixty editions in England and elsewhere within a year of its first appearance. The king became, for admirers, and for many later literary critics, an emblem of a dying order, a lost union of church, state and aesthetic beauty which had been disrupted by a brutal modern impiety and philistinism. The propaganda of the most high-flying royalists, however, should not be taken too readily at face value.

It is true that the loss of the monarchy disconcerted many even of Parliament's leaders. This was a republic reluctant to speak its name: it was some months after the regicide before the monarchy was abolished, and the regime's official utterances often tried to play down anti-monarchical sentiment. This inevitably inhibited the growth of a fully self-conscious republican rhetoric. Attempts by Marten and other militants to initiate a nation-wide oath of loyalty, ultimately modelled on Lucius Junius Brutus's policy after the overthrow of Tarquin, dwindled into the very cautious oath known as the 'engagement'.[1] The purged Parliament became derisively known as 'the Rump', and is often seen as defensively clinging to the political ways formed in the war conditions of the 1640s rather than radically breaking with tradition.[2] It is indeed misleading to describe all supporters of the government as 'republicans', given that many of them were waiting for some new form of monarchical settlement or had accepted the end of monarchy merely from fear of a worse outcome. If a new republic were one day to be established in England, and Continental styles of nomenclature adopted, perhaps the necessary term for its ancestor would be not the First but the Noughth Republic.

One may gain the impression from some accounts of the period that the English founded their republic, as they allegedly founded their Empire, in a fit of absence of mind. Yet this is to underestimate the extent to which confidently republican political, ceremonial and rhetorical forms did begin to emerge. Too often the rhetorical brilliance of Charles's strategy in the *Eikon Basilike* has allowed some of its premises to stand as facts rather than as polemical reworkings of a considerably different history. To take the state of England in the 1630s as the ideal base-line from which any deviation entailed total catastrophe, the assumption of the king's more rapturous elegists, is to give a very selective account of a past history that was marked by Harrington's repeated 'jumps' between different tendencies. The fact that a reply to *Eikon Basilike* was composed by England's leading poet should itself give pause to the idea that the monarchical order was inextricably bound up with poetry, and that the idea of a republic was beyond available linguistic resources.[3] As will be seen in this chapter, there was a significant continuity in the cultural politics of the new republic from the alliances that were being formed in the later 1640s. Once more Milton took

1 Sarah Barber, 'The Engagement for the Council of State and the Establishment of the Commonwealth Government', *Historical Research* 63 (1990), 44–57; see John M. Wallace, 'The Engagement Controversy 1649–52: An Annotated List of Pamphlets', *Bulletin of the New York Public Library* 68 (1964), 384–405.

2 This analysis predominates in what is still much the best study of the period's politics, Blair Worden, *The Rump Parliament* (Cambridge, 1974). For a different view, see Sean Kelsey, *Inventing a Republic: The Political Culture of the English Commonwealth 1649–1653* (Manchester, 1997).

3 For a recent statement of this argument see Kevin Sharpe, 'An "Image doting rabble"? The Failure of Republican Culture in Seventeenth Century England', in Kevin Sharpe and Steven N. Zwicker (eds.), *Refiguring Revolution: Aesthetics and Politics from the English Revolution to the Romantic Revolution* (Berkeley, Los Angeles and London, forthcoming). Elizabeth Skerpan, *The Rhetoric of Politics in the English Revolution 1642–1660* (Columbia and London, 1992), pp. 99ff, clearly brings out the difficulties faced by the republicans but overstates the extent to which they were arguing completely outside traditional discourses. Smith, *LR*, pp. 182ff, offers the fullest counterview to date.

the lead, but he was followed by several other poets in rallying to the young republic.

Of course, there was a central, and massive, discontinuity. Most attempted settlements of the 1640s had assumed that the king would be retained, albeit with limited powers. It had become increasingly clear, however, that he would never resign himself to a merely ceremonial role; still less would he grant the degree of religious toleration demanded by the Independents. His execution was an extreme measure which involved overriding the law, and it thus provoked opposition not only from the king's supporters but from Levellers and other civilian politicians who feared the power of the army. James Harrington, John Hutchinson, Algernon Sidney and Sir Henry Vane were amongst those who opposed the purge or the trial or both. Cromwell himself had been hesitant about extreme measures.[4] It is possible to distinguish between constitutional republicans and the 'regicides', those religious radicals, mainly in the army, whose main concern was the removal of Charles in person as an idolatrous 'man of blood', rather than of the royal office.

But that distinction had also become blurred in the crisis of 1648–49. As has been seen, Ludlow had urged Fairfax for military intervention in a situation which seemed to allow no other outcome but a return to an unfettered Caroline regime. Another staunch republican, Lord Grey of Groby, helped Pride to identify the Purge's victims, and Marten, after some apparent hesitation, fully endorsed it: the Purge can be read as a joint move of civilian and military republicans.[5] Though the regicide was an arbitrary act, it could also be seen as forming a continuity with earlier decisive actions, from the army's putting down of the Presbyterians in 1647 back to Strafford's trial. Justifications for that trial had been ultimately in the name of political necessity, to which the regicides also appealed. In Machiavellian terms, these events formed a succession of 'reductions' bringing the state back to its first principles; the trial and execution of the king formed a further stage in the process. Charles, like Strafford, became an exemplary sacrifice designed to stamp the need for justice in the popular memory. In staging his execution outside the Banqueting House where court masques had been performed, the regicides did indeed imprint his image on the public imagination – though they had severely miscalculated the spectacle's effects. At one stage a group of artists proposed to reinforce the message by redecorating the Banqueting House: at

---

4 However, Noel Henning Mayfield, *Puritans and Regicide: Presbyterian-Independent Differences over the Trial and Execution of Charles (I) Stuart* (Lanham, MD and London, 1988), pp. 18ff, argues that from Gardiner onward historians have exaggerated Cromwell's hesitations about the legitimacy, as opposed to the tactical timing, of the regicide.   5 See Sarah Barber, *Regicide and Revolution*, forthcoming.

8 Great Seal of the Commonwealth, 1651, reverse.

one end there would be a huge group picture of the House of Commons, with the Council of State at the other. The Banqueting House had been laid out during court masques in such a way that the king alone could see the perspective properly; in the new schema, images of collective, impersonal rule would have superseded the ruler's self-glorification.[6]

This message was central to the new Great Seal of the republic (figure 8). Here the king's image was replaced with an animated session of Parliament, with some members listening to a speaker while others are apparently exchanging their own responses. The seal draws on earlier printed and

6 The scheme foundered, mainly from lack of funds: Maija Jansson, 'Remembering Marston Moor: The Politics of Culture', in Susan D. Amussen and Mark A. Kishlansky (eds.), P*olitical Culture and Cultural Politics in Early Modern England* (Manchester and New York, 1995), pp. 255–76.

medallic images of Parliament, but moves far beyond them. Earlier images had normally reproduced the situation at a state opening, with the king in stately silence at the top, the House of Lords around and below him, and the Commons crowding towards the bar in the foreground. The new seal allowed the Commons to move into centre stage and crisply removed the upper hierarchical levels. Instead it presented a circular structure, with a speaker in the process of addressing the House, the clerks recording his speech, and the debate taken up by small groups of members. The title-page to Hobbes's Thucydides had counterposed the responsible debate of a monarchical assembly with democratic chaos; the new seal refused these alternatives.

This design shows signs of the influence of Henry Marten, who had long taken an interest in Parliamentary seals. He had been instrumental, against much opposition, in persuading Parliament to make its own seal back in 1643, risking charges of treason, and in negotiating with the engraver, Thomas Simon.[7] The accompanying inscription placed the seal within the framework of reduction or restoration. The regnal year was replaced by 'In the First Yeare of Freedome by God's Blessing Restored'. According to Aubrey, when it was objected how outrageous it was to present the regicide as a restoration, Marten retorted: 'there was a Text had much troubled his spirit for severall dayes & nights, of the man whose sight was restored that was blind from his mothers womb'.[8] Marten's joke fused the secular language of reduction with Christian terms in a way that was centrally important for the 'good old cause'. The miracle he alluded to, from John's gospel, is explicated by Christ in terms of the opposition between internal and external blindness (John IX.39–41): most people today think they can see but they are spiritually blind.[9]

Marten thus confronted the difficult situation of committed republicans who claimed to speak for the people but knew themselves to be a small minority, and were aware of the regime's imperfections. They could resort to paradox: the abolition of the monarchy was at once a radical innovation and an epiphany of the deeper nature of the nation's institutions. As the legal reformer John Warr put it:

> God sees good that *Liberty* should recover but by degrees, that so the world may
> be ballanced with light and knowledge, according to the advance thereof, and be
> more considerate in her *actings*. The deeper the *Foundation*, the surer the *Work*.
> *Liberty* in its full appearance would darken the eye newly recovered from

7 Alfred and Allan Wyon, *The Great Seals of England* (1887), p. 89.
8 Bodleian MS Aubrey 8, fol. 12v; *ABL*, II, 47. The objection is said to have been made by
  Sir Henry Vane, who would certainly have disliked Marten's facetious use of religious
  language, but there is no contemporary evidence.
9 The regime's supporters also invoked another Biblical restoration, 'Thou shalt be
  called, The repairer of the breach, The restorer of paths to dwell in' (Isaiah LVIII.12):
  Kelsey, *Inventing a Republic*, p. 8.

blindnesse, the principles thereof are infused to us by degrees, that our heads may be *strengthened* (not overturned) by its *Influence*.[10]

Here, as in Marten, the imagery of blindness is closely linked with the Machiavellian language of recovery of first principles. In similar vein, R. Fletcher proclaimed:

> Our fathers were
> Blinded, and we born heires of their feare.
> But our deliv'rance dawns; and Nature seems
> To joy there is a Seed that dare redeem's.

Fletcher viewed the republic as recovering not merely 'Roman hearts' but the natural freedom of Adam. His title, *Radius Heliconicus*, linked the new regime with the growing light of poetic as well as political inspiration.[11] Another of his pamphlets recycled an illustration of a pair of spectacles that had illustrated a pre-regicide tract: political change was leading to a growing recovery of lost sight.[12] Yet another republican graphically registered the effect of the regicide:

> I resolved to look back; as a man that is stunn'd with a stone, looks not after the stone, but after the hand that flung it.

Armed with these 'spectacles', he could reread English history and trace the kingdom's wrongs back to William the Conqueror. This treatise was introduced by engravings of a cat dourly eyeing a nervous King James (figure 9): where the masques had insisted that the king alone had true vision, here the view from below helps to overcome the blindness of self-delusion.[13]

Marten seems to have been behind a move that exemplified the republican strategy of sublime iconoclasm. Following Roman tyrannicidal precedent, the king's statue at the Royal Exchange was beheaded and replaced with the

---

10 John Warr, *The Priviledges of the People* (1649; E541.12), p. 7; also available in Stephen Sedley and Lawrence Kaplan (eds.), *A Spark in the Ashes: The Pamphlets of John Warr* (London and New York, 1992), pp. 80–1.

11 R. Fletcher, *Radius Heliconicus: Or, The Resolution of a Free State* (1651; 669f15.83); on Fletcher's ideology see Adriana McCrea, 'Reason's Muse: Andrew Marvell, R. Fletcher, and the Politics of Poetry in the Engagement Debate', *Albion* 23 (1991), 655–80, and for an interesting analysis of his anti-Augustan use of the couplet (cf. the enjambement of 'were/Blinded'), Roger Pooley, 'The Poets' Cromwell', *Critical Survey* 5 (1993), 223–34 (230–1).

12 R. F[letcher]., *Mercurius Heliconicus. Or, the Result of a Safe Conscience* no. 1 (1651; E622.14), illustrated by the 'paire of Cristall Spectacles' reproduced by Sharon Achinstein, *Milton and the Revolutionary Reader* (Princeton, 1994), p. 157; no. 2 repeated Achinstein's figure 7.

13 [Anthony Weldon], *A Cat may look upon a King* (1652; E1408.2), pp. 1–2. Worden, 'Wit in a Roundhead', in Amussen and Kirklansky (eds.), *Political Culture and Cultural Politics in Early Modern England*, pp. 301–7 (331 n. 73), attributes this tract to Nedham.

9 Title-page to Anthony Weldon [?], *A Cat May Look upon a King*, 1652.

inscription: 'Exit Tyrannus regum Ultimus, anno primo restitutae libertatis Angliae 1648' – 'Exit the tyrant, the last of kings, in the first year of England's restored liberty, 1648[/9]'. Rather than being offered a new statue of a civic leader, citizens were left to contemplate the absence of an image, to reflect on the deficiencies of their former perceptions, and to engage in a process of restoration.[14]

This rhetoric of blindness and iconoclasm had an especial relevance for Milton, whose sight was fading; but it offered a unifying point for many of the regime's supporters. It could bring together the themes of political and of poetic 'restoration'. Like the inhabitants of Plato's cave, the republic's enemies had become fixated on images which might be beautiful but were ultimately deceptive, falsely locating political virtue and agency in a tiny courtly elite. Those who had fought for the king's person while ignoring the public interest he represented, declared a republican judge, 'catcht at the shadow, but let goe the substance'. It was because they were 'looking thorow the false Glasse of their own self-Interest' that royalists saw 'imaginary shakings of Foundations,

14 *CSPD 1650*, p. 261; *JMLR*, II, 319.

overturning of Laws, and confused heaps of Ruines and Distractions.'[15] Milton had already used such language in *Areopagitica* when he wrote that the first appearance of truth comes to our eyes 'blear'd and dimm'd with prejudice and custom'. 'We boast our light,' he wrote; 'but if we look not wisely on the Sun it self, it smites us into darknes . . . The light which we have gain'd, was giv'n us, not to be ever staring on, but by it to discover onward things more remote from our knowledge' (*MPW*, II, 565, 550). Monarchists, he now declared, had been 'so dazzled by the very idea of gazing on the royal splendor that they can see no brilliance or magnificence in honest virtue and freedom' (*First Defence*, *MPW*, IV:1, 507). The regicides had made possible a restored vision:

> Their action endowed with new nobility the laws, the courts, which henceforth were restored to all alike, and above all the figure of justice herself, making her after this notable decision more glorious and precious than she had ever been before. (*MPW*, IV:1, 330).

The act was sublime because it defeated received expectations, and made its witnesses see beyond the external decorum that made the king insist on being treated differently from his subjects, to reveal or 'reduce' his common fallible humanity submitting to the awesome generality of the law. After such a deed, the people should 'plan and perform nothing low or mean, but only what is great and noble' (*MPW*, IV:1, 535). The regicide had set a marker that had to be lived up to. It had taught 'lawless Kings, and all who so much adore them, that not mortal man, or his imperious will, but Justice is the onely true sovran and supreme Majesty upon earth' (*The Tenure of Kings and Magistrates*, *MPW*, III, 237). The king, who had tried to make the law into 'his own privat reason', was reminded in the most forceful way possible that no citizen was above the law, which was 'public reason, the enacted reason of a Parlament' (*Eikonoklastes*, *MPW*, III, 360). A later republican, Catharine Macaulay, was recognizably in the same tradition when she wrote of the regicide: 'Fond and stubborn as are the prejudices of vulgar minds to precedent and custom, whatever is sublime in nature or in art is no sooner known than venerated . . . Monarchy, stripped of its trappings, and exposed to the eye of reason, becomes odious in the comparison'.[16]

The sublimity of the act was reinforced by its openness to the public sphere. The king had been brought down from the eminence of his mysteries of state and forced to engage in debate with his people. The trial formed the

---

15 *Sergeant Thorpe Judge of Assize for the Northern Circuit, His Charge* (1649; E558.6), pp. 1, 11.

16 Catharine Macaulay, *The History of England from the Accession of James I to the Elevation of the House of Hanover*, V (1771), 19. The occasion of this reflection is Owen Roe O'Neill's gravitating towards the republic in 1649 (see chapter 6 below).

occasion for Milton to break several years of public silence. His defence of the proceedings in *The Tenure of Kings and Magistrates* was begun before judgement had been passed on the king and appeared soon afterwards as one of the very first defences of the new regime in print. Milton insisted that the trial would give no offence 'to men whose serious consideration thereof hath left no certain precept, or example undebated' (*Observations upon the Articles of Peace*, MPW, III, 311). The regime was keen to emphasize that the execution of Charles differed from earlier regicides by not being committed 'in darkness, and in corners': rather than a private tyrannicide, this was an event in the public sphere – distorted though the communication might be by military force.[17] The deliberations of 'a *Publique State*', Henry Robinson insisted, were 'more open to the view of the world' than those of a monarchy.[18] This was one reason why the regime took the calculated risk of allowing full reporting of every stage of the trial in the newsbooks, even though this meant relaying Charles's sharp retorts against his judges. Both the trial and the execution, as Lois Potter writes, 'were dominated by a disagreement as to what constituted authentic speech'.[19] The king refused to recognize the authority of the court, and his comments then and on the scaffold were brief, maintaining the mystique and mystery of kingship, whereas the trial's organizers hoped for an open confrontation between opposing political philosophies.

In the week before the king's execution, the journalist Daniel Border had reflected on the steady emergence of a critical readership in a political public sphere. In the days of Elizabeth people had been

> rather guided by the tradition of their Fathers, than by acting principles in reason and knowledge: But to the contrary in these our dayes, the meanest sort of people are not only able to write, &c. but to argue and discourse on matters of highest concernment; and thereupon do desire, that such things which are most remarkable, may be truly committed to writing, and made publique, expecting to receive such satisfaction out of the variety of the present several actings, as may content all indifferent men, and stop the mouthes of wilful opposers.[20]

These remarks were an introduction to the new draft of the *Agreement of the People*. In this sense the medium was the message: the *Agreement* based its democratic case on the widespread politically literate audience to which Border was appealing.

The risk the government had taken was that the public would not share its

---

17 *A Declaration of the Parliament of England* (1649; E548.12), p. 14. Milton translated this into Latin.

18 [Henry Robinson], *A Short Discourse Between Monarchical and Aristocratical Government* (1649; E575.31), p. 12.

19 Lois Potter, *Secret Rites and Secret Writing: Royalist Literature, 1641–1660* (Cambridge, 1989), p. 168.

20 *The Perfect Weekly Account* no. 45, 17–28 January 1649, E540.2, p. 357.

view of the situation. The burgeoning sales of *Eikon Basilike* soon showed that this was the case. This, though, was not necessarily because the people were united in devotion to absolutism. Many of the book's purchasers would have been able paradoxically to assimilate Charles to another popular hero of 1649. John Lilburne's trial later in the year was cheered on by royalists even though he stood for principles antithetical to Charles's assertion on the scaffold that a subject and a sovereign were clear different things.[21] Lilburne had strongly opposed the king's trial and execution, which he saw as consolidating the army grandees' arbitrary power. For Lilburne it became an image of oligarchical injustice rather than republican heroism; appeals to its sublimity could look like an evasion of law rather than an appeal to higher laws. Having steadily dismantled older monopolies of trade and discourse, the House of Commons had ended up as the ultimate monopoly, with a power in many ways undreamt of by former monarchs. The constitutional innovation of a powerful Council of State aroused fears of an unaccountable oligarchy. In May 1649 Gilbert Mabbott, a long-serving licenser, was rebuked by the Council of State for allowing Lilburne's new *Agreement of the People* to appear, and for not being tough enough on the Leveller newsbook *The Moderate*; later in the month he resigned in protest.

The author of *Areopagitica* was defending a regime which had brought control of the press to a new height. This inconsistency was seized on by contemporary royalists and has been made much of by later commentators. Milton does seem to have been uneasy about Parliament's retention and strengthening of its licensing mechanism: he told Hartlib in 1650, quite wrongly, that licences were not needed for books, and was ready to defend the regime's openmindedness by appealing to *Areopagitica*.[22] As has been seen, however, *Areopagitica* was concerned with more general issues than press licensing; it was also a manifesto for the Independent party, defending a struggle for political liberty and religious toleration, with a strong republican colouring. When a German visitor noted in 1651 that *Areopagitica* had been a prophecy of the nation's coming freedom, he showed awareness of these continuities.[23] The republic of 1649, for all its shortcomings, was still closer to a defence of religious toleration than its main enemies, for whom toleration

---

21 On Lilburne and the public sphere see Achinstein, *Milton and the Revolutionary Reader*, pp. 42ff.
22 Hartlib's 'Ephemerides', 1650, *JMLR*, II, 278; Leo Miller, 'New Milton Texts and Data from the Aitzema Mission, 1652', *Notes and Queries* 235 (1990), 279–81. On the other hand, Rand, who wanted to use the press to propagate republican culture, believed that licensing was legitimate as part of the state's active intervention in literary culture (see below, pp. 282–3).
23 Christopher Arnold, letter to George Richter, 7 August[?] 1651, from *Epistolae selectiores* (Nuremberg, 1662), p. 491, cited by William Riley Parker, *Milton's Contemporary Reputation* (Columbus, 1940), p. 108.

opened up a terrifying abyss of blasphemous sedition. In *Areopagitica* Milton had expressed concern at the ready circulation of royalist newsbooks in embattled London and justified the state's seizing of dangerous writings. His concern was to create a space for religious dissent and republican politics, and with all its imperfections, the purged Parliament offered that space. Milton was thus ready to take on the role of hunting down Nedham's *Mercurius Pragmaticus*, which was fuelling the alliance between royalists and Levellers that seemed to threaten the regime's survival. *Areopagitica* had countered its democratic side with an implicit defence of strong checks to democracy; the Council of State now served as the Areopagus. In his defences of the republic Milton invoked Greek tragedians' praise of the Areopagus as an instrument of exemplary justice (*Eikonoklastes, MPW*, III, 589).

Milton aligned himself firmly with those like Marten who, while uneasy about the regime's oligarchical tendencies, placed the seizing of a republican *occasione* above short-term constitutional anxieties. The issues of representative government and freedom of speech, which loom so large today, were only beginning to emerge as crucial factors in this period, and for those like Milton who looked back to classical Rome, direct representation did not seem such an essential feature of republican government. The crucial point was that mechanisms should be guaranteed that would check the tendency of private interests to override the public good. Provided that the people's rulers and representatives were held to the public spirit, the mechanisms of their selection seemed less important, especially given the assumption that large sections of the population had been poisoned by monarchism. In Independent political thought, the stress on the sovereignty of a powerful legislature tended to outweigh concern for the details of representation or of a balance between opposing interests.[24] The reverse of the new Great Seal depicted a detailed map of England and Ireland with many place names spelled out: the clear implication was that the members depicted on the other side were representatives of these nations as a whole. But there is no close correspondence between the names shown and Parliamentary constituencies – and indeed since Ireland had currently no representation whatever, such correspondence was impossible other than on a level of vague future aspiration.[25] Nevertheless, those who designed the seal clearly believed that there was an appropriate relationship between the two sides. The map can be seen as continuing a seventeenth-century tendency in which cartographical representation was increasingly dissociated from regal representation.[26] Wither,

---

24 Tuck, p. 235, and on Milton's unusual lack of interest in representation, 252–3.
25 Kelsey, *Inventing a Republic*, pp. 97–98.
26 Richard Helgerson, *Forms of Nationhood: The Elizabethan Writing of England* (Chicago and London, 1992), p. 136.

who had long presented himself as a poet of the nation rather than the court, was to propose a new uniform for members of Parliament which incorporated the map from the Great Seal.[27] Where the monarchy had been a deceitful shadow of the people, Parliament would become visibly the image of the people. The crucial point, for the moment, was that open communication in Parliament had been redeemed from the corruptions of particular interests. Details of representation could be worked out in the longer term; the Levellers, to their republican enemies, were irresponsibly endangering the government's survival by raising relatively marginal issues.

There is some evidence, however, that Milton was aware of the new regime's shortcomings. He was rewarded for his support in *The Tenure of Kings and Magistrates* by being appointed Secretary for Foreign Tongues and given a series of important propaganda tasks. The first commission he was assigned was an attack on the Levellers; but he failed to produce it. It is impossible to tell how far this represented political scruple. In his first official pamphlet, *Observations upon the Articles of Peace*, published in May 1649, Milton threw his weight behind the forthcoming campaign to crush royalist forces in Ireland, which was being resisted by some soldiers and Levellers as likely to strengthen the influence of the grandees and Presbyterians. On the other hand, the theory of political power he advanced in *The Tenure of Kings and Magistrates* was as suspicious as the Levellers of any distancing of rulers from the people, and he never attacked them in later works.[28] In the *Observations* he attacked Presbyterians who complained that 'wee abolish Parlamentary power, and establish a representative instead thereof'; they 'would know the *English* of a Representative' (*MPW*, III, 328). Here he was on common ground with radicals for whom the word 'Parliament' was a badge of the Norman Yoke. In the preface to the *First Defence of the English People* he conceded that the new 'form of government is such as our circumstances and schisms permit; it is not the most desirable, but only as good as the stubborn struggles of the wicked citizens allow it to be', and ended with a warning that the English might revert to tyranny (IV:1, 316–7). These hints that the present constitution was far from perfect aroused Lilburne's warm admiration, and he quoted the passage at length.[29]

In the republic's first few years Milton turned his rhetorical powers not against the Levellers but against the royalists and in particular his old enemies, the Presbyterians. He became the republic's most celebrated champion in the public sphere. In *Eikonoklastes* he addressed an English audience

27 George Wither, *The Perpetuall Parliament*, in *The Dark Lantern* (1653; E1432.3; *WMW*, III), p. 71.
28 Martin Dzelzainis, 'Introduction', *John Milton: Political Writings* (Cambridge, 1991), pp. xiiff.　　29 *JMLR*, III, 217–19.

to counter the influence of *Eikon Basilike*, while in the *First Defence* he addressed the international republic of letters in Latin. He was immensely proud of these triumphs of republican rhetoric; but later commentary has often sounded a more jaded note. It is pointed out that these works scarcely deserve to be called fully republican, since they allow the legitimacy of monarchical rule in some contexts. The emphasis has been placed on passages in *Eikonoklastes* where Milton voices his disquiet at the people's devotion to the old idolatry of kingship. He seemed to admit defeat even in the process of writing, a pessimism only confirmed by the way sales of *Eikon Basilike* massively exceeded the two editions of *Eikonoklastes*.

These readings, however, are often heavily coloured by later traditions of monarchist literary history which have lost sight of an early modern humanist perspective. It is true that the cautious polemical brief imposed by the regime made Milton allow room for monarchical government, attacking Charles because he was a tyrant rather than because of inherent defects in royal power. Again and again in these works, however, clear connections are made between abuses of royal power and the very nature of the monarchical office, with its inbuilt tendency to aggrandize the personal will. In *The Tenure of Kings and Magistrates*, Milton ridiculed the idea that Parliament had been fighting for the king's office even if it had warred against his person. With grisly sophistry, he argued that the Scots and the Presbyterians had killed his office by subordinating him to their will, and that to kill his person was a mere afterthought. They should have welcomed the opportunity of removing 'the roots and causes' of the abuses they had long attacked (*MPW*, III, 191). In *Eikonoklastes*, insisting that power lies in the people, Milton finds it demeaning to derive from kings 'the right of our common safety, and our natural freedom by meer gift, as when the Conduit pisses Wine at Coronations' (*MPW*, III, 486). The provocatively irreverent simile here links Puritan suspicion of communion wine with a critique of regal ceremony: in each case hierarchical authority is shown to rest on a staged, ultimately tawdry miracle, and Milton's abusive rhetoric undermines any respect for regal traditions.[30]

Milton's attacks on the people's idolatry certainly mark a falling off from his rhapsodic praise of a nation of prophets in *Areopagitica*, and reflect the dark mood of the *History of Britain*. If Milton's political outlook was gloomy in the period around the regicide, it is not surprising that it took him some time to reach the greater republican enthusiasm of the *First Defence*. But as is by now clear, republicans were not necessarily given to political optimism; built into their vision of history was a model in which an inexorable drift

---

30 On Milton's critique of royalist structures of communication, see Lana Cable, 'Milton's Iconoclastic Truth', in David Loewenstein and James Grantham Turner (eds.), *Politics, Poetics, and Hermeneutics in Milton's Prose* (Cambridge, 1990), pp. 135–51 (143).

towards privilege and injustice could only be arrested by recurrent acts of forceful restoration. Princes had always 'sought meanes to abolish all ancient memory of the Peoples right by thir encroachments and usurpations' (*Tenure of Kings and Magistrates, MPW*, III, 201). Milton's belief in the people's readiness for republican civility was always precarious. And yet the very act of writing these treatises indicated the belief that further restoration was possible. His attacks on the people should not be taken entirely at face value: they have a rhetorical purpose in trying to shock readers out of identification with a royalist cause that has emerged as degenerate rather than refined, as it were bouncing them into the regenerate republican elite. Presenting the republican cause as a noble but beleaguered minority had a certain persuasive force. In fact, *Eikonoklastes* may have had more success than it is conventionally allowed. The two English editions 'were probably many times larger than each of the clandestine printings *Eikon Basilike* received'. The government circulated a French translation on the Continent and there seems also to have been a Latin version, though it has not survived.[31]

When Milton attacked 'an inconstant, irrational, and Image-doting rabble' (*MPW*, III, 601), he was aiming at one group in particular: the Presbyterians who had rallied to the king's cause. Milton uses the language with which the Presbyterians would themselves have denounced the superstitious masses to shame them for their apostacy. And there was some justification for the fury with which he rounded on the ideological somersaults involved in the new Presbyterian-monarchist alliance. This grouping now presented itself as a united front of monarchist tradition against the republicans' barbarous innovations. As Milton forcefully retorted, this involved much rewriting of history. In the early 1640s the Presbyterians still formed part of a common front of humanism and Protestantism which could be traced back to the sixteenth century, and which had consistently subjected absolutism to forceful critiques.

That common front had once linked English and Scots humanists, and Milton constantly returned to this theme. It was especially urgent because the English Presbyterians were in negotiation with the Scots government, which had declared for Charles II shortly after the regicide. This was another remarkable political *volte-face*. Scotland had long been in the vanguard of the campaign for religious and political reformation, and its people had arguably internalized the discourses of classical republicanism more than the English; the Latinity of figures like Buchanan was a source of national pride.[32]

---

31 Corns, *UV*, pp. 219–20; *JMLR*, II, 284.
32 On the dissemination of civic humanism in Scotland, see David Allan, *Virtue, Learning and the Scottish Enlightenment: Ideas of Scholarship in Early Modern History* (Edinburgh, 1993), chs. 1–2.

Buchanan had played a leading role in the deposition of Mary Stuart; his scathing denunciation of her tyranny, the *Detectio*, was one of Milton's major models in his attacks on Charles and was reprinted in 1651.[33] Mary's trial and execution with Elizabeth's approval provided a valuable precedent for the English regicides; Milton claimed that Charles had imitated Mary's exploitation of the rhetoric of martyrdom (*Eikonoklastes*, MPW, III, 597).

True to earlier political traditions, Scotland had taken the lead in the struggles of the Civil War. After rebelling against the king's ecclesiastical policies in the name of the National Covenant in 1637, the Scots had pioneered measures such as triennial Parliaments which were later to be taken up in England. In claiming their ability to govern their affairs in the king's absence, they had become a *de facto* republic. In 1646 the Scots Parliament baldly informed Charles that if he did not accept its terms, Scotland would 'continue the government of the kingdome without him, as hes bene done thir yeiris bygane'.[34] There was a certain truth in Milton's accusation that the Scots' imprisonment of Charles had 'extinguisht all that could be in him of a King', leaving him 'dead as to Law' (*Tenure of Kings and Magistrates*, MPW, III, 234). When their leader, the marquis of Argyll, declared for Charles II, it was partly for fear that the virus of popular revolution would spread. In 1648–49 the faction most sympathetic to Cromwell had opened both the Scottish Parliament and the General Assembly of the Kirk to wider democratic participation, so that 'Scotland teetered on the edge of political and social revolution'.[35] In constantly reverting to earlier periods of Scottish history, Milton was appealing to proto-republican traditions that could in principle be restored. Buchanan had been tutor to James VI and I; Milton views the passage from Buchanan to James to Charles, from humanist rhetoric to the mendacious beauty of court masques, as a clear intellectual deterioration.

Charles I, too, had drastically revised his earlier stance in forming an alliance with the Presbyterians. *Eikon Basilike* had been co-written with a Presbyterian clergyman, John Gauden, and though it made few substantive political concessions, its rhetoric struck a new note of Bible-centred piety that was calculated to appeal to a Presbyterian readership. *Eikon Basilike* had been composed at a time when the king's death already seemed possible; in the role of martyr he was in a position to gain far more public sympathy than he had done when alive. The government had in this sense played into his hands.

33 George Buchanan, *A Detection of the Actions of Mary, Queen of Scots* (1651; E1383.2).

34 Act of the Scottish Parliament, 24 December 1646, cited by David Stevenson, *Revolution and Counter-Revolution in Scotland, 1644–1651* (1977), p. 78. On Scots monarchism see also pp. 86–7.

35 Keith M. Brown, *Kingdom or Province? Scotland and the Regal Union, 1603–1715* (Basingstoke and London, 1992), p. 133.

'Remember' was his most forceful utterance on the scaffold; he was buried hurriedly and in secret. The government had thus put him in the same kind of position as those earlier victims of his power whose eradication from public memory had caused such resentment. Charles had suffered a fate reminiscent of Felton's; Caesar was casting himself as Pompey.

To his enemies, this self-portrayal was politically disingenuous. Even before the king's trial, Wither had criticized the emergent cult of Charles the Martyr, contrasting the honest humility of the prophet-poet with Charles's belying his self-image as a Christ figure by refusing to reduce his powers voluntarily. It was only when secret and often duplicitous negotiations had failed that Charles overcame his earlier resistance to lowering himself to engage with the public sphere. Yet *Eikon Basilike* continually betrayed the king's unease with the populace to whom he was appealing. He anticipated Burke's contempt for the 'swinish multitude':

> as Swine are to Gardens and orderly Plantations, so are Tumults to Parliaments, and Plebeian concourses to publique counsels, turning all into disorders and sordid confusions.[36]

He condemned Parliamentarians' tendency to

> suffer . . . their private dissenting in Judgement to be drawn into the common sewer or streame of the present vogue and humour, which hath its chief rise and abetment from those popular clamours and Tumults.[37]

Charles again and again sees Parliament as wrongly invading a sacred private space; his book is itself cast in a private genre, a letter to his son and personal meditations which are 'overheard' by the reader.[38]

Against these contradictory political alliances, Milton set himself to recover a clear public voice. The Presbyterians must be shamed into recovering their earlier commitment to Parliament. The king must be 'mett and debated with' (*Eikonoklastes*, III, 341) and made to face the arguments he had evaded at his trial. The disparity in rank between king and subject, while subverting a corrupt courtly decorum, is fitting for the sublime ethos of recovered liberty. Milton draws a direct parallel between the posthumous publication of *Eikon Basilike* and Mark Antony's cunning exploitation of Caesar's will to inflame the mob against the Roman republicans (III, 342); he thus aligns his own rhetoric with Cicero's. The comparison shows how short the king falls of the standards of humanist oratory: 'Kings most commonly, though strong in Legions, are but weak at Arguments; as they who ever have accustom'd from the Cradle to use thir will onely as thir right hand, thir

---

36 *Eikon Basilike: The Pourtraicture of His Sacred Maiestie* (1648; Wing E268), sig. C4r.   37 Ibid., p. 83.
38 Cf. Achinstein, *Milton and the Revolutionary Reader*, pp. 134–5.

reason alwayes as thir left. Whence unexpectedly constrain'd to that kind of combat, they prove but weak and puny Adversaries' (III, 337–8).

In choosing his title, Milton cast himself as the iconoclast, Charles as the artist, and in doing so he exposed himself to the misunderstanding of later generations.[39] Milton's aim was to restore poetry and rhetoric to a wider public function, to open them up in a potentially sublime direction from the closed world of courtly images. The best gloss on this process comes from Henry Parker:

> whereas the goodness, and beauty of government consists in the harmonious temperature of power, and obedience, of authority, and liberty, it hath been quite otherwise inverted by practise, and made apparent to lie in the Majestie, and greatness of the Monarch, and the absolute subjection, and servitude of the people; and the excellency, and sweetness of it rather to be seen in the presence-Chamber, and the magnificence, and grandeur of the Court, then in the Courts of Justice, and the rich and flourishing estate of the Kingdom, nothing being accounted more politicall, and glorious, then to have the Prince high, and the Subjects beggars[.]

The beauty which could be found in aspects of court culture was not wrong in itself, but it had been confined to the narrow channels of private interests rather than pervading the nation as a whole, and had thus helped to make injustice seem natural and even attractive. Those who attacked Parliament for turning the world upside down failed to see that it had already been 'inverted'. In 'cutting off that race of usurpers and tyrants', Parliament was being creative rather than merely negative, 'reducing affairs to their first naturall and right principle'.[40]

In Milton's chapter-by-chapter dissection, *Eikon Basilike* emerges as a work of specious beauty, in which harmony is a means of evading tough argument, like the Caesarian architecture of the *Pharsalia* and the Pandemonium of *Paradise Lost*. If it looks at first sight like a beautiful palace, the foundations are weak. The claim that Charles called the Short Parliament by his own inclination, 'his first foundation, and as it were the head stone of his whole Structure', is an 'unlucky and inauspicious sentence . . . betok'ning the downfall of his whole Fabric' (III, 350). Milton constantly tries to tie the king down to the historical details which his highly general narratives tended to blur. Milton does not deny that *Eikon Basilike* arouses strong emotions, but claims that the pity it engenders is a sentimental, manipulative emotion, masking rather than revealing the truth. *Eikonoklastes* establishes a model for a different kind of

---

39 Steven N. Zwicker, *Lines of Authority: Politics and English Literary Culture, 1649–1689* (Ithaca and London, 1993), pp. 37–59, argues that political pressure makes Milton cede the aesthetic to the royalists: these categories, I believe, distort the available options.

40 Henry Parker, *The True Portraiture of the Kings of England* (1650; E609.2), pp. 2–3, 15.

politics and of art: the truly virtuous 'need not Kings to make them happy, but are the architects of thir own happiness; and whether to themselves or others are not less then Kings' (III, 542). The regal monument of *Eikon Basilike,* which Milton claims to abound in craven borrowings from other writers, should give way to a nation of self-architects.[41]

If *Eikonoklastes* remained inescapably negative in rhetorical posture, Milton came to see his *First Defence* as the true monument both to the republic's aspirations and to his achievement as a writer. Though still hampered by the need for a point-by-point rebuttal of his opponent's arguments, he allowed himself a warmly positive note that had been lacking in *Eikonoklastes.* When he reissued the work in 1658, he added a coda describing it as a memorial which would not easily perish. These were the terms in which Horace had described his lyric poems; Milton set great store by the literary achievement of a work which, had he died before finishing *Paradise Lost,* would have stood as his most extensive memorial. This self-evaluation has often seemed surprising in a later age marked by a sharper split between the political and the aesthetic. And of course the status of the *Defence* in 'English literature' is made problematic by the fact that it was composed in Latin. But that medium still enjoyed great prestige in the international republic of letters, and its challenge galvanized him into some powerful writing.[42] Medium and message could coalesce: for central to the humanist enterprise had been the recovery not only of the Latin language in its purest form but of the political values it was believed to have embodied. As part of his duties as Secretary for Foreign Tongues, Milton took particular, indeed pedantic, care to restore specifically republican forms of language. Post-Ciceronian Latin, he believed, had lapsed into monarchical barbarism, and Milton always drew attention to such barbarisms when he found them in the writings of his adversaries. The lexicon of monarchical discourse – addressing the ruler not in the second person but as 'Your Highness', etc. – had entered Latin under the Empire; to strip away that language was also to strip away a set of political relations.[43] Linguistic and political restoration went together.

The very fact that Charles II had turned to a Continental scholar, Salmasius, to vindicate his cause in the *Defensio Regia* was itself to Milton a sign of the degeneracy of language under monarchy:

41 For a subtle discussion of the ways in which Milton forges new images out of his iconoclasm, see David Loewenstein, *Milton and the Drama of History: Historical Vision, Iconoclasm, and the Literary Imagination* (Cambridge, 1990), pp. 70–3.

42 Sharpe's claim that classical antiquity scarcely figured in arguments for the new republic ('An "Image doting rabble"?'), ignores this dimension of the culture.

43 Cf. Erasmus's satire of the pomposity of second-person forms in *De Conscribendis Epistolis,* in *Collected Works of Erasmus, vol. 25: Literary and Educational Writings* 3, ed. J. K. Sowards (Toronto, Buffalo and London, 1985), pp. 45–50.

you English deserters! All you bishops and scholars and jurists who assert that all the arts and letters fled from England in your company! Were you so utterly unable to find in your number anyone to defend the king's cause and his own with sufficient vigor and Latinity and to present it to the judgment of foreign nations ... (*First Defence*, IV:1, 527)

Salmasius was a noted classical scholar, and spent almost as much time denouncing the republicans' crimes against philology as against monarchy. Milton relished the task of outdoing him in linguistic virtuosity, demonstrating in Salmasius's intellectual decline the pernicious effects of monarchical influence on humanist values.[44] There was a direct parallel here with the Scots' betrayal of the values of Buchanan. Like Scotland, the Netherlands had been central to the axis of advanced Protestant powers in the sixteenth century. Salmasius taught at the University of Leiden, whose foundation had symbolized the Dutch rejection of Philip II's tyranny. He had previously attacked episcopacy; now his *Defensio Regia* reversed this position. He advanced an uncompromisingly absolutist theory which went further than many of Charles's advisers. Milton could easily show that this was a departure from the traditions of men like Erasmus and Buchanan who had championed limited monarchy. He must have been bribed: 'no free man in any free state, much less in the renowned university of the great Dutch republic, could have written books so slavish in spirit and design that they seem rather to emanate from some slave factory or auction block' (IV:1, 341).

This was a work with a message not just for Britain but for the whole of Europe. Although princely governments, worried about its seditious effects, tried to suppress the book, it enjoyed a large semi-underground circulation, and editions were widely pirated. In Germany, where there were many tensions between princes and city-states with parliamentary traditions, the events of the English Revolution were followed closely, and so many readers tried to get hold of the *First Defence* that it became hard to borrow a copy.[45] Milton could speak to a German intellectual world that was broadly hostile to absolutism – it had after all been the projected audience for the first translation of *Areopagitica*. German universities widely debated the *First Defence*; though published texts were always hostile to Milton, the very fact of raising anti-monarchical questions was important.[46] Sometimes Salmasius's and

---

44 For evidence that many contemporary humanists shared that view, see Leo Miller, 'In Defence of Milton's *Pro populo anglicano defensio*', *Renaissance Studies* 4 (1990), 300–28.

45 William Riley Parker, *Milton: A Biography*, second edition, 2 vols., ed. Gordon Campbell (Oxford, 1996), I, 387.

46 Günter Berghaus, 'A Case of Censorship of Milton in Germany: On an Unknown Edition of the *Pro Populo Anglicano Defensio*', *MQ* 17 (1983), 61–70, argues that many more editions were in circulation than the thirteen recorded by Madan for 1651–52; Berghaus, *Die Aufnahme der englischen Revolution in Deutschland 1640–1669, I: Studien*

Milton's works were issued together, permitting readers to stage their own debates *in utramque partem*.

Milton's triumph in the *Defence* helped to strengthen the prestige of the vulnerable young republic on the diplomatic stage. His nephew reported that its leaders

> stuck to this Noble and Generous Resolution, not to write to any, or receive Answers from them, but in a Language most proper to maintain a Correspondence among the Learned of all Nations in this part of the World; scorning to carry on their Affairs in the Wheedling, Lisping Jargon of the Cringing *French*, especially having a Minister of State able to cope with the ablest any Prince or State could imploy for the Latin tongue[.][47]

The attack on 'wheedling' and 'lisping' includes an ideological hit at the servility of Louis XIV's court as opposed to the generous openness of republican language. Though Milton's state letters have attracted little attention from modern readers with a narrower conception of the literary, they were much admired by contemporaries as belonging to the tradition of Cicero, Petrarch and Erasmus. When printed in 1676 they were given the defensive title of 'the letters of the pseudo-senate of England'; but that defensiveness was a way of trying to neutralize the fact that the letters themselves were considered to embody a true Latinity beside which it was courtly discourse that was 'pseudo-'.[48] As will be seen below, the regime courted supporters who would defend it in neo-Latin verse as well as prose.

The claims of the republic to represent some form of humanist civility were made easier by the activities of royalist ultras. In April 1649 Isaac Dorislaus was chosen as an envoy to the Netherlands, where he was promptly assassinated. As the republic's first martyr, he was given an elaborate funeral. An elegy contrasted his fate with Charles's:

> Judicio poenas solvit Rex magnus aperto:
> 　At tu larvatâ Proditione peris.[49]

The king had met his fate after an open trial; Dorislaus had been killed by masked treachery. The republican method boasts itself to be more civilized. The following year another ambassador, Anthony Ascham, was assassinated.

zur politischen Literatur und Publizistik im 17. Jahrhundert (Wiesbaden, 1989), demonstrates the extent of interest in English affairs in Germany. See also F. F. Madan, 'A Revised Bibliography of Salmasius's *Defensio Regia* and Milton's *Pro Populo Anglicano Defensio*', *The Library* 5th series 9 (1954), 101–21.

47　From the life by Edward Phillips, in Helen Darbishire, *The Early Lives of Milton* (1932), p. 69.

48　Leo Miller, *John Milton's Writings in the Anglo-Dutch Negotiations, 1651–1654* (Pittsburgh, 1992), pp. 4, 15–17.

49　Anon., *Epicedion in Dorislaüm* (n. pl., 1649; 669f14.49).

These events gave a certain propaganda advantage to the republic's Latin poets.[50] And they had a major impact on Thomas Hobbes. Though he strongly disapproved of the regicide, he was worried that his unorthodox political and religious views might prove dangerous in his exile amongst royalists: he began to 'Ruminate/On *Dorislaus*, and on *Ascham*'s Fate'.[51] The man who had been so terrified of the influence of the republican Trojan horse now chose to seek its protection. Government newsbooks began to run extracts from his writings, and it was from England that he published his great work, *Leviathan*. Had events worked out differently, the speech-act of its publication might have been strongly royalist; but the failure of the royalists to regain ascendancy left the work as a legitimation of the republic's *de facto* power. Though the tone of the work remained strongly opposed to civic humanism, Hobbes did make some compromises with rhetoric, and his impatience with traditional forms of monarchist discourse gave him some appeal to a republican audience. One member of the Hartlib circle wrote to a friend about *Leviathan*: 'if I mistake not there are many things to your palate, though some wch I thinke sufficient to procure a gentle vomit, where ye contemplation of royal majesty had dazeld ye good Gentlemans senses'.[52] Though Hobbes can hardly have been pleased with such tributes, he had lent even the most dourly pragmatic defences of the republic a new intellectual edge. His friend Edmund Waller also returned, though he was to bide his time before declaring himself in public. For all the success of *Eikon Basilike*, republican rhetoric was making an impact.

Hall, the republican sublime and the public sphere

One of the first writers to follow Milton's emphatic political lead was his long-standing admirer John Hall. Hall's writings of this period show how easy it was to develop the more radical Parliamentarian rhetoric of the 1640s into a spirited republican voice. He shows no sign of responding to the regicide as a cataclysmic break with the past; for him, it fulfils national aspira-

---

50 Thus *A Brief Relation* no. 57, 1–22 October 1650, E615.1, p. 869, saw the victory at Dunbar as a revenge for the assassinations:

> Marte iterum adverso pugnavit *Regius* ensis,
>   Ante *Doreslaî* victor & *Ascamii*[.]

51 Thomas Hobbes, *The Verse Life*, in J. C. A. Gaskin (ed.), *The Elements of Law ... with Three Lives* (Oxford and New York, 1994), p. 260.

52 William Rand to Benjamin Worsley, 11 August 1651, *HP*, 62/21/1A; Quentin Skinner, *Reason and Rhetoric in the Philosophy of Hobbes* (Cambridge, 1996), pp. 334ff, shows Hobbes's return to some engagement with rhetoric, though the shift was grounded largely in a pessimistic belief that political passions could not be avoided.

tions that have long been artificially held in check. He speedily greeted the change of government with *The Advancement of Learning*. This treatise has been discussed by historians of educational reform, but it should also be included in any canon of republican writing. Hall's title signalled his allegiance to the Baconian new science, and in a later work he complimented Hobbes; his attacks on the deceitful powers of language have been seen as linking him more closely with Hobbes than with classical republicanism.[53] But Hall saw no contradiction between the new science and a revival of rhetoric: just as the ancients' strategic wisdom had not been invalidated by the invention of gunpowder, so their rhetoric was still an important resource (sigs. A6r–v).[54] Language might deceive, but it could also unite and mobilize. In *The Advancement of Learning*, Hall brings out the political implications of *Areopagitica* and *Of Education* to give them an explicitly republican meaning. Hall in fact termed his tract an '*Areopagitick*', a coinage in English, and he directly imitated Milton at a number of points.[55] He took up the main concern of *Areopagitica* in attacking 'that hatefull *gagg* of licencing which silences so many Truths, and frights so many ingenuities, and makes them abhorre the publick' (p. 30). As with Milton, the emphasis is on the way licensing forces discourse into private space, so that this particular argument broadens into a wider reform of the old private monopolies of discourse. Hall constantly compares universities to monasteries which keep their learning 'in a few hands in a corner' (p. 18); now it must diffuse itself as widely as the ever-brighter sun of revealed Truth. Enlightened public patronage will gain a proper renewal of learning. And here his analysis of 'litterary Republicks' (p. 5) broadens into explicit republicanism. The republic had boasted that the king's trial had been in the public sphere, not in a corner. These educational reforms, he argues, will be of immense benefit in consolidating the regime. He spells out with great clarity the tactical basis of his arguments:

> What better means have you to confute all the scandalls and imputations of your deadly adversaries, who have not spared to speake you worse then *Goths and Vandalls*, and the destroyers of all Civility and Literature, then by seriously composing your selves to the designe of cherishing of either. (pp. 13–14)

53 J[ohn]. H[all]., *The Grounds & Reasons of Monarchy Considered* ([London], 1651; H348), pp. 49–50; Smith, *LR*, pp. 187ff.
54 J[ohn]. H[all]., *Peri Hypsous, or Dionysius Longinus of the Height of Eloquence* (1652; E1294.2), sigs. A6r-v.
55 John Hall, *An Humble Motion to the Parliament of England Concerning the Advancement of Learning* (1649; H350; ed. A. K. Croston, Liverpool, 1953), p. 28. Hall's comment that objections will 'according to the usuall ingenuity of Truth' further the argument (p. 16) echoes Milton's 'See the ingenuity of Truth, who when she gets a free and willing hand, opens her self faster, then the pace of method and discours can overtake her' (*MPW*, II, 521).

On one level, this argument is so pragmatic as to apply to any kind of regime, 'Kings' or 'Republicks' (p. 14). Parliament should support writers because they 'will embalme your memories' (p. 21, cf. pp. 8, 14 – here Hall echoes Milton's famous phrase in *Areopagitica* about the literary after-life, *MPW*, II, 493). But he goes further and, like Milton, draws a parallel between political innovation and sublimity in writing. Kingship, he assures Parliament, is linked with blindness and illusion:

> that great Bugbear of a continuall and shining power . . . though it endeavoured to seem a great light of it selfe, yet was onely an opake dense body, and had no other splendour but the reflection of yours[.] (p. 2)

Those who fail to see the grandeur of the king's sacrifice for the greater good are hampered by the 'prejudices' of their 'education': without education the nation would live in 'a darknesse worse then that of *Plato* his cave' (pp. 2, 9). Parliament's 'sublime mindes' have been carried 'above the extent of your owne designs, or almost the latitude of your own wishes, beyond the dictates of common Law and reason' (p. 15). Here Hall admits that the foundation of a republic had not been part of Parliament's original intentions but turns this into a virtue, a sign of its openness to futurity, its readiness to seize an *occasione* when it offered itself.[56] Hall takes up Milton's imagery in *Areopagitica* of the body that has yet to be reunited, implying a preference for the creatively incomplete over the neatly beautiful (p. 5: a reference to Medea's dismembered brother gives a decidedly grotesque twist to the image). Whereas in his *True Account* he had warned against pulling down an old building before the new one was ready, here he explicitly confutes such caution:

> For discomposition of the present frame, may not, I pray this be a Topicke for any Government, though never so ill grounded, never so irregular, or never so Tyrannicall? Should we sit still, and expect that those in whose hands it is, should quietly resigne it, or new-mould it themselves, or some fine chance should do it to our hands? or should we not out of this very reason, if our houses were all untiled and obvious to all injuries of the weather, forbeare to pull them down or mend them, because we would make no alteration, and so continue in our miserable patience, because we feare a change and some trouble . . .?[57]

And he praises Parliament for being 'as happy in re-erecting, as you were fortunate in pulling down' (p. 5).

As in *Areopagitica*, this boldness may mean accepting the need for military action in the defence of liberty. Hall directly echoes Milton's praise of the Romans who sold land even when Hannibal was at the gates (p. 23); this was one of several passages which he had already used in *Mercurius Britanicus*.[58]

---

56 Hall is following the language of the Declaration of 22 March 1649.
57 Hall, *The Advancement of Learning*, p. 20.
58 *MPW*, II, 557; *Mercurius Britanicus* no. 4, 8 June 1648, E 446.22, pp. [30]-31.

There is a parallel in the Dutch foundation of Leiden University during their struggle against Philip II. Peace might have softened and emasculated the people, while war has made them more agile and determined. Peace 'seems to smile on us againe, and promise us, that she will not flye away, for fear lest her snowy garments should be stayned in blood' (p. 23). This image of a peace ready to risk present stains for long-term prosperity contrasts with the monarchist 'White Peace' celebrated by Fanshawe's 1630 ode: beauty yields to sublimity. Hall makes learning as attractive as possible by linking it with the growth of empire. When he writes that England 'like a wakened Gyant begins to rowze it selfe up, and looke where it may conquer' (p. 19) he echoes *Areopagitica* (*MPW*, II, 558), but also gives a more specifically expansionist note: 'Nor doth she [knowledge] ever meet with any that would enlarge her Empire, but shee ambitiously encourages them, and willingly crownes them' (p. 19). Intellectual expansion will go hand in hand with political: Hall prophesies that Parliament will 'either enlarge our Territories with wide forraigne acquests, or else pull downe those powers which are now the hate and burdens of the face of the earth' (p. 15).

It is Parliament's action in sanctioning the regicide that proves it to be worthy of sublime actions in defence of learning. Like Milton, Hall sets the 'just violence' (p. 20) of the Purge and regicide in a longer-term context. He presents the purged Parliament as the elect body who, unlike the Presbyterians, have remained constant to their overall values even if the specific political means have changed. Their opponents lacked the courage to follow 'those opportunities wherewith Providence hath courted you' (p. 3). Here Hall gives the Machiavellian language of seizing the *occasione* a Puritan cast, disabling opponents' charges of self-interested opportunism by transferring the agency to God. Parliament understands that God's truth, 'as universall as his owne spirit' (p. 11), resists the bounds of received ideas. This openness to political change, to the universality of natural law over the defective traditions of the common law, puts Parliament in touch with a spirit of the age that also informs writers and other intellectuals. The 'highest spirits' are 'pregnant with great matters . . . labouring with somewhat, the greatnesse of which they themselves cannot tell'. The 'great and . . . restlesse Genius' of the time is bringing forth many a 'sublime and elevated spirit' (pp. 21–2).

The word 'sublime' here has a Longinian colouring, indicating that a reformed poetics implies a republican politics. The publication of his Longinus translation in 1652 was to make a strong political statement. In his preface Hall admitted that in a modern state it was impossible to recover the precise nature of ancient oratory, which functioned in small city-states where audience and speakers were scarcely separated; but he still believed that rhetoric could be adapted to the new public sphere. His dedication to

Bulstrode Whitelocke hoped that the translation would offer 'a short draught, or to speak rashly, a kind of prophecy of your own most excellent elocution'.[59] Whitelocke had drafted the republic's first Declaration of March 1649. He was, however, very cautious in his views, and the most vigorously ideological elements of that document, celebrating England's kinship with ancient Rome, Venice, the Netherlands, and Switzerland and adding a touch of social criticism, were probably contributed by figures like Marten and Chaloner.[60] Longinus as interpreted by Hall might, however, have served to radicalize Whitelocke's rhetoric.

Hall's experiments with sublime rhetoric helped to give the republic a rationale beyond mere expediency, and gained their reward. On 14 May Parliament paid him the high sum of £30 for *The Advancement of Learning* and a pension of £100 per annum 'to make Answere to such pamphletts as shall come out to ye preiudice of this Com[m]onwealth'.[61] Like Marten and Milton, Hall had set the survival of the republic against the fulfilment of the Levellers' more radical programme. His pamphlet appeared in May 1649, at a time when there was heated debate over the date when Parliament would dissolve itself.[62] As has been seen, Pride's Purge was a compromise which delayed new elections for a few months. Parliament showed increasing reluctance to hold those elections, fearing both radical and royalist influences, and by May was acting ruthlessly to suppress Leveller agitation, which had culminated in a military mutiny. The public sphere seemed to be getting out of control: a record number of twenty-six different newsbooks appeared in May. Preparations were made for new censorship measures, and on the day Hall was given his pension a draconian new Treason Act was introduced, threatening anyone who wrote against the government or army with execution.

These harsh realities contradicted the radical optimism of *Areopagitica*. Like Milton, however, Hall does seem to have tried to avoid severing links with those calling for further constitutional reform. His address to Parliament included a note of warning:

> unlesse you doe not also not rest here, but even run forward to the end of that course to which the divine will shall by apparent signes direct you, the worke will be taken out of your hands and put into others, who finishing it with the life and constancy which you ought to have done, must expect that reward and honour which waited on you.

59 Hall (trans.) *Peri Hypsous*, sig. A4v.   60 Worden, *The Rump Parliament*, p. 188.
61 PRO SP25/62, p. 303.
62 The treatise was entered in the Stationers' Register on 5 May and probably written close to that time, for he is said to have written it in four mornings: John Hall (trans.), *Hierocles upon the Golden Verses of Pythagoras* (1657; E1651.1), sig. b8v.

Parliament should 'absolutely alter the complexion and temper of the Commonwealth, and endeavour to your utmost to provide the best means to preserve it in the best constitution for the future' (p. 4). Hall concludes with an ecstatic vision of Parliamentarians in their old age looking indulgently on the reformed Commonwealth they have brought into being: 'you may see the reines also prosper in the hands of those that shall be your Successours, and melting away in a soft dissolution, finde that Crown above which is owing to fidelity . . .' (pp. 44–5). In a writer as witty as Hall, we may suspect in the word 'dissolution' a punning reminder of Parliament's promise to dissolve itself shortly.

In his subsequent work for Parliament, Hall, like Milton, concentrated his fire on the Presbyterians rather than the Levellers.[63] His first official pamphlet was a spirited attack on that Presbyterian stalwart William Prynne. At a point where Prynne cited Lilburne on his own behalf, Hall went out of his way to distinguish between them, rightly noting that they had 'different ends and principalls'.[64] Both Hall and Milton tried to maintain the provisional alliance between Independents and royalists sympathetic to religious toleration for which they had campaigned in the later 1640s. Hall presented himself as defending poetry against Presbyterian narrowness: 'Never durst any Tirant exercise these cruelties upon the bodies of men, that you have upon Meeter'.[65]

That immediate post-war era was recalled on the same day as *The Advancement of Learning* appeared, when Lovelace's *Lucasta* was finally published. Lovelace had been released from prison the previous month. The grounds for his imprisonment remain obscure, but it is possible that Henry Marten had something to do with his release. He was a distant kinsman, and he had a record of similar actions; he had helped Waller in 1643 and was to urge the release of another royalist poet, Sir William Davenant, in 1651. Milton may well have helped. And Hall, soon to join Milton as a government official, may have been in a position to put in a word. For Lovelace was later to write of him with gratitude, and Hall's and Marvell's commendatory verses were moved at a late stage of printing to the head of the volume. This move is often taken as a compliment to Marvell's literary abilities; but a more operative factor was surely the fact that their protest against licensing was highly topical. Marvell's association of licensing with the Presbyterians was no longer so appropriate given that they were so alienated from the regime, but

---

63 A 'Mr. Hall' was appointed in September to assist in the prosecution of Lilburne, *CSPD 1649–50*, p. 314, and David Masson, *The Life of John Milton*, 7 vols. (1859–94; rptd, New York, 1946), IV, 98, suggests that Hall may have helped to write some anti-Leveller pamphlets; in his known pamphlets however such attacks do not appear.

64 [John Hall], *A Serious Epistle to Mr. William Prynne* (1649; E575.4), p. 30. On 17 October the Council of State ordered this work to be translated into Latin, *CSPD 1649–50*, p. 345.

65 *A Serious Epistle to Mr. William Prynne*, p. 7.

the issue of censorship was being strongly contested. The appearance of *Lucasta* can then be seen as analogous to the kind of conciliatory gesture Hall had made in *Mercurius Britanicus* during the Second Civil War. The licenser of *Lucasta*, Sir Nathaniel Brent, had licensed Milton's 1645 *Poems*, and had perhaps been on his mind when he wrote *Areopagitica*. A few months later, Hall made a similar conciliatory gesture by appearing along with a mainly royalist company – including Denham, Fane, Herrick and Marchamont Nedham – in a collection of elegies for Lord Hastings. A poem by Marvell was inserted at a late stage just before Hall's elegy; as will be seen in the next chapter, before long Marvell was to align himself politically with Hall.[66]

Hall's skill as a witty pamphleteer soon put him not only in the literary but the military front line. By the spring of 1650, Cromwell had contained royalist opposition in Ireland, but Charles II had now made a deal with the Scottish leadership for a renewed invasion of England. As in the previous year there were fears that an incongruous union between Levellers, Presbyterians and royalists might cause serious danger. In June Milton was asked to search records of the 1648 risings in Kent and Essex, presumably to make it easier to prevent parallel cases in the future, and to search Prynne's rooms prior to his arrest.[67] One result of these fears was a convergence of the extra-Parliamentary opposition with the more militant Parliamentarians. These latter were keen to make a pre-emptive strike before the Scots could organize their campaign. Parliament took steps to win the propaganda war. Care was taken over the drafting of a declaration of war aims, whose Latin translation was entrusted to Milton and then, presumably because he was occupied with the reply to Salmasius, transferred to Thomas May.[68] Hall was commissioned to accompany the troops to Scotland and make such observations 'as might conduce to the settling of the Interests of the Common-wealth'.[69] Hall seized the opportunity to export England's republican rhetoric.

Hall's *The Grounds & Reasons of Monarchy Considered*, which was published in Edinburgh when English forces reached the Scottish capital, was in many ways an English-language equivalent of Milton's *First Defence*, and it was to acquire a lasting reputation in English and American republicanism.[70] Hall began by generalizing the specific question of why there was no Scottish

66 R[ichard]. B[rome]., ed., *Lachrymae Musarum* (1649; E1247.3), pp. 43–8, 40–2, 1–2, 38–9, 81–5; Marvell's verses, unpaginated, were inserted between Denham's and Hall's.

67 *JMLR*, II, 314.

68 *CSPD 1650*, pp. 216, 228; *Mercurius Politicus* no. 7, 18–25 July, 1650 E608.11, p. 109, praised the 'excellent penning' of the Declaration. The role of the writer was only secondary, however; a Council of State minute records that St John, Vane, and Scot were to prepare the heads of an answer to the Scots and then think of a fit person to pen it (*CSPD 1650*, p. 308).   69 PRO SP 25/9, p. 67; *CSPD 1650*, p. 325.

70 David Wootton, 'Introduction', *RLCS*, pp. 30–1.

republicanism into the more general issue of why republican principles were not universally accepted. He used the characteristic idiom of blindness and recovery: the people 'languish in a brutish servitude (Monarchy being truly a disease of Government' till better stars 'awaken them out of that Lethargy, and restore them to their Pristine Liberty, and its Daughter happinesse' (pp. 54–5). The people were superstitious, and 'a discovery or more refind reason' was 'as insupportable to them, as the Sunne is to an eye newly brought out of darknesse' (p. 4). Yet in fact, 'the people are the onely effective means, and the King onely imaginary' (p. 5). As with Milton, an interest in the poetics of the sublime underlies the political rhetoric, linking with a Machiavellian contempt for political orders based on a specious appeal to beauty and unity – the 'witty Barbarity of Courtiers' (p. 11). Like Milton, he calls for the recovery of the greater public spirit of 'the excellent *Buchanan*' (p. 119) against the inferior political thought and Latinity of '*Regious Defenders*' (i.e. Salmasius, p. 37).

Again in Milton's strongly humanist spirit, Hall attacks scholastic metaphysics: he has no time for the servile clergyman who 'vainly lavishes some Metaphysicks, to prove that all things have a naturall Tendencie to an *Onenesse*' (p. 13). Absolutists might indeed be fond of metaphor, but they abused it: the stock analogy between the king and the head was 'onely Metaphoricall, and proves nothing' (p. 40). In the same year Hall developed his scepticism about monarchist analogies when he published a paradox on the theme 'That an absolute Tyranny is the best Government'. Here he recycled many arguments that were familiar from high-flying royalists – that kings are images of God, that there must be a king amongst men just as the eagle was predominant amongst birds.[71] Hall relished the outrageousness of presenting what until recently had been public orthodoxy as an apparently absurd and far-fetched hypothesis which might just be worth giving at least semi-serious attention. In the treatise on monarchy he contrasted monarchists' obsession with unity to the sublime openness of republican liberty. An element of disunity was in fact a strength to a state: 'though among many joynt Causes, there may be some jarring, yet like crosse wheels in an Engine, they tend to the regulation of the whole' (*Grounds*, p. 50). Factions 'doe but poyse and ballance one another, and many times like the discord of humors upon the naturall Body, produce reall good to the Politicks [*sic*]' (p. 20), leaving republics 'sometimes gaining and advantag'd in their Controversies' (p. 54). Hall was close here to Machiavelli's argument that the young Roman republic's toleration of dissension from the lower orders had actually furthered its expansion.

Hall's treatise was a manifesto for transforming Scotland into a polity very

71 John Hall, *Paradoxes* (1650; w353), facsimile reproduction, ed. Don Cameron Allen (Gainesville, 1956), pp. 3–30.

much like the English one. As he recognized, however, such a transformation would be difficult. On his analysis, misled by 'a Tyrannizing Nobilitie and Clergie',

> the poore People are blindly led on by those affrighting (but false and ungrounded) pretensions of perfidy and perjury, and made instrumentall with their own estates and bloud, for the enslaving and ruining themselves. (p. 127)

A state in which the aristocracy continued to wield powerful influence over the middling sort and the lower orders and also over the church had not been able to develop the spirit of religious and civil liberty. The logic of Hall's argument was that in order to export their revolution the English would need to break the power of the aristocracy, bringing about a social as well as religious transformation. This policy was to be formulated by English republicans as an 'incorporation' of Scotland into England, a union which would be clearly on English terms but would help to propagate a republican culture which would be tied to England by its own interests. Machiavelli had counselled this as the strategy that fuelled the expansion of the Roman republic.[72]

It is not surprising that the policy failed. Republican politics became associated with subservience to England: the Scots were to be active citizens provided that they acted in England's interests. English Independents were too hostile to Presbyterians at home to understand how far the Scottish Kirk had virtually become a national public sphere. One political cartoon represented the Presbyterian clergy putting Charles II's nose to the grindstone: though the accompanying poem was a warning to the Scots to beware of Stuart tyranny, the image had the effect of arousing a certain sympathy for the king's fate at the hands of the zealots.[73] When Hall wrote that Ralegh's speeches at his trial under James I were 'too generous and English for the times' (*Grounds*, p. 117), he was losing sight of his notional Scottish audience and identifying republicanism with English nationalism. However, it is understandable that he should have believed Scotland to have strong republican potential. Even after turning to Charles II, the Scots' religious leaders remained deeply suspicious of monarchy. Before Charles was eventually crowned on 1 January 1651, a fast was held for the sins of the royal family. The coronation sermon was surely the most grudging in history, being distinguished by an attack on Salmasius, a defence of subjects' right to resistance, and a judicious weighing of the possibility that Charles's apparent godliness might be insincere.[74] Despite the ascendancy of the Kirk, there were religious radicals in the south-west who

---

72 Blair Worden, 'Marchamont Nedham and the Beginnings of English Republicanism', *RLCS*, pp. 45–81 (73–4).

73 'J. L. Philalethes', *Old Sayings and Predictions Verified* (1651; 669f16.13).

74 Robert Douglas's sermon in *The Forme and Order of the Coronation of Charles the Second* (Aberdeen, 1651; E793.2), pp. 9–10, 12.

were ready to challenge both the state church and king. Their nickname of the 'Whiggamores' was to pass into English political vocabulary; and already in 1648 an Irish observer was describing the Independents as 'master whigs'.[75]

Hall tried to build up in Scotland the kind of anti-Presbyterian – or 'Whig' – alliance in cultural politics with which he and Milton had been associated. The most prominent Scottish equivalent to the moderate royalists Hall was courting at home was William Drummond, the veteran poet who had died late in 1649. Hall undertook the publication of his prose works in 1655, while Milton's nephew Edward Phillips edited the poems the following year. Hall's selection carefully pointed those elements which could support his cultural politics. He omitted Drummond's writings against the Covenanters, in which he had adopted a militantly pro-monarchist rhetoric, but included a powerful attack on Charles's absolute measures in the 1630s. The main prose work, the *History of Scotland*, was strongly monarchist but it also included a powerful appeal for religious toleration, using imagery of fertile disunity comparable to Hall's.[76] Drummond would hardly have been pleased by this posthumous commandeering of his reputation, but it did have a political logic. Hall's republicanism, then, was much more than the pragmatic acceptance of a *fait accompli*; while firmly rooted in the principles of Renaissance humanism, it offered a major programme of social and cultural change.

Nedham joins the republic

It was in the summer of 1650, while Hall was working on his propaganda to the Scots, that a third powerful voice was added to the republic's defenders.[77] Back in 1648 Hall had audaciously appropriated the title of the newsbook that had been composed by Marchamont Nedham in his days as a Parliamentarian. In his first pamphlet of 1649 he concentrated his fire on one of Nedham's old targets, William Prynne.[78] Nedham will have read the propaganda for the new state with interest, for some of its champions were speaking

75 Patrick Crelly to the earl of Antrim, 16 September 1648, cited in Jerrold Casway, 'The Clandestine Correspondence of Father Patrick Crelly, 1648–9', *Collectanea Hibernica* 20 (1978), 7–20 (14).

76 William Drummond, *The History of Scotland*, ed. John Hall (1655; D2196), pp. 210–14; Hall emphasized Drummond's correspondence with English writers, sig. Bb2v. The toleration speech was printed separately (1655; E828.8); on Cromwell's admiration for this speech see Derek Hirst, 'The English Republic and the Meaning of Britain', *Journal of Modern History* 66 (1994), 451–86 (475 n. 114).

77 Nedham's writings on Scotland closely parallel Hall's: see the series of anti-Scots editorials published from April in *Mercurius Politicus*. On the government's uncertainty about Scotland, see Hirst, 'The English Republic and the Meaning of Britain', 456–8.

78 See [Marchamont Nedham], *The Lawyer of Lincolnes-Inne Reformed* (1647; E395.4).

a language that was familiar to him. He was still fighting a rearguard action for the king's cause with *Mercurius Pragmaticus*, but the republic's draconian measures against unlicensed newsbooks were starting to bite. In June 1649 he was imprisoned and after a further period at large was rearrested. He proceeded to make another of his extraordinary ideological somersaults. He returned to journalism on behalf of Parliament, this time under the title of *Mercurius Politicus*. Milton, who had been one of those charged with hunting him down and became licenser to the journal, may have had something to do with the change.

Nedham's move was explicable within the terms of interest politics. In the spring of 1650, Charles II was moving closer and closer to an alliance with Nedham's arch-enemies, the Scottish Presbyterians, and to return to Parliament's side was to campaign against them. At the same time, the fact that Nedham was known for a time to have been of different views, as he emphasized in the introduction to his new treatise *The Case of the Commonwealth . . . Stated* (May 1650), could be useful for propaganda purposes. He offers himself as a model for other writers who can decently change sides under his cover. In *Mercurius Politicus* Nedham addresses the cavaliers in rather the same terms that Hall had addressed them in 1648. Like Hall, he had drunk with these people, and he was able to use this sense of familiarity to appeal to them to change their loyalties. They should be taking up their time with learning and responsible activity, not with 'private *Luxurie*, or *publique* Conspiracie'.[79] And Nedham was quick to emphasize that their interests would be better served by a republic than by a king who was allying with the authoritarian Presbyterians. In effect, he was re-occupying the position that Hall had taken up in 1648.

One side of Nedham's case for the Commonwealth was merely pragmatic, in the normal vein of defences of the Engagement. He strongly attacked any challenge to the state's *de facto* authority, and was more vehement than Milton and Hall against the Levellers, whose cause he had championed the previous year. Like Milton and Hall he invoked the Athenian Areopagus, but in a more authoritarian spirit, citing it as one of his examples of an enlightened executive which prevented power from coming into the hands of the people.[80] And yet there was another, more positively and warmly republican, side to his writings. There had been republican flashes in his earlier Parliamentarian journalism, and now he could indulge them without inhibition. *The Case of the Commonwealth* ended with a demonstration of the superiority of a free state to kingly government. The second edition added

79 *Mercurius Politicus* no. 11, 15–22 August 1650, E610.3, p. 163.
80 Marchamont Nedham, *The Case of the Commonwealth of England, Stated* (1650; E600.7), ed. Philip A. Knachel (Charlottesville, 1969), p. 105.

extracts from Salmasius and from Hobbes, both strong supporters of absolute monarchy, to defend submission to the Commonwealth. On one level this was typical engagement-controversy pragmatism, but there was also a characteristic relish in the effrontery of mustering the republic's enemies in its defence.

Milton probably shared the joke. The opponent of licensing served as licenser for a newsbook which could veer dangerously close to opposition. It quickly overtook its lacklustre competitors as the best-written and best-informed newsbook. Just as when Nedham had earlier been working for Parliament in *Mercurius Britanicus*, he was sometimes allowed to sail close to the wind in the radicalism of the views expressed for the sake of his journalistic effectiveness. Nedham's successive newsbook titles expressed a kind of dialectical progression. If he had at first voiced British patriotism against the court (*Mercurius Britanicus*), his royalist phase could be seen as a merely tactical adjustment (*Mercurius Pragmaticus*), from which he emerged not just as a nationalist but a republican (*Mercurius Politicus*). He had chosen this title, he claimed, because the new government was a true *politeia* as opposed to a despotism.[81] He thus aligned himself with Milton in linking the English republic with the Greek *polis*. For Aristotle and other classical theorists, it was questionable whether a monarchy could be a polity, a state which permitted the full realization of a public life. In opposing the Commonwealth to despotism, Nedham effectively identifies monarchy with tyranny, as Milton had also come close to doing.[82] In rejoining Milton and Hall on the Parliamentarian side, Nedham was not simply recognizing necessity, though that was no doubt a factor; he was positively relishing the opportunities opened up for an uninhibited republican rhetoric. 'How sweet the Air of a *Commonwealth* is beyond that of a *Monarchy*!', he exclaimed in an early issue. He declared in his prospectus that his aim was 'to vndeceive the People' and that this meant he had to appeal to the 'Phantsie' more than to reason and thus write 'in a Jocular way'.[83] He indulged his talent for satire with irreverently demystifying comments on monarchy and aristocracy.

Mercurius Politicus in fact put its readers through a crash course in republican education. A commonwealth, the unfortunate cavaliers were told, was the only hopeful way for them to repair the ruins of their fortune.[84] The republic was presented as an experiment which would be not just pragmatically

---

81 *JMLR*, II, 311.

82 Cf. J. Fidoe et al., *The Parliament Justified in their Late Proceedings against Charles Stuart* (1649; E545.14), p. 9: 'when *Res Publica* comes to be *Res Privata*, it ceases to be a Commonwealth, and is then Tyranny'.

83 *Mercurius Politicus* no. 5, 4–11 July 1650, E607.12, p. 65; Joad Raymond, *Making the News: An Anthology of the Newsbooks of Revolutionary England 1641–1660* (Moreton-in-Marsh, 1993), p. 364; *JMLR*, II, 311.   84 *Mercurius Politicus* no. 1, 6–13 June 1650, E603.6, p. 10.

beneficial but imaginatively liberating to join. Another propagandist, Henry Robinson, had written that it would almost be worth hazarding the peace of one generation 'but to make an experiment of another *Government*, and spend our time in War (if it must be so) to procure peace for our Posterity, as our Ancestors have done in slavery, but to keep theirs'.[85] Nedham's initial issues used a jocular tone to win round readers unsusceptible to godly sermons; but from September he began to serialize editorials from *The Case of the Commonwealth*, which must be the first time 'high' political theory had been brought to a wider reading public in this way. He subsequently wrote a series of more radically republican editorials which could then be assembled as his treatise *The Excellency of a Free State*. This meant that theory and practice were conjoined in each issue. Though *Mercurius Politicus* was stronger on international than on domestic news, readers who approached the European scene through the republican editorials learned to see their own history as part of a wider process, going back to antiquity and being acted through on the European stage. The very first issue of *Mercurius Politicus* tells the story of a Dutch captain who 'wondred they would make such adoe about a King' – the Dutch had done much better under a republic. (There may have been a subliminal link with Shakespeare's *Much Ado About Nothing*, sounding the favourite 'king-thing' rhyme.) In France there was a rebellion against the young Louis XIV. Nedham writes that Bordeaux was once an English possession and 'retains to this day an *English* spirit, being resolved for a restauration of the Liberty of their Country . . . Oh, that my *Mercury* were there now for one twelve moneth, to teach them to spell the meaning of *Liberty*'.[86] He writes of the '*French Roundheads*' that as the English have been fools enough to follow French fashions, it is but just that the French should follow the English.[87]

Even the most quietist passages of *The Case of the Commonwealth* acquired a different aspect when circulated to a wide reading public. The newsbook itself stimulated political activism and awareness. Certainly it functioned differently from Leveller organs like *The Moderate*, which had been full of petitions from grass-roots organizations; *Mercurius Politicus*, like the political line it advocated, was the work of a vanguard which considered itself in advance of the people it aimed to educate. Yet Nedham's mercury was not entirely an organ of the ruling powers; he was to steer an independent course. Insofar as it did reflect official opinion, it was that of the more strongly republican groups in the government, who had been slowly chipping away at the symbolic remains of Stuart rule.[88] In January order had at last been given to

85 Robinson, *A Short Discourse*, p. 19.　　　86 *Mercurius Politicus* no. 1, pp. 10–11.

87 *Mercurius Politicus* no. 3, 20–27 June 1650, E604.8, p. 36.

88 Worden, 'Marchamont Nedham and the Beginnings of English Republicanism', pp. 60ff.

take down the royal arms from public places, and ships were renamed, with the *Charles* becoming the *Liberty*, the *Prince* the *Commonwealth*.[89] The effect was somewhat like Milton's republican sublimity, breaking out of a confining frame into a wider and more universal perspective. Time and space were symbolically reordered. Marten experimented with a practice that gradually developed of dating books not from the Christian year but from the first year of liberty – a practice that was to be resumed in France after 1789.[90] In the summer of 1650, order was given to throw down the statues of James I and Charles I at the west end of Paul's – the additions by Inigo Jones which Waller had so highly praised – and to erase the inscriptions as thoroughly as possible.[91]

The republican muse: Thomas May, 1649–1650

In the years after the regicide, there was an outpouring of elegies for the king and satires against the government. This evidence would seem to favour the traditional view of a natural association between poetry and monarchy. Yet in a broader picture of the public function of the writer, the balance was not quite so uneven.[92] By mid-1650, Milton, Hall and Nedham were disseminating a vigorous republican rhetoric throughout the British Isles and Europe. They could root their republicanism both in the civil war period and in longer traditions of Renaissance humanism. They were joined by Thomas May, whose Lucan translation had helped to fortify the world-view that culminated in the establishment of the republic. Like Milton, May was mainly occupied with prose defences of the republic, working until his death in 1650 on a Latin abbreviation and updating of his history of the Long Parliament for a European audience.

Before his death, however, May did seal his poetic allegiance to the republic. In 1650 there appeared a revised edition of his continuation of Lucan. The 1630 English-language edition had included a prefatory lament by Calliope, the muse of epic poetry, who lamented the tragic fate of the republican poet:

> Was not my *Orpheus* death (though long ago)
> Enough for me to bear, for you to do?

---

89 *CSPD 1649–50*, p. 482.   90 Marten, 'Opinions', ML, box 78 no. 10.
91 *CSPD 1650*, p. 261; *JMLR*, II, 319.
92 Joseph Frank, *Hobbled Pegasus: A Descriptive Bibliography of Minor English Poetry 1641–1660* (Albuquerque, 1968), offers a useful catalogue with brief extracts; but the exclusion of writings in Latin tilts the balance against pro-republican voices. The poetry of Thomas St Nicholas, a member of the republican Council of State, is being edited by Neville Davies.

> ... I saw his limbs (alas) scattered abroad
> On Hebrus banks, while down the silver flood
> His learned head was rowl'd, and all along
> Heard the sad murmurs of his dying tongue.
> No other Tragedie but *Lucan* slain
> By your untimely stroke could thus again
> Revive my griefe: Oh could you not prolong
> That thread a while, until the stately song
> Of his Pharsalia had been finish'd quite?

The poem had ended with a comparison between the ornate edifices of Augustan architecture and poetry and austere republican honour:

> Those stately Temples, where great *Caesar's* name
> Shall be by Rome ador'd, wanting the fame
> Which thy high lines might give, in time to come
> Shall envie *Pompey's* small Aegyptian Tomb.
> Had *Juba's* Tragick fall been sung by thee
> 'T had eas'd the loss of his great Monarchie:
> But that to them and us did Fate denie
> That we the more might wail thy Tragedie.[93]

In the 1640 Latin translation, however, May began to strike a new note. This version, published at Leiden, depicted Calliope in the underworld, giving Lucan's ghost a cup of sacrificial blood which would revive him for renewed poetic effort. This engraving was elucidated by a brief prefatory poem; engraving and poem also appeared in the English edition of the Latin *Supplementum*, which came out in 1646. The 1650 edition of the English *Continuation* was the first of four English editions to include the engraving (figure 10), along with a greatly expanded translation of the Latin prefatory poem. Calliope's lament in the earlier prefatory poem was now completed with a shift from pathos to action:

> But bootlessly thus to complain (quoth she)
> Is weak; to act is more befitting me.

The poem now ends with Lucan's obeying Calliope's command:

> Thou, once the Glorie of th'Aonian Wood,
> But now their sorrow, *Lucan*, drink this Bloud.
> No other Nectar *Phoebus* gives thee now;
> Nor can the Fates a second life bestow;
> A second voice by this charm'd cup they may,
> To give some progress to that stately Lay
> Thou left'st unfinish'd. End it not until

---

93 Thomas May, *A Continuation of Lucan's Historicall Poem* (1630; 17711), sigs. A3r–v; fourth edition (1650; M1401), sigs. A3r–v. This episode is patterned on Homer, *Odyssey* xi.

A
Continuation of
L V C A N S
Historicall Poem
till the Death of
IVLIVS CÆSAR
The 4.th Edition enlarged by
the Author T.M.

Printed for Will: Sheares at the Bible
in St Paules Church-Yard. 1650

(2)

10 Title-page of Thomas May, *A Continuation of Lucans Historicall Poem*, 1650.

The Senates swords the life of *Caesar* spil;
That he, whose conquests gave dire *Nero* Reign,
May as a sacrifice to thee be slain.
The Ghost receiv'd the cup in his pale hand,
Drunk, and fulfill'd *Calliopes* command.

In this grisly ritual, the writing of the *Continuation* now becomes a redemption of the deaths of Orpheus and of Lucan, and Lucan's ghost conflates the acts of writing and regicide.[94] Had the original prefatory poem been reprinted as it stood in 1650, the lament for Orpheus's severed head floating down the stream might have aroused associations with the elegiac cult of Charles the artist-martyr. By splicing in the story of Calliope's blood-sacrifice, May deflects such associations, and aligns the poem rather with the many defences of the regicide which presented it as a necessary sacrifice:

> I cannot but think that *Scaffold* sacred, and no other Sacrifice could have been so expiatory before God, or men, for that Blood which hath been shed in this *Nation*, then His who was the onely cause of it . . . We are now (through providence) on a new Foundation.[95]

The regicide had made possible a true renewal of the spirit of Lucan's poetry.

Cromwellianism and republicanism: Fisher, Wither and the problems of heroic poetry

May himself died before he could make any further contributions. And as was seen above, his prognosis for the Commonwealth in his *Continuation* retained a Lucanian pessimism. At its inception the Commonwealth seemed deeply vulnerable to domestic dissension and foreign invasion. Gradually, however, it wore down the royalists in Ireland and Scotland and expanded into a foreign war against the Netherlands. These achievements were acclaimed by supporters for their sublimity: breaking out of the narrow confines of dynastic policy, which had kept the Stuarts timidly safeguarding existing boundaries, the new republic had quickly established itself as a major European power. Hall's and Nedham's prophecies of expansion were being realized. In Machiavellian terms, Nedham specifically linked expansion abroad with republican values at

---

94 Thomas May, *Supplementum Lucani* (Leiden, 1640; 1646, M1413); *Continuation* (1650), sigs. A3v–4r. The engraving was by Frederick van Hulsen, who had also designed the title-page of May's 1627 Lucan and of two strongly Protestant works by George Carleton and Christopher Lever: see Sidney Colvin, *Early Engravings and Engravers in England 1545–1695: A Critical and Historical Essay* (1905), pp. 117–18. The 1646 translation refers to 'The Mind of the Picture, or Frontispiece', forming a link with the title of Ben Jonson's poem on the title-page to Ralegh's *History of the World*.

95 Robinson, *A Short Discourse*, p. 7.

home. Under the government of a '*standing Senate*', the Romans had 'made a shift to inlarge their bounds a little', but when the people were admitted to share directly in government, 'then it was, and never till then, that their thoughts and power began to exceed the bounds of *Italy*, and aspire towards that prodigious Empire: for, while the rode of preferment lay plain to every man, no publick work was done, nor any conquest made, but every man thought he did, and conquered all for himself, as long as he remained valiant and vertuous'.[96] England seemed on its way to becoming such a republic.

Paradoxically, however, these triumphs created problems of their own for the new state's poets. They could not be celebrated in the forms of demonstrative poetry and rhetoric that had become established under the monarchy. The old focus on a single person was precisely what the new regime tried to avoid: in its public commemorations of victories, idealized mythological pageants gave way to bare military parades.[97] As the republic prospered, however, more and more prestige accrued to the individual who had done most to consolidate those victories, Oliver Cromwell. Great though they were, his achievements formed – to an extent that is still often forgotten – part of a common agency, a shared purpose to which many others contributed. To compose a Virgilian epic in praise of Cromwell's victories would be violently inimical to the republicans' Lucanian suspicion of the cult of one man's glory. One writer did indeed compile a history of the republic's victories and intersperse it with frequent quotations from Lucan.[98] Yet the pressure in the Lucanian tradition to strip away myth and romance put strains on poets who had to develop alternative means of engaging their readers.

Defenders of the new republic sometimes preferred to gloss over these problems, but its critics constantly brought them to the fore. Leveller propaganda against Cromwell's Irish expedition betrayed a Lucanian scepticism about true greatness, attacking Alexander and other military heroes as 'so manie great and lawless thievs', and ridiculing him for his use of the royal 'we' in his statements as Lieutenant Governor.[99] His defenders instead invoked Roman history: 'being once embarqued, on he must, whether win or lose, with a *Caesarian* Confidence at the *Rubicon* and a *Spartan* resolution to go on with the Sword, or fal on the Sword'.[100] But comparing Cromwell to Caesar at

---

96 *Mercurius Politicus* no. 82, 25 December 1651–1 January 1652, E651.15, p. 1304.

97 Michael John Seymour, 'Pro-Government Propaganda in Interregnum England, 1649–1660', unpublished Ph.D. thesis, University of Cambridge, 1987, ch. 6.

98 Anon., *Britannia Triumphalis* (1654; B4817).

99 *Certain Queries Propounded to the Consideration of Such as were Intended for the Service of Ireland*, ed. Norah Carlin (1992), p. 15. The text is reconstructed from a lengthy reply that appeared in the newsbook *The Moderate Intelligencer* in May-June 1649.

100 *A Modest Narrative of Intelligence* no. 12, 16–23 June 1649, E561.7, p. 89; on Cromwell as Caesar cf. John Canne, *The Improvement of Mercy* (1649; E571.20), p. 23.

the Rubicon played into the hands of those who considered that the republic was merely a front for his ambition to be king. As Cromwell advanced on Scotland, a newsbook proclaimed:

> Our Armie is now before *Edinburgh*, the Citizens (as the *Romans* once [pardon the comparison, there being so great a disparitie betweene those diffident *Romans* and these cowardly *Calidonians*] at the approach of *Julius Caesar* to their very walls) have deserted their habitations . . .[101]

The comparison is with the vivid sketch in Book I of the *Pharsalia* of the panic occasioned by Caesar's advance on Rome. Though the writer's square brackets register that the comparison does not quite work, the only difference acknowledged is in the courage of the two generals' opponents. But in praising Cromwell as emulating the great destroyer of the republic, his panegyrists were giving a hostage to fortune.

Even some very militant republicans, however, were ready to use the analogy, expecting readers to be able to make a distinction between military and political factors: the extraordinary speed and decisiveness of Cromwell's victories recalled Caesar far more than the hesitant Pompey. '*Caesar*, and *Cromwell*', proclaimed the bombastic R. Fletcher, 'why, 'tis all but *C*.'[102] Yet the distinctive feature of republican thought, as Hobbes noted, was to set military virtues in specifically political contexts. Hall contrasted the deliberation and openness to disagreement required in a republican council with the virtues expected of military leaders, who must 'prevent occasions' (i.e. be ahead of events, seize the Machiavellian *occasione*) and who can 'scarcely be bounded while they stand levell, so that it is no wonder if they extinguish all emulations, by putting the power into the hands of one' (pp. 19–20).

This was of course the problem that had faced Lucan in portraying Caesar. There was a sublime element in his restless resistance to containment in set forms, yet because he carried this over into private political ambitions, his virtues were to freeze into imperial rigidity. Yet Pompey, the leader who did subordinate his individual military skill to the deliberations of the Senate, thereby became perhaps a more sympathetic but also a less imaginatively commanding figure. The young republic was confronting very similar problems in deciding how to represent its greatest commander. In the summer of 1650 it was in some ways Fairfax who was acting Pompey's role. He allowed constitutional scruples to stand in the way of military speed; the invasion of Scotland was indeed a case of preventing occasions.[103] On the other hand, it

---

101 *The Best and Most Perfect Intelligencer* no. 1, 1–8 August 1650, E609.6, p. 8. The style of this newsbook recalls John Hall.

102 Fletcher, *Radius Heliconicus* (l. 95).

103 The previous year a royalist newsbook had assigned them different roles, adapting Lucan:

was Charles II who was really playing the role of Lucan's Caesar in any topical analogue: in that sense Cromwell was redeeming past error by aiming to defeat Caesar before he had had a chance to cross the Rubicon. One pro-government poet published a series of Latin epigrams on the campaigns in Ireland and Scotland which went out of their way to defuse dangerous classical precedents by emphasizing the common interests of the two generals.[104] Fletcher could identify Cromwell's sublime transcendence of the pettiness of courtly culture:

> Our Resolutions strike a higher string
> Then *Tarquin's* Base, Tenor, or Minikin . . .

with the foundation of a new political order, parallel to the young Roman republic:

> *Rome's* Basis was as small, as this whereon
> We hope to raise our Fame's encomion[.] (*Radius Heliconicus*, lines 59–60, 97–8)

When projected back into an early republican history, Caesar-like virtues appeared unthreatening; but it was hard to exorcise the memory of the role they had played in destroying, rather than building, a republic.

The way in which the cult of Cromwell could blend into a new monarchism can be traced in the writings of the poet who became the main ceremonial laureate first of the republic and then of the Protectorate, Payne or Fitzpayne Fisher (1616–93). Though he has now disappeared almost without trace from literary history, in his day Fisher gained a considerable reputation, which has been eclipsed in part because most of his verse was written in Latin. With Milton and May gaining wide international recognition for their Latinity, however, the republican moment seemed a good one for the neo-Latin muse.

Fisher had begun his poetic career as a royalist. He fought with one of the armies opposing the Confederacy in Ireland[105], and was then transferred to help the besieged royalists at York in 1644. When that campaign ended in disaster, he began work on a heroic poem entitled *Marston-Moor*. Originally drafted both in Latin hexameters and in English blank verse – a rather

---

> Nec fert *Fairfaxve* Priorem,
> *Crumweliusve* Parem;
> *Crumwell* an *equall* neuer will abide;
> Nor *Fairfax* him that shall *more stately Ride.*

(*Mercurius Electicus* no. 12, 9–16 July 1649, E565.7, p. 92; cf. *Pharsalia*, i. 125–6).

104 Anon., 'Ad FARFAXUM Imperio post attritas regis copias usum', first poem of broadside, n. pl., n. d. [1651], 669f15.73.

105 Fisher should be noted as the author of *Hyberniae Lachrymae, Or, a sad contemplation on the bleeding condition of IRELAND* (1648; 669 f 12.84), which is an expanded version of 'The Cryes of Vlster', BL Additional MS 19,863, fols. 7–9.

unusual metre for that time – the poem grew until it was published in a greatly expanded version in 1650. By that time Fisher had been through a period of imprisonment, during which he apparently received help from Denzil Holles and other Presbyterian leaders. Fisher's immediate response to the regicide was strongly hostile – he published a broadside attacking the monstrosity of a headless body politic[106] – and when he published *Marston-Moor* in April 1650 he was heralded into the literary arena by writers with royalist sympathies. Edward Benlowes, a friend who helped subsidize the volume's printing, presented him as a soldier taking up the arms previously wielded by May in his Lucan translation, who had himself been reviving ancient Rome.[107] Benlowes was himself no republican, and several contributors to the volume dropped similar hints.[108] The Lucan comparison was made not so much on political grounds as because Fisher was writing of historical truth rather than epic fables. The poem was not very close to Lucan in its political analysis. It was closer to Cowley's *Civill Warre* in presenting pre-war England as an idyllic realm whose harmony was disrupted by external agency; there was praise of James I (which was dropped by the 1654 edition). Fisher tried to maintain a dramatic detachment, giving extensive speeches to figures from both sides, so that the poem avoided direct partisanship; but his dislike of Puritan iconoclasm was very clear.

Fisher's poem had drawn attention to the existence of a potential English Lucan, and its publication was probably designed to attract patronage. As

---

106 See his *Chronosticon Decollationis Caroli Regis* (1649; 669f14.24), which was reprinted the same year in two collections of royalist elegies, *Monumentum Regale* (E1217.5), sigs. A2v–3r, and *Vaticinium Votivum* ([1649]; E1217.2), pp. 48–50.

107

> In Te *Lucanans* MAYUS nova Tela videtur
> Sumere, & *Æmathios* iterum reserare Tumultus.
> Plura quid aggrediar *Veterum* vestigia *Vatum*?
> Mirer an *Italici* SILII, vel Plectra LUCANI
> Nominibus quorum mutatis, Fabula de Te
> Narratur, dum Tu *Scenam* variaveris omnem,
> Et *Latium, Briticis* hîc transplantaveris *Oris*.

Payne Fisher, *Marston-Moor, sive de Obsidione proelioque Eboracensi Carmen* (1650; E535), sig. A3v. Pierre de Cardonnel described the poem as a British *Pharsalia*, sig a1r, while Alexander Ross imitated Lucan's first line: 'Bella per *Eboracos* plus quàm Civilia Campos' (sig. a2v). The bibliographical problems presented by Fisher's writings are immense, since he specialized in preparing customized presentation copies in which preliminary matter was varied, and he repeatedly revised his poems; *Marston-Moor* went through at least three Latin versions: in the 'Fancies' manuscript, the 1650 edition, and *Piscatoris Poemata* (1656; F1034).

108 On Benlowes and Fisher see Harold Jenkins, *Edmund Benlowes (1602–1676): Biography of a Minor Poet* (1952), pp. 176, 260–1. There was even a quotation from *Eikon Basilike*, sig. O1r.

with Nedham, the fact that he had earlier held royalist views could be seen as an advantage, demonstrating the superior ideological appeal – and generosity as a patron – of the new republic. And indeed Fisher now embarked on a versified chronicle of Cromwell's next campaign which gained him a generous pension and a position as the regime's military laureate. *Irenodia Gratulatoria*, which appeared early in 1652, alluded in its title to courtly traditions of classical ceremonial poetry. King Charles's return from negotiations with the Scots in 1641 had been greeted by the University of Cambridge with a volume entitled *Irenodia Cantabrigiensis*; one of the contributors looked back to Charles's earlier return in 1623.[109] In 1643 the University of Oxford had greeted the queen's return from an arms-raising mission to the Netherlands with an uncharacteristically militant volume.[110] As in much Caroline ceremonial poetry, the leading model had been the odes of Horace, several of which were adapted to the king's praise.[111] In 1641 the praise of the king's power to bring peace had rung hollow. One contributor tried to ward off the threat of civil war by imitating the opening lines of the *Pharsalia* and then telling himself to stop, this being no time for erring poets like Lucan.[112] Cromwell's achievements lent themselves to hyperbole with a basis in reality.

Fisher's volume tried to adapt such courtly conventions to the new political order; and it revealed some of the difficulties in the way. In some respects the book directly imitated Caroline volumes. In the manner of the classical *epibaterion*, the oration greeting a hero's return, Fisher declares that '*Cromwells* return doth nought but raptures bring', and that the muses will now flourish.[113] Despite his credentials as an imitator of Lucan, the poet who

---

109 W. Fairbrother, in *Irenodia Cantabrigiensis* (Cambridge, 1641; E179.4), sig. K2r.

110 Cf. Henry Harington's contribution to *Musarum Oxoniensium Epibateria* (Oxford, 1643; E62.14), sig. C4v:

> Each coppy sent
> Of verse is Company, or Regiment,
> Verses are Files of Foot . . .

111 Samuel Collins adapted Horace's 'amatory dialogue 'Donec gratus eram' (*Odes*, III, 9) as a dialogue between England and Scotland, and added an imitation of *Odes*, I, 16, and P. Samwayes imitated IV, 4: *Irenodia Cantabrigiensis*, sigs. ¶4r–v, I1r–v.

112 R. Creswell, in *Irenodia Cantabrigiensis*, sig. I4r; for Creswell's later role as a panegyrist of Cromwell see below, chapter 7.

113 Payne Fisher, *Irenodia Gratulatoria* (1652; E796.30), translated by Thomas Manley as *Veni; Vidi; Vici. The Triumphs of . . . Oliver Cromwell* (1652; E1298.1), pp. 3–4. I quote for accessibility from Manley's translation, though it is very uneven, having apparently been rushed to the press (the Latin edition is dated by the publisher 1 January 1652, the translation 30 January). The only critical discussion this poem seems to have received is by Gerald M. MacLean, *Time's Witness: Historical Representation in English Poetry, 1603–1660* (Madison and London, 1990), pp. 226–33, though MacLean speaks of it as Manley's more than Fisher's poem.

turned epic into history, Fisher declares that it 'was not my purpose to write an elaborate *History*, but onely in brief in a *Panegyrick*' (p. 94). The main poem is an extended paean to Cromwell's virtues; it is Cromwell in person who receives the credit for the foundation of the republic:

> With safe and gentle gales you change the Scene,
> And make a S[t]ate where Monarchy hath beene. (p. 3)

The narrative is succeeded by a complimentary ode. In the English version which was published soon afterwards by Thomas Manley the metre is highly irregular, perhaps to give a sense of sublime breaking of forms; the original is in a Horatian metre and manner. The poet compares himself to Horace in directly addressing his hero and promising him immortality. In anticipation of his future title, Cromwell is acclaimed as the 'safe protector of our Land' (sig. H8r). The title of the English translation – *Veni; Vidi; Vici;* – directly quoted from Caesar.

Despite these Augustan elements, however, Fisher made some attempt to distance his own praise from monarchical conventions. Fisher does raise the difficulties of the comparison with Caesar. Most heroes have some stains (pp. 70ff). Though Caesar's conquests raised his honour, his treacherous dealing merited shame: he broke open the temple for gold. Fisher here alludes to the celebrated episode narrated by Lucan (*Pharsalia*, iii.112–68), and recently recalled by Sprigge, when with the robbery of the Temple of Saturn a Caesar first became wealthier than Rome. Cromwell's victories may be comparable to those of Hannibal, but the Carthaginian became corrupted by ease, whereas Cromwell

> hating idle sloth, and sinfull peace,
> By constant warfare th'*English* dost encrease. (p. 72)

Fisher presents Cromwell in Longinian manner as transcending space and time, as a flash of lightning (p. 64). But he also tries to show that Cromwell's military virtues are subordinated to the republic's needs. Though Manley's translation was dedicated directly to Cromwell, Fisher dedicated the original to Lord President Bradshaw and the entire Council of State, observing that he had said so much about Cromwell in the body of the poem that he did not need to dedicate it to him as well. Fisher even republicanized Heaven for Bradshaw's sake, prophesying that he would '*Praeside new* Councells *in a State* of Bliss' (p. 93).

A particularly significant aspect of the volume's prefatory matter was a commendatory poem by Marchamont Nedham. Though Nedham compared Fisher to the courtly Virgil, his own republican activities were most vigorous by 1651–52. In *Mercurius Politicus* he was running a series of radically democratic editorials which when published as *The Excellency of a Free State* in 1656 were to constitute a critique of Cromwell's Protectorate. At this time, Cromwell was playing a characteristic waiting game. He was lending his weight to reform proposals but simultaneously keeping more conservative options open, and some republicans suspected that he had deliberately allowed the king to escape after the battle of Worcester.[114] At this tense period, Nedham invoked May's Lucan in his campaign for a new 'representative'. In November 1651, at the time when the new elections for the Council of State were being held, he praised Pompey, who 'though he fell, yet he retained the name of *Pompey the great*, and still retains it to this day, to shew that it is not fortune, but a just and noble *Cause*, that makes men truely great, even after the greatest miseries and misfortunes'. Nedham quoted Cato's praise of Pompey in the words of '*Thomas May* our *English Lucan*, more excellent then the *Roman*'. Nedham was quoting here from his own epitaph for May, whose burial in Westminster Abbey had been organized by his friends Henry Marten and Thomas Chaloner as a major republican event.[115] Nedham seems to have been trying to conjure up an atmosphere of republican virtue for the elections.[116] The same issue ended with news that Parliament had voted to dissolve itself in three years' time, and that: 'There is coming forth also a *Latin Heroick Poem*, entituled *Irenodia Gratulatoria*, it being a congratulatory Panegyrick for my Lord Generall's safe return, summing up his Successes in so exquisit a manner, that I believe it excels all that hath been done in that kind for many years'. Nedham returned to May's Lucan a few weeks later, when discussing the corruption of political virtue under monarchy: 'take here the copy of old *Catos* countenance, as it was drawn by *Lucan*'. The same issue contained praise of Milton's *First Defence*, which had just appeared, and again advertised Fisher's *Irenodia*.[117] Fisher's poem was thus linked with a specifically republican ethos.

Lucan's elegy for Pompey acquired a new relevance when news arrived that Henry Ireton, who had succeeded Cromwell as Lord Deputy in Ireland, had died. Ireton had worked tirelessly for constitutional reform[118], and though he had often differed from the Levellers he was widely admired across a wide political spectrum for his integrity. Most uncharacteristically for one of the republic's leaders, he had turned down a large grant of money. According to Lucy Hutchinson, it was believed that at the point of his death he had been about to return to England to check Cromwell's ambitions.[119] Instead, the return of his corpse provoked a bizarre contest which dramatized opposing

---

114 Worden, *The Rump Parliament*, p. 265; Hutchinson, pp. 202–3.
115 *Mercurius Politicus* no. 76, 13–20 November 1651, E647.3, pp. 1205–7, 1220. Presumably the formulation plays on Lucan's own claim that he sings of wars more than civil.
116 Worden, *The Rump Parliament*, p. 281.
117 *Mercurius Politicus* no. 84, 8–15 January 1652, E651.25, pp. 1335, 1344, 1348.
118 Cf. Tuck, p. 246.   119 Hutchinson, p. 203.

conceptions of republican honour. His coffin was received in ceremony at Bristol and brought to lie in state at Somerset House. The contrast between this pomp and Ireton's personal austerity aroused much comment. Since Ireton's body, like May's, was exhumed after the Restoration, the inscription on his tombstone is uncertain. Hugh Peters published an elaborate inscription,[120] but Algernon Sidney, who believed that had he lived Ireton would have saved the republic, recorded that the tomb was inscribed: 'Rex Carlus nullo. Credimus esse Deos', in imitation of an epitaph made for Pompey, 'Pompeius nullo. Credimus esse Deos'. The inscription also alluded to the assassination of the republic's envoy Isaac Dorislaus.[121] Published elegies for Ireton struck a similarly anti-Augustan note. One elegist wrote:

> Here rests Dear *Iretons* Urne: who was as fit
> For th'Camp as *Julius*: yet abhorred it.
> He for the Pallace also was as fit,
> As wise *Augustus*: yet disdained it.
> Grandour by Him, as truly was eschewed,
> As tis by others eagerly pursued.
> Nor had it any power Him to inflate,
> But rather with sad cares to macerate.

The conclusion was the Lucanian: 'Pomp presses not the grave'.[122] Republican excitement at this time was heightened by cosmic factors: the astrologer Nicholas Culpeper welcomed an eclipse due on 29 March as manifesting God's impending judgement on monarchies. He quoted a dark prophecy from Lucan as continued by 'my friend and Country-man *Thomas May*', with an added line: '*All Monarchy it quite will overthrow*'.[123]

In this context, the manner in which Cromwell was to be praised was highly contentious. *Irenodia Gratulatoria* emanated from those circles which, while still believing Cromwell an agent of reform, were keen to keep him in a republican path. Fisher's dedication praised not only Milton's *Defence* but also, much more controversially, Lilburne's writings in defence of popular liberty. The English translation was dated 30 January 1652, the third

120 Hugh Peters, *Aeternitati Sacrum* (1649; 669f16.34). Peters declared that he was publishing the inscription at his own expense, lest Ireton's memory perish.

121 Jonathan Scott, *Algernon Sidney and the English Republic 1623–1677* (Cambridge, 1988), p. 105 n. 44, citing a manuscript by Sidney's friend Jean-Baptiste Lantin, Bibliothèque Nationale MS Fr. 32254, p. 100. The inscription would have alluded to a classical epigrammatic tradition contrasting the pomp lavished on the unworthy Licinus with the fates of Cato and Pompey; see T. P. Wiseman, 'Some Republican Senators and their Tribes: Addendum', *Classical Quarterly* 24 (1964), 132–3.

122 *The Weekly Intelligencer of the Common-wealth* no. 58, 27 January–3 February 1652, E652.15, pp. 341–3.

123 Nicholas Culpeper, *Catastrophe Magnatum: or, the Fall of Monarchie* (1652; E658.10), p. 48; adapting May, *Continuation* (1630 edition), sig. E5v.

anniversary of the regicide; the translator, Thomas Manley, had dedicated his previous poem to Chaloner, who was also close to Fisher himself.[124] Chaloner was particularly involved in the public imagery of the republic, having been asked at an early stage along with Selden to advise on the reception of ambassadors.[125] His interest in republican praise is indicated by his involvement in the engraved title-page of a work by Selden.[126] Fisher's title-page was dated, in appropriate republican manner, from the year of liberty as well as the calendar year. At the end of the volume Fisher added a *Propemptikon*, a formal ode of farewell, to Edmund Ludlow, who had been appointed Lieutenant-General of Ireland under Ireton after Cromwell's return. Cromwell was trying to reassure this committed republican of his good faith. Fisher's ode praised Ireton as well as Ludlow, so that his book's extravagant praise of Cromwell was bracketed by praise of figures who were scrutinizing his political ambitions very carefully.

Fisher's *Irenodia* was taken very seriously by the government. He was duly voted £100 to travel to Scotland and complete the promised second part of his poem, which, the Council of State declared, would be 'of great vse in all schools for the ye education of youth'.[127] The use of Fisher's poetry as a school textbook seems to have been the particular idea of Hugh Peters; a Dutch official recorded in January 1652 that he 'wants to introduce it into the Schools, doing away with Virgil as being outdated and fanciful; and he has almost succeeded in carrying his point'. The poem in fact found more favour with the Dutch than the paintings on recent battles which Peters had had commissioned: 'We had great difficulty in looking at them without laughing, although he in seriousness said each was worth more than £200'.[128] A painting of the king's trial which had been commissioned was locked up when Peters tried to show it, which perhaps reflects official unease about how far to publicize the regicide. The Dutch envoys' derision was doubtless in part politically motivated, for relations between the two powers were tense, and indeed had

124 Thomas Manley, *The Affliction and Deliverance of the Saints* (1652; E1318.2; dedication dated October 1651). Fisher presented a copy of *Marston-Moor* to Chaloner on 8 January 1652, with an inscription praising his learning and integrity (Edinburgh University Library DAV.II.3.4).   125 *CSPD 1649–50*, p. 14.   126 PRO SP 25/31, p. 29.

127 PRO SP 25/31, p. 19; *CSPD 1651–52*, p. 367, see also pp. 81, 152, 366–7. For evidence of his patronage by the army, see Worcester College, Oxford, Clarke Manuscripts, vol. 25, fol. 124r, Clarke to Gilbert Mabbott, 8 September 1653, recording that he has been in Scotland about ten months (cited by permission of the Provost and Fellows of Worcester College, Oxford; I owe this reference to Frances McDonald).

128 Lodewijck Huygens, *The English Journal 1651–1652*, ed. and trans. A. G. H. Bachrach and R. G. Collmer (Leiden, 1982), pp. 19, 50. Since this witness was the son of the strongly pro-monarchical Constantijn Huygens, there was no doubt a political element in the ridicule. Fisher's presentation copy to the Dutch envoy Scaeph has survived, Peter Wenham, *The Great and Close Siege of York, 1644* (Kineton, 1970), p. 140 n. 44.

they read to the end of Fisher's volume they would have encountered a warning of the possible need for military action.[129] Yet to write in Latin was also to appeal to the international republic of letters and recall the critical humanism on which it had been founded.

The English translation was designed to reach a wider audience; but the proposal to place the poem on the school curriculum, however far-fetched it may seem, shows how important the language of liberty was considered to be in political education.[130] In learning to imitate a poet who had something of Lucan's republican spirit as opposed to Virgil's courtliness, children would become better citizens. We can glimpse something of this process through the condescension of a hostile observer. The clergyman Thomas Thoroughgood discovered Colonel Pride, the architect of the Purge, drinking at an inn with a copy of Fisher's poems beside him. When asked if he was named in the poem,

> Very true saith he & tak^g ye booke, though no very good Scholler, he soone found his verse
>   Virtutem nec jam narrabo aut robora Pridi.
> [I shall not not narrate Pride's courage and strength] & while he prided himself in his praise, a witty man in ye company said to him, do not boast thereof, for thou art badly jeered & he made this construction, 'Neither will I now tell Virtutem, the villany, & robora, & the robbery & plundering of Pride.' This vexed him, but made others mery.[131]

The tendentious mistranslation of 'robora' ('strength, vigour') makes a stock social jibe designed to keep social barriers around classical texts erect, but Pride is genuinely proud of being brought into the world of classical learning. It helps to reinforce a sense that his is no mere mercenary army, that it is engaged in a great world-historical cause, and seeing his virtue as a classical *virtus* helps to give a universal lustre to his actions. What had made the joke irresistible, however, was the opportunity of displaying Pride's pride in a line which did no more than promise to mention him on some future occasion, and thus drew attention to the precariousness of his position on the edges of Parnassus. A regime that defined itself by its resistance to courtly self-display was always liable to charges of hypocrisy, and Lucan's iconoclastic poetics was uneasily suited to panegyric.

This was a problem to which George Wither was more acutely sensitive than Fisher. Though Wither had long called for a measure like Pride's Purge,

---

129 Fisher, *Veni; Vidi; Vici*, sig. H8r.
130 Kelsey, *Inventing a Republic*, pp. 211–14, rightly emphasizes the nationalist and populist aspect of the republic's use of the vernacular in political and legal transactions; but Latinity too could be a badge of national pride.
131 B. Cozens-Hardy, 'A Puritan Moderate: Dr Thomas Thorowgood', *Original Papers . . . of the Norfolk and Norwich Archaeological Society* 22 (1923–5), 311–37 (332).

he had initially opposed the regicide, petitioning Parliament to show mercy 'by reason the *rarity* of such an Act'.[132] Initially he confined his poetic addresses to Parliament to financial complaints.[133] But after his long campaign for drastically reduced powers for the monarchy, it was not difficult for him to adjust to a republican regime, and he became one of its earliest supporters in verse. He was named a trustee for the sale of the royal estate, a task he entered on with some animus against the royal goods' keepers.[134] Hall had called for the royal paintings to be kept in public ownership,[135] but Wither seems to have relished their dispersal:

> We have seen the pride of *Kings*,
> With those much desired things,
> Whence their vain ambition springs,
>   Scorn'd, despis'd, and set at nought.
> We, their *silk*, their *pearls*, their *gold*,
> And their *precious Jemms*, behold
> Scattred, pawned, bought and sold;
>   And to shame, their glory brought.[136]

Amongst such earthly vanities, however, Wither included the poetic forms in which court poets had celebrated their rulers. Wither's republicanism was more biblical than classical in inspiration, and he saw the fall of the monarchy as the occasion for national self-scrutiny and the scourge of personal vanity. He was careful to avoid any cult of personality in his praise of the republic's victories. Having long-standing Irish interests, he was acutely aware of the danger of the royalist advance in Ireland, and he first came to the state's defence in celebrating a victory gained by Parliament's commander there, Michael Jones, in the summer of 1649. Wither almost entirely subsumed Jones's personal achievement under divine Providence:

> *Mich'el*, and his *Angells*, there
> Threw their *Dragon-Cavaliere*,
> With his *Angells*, from our *Sphere*,
>   In confusion, to their owne . . .[137]

The play on Jones's first name transforms Parliament's soldiers into mere shadows of divine agents engaged in an apocalyptic struggle. As for

---

132 George Wither, *A Cordial Confection* (1659; E763.13), pp. 30–1.
133 Wither, *Carmen-Ternarium Semi-Cynicum* ([1649]; W3150), in J. Milton French, 'Four Scarce Poems of George Wither', *Huntington Library Bulletin* 2 (1931), 104–9.
134 Allan Pritchard, 'George Wither and the Sale of the Estate of Charles I', *Modern Philology* 77 (1979–80), 370–81.
135 Hall, *The Advancement of Learning*, pp. 30–1.
136 Wither, *Carmen Eucharisticon* (1649; E572.6; *WMW*, II), p. 4.
137 Wither, *Carmen Eucharisticon*, p. 2.

Cromwell, though Wither was to praise the victories in Ireland in general terms, he conspicuously refrained from praising him by name.

That absence is conspicuous in the poem he published in 1651 in response to a government call for commemoration of the second anniversary of the regicide. Wither proclaimed with pride that

> we, with *open face*;
> By *Publick Justice*; in a *Publick place*;
> In presence, of his *friends*, and, in despight
> Of all our *foes*, and ev'ry opposite,
> *Try'd*, *Judg'd*, and *Executed*, without fear;
> The greatest *Tyrant*, ever reigning here.[138]

But in his narrative of events since then he strenuously abstains from praise of personalities, and from the dedicatory poem onward he emphasizes the need for restraint in celebrations. The core of the book is a set of odes or hymns, which he also published separately. He leads up to them, however, in a long, characteristically meandering process of self-scrutiny and political critique. Wither's hymns strip away the accretions of classical myth and rhetoric to merge with the traditions of popular poetry; and he makes no apologies. He is deliberately challenging the modes of representation current at the Caroline court: encouraged by their 'Flattering *Priests*, and *Poets*', Charles

> and his *Queen* became
> So often represented by the name
> Of *Heath'nish Deities*; that, they, at last,
> Became (ev'n when their *Mummeries* were past)
> Like those they represented; and, did move,
> Within their Sphears like, *Venus*, *Mars*, and *Jove*. (p. 11)

Wither had been attacking courtly festivities for many years, but the speech-act involved was very different when the attacks were used to justify the monarchy's total abolition. Like so many republican writers, Wither seizes on the way in which flattering titles had become sealed off and reified into idols. He warns of the danger that public rejoicings may become deceitful, and gives the example of a much earlier occasion when there was a similar disparity, the return of Prince Charles from Spain in 1623 (see pp. 73–4 above):

> It fareth, now with me, as on that *morning*
> Which, first, inform'd us, of his *safe returning*[.] (p. 4)

Like Fisher, but more radically, Wither distances himself from the conventions of Stuart epideictic verse.

Wither does not repudiate titles altogether; but he insists that they should

138 Wither, *The British Appeals* (1649; W3143), p. 29.

bear a clear and accountable relationship to what they represent in the same way as Parliamentarians represent the people, and as Wither's poem represents his meaning. And all such representations must be regarded as provisional rather than being frozen into idolatry; they must be rescued from their superstitious accretions. Wither addresses his poem 'To the Soveraigne MAIESTY of the Parliament of the English Republike, (by the grace of God) Keepers of the Liberties of England; Protectors of the true Christian Faith, and (within their Territories) Assertors of all the just Priviledges of the Humane Nature, against the Usurpations of Domestick and Forraigne Tyrants, &c.' (sig. A2r). He acknowledges that these are 'such *New-titles*, and *high attributes/*As none have yet ascrib'd' (sig. A2v). But he makes them clearly conditional; throughout the poem he counterpoints the conventions of ceremonial praise with more personal and critical doubts and reservations. He does not allow himself to reach the formal odes until he has scrutinized very closely the grounds on which rejoicing is appropriate. Now as in 1623, Wither distances himself from public optimism. Even though he fully supports the regime, as he certainly did not then, he warns that without being subordinated to worthy ends,

> the formall observation,
> Of one *set-day* is but a *profanation*;
> Or, meer *hypocrisie*: It, makes men think
> They offer *incense*, when they offer *stink*[.] (p. 8)

Thanksgiving means little unless it is accompanied by good actions. Just as Milton attacks ceremonial set forms, so Wither makes his poem continually break out of its ceremonial bounds, so that the traditionally extravert form of the panegyric acquires a personal, introspective cast.

And after the climax of the ceremonial odes, Wither again allows doubts and uncertainties to intrude. He calls on his readers to retire into themselves and confess their failings (pp. 54–5), and concludes with a warning to Parliament:

> Yea, should you *conquer*, till, you did not know,
> *Abroad*, or, here *at home*, one able foe.
> Should all those *Princes*, and those powrfull *States*,
> Who court you now, prove firm *confederates*;
> Or, should you stand possesst of all their *powrs*,
> Of whom, you are, or may be *Conquerours*;

yet unless reformation proceeds, there will be calamity (p. 64). His poem celebrates the foundation of a new, less pompous, order on the ruins of a discredited architecture:

> My *Structure* therefore, shall be rather *strong*,
> Then *Lofty*; that, it may continue long[.] (p.2)

He draws a parallel with the building of the Temple in Jerusalem, comparing the publication of his poem to the raising of a stone.[139]

Like Milton and May, Wither used architectural metaphors to celebrate the construction of a new state, and yet was also hesitant about premature celebration. The foundations had to be built before the work could be completed. Waller's confident parallel between the courtly poet and the monarch as architect of the state could not be used so unproblematically by republican poets who were also alert to Lucan's figuring of the imperial state as a top-heavy, menacing edifice, and to his sense of the looming danger of Caesarian power. Under the new regime, both poetry and politics had to risk predictable beauty for uncertain sublimity. And yet Wither, like Milton, expresses confidence that in the long term he will be vindicated. Far from being inimical to the Muses, the republic will lay the foundations for poetic achievements greater than anything possible under the menacing embrace of Caesarian patronage. Out of this difficult but challenging context, Andrew Marvell produced his Commonwealth poems.

---

139 Wither seems to have been reading the *Defence*: compare his account of the death of
 the young Prince of Orange, p. 41, with *MPW*, IV:1, 312.

6

Double names: Marvell and the Commonwealth

Marvell and Commonwealth poetry I: the 'Horatian Ode'

In 1673 Andrew Marvell gave the following account of his relations with the English Commonwealth of 1649–53:

> I never had any, not the remotest relation to publick matters, nor correspondence with the persons then predominant, until the year 1657.[1]

Writing after the Restoration, Marvell was anxious to keep at bay any suggestion that he had been linked with the republic. The date of 1657 associated him with the last, and most conservative, phase of the Protectorate. And it is quite true that Marvell fully entered paid state employment only in that year. It is quite untrue, however, that he had no relation whatever with the Commonwealth; he defended it in verse and applied for an official post. Marvell was covering his tracks. He did so successfully: when he eventually became canonized as a poet of liberty, it was the monarchical liberty of 1688 rather than the republican liberty of 1649 that was invoked. And even when his 'Horatian Ode' was finally published more than a century after its composition, it was linked above all with his other poems to Cromwell, turning him into the court poet of a pseudo-king: the Marvell of 1657 rather than 1650. One edition classifies all his poems written during the Commonwealth under 'the Cromwell era'[2], following a larger historiographical tendency to efface the Commonwealth by turning it into a mere appendage of the Protectorate. Marvell's poetry of 1650 to 1653, however, is best understood not by reading backwards from his later Cromwellianism but by relating it to the very specific dilemmas of public poets under the Commonwealth.

If Marvell had obvious reasons for covering his tracks, later commentators have had their own ideological investments in wishing to stress Marvell's distance from the Commonwealth. The 'Horatian Ode' has received ironic readings which present the author as holding the republican discourse he uses at a

---

1 Andrew Marvell, *The Rehearsal Transpros'd and The Rehearsal Transpros'd: The Second Part*, ed. D. I. B. Smith (Oxford, 1971), p. 203.
2 Andrew Marvell, *The Complete Poems*, ed. George deF. Lord (1993), pp. 53ff.

fastidious distance. A tradition of criticism finds the essence of Marvell in his passive languishing with fruits and plants, and is all the more inclined to find irony in any overt expression of political commitment. But that tradition misses the sharply aggressive tone of so much of his writing in verse as well as prose. It comes as a salutary shock to find his career thus summarized in the official History of the House of Commons: 'Marvell was ineffective as a Member, partly because he was unable to control his temper'.[3]

The critical tradition is right, however, to find problems in interpreting Marvell's Commonwealth poetry. Marvell could not have covered his tracks so effectively if he had ventured into print; most of his public poetry of the Commonwealth period remained in manuscript, and the extent of its circulation is unknown. It is very difficult to find a consistent ideological pattern in the praise of Cromwell in the 'Horatian Ode', of the very different figure of Fairfax in 'Upon Appleton House', and the satire of the republic's laureate in 'Tom May's Death'. One response has been to present Marvell as ultimately standing above politics at a serene distance. Another has been to associate him not with the republicans but with the pragmatic supporters of the Commonwealth purely because it had *de facto* power – the kind of argument Hobbes used. Such readings grant him consistency, but at the cost of losing the passionate energy of these poems. I shall try to show that on the level of speech-acts, his poems of this period simply do not show consistency: with great force, they make incompatible utterances. Marvell proves to have something in common with a figure from whom idealizing pictures of his Olympian detachment have kept him far distant: the trimming Marchamont Nedham, who could tack between opposing sides with disconcerting dexterity.

To some extent, as was seen in the previous chapter, an ability to handle royalist and Parliamentarian discourses was a shared element of most propagandists for the new regime. Wither had not at first supported the regicide; Fisher had strongly attacked it. The habit of adopting different voices for public negotiations with the new state's leaders and for private discussion amongst friends would have been common – as it has been under more recent revolutionary orders. In Marvell's case, however, it is far from clear that the semi-public republican voice is an assumed mask while the royalist venom of 'Tom May's Death' is the real Marvell. Rather, the poems of this period show him testing out different voices, unsatisfied with a bland compromise but also keeping his options open with a certain tactical skill. He worked through his own argument *in utramque partem.* This is a continuation of the pattern we saw in chapter 4: Marvell responds to the republican sublime of Milton and

---

3 M. W. Helms and J. P. Ferris, 'Andrew Marvell', in Basil Duke Henning (ed.), *The History of Parliament: The House of Commons 1660–1690*, 3 vols., III (1983), 26.

Hall but retains a considerable engagement with the courtly beautiful. This may sound like another way of saying that he stands above politics; but the degree of detachment with which he viewed the regicide already distinguishes him from a significant spectrum of royalist opinion, and he showed no attachment to the old church. Marvell is interested in the phenomenon of ambiguity, whether verbal, political or sexual, but his poetry also shows a drive towards decisive alignment, and there are signs of a movement towards commitment during the Commonwealth period.

Marvell's first appearances in print after the regicide showed no enthusiasm for the new regime. As well as featuring prominently in the delayed Lovelace volume, he had contributed to a volume of elegies for the young royalist Lord Hastings along with Fane and the then-royalist Nedham. Even then, however, he was in the company of that 'forward youth' John Hall (above, p. 218). The following year he produced a pioneering poem which not only drew on some themes of the new republican literary culture but anticipated future developments. Until recently, however, the links of the 'Horatian Ode' with that culture have been obscured.[4] Indeed, the poem has often served as a central bulwark for a fundamentally royalist reading of literary history. Its sympathetic portrayal of the dying king's grace has been taken to epitomize the links between poetry and the muses in Renaissance culture. The poem's Cromwell, by contrast, appears as a figure of prosaic ruthlessness, and critics have found irony in the praise of his lawlessness and belligerence.

Most ironic of all, it is sometimes argued, must be the claim that the Irish praise him. Praise from an enemy was a recognized strategy of epideictic literature, and notably of Horace's odes[5]; but can praise by the Irish be taken seriously? The poem's occasion indeed pitches the issues of monarchism and republicanism at their sharpest. Cromwell's campaigns in Ireland in 1649 and 1650 were stained by the massacres of the garrisons at Drogheda and Wexford. He laid the foundations for a ruthless programme of resettling the Irish Catholics which amounted to large-scale ethnic cleansing and perpetuated the island's confessional antagonisms. The king, by contrast, had formed an alliance with Catholic leaders and in *Eikon Basilike* presented himself as a

---

4 'An *Horatian* Ode upon *Cromwel's* return from *Ireland*', *MPL*, I, 91–4. The breakthrough came with Blair Worden, 'Andrew Marvell, Oliver Cromwell, and the Horatian Ode', in Kevin Sharpe and Steven N. Zwicker (eds.), *Politics of Discourse: The Literature and History of Seventeenth-Century England* (Berkeley, Los Angeles and London, 1987), pp. 147–80, to which the present reading is complementary. The pioneering contextual reading of John M. Wallace, *Destiny His Choice: The Loyalism of Andrew Marvell* (Cambridge, 1968), ch. 2, is still valuable, though it gives the poem less ideological bite.

5 On the strategy in IV, 4, see *Bernardini Parthenii . . . in Q. Horatii Flacci Carmina . . . Commentarii* (Venice, 1584), fol. 143v. Parthenio states that such praise removes ambiguity, a comment that certainly provides a hostage to fortune in the case of Marvell criticism.

champion of mildness against the brutality of the Puritan settlers. Charles's fate was to be bewailed in Irish bardic verse, where the Stuart dynasty sometimes became an emblem of the traditional values being uprooted by the barbaric colonizers. English republicans, meanwhile, tended to find in Ireland the epitome of everything that was backward. 'I see in the generalitie of mens dispositions,' wrote Culpeper, 'an analogicall Irishe humor which nothing but an acte of [parl*iament*] can breake from drawinge by the horses tayle'.[6] Milton found the Irish 'indocible and averse from all Civility and amendment' (*Observations*, III, 304), heightening the charge by disseminating hugely exaggerated accounts of the atrocities against Protestants in 1641.[7]

The neat antitheses of Marvell's poem may indeed seem to invite a rigid opposition between a peaceful, monarchist, poetic order and a ruthlessly militaristic republicanism. But the monarchist readings of the 'Ode' rest on a series of premises, each open to question. Since the poem's full title brings the Irish campaign to the fore, it will be best to begin by scrutinizing its occasion. First of all, it is important to disentangle later responses to Cromwell's Irish career from those in the contemporary press. Though Cromwell's atrocities at Drogheda and Wexford were designed to inspire terror on the ground and no doubt did so, it was not until the nineteenth-century Irish nationalist revival that they began to play a major part in historical literature – and helped to fuel the quasi-Jacobite revival of monarchist literary history which T. S. Eliot canonized.[8] Though harsh even by seventeenth-century standards, Cromwell's tactics were not completely aberrant on either side in the period's European wars of religion. Contemporary Catholic commentators were more concerned with internal divisions on their own side. Remarkably, some wholly non-ironic praise of Cromwell can be found in an Irish Catholic source roughly contemporary with the 'Ode'.

This is the anonymous treatise written by a spokesman for the militant

---

6 Culpeper to Hartlib, 17 February 1646, *CL*, p. 264.

7 The growing literature on Milton and Ireland includes Willy Maley, 'How Milton and Some Contemporaries Read Spenser's *View*', in Brendan Bradshaw, Andrew Hadfield and Willy Maley (eds.), *Representing Ireland: Literature and the Origins of Conflict, 1534–1660* (Cambridge, 1993), pp. 191–208 and Norah Carlin, 'Extreme or Mainstream?: the English Independents and the Cromwellian Reconquest of Ireland, 1649–1651', ibid., pp. 209–26. On Milton's long-standing attacks on the Irish rebellion, see David Loewenstein, '"An Ambiguous Monster": Representing Rebellion in Milton's Polemics and *Paradise Lost*', *Huntington Library Quarterly* 55 (1992), 295–315; and for an Elizabethan anticipation of the republic's hard line against Ireland, see Markku Peltonen, *Classical Humanism and Republicanism in English Political Thought 1570–1640* (Cambridge, 1995), pp. 75–102.

8 Toby Barnard, 'Irish Images of Cromwell', in R. C. Richardson (ed.), *Images of Oliver Cromwell: Essays for and by Roger Howell, Jr.* (Manchester and New York, 1993), pp. 180–206 (181–4).

Catholic forces in Ireland some time after 1652, and known as the *Aphorismical Discovery* because each chapter opens with moral and political maxims. In recounting Cromwell's arrival in Ireland, the author launches into an extended comparison between Cromwell and the royalist leader Ormond:

> the one noted at home and abroade with a swip-chemny – character of perfidie and impeachment of covenant, the other a powerfull majestie to comaunde, and an awfull contenaunce to execute . . .

He places the main blame for the disaster at Drogheda on Ormond, who failed to outflank Cromwell in time. He begins the next chapter with some aphorisms in praise of 'celeritie' in a commander, and cites both Caesar's 'Veni, vidi, vici' and Lucan's description of Caesar advancing on Rome – the same passage that is alluded to, via May's translation, at the opening of the 'Horatian Ode'.[9] This author is certainly not apologizing for Cromwell, but as someone who has spent his life as a professional soldier he also finds in him virtues which he wishes the Irish possessed. Ormond is presented as a courtier-soldier, timid and theatrical; Cromwell gets down to the essentials. There is a remarkably close parallel with Milton's comparison, in the *Observations*, between Cromwell's practical achievements and Ormond's empty nobility (*MPW*, III, 312). Above all, this Cromwell knows how to 'prevent' his enemies, with astonishing speed to frustrate all their efforts. The Irish text carries with it much more than the 'Ode' of Lucan's condemnation of the imperial ambitions of Caesar; but the author does acknowledge, with a deep sense of shame, that Cromwell is a far more effective commander than most of the local leadership.

There is no evidence that the author of the *Discovery* had read the 'Horatian Ode', and he borrowed his Lucan allusion from another collection of aphorisms. The parallel may, however, remind us of unexpected links between English republican and Irish Catholic circles. In May 1649 the Council of State had asked Milton to investigate the 'Complicac[i]on of interest wch is now amongst the severall designers against the peace of the Comonwealth' in Ireland; Marvell would likewise have been aware, even if his poem does not itself make clear, that there were indeed immensely complicated balances of interests between contending parties.[10] The author of the *Aphorismical Discovery* belonged to a militant Catholic faction amongst the 'old Irish', the descendants of the island's traditional Gaelic-speaking

---

9 John T. Gilbert (ed.), *A Contemporary History of Affairs in Ireland from 1641 to 1652*, 3 vols. (Dublin, 1879–80), II: 1, 48, 53; the anonymous author borrows the Lucan tag from Robert Dallington, *Aphorismes Civill and Militarie* (1629; 6197), pp. 187–8. Forthcoming work by Deana Rankin will throw new light on this text.   10 PRO SP 25/62, p. 125.

inhabitants. Relative to the old Irish, both English royalists and republicans were innovators speaking alien political languages. The major difference was that the English monarchy had been settled in Ireland for many centuries, though its foothold was uncertain, and the 'old English' settlers had reached accommodation with the Gaelic-speaking culture. But under Elizabeth and James I a new breed of more aggressively Protestant settlers had arrived, and James had encouraged Presbyterians to settle in Ulster. These 'new English' and Scots were often at odds with the old English as well as the old Irish. The unpopularity of the king's deputy under his personal rule, Strafford, however, succeeded in uniting old and new English against Charles.

For their part, the old Irish were far from culturally static, being in the process of adapting to the new, militant piety of the Catholic Counter-Reformation and to humanist and absolutist political thought. Irish bardic poetry began to assimilate a new political lexicon including such terms as 'crown', 'majesty' and 'title', reflecting an accommodation with European courtly culture.[11] But republican ideas were disseminated too. In 1627 their exiled leader, Owen Roe O'Neill, had proposed that Ireland should become an independent Catholic republic. When in 1641 there was a rebellion of Catholics this was in some ways accomplished. Its leaders set up an Assembly – they held back from the title of Parliament – at Kilkenny, and conducted their own negotiations with Charles I. One tract published in 1645 called for an Irish republic, or at least a kingdom under O'Neill.[12] O'Neill, bent on a militant Catholic reconquest of the island, was often at odds with the old English royalists, who had their own reservations about traditional Gaelic culture. In a remarkable development in the late 1640s, his representatives opened negotiations with the English Independents. As Charles II moved towards the French, a tactical alliance with the Spanish-leaning Catholic militants in Ireland made some sense. Negotiations with O'Neill continued through the early part of 1649.[13]

In the long term, no more than tactical considerations were at issue in

---

11 Breandán O' Buachalla, 'James our True King: The Ideology of Irish Royalism in the Seventeenth Century', in D. George Boyce, Robert Eccleshall and Vincent Geoghegan (eds.), *Political Thought in Ireland since the Seventeenth Century* (London and New York, 1993), pp. 7–35 (14).

12 [Cornelius O'Malley], *Disputatio Apologetica De Iure Regni Hiberniae* (Frankfurt, 1645), appealing to the Romans' expulsion of kings (p. 76) and Buchanan (p. 85), see also pp. 117, 125; J. P. Conlan, 'Some Notes on the "Disputatio Apologetica"', *Bibliographical Society of Ireland* 6:5 (1955), 69–77. The tract was suppressed by the Catholic Confederacy, perhaps not so much for its republicanism as for its politically embarrassing calls for genocide against the Protestants; cold-blooded violence was not the monopoly of one side.

13 Jane H. Ohlmeyer, *Civil War and Restoration in the Three Stuart Kingdoms: The Career of Randal MacDonnell, Marquis of Antrim, 1609–1683* (Cambridge, 1993), pp. 220ff.

these brittle alliances. But a few visionary radicals were ready to extend toleration at home to Catholics and to argue that Ireland should become a 'free State'. Marten may have been swayed by these arguments.[14] He had long since argued that it was better to conciliate the Irish than to drive them into the king's arms by repressive policies, declaring that Charles's rebellion was more unjust and dangerous than the Irish one and ridiculing those who would try to make all Christendom a Protestant.[15] The more militant republicans consistently took a harder line on Scotland than on Ireland, and at one stage Ulster Presbyterians were included in the draconian legislation against Irish religious dissidents. O'Neill's successor, the marquis of Antrim, continued negotiations with the Independents, and at the time the 'Ode' was written was staying on friendly terms with Henry Ireton. Antrim linked the very different worlds of the old Irish and English poetry. He was the stepfather of Marvell's patron, the politically malleable duke of Buckingham; a great gambler, he had lost a lot of money to the cavalier poet Sir John Suckling.[16] Alliances between bards and monarchs, then, were under some strain on both sides of the Irish Sea.

It is, then, not self-evident that Marvell's lines about the praise from Ireland must be read ironically. That is not to say that his poem really contributes to an understanding of the 'complication of interest' in Ireland: 'his categories for Cromwell's enemies are curiously limited'.[17] The poem's polar oppositions here have themselves contributed to the critical paradigm of royalist civility versus republican violence, for Marvell allows little space for the important differences between civilian and military republicans. The focus is overwhelmingly on Cromwell and his achievements. There is a striking contrast here with Wither, who, as has been seen, rallied to the republic's support after Jones's victory but was consistently wary of celebrating any one individual. The regime's military triumphs would be meaningless unless they led to political reforms; otherwise they would merely serve to bolster the power of a tiny oligarchy. Culpeper was glad of Jones's victory insofar as it

---

14 *Certain Queries*, ed. Norah Carlin (1992), p. 17. See also Christopher Hill, 'Seventeenth-Century English Radicals and Ireland', in *A Nation of Change and Novelty: Radical Politics, Religion and Literature in Seventeenth-Century England* (London and New York, 1990), pp. 133–51.

15 ML78, fols. 13, 11, quoted in Williams, 'Marten', pp. 509–16; see also John Adamson, 'Strafford's Ghost: The British Context of Viscount Lisle's Lieutenancy of Ireland', in Jane H. Ohlmeyer (ed.), *Ireland From Independence to Occupation 1641–1660* (Cambridge, 1995), pp. 128–59 (133) and Sarah Barber, 'Scotland and Ireland under the Commonwealth: A Question of Loyalty', in Steven G. Ellis and Sarah Barber (eds.), *Conquest and Union: Fashioning a British State, 1485–1725* (London and New York, 1995), pp. 195–221 (209).

16 Ohlmeyer, *Civil War and Restoration in the Three Stuart Kingdoms*, p. 62.

17 Corns, *UV*, p.230.

might help to woo royalists from their beliefs, but the main gain for him was
that 'those whoe are nowe at sterne will be more likely to returne to theire
firste purity', that they would reduce themselves to 'a more equall & frequente
representatiue'.[18] Even Fisher's lengthy panegyric of Cromwell had been
accompanied by tributes to civilian republicans. By contrast, the 'Horatian
Ode' can be read as a straightforward glorification of Cromwell's power,
reverting to the courtly modes of panegyric of a single person. It bears noting
that Cromwell's victories, though they had a great impact, had not completed
the conquest: far from having tamed the Irish in one year (line 74), he left
plenty of work for Ireton and Ludlow to do.

But those who have found irony in Marvell's portrayal of Cromwell have
not been entirely governed by royalist wishful thinking. There are peculiarities in the poem's structure that mark it off radically from a traditional poetry
of praise. Rather than simply lamenting lost royalist traditions, however, the
poem calls for and embodies a 'recovery' of lost political and rhetorical energies in the spirit of the group of republican writers around Milton. Having
wavered in 1647–48 between Hall's calls for energetic 'forwardness' and the
ornamental beauty of cavaliers like Villiers, Marvell had decided to become a
'forward Youth'. He was joining another returning waverer, Marchamont
Nedham. The poem's implied date is between Cromwell's return to London
in early June 1650 and his departure in command of the Scottish army the following month. A day of thanksgiving for the victories in Ireland was proclaimed for July 26, and this might have seemed an appropriate target date, on
analogy with Wither's *Carmen Eucharisticon* the previous summer.[19] Milton's
first official pamphlet had addressed Irish politics, and Wither had chosen an
Irish occasion to 'appear' for the government.

Marvell would have been writing shortly after the publication of a poem by
another figure with Irish connections, Fisher's *Marston-Moor*, which had
opened the way to his appointment as a government poet. Marvell's poem
was not printed – unless it was published as a broadside that has since disappeared. Despite the weight of Marvell's poem, it was still left to Fisher to
announce to Cromwell:

---

18 Culpeper to Hartlib, 15 August 1649, *CL*, p. 356.
19 It has been suggested that the poem may have been written in August, for the Picts'
hiding in the brake (line 109) may refer to the Scots' evasive tactics in August: Derek
Hirst and Steven Zwicker, 'High Summer at Nun Appleton, 1651: Andrew Marvell and
Lord Fairfax's Occasions', *Historical Journal* 36 (1993), 247–69 (249 n. 9). It is impossible
to rule out the hypothesis that it could have been written, or at least revised, more than a
year later when he was seeking favour with the government after his period with Fairfax:
the forward youth could have made himself more forward than the others by projecting
himself back into that tense conjuncture and composing the kind of poem he might
then have written. On the dating see Corns, *UV*, p. 227.

Others may praise thee in a verse more high;
But none so *well*, since not so *soon* as I.[20]

The Latin, however, offers the more specific 'vates Latini' (sig. K3r), almost as if Fisher were acknowledging an English precursor, and a number of verbal analogies, which will be noted below, suggest that Fisher, Milton, and others had seen the 'Ode'. If Marvell was in search of patronage, manuscript circulation would still have been an effective medium. The patronage was not forthcoming, but perhaps it was forestalled by the invitation from Fairfax later in 1650 to act as tutor to his daughter. Since the 'Horatian Ode' was praising Fairfax's military and political rival without mention of his own achievements, it is understandable that Marvell did not seek its wide circulation.

Marvell's praise of Cromwell in the 'Ode' certainly soars higher than his contemporaries in the summer of 1650. Milton had praised him but briefly in the *Observations*; Nedham did not mention him in *The Case of the Commonwealth Stated*. On the other hand, Cromwell had been the central target of abuse of the regime, and coming to his rescue did confer dignity on the state as well as on the commander. In the early months of 1649, royalist newsbooks had combined eulogies of the martyr-king with stock vituperation of Cromwell's low birth and huge nose and prophecies that Ormond would soon reconquer Ireland. News travelled slowly from Ireland and reports and counter-reports undermined confidence in the government's official accounts. Rumours about Ireland were one factor in the government's major crackdown on the opposition press in the summer of 1649.[21] Jones's victory was not enough to convince the regime's enemies that its position was safe. The Council of State had decreed that ministers should read out Jones's report of his victory in the pulpit, but responses were muted, and Wither was alone in celebrating in verse. As Cromwell prepared to join Jones, government newsbooks were forced on to the defensive in answering Leveller criticisms of the expedition's justice, while royalists exultantly prophesied his defeat.

The joke, of course, turned out to be on the royalists. The newsbooks' uncertainties gave way to the firm republican voice of *Mercurius Politicus*; at the same time, Marvell exposed the hollowness of royalist satire of Cromwell by placing him at the centre of his triumphal ode. Cromwell's return from Ireland was an appropriate nodal point for exploring those problems. It

---

20 Payne Fisher, *Veni; Vidi; Vici. The Triumphs of . . . Oliver Cromwell*, trans. Thomas Manley (1652; E1298.1), sig. I1r, see also n. 57 below.

21 It is improbable, however, that the suppression was designed to stifle news of Cromwell's brutality in Ireland, which was lamentably unlikely to sway English readers; for discussion see Joad Raymond, *The Invention of the Newspaper: English Newsbooks 1641–1649* (Oxford, 1996), pp. 73–6.

occasioned the most elaborate public festivities since his return from crushing the army mutiny, and perhaps since the regicide itself. Had the commander been Charles, the result would surely have been a series of commemorative volumes. So conventionally had the poetry of return become linked with royal occasions that when Charles I returned from Scotland in 1641 an Oxford poet asked:

> And when from juster Empha'ses could we Greet,
> Then when, *Prince, Such, Return'd,* in one Theam meet? [22]

The republic, as has been seen, was less sure of how to commemorate its heroes, nor had it yet gained enough support to be able to expect an outpouring of verses. But Cromwell's victory had made much previous Caroline panegyrical poetry retrospectively look hollow. Marvell's ode of return, in a more sophisticated way than Wither's *Carmen Eucharisticon*, provocatively rewrites that entire tradition.

The 'Horatian' of his title is one of the generic signals that might arouse expectations of a royalist poem. Sir Richard Fanshawe, who had affirmed his royalism with versions of Horace in 1647, went on to translate further odes, one of which uses the same stanza-form as Marvell; this has led to speculation that the two men may have been in contact. But the way in which Marvell reworks Horatian and panegyrical conventions would have been deeply disturbing to loyal supporters of the king. Just how radically his poem differs from royalist Horatianism emerges in a comparison with poems by another writer sometimes claimed to have been one of Marvell's imagined audience, Mildmay Fane, second earl of Westmorland (1601/2–66). [23]

Fane was a veteran of the poetry of royal return. In 1648 he had reprinted poems on Charles's return from Scotland in 1641 and published an appeal for his son's return from his exile. [24] Fane was a friend of Herrick's, and despite his normally retired life he had contacts with London literary circles, taking part in the Horatianizing circle of the late 1640s which was discussed in chapter 4. He was also the brother-in-law of Marvell's future employer Lord Fairfax, and addressed a poem to Oliver St John, a statesman whom Marvell praised in 1651. [25]

22 Jos. Howe, in *Eucharistica Oxoniensia* (Oxford, 1641; 0883), sig. c4r.

23 R. I. V. Hodge, *Foreshortened Time: Andrew Marvell and Seventeenth Century Revolutions* (Cambridge, Ipswich and Totowa, 1978), p. 118, suggests Fane and Fairfax as readers of the 'Ode'. We cannot be sure that the 1681 title was the original one.

24 Mildmay Fane, second earl of Westmorland, *Otia Sacra Optima Fides* (1648; w1476), pp. 141–3, 147, 166, 86–7. See also James Turner, *The Politics of Landscape: Rural Scenery and Society in English Poetry 1630–1660* (Oxford, 1979), pp. 151–2.

25 Mildmay Fane, 'Thorp Palace: A Miracle', in Alastair Fowler (ed.), *The Country House Poem: A Cabinet of Seventeenth-Century Estate Poems and Related Items* (Edinburgh, 1994), pp. 220–2. For possible echoes of Fane in Marvell see J. B. Leishman, *The Art of Marvell's Poetry*, second edition (1968), p. 284.

Whether or not Marvell was aware of the fact, in 1649–50 Fane was meditating on Horace in ways that are highly revealing of royalist responses to the regicide.[26] Some of his poems imitate Horace's most famous public odes: thus I, 2, which Marvell had imitated in his youth, is adapted to make punning attacks on 'Micae-fons' – Crumb-well – St John, Vane and other republican leaders, and ends with a call for the return of Charles II (p. 83). A poem dated 7 January 1650 adapts Horace's famous invocation of spring:

> diffugere niues, redeunt iam gramina campis
> arboribusque comae

('the snows disperse, and now grass returns to the fields and leaves to the trees') to prophesy a change in the political climate when Charles returns:

> diffugere Ciues redeunt iam fausta vicissim
> Numina Nobilibus

('the citizens disperse, and now good fortune returns to the nobles') (IV, 7; p. 77). Here the republic's civic humanism is seen as a disruption of a traditional aristocratic order; Fane, whose father had bought his title from Buckingham, had a high sense of aristocratic honour. In another imitation of a spring ode (IV, 12) the royal return is anticipated by victories for Ormond in Ireland (p. 82). Ireland recurs in an ode imitating II, 11, where Horace tries to divert an anxious friend's mind from politics; Fane declares that it does not matter whether the bellicose brewer (a stock social sneer at Cromwell) is machinating divisions in Ireland (p. 68). A poem for the king's birthday in May 1650 calls for drinking and rejoicing (p. 91). An inscription composed in August 1650 laments the state of the kingdom as a world turned upside down (p. 92). Later the same month, however, he was so confident that the Scots' alliance with Charles II would redeem the situation that he placed at the centre of his manuscript a poem on the king's return headed by a sketch of an empty throne, with a kneeling Charles being helped to his feet and his throne by Britannia. The poem prophesies that the doors of the Temple of Janus will be closed and the people united with their king (p. 95).[27] Had Charles's campaign prevailed, there would doubtless have been an outpouring of similar

26 Mildmay Fane, 'Fugitive Poetry', Harvard University Library fMS Eng 645, pp. 65–6. References in the text are to this MS. Horatian imitations are also found in the 'Middle Manuscript' of the Fulbeck MSS which was begun about 1649, and which is to be issued in facsimile in the *Renaissance Text in Manuscript* series, ed. T. C. S. Cain; I am grateful to Dr Cain for providing transcriptions of the MSS, which I cite by permission of Mrs Mary Fry. See also Eleanor Withington, 'The "Fugitive Poetry" of Mildmay Fane', *Harvard Library Bulletin* 9 (1955), 61–78, and 'Mildmay Fane's Political Satire', ibid. 11 (1957), 40–64.

27 The theme of return figures prominently in Fane's manuscript autobiography, which ends with the Restoration and the arrival of Charles II's queen in England, BL Additional MS 34,220, fol. 20.

odes. The opening of the famous 'Cleopatra' ode (1, 37), often cited as a parallel with Marvell's ode, is inverted from 'Nunc est bibendum' to 'Nunc est
Lugendum', festive drinking being turned to mourning as the poet laments
the kings' fall from their Capitol (p. 64).

Fane had confidently made Horace a royalist symbol. Familiarity with his
odes offered his elite circle of alienated royalists a coded language of bonding
and renewal until the political climate changed. Marvell's 'Ode' rudely shatters that whole ethos. Most obviously, it nowhere mentions Charles II; the
only return at issue is Cromwell's. Marvell's poem affirms the severing of old
loyalties that Fane's odes denounce; it looks forward to further wars where
Fane calls for peace. Both poets imitated the fourth ode of Horace's fourth
book, in which Drusus is compared to an eagle attacking a serpent and a lion
hunting a deer, and which ends with the defeated Hannibal paying tribute to
the Romans. Marvell's images of Cromwell as hunter may have their ominous
side, but they are as nothing to Fane's reworking of the opening stanza to have
Cromwell not an eagle but an agent of Satan. Fane glosses the opening with 'O
braue Ol:'.[28]

Like the royalist newsbook-writers, Fane would grant no kind of dignity,
even a negative one, to the republic's leaders. In July 1650 he wrote a bitter,
irreverent satire on Fairfax's yielding his command to Cromwell – 'When
Theeus fall out one comes by good' – and suggested that both men needed
hanging (p. 89). Marvell ignores stock sneers at Cromwell's low birth, both
granting him a space in 'private Gardens' of the kind Fane praises and elevating the public far above the private to align him with the greatest classical
heroes. In the classicizing royalist tradition to which Fane belonged, festivities for a return might be represented by classical imagery of sacrifice.[29] In
Marvell, in a piece of particularly grim wit, the only sacrifice is the past one of
Charles I.

Marvell's strategy invites comparison with a militantly republican poem
by Henry Marten, who certainly knew Fane. At the time when Marten and
Fane were on their youthful travels, Fane had addressed Latin poems to
Marten and/or his father.[30] Marten reciprocated some time later with a

---

28 Harvard University Library fMS Eng 645, p. 73. Contrast Fisher's description of
   Cromwell's Scottish foes

>   beset
>   By barking Hounds, intangled in a net (*Veni; Vidi; Vici*, p. 32).

29 For example, Robert Herrick, 'To the King, upon his welcome to *Hampton-Court*', *The
   Poetical Works of Robert Herrick*, ed. L. C. Martin (Oxford, 1956), p. 300.

30 Fulbeck 'Small MS': 'Ad Hen: Martin', p. 11, 'In H. M.' and 'De seipso ad Dom[inum]
   Martin', p. 14. The title 'Dominus' may refer to Marten senior's recent elevation to the
   Court of Arches, but the other poem seems to refer to Marten junior.

caustic response to the royalist cult of peaceful retirement. His 'Antepod[um] Horatian[um]: Vitae civicae Laudes' inverted Horace's most celebrated epode, the second, 'Beatus ille qui procul negotiis', which had been translated by Jonson and echoed by innumerable cavalier poets.[31] Marten inverts Horace's opening to attack rural retirement as a cowardly shunning of public business:

> Ignavus ille qui sepultus ocio
> (Vt bruta gens animalium)
> Materna bobus rura vexat pigrior,
> Inhians decuplo foenori
> Rostris ineptus, impar et se iudice
> Civis, cliensq[ue] civium.[32]

[Cowardly, slothful is he who buried in leisure, like the brute race of animals, more sluggish than his oxen, vexes his mother lands, gaping for tenfold increase, unfitted for the rostra, even in his own judgement unequal to a citizen, and a dependent of citizens.]

Fane had called for the citizens to be dispersed so that the nobility could resume their reign; Marten attacks this kind of idealization of the retired life as a falling-off from the highest realization of humanity in civic life. By writing in Latin himself he aims to refute royalist charges against the rebels' barbarism: instead, the republicans are recovering the values inherent in the Latin language at its greatest point.

Marvell's ode is in many ways an anti-ode parallel to Marten's anti-epode: a Horatian poem of royalist return viewed through a violently distorting mirror. Not all readers would have accepted Marten's attack on Horace's political regression: the poet had fought for the republicans in his youth and May's friend Daniel Heinsius saw him as maintaining a humanist commitment to the active life.[33] Caroline Horatianism, however, was more liable to Marten's strictures. The poetry of royal returns – including Marvell's own – had often heightened Horace's mythologizing tendencies. Unlike Charles, Cromwell made much of his refusal of elaborate ceremony on his return. Marvell's poem rises to such sobriety, but pushes far beyond it. Had it been

---

31 Fane imitated the poem in a religious rather than political direction, 'Fugitive Poetry', p. 67.
32 ML78, fol. 4v; cited in Williams, 'Marten', p. 217. Williams states that this poem was written to mark the dissolution of the Long Parliament in 1653, but the grounds for this dating are unclear.
33 Heinsius dedicated one Horace edition to a Venetian statesman, drawing a parallel between the activism of his own nation's struggle against the Spaniards and the Venetians' defence of their republican liberty; *Quintus Horatius Flaccus*, 3 vols. (Leiden, 1629), fol. 8r; May's inscription to Heinsius (see above, p. 81 n.) notes his membership of the Venetian Order of St Mark.

issued as a broadside in July 1650, its opening would immediately have come as a shock. Horace's odes and their Caroline imitations lingered over the peaceful ceremonies appropriate to a returning hero. One poet wrote in 1641 that had there been such peace in his time, Hannibal would never have crossed the Alps; another, imitating the end of *Odes* IV, 4, claimed that all Europe would follow Charles's example of peace.[34] Cowley wrote of the anticipated avoidance of war:

> Their Armour now may be hung up to sight,
> And onely in their Halls the children fright.[35]

Even Fisher's Cromwell, on his return from Scotland,

> With the same sword that he before did cut
> Ope *Ianus* gates, again the same doth shut.[36]

Fisher did, however, share with Marvell a polemical attack on the Stuart cult of 'sinfull peace'.[37]

Marvell's poem urges its readers to abandon the inglorious arts of peace; the word 'Must' is an abrasively unusual word for the opening of a festive poem. Where Fisher wrote in his ode to Cromwell that

> I humbly do appear
> Thy *glories* trumpet, and *Thy* Honorer[38]

this narrator disappears behind a hypothetical youth who only 'would' appear.

The first reference to Cromwell is not to his present return but is offered as an analogy with the 'forward Youth' in his haste to fight for Parliament, and we are then given a very long flashback through his career. Readers may well think that they have strayed into the wrong poem, until at line 73 they return to the initial 'now', the present tense traditionally deemed appropriate for ceremonial poetry.[39] Here again ceremonial elements are downplayed. We are given not a speech of welcome from the English but, startlingly, a reported speech by the Irish he has left behind. The poem does then offer an image of Cromwell's handing over his 'Sword and Spoyls' to the public, but this gesture has already been undermined by the opening injunction to the forward youth to take up arms. Only now, when Cromwell is imagined as having removed his sword and armour, does the poem offer a moment of repose, mirrored in the simile of the falcon perching on a 'green Bow'. Ceremonial poetry would normally be expected to excel in colourful description, but 'Green' is the first colour word apart from the references to blood.

---

34 James Duport, *Irenodia Cantabrigiensis* (Cambridge, 1641; E179.4), sig. F1v; P. Samwayes, sig. I1v.

35 Abraham Cowley, 'An Ode upon the return of his Majestie', *Irenodia Cantabrigiensis*, sig. K1r.   36 Fisher, *Veni; Vidi; Vici*, sig. I3r.

37 Fisher, *Veni; Vidi; Vici*, p. 72.   38 Fisher, *Veni; Vidi; Vici*, sig. H7r.

39 Aristotle, *Rhetoric*, I, 3.

And the rest does not last long; the poem proceeds to look forward to the Scottish campaign and beyond. After a prophecy of major European victories in the future, the poem reverts to a 'now' that is not ceremonial but persuasive, the immediate urgency of the war with the Scots (line 105). In the end, the poem is more concerned with Scotland than with Ireland; so much emphasis indeed is placed on the Scottish war that it was perhaps written not immediately on Cromwell's return but after his appointment as commander, the period when the press was stepping up its propaganda, and when Hall and Fisher were preparing to cover the campaign. The poem's 'now's can perhaps be linked with a portrait of Marten by Lely which had 'now' inscribed on it (figure 11). This seems to have been a Machiavellian injunction to decisive action, to seize the *occasione*, perhaps linked with the regicide. The war against the Scots, while disturbing royalist-leaning Presbyterians in both countries, had reunited many radicals with the republicans: Lilburne went to see Cromwell off to the war and appeared satisfied with his assurances that he would use any victories he gained to establish a reformed political settlement.

If the poem lacks any sympathy with the Irish, it treats them as enemies worthy of respect, and of having a voice in the poem, tendentiously though it may be manipulated. Many leading republicans displayed more animus against the Scots, as renegades from the cause, than the Irish, and the 'Ode' falls in with this pattern. Cromwell's 'Valour sad' (sober, serious) is directly contrasted with the Scots who shrink under their plaids with their 'party-colour'd Mind'. The Scots Presbyterians, who prided themselves on having elevated themselves above superstition, are punningly linked with a primitive taste for garish colours – a taste that also aligns them with courtly luxury. The sobriety of the Commonwealth's man versus Presbyterian duplicity had become an established theme (see figure 12).[40] The Scots' gesture of hiding under their plaid recalls Spenser's hostile accounts of Irish mantles in his *View of the Present State of Ireland*, a work that was currently in Milton's mind (*Observations, MPW*, III, 303 n. 10). The taunt forms a reminder that the Scots' Presbyterian allies in Ulster had allied themselves with the king's Irish supporters. The poem's praise of Cromwell parallels the excited tone of a newsbook: 'And now what glory shall we give unto him? shall we erect him a Statute[sic]? why that will prove as mortall as his Body? shall we lay up his sword like the sword of *Goliah*? Alas that will preserve rust as much as fame'. Marvell's forward youth is urged to oil his rusty armour and join this army whose enemies were 'amazed at the forwardnesse of their march'.[41] The effect

40 The illustration, here shown as it appeared in Samuel Chidley, *The Dissembling Scot* (1652; E652.13), had already been used in *A Cloak for Knavery* (1648; C4718), an attack on the invading Scots during the Second Civil War.

41 *The Weekly Intelligencer of the Commonwealth* no. 1, 16–23 July 1650, E608.9, pp. 2, 4.

11 Henry Marten, by Sir Peter Lely.

of all this emphasis on the forthcoming war is of a kind of skewed perspective, with the poem demonstrating its own forwardness while ceremonial that would be expected to be at the centre of the poem is virtually edged out.

Up to a point, it is true, prophecies of conquest were conventional in panegyrical verse, but they had become unusual in Caroline *prosphonetika*, which regularly ended with praise of the peace enjoyed by Britain while war raged elsewhere. Marvell was in one sense here going back more rigorously than the Carolines to the Horatian model; for many of Horace's poems of return ended with prophecies of future campaigns. But here as so often he

Religion is made a Covering
For every wicked and Rebelious thing,
Errors are hid heer on the right and left
Rebelion, Idolitry, and Theft,
Plunders, and Rapins, Whordoms, Fornications,
Dissimulations, Flateries, and Invasions,
By Time, this Cloake is worn fo of their Back
So their's discover'd many a Knavish Knack.

12 Engraving prefatory to Samuel Chidley, *The Dissembling Scot*, 1652.

radically revises the Horatian model. Where Horace celebrates campaigns that will consolidate the power of Augustus's dynasty against the remaining institutions of the Roman republic, Marvell celebrates wars that are specifically directed by the newly founded republic against monarchies and in defence of republican values. *Mercurius Politicus* constantly reminded its readers of anti-monarchical risings in many parts of Europe.[42] Horace's odes frequently prophesied victories against the Britons,[43] and Lucan's narrator had lamented that Caesar had turned his arms against his own people instead of properly subduing Gaul and Britain (iii.73–8). Marvell's poem celebrates an English republic that is able to outdo the tottering Roman republic.

The jingoism of the poem's ending has been assumed by some critics to be self-evidently ironic; but there are parallels in other verse tributes to the new state. After the Battle of Worcester, one 'Franciscus Nelson, *Miles Academicus*' – a signature yoking together arms and arts – published a Horatian ode in praise of Cromwell which echoed Horace, *Odes* I, 2, and an English poem with the militant ending:

> Woe to all Monarchs, woe; thrice woe to *Roome*;
> Ev'n from the *North* proceeds her fatal Doom:
> Let free-born *Brittains* now triumph and sing,
> Let CROMWELS Fame amongst the Nations ring.[44]

R. Fletcher prophesied English expansion:

> Then *Thames* as *Tybur* shall rejoice to be
> Crown'd with the spoiles of the worlds royaltie:
> And all the neighb'ring Continents implore
> To be imbrac'd under the British lore.[45]

Another poet urged of the new republic that

> Sea-Dominion may as well bee gain'd
> By new acquests, as by descent maintain'd[46]

in terms very close to Marvell's

> The same *Arts* that did *gain*
> A *Pow'r* must it *maintain*. (Horatian Ode, lines 119–20)

The baldness of this formulation has been taken to indicate ironic exposure of Cromwell's brutality; but such antitheses were very much in the air amongst

---

42 Christopher Hill, 'The English Revolution and the Brotherhood of Man', in *Puritanism and Revolution*, revised edition (Harmondsworth, 1986), pp. 126–53; see also Worden, 'Andrew Marvell, Oliver Cromwell, and the Horatian Ode', pp. 160–2.

43 For patriotic retorts to Horace's anti-British sentiments see J[ohn]. S[mith]., *The Lyrick Poet* (1649; H2772), p. 22, and *The Poems and Translations of Sir Richard Fanshawe*, vol. I, ed. Peter Davidson (Oxford, 1997), 210.

44 *The Last Newes from the King of Scots* (1651; E641.24), pp. 4–5. Nelson's 'Te Duce CROMWELL' adapts Horace's 'Te duce Caesar'; he also cited parallels from Athenian history.

45 R. Fletcher, *Radius Heliconicus: Or, The Resolution of a Free State* (1651; 669f15.83).

46 John Selden, *Of the Dominion, or Ownership of the Sea*, trans. Marchamont Nedham (1652; S2432), verses facing title engraving.

the regime's supporters. A pamphlet supporting the Irish campaign complained that 'the Art of keeping that which the sword bequeaths' had decayed since Roman times.[47] Another republican asked the Presbyterian royalists: 'tell me, why a Reformation gained, and maintained by the Sword in *England*, is so unlawfull, which in other places is so just and pious?'.[48] There may have been a common source for the antithesis in Machiavelli.[49] But there may also be a glance back at Lucan's narrator's ominous warning to the Roman people: 'O faciles dare summa deos eademque tueri/Difficiles!', 'You gods that easily giue prosperity,/But not maintaine it'.[50]

Part of the poem's wit is to set up expectations of a conventionally Horatian poem and offer something much closer to Lucan instead, a kind of mini-*Pharsalia*.[51] As many critics have noted, there are close parallels between lines 9–16 and Lucan's celebrated initial portrait of Caesar:

> restlesse valour, and in warre a shame
> Not to be Conquerour...
> Ready to fight, where hope, or anger call,
> His forward Sword...
> And loues that ruine should enforce his way;
> As lightning by the winde forc'd from a cloude
> Breakes through the wounded aire with thunder loud,
> Disturbes the D[a]y, the people terrifyes,
> And by a light oblique dazels our eyes,
> Not *Ioues* owne Temple spares it; when no force,
> No barre can hinder his preuailing course... (*Pharsalia*, i. 144–56; May, sig. A3v)

The parallels are at least as close with Lucan's tightly condensed Latin: Caesar has 'nescia virtus/Stare loco' (i.144–5), a courage that cannot stay in one place;

---

47 *A Discourse Concerning the Affaires of Ireland* (1650; E619.7), pp. 1, 2.

48 G[eorge]. W[alker?]., *Republica Anglicana* (1650; E780.25), p. 43. For reasons against the attribution of this work to Wither see David Norbrook, 'Some Notes on the Canon of George Wither', *Notes and Queries* 241 (1996), 276–81 (279–80); I now believe that many analogies with Walker's *Anglo-Tyrannus* (1650; E619.1), which had the same publisher, suggest a common authorship. Cf. John Canne, *The Improvement of Mercy* (1649; E571.20), p. 24, on Jones's victory in Ireland: 'we hope our Army there, will use this victory to purpose, and be carefull still to maintaine that which they winne'.

49 On the Machiavellian coupling of 'acquistare' and 'mantenere' see Brian Vickers, 'Machiavelli and Marvell's "Horatian Ode"', *Notes and Queries* 234 (1989), 32–8.

50 *Pharsalia*, i.510–11; May, sigs. A8v-B1r.

51

> What Field of all the Civil Wars,
> Where his were not the deepest Scars?

echoes Lucan's 'alta sedent civilis volnera dextrae', 'Deepe pierce the wounds receiu'd in ciuill warre' (i.32; May, sig. A1v).

'virtus' could also be rendered as Machiavellian *virtù*, and Marvell develops Cromwell's spatial restlessness throughout the poem:

> So restless *Cromwel* could not cease
> In the inglorious Arts of Peace,
>   But through adventrous War
>   Urged his active Star.
> And, like the three-fork'd Lightning, first
> Breaking the Clouds where it was nurst,
>   Did thorough his own Side
>   His fiery way divide.
> For 'tis all one to Courage high
> The Emulous or Enemy;
>   And with such to inclose
>   Is more then to oppose. (lines 9–20)

The analogy with Lucan's Caesar is extended by the play on 'inclose/oppose', which recalls Caesar's word-play when the besieged inhabitants of Marseilles ask him to lay down his arms and enter the city: 'Iam non excludere tantum,/ Inclusisse volunt', 'now they want not to exclude me but to have inclosed me' (*Pharsalia*, iii. 368).[52]

Just which political events Marvell's enigmatic lines refer to remains obscure: neither the lethargic aristocratic commanders of the pre-New Model Army era nor the Levellers Cromwell had crushed in 1649 were precisely emulous.[53] But they carry a possible warning for the future. Marvell's Cromwell has not only the restless energy of Lucan's Caesar but his cunning. The first thing we learn is that he turned against those on his own side who were emulous of him. There is no evidence for the poem's claim that he contrived Charles's escape to Carisbrooke in order to entrap him, a charge made with different motives by royalists and Levellers. For most of the poem the emphasis is on his destructiveness; and though at times he is associated with providence, at the climax he is 'the Wars and Fortunes son'. The state as a whole may be a hunter just as much as Cromwell; but it will need all its political skills to 'lure' such an energetic figure back to its perch (line 95). Wither was to use a similar animal figure to bring out the mingled admiration and unease that Cromwell aroused:

> A *homebred Lion* (of a hair unknown
> In *Africa*) by being overgrown,

---

52 The resemblance is not so striking in May's version, 'they desire/Not to exclude, but take me prisoner' (sig. E1v).

53 Michael Wilding suggests an allusion to the crushing of the mutiny in *Dragons Teeth: Literature in the English Revolution* (Oxford, 1987), pp. 122–4. He forcefully draws attention to the elements that mark the poem off from more radical groupings.

And dreadfull to his *Keepers*, will thereby
Awake the rage of *smother'd jealousie,*
And lose his *tail*; except within his *pawes,*
He couch his head, and hide his *teeth* and *clawes*;
Or *Rampant* grow . . .
But that stout *Lion* by his prudency
May easily improve this *jealousie,*
Both for the *Publike safety,* and th'increase
Of his own *honor . . .*[54]

These negative hints may seem to align Marvell with royalist critics of
Cromwell the usurping Caesar, thus turning the poem into an equivalent of
Cowley's *Civill Warre,* with Charles as the lamented Pompey. There are
indeed overtones of Pompey's composed and dignified death (*Pharsalia,*
viii.613ff) in Charles's demise. And possible parallels between Cromwell and
Caesar do cast an ominous shadow. Nevertheless, in the summer of 1650 the
obvious equivalent to Lucan's Caesar at the Rubicon was the young Charles
II, poised to invade England.[55] And as was seen in the previous chapter,
analogies between Cromwell and Caesar could work at very different levels of
ideological sophistication. For the more self-consciously republican writers,
it was perfectly possible to make a distinction between Caesar the general
and Caesar the enemy of liberty. If in royalist panegyric moral virtue is
related to a timeless, mythical realm, in republican writing it is assessed in
relation to specific political contexts. Cromwell is praiseworthy because he is
'still in the *Republick's* hand' (lines 81–2), and his victory is given an ideological charge by the fact that he offers a '*Kingdome*' for the disposal of the
republic.

In this context, some of the paradoxes in the presentation of
Cromwell begin to make more sense. Like many of Hall's and Nedham's
writings, the 'Ode' straddles the divide between the highly moralistic
language of civic humanism and the more self-consciously 'scientific' language of those who defended the regicide by an appeal to practical necessity. On the one hand, the poem gives a powerful sense of Cromwell's
agency, as in

But through adventrous War
Urged his active Star (lines 11–12)

---

54 George Wither, *The Dark Lantern* (1653; E1432.3; *WMW*, III), p. 27. Wither later
explained that 'This was interpreted as a Relative to *Oliver Cromwel*, then Lord General
of the *Army*, whose Arms was a *White Lyon*': *Ecchoes from the Sixth Trumpet* (1666;
WMW, VI; W3155), p. 64.
55 Nicholas Guild, 'The Context of Marvell's Allusions to Lucan in "An Horatian Ode"',
Papers on Language and Literature 14 (1978), 406–13.

where the emphatic initial vowels heighten the complex idea of Cromwell as both determined by and determining his active star.[56] He 'Could by industrious Valour climb' (line 33), and shows us how

> much one Man can do,
> That does both act and know. (lines 75–6)

Moreover, his agency, in classic republican manner, is seen as an aspect of his self-control, his self-rule: he 'can so well obey' (line 84), and

> what he may, forbears
> His Fame to make it theirs[.] (lines 87–8)

On the other hand, Cromwell's vigour is repeatedly seen as the mere effect of an external force. Marvell shares with Nedham a fondness for stating the republic's case with a provocatively extreme edge:

> Though Justice against Fate complain,
> And plead the antient Rights in vain:
>   But those do hold or break
>   As Men are strong or weak.
> Nature that hateth emptiness,
> Allows of penetration less:
>   And therefore must make room
>   Where greater Spirits come. (lines 37–44)

No sooner does Justice appear as a personification than she collapses into an arbitrary label. The emphasis on physical necessity here is Hobbesian in spirit, and recalls Nedham's publication of extracts from Hobbes in *The Case of the Commonwealth*. A humanist, moralizing discourse of justice and virtue gives way to a harsh pragmatism. Similar effects are to be found throughout much of the literature defending the new state. The republic is a 'forced Pow'r', at once agent and instrument of necessity (line 66). But what unites Marvell's ode with works by Milton, Nedham, Hall and Fisher is the ability to combine a self-consciously unillusioned realism with an activist republicanism. Fisher – or Manley – seems in fact to be echoing Marvell's scientific language in his portrait of Cromwell's assaults on the Highlanders:

> So do those towring lightnings sadly cleere
> The place from Troopes, and make a *Vacuum* there[.] (p. 64)

---

56 There seems to be a crude inversion of this kind of effect in Manley's translation of Fisher:

> When the unhappy Kings ill luck
> The State into a storm did pluck

(*Veni; Vidi; Vici*, sig. H7v).

while his 'Of that which heaven withstands, 'tis vain to treat' may echo ''Tis Madness to resist or blame/The force of angry Heavens flame' (lines 25–6)[57]. The mediating term between necessity and virtue is a republican analysis of history. Hobbes was very reluctant to see virtues as changing according to the political form under which they occurred; Nedham takes it for granted that a republican form will allow virtues unknown to monarchy. Political forms mould and facilitate virtue; at the same time, they cannot entirely determine it, for great men can still help to change from one form to another. Machiavelli argued that only a single great individual could successfully create liberty where it had not previously existed. But such changes would be immensely difficult, and the very qualities that helped to create liberty might also destroy it. Lucan's Caesar had possessed many qualities that might have been admirable in one founding a republic; the wager of the 'Ode' is that a kind of positive rewriting of the *Pharsalia* may now be possible, yet that poem's tragic resonances are not lost.

When seen in this light, the exposure of Cromwell's potential dangers appears less ironic than carefully analytic, exploring these complexities of agency.[58] The stress on natural laws retrospectively raises questions about the 'Must' of line 2: what at first sounded like a moral imperative turns out to be no more than an impersonal necessity.[59] We are reminded that Cromwell 'could not cease' in the arts of peace. He is associated with the natural violence of lightning (line 13). When we are told that like a falcon he 'Falls heavy' (line 92), the agency of hunting blurs into a sense of gravitational inevitability. The 'must' of the poet's concluding reminder about maintaining power seems to box Cromwell into a corner. He must keep his sword erect 'for the last effect'. This phrase may have been suggested by Fanshawe's translation of the Horatian ode that is Marvell's closest model:

> What is't but *Neros* can effect,
> Whom Heav'ns with prosperous Stars protect,
> And their own prudent care
>   Clews through the Maze of War.[60]

But where Fanshawe, like Horace's 'perficiunt manus', stresses powerful agency, Marvell's 'last effect' inserts Cromwell into a much larger pattern of

---

57 Fisher, *Veni; Vidi; Vici*, pp. 64, 8; Payne Fisher, *Irenodia Gratulatoria* (1652; E796.30), sig. G2r: 'Sic per densatas acies glomerata vagantur/Fulmina, & excussis apparet *Inane*, Catervis'. Compare 'sadly' with Marvell's 'Valour sad', l. 107.

58 Marvell's 'Ode' can be fruitfully read against Victoria Kahn's sophisticated analysis of the complexities of agency and intentionality in the Engagement Controversy: *Machiavellian Rhetoric: From the Counter-Reformation to Milton* (Princeton, 1994), pp. 156–65.   59 I am grateful to Sharon Achinstein for this point.

60 Fanshawe, *Poems and Translations*, I, 200, translation of IV, 4.

causation; it seems to be an austerely secular term for the apocalypse. As in many pragmatic defences of the republic, we are referred to an inscrutable divine will: Cromwell carries through a providential pattern outside his individual control.

And although the poem lays the emphasis on Cromwell's actions, his is not the only agency. He is part of a common undertaking which indeed involves destroying time-hallowed institutions, and even the political vocabulary that accompanies them, but is also a new creation. Cromwell has

> cast the Kingdome old
> Into another Mold. (lines 35–6)

This claim is slightly qualified later in the poem:

> So when they did design
> The *Capitols* first Line,
> A bleeding Head where they begun,
> Did fright the Architects to run;
> And yet in that the *State*
> Foresaw it's happy Fate. (lines 67–72)

Here a distinction is made between the architects of the new state, those responsible for its design, and the soldier who put the plan into practice. Marvell's analogy of the frightened architects presents accurately enough the reaction of many members of the Rump Parliament who were backing away from the radical implications of the regicide. Marvell may also recall Milton's denunciation in *The Tenure of Kings and Magistrates* of those who

> comming in the cours of these affaires, to have thir share in great actions, above the force of Law or Custom, at least to give thir voice and approbation, begin to swerve, and almost shiver at the Majesty and grandeur of som noble deed, as if they were newly enter'd into a great sin; disputing presidents, forms, and circumstances, when the Common-wealth nigh perishes for want of deeds in substance, don with just and faithfull expedition. (*MPW*, III, 194)

The omen, however initially disturbing and violent, has to be seen in a longer-term pattern: it anticipates a decisive historical break, the transition from monarchy to freedom in Rome. The poem's claim is that England is at just such a stage.

This imagery of foundation needs to be set against the poem's sympathetic portrait of the dying king's grace. It was possible to acknowledge the elements of beauty in pre-war courtly culture, as did other republican writers like Robinson, Warr, Harrington and Lucy Hutchinson, and still insist that the beauty should be considered in relation to the society as a whole. In the 'Ode', courtly elegance is associated with a certain evasion of difficult realities, as in the weak rhyme of 'sing' with 'languishing' (lines 3–4);[61] the youth must 'appear' (line 1), enter the public realm, to be in tune with the spirit of the times. Though the king is forced into his 'narrow case' (line 52), and only under compulsion does he bow his head 'Down as upon a Bed' (line 64), the retreat into privacy and passivity is consistent with a general republican critique of courtly culture: Cromwell places it under sufficient pressure to reveal both its beauty and its limitations. The stock erotic analogies between love and death are pushed to a grisly extreme as this last of Marvell's recent sequence of beautiful young royalists sinks into bed. And Cromwell turns the king's fate into a tragedy that grotesquely breaks the frame of art, with the soldiers clapping their bloody hands (line 56); however grisly, that breaking of the frame is also the sublime moment celebrated more directly by Milton and others. Marvell does not follow Milton in insinuating that Charles's beautiful end was a more banal figure's sentimental claim for tragic status; but by placing so much emphasis on Cromwell's individual role in the regicide, he makes the two men artistic as well as political antitypes.[62] The poem is as free as the *Pharsalia* of conventional mythology, preferring a self-conscious tough-mindedness and austerity that verges on undermining the compliments it bestows.

The regicide may have destroyed some forms of beauty, but it has opened the way to the sublime. The poet of the poem's opening becomes suddenly yoked to Cromwell at the ninth line by a decisive 'So' that lifts him out of traditional frameworks. The poem's diction again and again parallels not only Hall's political writings but his *Advancement of Learning* and Longinus translation: the preference for being 'forward' over 'languishing', the sense of being present at a restless new birth, the preference for a risky new experiment even at the cost of violence over a safe, received beauty, the preference for apparent discords making possible a higher kind of unity over a narrowly contained beauty.[63] It is possible that, not for the last time (see chapter 8), Marvell engages with that kind of narrow concord in the form of lines by

---

61 Languor is a distinct target of republican thought: see, for example, Cicero, *De Natura Deorum*, I.iv.7; see also *De Officiis*, 3.1.3, *Academicus*, 2.2.6, *Orator*, 2.6, *In Pisonem*, 33.82, and for contemporary examples, Worden, 'Andrew Marvell, Oliver Cromwell, and the Horatian Ode', pp. 167–8.

62 For some interesting observations on this point see Thomas R. Edwards, *Imagination and Power: A Study of Poetry on Public Themes* (1971), pp. 66–82.

63 To Marvell's association of Cromwell with 'three-fork'd Lightning' 'burning through the Air' (l. 21) compare Hall's Longinus: sublime poets '*burn* up all before them'; Demosthenes '*thunder-strikes* and in a manner *enlightens* the Oratours of all ages' (J[ohn]. H[all]., *Peri Hypsous, or Dionysius Longinus of the Height of Eloquence* (1652; E1294.2), pp. 62, 64). Compare also Hall on the victories of the 'sur-humane' Parliament: 'You gathered strength at the Center, and burned through them like stubble': *A Gagg to Love's Advocate* (1651; E640.28), sigs. A2r–v.

Edmund Waller: a significant number of rhyme-words coincide with those in Waller's 'Upon his Majesties repairing of Pauls'.[64] Marvell's architects draw the lines of their state's 'happy Fate' just as Hall's Parliament is urged to 'lay a modell, and draw the lines of happinesse and security for all posterity'.[65] Cromwell's 'wiser Art' is in the first instance a political skill that is needed to turn such plans into reality, but it also directly confronts the arts of the Caroline court.

Marvell effects the transition between destruction and new beginning by the analogy of the bleeding head. It was perhaps in Machiavelli's admired Livy that Marvell found the story of the head whose discovery gave new hope to the builders of the Temple of Jupiter; Marvell adds the blood to intensify the link with the regicide, and with the defences of Charles's execution as an exemplary or expiatory sacrifice. Cromwell does not go so far as May's ghost of Lucan in drinking sacrificial blood to renew republican discourse, but it is his refusal to shrink from such grotesque but sublime images that enables him to carry through the victory. Strongly though the central placing emphasizes Charles's death, in terms of rhetorical argument it constitutes a digression, and Marvell meshes it in with his narration, beginning with a 'that' taking up from Cromwell's actions and ending with a 'So' leading on to the new foundation. If the poem's first sixty lines embody in their form the 'memorable hour' of the execution, the 'Ode' moves on to a new political world: its structure is centrifugal, not symmetrical, moving out both at the beginning and end from the encomiastic present to the uncertain but urgent future.[66]

And there is a moment of empathy between the soldier and the poet: for Marvell too is moving out of the Horatian paradigm and claiming for the young republic a literary greatness and originality equal to the ancients. Lucan's audacious claim of affinity with Caesar, 'Me teque legent', here takes on a new kind of resonance. Like d'Aubigné, Marvell is able to appropriate the spirit of Lucan's Caesar to prophesy a very different, Protestant conquest of Rome; and he has already engaged in his own, poetic conquest. Hall had observed that when knowledge met those who would enlarge her empire, 'shee ambitiously encourages them, and willingly crownes them'.[67] A newsbook commented in August 1650 that '*Scotland* (it seemes) hath its *Crisis*, as well as *Ireland*'[68]; Hall proclaimed in his Longinus translation that Europe

64 Paul Hammond, 'Echoes of Waller in Marvell's "Horatian Ode"', *Notes and Queries* 236 (1991), 172–3.

65 John Hall, *An Humble Motion to the Parliament of England Concerning the Advancement of Learning* (1649; H350; ed. A. K. Croston, Liverpool, 1953), p. 23.

66 Alastair Fowler, *Triumphal Forms: Structural Patterns in Elizabethan Poetry* (Cambridge, 1970), pp. 78–81.   67 Hall, *The Advancement of Learning*, p. 19.

68 *The Best and Most Perfect Intelligencer* no. 1, 1–8 August 1650, E609.6, p. 3 (this is the only surviving issue).

was encountering 'the *Crisis* of eloquence'[69]; the '*Clymacterick*' of Marvell's poem relates to literary as well as political culture. Finding his poetic *occasione*, he had seized it; like Wither, he had helped to lay new foundations, to open up the space for a new or recovered form of writing.

The poem's sublime aspirations break its Horatian framework. In one of his odes (IV, 2), Horace declares that he is unable to imitate Pindar, that he is more like a bee than a soaring bird. This is in part a mock-modesty, for *Odes* IV, 4 was widely praised as a fine imitation of Pindar. But Renaissance readers noted, and were intrigued by, the difference between Horace's measured rationality and the unusual transitions, half-understood metres, and unexpected digressions of Pindar's odes[70] – qualities that made Longinus admire him as a prototype of the sublime poets who '*burn* up all before them'.[71] As in Milton's ode to Rous, the Horatian ode has a Pindaric ode inside it, struggling to escape. Milton was acknowledged by early readers to be especially close to Pindar in his lyrics, especially in a poem like *Lycidas*, with its strong tension between conventional rhyme scheme and centrifugal digressions.[72] Poetic and political liberty were paralleled. Milton's sonnets too became known for their sublime effects. Learning after the Restoration that Milton had written some 'admirable Panegyricks (as to sublimitie of Witt)', on Cromwell and Fairfax, John Aubrey eagerly sought them out: even if they were in praise of the devil, 'tis the *hypsos* [sublime] y^t I looke after'.[73] Significantly, he added that ''tis beyond Waller's, or any thing in that kind': Aubrey readily thinks of Milton as engaging in a contention with Waller, and as outdoing him in sublimity. Milton's Cromwell sonnet, with the hero emerging from a 'cloud' of war and detractions, seems to reflect knowledge of Marvell's ode.[74] Marvell's elliptical account of Cromwell's career, with its sublime imagery and its long digression about Charles, parallels Milton's experiments with the sublime lyric. It also counters royalist modes of the sublime. In 1647 Cowley had published a poetic manifesto which announced his intention of aiming higher:

---

69 Hall, *Peri Hypsous*, sig. A7v.
70 *Bernardini Parthenii... Commentarii*, fol. 67r.
71 Hall, *Peri Hypsous*, p. 62.
72 John Beale, letter to John Evelyn, 31 August 1667, BL, Evelyn Collection, fol. 2v; Nicholas von Maltzahn, 'Laureate, Republican, Calvinist: An Early Response to Milton and *Paradise Lost* (1667)', *Milton Studies* 29 (1992), 181–98 (184).
73 Bodleian MS Wood F. 39, fol. 372r; *ABL*, II, 70.
74 David Crane, 'Marvell and Milton on Cromwell', *Notes and Queries* 231 (1986), 464. The Fairfax sonnet may also be echoed in [Walker?], *Respublica Anglicana*, p. 23: 'The Lord Generall *Fairfax*, a man whose Fame rings through all *Europe*'; *The Tenure of Kings and Magistrates* is quoted on p. 41.

> Unpast Alps stop mee, but I'le cut through all;
>   And march, the Muses Hanniball.[75]

Cowley, who had written many Horatian odes, including several on royal occasions, was to turn increasingly to translating and imitating Pindar; Marvell's Cromwell takes up Cowley's challenge.[76]

But there were inevitable difficulties in taking a single person as the muse of a new republican sublime, and the 'Ode' does not entirely suppress them. Cromwell's sublimity involves an impatience with established limits and laws; and this necessarily sets up a tension with the demands of a republic to avoid cults of personality. Fisher tried to compensate for his praise of Cromwell by addressing other leading republicans; Wither played down personalities altogether; Marvell is content with assertions that Cromwell will remain loyal to the state. However much he holds back from conventional language of monarchical praise, Marvell lays so much emphasis on Cromwell's agency in establishing the republic that the other protagonists remain in the shadows, or appear only as the frightened architects. And we are led to ask whether the architects have yet recovered from their fear. The purged Parliament was still a provisional constitutional settlement, with an undertaking to dissolve itself at some stage. John M. Wallace has suggested that Marvell's 'Ode' implies the need for Cromwell to assume supreme powers to remould the state more completely, playing the role sketched out by Machiavelli for the founder of liberty.[77] It is hard to find any specific grounding for this programme in the ode, beyond a generalized praise of his ability to 'sway' (line 83); but within a few years Marvell was indeed to approve Cromwell's rule in these terms, after Cromwell had divided his way through his own side by dissolving the Rump in April 1653. The personal enthusiasm for Cromwell in the 'Ode' is compatible with Marvell's later career, and marks it off from much republican writing.

At this stage, however, there are still reservations about personal rule. And insofar as the poem does leave open the way for Cromwell to take further providential actions, it is not because it is nostalgic for monarchy but because the republic's foundations have not yet been completed. In November 1650 the reformer William Hickman wrote to Cromwell that the Irish campaign must be the basis for radical political change:

> hetherto in the chandge of our Government nothinge materiall as yet hath bin done, but a takinge of the head of monarchy and placing uppon the body or trunck of it, the name or title of a Commonwealth, a name aplicable to all forms

75 Abraham Cowley, 'To the Reader', in *The Mistresse* (1647; E1149.1), p. 115.
76 When Cowley returned to England and made his peace with Parliament he began work on a Pindaric ode in praise of Brutus and the Roman republic. On Cowley and Pindar see David Trotter, *The Poetry of Abraham Cowley* (London and Basingstoke, 1979), pp. 109ff.   77 Wallace, *Destiny His Choice*, pp. 89ff.

of Government, and contained under the former . . . [there was a need for new laws] not superstructed uppon the same foundation, and so will no better consort together, then a new peece in an ould vestment, but clash one with the other . . . the onely way to make this a happy Government, is not onely to abolish all things that weare constituted under monarchy, though very good in themselves, yet the best of them have relation and dependancy one way or other to it . . . But to sett upp a Government in all the parts of it sutable to our republike.[78]

This was, perhaps, the kind of building that Marvell's frightened architects were resisting.

'Tom May's Death' and anti-Commonwealth poetry

The 'Horatian Ode' might have been expected to open for Marvell the kind of career with the new state that Milton, Hall and Fisher were pursuing. It was rather ironic that at the moment of completing this masterpiece of anti- or semi-Horatianism, Marvell should have been plunged into the classic situation of Horatian retirement. But the offer of tutoring Fairfax's daughter must have looked hard to refuse. The position may have come to him through Yorkshire connections.[79] Even after he resigned his command, Fairfax remained a figure of great influence and standing, whose favour might be very valuable in the long term; and he had literary interests harmonious with Marvell's own. Hobbes had been content to spend his life in such a tutorial role. The creative energies involved in the 'Ode', however, do seem to have experienced a kind of stifling, as can be seen in its odd after-life. First of all, Marvell attacked its own assumptions in 'Tom May's Death'; then he reworked it in *The First Anniversary*. Repressed by circumstance, the 'Ode' returned.

The attack came first. On 13 November 1650, Thomas May died. As has been seen, he was given a major state burial, and his Lucan became an emblem of *Mercurius Politicus*'s radical republicanism. It appears that not long after this Marvell composed a viciously witty satire on May's classical republicanism. Some doubts remain about the authorship of 'Tom May's Death', but the poem's language is so close to Marvell's that there remains a strong presumption in his favour.[80] It will be clear, however, that on the basis of what has been

78 John Nickolls, Junior (ed.), *Original Letters and Papers of State* (1743), pp. 31ff.
79 Christopher Hill, 'John Milton (1608–74) and Andrew Marvell (1621–78)', *WR*, pp. 157–87 (161–2).
80 *MPL*, I, 94–7. 'Tom May's Death' was one of three poems excluded from Bodleian MS Eng. poet. d.49, a copy of the 1681 'Poems' with added manuscript verse. This exclusion, however, can probably be explained by the embarrassment caused a Whig editor of the late seventeenth century who was planning a new edition: Nicholas von Maltzahn, 'Marvell's Ghost', in Warren Chernaik and Martin Dzelzainis (eds.), *Marvell and Liberty* (Houndmills, 1999), pp. 50–74 (64–5).

said above about May and about the 'Horatian Ode', the new poem constituted a staggering reversal. Some critics have argued that there is no ideological incompatibility between the poems because they are concerned with moral or personal rather than political issues; but such judgements tend to assume the traditional royalist view of May as turncoat and time-server, and critical demands are satisfied if it can be proved that Marvell was a man of integrity and May the reverse.[81] In such judgements, however, a curious displacement occurs. May becomes the whipping-boy for faults which critics are uneasily aware might otherwise be imputed to Marvell. The latter displayed a transcendence of narrow partisanship by being able to hold pro- and anti-monarchist perspectives simultaneously in his mind; the former was a despicable traitor. One critic writes of May's 'defection to Parliament', another that he 'notoriously deserted his royal master'; another that he supported Parliament 'for money, of course'.[82] The discourse of seventeenth-century monarchist propaganda enters the language of literary criticism without any significant change. 'Tom May's Death' has become the main authority on Thomas May's life. If May was indeed such a low form of humanity, Marvell's attack on him is understandable quite independently of political considerations; while critics arguing for a crypto-royalist 'Horatian Ode' are glad to find Marvell vituperating republicanism.

One well-informed and acute early reader, however, was interestingly puzzled. Some of John Aubrey's notes on May are worth quoting:

> clap. Came of his death after drinking w[th] his chin tyed w[th] his cap (being fatt) suffocated.
> M[r] E. Wyld told me that he was acquainted w[th] him when he was younge and then he was as other young men of this Towne are, sc: he s[d] he was debacht *ad o[mn]ia*. but doe not by any meanes take notice of it: for we have all been young. But M[r] Marvel in his Poëms upon Tom May's death, falls very severe upon him . . . A great acq[uaintance]. of Tom. Chaloner. would when (inter pocula) speak slightly of the Trinity.[83]

Aubrey's vignettes show how May offered a handle for the satirist: we have the sense of an incongruous combination of republican *gravitas* and Falstaffian

---

81 In a variant of standard arguments, Gerard Reedy, S. J., ' "An Horatian Ode" and "Tom May's Death" ', *Studies in English Literature* 20 (1980), 137–51, argues that Marvell finds May a turncoat because he had moved from a pro-Presbyterian position in the *History* to an Independent one in the *Breviary*. It is hard to find support for this reading in the poem.

82 Margarita Stocker, *Apocalyptic Marvell: The Second Coming in Seventeenth Century Poetry* (Brighton, 1986), p. 69; Robert Wilcher, *Andrew Marvell* (Cambridge, 1985), p. 111; William Empson, 'Natural Magic and Populism in Marvell's Poetry', in R. L. Brett (ed.), *Andrew Marvell: Essays on the Tercentenary of his Death* (Oxford, 1979), p. 39.

83 Bodleian MS Wood F.39, fol. 414r, MS Aubrey 8, fol. 27r; *ABL*, II, 55–6. Aubrey speaks of 'Poëms' in the plural; it is not clear what else he may be referring to.

insobriety. Aubrey, however, takes a tolerant view, sympathetic to May's love for the republic, and he is puzzled as to why Marvell should have thought differently. Aubrey probably did not know about Marvell's Cromwellian past, the 'Ode' and other Cromwell poems having remained anonymous or unpublished; but he did know that Marvell had composed an epitaph for another leading republican, James Harrington, which was not used on his tomb as it 'would have given offence'.[84] Christopher Hill, likewise rightly troubled, tries to explain the incongruity between the 'Ode' and 'Tom May's Death' by the fact that the satire was written or revised after 1660, or possibly even after Davenant was himself buried in the place left vacant. This is possible, but it does not necessarily make the latter poem 'less unpleasant'.[85] Amongst those exhumed in 1661 was Cromwell's mother, on whom Marvell had written affectionately in 1655; it seems if anything more damaging to Marvell to have him finding the occasion of her exhumation uproariously comic. Payne Fisher, though he recanted his support of the Commonwealth after 1660, was nevertheless ready to stick his neck out with a generous tribute to his former friend:

> that most Memorable Poet of his Time, who (abstracted from his sullen siding with the late long Parliament,) hath done that for the Honor of this Nation was never paralel'd by any English Man before, witness in his elaborate pains, and successful lucubrations in his *Supplement of Lucan*, written in so lofty and happy Latine Hexameter, that he hath attain'd much more reputation abroad, than he hath lost at home; and though he dyed a Batchelor without Bodily issue, yet will he for ever live, and be perpetuated to posterity, in the lovely and lively issue of his Brain...[86]

Fisher's opening words here directly translate from the epitaph which Nedham had composed for May in Westminster Abbey and which had been subsequently destroyed. He was obliquely contrasting the violence done to May's tomb with the true immortality of his writings. It was perhaps the contrast with this graceful tribute that led Aubrey to express surprise over 'Tom May's Death': he and Fisher were on friendly terms and were in a position to discuss May's reputation.

If the poem as we have it does date from 1650, however, the incongruity is striking, for its closest equivalent is a mock-epitaph whose militant royalism is beyond question. There May was presented as even worse than Lucan: if

84 Bodleian MS Aubrey 6, fol. 99bv; *ABL*, I, 293.
85 Hill, 'John Milton and Andrew Marvell', pp. 157–87 (160). William Raymond Orwen, 'A Study of Marvell's "Horatian Ode"' (Syracuse University Ph.D. dissertation, 1956), pp. 213ff, had earlier argued for a post-Restoration revision.
86 Payne Fisher, *The Tombes, Monuments, And Sepulchral Inscriptions, Lately Visible in St Pauls Cathedral* ([1684]; F1041), p. 103. Aubrey's note on Marvell dates from 1691; Fisher praises Aubrey (p. 139).

Lucan had ungratefully betrayed the tyrant Nero, May had betrayed in Charles the best of princes. Lucan, the epitaph declared, repented his betrayal before his death, while May died suddenly before he could repent. He was as pertinacious an accomplice of the rebel Parliament as he was a sacrilegious enemy of the muses whom he had once religiously cultivated. But he did not entirely lay aside the art of fiction, for he lyingly wrote and printed their deeds. Even the marbles seemed amazed that the rebels had placed such unworthy ashes amongst such noble heroes.[87]

Marvell's poem, though far more sophisticated, shares this basic diagnosis. It was written shortly after some of the leading architects of the republic's Dutch policy, Marten and Chaloner, had arranged May's burial. Marvell's response to the burial, if it was indeed his and contemporary, amounted to a demolition not only of one of the republic's new icons but of the intellectual foundations of the 'Horatian Ode'. The discourse, the political frame of reference, of the May poem is radically different from that of the ode. This does not mean the same man cannot have written them; discourses generate their own internal logic, and each poem follows through its logic with immense skill. But it will not quite do to say that the May poem attacks the poet on personal rather than political grounds, for the way in which the poem personalizes May's political views is itself part of a specific political discourse. Like the mock-epitaph, the poem holds May up to a standard of personal fidelity and service to a prince. The poet himself does not attack May; this task is entirely delegated to the shade of Ben Jonson. To some extent, this distancing allows Marvell to detach himself from Jonson's views. He certainly enjoys playing with a variant on the old Horatian model of the garrulous bore and taciturn poet, which he had imitated in 'Flecknoe'. We are allowed a moment of sympathy with the hapless May when Jonson undertakes 'Gently to signifie that he was wrong' (line 20), and we know that the stammering poet is in for an uninterruptable blast of invective. Jonson's literary dictatorship, belabouring Virgil and Horace, is given some satirical treatment. The fact that Jonson is chosen at all, however, is heavily weighted in ideological terms, for he had been the poet laureate, and charges of May's infidelity and ingratitude centred on the idea that he had supported Parliament in bitterness because he had been turned down in favour of Sir William Davenant as Jonson's successor.[88] Allegations that the two men were rivals for the laureateship go back before 'Tom May's Death', and are hard at this distance either to prove or to

---

87 Bodleian MS Wood F.39, fol. 154. A note by Wood cross-refers to Fisher's comment on May.

88 Howard Erskine-Hill, *The Augustan Idea in English Literature* (1983), pp. 192ff, emphasizes Jonson's role as a dramatic character, but also concludes that Marvell would have endorsed much of what he is made to say.

disprove. The elegy that May composed for Jonson did not perhaps strike the most tactful note for an aspiring laureate in that he compared himself to Statius as writer of an elegy for Lucan, whose death had of course come after his plot against Nero.[89] As for May's jealousy of Davenant's superior skills, posterity has not left this a particularly uneven contest.

Whatever personal elements entered into May's quarrels, rivalry certainly does not constitute a full explanation for his career, especially given the earlier interest in republicanism shown by the Lucan translation. As has been seen, it could be argued that his inconstancy was in becoming a panegyrist of the king during the 1630s. But the idea that having once sought royal patronage May was obliged to share the king's political views for the rest of his life assumes an absolutist model of personal political loyalty to which he gave no sign of subscribing. According to such a model, Parliament itself was a grace passed down from the king rather than a constitutional right, and the House of Commons from the Petition of Right onwards had been consistently ungrateful. By contrast, republicans saw courtly patronage as illegitimately subordinating the public interest to private, personal considerations. In the spring of 1652 *Mercurius Politicus* devoted itself to refuting the common allegation that governments by the people were prone to ingratitude by retorting that princes were more often ungrateful to subjects who did them good service, as in the case of Cicero and Augustus.[90]

'Tom May's Death' alludes to an earlier debate, in 1645, when May had been specifically taxed with the charge of ingratitude. May had intervened in a battle of words between Berkenhead's *Mercurius Aulicus* and Nedham's *Mercurius Britanicus*, which was moving towards its most militantly anti-monarchical posture, and other Parliamentarian newsbooks.[91] A moderate satire, *The Great Assises Holden in Parnassus*, came to May's defence. The satire anticipates 'Tom May's Death' in many features, including the prominent role given to Ben Jonson. It is interesting in its tolerant acceptance of the public sphere, of

> the literary Presse,
> A priviledge which our forefathers wanted

and which is hailed as 'This engine of the *Muses*'. The satirist's attack on newsbooks reveals that he nevertheless reads them carefully and expects his own readers to have done so. Many of the judges in this mock-trial are traditional poets and humanists, and the satire accepts that newsbooks are a logical extension of the humanist republic of letters. In this context, May emerges

---

89 *Ben Jonson*, ed. C. H. Herford and Percy and Evelyn Simpson, 11 vols. (Oxford, 1925–52), XI, 443.   90 *Mercurius Politicus* no. 97, 8–15 April 1652, E659.28, p. 1525.
91 [Thomas May?], *The Character of a Right Malignant* (1645; E27.3).

sympathetically. *Mercurius Aulicus* complains that May should not be on the jury because he is motivated by 'private spite' and 'ingratitude'. May pleads his own innocence and asks to feel '*Ixion's* wheele' if he is guilty, and Apollo agrees that the charge of 'meere malice' should be turned against *Aulicus*.[92] 'Tom May's Death', however, takes the position of *Aulicus*, declaring that it is May who is governed by 'malice' (line 56) and that he should indeed be 'rivited unto *Ixion's* wheel' (line 93). The satire is much closer to the position of earlier militant royalists such as John Taylor, who had linked May with Nedham by suggesting him as a possible author of *Mercurius Britanicus*, though he ruled him out because 'he was better at Translation then Invention'.[93] Similarly, 'Tom May's Death' points the contrast between May's original verse and his translation: 'Those but to *Lucan* do continue *May*' (line 54).

The debates of the mid-1640s were still alive in the early 1650s. Berkenhead was continuing to take a critical view of May and of Lucan. In 1651 he contrasted the royalist poet William Cartwright with those who were 'shouldering . . . To follow *Lucan* where he trod amiss',[94] and ridiculed May's *History* as no more than '*All the* London *Diurnals bound together*'.[95] Marvell's poem is in tune with royalist themes here; Jonson ironically sees May's death as renewing 'Right Romane poverty and gratitude' (line 80). Jonson keeps him out of his courtly heaven because he is 'Sworn Enemy to all that do pretend' (line 30); 'pretend' is the equivalent of being 'forward', the public-spiritedness of the 'Ode' which in this world is an impermissible ambitiousness parallel to regal usurpation. May had to some extent brought such criticisms on himself by continuing to reprint his original dedication of the continuation of Lucan to Charles I, which did indeed present him in very extravagant terms as a humble subject; but this could be viewed as a more honest policy than simply suppressing his past. The poem's Ben Jonson gloats that he was

> taken hence with equal fate,
> Before thou couldst great *Charles* his death relate. (lines 75–6)

---

92 *The Great Assises Holden in Parnassus* (1645; E269.11), ed. Hugh MacDonald (Oxford, 1948), pp. 1, 13–14. MacDonald rightly rejects the common attribution to George Wither; see Raymond, *The Invention of the Newspaper*, pp. 210–25.

93 [John Taylor], *Mercurius Aquaticus* (1645; E29.11), sig. B2r.

94 William Cartwright, *Comedies, Tragi-Comedies, with Other Poems* (1651; E1224), sig. *8v. Another contributor, W. Waring, praised Cartwright as 'A wit that ne'r broke loose/To reach bold *Lucan's* Muse' (sig. ‖4r); though Cartwright himself was compared by Sir Edward Dering to Cato (head of volume, no signature), somewhat as Cato is evoked in the presentation of the ideal poet in 'Tom May's Death'. Another contributor attacked those who 'taught the Rowt to rave *Euripides*' (Robert Waring, sig. *7r): could this be a hit at Milton? On this volume's status as a 'reaffirmation of Cavalier ideals' see P. W. Thomas, *Sir John Berkenhead 1617–1679: A Royalist Career in Politics and Polemics* (Oxford, 1969), p. 177.

95 [Berkenhead], *Paul's Churchyard* (1651; E989.7), sig. A2v.

But May had already had an opportunity to narrate the death and had very conspicuously refrained from doing so. The *Breviary* which had appeared in June 1650 had ended by declaring that there was not enough space to narrate the events leading up to the regicide, but there is no obvious reason why he could not have done so. Overall his writings refrain from personal attacks on Charles, and indeed Lucy Hutchinson blamed him because he showed 'more indulgence to the King's guilt than can justly be allow'd'.[96] He may have had his doubts about the regicide, as did many people of widely differing political views, and certainly did not rush into print with anything like Milton's alacrity. There is all the less reason for believing that his support of Parliament was motivated by nothing but personal spite. But the poem specifically rules out the alternatives of 'Ignorance' or 'seeming good' and offers only 'malice fixt and understood' (lines 55–6).

The poem's courtly discourse is reinforced by its allusions to masques. Jonson was of course the leading masque-writer, and Davenant had also written masques. Marvell recalls the episode in 1634 when the earl of Pembroke, then Master of the Revels, quarrelled with May and broke his staff over his shoulders. After the abolition of the House of Lords, Pembroke had been elected to the Commons as one of the peers who became 'reduced' to the people, and his death in 1650 had been marked by Parliament with rituals of respect and by royalists with a wave of satires. One of them has him declare: 'To *Tom May* (whose pate I broke heretofore at a *Masque*) I give Five Shillings; I intended him more, but all that have read his *History of the Parliament* thinke Five shillings too much'.[97] At the end of the poem Jonson tells May to descend to the underworld and, 'only Master of these Revels', he vanishes in a 'Cloud of pitch'. At the finale of Stuart masques the heroes would ascend to the heavens on cloud-machines; May's undignified descent, to Davenant's laughter, casts him with the antimasque figures who must be banished from an orderly court. In this Elysium poets sing of 'The Subjects Safety, and the Rebel's Fear' (line 16). There is no space in this opposition for citizens: men are rebels – '*Brutus* and *Cassius* the Peoples cheats' – or they are grateful and obedient subjects.

The poem was written at a time when this courtly world did not have an embodiment in England, but it does allude to the surviving laureate, who was about to publish *Gondibert*, an ambitious attempt at formulating a new royalist poetics for the changed political circumstances. Davenant published the preface in advance of the poem in 1650, with a reply by Hobbes, with whom he had talked frequently during his exile at the English court in Paris. Davenant presented a theory of poetry as a kind of manipulative image-making which would quell popular disorder by the pleasure it offered. The people, he wrote,

> looke upon the outward glory or blaze of Courts, as Wilde beasts in darke nights stare on their Hunters Torches . . . the expences of Courts (whereby they shine) is

96 Hutchinson, p. 53.   97 Anon., *The Earle of Pembrokes Last Speech* (1650; E593.16), p. 3.

that consuming glory in which the people think their liberty is wasted (for wealth is their liberty and lov'd by them even to jealousy . . .

Such jealousy is best contented not by changing the political order but by offering placatory images: Davenant compares political poets to farmers who whistle to their beasts to encourage them to work. Davenant gave a lengthy critique of Lucan, who was quite unsuitable as a model for heroic verse because of his confusion of poetry and history and his hyperbolic style. His admirers 'mistake him in his boyling Youth (which had merveilous forces) as wee disrellish excellent Wine when fuming in the Lee'.[98] As in 'Tom May's Death', a link is made here between excess in drink and political sedition. Soon after formulating these views, Davenant was captured and brought back to England, and in the summer of 1650 *Mercurius Politicus* covered his case with amused sympathy: here was another possible writer to be converted to the republic's cause.[99] And indeed he was eventually released, with the help of Marten and possibly Milton. His theory and that of his mentor Hobbes, who was soon to return voluntarily to acknowledge the *de facto* power of the republic, could be used to legitimize any established regime – as has been seen, Nedham recycled Hobbes in *Mercurius Politicus*. There was an overlap between this position and the more deterministic side of the 'Horatian Ode', but not with its elements of republican humanism; and Marvell was to attack Hobbes and Davenant's poem together twenty years later in *The Rehearsal Transpros'd*. The praise of Davenant in 'Tom May's Death' is then anomalous.[100]

If 'Tom May's Death' offers a future for poetry beyond nostalgia for the old courtly world, it is Davenant towards whom it specifically points, while May's discourse is relegated to the grubby London world in which he aggrandizes the 'novice Statesmen' of the new regime by drawing classical parallels. The detail by which May finds himself baffled at his whereabouts when he awakes, 'For Whence in Stevens ally Trees or Grass?', has rightly been seen as distinctively Marvellian.[101] It also establishes a contrast between the sordid, mercenary world of the city and the pastoral, contemplative surroundings appropriate to poetry – the kind of contrast established by Fane's odes and Marten's 'Antepode'. This is the appropriate milieu for the new republican poetry:

> Cups more then civil of *Emathian* wine,
> I sing (said he) and the *Pharsalian* Sign,
> Where the Historian of the Common-wealth
> In his own Bowels sheath'd the conquering health. (lines 21–4)

98 *Sir William Davenant's 'Gondibert'*, ed. David F. Gladish (Oxford, 1971), pp. 12, 40, 5.
99 See, e.g., *Mercurius Politicus* no. 4, 27 June – 4 July 1650, E607.4, p. 64.
100 Smith, *LR*, pp. 87–8, 239–41; Marvell, *The Rehearsal Transpros'd*, ed. Smith, pp. 8, 47, 143.
101 Elsie Duncan-Jones, 'Marvell: A Great Master of Words', *Proceedings of the British Academy* 61 (1975), 267–90 (283).

The cup recalls the engraving on the *Supplementum* title-page of Lucan's ghost drinking the sacrificial blood (figure 10). This sacred republican rite becomes conflated with the wine on which May fatally choked and with the sword of Roman discord, revealing the destructiveness of republican discourse to May's body as well as the body politic. The poem's repeated references to translation present this urban republican culture as irredeemably second-hand, deluding itself that it can emulate classical heroism:

> Foul Architect that hadst not Eye to see
> How ill the measures of these States agree.
> And who by *Romes* example *England* lay,
> Those but to *Lucan* do continue *May*. (lines 51–4)

May's much-vaunted *Supplementum*, which had been presented in 1650 to the English public as successfully reviving Lucan's ghost, epitomizes the vainglory of trying to revive classical republicanism. The poem's finale satirizes Lucan's claims to strip poetry away from myth by placing May in a real rather than feigned underworld:

> 'Tis just what Torments Poets ere did feign,
> Thou first Historically shouldst sustain. (lines 95–6)

Although Lucan is thus disparaged, he nonetheless plays a hidden role in the poem. In the most powerful lines, Jonson rises to a celebration of poetic integrity:

> When the Sword glitters ore the Judges head,
> And fear has Coward Churchmen silenced,
> Then is the Poets time, 'tis then he drawes,
> And single fights forsaken Vertues cause.
> He, when the wheel of Empire, whirleth back,
> And though the World's disjointed Axel crack,
> Sings still of ancient Rights and better Times,
> Seeks wretched good, arraigns successful Crimes. (lines 63–70)

The glittering sword recalls the 'gladii ... micantes' of Pompey's troops invading the courts (*Pharsalia*, i.320). The poem proceeds to echo Lucan's images of cosmic discord. In fact, the poem directly echoes Jonson's commendatory poem for May's Lucan translation:

> When, *Rome*, I reade thee in thy mighty paire,
> And see both climing vp the slippery staire
> Of Fortunes wheele by *Lucan* driu'n about,
> And the world in it, I begin to doubt,
> At euery line some pinn thereof should slacke
> At least, if not the generall Engine cracke.[102]

---

102 *Ben Jonson*, VIII, 395; see below, chapter 10 n. 117.

Jonson's privately-expressed opinions of Lucan were not in fact so favour-able[103], but by the 1650s, poets across a wide spectrum from Anglicans to Presbyterians found themselves in an oppositional position, and certain aspects of the *Pharsalia* could speak to their situation. The political context would seem to imply that the 'Coward Churchmen' are those Presbyterians who were conforming to the regime and taking the Engagement rather than actively opposing it. Lucan's imagery of discordant concord was being appropriated by Hall to image a complex, Machiavellian model of republi-can unity-in-diversity, and had a somewhat similar role in the 'Horatian Ode'; but in 'Tom May's Death' there is a more conventional image of a tradi-tional royalist order falling into ruin. The poet here pleads for the very 'ancient Rights' which the poet of the 'Horatian Ode' was invited to move beyond; he looks back to 'better Times' rather than forward to a 'happy Fate'.

It is very hard, then, to see the two poems as easily compatible. Perhaps we should see them as rival experiments, exploring the challenges of different poetic modes both for opening alternative worlds of political connection and for their own linguistic challenges. In a year when Nedham had drawn atten-tion to the virtuosity with which he could excel in both royalist and republi-can discourses, and indeed made his empathy with royalist discourse a leading argument for his authority in drawing others to the new cause, there was a particular pertinence in such an experiment. Or in a less elevated way, we can see him as keeping his options open. Another fascinating detail that Aubrey tells us about May is that he shammed – that is, told lies with an utterly straight face.[104] Perhaps Marvell took a leaf out of May's book in more ways than one, composing these two poems as exercises in differing discourses and sustaining them so long that he himself found it hard to be sure which one was shamming.

Marvell and Commonwealth poetry II: the poem to St John

What is clear is that Marvell had not abandoned republican options. It must have been around the time of 'Tom May's Death' that he composed a Latin poem for the departure of the English mission to the Netherlands. He praised

---

103 *Ben Jonson*, I, 134, 149.
104 Bodleian MS Aubrey 8, fol. 27r, *ABL*, II, 55. Aubrey implies that May learned his 'sham-ming' from Thomas Chaloner, whose most extreme example of the genre was the deadpan religious imposture, *The Strange Finding Out of Moses His Tombe* (1657; c1805; ed. C. H. Wilkinson, Oxford, 1958): Bodleian MS Aubrey 7, fol. 19r, *ABL*, I, 159–60. Aubrey's MS reads 'shamed', and Dr Kate Bennett, who is working on a new edition of the 'Brief Lives', understands it in the sense of dishonouring as opposed to Clark's 'shamming'.

its leader, Oliver St John, as the man in whom alone the republic had placed its trust, 'cui soli voluit *Respublica* credi'.[105] Two years later he was to compose an anti-Dutch satire as part of a bid for public office, and this poem would suggest that he was considering this option much earlier. If he was indeed considering entering the public's service at the same time as he was lampooning May, it is not surprising that the St John poem should be so centrally concerned with the issue of linguistic duplicity. It can be seen as sketching some kind of synthesis between the different political options he had been exploring. Like the *prosphonetikon* of the 'Horatian Ode', this *propemptikon* adapts the conventions of epideictic poetry to new political conditions. It is a poem about a republican speech-act which implicitly considers its own relationship to republican speech-acts.

Marvell writes that St John's mission is encoded in his name: fate has provided him with a double name, '*ancipiti Nomine*'. The Oliver evokes the olive of peace, while the St John evokes war. And that is appropriate to his mission, which is to offer peace to the Netherlands if they support England's goals, but war if they refuse. He holds the key to the iron gates of Janus. It is not necessary to commit arcane senses to paper and engage in legitimate deceptions with shifting guile, for his name carries words like secret writing. Do the Dutch want Oliver or St John? Marvell concludes with an allusion to the Roman consul Popilius, who drew a circle around King Antiochus in the sand and told him he could not step out of it until he had made a commitment not to attack the Romans' allies in Alexandria. The Dutch, he says, are in as small a circle.

In this poem Marvell draws attention to the links between poetic and diplomatic language. He goes out of his way to declare that diplomatic language involves licensed fraud, deceit, perhaps recalling Sir Henry Wotton's famous pun that an ambassador is someone who lies abroad for his country. St John's message is compared to a classical form of secret communication, the *scytale*, a stick that was divided to split the letters. The image of the double locks of Janus takes up the theme of doubleness from the reference to St John's two-headed name. Another image for such doubleness is that of the two names as keys of the iron locks of Janus. Conventionally, of course, closing the gates was favoured by court poetry; the previous August Fane had prophesied that Charles's return would close the gates. In his emphasis on the choice of opening them or not, Marvell perhaps had in mind Milton's provocative comment in *Areopagitica* that 'The Temple of *Janus* with his two *controversal*

---

105 'In Legationem Domini *Oliveri St John* ad Provincias Foederatas', *MPL*, I, 99. Initial preparations for the embassy were made in December 1650, around the time of May's funeral. On the ceremonial aspect see Sean Kelsey, *Inventing a Republic: The Political Culture of the English Commonwealth 1649–1653* (Manchester, 1997), pp. 65–7.

faces might now not unsignificantly be set open' (*MPW*, II, 561). The English were exporting their own debate between republicanism and monarchism, and pressuring the Dutch to take a decision. Marvell was to return to the Antiochus-Popilius story in a post-Restoration controversy, and there he drew a direct analogy with humanist disputation: each disputant in turn was Popilius to his adversary's Antiochus.[106] Ideally, then, such disputes could be resolved through the pen rather than the sword. But under certain circumstances rhetorical debate might depend on military victory – *Areopagitica* had amongst other things been a call to arms. The Greek word *scytale* could refer both to a poisonous snake, in which form it appears in the snake catalogue in the *Pharsalia* (ix.717), and to a club. St John's language, for all its doubleness, performs a very decided speech-act. One of the heads of the two-headed Janus will need to be cut off. There may be a very oblique glance at the regicide in the choice of the word 'anceps' for an ambiguous or double name, and certainly decapitation was to figure prominently in his later Dutch poem, 'The Character of Holland'.

The concluding allusion brings out the military menace and republican aspiration behind the poem's language. Both Livy and Polybius, the two great historians of the young Roman republic, tell this story and emphasize that Popilius was widely condemned for his harshness of temper.[107] Marvell's Antiochus may seem to be in the position of a humanist dialectician, engaged in an open-ended debate *in utramque partem*, but he is forcibly aware of the need for decision: his hermeneutic circle is being used by Roman political power as a noose. Marvell was to use a similar analogy for the force of republican speech-acts in his praise of Milton's *Second Defence*: Trajan had driven Decebalus to suicide, Milton's rhetoric had the same power.[108] Here the stakes have been raised from the St John poem: Salmasius is driven to suicide where Antiochus was merely driven into a circle. But in each case the speech-act is militantly republican. Marvell is invoking the spirit of the young Roman republic as it was chronicled by Livy.

Later in 1651 a member of the Hartlib circle lamented that not enough use was being made of the printing press: more books should be translated into English and Livy's *History* should be made available in a cheap, compact edition to instil a cult of liberty. Rand was 'of opinion [&] have long bin with

---

106 [Andrew Marvell], *Mr. Smirke, or the Divine in Mode* (1676; M873), p. 20.
107 Livy, *History*, 45.10; Polybius, *Histories*, 29.27. William A. McQueen and Kiffin A. Rockwell (eds.), *The Latin Poetry of Andrew Marvell* (Chapel Hill, 1964), p. 51, trace the Popilius reference to the hack writer Valerius Maximus. The sarcasm of Marvell's 'a most apt and learned resemblance, and which shews the Gentlemans good reading' (*Mr. Smirke*, p. 20) may suggest that he imagines his adversary as finding it there, but readers of Latin poetry would surely have the more prominent republican texts in mind.   108 Marvell to Milton, 2 June 1654, *MPL*, II, 306.

Mr Hobbs, that ye reading of such bookes as Livy's History has bin a rub in the way of ye advancment of ye Interest of his Leviathanlike Monarchs'.[109] Marvell's choice of medium restricted his audience, but he was likewise contributing to the growing force of the parallels between the young republics. There are interesting parallels between the St John poem and Milton's sonnet to Vane, written the following year. Milton had been commissioned by Sir Henry Vane to translate a document in support of St John's mission. Whether or not he had seen Marvell's poem, Milton likewise links his addressee with the heroes of the early Roman republic in the Punic wars, draws punning attention to the ambiguities of diplomatic language, 'The drif*t*s of hollow states hard to be spelld', and presents the statesman he addresses as equally poised between peace and war, though ready to act resolutely once the choice has been made.[110]

Marvell knew Dutch and had travelled in the Netherlands on his European tour, and his poem shows a strong awareness of the ideological stakes of St John's mission.[111] There were close parallels between the republic's relations with Scotland and with the Netherlands. In each case, it confronted a political culture with strong proto-republican elements but also monarchist traditions. The office of Stadholder had been passed down in the Orange dynasty, and the recent incumbent, Willem II, had married Charles I's daughter Mary. Many Dutch poets, led by the celebrated Constantijn Huygens, greeted the regicide with the same kind of outrage as the Scots.[112] English republicans, with Nedham in the vanguard, responded to this situation with two alternative strategies. They urged a closer alliance, culminating eventually in a proposal for one of the most remarkable and visionary projects of the century, a complete political union with a common Parliament. That union would strengthen republican elements in both polities and allow monarchist elements to wither away. If the republicans were prone to see Ireland as more politically backward than they were, they might well see the Netherlands as more advanced. Ideological considerations overshadowed merely national ones. But it was characteristic of republicans to see all states as combining contradictory cultural and political forms

109 William Rand to Benjamin Worsley, 11 August 1651, HP, 62/21/2A.

110 *CSPD 1651*, p. 116; Leo Miller, *John Milton's Writings in the Anglo-Dutch Negotiations, 1651–1654* (Pittsburgh, 1992), p. 8; Trinity MS text, *John Milton: Poems* (Menston, 1972), p. 48.

111 Steven C. A. Pincus, *Protestantism and Patriotism: Ideologies and the Making of English Foreign Policy, 1650–1668* (Cambridge, 1996), pp. 15ff.

112 'To the Lady Luchtenburgh, with my Poems Translated from the English of Donne', in Peter Davidson and Adriaan van der Weel (eds.), *A Selection of the Poems of Sir Constantijn Huygens* (Amsterdam, 1996), pp. 164–5. For Marvell's possible Dutch connections, with special reference to 'Upon Appleton House', see pp. 208–14.

which would need careful strategic action to bring to fruition; the union offered a golden opportunity.

At the time Marvell wrote his poem, *Mercurius Politicus* was striking a particularly strident republican note. Willem had just died, dealing a severe blow to the monarchist cause. *Mercurius Politicus* printed a poem which greeted his 'Most Timely Death' with nothing but indecorous enthusiasm, and urged the Dutch to seize this republican *occasione*, the 'fit opportunity . . . which God hath now put into their hands for the redeeming of their former Liberties, which the Prince of *Orange* had so ingrossed to himself'.[113] Nedham was equally irreverent about his widow, '*Mal. Tarquin*'.[114] One role of the English embassy was to urge the authorities to take action against the English royalists who had assassinated Dorislaus. In early 1651 *Mercurius Politicus* was running frequent references to Milton's recently published *First Defence*, which had rejoiced in the providential death of Willem II and expressed the hope that Salmasius would not teach Dutch youth to return to tyranny (*MPW*, IV:1, 312, 430). The English embassy's role was to urge closer union. It was welcomed in that spirit by a Dutch poet who prophesied that the two nations would come closer in a divine union and emphasized his country's status as a republic and the free laws of the English.[115]

Many of his countrymen disagreed, however. If union were refused, it would be a sign that their monarchists had prevailed, and the alternative strategy was to be military action. When the mission's failure did eventually lead to war, Marvell made the point with a telling pun on 'Hol-land':

> For these *Half-anders*, half wet, and half dry,
> Nor bear *strict service*, nor *pure Liberty*.[116]

The Dutch should make a proper choice, as the English had done, rather than trying to be royalists and republicans at the same time. What was at issue in 1651, then, was a practical decision with much wider ideological implications.

---

113 *Mercurius Politicus* no. 33, 16–23 January 1651, E622.8, p. 542, no. 31, 2–9 January 1651, E621.10, p. 512.   114 *Mercurius Politicus* no. 45, 10–17 April 1651, E626.28, p. 724.
115

> Jamque adeò propriùs regnatrix Anglia Belgis
>   Et septem-geminae concilietur humo.
> Vincula tantarum latè certissima rerum
>   Et coelum & veri sacra Tonantis erunt;
> Liberaque invicto longùm Respublica bello
>   Gestiet Anglorum libera jura sequi.

A. S., *Magnificentiss. Dominis, Dominis OLIVERIO ST. JOHN GVALTERO STRIC-LAND Ser. Reipublicae Anglicanae ad Foederatos Belgas Legatis* ([London, 1651]; S7A).
116 Marvell, 'The Character of Holland', lines 53–4, *MPL*, I, 101.

The embassy placed a strict time-limit on the decision, prompting the Dutch to complain that 'it was unusual amongst us and other nations, that any one, that pleases to treat, should of himself set a precise time; and more that great treaties should be bound to time; and yet stranger, that such treaties should be bound to a day, or a few days'.[117] But time was of the essence for the English. Charles II was mustering forces in Scotland for an invasion, rumours were circulating that Cromwell had been killed, and many of the Dutch were clearly waiting to see which way things went in England before committing themselves to the republic. The Dutch were being invited, with military threats behind the invitation, to accelerate their national debate *in utramque partem* and reach a republican conclusion. St John declared that the Anglo-Dutch union was desirable because neither state depended upon the uncertainties of the life, allegiance, change of affections, and private interest of one person.[118] *Mercurius Politicus* reported that at the moment St John entered the Great Hall at The Hague the infant Prince of Orange was thrown into convulsions.[119] Contemporary records and later historians emphasize how angry St John was during this mission. Marvell's poem indicates that a lot of that anger was pre-scripted for political purposes, and that Marvell was in on the script.

Marvell conveys the tremendous urgency with which the republic wished to box the Dutch into their circle. The apparent open-endedness of the poem's options is counterbalanced by the insistence on a timescale that would serve the republic's interests. The imagery anticipates his paean in *The First Anniversary* to Cromwell as transcending the weak circles of succeeding years by contracting the force of scattered time. It is tempting also to notice the poem's reference to opening iron gates and recall that iron gates are invoked in 'To his Coy Mistress' by a speaker urging haste in an amatory *occasione*. That lyric is no political allegory, but its wit consists partly in transferring a recognizable political discourse to the erotic sphere.[120] If the lyric playfully

---

117 *TSP*, I, 192.
118 PRO SP108/46, p. 24, cited by Pincus, *Protestantism and Patriotism*, p. 26 n. 58.
119 *Mercurius Politicus* no. 45, p. 722. Years later, Marvell quoted an account of the Prince's illness by Leo van Aitzema, who wrote an account of the Anglo-Dutch negotiations and became a friend of Milton: *The Rehearsal Transpros'd*, ed. Smith, p. 149.
120 'Grates' is the reading of Bodleian MS Eng. poet.d.49, favoured by Elizabeth Story Donno (ed.), *Andrew Marvell: The Complete Poems* (Harmondsworth, 1972), p. 235. The evidence she offers, that in associating iron gates with life rather than death Marvell would be inverting normal expectations, seems an argument for rather than against that reading. Stocker, *Apocalyptic Marvell*, pp. 202–34, offers an elaborate apocalyptic reading of 'To His Coy Mistress'.

invokes the millennium, in the St John poem the apocalyptic implications are overt.[121]

The St John poem, then, brought Marvell into the very republican world which he had pilloried in 'Tom May's Death'. But there are further complexities in its allegiances. When Marvell wrote that St John was the man to whom alone the republic wished to be entrusted, he was almost certainly aware that this was very much a double-edged comment as far as St John was concerned. He had in fact petitioned Parliament not to be sent on this mission, 'considering, that *Dorislaus* sent thither before, was killed; and the losse of a good part of the profits of my place, as Judge, in my absence'.[122] His fears were not ungrounded: an attempt was made on his life. There may, however, have been ideological hesitations as well. St John had been a leading member of the Parliamentary 'middle group', and Valerie Pearl has spoken of his 'Janus-faced reputation'.[123] Royalists did not agree that he was a man of the middle: he had urged resolute pursuit of the Civil War. But he did try to keep together different groupings on the Parliamentary side and had not supported the regicide. Though he continued his legal office under the republic, by later in 1651 he was discussing with Cromwell the re-establishment of some kind of monarchy. On his return from the Netherlands he was more interested in designing his new country house than in republican politics, and in this role he was praised by the retired royalist Mildmay Fane.[124] After the Restoration, St John wrote that he went to the Netherlands because he was commanded by the *de facto* supreme power.[125]

Like all such post-Restoration comments, however, this may need to be read with a certain amount of scepticism. Pincus aligns St John with those who favoured a strong stance against the Dutch not so much on republican as on religious grounds, hoping to further the apocalyptic struggle against Antichrist which had also motivated the militancy in Ireland.[126] St John's wife

---

121 It is hard to see why the commentary in *MPL*, I, 308, denies an association with Revelation. *A Perfect Diurnall of Some Passages and Proceedings* no. 60, 27 January–3 February 1651, E784.1, p. 804, prints an advertisement for a new edition of Joseph Mede's *The Key of the Revelation of Saint John* just below the report that 'The Parliament have ordered the Lord St *John* and Mr. *Strickland* to goe as Embassadors extraordinary to the Assembly of the united Provinces'. When St John showed signs of changing sides in 1660 a ballad mocked that 'He turn'd o're a new leaf in *St John*'s Revelation': *Arsy Versy: Or, The Second Martyrdom of the Rump* (1660; 669f24.31).
122 *The Case of Oliver St Iohn* (1660; E1035.5), p. 5.
123 Valerie Pearl, 'Oliver St. John and the "Middle Group" in the Long Parliament: August 1643–May 1644', *English Historical Review* 81 (1966), 490–519 (516).
124 Timothy Mowl and Brian Earnshaw, *Architecture without Kings: The Rise of Puritan Classicism under Cromwell* (Manchester and New York, 1995), pp. 111–13; Fane, 'Thorp Palace: A Miracle'.   125 *The Case of Oliver St Iohn*, p. 5.
126 Pincus, *Protestantism and Patriotism*, pp. 24–5.

was strongly evangelistic: a royalist later reported that she and her friends 'assemble 3 tymes each weeke And Sing to God & each Other extempory in Rhyme 6 howers together'.[127] Marvell hints at St John's godly sympathies in his emphasis on Revelation. St John also had secular grounds for supporting the war: he was one of the architects of the Navigation Act, which challenged Dutch supremacy in trade. Figures like St John might support this regime not because they were committed republicans, and not necessarily on religious grounds, but because it seemed to be extremely vigorous in defence of the nation.

Nevertheless, the republic was still such an unstable formation that to act on its behalf was a momentous step, laying one open to long-term reprisals should the monarchy return, and much more immediate dangers if one took up a diplomatic post. Being ready to die for a regime about which one has serious reservations is a particularly difficult test of conscience. In agreeing to go on the mission, St John was agreeing to participate in a republican speech-act. His intentions then became subsumed under the republican intentions of the speech-act, even if his motives for accepting the mission were mixed and equivocal. Had he been assassinated, he would have been consecrated as a republican martyr even if that simplified his actual stance. In addressing St John, Marvell was able to work out some of the complexities of his own relationship to the Commonwealth. On one level, his relation to St John parallels St John's to the Dutch: his message manoeuvres him into a circle. When Milton wrote on Marvell's behalf in 1653, he prophesied that he 'in a short time would be able to doe them [the Council of State] as good service as M^r: Ascan' (*MPW*, IV:2, 860). Marvell had decided by 1653 to take the kind of risk of assassination that St John had taken in 1651. However equivocal he might feel about the republic, he was prepared to die for it. The ideological crisis shown by the poems of 1650–51 had caught Marvell in a circle as tight as Antiochus's; but the St John poem perhaps points to a decision to find his way out.

Retirement from the Commonwealth: 'Upon Appleton House'

It was to be two years, however, before Marvell returned actively to the search for public office. At the time he wrote the St John poem, he had entered the service of Lord Fairfax as tutor to his daughter Maria. The ideological complexities were immense. Fairfax had opposed the very Scottish war

---

127 Broderick to Hyde, 24 June 1659, Bodleian MS Clarendon 61, fol. 321r; *Calendar of the Clarendon State Papers, vol. IV: 1657–1660*, ed. F. J. Routledge and Sir Charles Firth (Oxford, 1932), p. 248. Later in the 1650s Marvell lodged with her brother John Oxenbridge.

Marvell celebrated in the 'Ode', and he may have had mixed feelings about the commitments that Marvell was urging on St John. Yet Marvell's next poem was a celebration of Fairfax's withdrawal from public life. 'Upon Appleton House' was probably written in the summer of 1651, at a time when the Council of State was anxious about Fairfax's loyalty. He had been disturbed by the regicide, even though he had done nothing to prevent it. His muffled unease is revealed by his own poem 'On the Fatal Day Jan: 30 1648[/9]':

> Oh Lett that Day from time be blotted quitt
> And Lett beleefe of 't in next Age be waued
> In deepest silence th'Act Concealed might
> Soe that the King-doms – Credit might be saued[.]

Fairfax's protest turns into acceptance, albeit on very limited terms:

> But if the Power deuine permited this
> His Will's the Law & ours must acquiesse.[128]

The fact that he could invoke a factor as secular as 'the King-doms Credit' to counterbalance the regicide shows that he could live with *de facto* allegiance. But his wife's overt hostility to the regicide led to fears that Fairfax might fail to throw his weight behind opposition to an impending Scots invasion or even side with the enemy.[129] In July–August, when there is good evidence that the poem was written, the government was in an agony of indecision over whether to execute the Presbyterian minister Christopher Love, who had been found guilty of intriguing with the king; Hall wrote a defence of the execution.[130] In the Scots camp was Marvell's old acquaintance the duke of Buckingham, who was characteristically operating a trimming policy, trying to move Charles closer to the Argyll regime. Parliament had rewarded Fairfax with Buckingham's confiscated lands after the Second Civil War. Fairfax kept them intact, and may even at this stage have had in mind the match of his daughter with a man who, should political conditions change, would muster immense wealth again. Had Buckingham prevailed with Charles, some kind of moderate royalist settlement might have been conceivable.

Marvell, then, found himself in political company that can scarcely be described as republican. And the main poem he wrote for his new patron, 'Upon Appleton House, to my Lord *Fairfax*' (*MPL*, I, 62–86), celebrates the very kind of Horatian retreat that Marten ridiculed in his 'Antepode'. This poem does not belong as directly to a republican canon as the other poems to

---

128 Bodleian MS Fairfax 40, p. 600; *The Poems of Thomas Third Lord Fairfax*, ed. Edward
   Bliss Read, *Transactions of the Connecticut Academy of Arts and Sciences* 14 (1909),
   281–2.
129 Hirst and Zwicker, 'High Summer at Nun Appleton, 1651', p. 255; *CSPD 1651*, pp. 323–4.
130 [Hall], *A Gagg to Love's Advocate*.

be considered here, and it will thus be treated briefly. But a few points need attention in any study of the development of Marvell's political poetry.

First of all, the poem is cast in such a way as to resist any easy nostalgia for an old rural order; in a gentler manner than Marten's 'Antepode', it revalues the cult of rural peace found in such poems as Jonson's 'To Penshurst'. Though the poet laments England's paradisal pre-war peace (lines 329–36), he completes the rhyme with a direct echo of 'Horatian Ode': 'His warlike Studies could not cease' (line 284). Fairfax is praised for not allowing himself to slough off his public responsibilities lightly, though there is a discreet reminder that his retirement prevents him from making the nation's garden spring 'Fresh as his own' (line 348). The contemporary poet and artist Ian Hamilton Finlay has created a formal landscape garden in which the picturesque is constantly disrupted by images of the sublime in the form of symbols of the revolutionary justice of the French Revolution. The Nun Appleton garden may be less militantly republican than Hamilton Finlay's at Little Sparta, but his maxim that 'certain gardens are described as retreats when they are really attacks' could apply, in its slightly more muted way, to 'Upon Appleton House'.[131]

Appleton House had been built at the Reformation out of the ruins of a nunnery; the opening of the poem is an extended warning, if a playful one, of the dangers that the old religious order might return. The satire of the lesbian nuns hits at the female Catholic patronage of Henrietta Maria, while Fairfax's daughter Maria offers a counter-pattern, of a woman distinguished by her skill in languages (lines 705–12), which, we are led to understand, would arm her against the kinds of temptations Isabella Thwaites had been unable to resist. Parliamentarian propaganda was constantly warning against the dangers that the king's return would reinstate the Roman church.[132] At one point in the poem (lines 361–8), the reader's eyes, which have been straying over the pleasures of the landscape, are disconcertingly wrenched into weapons, engaging in a siege against the castle of that '*Prelate* great', John Williams, archbishop of York. Marvell's legitimation of the seizure of Catholic property also justified the Irish campaign.[133] The allusion to recent church politics qualifies the poem's nostalgic backward glances, evoking rather Milton's claims that the bishops had already been engaged in a civil war long before 1640.

Despite its Horatian manner, moreover, 'Upon Appleton House' shows a continuing interest in an anti-courtly poetics. Just as he shows more

131 Yves Abrioux, *Ian Hamilton Finlay: A Visual Primer*, second edition (1992), p. 40.
132 Gary D. Hamilton, 'Marvell, Sacrilege, and Protestant Historiography: Contextualizing "Upon Appleton House"', in Donna B. Hamilton and Richard Strier (eds.), *Religion, Literature and Politics in Post-Reformation England, 1540–1688* (Cambridge, 1996), pp. 161–86.   133 Wilding, *Dragons Teeth*, p. 149.

independence from Jonson here than in 'Tom May's Death', so he also takes a less sympathetic view of Davenant – though given the reformed royalist's sympathetic treatment by the republic, the teasing remains affectionate. One of the heroes of Davenant's *Gondibert* lived in a palace

> So vast of height, to which such space did fit
> As if it were o're-cyz'd for Modern Men;
> The ancient Giants might inhabit it;
> And there walk free as windes that passe unseen.[134]

Marvell demolishes the presumption of 'Man':

> But He, superfluously spread,
> Demands more room alive then dead.
> And in his hollow Palace goes
> Where Winds as he themselves may lose.
> What need of all this Marble Crust
> T'impark the wanton Mote of Dust,
> That thinks by Breadth the World t'unite
> Though the first Builders fail'd in Height? (lines 17–24)

The allusion to the Tower of Babel reminds us of its builder Nimrod, a central symbol of monarchical tyranny. By contrast Fairfax's residence recalls '*Romulus* his Bee-like Cell': as in the 'Horatian Ode', Marvell compares the present of the English republic with the early days of Rome. And as in that poem, the architecture of his own poem parallels that he describes:

> *Humility* alone designs
> Those short but admirable Lines,
> By which, ungirt and unconstrain'd,
> Things greater are in less contain'd.
> Let others vainly strive t'immure
> The *Circle* in the *Quadrature*!
> These *holy Mathematicks* can
> In ev'ry Figure equal Man. (lines 41–8)

The short lines are in part those of his own poem, two syllables shorter than Davenant's pentameter. As in the 'Horatian Ode', Marvell is interested in a form of art and politics that can recover 'Man' not necessarily as he has become in courtly culture but when stripped of the 'Marble Crust' of ritual. The architecture implied in his poem is that of the 'Puritan minimalism' so common in the 1650s, where Inigo Jones's court-sponsored classicism is 'reduced' to a dignified simplicity.[135] There is a strong contrast with the nuns' courtly flattery, idolizing Isabella Thwaites as 'something more then humane'

---

134 Davenant, *Gondibert*, II.ii.7; Gladish, p. 126; the allusion is noted by Wallace, *Destiny His Choice*, p. 239.   135 Mowl and Earnshaw, *Architecture Without Kings, passim*.

(line 144). To the claustrophobic order of the nunnery the poem opposes an art subordinate to Nature:

> Art would more neatly have defac'd
> What she had laid so sweetly wast[.] (lines 77–8).

To 'lay waste' becomes an active, constructive activity rather than a negative one.

Marvell returns to his critique of Davenant at the centre of the poem, where we move to a common, 'a new and empty Face of things', a 'levell'd space' like a cloth on which Lely will paint (lines 441ff). The cattle on the meadow remind the poet of Davenant's description of a temple of praise decorated by paintings of the seven days of creation; Marvell joins the other wits who were teasing Davenant at this stage by making him appear as amongst his own fictitious cattle.[136] The 'naked equal Flat', we are told, is a pattern for the Levellers. This is sometimes taken as a routine jibe against radicals, but the effect may be more complicated. Marvell is glancing at the Diggers or 'True Levellers' who were active in the vicinity;[137] but the idea of going back to a more equitable mode of representation was built into the Leveller political programme. This passage juxtaposes two different forms of experiment with representation. Davenant's poetics at this stage would have been closely associated with Hobbes's politics, after the publication of *Leviathan* in the spring of 1651. In that work Hobbes, who had earlier been very dubious about speaking of the government as representing the people, had moved to using the language of representation; but he did so merely to outflank its democratic potentialities and reclaim it for absolutism.[138] Davenant's manipulative, Hobbesian poetics, like the deceptive artifice of the nuns, becomes a parody of the openness and sublimity of divine creation which Marvell evokes, however obliquely, in his images of a paradisal Nature. The flatness of the meadow scene, for all its austerity, has a utopian quality, a sense of returning to origins both in nature and in art. Lely is in a position analogous to Marvell's Cromwell as architect of a new state: the political upheavals have permitted a new clarity of vision, a new sense of possibility. Lely and other artists would soon be planning to seize this opportunity with their designs for huge paintings depicting Parliament and the Council of State.

Having sported with Davenant, Marvell now unleashes on the meadows a flood that plays something of the role of Machiavellian *Fortuna*. These elaborate schemes of control, trying to bring politics into the realm of the exact science of optics, are always vulnerable to contingency. The flood provides Marvell with

---

136 *Gondibert*, ed. Gladish, II.vi.60, p. 166.
137 Hirst and Zwicker, 'High Summer at Nun Appleton, 1651', 252–3.
138 Tuck, p. 328; on political theory as aesthetics in Hobbes, see Smith, *LR*, pp. 154ff.
    Hobbes had himself written an estate poem, *De Mirabilibus Pecci* (*c.* 1636; 13537).

images of the world turned upside down, the kinds of image which for Fane had signified the disorder of the republic. In this case, however, the turbulence proves to lead to renewal, leaving the meadows 'fresher dy'd'. The flood can be seen as echoing the end of Denham's *Coopers Hill*,[139] where, as has been seen, Denham had adopted a more pessimistic view than Machiavelli of the power of human agency to control an unacceptable constitutional situation; Marvell as it were re-Machiavellianizes the figure. The poem's ending, charged with apocalyptic echoes, further revalues the idea of the world upside down.[140] It returns us to the beginning, to the valorization of natural economy over artificial excesss, and Marvell transforms the conventional ending of the pastoral with the shepherds returning home at evening (lines 769–76). The shift from shepherds to fishermen evokes the Christian symbolism of fishers of men. They have been at work and their relationship with their boats, which at first links them with the world-turned-upside-down section, then becomes a greater link with the structure of the macrocosm. Marvell has turned the country-house poem upside down, just as the upheavals of the Puritan revolution had done; but the poem raises questions about just when in English history things have ever been the right way up.[141]

Marvell and Commonwealth poetry III:
'The Character of Holland'

If 'Upon Appleton House' reveals a certain independence from its patron, it should be remembered that even during his two-year stay with Fairfax, Marvell had tried to keep other options open. In February 1653, Milton wrote a letter on his behalf to the Council of State stating that Marvell had 'lately' left Fairfax's service (*MPW*, IV:2, 860). Weckherlin, who had given him some help in his secretarial office, had just died. Milton wrote, amidst high praises, that he admired Marvell enough to dismiss 'those Jealosies & that æmulation w^{ch}: mine owne condition [i.e. his blindness] might suggest to me by bringing in such a coadjutor'. Milton evidently respects Marvell so much that he fears he may become a rival. Modesty was never one of Milton's most striking characteristics, and this acknowledgement that Marvell might be a serious cause for worry to him deserves more attention than it has received. Marvell had published no prose and very little serious poetry. To have regarded Marvell as such a serious competitor, it seems possible that Milton may have

139 Thomas Healy, ' "Dark All Without it Knits": Vision and Authority in Marvell's *Upon Appleton House*', in Thomas Healy and Jonathan Sawday (eds.), *Literature and the English Civil War* (Cambridge, 1990), pp. 170–88 (180).
140 Stocker, *Apocalyptic Marvell*, pp. 46–66, 137–64, charts the apocalyptic dimension.
141 Stocker, *Apocalyptic Marvell*, p. 163.

read some of his poetry and recognized in him a younger and potentially ago-
nistic talent, one that had drawn on his own poetry but done something new
with it; as has been seen, there are possible verbal links. There was even a
rumour, which has not been substantiated, that Marvell had collaborated
with Milton over *Eikonoklastes*.[142] The reference to Ascham shows that Milton
envisaged for Marvell a leading career in the republic's diplomatic service.

Marvell backed up his application by the publication of a vigorous pro-
government satire, 'The Character of Holland' (*MPL*, I, 100–3). By now, the
tensions between England and the Netherlands had erupted into wholesale
war. Paradoxically, as Marvell's St John poem had shown, some of those who
most favoured union with the Dutch were also keenest on war, which stood to
eliminate monarchical interest. There were also economic factors. In October
1651 Parliament had passed the Navigation Act, which cut off Dutch trade
with English colonies. Amongst the architects of the Act were St John and two
members of the Hartlib circle, Worsley and Culpeper. Though the republic
did not carry through a vigorous anti-monopoly policy, it did attend strongly
to trading interests.[143] Hall, recycling an old atrocity story about the Dutch,
proclaimed that although James and Charles had neglected English commercial interests, 'since that yoak of Kingship is taken off our necks, me thinks we
should like men, whose shackles are taken off them while they are asleep, leap
up nimbly, and make use of our Liberty'.[144] In May 1652 Anglo-Dutch tensions
flared up into open war. This was in part a war of trade but it was also an ideological, republican war, designed to prevent an alliance between the royalist
parties in England, Scotland and the Netherlands. Nedham gave a strongly
ideological cast to the campaign. He praised Parliament for its courage in exe-
cuting Charles I and called on it to display equal courage in foreign policy: 'It
is your honor, that God hath made you Founders of the most famous and
potent Republick this day in the world; and your felicitie, that all your
Enemies have no other Ground of quarrel, but that you are a Republick . . . It is
just as if *Hannibal* were again in *Italy*, or *Charls Stuart* at *Worcester*'.[145]

Nedham tried to enlist poets in the cause. In November 1652, in a translation of Selden's *Mare Clausum*, he wrote that 'It is a gallant sight to see the

142 William Riley Parker, *Milton: A Biography*, second edition, 2 vols., ed. Gordon
   Campbell (Oxford, 1996), II, 1022.
143 Robert Brenner, *Merchants and Revolution: Commercial Change, Political Conflict, and
   London's Overseas Traders, 1550–1653* (Cambridge, 1993), pp. 625–8. It is unfortunate
   that this Marxist study of commercial policy gives such brief attention to the revolutionary period, and Pincus, *Protestantism and Patriotism*, pp. 40ff and *passim*, qualifies
   Brenner's analysis by a detailed demonstration of the significance of ideological
   factors.
144 [John Hall], *A True Relation of the Unjust, Cruel, and Barbarous Proceedings against the
   English at AMBOYNA* (1651; E1311.1), sig. *5v.
145 Selden, *Of the Dominion, or Ownership of the Sea*, sigs. c1v, d1r.

Sword and *Pen* in victorious Equipage together . . . the *Pen* Militant hath had as many sharp rancounters as the *Sword*, and born away as many Trophies from home-bred Enemies in prosecution of your most righteous caus by Land.' It was specifically as an image of the English republic, treading down the Stuart crown, that Britannia made an early appearance as the symbol of an emergent naval empire (figure 13). In the accompanying verses Neptune likened the young republic to Venice and proclaimed:

> Go on (great STATE!) and make it known
> Thou never wilt forsake thine own,
>   nor from thy purpose start:
> But that thou wilt thy power dilate,
> Since Narrow Seas are found too straight
>   For thy capacious heart.
> So shall thy rule, and mine, have large extent:
> Yet not so large, as just, and permanent.[146]

Mercurius Politicus serialized anti-Dutch poems such as *Anglia Victrix*, a neo-Latin celebration of a British victory in February 1653. Though Nedham says that these verses come from abroad, their use of the figure of Britannia and reference to *Mare Clausum* might make one suspect them for Nedham's own.[147] Nedham also reported on volumes of celebratory verse being produced in the Netherlands to show how the Dutch had cravenly submitted to a sentimental cult of the English monarchy.[148]

Another pro-war poet invoked Lucan. This was particularly appropriate because a war between two republics which had negotiated union verged on civil war: to fight the Dutch was in some sense to attack English monarchists. Furthermore, Lucan was regarded as a pioneer in the poetry of naval warfare, a theme, May had argued in dedicating the third book to a veteran of Elizabethan wars, 'on which no other Poet light'.[149] This author began with a lengthy imitation of the opening of the *Pharsalia*:

> Wars, worse then Pitch-feilds, on a moving plaine,
> We sing, and for it; where two States retaine
> In their owne bowels their victorious shot,
> Fast Wounds, and horrid Death, yet feele them not.

---

146 Selden, *Of the Dominion, or Ownership of the Sea*, sigs. b1r–v, verses opposite engraving. The verses are signed 'Klareamont'; might this be some kind of anagrammatic sobriquet for Thomas Chaloner, who was involved in publishing the engraved frontispiece (*CSPD 1651–52*, p. 358)? See David Armitage, 'The Cromwellian Protectorate and the Languages of Empire', *Historical Journal* 35 (1992), 531–55 (533).
147 *Mercurius Politicus* no. 144, 10–17 March 1653, E689.26, pp. 2295–7; English translation reproduced by Smith, *LR*, p. 282.
148 *Mercurius Politicus* no. 145, 17–24 March 1653, E689.30, pp. 23[20]–21.
149 May, *Lucan's Pharsalia* (1627), sig. D5r.

13 Title-page of Marchamont Nedham's translation of Selden, *Of the Dominion, or Ownership of the Sea*, 1652.

And, as *Romes* paire with this point dig'd their grave,
Caesar no first, *Pompey* no Peere would have:
Just so tis here with us; *Van-trump* allowes
No State to his Superiour; and *Blake* vowes,
Ours hath no equall: neither thus will vaile,
[B]ut loose a Fleet, rather then strike a Saile.[150]

In this comparison, Caesar is presumably the Dutch admiral, Van Tromp, who had triggered the war by refusing to lower his sails; he was a strong Orangist and was specifically refusing to acknowledge the republic as opposed to the monarchy – some of his ships flew Charles II's colours.[151]

Marvell's 'Character of Holland', probably written to commemorate a day of thanksgiving on April 12 1653, joins in this poetic campaign, and reveals some of the tensions involved in praising a war by one republic against another. Marvell had recently returned from celebrating a flat, easily-flooded piece of land in Yorkshire and praising his patron for his humility, the way in which his artifice mirrored the world of animals and birds. In 'The Character of Holland' he inverts the values of these topoi, giving a satirical myth of the foundation of the Dutch republic:

Collecting anxiously small Loads of Clay,
Less then what building Swallows bear away;
Or then those Pills which sordid Beetles roul,
Transfusing into them their Dunghil Soul.
How did they rivet, with Gigantick Piles,
Thorough the Center their new-catched Miles;
And to the stake a strugling Country bound,
Where barking Waves still bait the forced Ground;
Building their *watry Babel* far more high
To reach the *Sea*, then those to scale the *Sky*. (lines 13–22)

The architectural imagery that pervades Marvell's poetry at this time is devoted to negating the Dutch achievement; the Babel comparison invokes the tyrant Nimrod. Yet there is a certain grudging admiration in Marvell's portrayal of Dutch ingenuity and industry: the swallow is not conventionally negative in association, and the image of the land as a bear being baited invokes some sympathy.

The poem as a whole, however, is militantly pro-war. Critics who argue that the end of the 'Horatian Ode' must be ironic fail to acknowledge that Marvell is frequently belligerent: more so than Milton. Milton had in fact shown considerable unease about the war. His sonnet to Cromwell, if it echoes Marvell, turns from the ode's martial concerns at the end to religious

---

150 I. D., *Concordia Rara Sonorum* (1651; E689.31), pp. 1–2.
151 Pincus, *Protestantism and Patriotism*, p. 71.

toleration at home. His sonnet to Vane would have been written at a time when he was voicing opposition to the war, and the poem was taken by an early republican commentator to illustrate Vane's dislike of those 'that too much turned War into a Trade'.[152] Marvell registers no such doubts, though his commitment to the war is as much patriotic as specifically republican.[153] The poem continues with a great deal of conventional ethnic abuse, and the first hundred lines were sufficiently lacking in overt republican language to be reprinted after the Restoration. The attack on Dutch sects could have appealed to religious conservatives.

As the poem reaches its climax, however, republican overtones become more explicit. Like the *Mercurius Politicus* poem, Marvell alludes to Grotius's *De Jure Belli ac Pacis* (line 113). When he claims that the Dutch have slighted England's 'ancient Rights' in refusing to salute her ships (line 107), he is giving a new twist to this phrase. In the 'Horatian Ode' and 'Tom May's Death' it had signified the old monarchical order, but here English rights have been separated from the monarchy, as they had been by Nedham in his Selden edition. Though less explicit than *Anglia Victrix* in linking van Tromp with 'th'*Orange* faction', Marvell ridicules him as this '*Burgomaster of the Sea*' (line 114). Republican language emerges as he praises a strenuous commission of inquiry into the English fleet:

> The *Common wealth* doth by its losses grow;
> And, like its own Seas, only Ebbs to flow.
> Besides that very Agitation laves,
> And purges out the corruptible waves. (lines 131–4)

The language here is Machiavellian: turbulence serves in the long term as a source of strength.

The poem now builds up to a climax as jingoistic as that of the 'Horatian Ode':

> And now again our armed *Bucentore*
> Doth yearly their *Sea-Nuptials* restore.
> And now the *Hydra of seaven Provinces*
> Is strangled by our *Infant Hercules.*
> Their Tortoise wants its vainly stretched neck;
> Their Navy all our Conquest or our Wreck:
> Or, what is left, their *Carthage* overcome

152 [George Sikes], *The Life and Death of Sir Henry Vane, Kt.* (1662; S6323C), p. 96. On Milton's unease about the Dutch war see Parker, *Milton*, I, 415–16.
153 For discussion see Richard Todd, 'Equilibrium and National Stereotyping in "The Character of Holland"', in Claude J. Summers and Ted-Larry Pebworth (eds.), *On the Celebrated and Neglected Poems of Andrew Marvell* (Columbia and London, 1992), pp. 169–91 (190–1).

Would render fain unto our better *Rome.*
Unless our *Senate,* lest their Youth disuse,
The War, (but who would) Peace if begg'd refuse.
    For now of nothing may our *State* despair,
Darling of Heaven, and of Men the Care;
Provided that they be what they have been,
Watchful abroad, and honest still within.
For while our *Neptune* doth a *Trident* shake,
Steel'd with those piercing Heads, *Dean, Monck and Blake.*
And while *Jove* governs in the highest Sphere,
Vainly in *Hell* let *Pluto* domineer. (lines 135–52)

The Bucentaur was the Venetian state barge, used in that republic's ritual of marriage to the sea. *Mercurius Politicus* had been rehearsing the common republican contrast between the aristocratic constitution of Venice, which was suitable for stability and longevity, and ancient Rome's more unstable contention of democratic and aristocratic elements, which had been more appropriate for colonial expansion. Marvell presents England as a fusion of Venetian and Roman elements. The rivalry with the Netherlands is paralleled to ancient Rome's with Carthage; as has been seen, Nedham had argued that the conflict reflected credit on both parties because their republican liberty gave them strength. Marvell is indeed confident that the Dutch will soon bow to England's superior energy. The tortoise, which Marvell had so recently used in 'Upon Appleton House' to connote natural simplicity, now figures in its Roman sense as a siege-engine, and the idea of cutting off its head seems to glance at the regicide. *Anglia Victrix* had referred to the three English commanders as *'Triumvirs'*; in a less directly politicized but still militant image, Marvell makes them the three heads of Neptune's trident.

'The Character of Holland' shows how far republican propaganda had come in three years. The initially beleaguered state was constructing an image of its youthful strength that had an imaginative as well as pragmatic appeal. Marvell compares the Dutch republic to a small boat towed behind 'some greater Vessel' (line 110): the English republic is not a static, traditional entity but a project still in process. He could not have known how soon it was to hit the rocks.

King Oliver? Protectoral Augustanism
and its critics, 1653–1658

Waller and the trend towards monarchy

On 20 April 1653 the republic died. Or did it?

On that dramatic day, Cromwell stormed into the Parliament, declaring that it had sat long enough, summoned some troops and had the House cleared and locked. For many republicans, this was an act more momentous than the regicide, a flagrant assertion of arbitrary power and personal ambition. Later historians have in general been concerned to vindicate Cromwell from such charges. His motives were too complex and ambiguous to be reduced to a simple bid for kingship. Parliament was about to vote on a bill for its dissolution and the election of a new 'Representative': might this bill not have buttressed oligarchy, or risked letting royalists flood back to power? Since Cromwell snatched the bill away and it has never been seen since, this gives him the benefit of the doubt he created.[1] Whatever the complexities of his motives, to many contemporaries his actions looked like those of a Caesar – as has been seen, the Commonwealth's poets had already taken to making the comparison. Within a month an anonymous poet had displayed at the New Exchange a panegyric of Cromwell which ended 'God Save the King'. Did not, asked one enthusiast, 'the *Roman* Commonwealth flourishe more under *Julius Caesar* and *Augustus*, then ever it did either before or after their times?'[2]

Such celebrations of Cromwell as Caesar were premature, however. At first the new military-dominated regime made reassuring noises and tried to

---

1 On the historiography, see Sean Kelsey, *Inventing a Republic: The Political Culture of the English Commonwealth 1649–1653* (Manchester, 1997), pp. 12–13.

2 *To his Excellency Oliver Cromwell* (1653; 669f17.8). For other versions see Samuel Rawson Gardiner, *History of the Commonwealth and Protectorate*, 4 vols. (1903; rptd, Adlestrop, 1988–9), II, 279, and Wilbur Cortez Abbott, *The Writings and Speeches of Oliver Cromwell*, III (1945; rptd Oxford, 1988), III, 28–9; as Abbott says, it is unclear whether this was a pro- or anti-Cromwell gesture; *Reasons why the Supreme Authority of the Three Nations (For the Time) is not in the Parliament, but in the new-established Councel of State* (1653; E697.19), p. 4.

establish political continuity. One poet, John Ward, continued the characteristic republican imagery of blindness and reduction, arguing that the Long Parliament's leaders had been more culpable than Charles precisely because they now had more light, urging the people not to be blinded by custom to the need for 'Vicissitude', and optimistically telling England that

> Theres not a land beneath a vaulted sky:
> So free as thou art now from Monarchy.[3]

Ward's praise went to the army without mentioning Cromwell in person. To palliate such opinion, rather than declaring himself emperor, Cromwell tried to delegate decisions to a nominated assembly. This was an experiment in godly republicanism, with the standard system of election giving way to nomination by Cromwell in consultation with Independent churches. The assembly had a reforming agenda and was warmly greeted by many religious radicals. Particularly enthusiastic were the 'Fifth Monarchists', who retained some of the social and economic radicalism of the 1640s but had given it a more emphatically apocalyptic cast. They drew inspiration from the prophetic books of the Bible for their belief that after the demise of the four great empires of the earth – Babylon, Assyria, Greece and Rome (including the Holy Roman Empire) – Christ alone would be king and preside over a thousand years of justice. Though the Fifth Monarchists regarded kingship as idolatrous, they did not have a consensus on which constitutional forms should succeed it, and were at first ready to praise Cromwell as an agent of the millennium.[4] Before long, however, Cromwell dissolved the Nominated Parliament, and in retrospect it looked to his opponents like a mere plaything for an autocrat. Cromwell now assumed power under a constitution drafted by a group of army commanders.

On 16 December Cromwell was proclaimed Lord Protector, and installed, according to one eyewitness, 'with no less state and magnificence than any former Kings have used'. The same baffled observer reported that 'he ratified (I know not what to call it) an instrument of three or four skins of parchment, covenants, I suppose, for his government'. This was a menial description for England's first written constitution, the Instrument of Government. But since its details had not yet been printed, the ceremony could not be fully understood: 'This is all the certainty I can pick out of the confused discourses among men in a maze, as are most'.[5] As will be seen, the Instrument was not an

---

3 John Ward, 'The Changes Or a Vicissitude of Change of Gouerment Being a Vindication of the present Actings of the Army in dissoluing the late Parliament', Bodleian MS Ashmole 49, fols. 4r, 5r, 9r–v; *The Seventeenth Century* 13 (1998), 185–211.

4 Bernard Capp, *The Fifth Monarchy Men: A Study in Seventeenth-Century English Millenarianism* (1972), pp. 62–3.

5 *H. M. C. Egmont*, I, 532 (Samuel Percivall to John Percivall, December 17 1653).

unequivocally monarchical document, even though it had initially termed Cromwell a king; its intellectual origins lay in the army-Leveller constitutional proposals of 1647. However, it was characteristic of the Cromwellian era that even a notionally democratic constitution should have been ratified by a tiny elite before the people had any chance of understanding its terms. Nedham's report had to admit that many details of the Instrument had 'slipt my memory'.[6] Ludlow later complained that 'this important business that so highly concerned the nation, and in some measure all Europe', was 'in a clandestine manner carried on and huddled up by two or three persons; for more they were not who were let into the secret of it, so that it may justly be called a work of darkness'.[7]

The impression that Cromwell had become a kind of king would certainly have been understandable. Early drafts of the Instrument of Government had given that title, though Cromwell himself demurred. He was from now on referred to as 'His Highness', and soon there were rumours that he would be proclaimed as Emperor.[8] On 8 February 1654 he made a formal entry to London, reviving a practice of former monarchs, and poems marking the occasion took a strongly Augustan tone.[9] A continuation of May's *History* published in April, having celebrated the Commonwealth's deeds with frequent quotations from Lucan, concluded somewhat incongruously: 'now Reader have I brought my story from the end of one Monarchy to the beginning of another'.[10] When a peace treaty with the Netherlands was signed in the summer, Oxford and Cambridge Universities marked the occasion by reviving the discontinued custom of ceremonial verses. The first poem in the Oxford volume, by John Owen, Cromwell's appointee as Chancellor, noted that Augustus's peace had been beneficial to poetry, and another poet compared Cromwell to Augustus shutting Janus' temple: 'We can be Poets when you make us so'.[11] New coins were struck which depicted Cromwell in an imperial guise. On the new Great Seal, the map was replaced by Cromwell's coat of arms and the session of Parliament gave way to an image of the Protector on horseback modelled on Charles I's seal. The structure of government began to move closer to the pre-war system, with greater emphasis on personal patronage than on impersonal committees.

6 *Mercurius Politicus* no. 184, 16–22 December 1653, E725.6, p. 3053.

7 *The Memoirs of Edmund Ludlow*, ed. C. H. Firth, 2 vols. (Oxford, 1894), I, 371.

8 David Armitage, 'The Cromwellian Protectorate and the Languages of Empire', *Historical Journal* 35 (1992), 531–55.

9 For example, Edmund Litsfield, *Triambeisis Celsissimi Domini Oliverii Cromwelli* (1655; E1069.1).

10 Anon., *Britannia Triumphalis* (1654; B4817), p. 207; see Smith, *LR*, p. 344.

11 *Musarum Oxoniensium Elaiophoria* (Oxford, 1654; E740.1), pp. 1, 59.

The way was open for a renewed form of literary Augustanism.[12] And it was during this drift towards monarchism that Edmund Waller re-entered the public sphere. As was seen in chapter 3, his divided allegiances in the early period of the Civil War had silenced him poetically and politically. This new, reformed monarchy offered Waller the kind of synthesis between social conservatism and economic and intellectual innovation that he had been unable to find under either Charles I or the Commonwealth. He was a kinsman of Cromwell, and by 1653 Evelyn was turning to him as an intermediary because of 'your authority with his Excellency'.[13] His *A Panegyrick to my Lord Protector* appeared in May 1655, at a time when Cromwell had strongly affirmed his personal rule. In February he had dissolved his first Protectoral Parliament, which had proved unexpectedly contentious; under the Instrument of Government it would be more than two years before he had to summon another. Proposals had been made to have him declared king, and though in his closing speech Cromwell affirmed his personal opposition to kingship, his critics pointed out that he still left the option open. Major decisions would for some time be taken by the Protector and his Council without causing turbulence in the public sphere, and indeed later in the year all newsbooks but two official ones were closed down. The commotions of political rhetoric, which had long disturbed Hobbes and Waller, had been steered into calmer channels.[14]

Cromwell's influence was greatly strengthened by his ability to draw on England's military prestige on the international stage. England had brought the Dutch to a favourable peace settlement, and during 1655 Cromwell was being courted by the rival governments of France and Spain to form an alliance with them. He drove a hard bargain. He tried to gain substantial financial as well as political concessions from Spain, and when these failed – indeed before the negotiations were over – he was to launch his 'Western Design', an assault on Spanish territories in the New World, camouflaged by a feint against the Netherlands. Gardiner declared these dealings 'a sorry spectacle', and saw them as marking a decisive shift towards the secularization of the Puritan Revolution.[15] There were religious grounds for attacking a Catholic power long suspected of harbouring designs for a Satanic universal monarchy; Campanella's treatise on that subject appeared in an English translation in November 1653.[16] A major motive for the war, however, was to

12 Howard Erskine-Hill, *The Augustan Idea in English Literature* (1983), pp. 199ff.

13 British Library, Evelyn Collection, MS Letters, Evelyn to Waller, 12 November 1653.

14 On Cromwell's curbing of the press see William M. Clyde, *The Struggle for the Freedom of the Press from Caxton to Cromwell* (1934), pp. 243ff.

15 Gardiner, *History of the Commonwealth and Protectorate*, III, 163, 165–6.

16 On the significance see Steven C. A. Pincus, *Protestantism and Patriotism: Ideologies and the Making of English Foreign Policy, 1650–1668* (Cambridge, 1996), p. 185.

seize Spanish silver, gold and territory, to continue to build the foundations of a great naval empire. This was, says David Armitage, the 'imperial moment of the English republic'.[17]

For more secularly minded republicans, colonial expansion was perfectly desirable in a 'commonwealth for increase'. The Stuarts, with their policy of accommodation with Spain, had been slow to take such opportunities; the republic's Navigation Act had reclaimed them. But there remained within republican ideology a sharp tension between the austere activism of civic virtue and the tendency of commerce to lead to luxury and quietism. As Steven Pincus has shown, the republic's anti-Dutch war had had ideological as much as commercial motivations. Republicans might favour alliance with Spain as opposed to France, so that support could be given to Protestant and anti-courtly forces there: Marten's Leveller friend Edward Sexby was trying to disseminate republican principles in south-west France. A raid against the Spanish Empire offered financial gains but might not be so effective in ideological terms. In the spring of 1655 Harrington was probably already drafting the argument that England could achieve increase as well as permanence only if it adopted substantial social and political reforms. Much therefore hinged on the direction taken by Cromwell's policy.

Gardiner wrote that Waller 'celebrated in his facile verse, not the spiritual hopes and fears, but the earthly glory of the Protector'. As ever in Waller, the verse has been carefully crafted to give its sense of facility; but the *Panegyrick* certainly distances itself from Puritan idealism.[18] Waller begins by exploring England's status as 'the seat of Empire' (line 15).[19] He does advance an ethical justification for empire when he declares that foreigners will crave justice from England as 'the Sacred Refuge of Mankind' (line 28). Here he anticipates Harrington, whose Archon declares that his commonwealth is 'a Minister of God upon earth' which offers 'an holy *Asylum* unto the distressed world'.[20] This ethical imperative, however, soon gives way to more material concerns. The poem is conspicuously silent on apocalyptic motives for overseas war: it uses the word 'Fate' (line 121), which Cromwell had specifically denounced for

17 Armitage, 'The Cromwellian Protectorate and the Languages of Empire', 533.
18 Gardiner, *History of the Commonwealth and Protectorate*, IV, 193.
19 Quotations are from the second of the two 1655 editions, *A Panegyrick to my Lord Protector* (published by Thomas Newcomb, 1655, w507); *WP*, II, 10–17; on the different texts see David Norbrook, 'Lucy Hutchinson versus Edmund Waller: An Unpublished Reply to Waller's *A Panegyrick to my Lord Protector*', *The Seventeenth Century* 11 (1996), 61–86 (86). Thorn Drury suggests that the poem had been written as early as 1653 and subsequently revised, but evidence is lacking.
20 *James Harrington's 'Oceana'*, ed. S. B. Liljegren (Lund and Heidelberg, 1924), p. 11; *HPW*, p. 323; echoing Cicero, *De Officiis*, 2.27.

paganism in his address to Parliament.[21] The word 'piety' was apparently changed in revision to the more secular 'Clemency' (line 124). The emphasis is on luxuries like spices and silks: gold, though the heaviest metal, comes swimming to England (line 62). When Waller then proceeds to denounce the greed of England's enemies, there is therefore a certain tension. The Scots are denounced for being bribed to war by 'forraign Gold' which is kept at bay by 'Our *English* Iron' (lines 87–8). Waller here probably has in mind Machiavelli's claim that iron, republican military strength, rather than gold provides the sinews of war (*Discourses*, II.10). An anti-Spanish pamphlet later in the year declared: 'These Silver Sinews, and Golden Nerves, are the strength of the Man of sin; as to his external part, which to destroy is (instrumentally) the work of the Sword'.[22] In similar vein, in a poem on a 1656 victory over the Spanish fleet, Waller decreed the Spaniards doomed because their 'chiefe support and Sinewes are of Coine', as opposed to England's 'solid vertue'.[23] Here again, however, there was an ethical tension, for having denounced gold for fuelling 'the Pride of Courts' he ended by proposing that the state should be 'fix'd' by making Cromwell a crown:

> With *Ermyns* clad and *Purple*, let him hold
> A Royall Scepter made of *Spanish* Gold.

By 1658, when this broadside was published, the Protector had entered a second term of office in which he took on a still more regal tone, nominating an 'other house' that was effectively a House of Lords, amidst growing expectation that he would declare himself king.[24] In 1655 Waller was already hinting that his 'Princely vertues' (line 135) needed a special reward. He still, admittedly, paid lip-service to the formal republicanism of the Instrument of

---

21 Abbott, *Writings and Speeches*, III, 590. Waller's reluctance to invoke apocalyptic language can be contrasted for example with [George Tooke], *An Encomiastck [sic] ... of ... Robert Blake* (1658; T1897), p. 22, with its references to Baal and Babel, and its concluding invocation to Cromwell (p. 28):

> And thou great *Oliver*, thy sword gird on ...
> Yet crowned with this Epinicion be
> Great *Babilon* is fall'n, and that by thee.

On this poem see Margarita Stocker and Timothy Raylor, 'A New Marvell Manuscript: Cromwellian Patronage and Politics', *English Literary Renaissance* 20 (1990), 106–62 (138–43).

22 *A Dialogue ... concerning the Present Designe in the West-Indies* (1655; E1619.2), p. 12.

23 Quotations are from the 1658 edition, *A Lamentable Narration of the Sad Disaster of a Great Part of the Spanish Plate-Fleet* (669f21.2), dated 13 April by Thomason (also in *WP*, II, 23–7). Oddly, this edition dates the battle to 1657: perhaps this was to blur it in the inattentive reader's mind with the greater victory won by Blake at Teneriffe the following year, and celebrated by 'R. F.' in his poem (see below, n. 35).

24 Roy Sherwood, *The Court of Oliver Cromwell* (1977), pp. 158ff.

Government. The sub-title, in one edition, was 'Of The present Greatness and joynt Interest of His Highness, and this Nation'.[25] Cromwell in his dissolution speech had emphasized that there was a 'true and equal balance' between Protector and Parliament.[26] As has been seen, Waller had long sought a balance in politics analogous to the balance he sought in poetry; and it tended to involve a restriction on the turbulence of the public sphere, a shift from Parliamentary rhetoric to courtly poetry. In the Protector he finds a man who can 'balance *Europe*' (line 22) as well as his nation.

Throughout the poem the idea of political balance is worked through by recurrent oscillations between the 'you' of the Protector and the 'we' of the people. In practice, however – as was, arguably, the case in political reality – the Protector has a massive preponderance. He can 'Protect us from our Selves' as well as from the foe (line 3): already agency shifts from subject to ruler, for Cromwell is granted a privileged insight that can overrule the individual's erroneous judgements. Those who are discontented with the Protectorate are seen in Hobbesian terms as bringing the nation back to a state of nature, where they can 'Without controule upon their Fellows prey' (line 8). Waller returns to the Virgilian imagery of stilling storms that he had been exploring since the political crises of the 1620s: Cromwell is a Neptune calming the waves of ambition (line 9). The country has been 'Restor'd by you' (line 14): if there has been a Machiavellian reduction, it has depended on Cromwell alone. It is precisely because Cromwell is 'rais'd above the rest' at home (line 11) that the nation can 'lift her Head above the rest' (line 38). Again and again Cromwell's agency is seen as underlying that of his armed forces: he can 'make us Conquer' (line 4). Like Augustus, he is active so that the people may achieve 'repose' and 'rest' (lines 169–72).

The balance the poem seeks, in fact, is one of submission. The Scots have been 'happily o'rethrowne' (line 93), and it would appear that the English are in a somewhat similar position in relation to Cromwell. Where Marvell had seen Cromwell as rejecting the arts of peace, Waller's Cromwell can 'heale us with the arts of Peace' (line 110). The traditional social structure has been restored: 'The noble rest secured in your Blood' (line 128). It is striking that Edmund Burke in his most militantly conservative phase could find something to praise in Waller's Cromwell. Waller uses the stock monarchical image of the rising sun:

> Still as you rise, the State exalted too,
> Finds no distemper, while 'tis chang'd by you.
> Chang'd like the Worlds great Scene, when without noise,
> The rising Sun Nights vulgar Lights destroyes. (lines 141–4)

25 Title-page of the edition published by Richard Lowndes (1655; E841.2).
26 Abbott, *Writings and Speeches*, III, 588.

Burke writes that men like Cromwell were

> not so much like men usurping power, as asserting their natural place in society.
> Their rising was to illuminate and beautify the world . . . I do not say, that the
> virtues of such men were to be taken as a balance to their crimes; but they were
> some corrective to their effects.[27]

The great theorist of the sublime finds that Cromwell has managed to transform his sublimity into the beautiful, to naturalize his power.

Having installed the Protector into the monarchical cosmos, Waller now
compares him to Caesar in a warning against any possible Brutus who might
be tempted to assassinate him. The government was concerned about plots,
and indeed Waller's old poetic ally Denham was arrested soon after the
Panegyrick appeared for involvement in a royalist conspiracy. Waller tries to
outflank the royalists by presenting Cromwell, not Charles, as the true
Augustus. His classical analogues now grow blurred as Caesar becomes the
setting sun, a night from which Cromwell alone can redeem the state:

> That Sun once set, a thousand meaner Stars,
> Gave a dim light to Violence and Wars,
> To such a Tempest, as now threatens all,
> Did not your mighty Arm prevent the fall. (lines 152–6)

It would appear that Caesar here figures Charles I and Cromwell steps in as
Augustus.[28] In a kind of rhetorical sleight of hand, Waller manages to make
Cromwell the true heir of the Roman emperors and of the Stuarts.

Having subordinated the nation's military and political achievements to
Cromwell, Waller subordinates the active life to the contemplative, to the
'rest' that Cromwell gives the state. The Muses will celebrate his peace.
Though the poem does then look forward to future successful campaigns, the
emphasis is on Cromwell's personal role in writing history: 'every Conqueror
creates a Muse' (line 182). The values of civic humanism are inverted: the
movement is from the active life to the calm of the contemplative life, surren-
dering authority and judgement to the ruler. In the same way, political virtue
has been subordinated to the more private priorities of commerce. And the
poem's conclusion clinches the Augustan emphasis with a prophecy of
monarchical power:

> Here in low Strains your milder Deeds we sing,
> But there (my Lord) wee'll Bayes and Olive bring
> To Crown your Head, while you in Triumph ride

27 Edmund Burke, *Reflections on the Revolution in France*, ed. Conor Cruise O'Brien
   (Harmondsworth, 1969), p. 137.
28 Erskine-Hill, *The Augustan Idea in Stuart England*, p. 202, suggests that the parallels are
   not exact and that Caesar and Brutus 'do not appear to have English counterparts'.

> O're vanquish'd Nations, and the Sea beside;
> While all your Neighbor Princes unto you
> Like *Joseph*'s Sheaves pay rev'rence and bow. (lines 185–8)

A very rare enjambement breaks through the poem's closed couplets to place the emphasis on crowning. And the final lines allude to Joseph's dream of a single sheaf standing above the rest, which his brothers jealously read as an aspiration to becoming king.[29] The day after Thomason bought his copy, a crowd gathered in Westminster Hall in the expectation that Cromwell would be declared king.[30]

Waller's *Panegyrick* aroused a great deal of public attention. As a poet of acknowledged though controversial standing, his endorsement of the regime after a long period of withdrawal from public life carried some weight. Waller had deftly dissociated Augustan poetic culture from the Stuarts and found an idiom for supporting the Protectorate which could appeal to a traditional political elite that was weary of years of tumult. There was a price to be paid: the abandonment or diminution of some of the wider ethical and religious claims for the regime's legitimacy in favour of a bland pragmatism. But there were people to whom such a message would appeal – even though Waller's image of the Protector was very different from Cromwell's self-image.[31] Waller was warmly praised by Payne Fisher, who had by now become a firm supporter of the Protectorate, celebrating Cromwell as Augustus and even declaring that Brutus himself would have been happy to live under such a prince. Fisher praised Waller as the English Virgil who made his native Buckinghamshire into Mantua.[32]

Other admirers of Waller's shared his project of Protectoral Augustanism. Robert Creswell issued a copiously annotated edition of a Latin panegyric on Cromwell's installation as Protector which seems to have been intended as a possible school textbook, bringing the new Augustanism to a wide public.[33]

---

29 The analogy was applied to Cromwell's son Richard in January 1658: 'I hope God has fitted him, and if his sheaf be not as Joseph's, to which all the rest bow, I shall not receive much joy from what has passed' (Sir William Lockhart to Viscount Falconbridge, 16 January 1658, *CSPD 1657–58*, pp. 266–7).

30 Gardiner, *History of the Commonwealth and Protectorate*, III, 304; newspaper reports anticipating a Cromwellian monarchy had been appearing for some time, see *Certain Passages of Every Dayes Intelligence* no. 188, April 27–4 May 1655, E835.9, sig. A3v.

31 *WP*, I, lxi, prints a letter from Cromwell dated 18 June 1655 which mock-modestly rebukes him for 'your soe willinglye mistakinge mee in your verses' (also in Abbott, III, 748–9). Beal, 553–4, expresses doubts about its authenticity.

32 Payne Fisher, 'In . . . PANEGYRIM *OLIVERIANUM* . . . Dom. ED. WALLERI', in *Piscatoris Poemata* (1656; F1034), sigs. A1r–2r.

33 Augustine Wingfield, *Carmen Panegyricum, sive Paraeneticum* (1656; W3027, pp. 3, 12, 17–18). The Bodleian copy has a note attributing the annotations to Robert Creswell, a member of Waller's circle: Christopher Wase (trans.), *Grati Falisci Cynegeticon* (1654; E1531.3), sig. a6v, praise of Waller by Creswell; see also verses by Waller, sigs. a5r–6r.

The poem in question had been composed by Augustine Wingfield, a member of the Nominated Parliament with strong views on legal and ecclesiastical reform. Though Creswell alluded to Lucan's unmasking of tyranny in Photinus's speech, he gave more attention to Virgilian analogues, effectively Augustanizing Wingfield's strongly biblical language. Thus where Wingfield had compared Cromwell to Moses and even, audaciously, credited him with ushering in the Fifth Monarchy of Christ on earth, Creswell emphasized the parallels between the Protector's installation and regal anointment, and stressed that the coming millennium was a matter of inner, spiritual renewal more than of social change.

In September 1656 members assembling for the new Parliament were greeted with a fawning panegyric which claimed to be a 'little medal and Image of his Highnesse', thus evoking memories of the *Eikon Basilike*.[34] Like Waller, however, 'H. H.' presented Cromwell not only as a king but as a better one than his predecessors precisely because he was new to the job and could offer a modern form of polish: 'He is a *new Prince*, but hath the beauties and features of all the old-spirited Gallants . . . he hath [taken away all its rudenesse, and] put a new glosse upon *Monarchy*, which was so spotted and sullied, that it was quite cast off and rejected' (pp. 11, 19, brackets in original). He is thus presented as a kind of living equivalent of a Waller poem with its reformed and refined numbers. Well might 'H. H.' claim that 'this *Panegyrick* had been more fitly exprest in the sweet odors of Incense' (p. 20): he was even 'sometimes willing to scruple His mortality' (p. 44). He concluded his tract with a verse panegyric of Cromwell which was clearly modelled on Waller's, with the same stanza-form and some verbal borrowings: the Protector could 'save us from our crimes' (sig. I3v). He put a brave face on the Western Design, which had already proved to be a disaster:

> You needed not have sent so far about
> To fetch the mines & beat the *Spaniards* out
> This Island scornes *Spaine* and *Domingo* to
> She'l want no treasure can she keep but you. (sig. I4v)

Later Protectoral poetry by Waller and others carried these emphases further. Increasingly, naval victories were ascribed to the agency of the Protector rather than of individual commanders. The process can be traced in fascinating detail in different drafts of a poem by 'R. F.' about a naval victory of 1657, where the claim that the Spaniards 'only labour to exalt Our prayse' (line 60) is transferred to 'your praise' (line 94), and Blake's fleet rides first for 'Englands Fame' (line 67) and then for 'your renown' (line 101).[35] The cult of

---

34 'H. H.', *The Unparalleld Monarch* (1656; E1675.1), sig. a1r.
35 'To his HIGHNESSE. In his late Victory in the Baij of Santa Cruz, in the Island of Tenariff', printed in Stocker and Raylor, 'A New Marvell Manuscript', 147–62. The

personality had advanced so far by 1658 that another poet went to the lengths
of publishing an imaginary scenario in which Cromwell is chosen as king and
makes a triumphal entry to London. In this poem contempt for republicanism was open and traditional monarchical imagery was fully adapted to
Cromwell. A note attacked '*Catos* unseasonable constancy, struggling so long
against Authority . . . Or, *Cicero's* as unseasonable eloquence, who talkt so long
against the Conquering side, till he was proscribed, and lost his head at last'.
The poet called for all books teaching anything but obedience to the magistrate to be forbidden to the common people.[36]

If the republic had briefly tried to make itself a vehicle for national identity, the Protectorate seemed to be moving back towards identifying a
national with a dynastic interest. There are revealing tensions in another
publication of 1658, which Richard Hawkins proclaimed to be the very first
book in praise of the English nation. The author placed the emphasis on
military achievement. Though he celebrated the end of the Civil War, he
saw the valour there shown as redounding to the nation's credit and as
prophesying further victories abroad; rather than stressing an Augustan
peace he studded his treatise with lengthy quotations from 'the pious
Lucan'. Though ready to celebrate the pre-republican era because it offered
'freedoms' that were normally 'incompatible with a Monarchy', he declared
that the republic 'outwent in warlike Atchievements all other Common-
wealths'. Having lamented its passing, Hawkins said nothing whatever
about the Protectorate (two quotations from Waller's *Panegyrick* referred
to English rather than specifically Protectoral achievements). The book's
political section breaks off with the comment that the 'Humble Petition
and Advice' has just appeared and he will say no more at present. This
author's historical self-consciousness is striking: the fall of the monarchy
makes possible a new variety of epideictic literature, a founding document
of English nationalism; but the tendencies towards a Cromwellian monarchy were forcing epideictic literature back into dynastic, Augustan
moulds.[37]

poem's title itself elides Blake's agency. Though this poem appeared in the 1681 Folio of
Marvell's poems (*MPL*, I, 119–24), Elsie Duncan-Jones, 'Marvell, R. F. and the
Authorship of "Blake's Victory"', *English Manuscript Studies 1100–1700* 5 (1995), 107–26,
has revealed a different manuscript version attributed to an unidentified 'R. F.'; and the
manuscript printed by Stocker and Raylor has no signature. Verbal affinities between
the differing versions of this poem and of Waller's poem on the victory at Santa Cruz
suggest that there was close collaboration between the Protectorate's poets. Duncan-
Jones argues that the version printed in the 1681 folio antedates the other two MSS; but
the political arguments offered by Stocker and Raylor still seem persuasive.
36 *Anglia Rediviva* (1658; A3180), pp. 54–5.
37 R[ichard]. H[awkins]., *A Discourse of the Nationall Excellencies of England* (1658;
E1583.2), sig. A4r, pp. 83, 86, 96, 224–5, 232.

Oppositional poetry: The contest for Augustanism and republican anti-Augustanism

Cromwellian Augustanism was a precarious formation. In trying to span widely differing political interests, it risked alienating them all, and Waller's *Panegyrick* became a central point of reference for the Protectorate's opponents as well as its supporters.

One source for attacks on Cromwellian monarchism was of course Stuart monarchism. Waller and 'H. H.', in giving a fresh gloss to the Cromwellian image, were obscuring the Stuart image. However, attempts were made during the 1650s to retain associations between Augustanism and the Stuarts. When John Ogilby brought out a sumptuously produced translation of the *Aeneid* in 1654, most of the subscribers were strong royalists and the annotations indicated his political sympathies.[38] Denham was not won round by Waller to supporting the regime, even though his *Coopers Hill* had been adapted to the praise of Cromwell in the Oxford ceremonial volume.[39] Indeed, he may have been one of the 1655 rebels whom a royalist satirist had in mind for inclusion in a future poem:

> For the rest nott here nam'd I would not bee blam'd,
>   As if they were scorn'd by our Lyricke,
> For Waller intends to use them as ends
>   To patch up his next Panegyrick.[40]

In 1656 Denham brought out a translation of Virgil's narration of the fall of Troy which pointedly concentrated on the death of King Priam:

> On the cold earth lyes this neglected King,
> A headless Carkass, and a nameless Thing.[41]

The second line anachronistically drew attention to the death not only of the monarch but of the monarchy by using the favourite republican 'king-thing'

---

38 *The Works of Publius Virgilius Maro*, trans. John Ogilby (1654; v610); Annabel Patterson, *Pastoral and Ideology: Virgil to Valéry* (Berkeley and Los Angeles, 1987), pp. 170ff; Derek Hirst, 'The Politics of Literature in the English Republic', *The Seventeenth Century* 5 (1990), 133–55 (148). On Ogilby's royalism see below, chapter 9 at n. 157.

39 William Godolphin, in *Musarum Oxoniensium Elaiophoria*, pp. 97–9; Brendan O Hehir, *Expans'd Hieroglyphicks: A Critical Edition of Sir John Denham's 'Coopers Hill'* (Berkeley and Los Angeles, 1969), pp. 284–8, 227–56.

40 *The Poetical Works of Sir John Denham*, ed. Theodore Howard Banks, second edition (n. pl., 1969), p. 140. Brendan O Hehir, *Harmony From Discords: A Life of Sir John Denham* (Berkeley and Los Angeles, 1968), pp. 117ff, questions Banks's attribution of this poem to Denham; on the poets' relations see also p. 102 n. 40.

41 [Sir John Denham], *The Destruction of Troy* (1656; E880.4), p. 28, line 549. See Lawrence Venuti, '*The Destruction of Troy*: Translation and Royalist Cultural Politics in the Interregnum', *Journal of Medieval and Renaissance Studies* 23 (1993), 197–219.

rhyme. Denham thus signalled his constancy to the Stuarts in contrast with Waller, a point emphasized by a title-page which dated the translation to 1636.

Something of an ideological tug-of-war was developing, for two years later, nothing daunted, Waller issued a Virgil translation of his own. This had likewise been begun before the Civil War with the aid of Sidney Godolphin, to whose memory Hobbes had dedicated *Leviathan*.[42] Waller thus signalled the availability of Virgil to those who had followed Hobbes into submission to the new regime. And he was sending his signal to close acquaintances: his friend Christopher Wase was sharing with Denham the patronage of the earl of Pembroke. Such lovers of Virgil, his example proclaimed, need not feel that they had to remain devoted to a defunct dynasty. His patronage by Cromwell was indeed to become acclaimed as one of the leading achievements of the Protectorate. Henry Dawbeny, in a panegyric he described as 'a piece of an *Aenead* (some will think of flattery)', exclaimed:

> What obliging favours has he cast upon our *English Virgil* here (I mean Mr. *Edm. Waller*) and meerly for that [poetry], and his other vertues, having in some other relations, little capacity enough to deserve them. My Lord has sufficiently shewed his own most excellent judgement in Poetry, by his approbation and election of him, to be the object of his great goodnesse, who is clearly one of the ablest, and most flourishing wits, that ever handled a pen ... his words glide along like a river, and bear perpetually in them, some flashes of lightning, at the end of each period ... [Let us] adore the judgement of our great *Augustus*, who alwayes chose him out, and crowned him for the *Virgil* of this Nation[.]

For this panegyrist, Lucan had things completely the wrong way round. It was praiseworthy for Cromwell to be 'like a *Caesar* indeed ... resolved to break through all obstacles, to Crown his inspired purposes'. As for Pompey, 'what memory have all his great actions acquired to him, but of a proud, bloody, imperious Common-wealths-man, that could endure no corrival in great-nesse.'[43]

The smooth Virgilian flow of Waller's words may have been more effective as propaganda than more contentious defences of the Protectorate. In a 1659 volume which collected a number of parodies of his panegyrics, and which seems to have echoed Dawbeny's language, Richard Watson complained that 'tender Hearts are addouced rather by ye smoothnesse of his straine, then honourably incensed at the severity of his matter, which, like a deluding streame, more dangerously undermines the bankes of his *Prince's* interest, then a bolder torrent that attempts to invade his territories by a deluge' (sig. [A2r]). Waller might charm people 'into the ... declension of any enterprize

---

42 *The Passion of Dido for Aeneas* (1658; v633).
43 Henry Dawbeny, *Historie & Policie Re-Viewed* (1659; E1799.2), sig. A3r, pp. 207–9, 298, 300.

with hazard in behalfe of their exild' King' (sig. F3r). The editor warned that the 'slie artifice of y^e *Poëtike Rebell*' was in danger of obscuring the 'image' of Charles II (sig. B2v), and listed sixteen different points in which the poem was sinful and seditious (sig. [A]2vff).[44] The *Anti-Panegyrike* hammers home at every opportunity Waller's disloyalty to the House of Stuart and uses biblical parallels to denounce the monstrous sin of rebellion against monarchy. The sun is straightforwardly identified with the Stuart monarchy, and Charles II is 'our *Augustus*' (p. 20). Interestingly, however, the author displays a certain ambivalence towards Waller. At one point he retracts his call for him to be hanged and suggests that he may after all repent and be drawn back to the royal cause. At another he says he thought that Waller, being notoriously cowardly, had been 'awed into an ungenerous submission' by hopes of reward. After reading his elegy for the Protector, however, he reverted to the view that he was no better than 'the *Desperados* such as *Milton* and *Britannicus* [Nedham]' (sig. F2r), even though he granted that he had 'more *wit*, though not more *honesty* in keeping distance' from those writers' attacks on Charles I and Charles II: as has been seen, his handling of the regicide was indeed oblique. Waller provided a problem for Stuart royalists because the dividing-line between his position and theirs was in some ways a very narrow one. Watson's alarm that Waller might win over his friends was counterbalanced by the remote possibility that Watson might be able to win him over.

Ironically enough, one of the wrongs for which Watson denounced the Protectoral regime was censorship. Because of pressure from England he had been unable to get his book published in the Netherlands, and he chided the hypocrisy of the 'poëtike *Areopagite*', '*Milton* who publish'd a speech for the libertie of unlicens'd printing' ('To the Pvsillanimous Authour of the Panegyrike'). Waller supported religious toleration and probably did have some sympathy with Milton's desire for openness of the press to heterodoxy, but his career in the 1640s had made it clear that as far as he was concerned there were definite limits to the expansion of the public sphere, and the Protectorate was providing just such limits. For Watson's part, it is unlikely that his enthusiasm for press freedom would have survived the Restoration when Charles introduced much more draconian restrictions. Where Milton had celebrated the emergence of civic and martial virtue in the image of dragons' teeth, Watson complains that

> The Land unnaturally beares, by charmes,
> From serpents teeth *Cadméan* men in armes. (p. 7)

44 [Richard Watson], *The Panegyrike and The Storme* (n. pl., 1659; W1092); pagination is irregular, and different copies vary in content. There is a further manuscript reply to the *Panegyrick* in the margins of a Bodleian copy, 4° Rawl. 219 (I owe this reference to Nicholas von Maltzahn).

For Watson, natural order is monarchical order, and Cromwell is its antitype. Waller occupied some kind of middle position between the two men, a position that was in some ways more dangerous to Stuart sympathizers than Milton's.

That position left him vulnerable to attack from very different quarters. The *Panegyrick* received another stanza-by-stanza refutation, this time from a republican point of view. The author seems to have been Lucy Hutchinson, whose husband had retired from public life in protest at the dissolution of the Long Parliament and never accommodated himself to the Protectorate. Lucy Hutchinson had a particular interest in poetic Augustanism. She regarded Waller as a shameful turncoat but also took the trouble to transcribe in her commonplace book two of his poems, including the *Panegyrick*, and extracts from Denham's and Godolphin's Virgil translations.[45] In her later account of the Protectorate she attacked what she saw as the prevalent atmosphere of servility, of sacrificing liberty for empty titles. The contrasts between her poem, Watson's, and Waller's provide a revealing index of the contending political discourses of the 1650s.[46] In some respects Hutchinson's criticisms converge with Watson's. She too finds Waller dangerous because of his insinuating sweetness: he has a 'smooth but yet a fertile Tongue' (line 1). But where Watson was worried that this sweetness would provide a substitute for true courtly language, attracting readers to a false rather than a true image, Hutchinson is iconoclastic, opposed in principle to the structures of political power that substitute courtly sweetness for free rhetoric, that seek luxury and glory abroad at the cost of servility at home.

Hutchinson points to the negative side of Cromwell's foreign policy, which had begun to emerge soon after Waller's *Panegyrick* was published. The expedition to the West Indies suffered huge losses from battle and disease. Since Cromwell alone had taken the initiative, and had been confident of divine endorsement, the failure was a deep blow to the prestige of the Protectorate. Hutchinson's poem attacks the whole direction of Cromwellian foreign policy. The treaty with the Netherlands which had been greeted by the universities as ushering in an Augustan peace becomes for her a shameful sell-out:

> Holland courted his friendship to prevent
> Their dreaded just impending punishment
> Which while the Commonwealth intirely stood

---

45 Hutchinson, p. 78; Nottinghamshire Archives, DD/HU1, pp. 251–8, 236–7 (the poem to Lady Morton on New Year's Day 1650), 5ff, 207ff.

46 British Library Additional MS 17,018, fols. 213–17; printed with the Waller text and discussion of authorship in Norbrook, 'Lucy Hutchinson versus Edmund Waller'. Some doubts remain about authorship, but for brevity's sake I shall refer to this poem as Hutchinson's.

Threatned their falshood and Ingratitude . . .
His Exaltation only gave delight
To such as the States Anger did affright
The Belgick Lords into distresses brought
Obtain'd a League who would haue pardon sought[.]

Waller had alluded to a section of the treaty in which the state of Holland for-
swore the succession of the House of Orange.[47] This was a republican gesture,
but Hutchinson sees it as not going far enough: the war should have been continued, presumably to force the Dutch into the more radical union that had
been called for by some republicans. Instead, Cromwell had turned against
Spain. Hutchinson ridicules his attempts to keep his design secret ('Fame . . .
tells th'Iberian his Deepe Policies', lines 33–4)[48] and complains that

> free born English sent to other Soyles
> Are there kill'd vp with Sicknesse and vaine Toyles
> To augment his Highs. Treasure and his Name
> Not satisfi'd with any Wealth or Fame. (lines 61–4)

Cromwell did indeed exile some of the politically disaffected to the West
Indies. Hutchinson inverts the procedure of Protectoral poets, condemning
the process by which others' agency is turned into Cromwell's fame. England's
Empire cannot possibly be a benign protection because she can only export
her own political corruption: Cromwell

> The enclosed Isle with sadd Exactions greiues
> And forreigne Lands more troubles then Releiues.(lines 43–4)

The traditional poetic celebration of Britain as an island splendid in its isolation becomes the political claustrophobia of being 'enclosed'. The island's
natural richness simply 'supplies' his greedy ambition – there is a glance here
at Parliamentary supplies (line 55). The 'bright Silkes' gained by overseas
empire merely line 'our Scorned fetters' (line 58). Hutchinson is equally dis-
missive of other prized aspects of the Cromwellian imperial policy. Waller
had celebrated the incorporation of the Scots and Irish; Hutchinson says that
these people rejoice only because they are now treated no more tyrannically
than the English themselves.

The final part of the poem savagely deflates the entire Augustan mythology
with which Waller was surrounding the Protectorate. But where Watson

---

47 Pincus, *Protestantism and Patriotism*, p. 182.
48 The former Leveller Edward Sexby had spread word of the Western Design in Spanish
 Flanders with a view to discrediting Cromwell: Olivier Lutaud, *Des Révolutions
 d'Angleterre à la Révolution Française: le tyrannicide et 'Killing No Murder' (Cromwell,
 Athalie, Bonaparte)* (The Hague, 1973), p. 53.

attacks Cromwell for differing from Augustus, Hutchinson's complaint is that he is just like Augustus, an enemy to his country's freedom. She offers a narrative of the regicide very different from Waller's or Watson's:

> This Caesar found in our dissembling Age
> Which made him desperately himselfe engage
> When the Mistaken Senators who broke
> His fetters fear'd no other galling Yoke.
>
> And in the darke night like the radient starrs
> Shin'd forth after the Tempest of our Warrs
> Till this new Mist did from this Earth arise
> Blacking againe the Lustre of our Skyes[.] (lines 149–56)

Parliament is mistaken in its execution of Charles, not necessarily because it was wrong in itself – Hutchinson allows the possibility that the dynasty may have been removed by divine judgement (line 25) – but because not enough care was taken to secure the institutions of power against future tyranny. For Hutchinson, the death of the king means the possibility of future glory, and she tries to make the image of the stars positive, as the emergent light of a new beginning. Waller had declared the Senate unable to wield the sword; Hutchinson condemns them for parting with it. And she has no time for the Augustan celebration of the 'arts of peace':

> Our soft Remorce made Civill Warrs to cease
> And Wee are heal'd now with the Axe of Peace,
> Which doth our quiet Spirits disingage
> Turnes our affections and reviues our Rage[.] (lines 109–12)

'Axe of Peace' is a brilliantly compressed rendition of a whole tradition of Roman republican thought which sees the imperial peace as a specious façade for the threat of violence. No more than for the Marvell of the 'Horatian Ode' are the arts of peace necessarily glorious: on the contrary, in seeking a premature peace both at home and, in the treaty with the Netherlands, abroad, the people has brought tyranny on itself. As for the future under this new Augustan dynasty, the prospects are as bad as they were for Roman republicans:

> As by severe Augustus Rome at last
> Into Tiberius grinding Iawes was cast;
> So England now opprest with the like curse
> Groanes vnder him, feares his Successors worse. (lines 169–72)

Provocatively, and with overtly seditious intentions, Hutchinson calls on 'True English hearts' to 'Storme his Townes, his Armies overcome' (lines 175, 177).

But the poem's final animus is reserved not for Cromwell but for Waller.

While Waller ended two of his poems by suggesting that the Protector should wear a crown, Hutchinson contemptuously offers a crown to him:

> Chang'd Acts and Powers chang'd Raptures will Infuse
> Till Men at length detest soe base a Muse
> As vnto all Heads Bayes and Olives brings
> Those who vphold and those who pull down Kings.
>
> No generous hearts will enuie his Renowne
> That Rides triumphant in the paper Crowne.
> A Modest Scorne perhapps may bend those Eyes
> Which you and him doe equally despise. (lines 181–8)

The poem vigorously asserts agency, 'Chang'd Acts and Powers', and proclaims the strength of its own speech-act. But Hutchinson is also aware that

> while Tyrants Liue
> Their fowle Deeds still a flattering Glosse receive. (lines 147–8)

Lucan was a reminder that tyranny might nearly succeed in obliterating the memory of liberty. If Watson had feared that Waller might win over royalists with his insinuating lines, the violence of Hutchinson's attack betrays a similar fear from the opposite direction. Her poem acknowledges that poetic agency will not in itself bring about change: only 'Chang'd Acts' will make it possible for language to regain its freedom.

Action, however, was difficult without good communication. It was a time, wrote Hutchinson, when 'it was not safe to speake to any man'[49]; the most forceful statements of opposition had to be clandestine, which means that some of them have remained obscure, even the responses of so prominent a figure as Henry Marten. Marten had been the object of much abuse from Cromwell when he dissolved Parliament and counter-attacked by refusing or parodying the terms of Protectoral discourse. It is not surprising to find Marten in the vanguard of republican anti-Augustanism. As has been seen, he had been keen to shape the republic's literary culture. He met Cromwell's dissolution of Parliament with unrelenting hostility. Cromwell seems to have tried to win him round by offering him a seat in the Nominated Parliament, but Marten refused in a letter which directly challenged the legitimacy of the dissolution. As will be seen below, some republicans accommodated themselves to the Protectorate by the Machiavellian belief that a single great legislator could restore liberty at a stroke. Marten disagreed:

> as for the . . . framing a new modell sutable to the intenc[i]on and genius of a Com[m]onwealth though it bee an Excellent designe, yett it cannott bee the worke of one age . . . if ever there were a frame of lawes cast in a mould, first they

49 Hutchinson, p. 211.

have been contrived by the wisest of men as Solon, Lycurgis [*sic*] and some few others (whome these legislators are not like to resemble) and then they suddenly altered with the humour of the people and in few yeares became impracticable and more like Romanza's then prudent constituc[i]ons[.][50]

Marten complained that Cromwell had concluded the people were incapable of liberty before he had given them a chance.

Marten may have written his polemically anti-Augustan 'Antepodum Horatianum' to mark the dissolution, and a few months later he composed a sharp parody of the Latin poems that were greeting the Protectorate.[51] His own poem (figure 14) reads at first sight like a straightforward celebration of Cromwell's installation in office, praising Cromwell for excelling all past heroes. He goes on, however, to praise Cromwell for gaining office by his military virtues rather than by buying the votes of the people, and contemptuously dismissing the political worth of the 'Mobilis . . . plebis'. This sentiment runs directly counter to his insistence on popular participation in his letter to Cromwell, but it does parallel the anti-democratic tone of some of the Protector's propagandists. Cromwell is said to 'compescere', restrain, the citizens: the word could be used relatively benignly to refer to pruning plants, but the basic association was of chains. Marten uses the terms 'exspatiata' and 'distenda' to characterize Cromwell's expansion of British rule. These are negative terms, the latter connoting the swelling of disease, and thus link with criticisms of Cromwellian foreign policy. That sense of improper swelling – the Protector's cheeks are described as puffed up – is enacted in the poem's language of praise. Marten describes Cromwell as a 'Dynasta', a borrowing from Greek which had been used by Cicero as a contemptuous term for the quasi-monarchical Triumvirate.[52] Foreigners are said to whisper his praises, a deflation of the expected hyperbole. What they whisper is 'Vnde Sua? Quantus homo! quò demùm? vbi sistere fas est?' ('Where do his achievements [?] come from? What a great man he is! Where will he go in the end? Where is it right for him to stop?'). There may be an echo here of a famous moment in the first book of the *Pharsalia* (i.190–92) where a vision of Rome asks Caesar as he approaches the Rubicon:

> Quo tenditis ultra?
> Quo fertis mea signa, viri? si iure venitis,
> Si cives, huc usque licet.
> oh whither carry yee,
> My Ensignes Souldiers: If you come as friends,
> As Roman Citizens, your march here ends. (May, sig. A4r)

50 ML93/39–40, fol. 4r, cited by Williams, 'Marten', p. 558.
51 BL Additional MS 71,532, fol. 16r; the Latin text, which is a chaos of second thoughts, is reproduced as figure 14, with a very tentative translation in the Appendix.
52 Cicero, *Ad Atticum*, 2.9.1.

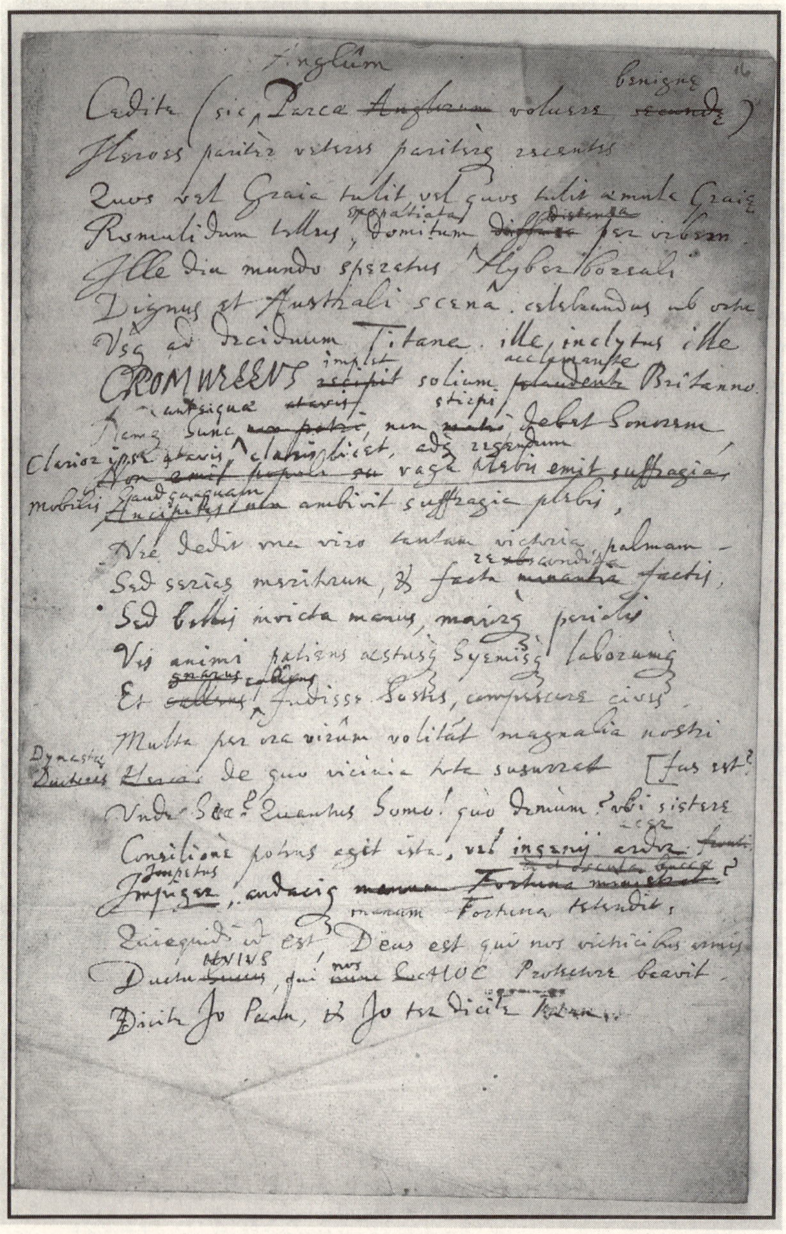

14 Henry Marten, manuscript poem to Oliver Cromwell.

If Caesar goes any further he will abandon the obligations of republican citizenship and prove himself to be pursuing only a private interest. (In the same spirit, Edmund Ludlow later wrote that in dissolving Parliament Cromwell had 'passed the Rubicon'.[53]) In his 'Antepode' Marten had vindicated a similar conception of citizenship; the mock-panegyric shows how Cromwell is coming to be praised for repressing citizens. Marten does indeed seem to have associated the ambitious Cromwell closely with Lucan's Caesar:

> when ye hill was climbed & ye valley beyond it shewed it self, ye lovelynes of ye prospect might putt things into his head that he never dreamed [of?] ambition & covetousnes being allwayes ready in ye best of vs to embrace their food, & yet dresse themselves vp in ye likenes of better creatures.[54]

Marten seems to have in mind Lucan's portrayal of Caesar as he first catches sight of Rome (*Pharsalia*, iii.84ff).

Marten's and Hutchinson's poems show how important language was for the republican opposition. Characteristically, however, they tended to view language in a broader social and political context than the regime's supporters. There was a profound imbalance in society if its leader was being celebrated in melodious compliments while open debate of public issues was being stifled. The republicans championed open communication and public accountability against the confinement of political discourse to a tiny courtly elite. They shared Milton's commitment to a political public sphere which might not be fully democratic but was broader than anything traditionally tolerated under monarchy. It is perhaps difficult today to reconstruct what an affront the title of 'Protector' would have been to their central principles, which implied that the people were incapable of looking after themselves without a supremely enlightened superior.

At the time of *Areopagitica*, Milton's classical republicanism may have seemed distant from popular political movements; but by the 1650s, many links were being forged. The most remarkable example is the career of John Streater. Streater had worked as a printer and fought in the army. He had served in Ireland, where Ireton and his successor Ludlow had provided a focus for suspicion of Cromwell's political ambitions.[55] Streater returned to England in 1653 and began to campaign against Cromwell's authoritarian tendencies. Already before the dissolution of the Long Parliament he was warning against the dangers of a monarchical coup. Streater explicitly linked republican politics with the maintenance of a vigorous public sphere, insisting that the people should take an interest in liberty rather than leaving public

---

53 Ludlow, *Memoirs*, I, 354.   54 BL Additional MS 71,532, fol. 18r.
55 Sarah Barber, 'Irish Undercurrents to the Politics of April 1653', *Historical Research* 65 (1992), 315–35; Ludlow, *Memoirs*, I, 318–19.

affairs to statesmen. Rome was greatest 'when every Member of that Common-wealth perfectly understood the mysteries of State . . . They never received such a stroak at their Libertie, as when *Caesar* was made perpetual Dictator'. For Streater, there was always a close link between language and politics, inflated titles being a mark of the loss of freedom: 'Flatter none of thy fellow-members of the Commonwealth with Titles, as, *High and Mighty*, or *Excellent*; The Title of *Honor*, or *Honorable*, is the highest mark of desert that a Member of a Commonwealth is fit to attain unto or bear'.[56] In one pamphlet possibly written by him, Cromwell is contemptuously described as 'his Talnesse' and the author feels it necessary to add a postscript apologizing for the occurrence of 'his Highness' in his tract, justifying it as the kind of thing time-servers would say.[57]

Streater was quick to proclaim that the dissolution of Parliament had led to a military oligarchy that was 'next doore to monarchy'.[58] He carried his opposition into the public sphere by launching a series of newsbooks which invoked the spirits of Tacitus and Livy and attacked Cromwell as a Nero.[59] Streater had high expectations of his readers: his longest-running newsbook bore the title *Observations Historical, Political, and Philosophical upon Aristotles first Book of Political Government*. Another journal moved more boldly towards personal allusions by offering a serialized commentary on Suetonius's life of Julius Caesar which bitterly denounced him as a usurping tyrant. With extreme provocativeness at a time when Cromwell was regularly being compared to Caesar, he proclaimed that 'to be like *Caesar* is in effect to say they deserve to be killed by a *Brutus* as he was'.[60] He certainly worried the authorities enough to provoke both repeated arrests and a series of counter-newsbooks.[61]

Streater's newsbooks formed part of a growing republican campaign in the run-up to the first Parliament of the Protectorate, which assembled in September 1654. Parliament proved no mere rubber-stamp and a republican faction immediately began to challenge Cromwell's powers as Protector. On

---

56 John Streater, *A Glympse of that Jewel, Judicial, Just, Preserving Libertie* (1653; E690.11), sig. A2r, pp. 1–2, sig. A4r.

57 I. S., *The Picture of a New Courtier* (1655; E875.6), pp. 3, 15. For the attribution to Streater, and an excellent study of his career, see Nigel Smith, 'Popular Republicanism in the 1650s: John Streater's "Heroick Mechanicks"', *MR*, pp. 137–55 (139 n.4).

58 [John Streater], 'Ten Queries' (Thomason MS, E693.5), fol. 1v.

59 *A Further Continuance of the Grand Politick Informer*, 31 October 1653, E221.4, pp. 42–43. I owe this reference to Joad Raymond: this newsbook, apparently the fifth of the series, has been missed by previous commentators on Streater.

60 *A Politick Commentary on the Life of Caius July Caesar* no. 1, [May 23 1654], E 735.17, p. 8.

61 *The Politique Informer* no. 1, 23–30 January 1654, E223.28, p. 2; [Marchamont Nedham], *The Observator* nos. 1 and 2, 24–31 October and 31 October–7 November 1654, E814.4 and E816.4.

the day Streater gained his freedom by an undertaking to refrain from further criticism, the torch of printed opposition was taken up by a petition by three military men which was widely distributed.[62] Opposition in the army was spreading, and in December Robert Overton (*c.*1609–72?), the governor of Hull who was now a military commander in Scotland, was arrested on the charge of fomenting a conspiracy.

Overton's republicanism had a slightly different, less secular basis from Streater's, and far from condemning the dissolution of the Long Parliament, he had at first welcomed it.[63] He was on close terms with John Canne, a leading member of the Fifth Monarchists, who had become convinced after the dissolution of the Nominated Parliament that Cromwell was impeding the millennium by usurping kingly power. Their campaign against him involved hymns and versified prophecies, most notably those of Anna Trapnel, who repeatedly reminded Cromwell of the example of Gideon, the Old Testament judge who had resisted calls to become king.[64]

Overton's career, however, is a reminder that during the 1650s secular and biblical republicanism could not be easily separated. His garrison had long been accustomed to reading English history through Roman republican eyes.[65] Overton also had connections with figures like the ex-Leveller John Wildman, who had been rallying such figures as Bradshaw and Marten, and the opposition to Cromwell even brought loose alliances with former royalists. One of the charges against Overton was that he had composed a satire against Cromwell. Overton strongly denied that he had written this poem, and claimed that the Protector only laughed at such libels,[66] but the fact that he had circulated it indicates the complex overlappings of political discourses in the opposition politics of the 1650s:

> A Protector, Whats that? Tis a Stately thing
> That confesseth itselfe but the Ape of a King
> A Tragicall Caesar acted by a Clowne
> Or a Brass farthing stamp'd wth a kinde of a Crowne . . .
> The Ecchoe of Monarchy till it come
> The Butt End of a barell in the shape of a Drum[m]
> A Counterfeit peece that wodenly showes
> A Golden Effigies with a Copper noase
> The fantastick shadowe of a Soveraigne head

62 Barbara Taft, '*The Humble Petition of Several Colonels of the Army*: Causes, Character, and Results of Military Opposition to Cromwell's Protectorate', *Huntington Library Quarterly* 42 (1978–9), 15–41.
63 [Robert Overton], *More Hearts and Hands Appearing for the Work* (1653; E699.7).
64 Anna Trapnel, *The Cry of a Stone* (1654; E730.3), p. 29.
65 *The Declaration of the Officers of the Garrison of Hull* (1649; E545.17), pp. 11–12, cites Tacitus on the tendency of tyrants to efface the people's memory.
66 *Two Letters from Major General Overton* (1655; 0643A), p. 5.

The Armes Royall reversed and disloyall in stead
In fine hee is one wee may Protector call
From whom the King of Kings protect vs all.[67]

It is unlikely that Overton himself wrote the poem: its animus against Cromwell is in some ways closer to Watson's than to Hutchinson's. Some familiar themes of royalist satire are recycled. Cromwell is condemned for being unable to live up to an ideal of legitimate kingship, not for being Caesar but for impersonating him, and the suggestion is that monarchy will eventually return and the royal arms be restored to their rightful position. In a different version circulating amongst royalists, this theme was more explicit: Cromwell was 'Charles his Effigies' and the shadow not merely of a 'Soveraigne' but a 'Royall' head.[68] In the conditions of the Protectorate, however, different forms of opposition to Cromwell shared common ground. The satire's deliberately rough metre is appropriate to the attack on Cromwell's vain attempts to present a glittering surface of legitimacy. Although Overton was found guilty of no charge he was kept imprisoned for the rest of the Protectorate, becoming celebrated as a '*Cato*' who refused to be 'any *Caesars* slave'.[69] He compared his own lot to that of Cremutius Cordus, the truth-telling historian who was suppressed by Tiberius.[70]

The coalition of opposition forces was further strengthened when later in 1655, in an attempt to crush royalist conspiracy and engineer moral reform, the country was placed under the local rule of Major-Generals, funded by a draconian tax on royalists. The dubious legality of these measures had the effect of uniting royalist and republican opposition to the regime. It was further discredited by the palpable failure of the Western Design on which Cromwell had staked so much. The failure had constitutional implications, since the Design had in September 1655 become a full-scale war with Spain which according to the Instrument of Government should have received Parliament's approval.

Eventually, in the summer of 1656, the costs of the war with Spain led Cromwell to summon another Parliament. The rising political excitement saw a powerful revival of the republican press which could not be dampened by panegyrists like Waller and 'H. H.'. The harbinger, a letter by one 'R. G.' in which Streater may have had a hand, may have been written earlier, but it can also be seen as a sharp retort to semi-royalist works like Waller's *Panegyrick*.[71]

67 Bodleian MS Rawlinson A.21, p. 576; *TSP*, III, 75–6; see also Thomason E753.2.
68 Bodleian MS Clarendon 92, fol. 21ᶜr.
69 J. R[ye?]., *The Sad Suffering Case of Major-General Rob. Overton* (1659; E972.4), p. 2.
70 Overton to Cromwell, ?January 1655, *TSP*, III, 67.
71 R. G., *A Copy of a Letter from an Officer of the Army in Ireland* ([1656]; E881.3). This tract, sometimes ascribed to Richard Goodgroom, is dated 24 June 1654. Thomason believed this date to be false, and he is supported by John H. F. Hughes, 'The

The best monarchies, the author insisted, are 'but perpetuall contests between the interest of Mankind, and that of one person' (p. 4); he could not share Waller's belief in the possibility or desirability of an equitable balance between the two. Far from welcoming the ease and peace of the Protectorate, he affirms that 'it is a vile and an unnatural Passion in us which makes us prefer estate, much more a little quiet or ease, before that liberty which is so essential to us' (p. 18). And in a self-conscious paradox he proclaims that nothing could be worse for the nation than for Cromwell to govern well, for it would palliate the illegitimacy of his power and

> hide it from the just indignation of this age, and prove like the guilding of poysonous pills, or Painting of Sepulchers, and be a bribing us out of our Rights and Liberties with a seeming justice, nothing but this can lull asleep so many Patriots, who have been often awakened with Drums and Trumpets, to adventure their lives against a Tyrant; neither indeed could any other thing then the just and happy Reign of *Augustus Caesar*, have given the last defeat to the Roman liberty, or made way for those Monsters who succeeded. (p. 19)

The language here is close to the conclusion of Hutchinson's retort to Waller: regal power is seen as a kind of deception which is closely linked with a facile elegance of language. Like May in his *Discourse* of 1642, 'R. G.' makes a hard-headed distinction between persons and institutions. Conventional pane-gyric of a great ruler's virtues is fatally flawed in blurring the boundaries between public and private. The postscript seems to have marked the first appearance in print of the phrase '*the good old cause*' (p. 22), in the sense of the 'good old principle of common justice, equity and liberty' as embodied in the 'peoples representative'. Republicanism was retrospectively established as the goal which had been fought for over many years. As the Protectorate's defenders repeatedly pointed out, that was a major simplification; but the rallying-cry clearly carried conviction for many.

The elections for the Parliament became an opportunity for open political agitation. A visit to Hull by Overton's wife Ann aroused suspicion that she might be organizing opposition.[72] Cromwell tried to ensure that this Parliament went smoothly by the detention of some republicans and by excluding more than a hundred politically suspect candidates. He was helped by the good news of the victory by Blake and Montague over the Spanish trea-sure-fleet, and Waller may have composed the first draft of his poem of

Commonwealthmen Divided: Edmund Ludlowe, Sir Henry Vane and the Good Old Cause 1653–1659', *The Seventeenth Century* 5 (1990), 55–70 (67), who notes two contem-porary attributions to Ludlow. However, Blair Worden, 'Harrington's "Oceana": Origins and Aftermath, 1651–1660', *RLCS*, pp. 111–38 (116), argues that the date is genuine; certainly the author's anxiety about being sent to Scotland to impose a settle-ment (p. 20) is more relevant to 1654. The text's speech-act, however, is one of mid-1656.
72 PRO SP18/129/91.

celebration at this time. Certainly this Parliament saw a sustained campaign to offer Cromwell the crown, and though after a cliff-hanging period of hesitation he demurred, he did accept other proposals in the 'Humble Petition and Advice' which made his office more monarchical: the 'other house' and hereditary succession.

This drift towards kingship provoked the most brilliant republican polemic of the 1650s, Edward Sexby's *Killing Noe Murder*.[73] Sexby had been involved in a series of plots against Cromwell, and had enlisted the aid of the Spanish and of exiled royalists in an assassination plot. It is noteworthy that he makes a concession to royalist sentiment by suggesting that it would have been better to have endured Charles than to have become subject to a mean tyrant (p. 398). The rest of the pamphlet, however, is uncompromisingly republican, drawing on biblical and classical models for tyrannicide. Sexby draws a sharp distinction between a true *polis* and tyrannical rule under which the state becomes no more than a family or household. Sexby repeatedly alluded to the classical cult of tyrannicide, and the pamphlet is in part an elegy for his colleague Miles Sindercombe, who had been captured while plotting to kill Cromwell. In a familiar tradition going back to the cult of Felton, whom Sexby much admired, the 'official' memory maintained by tyrants is contrasted with the 'Statues rear'd to *Sindercombe*' in 'every vertuous Mind' (p. 399). Sexby also sardonically proposes that Cromwell erect for Sindercombe a monument of pillows and featherbeds, the instruments which were allegedly used to stifle him (p. 400). Links with earlier republican propaganda are seen in Sexby's agreeing with 'R. G.' that even if Cromwell ruled justly, as with Augustus the ultimate condition of the nation would be worse (p. 396). Behind the text's bravado, however, there is political gloom: such desperate remedies were essential because constitutional opposition had been ineffective.

It is hard to tell how far Sexby's pessimism was justified. In the last period of Cromwell's rule, he seemed in many ways in an unprecedentedly strong position, and opposition was effectively contained. On the other hand, there remained a crisis of legitimacy. If Cromwell became king he would alienate much support and strengthen republican opposition, but as long as he refused the crown his status remained too equivocal to become an effective focus for political loyalty. The difficulties faced by his apologists can be seen in a reply to Sexby by Michael Hawke. Hawke reported that the people had

---

73 William Allen [Edward Sexby], *Killing Noe Murder* ([1657]; E501.4); the text is cited from Lutaud, *Des Révolutions d'Angleterre à la Révolution Française*, pp. 371–405. The authorship of this work is uncertain, and may have been collaborative; for discussion see C. H. Firth, '*Killing No Murder*', *English Historical Review* 17 (1902), 308–11, and James Holstun, 'Ehud's Dagger: Patronage, Tyrannicide, and *Killing No Murder*', *Cultural Critique* 21 (Fall 1992), 99–142 (139 n. 8).

greedily swallowed the pamphlet, and that he felt constrained to reply to show the world that 'a general silence had not begotten a general consent'.[74] Sexby, he complained, 'secretly steals into the easie People, whose ears are more open to Rhetorique, then Logick' (p. 2). Hawke responded by an uncompromising defence of the Augustan tradition. He followed through the parallel between Cromwell and Caesar in great detail: just as Caesar had not been content to defeat Pompey at Pharsalia but had made sure of Pompey's death, so had Cromwell done with Charles. Like Caesar in his raid on the Roman treasury, Cromwell had had to raise money by unconstitutional means on the grounds of 'Necessity' (pp. 17–18). Hawke felt compelled to reply to Machiavelli's much-cited comment that to learn what people really thought of Caesar one could not rely on historians with a vested interest in praising him. His not very impressive response, however, is to refer to the praise of Caesar in Florus, the minor anti-republican historian whose works had been popularized at the expense of Tacitus's under Charles's personal rule (pp. 13–14). The treatise's distinctly uninspiring conclusion was that even if Cromwell's power had no further legitimacy than conquest, it would be in the people's interest to submit. Equally uninspiring was his response to the provocative irony of Sexby's title with the flat-footed *Killing is Murder*. Silas Titus, a royalist who claimed authorship of *Killing Noe Murder*, called the reply 'such a peece that 'tis wonder Cromwell, as impudent as he is, would give allowance to come forth, for it is to make him as absolute as the Great Turke'.[75]

---

74 Michael Hawke, *Killing is Murder* (1659; E925.12), p. 1. Hawke had earlier published a Hobbesian-Augustan defence of the Protectorate, *The Right of Dominion, and Property of Liberty* (1656; E1636.1). He complained that his writings had brought him no reward but hatred and vengeance (letter of 28 May 1656, *CSPD 1655–6*, pp. 338–9).

75 Titus to Hyde, 7/17 December 1657, *Calendar of Clarendon State Papers, Vol. III, 1655–1657*, ed. W. Dunn Macray (Oxford, 1876), 397. I owe this reference to James Holstun.

8

Republicanizing Cromwell

Nedham and Milton

Milton and Marvell are well known for their writings in praise of Cromwell. The political contexts of that praise, however, have often been presented in an unduly bland way. These lofty idealists, we are given to understand, would not have troubled themselves with the mundane details of constitutional propriety. Critical appreciations of their texts thus blend imperceptibly into apologias for the Protectorate, and the poets' enthusiasm for the great law-breaker can come to seem uncomfortably akin to more modern paeans of strong military rulers. The previous chapter tried to show just how much public opposition could be encountered by those who championed the regime. Waller became a by-word for shameful flattery. Milton and Marvell cannot have been unaware of these pressures. They were on friendly terms with some leading republicans; and figures like Streater were constantly drawing attention to the links between republican liberty and a revival of rhetoric that had been so crucial to Milton. It is well to be aware of the political unease that could be aroused by panegyrics of Cromwell. And yet it is possible to find a rationale for pro-Protectoral writings in this period that involves more than a compliant drift back to monarchism. The rationale involves a certain aspect of republican ideology, and a characteristically humanist commitment to active involvement, rather than apolitical idealism. It thus resulted not in bland panegyrics but in writing that stands out from Waller's not only in political complexity but in poetic subtlety. The space between Waller's panegyrics and the republican opposition was indeed a difficult one to occupy, and yet even the most celebrated republican treatise of the century, Harrington's *Oceana*, has points in common with this 'republicanizing' Cromwellianism.

There were personal and political reasons for holding back from the more militant republicans' criticisms of Cromwell. On a personal level, his complex, sometimes tortured personality did not fit into the conventional mould of Roman tyrant which many republicans tried to impose on him. One reply to Waller's *Panegyrick* went so far as to make a sharp distinction between poet and Protector: Waller could indeed emulate Cromwell's recent 'cheating elloquence' and frivolous pillow-fights but not his early struggles for liberty. Interestingly, this poet sets up as an antitype to Waller's Virgilianizing rhetoric the example of Lucan:

> Lucan who writt the Civill warrs of Rome
> Did not like you receive his fatall doome
> Nor pardon with a servile breath implore
> But with high courage his misfortune bore
> And in a noble death contemning pride
> Like Pompey or unvanquisht Caesar died[.][1]

There is more sorrow than anger in this attack on Cromwell; Waller is much more culpable because he is bringing Cromwell down to his own trivial level. Even Henry Marten was ready to acknowledge that Cromwell was not quite the single-minded power-grabber of hostile stereotype, to see in him some of that 'height of minde' which he had traced back to Ovid's Golden Age.[2]

Might not those qualities qualify him, despite Marten's scepticism, for the Machiavellian role as the single person in a unique position to effect a reduction of liberty? The Long Parliament, though energetic in foreign policy, had been dilatory over legal and social reforms. Marten was one of many of its leaders who had used his power to divert favour to close associates. In the digression to the *History of Britain* Milton had shown his awareness of the republican impasse: where could the agency be found from within a far from civil nation to make republican civility possible? He had supported the military force of Pride's Purge as the only possible solution. In the *First Defence* he had indicated that the present constitutional settlement was inadequate; a further stage of military intervention might perhaps provide the momentum for fuller structural reforms. The republicans who attacked Cromwellians' blatant appeals to necessity could be accused of having short memories. After all, some of Parliament's most important measures from the early 1640s onward had been justified by necessity and political emergency. Marten had entered the Commons side by side with Cromwell after Pride's Purge. The Instrument of Government, though certainly diluted in comparison with earlier Agreements of the People, was not in any simple sense a return to the old order. The very fact that it was England's first – and so far only – detailed written constitution marked a radical break with tradition. Its attempt to separate legislative and executive branches of government looked forward to the American republican constitution. Whatever its ambiguities, it constituted an imaginative constitutional experiment. And in 1653–4, just as in

---

1 BL Harleian MS 7,316, fols. 1r–v. This is an early eighteenth-century MS and I have been unable to trace an earlier version, but the poem seems to date from the 1650s.
2 BL Additional MS 71,532, fol.18r.

1649–50, we find Milton, Hall and Nedham enthusiastically welcoming the change of government precisely because it offered an opportunity for experiment. Once again, Marvell transferred that experimentation to an anti-Augustan poetics.

Nedham's career throughout the Protectorate was a characteristically daring balancing-act, oscillating between quasi-monarchist and quasi-republican languages according to his analysis of the overall balance of power. If Waller aimed at a steady but somewhat pedestrian balance, Nedham always balanced on a tightrope. In the autumn of 1653 he had hinted that a stronger hand at the helm might be needed to counteract the religious radicals who were influential in the Nominated Parliament, and who seemed to him intent on establishing a theocracy.[3] Nedham willingly provided the fullest formal defence of the Protectorate, *A True State of the Case of the Common-wealth.* Here he equivocated on the status of kingship. Initially he seems to be leaving open the way for Cromwell to make himself king, by roundly retorting to the republicans that 'we never fought against the King, as King; nor for the Parliament or Representative consider'd purely as such'. Later in the pamphlet, however, he argues that 'the Kings of this Nation . . . maintained an Interest of their own, as they were Kings, distinct and superior to that of the People', and that the Instrument of Government will provide previously unknown safeguards of liberty. Nedham also recycled material on the separation of powers from *Mercurius Politicus* at its most republican phase.[4]

Nedham performed a similar balancing-act, on a smaller scale, in a poem which appeared at the same time, marking the Protector's inaugural entry to London in February 1654.[5] This occasion was modelled in part on the traditional royal entry, but Cromwell tried to avoid too overtly regal a posture. One panegyrist, however, hailed him in terms indistinguishable from a monarch, using the traditional analogy with the sun.[6] Nedham's poem, by contrast, began on a boldly and provocatively anti-Augustan note: 'Barbara Caesareae sileant Magnalia *Romae*' ('Let the barbarous achievements of Caesarean Rome be silent'). Since Augustan writing claimed to have gained the highest degree of polish under the Caesars, to equate their reign with barbarism was

---

3 Joad Raymond, 'Framing Liberty: Marvell's *First Anniversary* and the Instrument of Government', forthcoming.

4 [Marchamont Nedham], *A True State of the Case of the Common-wealth* (1654; E728.5), pp. 5, 29. There remains some uncertainty about the authorship of this pamphlet, which may have been a composite work.

5 '*Latin* Epigram . . . made upon his Highnesse's entertainment in the City', *Mercurius Politicus* no. 192, 9–16 February 1654, E729.14, p. 3270. The poem is unsigned but appears as by 'M. N.' in Payne Fisher's *Inauguratio Oliveriana* (1654; F1027), pp. 89–90.

6 Edmund Litsfield, *Triambeisis Celsissimi Domini Oliverii Cromwelli* (1655; E1069.1), p. 1.

an extreme reversal worthy of Henry Marten. Nedham went on to recuperate something of the Augustan myth, but with a distinctive twist:

> *Caesar* adest melior. Sidus ut orbe novum.
> *Caesare* major adest, quia noluit esse: Coronam
> Arripiant alii: Se potuisse sat est.

('A better Caesar is approaching, like a new star to light up the world. He is a greater Caesar because he did not want to be one; let others seize the crown, it was enough for him to have been able to do so.') Against those who saw the Protectorate as a regression into kingliness, Nedham found in it precisely the heroic renunciation of conventional splendour that Cromwell's critics were urging on him. And his assault on Roman barbarism has a Puritan as well as republican edge. This Caesar will destroy the profane gods of Rome:

> tua jam capitolia posse
> Scandere, & hinc *Britico* subdere colla jugo . . .

('able to climb your Capitols, Rome, and subdue your necks under a British yoke'). There are multiple ironies here. Lucan had condemned Caesar for his impious descent on Rome; but since Rome is now the centre of idolatry and superstition, this Caesar's destructiveness can be applauded – as in d'Aubigné's prologue to *Les Tragiques*. Nedham seems to be echoing the famous ode (III, 30) in which Horace declares that his verse will live

> dum Capitolium
> scandet cum tacita virgine pontifex

– as long as the High Priest and Vestal Virgin climb the Capitol. He is inverting Horace quite as boldly as Marten had done.[7]

Nedham goes on to introduce the figure of Britannia as an emblem of future naval victories. He celebrates Cromwell as a prince but also praises him for rejecting a crown: he prefers the hearts of men to scaffolding rising in the middle of the street. Here Nedham is echoing an epigram of Martial (*De Spectaculis*, 2.1–4) which contrasted the benevolent architecture of Domitian with a colossal statue of the hated Nero: Cromwell is superior to both emperors.[8] In another bold paradox, Nedham claims:

> Nunc primùm Cives estis, qui Regibus olim
> Servi, ut Concives discite fraena pati[.]

---

7 Nedham may also have been thinking of Wingfield's poem for the investiture (above, p. 308), which had represented Cromwell as climbing the sacred heights over the necks of tyrants ('Faelix per Colla Tyrannûm/Ascendas clavi culmina summa Sacri'). 'Clavus' is taken by Creswell, p. 5, as referring to the helm of the ship of state, but it could also refer to a sacred nail driven into the wall of the Temple of Jupiter.

8 I owe this point to Ben Tipping.

The people are only now citizens, and as fellow-citizens they must learn to bear the reins of obedience. Where Marten had seen the dissolution of the Long Parliament as the end of citizenship, Nedham sees the Protectorate as making citizenship a reality, but only on the provision that the people are disciplined enough to make use of the opportunity. The climax of the poem returns to the idea of Cromwell as a new force in the cosmos. God-like, he will bring order out of chaos. He will bring round the Platonic year and restore the first, golden age: 'cum aeternis solibus *Annus* eat', 'Let this year go out with eternal suns!'.[9] The end of the poem uses the traditional solar imagery only to contrast Cromwell with all previous rulers.

Nedham's poem contains the germ of a new, Cromwellian poetics which was to be emulated by Milton and Marvell. His emphasis on an energetic tension between republican and monarchical elements marks out a distinctive group of texts. John Hall addressed a poem to Fisher which shared the imagery of Cromwell as creative, God-like sun, and contrasted his self-mastery with the people's fickleness.[10] In May 1654 there appeared two prose panegyrics of Cromwell which were attributed to a Portuguese envoy. A later scholar ascribed these texts to Milton, and though there is no evidence for this, there are striking affinities between them and writings by Milton and Marvell which indicate a conscious collaborative effort at a carefully revised form of Augustan praise.[11] The author of the second panegyric in particular is keen to emphasize the democratic nature of the Cromwellian regime, stressing that the people are the foundation of power (p. 72). Though Cromwell is occasionally compared to Caesar (p. 93), an attempt is also made to link him with such republican paragons as Brutus and Pompey (pp. 79, 90), while it is the power-hungry Parliamentarians who are likened to Caesar (p. 112). Cromwell is compared to a bold charioteer who drives up to the edge of the arena but just avoids crashing: his audacious virtues come close to vices (p. 105). There is a parallel here with the double-edged praise of Marvell's 'Horatian Ode'. The panegyrist even risks invoking Lucan's 'Victrix causa deis placuit, sed victa Catoni'. Providence, he declares, has clearly endorsed

---

9 Nedham used the same imagery in a letter to Bulstrode Whitelocke on 6 January 1654: 'we have a new world formed (like the old) out of Chaos, by the prudence and industry of that excellent person [Cromwell]: . . . I would chuse much rather to serve him upon any Terms, than be a Favourite to any of those golden Things that are drop't at adventure into the world, with Crowns upon their heads': Ruth Spalding, *Contemporaries of Bulstrode Whitelocke 1605–1675* (Oxford, 1990), p. 217.

10 J. Hall, in Fisher, *Inauguratio Oliveriana*, sigs. a1v–2r; Hall also contributed a Greek poem.

11 *Panegyrici Cromwello Scripti* ([Leiden], 1654; E231.1); Francis Peck, *Memoirs of the Life and Actions of Oliver Cromwell* (1740). William Raymond Orwen, 'A Study of Marvell's "Horatian Ode"' (Syracuse University Ph.D. dissertation, 1956), pp. 189ff, discusses the panegyrics in relation to Marvell.

Cromwell's rule; but he leaves open the question of whether it is truly just (pp. 80–81).

In the same month, Milton declared his position on the Protectorate. He had not joined the opposition and had continued in his official post. But he did not follow his colleagues Nedham and Hall in issuing an official defence. Instead, he included his discussion of the Protectorate in a work whose origins went back to the republic. His *Second Defence of the English People* was a riposte to *Regii Sanguinis Clamor*, a defence of Salmasius which had appeared anonymously in the Netherlands in 1652. Much of the *Second Defence* is devoted to personal vituperation, which proved to be misdirected since the hapless Alexander More was not its real author – though his touchiness is understandable, given that his opponent had expressed the wish that not just Milton's book but its author should be burned (*MPW*, IV:2, 1072). Milton's polemical purpose draws him back to the time of the Commonwealth. It was, however, inevitable that his book would attract scrutiny as his first public statement since the establishment of the Protectorate. Would Milton throw his weight behind the emergent cult of Cromwell as Augustus? Or would he signal support for the militantly anti-Augustan opposition?

Milton kept his readers in suspense. The first part of the book plunges into the controversy over the regicide without making any mention of the changed political circumstances, and discussion of Cromwell is withheld until nearly the end. The magnificent peroration develops and extends Milton's adaptation in *Areopagitica* of classical rhetoric to modern conditions. He addresses the international republic of letters, a vast forum that breaks through the boundaries of any one nation or dynasty (IV:1, 554–5). Milton is unflinching in his defence of the regicide, including it amongst 'the most heroic and exemplary achievements since the foundation of the world' (549); it is a restoration, reviving liberty after its degeneration into church-dominated tyranny (550–2, 555).

This restoration is sublime. As in *Areopagitica*, Milton claims to find it hard not to fly to 'loftier and bolder flights than are permissible in this exordium'. His eloquence and style may not match the ancients but his subject-matter soars above them (554). This superiority lies in the fact that the English did not merely kill a tyrant but put him formally on trial (638). He vindicates the magnanimity and universality of humanist rhetoric against the narrow constraints of courtly discourse, which favour King Charles over Queen Truth (628). The royalists' claim that the regicide was a tragic event merely demeans tragedy, whose authors down to Buchanan have attacked tyranny (592). At the end of the treatise he celebrates the foundation of the republic as an achievement truly epic in its grandeur:

... just as the epic poet, if he is scrupulous and disinclined to break the rules, undertakes to extol, not the whole life of the hero whom he proposes to celebrate in his verse, but usually one event of his life (the exploits of Achilles at Troy, let us say, or the return of Ulysses, or the arrival of Aeneas in Italy) and passes over the rest, so let it suffice me too, as my duty or my excuse, to have celebrated at least one heroic achievement of my countrymen. (685)

This sentence has been much quoted, but its wit has been missed. It may be seen as giving the book an Augustan tone, especially when it comes after his boast in an echo of Horace that he has erected a lasting monument. (Nedham had echoed the same passage in his 'Augustalia'.) But in the context of mid-1654, when Virgil was being invoked by Stuart or Cromwellian royalists, to compare the execution of Charles with the subject-matter of the *Aeneid* was an extreme provocation. Royalists were casting Charles II as the wandering Aeneas, and Denham was soon to link the death of Priam with the regicide; Milton inverts these political values. He presents a speech-act which royalists regarded as outrageously transgressive as a pedantically faithful observance of the rules. It is true that earlier in the *Second Defence* he alludes to the vision of Roman history in Book VI of the *Aeneid* (555)[12], and there are other brief Virgilian echoes (639, 653); but he also relishes having been attacked as Virgil's Cyclops. His adversaries invoked Virgil to present violations of monarchical order as physical deformity (559, 582); Milton seizes on this royalist obsession with externals to emphasize his spiritual insight, developing the dialectic of blindness and vision which he had explored in *Areopagitica* and the *First Defence*. He cites Christ's healing of the man who had been blind from birth, which had been offered by Marten as a precedent for his republican 'restoration' (587). He sees the loss of his eyes not as a divine punishment but as the cost of his service to the republic, which he links with the heroism of Achilles at Troy (588). Here again a traditional epic exploit is redefined in terms of republican virtue. And at another point he proclaims the traditional humanist preference for the eloquent Ulysses over the martial Achilles (595). He praises the republic for rivalling the enlightened support given by ancient Athens to distinguished citizens, thus challenging royalist attacks on republican philistinism (591).

In the *Second Defence* Milton was developing the persona of the blind, sublime republican poet which culminated in the proems to *Paradise Lost*. Yet

12 Andrew Barnaby, ' "Another Rome in the West?": Milton and the Imperial Republic, 1654–1670', *Milton Studies* 30 (1993), 67–84 (74–7), noting the use of the name Liber in Milton and at *Aeneid*, vi.805. The lengthy parallels he finds between the episodes, however, seem to me less striking than the differences: Virgil is more concerned with conquest than with liberty; Milton declares that he is bringing liberty back after a long interval, recalling Lucan's lament that it had fled beyond the Rhine and the Tigris (*Pharsalia*, vii.433–4).

there were complications in this decided republicanism. Milton presents a portrait of a good monarch, Queen Christina of Sweden, who is praised for her good judgement in admiring the *First Defence* and seeing that it was not inimical to all monarchs (604). Joining a European chorus of panegyrists, Milton addresses her in rapturous terms as 'Augusta' and 'most august queen' ('augustissimam reginam' in the original) (604, 655).[13] On closer inspection, however, the praise of Christina looks a little double-edged. She is praised in the first instance because she had banished Salmasius from her court: her wisdom consists above all in rejecting monarchist propaganda, even when her own power is at stake. Milton remarks that he is extremely fortunate to have been praised by her because she can substantiate in her person the distinction he was making between kings and tyrants – the implication being that a good monarch is a rare and fortuitous phenomenon (604). Moreover she was a particularly useful model to hold up under the Protectorate because, as had been rumoured since 1651, she was planning to abdicate, which would be more sublime (*sublimius*) than to reign (606): a perfect example of a true 'reduction' of power back to the people, especially since she then planned to maintain a millennial role in her personal rather than regal capacity.[14] Christina was a great admirer of Lucan, possibly through her friendship with Grotius, and one English poet wrote verses which wittily presented the abdication in Lucanian terms as an inner civil war, an auto-tyrannicide.[15] In a similar vein, Milton's praise of monarchy has been sublimated away from the institution of kingship so far that it is indistinguishable from Stoic praise of the good man as king over himself, a sense in which every good man is a king (562). Christina has effectively become a personification of the Queen Truth who is to be preferred to King Charles. Milton's praise of her learning may also be double-edged: humanists often lavished extravagant praise on learned women as exceptions to the general rule, and Milton places a virtuous monarch in the same kind of category.[16] He signals the fact that his

---

13 Further English examples are added below to Iiro Kajanto, *Christina Heroina: Mythological and Historical Exemplification in the Latin Panegyrics on Christina Queen of Sweden* (Helsinki, 1993).

14 Susanna Åkerman, *Queen Christina of Sweden and her Circle: The Transformation of a Seventeenth-Century Philosophical Libertine* (Leiden, New York, Copenhagen and Cologne, 1991), pp. 157ff.

15 Walter Fischli, *Studien zum Fortleben der Pharsalia des M. Annaeus Lucanus* (Luzern, n.d.), p. 57; *A Journal of the Swedish Embassy [sic]*, ed. Charles Morton, 2 vols. (1772), I, 508–10, II, 474–5; the poem is by Dr Daniel Whistler, who accompanied the embassy as a surgeon. Parallels include 'In te magna ruis' (cf. 'In se magna ruunt', *Pharsalia* i.81), 'propriae sed vulnere dextrae/Occumbit' (cf. 'In sua victrici conversum viscera dextra', i.3), 'Serius in Coelum redeas' (cf. 'astra petes serius', i.46).

16 For many parallels – and a striking exception – see Kajanto, *Christina Heroina*, pp. 80ff, 91–5.

encomium is a digression from his main theme (606). And in fact, far from appeasing monarchists, his praise of Christina came under attack by Alexander More for its audacity in claiming a personal affinity with a monarch (IV:ii, 1106–07).

More's hostility to the praise of Christina is understandable, for it certainly does serve mainly to reflect praise back on Milton. The book is a defence at least as much of Milton as of the English people, though Milton pauses at one point to explain that the people as a whole would be discredited if their most celebrated international defender were slandered (IV:1, 611). He gives a lengthy defence of his own interventions in the polemics of the 1640s; and it is only when he comes to his refutation of some of Salmasius's historical arguments that he engages at length with other individuals. In the course of a discussion of the events of 1648, Milton mentions that Salmasius attacks Cromwell but declares that he will postpone consideration of this issue (636). English readers were thus still kept in suspense as to where Milton would come down on the question of the Protectorate. They would have been intrigued when immediately after this reference to Cromwell Milton launched into a panegyric of Bradshaw, celebrated as an outspoken opponent of the dissolution of the Long Parliament. Milton sees his participation in the regicide as particularly praiseworthy: 'you would say he was judging the king, not merely from the tribunal, but throughout his entire life' (638).

After defending various sections of the republic's support, Milton returns briefly to his praise of Christina as part of an argument that monarchs do in fact favour the republic (655–6). But soon afterwards Milton is reiterating his earlier arguments in defence of tyrannicide. If the English are the first people to have put a tyrant to death, it is because they are the first people for whom the course was possible (658). Just as at points in the *First Defence*, Milton abandons justifications for the regicide on the grounds of legal precedent and asserts a universal human right to oppose tyranny (658). This was the kind of argument Sexby was to draw from Milton in *Killing Noe Murder*. It is only after thus restating arguments that were already starting to make some Cromwellians uneasy that Milton comes at last to the refutation of Salmasius's charges against Cromwell.

Milton's first comment is adapted to the new climate of the Protectorate: it is quite false to claim that Cromwell ever attacked monarchy in general, and foreign princes should ignore Salmasius's distortions. After chronicling some of Cromwell's actions in 1648, Milton ostentatiously passes over his involvement in the regicide. And he now launches into a lengthy panegyric of Cromwell. Though fulsome in its praise, this panegyric is conspicuous for what it omits. Like the panegyric of Christina, it is offered in the first instance as a justification of Milton himself, whose character would be tarnished if abuse of Cromwell were credited (666). Unlike Nedham, Milton refrains from comparing him to Caesar, and though Lucan's hero-villain may be briefly evoked by the praise of his remarkable speed, Milton goes on to lay claim to a comparable brevity in chronicling Cromwell's achievements (670): where Caesar had written of his own deeds, Cromwell relies on Milton.

Milton's praise comes closest to stock Protectoral propaganda when he deals with the demise of the Long Parliament and its successor. At this point, Milton declares, Cromwell alone could save the state, and he impugns his republican critics as motivated by envy or by failure to understand that 'there is ... nothing in the state more just, nothing more expedient, than the rule of the man most fit to rule' (671–2). This comment stands out the more glaringly from the surrounding republican context because there is no mention of the Instrument of Government with its at least notional constraints on Cromwell's power. But he does go on to activate the recurrent evocations of an anti-courtly sublime:

> For what is a title, except a certain limited degree of dignity? Your deeds surpass all degrees, not only of admiration, but surely of titles too, and like the tops of pyramids, bury themselves in the sky, towering above the popular favor of titles ... You suffered and allowed yourself, not indeed to be borne aloft, but to come down so many degrees from the heights [*ex sublimi*] and be forced into a definite rank, so to speak, for the public good. The name of king you spurned from your far greater eminence, and rightly so ... By your deeds you have outstripped not only the achievements of our kings, but even the legends of our heroes. (672)

At a time when some Cromwellians were hinting at a return to kingship, Milton firmly rejects such a course as an idolatry inimical to a true republican literary as well as political culture, a return to empty names from bound-breaking achievement. Milton's praise of Christina comes in retrospect to seem something less than a digression. For it has gone as far as Milton is prepared to go in defence of monarchy, only to suggest that the best monarch is one who is ready to abdicate. Cromwell's praise is allowed to outshine Christina's precisely because of his greater distance from monarchy.

By the same token, however, he must permit his people a greater degree of critical judgement of his actions. Milton's praise of Cromwell is conditional on his continual self-scrutiny and commitment to the principles of liberty. His rule will be a republican *ridurre ai principii*: he will 'restore [*reddere*] to us our liberty, unharmed and even enhanced' (674). The parallel with Christina hints that Cromwell should be preparing to lay down power once he has secured liberty. As a first step, he should admit good men to his counsels. Again, Milton is oddly blurred on constitutional issues: if he is referring to the Council of State, which was given great authority by the Instrument, then he is largely urging Cromwell to do what he has done already, for nine of those he names were already on the Council. However, there was scope for six vacancies to be filled. Of those Milton mentioned, Whitelocke, the dedicatee of

Hall's Longinus translation, had come under attack by Cromwell at the dissolution of Parliament, though he had subsequently made his peace. A much more controversial nomination was Robert Overton, who was becoming a thorn in the Protector's side.[17] It is true that Milton made no attempt to enlist such a staunch republican as Sir Henry Vane. And yet when he turns from personalities to programmes, he does outline an agenda that would have been acceptable to many opponents of the Protectorate. He insists on the separation of church and state, running counter to Protectoral championing of a state church, and on the need for freedom of the press, thus addressing the criticisms of republicans like Streater. Like his advice to Cromwell, this passage again provoked More into attacking Milton's laying down of the law to rulers (IV:ii, 1109).

Milton does not, however, end the book on this note of criticism of the Protector; instead, he turns to the people he has been defending, and gives a highly critical account of their past conduct. He comes closer here than in the *First Defence* to making public the deep reservations about the people's readiness for a republic which he had voiced in the 'Digression' and in personal comments. Milton's readiness to accept the Protectorate at all was governed by his unease about the public's civic virtue. As in the 'Digression', at the end of the *Second Defence* he warns the people that success in war is not enough unless they can also pursue the arts of peace. If they favour foreign conquest and unjust taxes over the pursuit of justice, they will ruin themselves; if they pursue vanity and excess, they will themselves become royalists (681). At a moment when he is voicing his deepest reservations about the English people, Milton is simultaneously broadening the concept of royalism so that it becomes virtually identical with vice and republicanism with virtue. But his warning against what might happen amounts to a scathing indictment of the previous Parliaments: private interests had completely overcome the public good, and brought the nation to a point at which it was impossible to restore liberty. Where a nation is totally corrupt, neither a Cromwell nor a whole nation of Brutuses can deliver it. The equation of Cromwell with Lucius Junius Brutus, the destroyer of the Roman monarchy, once more casts Cromwell in opposition to the spirit of monarchy; Milton later invokes another republican hero, Cola di Rienzo, who had restored the Roman republic in the fourteenth century.

Readers scrutinizing the *Second Defence* to find Milton's judgement of the Protectorate had, then, been given a perplexing series of twists and turns. The praise of Cromwell, deferred so long, had been qualified enough to give some heart to republicans, but the denunciation of the people had been calculated to cool their ardour and instil patience. The only figure not subject to such

17 The Yale translation of the *Second Defence*, IV:1, 677 n. 524, glosses 'Sidney' as the republican Algernon Sidney, but Philip Sidney, Viscount Lisle, was on the Council.

reservations is Milton himself, whose confidence in his own rhetorical skill is unalloyed. Having just congratulated himself on having erected a lasting monument in prose, he gives his countrymen a warning. Posterity may complain that they had laid the foundations but that there were not enough people to complete the structure. And yet the antithesis of political incompletion and literary completion is not quite absolute: Milton's sublime rhetoric has always pushed against the limits of traditional forms and titles, and his aim from the beginning has been to create a readership which will not remain satisfied with the literary or political status quo.

Marvell's 'The First Anniversary' and Wither's Protectoral poems

One of the first admirers of the *Second Defence* was Andrew Marvell. In June 1654 he wrote to Milton praising the work in the highest terms:

> I shall now studie it even to the getting of it by Heart: esteeming it according to my poor Judgement (which yet I wish were so right in all Things else) as the most compendious Scale, for so much, to the Height of the Roman eloquence.[18] When I consider how equally it turnes and rises with so many figures, it seems to me a Trajans columne in whose winding ascent we see imboss'd the severall Monuments of your learned victoryes. And Salmatius and Morus make up as great a Triumph as That of Decebalus, whom too for ought I know you shall have forced as Trajan the other, to make themselves away out of a just Desperation.

Marvell catches astutely the complexities of Milton's work. It is a monument, and comparable to a monument raised by a Roman emperor. But the emperor in question, Trajan, had been praised in the *First Defence* for staying within the laws, for recovering and restoring ancient Roman liberties (*MPW*, IV:1, 465). Milton's stance towards Cromwell in the *Second Defence* is analogous to that of Pliny towards Trajan. Milton had several times quoted from Pliny's panegyric to his emperor in the *First Defence*, noting that he had reminded Trajan that bad rulers deserved to be killed and judged it almost a crime not to have killed Nero. Pliny had chronicled tyrannicide with a distinctively Roman relish:

> It was a joy to hurl that haughty visage to the ground, to set on with the swords and swing the axe as if each blow brought him bloody torture: no one so checked his delight as to feel that the sight of his torn and bleeding joints and limbs, his grim and terrible statues cast down and thrown into the flames, was anything but vengeance overdue. (Pliny, *Panegyricus*, 52.4; *MPW*, IV:1, 446, reading 'statues' for 'statutes')

18 *MPL*, II, 306. The syntax here seems garbled; perhaps there has been an omission in the transcription from the original letter, which has not survived.

Marvell savours Milton's tyrannicidal enthusiasm; and he links it with his sublimity. Great as it is, the *Defence* is valuable above all not as a static monument but as leading its readers towards 'the Height of the Roman eloquence' – Marvell perhaps glances at the title Hall gave to his translation of Longinus. Marvell notes the text's 'turnes', its sense of an ongoing process. 'When I consider' is a common enough phrase but we may wonder whether in an address to Milton it is not intended to echo the sonnet 'On his Blindness', which was probably composed around this time, given that blindness, and its sublime compensations, were such a theme of the *Second Defence*. Marvell follows his praise of Milton by enquiring after the fate of Overton: he has signalled that he has picked up Milton's provocative insertion of Overton in the list of prospective councillors.

Marvell's admiration for the *Second Defence* was palpably genuine, for the work left its mark on his own writings, but by now the two men's relationship seems to have been close enough for reciprocal influence. Despite Milton's intercession, Marvell's bid for office in the Commonwealth had not been successful; but he gained important connections with Protectoral circles by being appointed tutor to William Dutton, who was spoken of as a possible match for Cromwell's daughter Frances. Dutton was the son of a royalist and Marvell was clearly considered trustworthy enough by Cromwell to be given the charge of keeping this potentially significant young man on the path of true religion. It is possible that this charge was a belated fruit of his approach to St John back in 1651, for Dutton was housed at Eton with John Oxenbridge, St John's brother-in-law. Hull connections may also have been involved, for Oxenbridge had served as chaplain to Robert Overton, who had been reluctant to lose him from Hull.[19]

Whatever its origins, the position gave Marvell personal contact with Cromwell, and by the following year he seems to have been considered worthy of considerable political confidence. He anticipated Milton in neo-Latin praises of Cromwell and of Queen Christina in a verse letter to his friend Nathaniel Ingelo, who was a chaplain to Bulstrode Whitelocke, the envoy to the Swedish court.[20] Marvell's poem seems, like other English verses, to have been circulated at court.[21] Though Marvell adopts many themes that were to become familiar in Protectoral poetry, he gives the Augustanism of his poem an ideological tinge. He is closer than Milton to the more mystical, millenarian cult surrounding the queen. Christina is praised as 'Augustam' (line 27),

19 *HMC Various Collections*, I, 17.   20 'A Letter to Doctor *Ingelo*', *MPL*, I, 104–7.

21 W. Hilton Kelliher, 'Marvell's "A Letter to Doctor Ingelo"', *Review of English Studies* N.S. 20 (1969), 50–7; Christine Rees, 'Some Seventeenth-Century Versions of the Judgment of Paris', *Notes and Queries* 222 (1977), 197–200 (200) suggests that Milton's allusion to the Judgment of Paris in praising Christina may have been borrowed from Marvell (*MPW*, IV:1, 656; lines 59–60).

but the emphasis is not only on her learning in the arts of peace but also on her pivotal role in a forthcoming Protestant alliance which Cromwell is to champion. There is a strong contrast here with a poem addressed by an English writer to Whitelocke at this time, which ended by praising the ambassador for helping to close the gates of Janus. (Marvell had already inverted that stock figure in his earlier poem to St John).[22] Marvell imitates Virgil most directly at the point where the speaker in the fourth eclogue self-consciously raises his style above the surrounding panegyric, and marks out Christina as one of the godly elect. This passage leads into a comparison of Cromwell with Geoffrey of Boulogne, the hero of Tasso's *Jerusalem Delivered*; pastoral retreat is ultimately to give way to godly warfare.[23] Marvell enacted a similar complex tension between Augustan and Puritan emphases in two epigrams supporting Cromwell's bid for a northern alliance. The first poem puns on the 'umbra' provided by Augustus for his poets:

> Haec est quae toties *Inimicos* Umbra fugavit,
>   At sub qua *Cives* Otia lenta terunt. (*MPL*, I, 108)

Unlike Marten's 'Antepode', this epigram praises the leisure offered by the Protectorate. But the shadow cast by Cromwell is also militant and menacing, like the shades against which Cromwell contends at the end of the 'Horatian Ode'. The second epigram ends by proclaiming that Cromwell's face is not always inimical to princes, but the rest of the poem recalls the 'Horatian Ode' by emphasizing the scars he has gained in the struggle for liberty (*MPL*, I, 108).

Marvell was experimenting earlier than Milton with a poetic language for the Protectorate that would offer a complex synthesis of courtly and apocalyptic elements, and might thus potentially unite more radical friends like Robert Overton with Protectoral monarchists. Only after the appearance of *The Second Defence*, however, did he venture into print. *The First Anniversary of the Government under His Highness the Lord Protector*[24] is the most remarkable of Protectoral poems, an experiment whose very boldness and brilliance worked against its having an immediate political impact (though as will be seen, there are signs that it had some careful readers).[25] Published in mid-January 1655, the poem was subsequently entered in the Stationers' Register at the same time

---

22 Morton (ed.), *A Journal of the Swedish Embassy*, II, 10–11, 476.
23 Margarita Stocker, 'Remodelling Virgil: Marvell's New Astraea', *Studies in Philology* 84 (1987), 159–79.
24 The title of the first edition (1655; E480.1); *MPL*, I, 108–19, gives the Folio title.
25 Annabel M. Patterson, *Marvell and the Civic Crown* (Princeton, 1978), pp. 68–90; Steven N. Zwicker, 'Models of Governance in Marvell's "The First Anniversary"', *Criticism* 16 (1974), 1–12; Derek Hirst, '"That Sober Liberty": Marvell's Cromwell in 1654', in John M. Wallace (ed.), *The Golden and the Brazen World: Papers in Literature and History, 1650–1800* (Berkeley, Los Angeles and London, 1985), pp. 17–53; Nigel Smith, forthcoming edition; Raymond, 'Framing Liberty'.

as Waller's *Panegyrick*, and later seventeenth-century manuscripts attributed it to Waller. That conflation might have irked Marvell, for the poem is in one sense a sustained critique of the direction in which Waller had been leading English poetry and politics. The two poems have so many common concerns that the one is likely to have been a response to the other; Marvell's poem was published first but the *Panegyrick* may have already circulated in manuscript. In the event it was Waller's poem that prevailed with contemporaries and for many years afterwards: whether admired or reviled, it caught the public imagination. As late as 1928, the French critic Pierre Legouis could judge the *Panegyrick* preferable because it answered to critical standards of classical sobriety and clarity.[26] Against such a background, *The First Anniversary* is a wild and tormented poem. But Marvell was trying to create a different kind of readership, one that was wary of Augustan cliché and open to religious enthusiasm and to Milton's calls for a radical sublime.

Marvell himself had of course already experimented with the sublime in the 'Horatian Ode'. *The First Anniversary* is perhaps the only instance in English literature of a poet's cannibalizing one major poem so extensively to produce another poem of such accomplishment on the same theme. This strategy enables Marvell to cut across the huge political gulf that for some republicans had opened up between Commonwealth and Protectorate. Here again, the indefatigable Cromwell (line 45) who can achieve so much 'in one year' contrasts with the timidity of conservatives who hold to a more conventionally beautiful form of state. The earlier poem tells Cromwell to keep his sword erect in moving towards 'the last effect'; here he 'Girds yet his Sword, and ready stands to fight' (line 148), and 'we might hope' some 'wonderfull Effect' (line 135). The regicide had shown that

> 'Tis Madness to resist or blame
> The force of angry Heavens flame:

now,

> What since he did, an higher Force him push'd
> Still from behind, and it before him rush'd[.] (lines 239–40)

The uncompromising declaration that

> restless *Cromwel* could not cease
> In the inglorious Arts of Peace,

is only partly qualified:

> 'Twas Heav'n would not that his Pow'r should cease,
> But walk still middle betwixt War and Peace[.] (lines 243–4)

---

26 Pierre Legouis, *André Marvell: poète, puritain, patriote 1621–1678* (Paris and London, 1928), p. 208.

In both poems, moreover, artistic analogies make possible a continuous parallel between Cromwell and the figure of the innovative poet. Cromwell 'in his Age has always forward prest' (line 146), like the 'forward youth' of the earlier poem. The Cromwell of the 'Ode' had been ready to carry through what the frightened 'Architects' could do no more than 'design'; now Cromwell the 'Architect' transcends earlier 'Authors' of 'good Designes', being formed out of a better 'Mold' (lines 84, 158, 160). In each poem destruction leads to renovation: Cromwell may 'ruine the great Work of Time' but he can cast it into a new mould, and now his 'great Work' is to 'rase and rebuild' the state (lines 56, 352). The occasions of the two poems run parallel. In 1650 Cromwell had returned from a campaign in Ireland that had threatened to enmire him like so many commanders before him. In 1655, in Marvell's presentation, he had confounded his enemies by 'return-ing yet alive' from a coaching accident and a series of political crises, his energy contrasting with the 'wide Return' of monarchs (lines 323, 15). In political terms, Cromwell's new return from jeopardy marks him as a Machiavellian legislator, one who is able to return the state to its best princi-ples by decisive innovation. In poetic terms, his confounding of conven-tional expectations marks him as sublime. Like the 'Horatian Ode', *The First Anniversary* constantly looks forward from the present tense of epideictic verse to the future:

> Till then my Muse shall hollow far behind
> Angelique *Cromwell* who outwings the wind[.] (lines 125–6)

A major index of sublimity is the poem's reworking of solar and circu-lar figures. The concern with circles develops his response to the *Second Defence* with its 'turns and rises' and 'winding ascent'. The poem opens with a haunting evocation of the mutability of human actions as 'vain Curlings' disappearing in 'weak Circles' (lines 1–4). The poem's own structure breaks through such circles; it can be seen as an ascending spiral, repeatedly covering similar ground but constantly moving upward. Like the 'Horatian Ode', it conveys a strong sense of symmetry. Ringing the poem are the evocations of troubled water; within them are satirical portraits of princes who are incapable of understanding Cromwell's greatness; within these are accounts of Cromwell's career as constitution-founder and as godly ruler; and at the centre is an account of his accident and the disastrous effects his death would have had. Cromwell's fall is at the centre of *The First Anniversary* as Charles's decapitation had been at the centre of the 'Horatian Ode'. As in the earlier poem, however, Marvell makes Cromwell's energetic movement cut across formal patternings, and possibly intends to evoke Pindar's unexpected, sublime transitions.[27] He impudently borrows the traditional simile of the sun as king and transfers it to Cromwell, relegating monarchs to the sluggish outer planets. He then proceeds to qualify the expected associations of the sun with cyclical repetition:

> *Cromwell* alone with greater Vigour runs,
> (Sun-like) the Stages of succeeding Suns:
> And still the Day which he doth next restore,
> Is the just Wonder of the Day before. (lines 7–10)

The word 'restore' here functions very differently from Waller's appeal to Cromwell to 'Restore us to ourselves': involving exciting change, the restoration is more like a Machiavellian *ridurre ai principii*. Cromwell's revival of fortunes after the travails of his first year is compared to the first sunrise seen by Adam, for whom it had seemed that night would last forever and who had looked for it where it had set. The sudden surprise when he turns and sees it 'Smiling serenely from the further side' (line 342) enacts the sublime process of returning to and restoring lost perceptions: the monarchical sun imagery had become banal and stereotyped, but in the Cromwellian/Marvellian reworking it gained a new lustre. Readers of Hall's Longinus might have found a strong association between Cromwell and the poet who, having made the auditor fear by his wanderings that the whole oration may fall apart, '*unexpectedly* after a long time... handsomely *returns* to his *first point* and *finishes* it; with these *adventures* and *excursions*, leaving the Hearer in much more *astonishment*'.[28]

Cromwell's sublimity, however, is politically ambiguous: if it marks his regime off from monarchical ones, it also marks his personal greatness off from his peers. In the 'Ode', Cromwell had been 'still in the *Republick's* hand'; now his 'gentle hand' had moulded the state anew (line 50). He had laid Ireland at the Commons' feet; now the state existed as a place to plant his foot as he threatened the world (line 99). He had forborne his fame to make it the republic's; now his republican critics were attacked at length as 'thankless Men' who failed to acknowledge his divine mission and whose sins might kill him (line 217). The agency for the revolution is transferred to '*Cromwell* alone' (line 7).

Marvell is careful to allay some of the unease this adulation would arouse by placing vigorously anti-monarchical language at the poem's threshold. The satire of the kings' slowness and lack of *virtù* is linked with a critique of their dependence on the actions of others which they then appropriate for their private interests (lines 23–30). Where the Marvell of the 'Horatian Ode'

27 Stella P. Revard, 'Building the Foundations of a Good Commonwealth: Marvell, Pindar, and the Power of Music', in Claude J. Summers and Ted-Larry Pebworth (eds.), '*The Muses Common-weal*': *Poetry and Politics in the Seventeenth Century* (Columbia and London, 1988), pp. 177–90.   28 J[ohn].H[all]., *Peri Hypsous, or Dionysius Longinus of the Height of Eloquence* (1652; E1294.2), p. 46, ch. 22.

was at least ready to grant Charles an admirable beauty, here such beauty is dismissed as merely ornamental:

> Thus (Image-like) an useless time they tell,
> And with vain Scepter, strike the hourly Bell;
> Nor more contribute to the state of Things,
> Then wooden Heads unto the Viols strings[.] (lines 41–4)

Marvell's language here is close to Hall's satires on monarchy; and its emphasis on speed and energy enables him to modulate from a critique of kingship to a critique of the Long Parliament. Hall had defended the dissolution on the grounds that they worked with 'such a *Spanish* slownesse, that unlesse either some particular Interest, or some immediate Necessity enforc'd them to hast, it was a common difficulty of a year or two to get passe an *Act*'; they would '*spin* out the time'. Just as 'all *sedentary* Bodies are slow and *unactive*) there appear'd such a lazinesse in the execution of that power, such a *Lethargy* as to Act in the *right* of the *Nation,* that *these* immortal persons, whose blood had been stirr'd or spill'd in their *Cause,* began to awake'. Hall had at first suggested that the dissolution would make possible a more thoroughgoing republican settlement:

> What these men have done as to *Establishment* and *Liberty,* I am to confesse they have altered the Titles of *Writs,* they have told us we have a *Commonwealth,* but for any *essential* fruits thereof, a man may (*drolling*) say, they have cut off the head of a *King,* and set a *Commonwealth* upon his shoulders, which like *Epistemon* in *Rabelais* (who was beheaded in a fight) are so finely *sewed* together, that they return out of *Hel,* and tell things that they did there.[29]

On the establishment of the Protectorate, he had repeated his condemnation of the Long Parliament as a drowsy giant, its power grown corrupt like standing water. Hall now diluted his republican language. He headed a new pamphlet with a quotation from Tacitus, previously used by Hobbes in an early anti-republican work, on Augustus's taking power to quell civil discord. He redefined a '*Re-publick*' as 'the Supreme Power in any Government'.[30] But he maintained his long-standing enthusiasm for sublime radical energy as opposed to customary inertia, and Marvell sustains this note. He does not go so far as Hall in invoking Augustus, and presents Cromwell as the kind of supreme legislator canonized in republican tradition, seizing a unique *occasione* for constitutional reform.

29 [John Hall], *A Letter Written to a Gentleman in the Country, Touching the Dissolution of the Late Parliament* (1653; E697.2), pp. 5, 6, 13–14. Thomason believed this tract to be by Milton.

30 [John Hall], *Confusion Confounded* (1654; E726.11), pp. 2, 9; Noel B. Reynolds and Arlene W. Saxonhouse (eds.), *Thomas Hobbes: Three Discourses* (Chicago and London, 1995), p. 37.

The interest in legislation forms a striking contrast with Waller's *Panegyrick* – and with the *Second Defence*. Marvell's poem is not simply a personal panegyric of the triumphs of Cromwell but is specifically concerned with the first year of a new political order with a written constitution and clearly delimited powers for the head of state. The image of the sun as restoring each day prepares us for a lengthy description of Cromwell as Machiavellian legislator. And, as in the 'Horatian Ode', echoes of Waller pointedly contrast monarchical with Cromwellian agency.[31] Waller's Charles-Amphion could

> higher clime,
> And things halfe swallow'd from the jawes of time
> Reduce[;] an earnest of his grand designe,
> To frame no new Church, but the old refine[.]

Charles's reduction had been much less radical than a Machiavellian *ridurre ai principii*; Cromwell is more truly like Amphion in being ready to found a new state from the beginning. In terms very close to Hall's, Marvell transfers the imagery of devouring to the leaders of the Rump Parliament. They looked only to the past to restore an inert ancient constitution and were not ready for drastic innovation:

> While tedious Statesmen many years did hack,
> Framing a Liberty that still went back;
> Whose num'rous Gorge could swallow in an hour
> That Island, which the Sea cannot devour[.] (lines 69–72)

Their attempt to frame liberty marks them out as failing to understand how political sublimity breaks through frames – just as the speaker of Marvell's lyric 'The Coronet' was ready for God to shatter the poem's more conventional frame. On the other hand, Cromwell's innovation is not crudely absolutist. The people are not merely an amorphous mass on whom the sovereign imposes order; their differences are to be respected and made into forces for political cohesion. There is thus a conspicuous difference between Waller's description of Charles demolishing the old buildings around Paul's:

> So ioyes the aged oak when wee divide
> The creeping Ivy from his injur'd side.

and Marvell's account of Cromwell's more sophisticated political architecture:

> The Common-wealth does through their Centers all
> Draw the Circumf'rence of the publique Wall;

31 Hirst, ' "That Sober Liberty"', p. 34, notes that Waller's Paul's poem would have been newly topical since the building was precarious and proposals were being made to demolish it; see also Smith, *LR*, p. 283.

The crossest Spirits here do take their part,
Fast'ning the Contignation which they thwart;
And they, whose Nature leads them to divide,
Uphold, this one, and that the other Side;
But the most Equal still sustein the Height,
And they as Pillars keep the Work upright;
While the resistance of opposed Minds,
The Fabrick as with Arches stronger binds,
Which on the Basis of a Senate free,
Knit by the Roofs Protecting weight agree. (lines 87–98)

'Divide', in the context of Amphion's lute-playing, becomes a musical pun which tempers the harshness of Marvell's earlier comment that he

Did thorough his own Side
His fiery way divide. ('Horatian Ode', lines 15–16)

The geometrical figure here links Protector and people as common centres of the new commonwealth's circle. There is a place in this political order for resistance and opposition. This concord is based on such complex discords that it resists easy representation. The monarchical circles of the beginning are so weak that they become a maze and their 'short Tumults' dissipate themselves (line 5). Cromwell, like a Machiavellian leader, accepts the need for tumults as a firmer basis for liberty:

And as the *Angel* of our Commonweal,
Troubling the Waters, yearly mak'st them Heal. (*First Anniversary*, lines 401–2)

The regicide, which Waller was to describe in terms of a calamitous sunset, is no more than a 'fertile Storm' that redeemed the state even though it 'o'r-took and wet the King' (lines 237–8). The oxymoronic formulation recalls Milton's 'healthfull commotions' in *Areopagitica*. The healing process here is much more strenuous than Waller's appeal to Cromwell to 'heale us with the arts of Peace', recalling rather Hall's condemnation of Parliamentary inertia as standing water. Cromwell's power to encourage a fertile rain sets up another contrast with Waller's Paul's poem, where the rebuilding is said to have helped to end a long drought, and identifies Charles, with a remarkably offhand dismissiveness, with the tyrannical King Ahab. Protectoral propaganda often used the language of healing in a distinctly bland manner. When Sir Henry Vane styled an oppositional work *A Healing Question* he was, like Hutchinson in her parody of Waller, glancing ironically at the Protector's premature or false claims to bring healing and harmony. Marvell presents Cromwell's healing in a way that might be somewhat more sympathetic to republicans, even as he hints at a near-blasphemous association with Christ himself: the tensions are high indeed.

Marvell's architectural figure emphasizes Cromwell's role in founding the state but leaves his function within that state more vague. The protecting roof knits the building together but it is the Senate that is its foundation. The syntax does, however, hint that the Senate's conclusions are reached only after strong pressure from above. Marvell proceeds to move beyond the architectural figures, which give the Protector too static a role. But his activity is conceived as directed largely towards foreign affairs, in which the Instrument of Government gave him a leading role, while Marvell defers comment on domestic policies:

> When for his Foot he thus a place had found,
> He hurles e'r since the World about him round;
> And in his sev'ral Aspects, like a Star,
> Here shines in Peace, and thither shoots a War. (lines 99–102)

All citizens are centres of the commonwealth, but Cromwell as Protector is the axis of world politics.

Marvell's treatment of foreign policy is very different from Waller's straightforward celebration of overseas conquests. Marvell develops the distinctly apocalyptic transformations of Augustanism which he had explored in the Latin poems. At this point, however, he begins to moderate the republican militancy of the opening. As in the *Second Defence* and in Marvell's poem to Christina, exceptions are made for wise and godly princes who are willing to follow Cromwell in an anti-Catholic crusade. Their defects are now seen not as intrinsic to monarchy but as the product of bad education even in their own best interest:

> Unhappy Princes, ignorantly bred,
> By Malice some, by Errour more misled[.] (lines 117–18)

They are 'mad with Reason, so miscall'd, of State' (line 111); but Marvell promises for them his most ambitious poem to date. As in the Christina poem, he raises his style in Virgilian manner to prophesy an apocalyptic epic that will shake the kings' 'Regal sloth' with 'graver Accents' and rally them to Cromwell's cause (lines 121–4). As he moves closer to the poem's central rings, Marvell moderates his satire and urges a momentous solemnity. It is at this point that he comes closest to identifying the spirit of his poetry with that of Cromwell's government: Cromwell the artist has favoured 'graver Notes' (line 63), and now Marvell matches his expectation of a supreme prophetic poem with a prophecy of Cromwell's ushering in a millennial deliverance when

> Fore-shortned Time its useless Course would stay,
> And soon precipitate the latest Day. (lines 139–40)

Circular and linear energies both buckle before divine immediacy; Marvell shifts the courtly devices of perspective art from the spatial to the temporal planes. He quickly qualifies this expectation, but it has served to confirm

Cromwell in the dual roles of classical legislator and agent of apocalypse.[32] His opponents can be presented as actively impeding rather than furthering the millennium:

> Hence that blest Day still counterpoysed wastes,
> The Ill delaying, what th'Elected hastes[.] (lines 155–6)

If the syntactic balance here parallels Waller's, it embodies a forward progression rather than a stable equilibrium.

It is at this point, having tried to present Cromwell as meeting the expectations of both secular republicans and millennialists, that Marvell starts to turn more directly on the opposition. The apocalypse would be hastened only if 'a seasonable People' should 'bend to his, as he to Heavens will' (line 134). This is a simpler expression of the relation between governor and people than the earlier demand that some should 'bend' to be 'sunk in the Foundation' (line 81). From now on, we hear less of the Instrument of Government and more of the threat to all civil order caused by any threat to Cromwell's person. In a remarkable passage, Marvell writes the kind of poetry that it would have been necessary to produce had Cromwell perished in his coaching accident. Here he resorts to hyperboles that might have been found in an elegy for Charles I:

> It seem'd the Earth did from the Center tear;
> It seem'd the Sun was faln out of the Sphere . . .
> A dismal Silence through the Palace went,
> And then loud Shreeks the vaulted Marbles rent. (lines 205–6, 209–10)

The imagined death is blamed on the people's sins: this is the reward for being 'the headstrong Peoples Charioteer' (line 224). The language here seems inconsistent with the Instrument's insistence that the Protector's role is a publicly defined office rather than depending on the personality of a single individual.

As so often, however, condemnation of the people is immediately followed by a condemnation of kingship:

> For to be *Cromwell* was a greater thing,
> Then ought below, or yet above a King:
> Therefore thou rather didst thy Self depress,
> Yielding to Rule, because it made thee Less. (lines 225–8)

Having rebuked the people, Marvell reassures them, as Milton had done in the *Second Defence*, that Cromwell is great enough not to become king. In the recapitulation of his career that follows, Marvell emphasizes Cromwell's affinity with judges like Gideon – 'Yet would not he be Lord, nor yet his Son'

---

32 On the strength of the poem's millenarianism, see Hirst, ' "That Sober Liberty" ', pp. 35ff.

(line 256). A contemporary pamphlet spoke of the regime as 'Gods cutting down *Monarchs*, his Adversaries, and making way for restoring of his Judges as at first'.[33] Still looking back to the time of the judges, Marvell then retells an anti-monarchical fable of the olive and the bramble. In this version, the bramble would have 'Levell'd every Cedar's top' (line 262): Marvell links monarchist and Leveller opposition to Cromwell's authority. If such opposition could only be stopped by Cromwell's 'growing to thy self a Law' (line 263), it was for the first time and in circumstances of political emergency when those in power were 'artless'.[34] Marvell now returns to satiric mode, and this time his satire is directed against the Fifth Monarchist opposition. The force of his attack, however, is somewhat mitigated by the fact that he has himself risen to fervently apocalyptic heights at an earlier point of the poem.[35] Whereas Hall and Nedham had attacked the Fifth Monarchists from a mainly secular point of view, Marvell has already gained credentials as a godly prophet and thus as one able to distinguish between true and false prophecy. The false prophets are accused of seeking a kingship of their own under the mask of ushering in Christ's kingship:

> their new King might the fifth Scepter shake,
> And make the World, by his Example, Quake[.] (lines 297–8)

They parody Cromwell also in offering a form of 'reduction', but theirs degenerates into an absurd primitivism:

> You who the Scriptures and the Laws deface
> With the same liberty as Points and Lace;
> Oh Race most hypocritically strict!
> Bent to reduce us to the ancient Pict;
> Well may you act the *Adam* and the *Eve*;
> Ay, and the Serpent too that did deceive. (lines 315–20)

Marvell links the Fifth Monarchists with those radicals who liked to go naked for religious reasons and with the purists who regarded buttons as an ungodly artifice. Here – as in mocking defence of 'points' in his poem on *Paradise Lost*, see chapter 10 below – his voice is that of reassurance to sober men of property and even of fashion; earlier he had compared his own poem to a gold tapestry interwoven with silver (line 184).

Having dismissed the radical opposition, Marvell introduces the climactic sun image and returns to the vigorously republican outer circle of his poem: this sun's light starts aggressively through the slothful princes' windows. Now

---

33 Anon., *A Full and Perfect Relation of the Great Plot* (1654; E730.1), p. 5, cited by Hirst, '"That Sober Liberty"', p. 49 n. 42.

34 Hirst, '"That Sober Liberty"', p. 37, glosses the phrase as defining a 'legally self-limiting ruler' who imposed the Instrument '*on himself*'.

35 Hirst, '"That Sober Liberty"', p. 42.

the princes themselves speak, and offer baffled praise of the new state. It is above all its unrepresentability that concerns them; the categories they have inherited from courtly culture leave no room for understanding this new phenomenon. The first part of their speech pays tribute to the nation as a whole, not just to Cromwell, cowering before its awesome speed and military force. The beneficial effects of the complex, innovative form of political unity that Cromwell has brought can be seen in their 'Union of Designes' (line 354). Marvell's language here falls into the jingoistic note of so many of his poems of the 1650s, and he portrays the process of colonial expansion with far more imaginative energy than Waller: the ships are paradoxical 'Arks of War', 'wood-Leviathans' that can 'sink the Earth that does at Anchor ride' (lines 357, 361, 364). 'Leviathan' would have had inevitable associations with Hobbes at this period, but Marvell seems to have been the first to transfer the word to a battleship, a usage not recorded in the *OED* before the nineteenth century. The monarchs now declare that they could have defeated the nation had it not been for Cromwell, the soul who animated the whole nation. In declaring that 'still his Fauchion all our Knots unties' (line 384), they associate him with Alexander the Great. This sword, however, like the erect sword of the end of the 'Ode', is a menacing nightmare to all monarchs, and recapitulates the opening imagery of Cromwell's linear movement cutting through monarchical circles. They acknowledge that he, like the nation, eludes their normal categories:

> 'He seems a King by long Succession born,
> 'And yet the same to be a King does scorn.
> 'Abroad a King he seems, and something more,
> 'At Home a Subject on the equal Floor.
> 'O could I once him with our Title see,
> 'So should I hope yet he might Dye as wee. (lines 387–92)

This is the poem's climactic *concordia discors*: the balanced couplets register not an easy harmony but a teasing elusiveness. Like Milton, Marvell locates Cromwell's sublimity in his refusal to accept the title of king. Marvell has given him various styles ranging from the secular – 'Captain' (line 321), 'lusty Mate' (line 273), 'Father' (line 282) – to the classical – 'our *Amphion*' (line 73) – and religious – 'Angelique' (line 126) – but he has steered clear of conventional titles. Remarkably, he has never directly termed him 'Protector'. The kings' final comment is double-edged. On the surface, it enables Marvell to pay a compliment to Cromwell's immortality. But this hyperbolical, and patently untrue, praise betrays the kings' limited mental world. The centre of Marvell's poem has not flinched from drawing attention to the fact that Cromwell is indeed mortal. Triumphs conventionally included a reminder that the triumpher is mortal; Marvell describes Cromwell as 'triumphant' only in his death (line 215). 'So with more Modesty we may be True' (line 187): it is only now, when Cromwell has been carefully separated from kingship, that Marvell ventures to address him, for the first and only time, as 'great Prince' (line 395). And he immediately declares all such titles to be inadequate to Cromwell's sublimity:

> thou thy venerable Head dost raise
> As far above their Malice as my Praise. (lines 399–400)

It is as the active, renovating '*Angel*' of a kingless 'Commonweal' – 'which, it need hardly be said, is no civic office' – that Cromwell finally moves out of the poem's frame.[36] The claim that he makes the waters heal 'yearly' is a reminder that the Instrument had not been fully defined at the time the poem was published, some details having been left to Parliament; like Cromwell, the Instrument is an agent of restoration which may never take a completely fixed and final form.[37]

Marvell's strategy in the *The First Anniversary*, then, is significantly different from that of the Protectoral Augustans. The poem is addressed not only to former royalists but also to disaffected secular or apocalyptic republicans, aiming to answer their anxieties by showing that the Protectorate offers an occasion which it would be merely perverse to miss. His swingeing assaults on the Fifth Monarchists recapitulate stock conservative smears against radical groups and would have given offence to many. But there is no evidence that this poem aroused the same hostility as Waller's – though this may be partly because it was published anonymously. It could adopt the political language of figures like Overton and Canne, whom Marvell knew from Hull, and both of whom had been ready to go some way with the Cromwellian regime. It also adopts something of Overton's favoured poetic language. As well as sharing the Puritans' conventional regard for Wither and Quarles, Overton was a great admirer of Donne; a decade later, when in prison under the Restoration regime, he adapted many of the *Songs and Sonets* as a memorial to his wife. The 'affectionate curiosity' which Marvell had expressed to Milton, in the context of praise of Cromwell, suggests that Marvell was close enough to Overton to be acquainted both with his poetic interests and his political reservations. One of Overton's favourite Donne poems was 'Love's Growth', which he adapted in a godly direction, with

> Love's not so pure, and abstract, as they use
> To say, which have no Mistresse, but their Muse

becoming

> This Loue's a purer abstrac^t then they use
> whoe have no other M^{rs} then theire Muse (p. 162)

---

36 Hirst, '"That Sober Liberty"', p. 25.   37 Raymond, 'Framing Liberty'.

The imagery of this poem, with its concentric circles which constantly expand without ever losing their purity, seems to have left its mark on *The First Anniversary*, along with the invocations of the sun in 'The Sun Rising'. Overton was also to adapt Donne's *First* and *Second Anniversaries*, with their combination of hyperbolical praise and unease at cosmic dissolution.[38] Marvell of course had an independent interest in Donne, but Overton is a reminder that the fusion of metaphysical imagery with republican and apocalyptic politics was a shared concern in the 1650s. That conjunction also ensured the poem's speedy eclipse relative to Waller's, later in the century. Or its confusion with Waller's – by the end of the century when both apocalyptic enthusiasm and the taste for metaphysical poetry were on the wane, the important distinctions between the poems became blurred.

Even in its own time, the poem may be said to have missed its occasion. Not only was it printed too late for the Instrument's anniversary, but the concord it called for was becoming harder and harder to maintain. The same issue of *Mercurius Politicus* that advertised *The First Anniversary* also recorded Overton's imprisonment. In another sense, the poem was too accurate for its own good: Cromwell had outrun the poet and the politicians. Increasingly angry with the republican opposition, he decided that the five months specified for Parliament by the Instrument alluded to lunar rather than solar months, and duly dissolved it on 22 February 1655.

Cromwell's celerity, however difficult it might prove, served as a stimulus to Marvell's imagination. It was more of a perpetual vexation for another of Cromwell's non-monarchical poets, and a great favourite of Overton's, George Wither. The confusions of the times, he wrote in a poem written around the time of the Protector's first anniversary,

> make it difficult to know
> What, really *he is*; what *he would do*[.][39]

For Wither, Cromwell posed equally difficult problems of political and of poetic representation. He welcomed Cromwell's speed and energy but was troubled by his unpredictability, and his own status as poet-prophet was continually confounded during the 1650s by Cromwell's leaping ahead of his expectations. He had been taken by surprise by the dissolution of the Long Parliament, which rendered obsolete in advance a poem he published a few days later that had called for radical Parliamentary reform. Sharing other reformers' disillusion with the purged Parliament's dilatoriness and favouritism, Wither had called for a permanently rotating system of Parliamentary

---

38 David Norbrook, "This Blushing Tribute of a Borrowed Muse": Robert Overton's Overturning of the Seventeenth-Century Canon, *English Manuscript Studies 1100–1700*, 4 (1993), 220–66.

39 George Wither, *The Protector*, second edition (1655; E1597.3), p. 18.

representation. An elaborate system of monthly elections would ensure that representatives did not cling to power and that they represented their people as transparently as possible. This would be a 'course of *restauration*', returning the nation's liberty to first principles by a bold innovation. Parliament would thus purge the arbitrariness of its political actions and

> restore
> Those *rights* which they usurped heretofore[.][40]

Wither indulged in a fantasy of a rebuilt Whitehall, anticipating Harrington's political imagery, with the twelve houses for representatives elected in each month mirroring the orderly progression of the signs of the zodiac. Undermining this republican settlement would be punishable with exile or death.

Wither himself recognized, however, that there was a huge gulf between this proposal, heavily coloured as it was by Venetian ideals of balance and stability, and the conditions of England in the 1650s. Cromwell rudely shattered that balance, and made Wither seek new solutions. He came to terms with the idea that Cromwell might have been providentially sent to establish a new political order. He urged Cromwell to reassure the public by issuing a declaration of his political principles. He should show himself 'industrious to reduce all things to their *pristine orderly Course*, as soon as the necessity which constrained his irregularity, is so evidently removed, that it may be safely done'. Cromwell met this proposal sympathetically, declaring that Wither's draft declaration 'answered to his heart, as the *shadow of his face* in the Glass (then hanging before him in the room) answered to his *face*'. He gave Wither the keys to his study with his private papers, and Wither enthusiastically set about certain revisions that Cromwell had proposed. However, Cromwell and his secretary Thurloe became increasingly evasive and the project went no further. The turning-point for Wither, according to his own later account, came on the day when Cromwell fell from his coach after rashly taking the reins, an 'imprudent, if not disgraceful attempt mis-beseeming his person'.

Yet Wither refused to give up hope in the Protectorate. This was, after all, the only time in his life his prophetic and political skills were taken seriously by someone in government. Here as on so many occasions Cromwell showed his skill in defusing political opposition by his readiness to listen sympathetically to adversaries on an individual basis. And he was genuinely interested in those who claimed prophetic powers. Though Wither left Whitehall on the day of the coaching accident in an angry mood, he proceeded to publish a poem in the Protector's defence, feeling obliged 'to prevent as much of the dishonor, as I might ... in regard he executed the *Supreme Office* at that time'.[41]

---

40 George Wither, *The Perpetuall Parliament*, in *The Dark Lantern* (1653; E1432.3; *WMW*, III), pp. 44, 49.   41 George Wither, *A Cordial Confection* (1659; E763.13), pp. 6–8.

In *Vaticinium Causuale*, Wither defended riding in uncharacteristically courtly terms. But he also called on Cromwell to defend liberty; like Milton in the *Second Defence*, he balanced an appeal to the people with an appeal to the Protector. Comparing himself to the figure at a triumph who reminded the emperor of his mortality, he called on Cromwell to 'redeeme, and husband well, his *Time*'.[42] Going further, he declared that in fact the title of emperor must be rejected:

> *Emperour* to stile him, should not better
> His happy *Lot*, or make him ought the greater;
> But, rather seeme, a foolish over-lay
> Of purest *Ophir Gold*, with *common Clay*. (p. 9)

Rather than seeking such vainglory, Cromwell would make the people truly free and become

> *first-borne*, of those *Viceroyes*, who, shall take
> Their *Throns* from HIM, whose *Kingdom* down will break,
> All Monarchies of *Tirants*; with all those,
> Who, help patch up, the *Clay and Iron toes*,
> The Reliques of that *Image*, which hath bin
> The prop of him, that's call'd, *the man of sin*. (p. 13)

Rather than becoming king, Cromwell would usher in the reign of King Jesus.

Wither's association of idolatrous monarchies with clay may have helped to shape Marvell's more secular reference to 'the *China* clay' in *The First Anniversary*. There are indeed several indications of links between Marvell and Wither. Marvell may have gained from Wither the idea of linking the coaching accident with images of good government. Wither in turn seems to have drawn on *The First Anniversary* in his own poem in honour of the new regime, *The Protector*. Like Marvell, Wither calls on Parliamentarians to cease their bickering and rally behind their leader, whose 'hands must tune so many *diff'ring strings*' (p. 27). Cromwell may inaugurate apocalyptic deliverance:

> *Room*, therefore; and henceforth let *Names of Powr'* . . .
> Descend; that in their place I may enthrone
> The Title of PROTECTOR . . .
> Till He, who these *Dominions* doth protect,
> Hath by *example*, taught, how to reduce
> All *Governments* to their intended use;
> Or, broke them into pieces, who, persist
> To tyrannize, and rant it, as they list. (p. 17)

---

42 George Wither, *Vaticinium Causuale* [*sic*] (1655; E813.14; *WMW*, I), p. 6.

Like Marvell, Wither holds back from specifying apocalyptic possibilities:

> But, whither, do my *Contemplations* fly?
> I may, perchance, unseal a *Mystery*
> Before the time; my *Muse*, therefore, descend . . . (p. 13)

And Wither shares with Marvell an attempt to cast his praise in a hypothetical mode to avoid charges of flattery:

>   though none
> Should give their *Plaudits*, till the *Play* be done;
> (Or, crown men, till the *Coronation-day*,
> Which is their last) yet, somewhat I will say
> To hint, in brief, what, more at large, I might
> Express, should I, a *Panegyrick* write[.] (p. 30)

Wither boldly makes more explicit a point that Marvell only hints at: true coronation comes only with the heavenly crown, so that all secular cere-monies – and poems – are vain attempts to cheat mortality.

As in *The First Anniversary*, religious language is combined with secular Machiavellianism: Wither transfers from Parliament to Cromwell the role of reducing the state to its first principles. Like Marvell and Milton, Wither insists that Cromwell transcends the title of King, a name which

>   makes him to be rather *less*, then *greater*,
> (As in himself) and rather *worse* then *better*
> As to his *People* . . .
> At best, it mixeth with it, but as *Clay*
> With *Iron*, which, both takes the *strength* away,
> And *value* of it: adding thereunto,
> Nothing, but what that *structure* may undo.
> It cracks the *Instrument*, which doth invest
> Him in his *Pow'r*; and lames his *Interest*[.] (pp. 4–5)

Again, monarchy is associated with inferior clay. Like Marvell, Wither calls for vigorous new building:

> Why then should we of *Scarcrows* be afraid?
> Or on *Foundations*, by GODS own hand laid,
> Rebuild again old *Babylon*? or fix
> To *Sion's* firm stones, her untemper'd *bricks*? (p. 9)

Wither's uncharacteristic use of astronomical imagery may derive from *The First Anniversary*:[43]

---

43 Charles S. Hensley, 'Wither, Waller and Marvell: Panegyrists for the Protector', *Ariel* 3 (1972), 5–16 (8).

Thou, who art now, the worlds new *Northern Star*,
Let, in thine *Orb*, no *Course irregular*
(*Oblique* or *Retrograde*) divert thee from
Those *motions*, which, thy *Circle* best become;
Lest, from that *Heav'n*, in which thou now dost shine,
Down to the *Earth*, thou back again decline,
And, like the *Star* call'd *Wormwood*, bitter make
Those *waters*, whence, we now *refreshments* take. (pp. 25–6)

Differences from Marvell, however, are also evident in this passage. Marvell never entertains any doubt about Cromwell's magnificent, circular perfection: apparent difficulties are merely the product of a limited imagination that fails to grasp his sublimity. Wither is worried that Cromwell's status may instead be an optical illusion, and wants his motions to conform to the cosmic cycles rather than defiantly transcending them. The fear that his apotheosis may be transitory, that he may fall back to earth, arouses troubling memories of the invocation to Nero at the opening of the *Pharsalia*, and Wither ends by implying that he may be a false prophet (cf. Revelation VIII.11). Wither is perplexed rather than stimulated by Cromwell's transcendence of normal categories of representation. Cromwell had claimed that Wither's image of him in an earlier writing was as transparent as a mirror, yet the relations between text and Protector had proved bafflingly opaque. He could only hope that negative views of the Protector were '*Mis-representings*' (p. 18), and that we

> (by what we discern,
> Without suspect) as perfectly might learn,
> How, by his *Foot*, a harmless *Lamb* to draw,
> As to describe a *Lion*, by his *Paw*. (p. 19)

Wither tries to bring Cromwell into a stable world of representation in which he is clearly subordinate to 'that *Heav'nly King*,/Whom, he but represents' (p. 15); he ushers in the way for the heavenly king by breaking down 'Both our *Self-confidences*, and his *own*' (p. 28). It will be a time when

> *Kings* and *Emperours*
> Hav lost their *Names*, their *Kingdoms*, & their *Pow'rs*:
> And . . . here, that *King of kings* doth raign[.]

In that spirit, the title of Protector has no 'stamp of *Self-relation*' (p. 14).

But Cromwell was very hard to contain; he kept the nation in continual suspense as to how far he would be willing to lose his name rather than aggrandizing it. By the time Wither had completed *The Protector*, Parliament had been dissolved and Wither withheld publication to see what would happen next. He did not bring it out until mid-summer, perhaps stimulated by rumours that Cromwell was to make himself king, a prospect Wither was anxious to prevent. It may be that his reference to what he would say if he wrote a '*Panegyrick*' was inserted later, in response to the appearance in the meantime of Waller's *Panegyrick*. He was still declaring his readiness to write a panegyric, but failing actually to do so, two years later. Once again, his hesitation was affected by Cromwell's refusal to be bound by public expectation. The campaign for Cromwell to be crowned, to which Waller lent his voice, was reaching its height. Wither was delighted when Cromwell refused the crown after all, and *A Suddain Flash* reaffirmed his opposition to kingship. But he had so little confidence in Cromwell's keeping to this resolution that he withheld publication for several months, and voiced, even while rejecting, the fear that the refusal might have been a mere '*Trick of State*'.[44] He left matters as open as possible by declaring that titles were in the end things indifferent: if Parliament could find a candidate for kingship who willingly limited his own powers, Wither would

> sing a *Panegyrick* in their praise
> Who mov'd it, that should long out-last my daies. (p. 12)

Wither made it clear, however, that the 'if' was a very big one. He reiterated his old arguments against kingship, recalling the precedent of Gideon. He recollected his prophecy in *Prosopopoeia Britannica* that a king would grow greater by unkinging himself (p. 4). Cromwell is likened to Christ being tempted by Satan with earthly crowns (p. 5). If there must be a new title – and he preferred a less overtly regal formulation like '*Soveraign Protector*, or, *Protector Imperial*' (p. 42) – it would only be because of Cromwell's transitional political status, as someone to whom God had transferred absolute power in the expectation that he would use it to restore liberty. Like the world before its creation, the commonwealth must be the work of one man:

> This One, GOD, hath provided to restore
> All, that our *Kings* usurped heretofore
> (Or, our Sins forfeited) And to resetle
> On us, those *blessings*, by a *stronger Title*[.] (p. 47)

The result would be

> Things ballancing, so evenly, betwixt
> *Prince, Peeres*, and *People*, that, each may subsist,
> And not infringe each others *Interest*[.]

Wither did not radically revise the conception of the balanced constitution in the manner of Harrington's republicanism, for he still left a role for the prince, but he strongly opposed measures to reinstate a hereditary upper house, which would be inimical to the balance of a '*Free Republicke*' (p. 33).

---

44 George Wither, *A Suddain Flash* (1657; E1584.3; *WMW*, II), p. 2.

Until such a balance was established, Cromwell had to have a degree of arbitrary power, however it was termed. Foundations must be laid for future generations: the Protector must be

> the *Stone*
> First laid, to build their *new fram'd work upon*[.] (p. 16)

Like Marvell, Wither insisted that this required demolition as well as construction:

> In which *work*, if they should
> Leave any *Arch*, or *Pillars*, rais'd of old,
> *Mis-laid*, or *Crooked*, *Rotten*, or *Mis-wrought*,
> It would, at last, bring all the Pile to nought. (pp. 37–8)

Wither tried to persuade himself that the contention between pro- and anti-monarchists might itself be a form of strength, for

> those things which bee
> Well done, are *Best done*, when, some disagree:
> And . . . *Truth* doth appear in her perfection
> When she is polished by *Contradiction*[.] (p. 53)

Those contradictions appeared in the toings and froings of his own poem. But Wither could not be as sure as Marvell that these twists and turns could nevertheless resolve themselves into a sublime unity. *A Suddain Flash* was his last attempt to address Cromwell in public, though he continued to try to influence him by means of annual private addresses on 3 September, a day which had special significance for Cromwell as the anniversary of his victories at Dunbar and Worcester. The date of the second address proved to be the date of Cromwell's death. Wither believed that there had been plans to crown Cromwell on that day; his death showed how strongly the Almighty disapproved of Cromwellian kingship.[45]

From Cromwell to Virgil: James Harrington and republican literary culture

In different ways, Milton, Marvell and Wither tried to bridge the widening gulf between republicans and Cromwellians. There are close, and little-recognized, affinities between their defences of Cromwell and the most important text of English republicanism, Harrington's *Oceana* (1656). The relationship may also be reciprocal: Harrington emerged from the same literary culture, and its traces are to be found in his writings.

45 George Wither, *Fides-Anglicana* (1660; W3157; *WMW*, V), p. 93; *Salt upon Salt* (1659; E1827.2; *WMW*, IV), pp. 31–3.

Little is known about Harrington's life in the early 1650s. Almost all authorities quote Aubrey's claim that he was plunged into depression by the death of Charles I, having been present on the scaffold. Aubrey tells us that Harrington himself testified to this at the Rota Club meetings.[46] This narrative has been seized on as confirmation for the retrospective nature of English republicanism: having suffered traumatic shock from the king's death, Harrington can open himself to a new political order. It would be easy to link this with another narrative, of the transition from poetry to politics. According to Aubrey, 'his Muse was rough' and it was a fellow-republican, Henry Neville, who 'disswaded him from tampering in Poetrie, wch he did invitâ Minervâ [against the Muse's will]', and made him recognize that his true talent lay in political thought, which led him to write *Oceana*.[47] Harrington would thus appear to conform to the paradigm in which a prosaic republicanism shatters an old monarchical order.

Both politically and chronologically, however, that account is suspect. As regards the alleged incompatibility between republicanism and poetry, Aubrey considered that his informant Neville was himself 'an excellent (but concealed) Poet' – unfortunately his verse was so well concealed that we can no longer judge of its excellence. Harrington's poetry has been ignored by historians of political thought because it is not political, and by literary historians because it is not properly literary. If we situate him in the context of mid-century republican culture, however, these sharp distinctions become blurred. There is no evidence that Harrington straightforwardly shifted from poetry to prose: he took an interest in both media throughout his short writing career. The *Oceana* is in some ways a classic humanist work in exploiting wit and imagination to convey its abstract ideas. Commentators in the discipline of the history of political thought have tended to pass over this aspect of his work, but his writing, however idiosyncratic, is striking and forceful.[48] As for his politics, Aubrey himself says that he had been interested in republicanism before 1649. His late-seventeenth-century editor, John Toland, who had access to papers that are now lost, gave a slightly different story from Aubrey's:

> After the King's Death he was observ'd to keep much in his Library, and more
> retir'd than usually, which was by his Friends a long time attributed to
> Melancholy or Discontent. At length when they weary'd him with their importu
> nitys to change this sort of Life, he thought fit to shew 'em at the same time their
> mistake and a Copy of his *Oceana*, which he was privately writing all that while[.][49]

46 *ABL*, I, 289.   47 Bodleian MS Aubrey 6, fol. 98v; *ABL*, I, 289.
48 Jonathan Scott, 'The Rapture of Motion: James Harrington's Republicanism', in
   Nicholas Phillipson and Quentin Skinner (eds.), *Political Discourse in Early Modern
   Britain* (Cambridge, 1993), pp. 139–63, emphasizes the differences that mark off
   Harrington's political determinism from humanist civic virtue; the status of *Oceana* as a
   humanist text may at least qualify this analysis.
49 *The 'Oceana' of James Harrington, and his Other Works*, ed. John Toland (1700), p. xvii.

Toland had a propensity for editing texts to give them a more clearly upbeat republican message, and perhaps that is what he is doing to his sources here. But his version at least deserves to be set in the balance with Aubrey's. The work with which Harrington emerged, *The Common-wealth of Oceana*, shows no sign of nostalgia for the old political order. It is in many ways a comic, cheerful book. In Harrington there is sometimes a manic quality to the wit, and he did lose his sanity later in life, so perhaps his depression was the inverse of the wit.

There is no reason to doubt that Harrington was shaken by Charles's execution. He had built up a close personal relationship with the king. And his contribution to Lawes's *Psalmes* – if it is indeed his – brought him into a circle of royalist poets. But as has been seen, there were opposing cross-currents in the literary culture of the late 1640s, with Milton pointing the way to a new sublimity that would transcend the limited beauty of courtly verse. Harrington said that Lawes showed how music's power

> To chaine wilde Winds, calme raging Seas, recall
> From profound Hell, and raise to Heav'n, are all
> Of Harmony no fables, but true story[.] (figure 7)

This tribute may have been suggested by Milton's tribute to Lawes in *Comus*.[50] Direct influence is hard to prove – Harrington's tribute is in line with conventional praise of art as bringing concord out of discords – though there is a characteristic interest in revealing the truth behind myth. But if Aubrey is right to say that Harrington tried to debate republican constitutions with the king, he is likely to have been open also to less courtly forms of poetry. The violence with which the king's execution was engineered was of course disturbing to many who wished for constitutional reform and came to support the republic.

There is evidence that Harrington began work on *Oceana* a long time before its publication. Blair Worden has pointed out that some sections bear traces of the debates of the Commonwealth period. Scotland (Marpesia) is said at some points to have been conquered, but elsewhere still to await liberty (10/159, 196/331), and there are other oscillations between points of view before and after the dissolution of the Long Parliament.[51] Much of the opening is a polemic against Hobbes, whose *Leviathan* was more immediately topical in 1651 than 1656. And much of that polemic is a defence of humanist rhetoric and interpretation. To that extent, Harrington was lining up with Milton in associating the new republic with humanist tradition. As Quentin

50 Willa McClung Evans, *Henry Lawes: Musician and Friend of Poets* (New York, 1941), p. 180.
51 Blair Worden, 'Harrington's *Oceana*: Origins and Aftermath, 1651–1660', *RLCS*, pp. 111–38 (114–15).

Skinner has shown, in *Leviathan* Hobbes drew back from some of his earlier violent repudiation of rhetoric. The fact remains that he was deeply suspicious of the power of language to override the rational case for political obedience; and this made him dubious about the value of literary education. Harrington rejects Hobbes's anti-republican mode of reading:

> [Hobbes] insinuates, that [the great prosperity of ancient commonwealths] was nothing else but the emulation of particular men; as if so great an emulation could have been generated without as great virtue; so great virtue without the best education; the best education without the best Lawes; or the best Lawes any otherwise then by the excellency of their policy (130/178).[52]

For Harrington, then, a republican reading involves looking at moral issues in explicitly political terms.

Harrington gave an example of this mode of reading in his commentary to a translation of Virgil's first and ninth eclogues. These translations were published, and probably composed, later in the decade, and the commentary takes for granted his mature political system. But it is not difficult to see how the analysis could have emerged from earlier radical humanist readings. As Annabel Patterson has shown, the poems had long been used to explore 'What kind of thing it was call'd Liberty'.[53] The speakers in the first eclogue represent different outcomes of the Roman civil wars: Tityrus has been granted land and leisure by Augustus, but Menalcas has been driven from his lands by soldiers who have to be rewarded for their service. As has been seen, Fanshawe had drawn parallels between this period of Roman history and his own times, and drawn the conclusion that the king should be restored to full powers. In translating the first eclogue, Harrington could be seen as expressing some sympathy with those royalists who were discontented at the expropriation of their estates. However, he gave his reading of Virgil a more radical cast by adding a further note which set the poems in a much longer time-scale of republican analysis (sigs. A8r–v). Monarchist readings found in Virgil's poetry a balance and harmony that reflected the harmony of rule under a benign emperor. Harrington's note baldly begins: 'That the *Roman* Empire was never founded upon a sufficient ballance of absolute Monarchy, is very true; but not truer then that this was the cause of that impotency and misery in the same, which oppressed both Prince and people'. He proceeds to give a highly condensed analysis of Western history, tracing a deep-rooted structural defect: from the later Roman republic onwards, too much preponderance of the power of the

---

52 James Harrington, *The Common-wealth of Oceana* (1656; H809, –9A); ed. S. B. Liljegren (Lund and Heidelberg, 1924); references in parentheses to Liljegren and *HPW* in turn.

53 James Harrington, *An Essay vpon Two of Virgil's Eclogues, and Two Books of his Aeneis* (1658; V627), sig. A5r (Eclogues, i.27; *HPW*, pp. 580–1); Annabel Patterson, *Pastoral and Ideology: Virgil to Valéry* (Berkeley and Los Angeles, 1987), *passim.*

nobility had opened the way to a monarchy that allied with the nobility against the people. Sulla had precipitated the Roman crisis by planting huge numbers of veterans on confiscated lands, and first the triumvirs and then Augustus had followed his precedent, 'as in these Eclogues'. These grants had become hereditary, and the nobility thus formed became more independent of the emperors, who had to consolidate their power instead through grants to mercenary Goths and Vandals. This top-heavy structure collapsed, and the Goths and Vandals took over but reduplicated the same power structures.

In this historical perspective, the eclogues began to look very different. The debate between Menalcas and Tityrus was not one that could be resolved by the advent of a benign monarch. Augustus was struggling between the conflicting demands of traditional land rights and the military following which he needed to secure supreme power. His dilemma testified to a structural fissure in Western political culture; Virgil's elegantly balanced dialogue might point to a provisional, poetic resolution, but at a deeper level the fissure had never been healed. Harrington was calling for a new way of reading the classic texts, and a new conception of balance:

> The doctrine of the ballance not sufficiently discover'd or heeded by ancient Historians and Polititians, is the cause why their writings are more dark, and their judgement less steddy or clear in the principles of Government then otherwise they would have been[.] (sig. A8v)

Harrington was convinced that his great contribution to political theory was a new concept of political balance. The idea that a good state rested on a balance between the one, the few and the many could be found in classical theory. It was possible to graft this on to the English constitutional framework, but the role of a personal monarch immediately became more problematic – as was seen in the case of Milton's early pamphlets. By the late 1640s, the concept of balance in English political debate had been further complicated by the terms of interest theory, which emphasized the variety of opposing factions in the state and made it seem much harder to achieve a balance that would do justice to them all. Hall, in his *True Account* of 1647, had compared the state to a watch that had come to pieces and was hard to reassemble. The more complex the balance, the more the coherence of the state was seen as the product of artifice rather than the natural harmony of the body politic. Harrington developed the concept of the balance still further by claiming that England could be brought into a new balance only through thoroughgoing constitutional reform and an agrarian law that would drastically curtail the size of landed estates.

Harrington could have developed his ideas without reference to literature, but his literary interests would not necessarily have worked against them. He was on friendly terms with writers who longed for a return to the Caroline system, but there was also the example of Milton, who was offering a very different kind of response to events. If for some royalist poets an ease and balance of writing could be equated with a return to the traditional political order, Milton's move towards a much more complex model of balance in poetry had its political equivalents. Harrington's intellectual development may have run parallel to that of Hall and Marvell, who negotiated in different ways with these contending influences. Marvell was a close friend of Harrington's by the time of the latter's death; we do not know when the friendship began, but their circles certainly overlapped by the late 1640s.

Harrington maintained contact with royalist literary circles throughout the period in which he developed his republican theory. In 1655 he contributed two pastoral dialogues to Lawes's *The Second Booke of Ayres, and Dialogues*.[54] This volume was in many ways a public manifestation of royalist sentiment, but it also showed the possibility for artistic interests to override political differences. In his dedication, Lawes again lamented the king's fate. Amongst the contributors was the fiery royalist Sir John Berkenhead, who protested against the banishment of royalists from London. His reference to the Roman dictator Sulla, 'Whose *Fire* and *Blood* met in his *copper face*', would probably have been taken as a glance at Cromwell (sig. B4v).[55] But Lawes also included a setting of a tribute by Edmund Waller, in the year of his *Panegyrick* to Cromwell. Waller noted that his poem had been written back in 1635, perhaps obliquely reminding readers of the changed circumstances that accounted for his changed allegiances.[56] Harrington seems to have tried to involve Waller in a constitutional commission for a republic.[57] Other contributors were Milton's nephews, Edward and John Phillips. Assuming that the 'James *Harrington Esq*' who contributed two pastoral dialogues was the republican[58], he was entering

---

54 Henry Lawes, *The Second Booke of Ayres, and Dialogues* (1655; L641), pp. 33, 38. Worden, 'Harrington's *Oceana*: Origins and Aftermath, 1651–1660', p. 432 n.42, identifies this Harrington, independently of Evans, as the republican political theorist.

55 Berkenhead attended meetings of the Rota Club in 1659–60, albeit possibly as a royalist spy: P. W. Thomas, *Sir John Berkenhead 1617–1679: A Royalist Career in Politics and Polemics* (Oxford, 1969), pp. 185–9, 204–5.

56 The *Second Booke of Ayres* includes a reference to a death that took place on 11 April 1655 (p. 28); Waller's *Panegyrick* was entered in late May, so the *Ayres* volume is likely to have come out later.

57 *A Proposition in order to the Proposing of a Commonwealth or Democracie* (1659; 669f21.49), proposes 'Mr. *Edward Waller*' to join a legislative committee headed by the earl of Northumberland and covering a wide spectrum of opinion; given Waller's previous associations with Northumberland it may be that 'Edward' is a mistake for 'Edmund'. Pocock, *HPW*, p. 111, suggests that this tract was in any case a satire.

58 Another contributor, Henry Harrington (p. 14), was listed in Lawes's *Ayres and Dialogues* of 1653 as the son of Sir Henry Harington, but his family does not seem to have included a James. For the family's different branches see Ian Grimble, *The Harington Family* (1957).

mixed political company, but not crossing an otherwise impermeable barrier. His praise of the shepherd's simple life above 'purple Robes, and Crowned heads' should probably not be taken too seriously as a critique of the Protectoral court, but places Harrington on common ground with Milton in looking behind current poetic fashions to an idealized Elizabethan age. Harrington regarded Elizabeth's government as virtually republican. In 1653 Milton's amanuensis transcribed a fair copy of his sonnet to Lawes with the new title 'To M^r: H*en*. Lawes on the publishing of his Aires': this was presumably intended for the first volume of *Ayres and Dialogues*, which appeared in 1653.[59]

For reasons unknown the poem did not appear, but there is other evidence of Milton's involvement in this circle. Another contributor to the 1655 volume was Sir William Davenant, who like Milton had collaborated with Lawes as a masque-writer in the 1630s. In 1653 he had drafted a manifesto for dramatic spectacles. The influence of Milton, who had interceded on his behalf in 1651, has been detected in this scheme; it was patronized by Whitelocke, the dedicatee of Hall's translation of Longinus.[60] Milton and Davenant both addressed poems around this time to their friend Edward Lawrence.[61] In 1656, the year *Oceana* was published, Lawes returned to his pre-war partnership with Davenant, collaborating on the first of a series of quasi-operatic spectacles which effectively launched the public re-opening of the London stage. This development had a political rationale: in a manifesto of 1656 Davenant argued that royalists who had been banished from the city under political suspicion should be encouraged to return for economic reasons and to dissuade them from rebellion.[62] Several of the poems set by Lawes addressed the dilemma of royalists fallen on hard times. Such dramatic schemes were not exclusively the product of the conservative ambience of the Protectorate, however. An interest in the theatre was found amongst some committed republicans, including Marten, who interceded for Davenant, and Streater, who had campaigned for the public theatre as early as 1654.[63] Hall had called for the re-opening of the theatres back in 1647.

Harrington's contacts with royalist literary culture, then, did not contradict the urgency of his republican convictions; like Milton, he hoped to

---

59 Parker, *Milton*, II, 1026.

60 James R. Jacob and Timothy Raylor, 'Opera and Obedience: Thomas Hobbes and *A Proposition for Advancement of Moralitie* by Sir William Davenant', *The Seventeenth Century* 6 (1991), 205–50.

61 Milton, Sonnet 17, '*Lawrence* of vertuous Father vertous son'; Davenant, 'To Mr. Edward Laurence', in *The Shorter Poems and Songs from the Plays and Masques*, ed. A. M. Gibbs (Oxford, 1972), p. 156.

62 C. H. Firth, 'Sir William Davenant and the Revival of Drama during the Protectorate', *English Historical Review* 18 (1903), 319–21.

63 John Streater, *Observations*, no. 4, 25 April–2 May 1654, p. 30, cited by Nigel Smith, 'Popular Republicanism in the 1650s', *MR*, pp. 137–55(151).

counter royalist accusations that republican government undermined literature. When *Oceana* appeared in 1656, it made this point very strongly. In his
concluding prophecy of the foundation of his ideal commonwealth, we are
told that the drama flourishes in state-built theatres, from whose profits a
'Poet *Laureate*' receives 'a wreath of five hundred Pounds in Gold' (221/354).
Davenant, who had been Charles's laureate, might have had the same
expectations in Harrington's republic. 'Wit and Gallantry' were valued, for 'to
tell men that they are free, and yet to curb the genious of a People in a lawfull
Recreation unto which they are naturally inclined, is to tell a tale of a Tub'
(220–1/353–4). In a witty riposte to Puritan denunciations of the drama's
immorality, Harrington invents a law which would forbid women found
guilty of sexual immorality from attending public recreations. The love of the
theatre is thus ingeniously turned into an incentive for moral virtue. In a
broader sense, Harrington turned the whole republic into an elaborate piece
of public theatre. Drawing heavily on his memories of Venetian political
rituals, Harrington created a realm in which the kind of balletic grace that had
been cultivated in court masques became democratized and extended to the
nation as a whole. Ceremonial beauty, he believed, could be a spur to virtue
(104/247). One satirist complained that he expected all who would 'hear and
see his *Puppet-play* of a new *Commonwealth*' to be brought at first sight to a
'*Popish blinde obedience*'.[64]

That was a shrewd hit: some later commentators have complained that
Harrington drained the republican idea of its broader social vision by pla-
cating the advocates of aristocratic stability.[65] Like Waller, Harrington presents an idealized version of Cromwell in the Lord Archon, as the man who
can supremely balance opposing interests. During the 1650s Waller was said
to be working on a 'Romance . . . of Our Warr's'.[66] The allegorical romance
was a favourite royalist genre in the 1650s, and the *Oceana*, if not fully a
romance, does appeal to something of the romance-reader's love of fantasy
and spectacle.[67] The republican sublime, it could be argued, had been
reduced to a quasi-courtly beautiful. The book's tone is radically different
from the anti-Augustan diatribes of Streater and his allies. It is playful,

64 *An Answer to a Proposition . . . Proposed by friends to the Commonwealth by Mr.
    Harringtons Consent* (1659; E986.24), title-page.
65 Scott, 'The Rapture of Motion', p. 32, see also Scott, 'The Peace of Silence: Thucydides
    and the English Civil War', in Miles Fairburn and Bill Oliver (eds.), *The Certainty of
    Doubt: Tributes to Peter Munz* (Wellington, 1996).
66 Dorothy Osborne, 24/5 September 1653, *Letters to Sir William Temple*, ed. Kenneth
    Parker (Harmondsworth, 1987), p. 132.
67 Annabel Patterson, *Censorship and Interpretation: The Conditions of Writing and
    Reading in Early Modern England* (Madison, 1984), pp. 190–202; Smith, *LR*, pp. 233–49.
    Romance could however be a genre for utopian speculation, as it had been for John
    Hall.

witty, and self-consciously aristocratic. One of his central tenets is the need for a clear distinction between 'debate' and 'result', between a policy-making senate elected from a landed aristocracy and a popular assembly whose role is to vote on decisions made by the upper house. Here Harrington departs radically from many of the republican opposition of 1656 who were agitating for a return of the old one-chamber Parliament. Where some republicans demanded the exclusion of former royalists from the political process, at least for a lengthy period, Harrington insists on the need to include them, and attacks the decimation tax, a levy on former royalists (50–51/199). He attacks the parsimony which had led the government to sell off cathedrals and palaces that could lend lustre to public affairs (158/295). The aristocracy has an important role in the cultural and political 'superstructure': 'where there is not a *Nobility* to bolt out the people, they are slothfull' (35/183). Harrington here seems to invert the assumptions of Machiavellian civic humanism, which associated aristocratic pre-dominance with sloth and celebrated the energy of urban culture (as in Marten's 'Antepode'). He fears the popular dissension that might ensue from the lack of a 'natural *Aristocracy*' (123/262, cf. 479). For all his differences from Hobbes, Harrington greatly admired him – and his Thucydides translation – and he shared Hobbes's and Davenant's unease at the disruptive effects of uncontrolled popular rhetoric. Another way of putting this would be to say that Harrington Virgilianized republicanism: he offers an ideal commonwealth characterized by agrarian balance rather than civic dissension. Archon frames his summary of the new constitution with two quotations from the *Aeneid*, the first from Deiphoebus's address to Aeneas as he moves towards Elysium (vi.546; 197/333), the second from the description of the safe cove in which the Trojans land after the storm that opens the poem (i.159–64; 203/337). Harrington would have reminded some readers of Denham's figure of the monarchically contained river when he asked '*whether our Rivers do not enjoy a more secure and fruitfull raign within their proper banks, then if it were lawful for them, in ravishing our harvests, to spill themselves?*' (84/230).

But if Harrington Virgilianized republicanism, he could also republicanize Virgil, as will be seen below. For all its conciliatory gestures towards royalists, *Oceana* presents a challenge to readers desiring an easy political haven. They are asked to share the 'Courage' which one of Harrington's poems called for in an author:

> Who writes doth launch a ship, that should not pray
> For calms, but winds to make her streamers play[.][68]

68 Harrington, *An Essay . . .*, sig. A3v.

Readers must be prepared to go beyond the kind of direct identification with timeless virtues which Hobbes had proposed, and instead to set virtue in institutional contexts. Waller had presented the Protectorate as a balance between the Protector's interest and the people's. Harrington presents a new theory of political 'balance' which is designed to show that both monarchical government and the current structure of the aristocracy are totally incompatible with England's economic development. Any balance that does not place the popular interest to the fore will be ultimately unstable, whatever its specious beauty. The end of England's civil wars must then be radically different from the end of Rome's, and Cromwell must be an anti-Augustus. He must indeed, like Waller's and Marvell's Cromwell, be an artist, a creator: 'And, whereas a Book or a Building hath not been known to attaine to perfection, if it have not had a sole *Author*, or *Architect*: a *Common-wealth*, as to the Fabrick of it, is of the like nature' (59/207). But this process of authorship is both critical and collaborative; and it will end up with Archon's recapitulating Harrington's own intellectual development.

At the centre of *Oceana* is a process of humanist self-education: it is here, not in his military achievements, that Archon's true glory is found. In Harrington's imaginary reconstruction of history, the failings of the Commonwealth Parliament 'cast him upon *books*' (58/206) and in particular on Machiavelli's portrait of Lycurgus. He responded to the glory of the founder of a republic as being 'much greater' than military heroism. In language close to the 'Horatian Ode', Cromwell is said to have been 'almost wholly deprived of his naturall rest' by his 'debate . . . within himselfe', and touched by 'the *misery* of the *Nation*' which seemed 'ruined by his *Victory*'.[69] He comes to see that it may be justifiable for one man to use 'extraordinary meanes' to 'get the soveraigne *power* into his own hands' provided that he can use it to gain liberty. Having taken power, he chooses 'fifty select persons to assist him (by labouring in the Mines of *ancient Prudence*, and bringing her hidden *Treasures* unto new light' (59/206–7). The echo here of *Areopagitica*, 'labouring the hardest labour in the deep mines of knowledge' (*MPW*, II, 562), shows how deeply Harrington is concerned with humanist processes of reading. The '*Archives* of *ancient prudence*' are duly 'ransackt', each counsellor choosing a particular constitution for study, and a mechanism is established by which 'the pulse of the people' could be taken by popular participation, so that they 'verily believe when it came forth, that it was no other than that, whereof they themselves had been the makers' (60/209). This process of consultation may indeed look rather manipulative, a little like Plato's 'noble

69 James Holstun, *A Rational Millennium: Puritan Utopias of Seventeenth-Century England and America* (New York and Oxford, 1987), p. 223, speaks of *Oceana* as an 'ode in prose'; I am much indebted to his pioneering reading.

lie'.[70] Once this great debate has taken place, no further deviation from its conclusions will be allowed. All the same, the architecture of this new commonwealth is less of a top-down process than the emphasis on one founder at first suggests, and somewhat closer to the collaborative building of *Areopagitica* which Marvell had tried to adapt in *The First Anniversary*. Harrington's description of the workmen who 'squared Every stone unto this Structure in the quarries of *Ancient Prudence*' (62/210) recalls both Milton's workmen 'squaring the marble' and making 'dissections . . . in the quarry and in the timber'[71] and also Marvell's stones which 'Dans'd up in order from the Quarreys rude' (*The First Anniversary*, line 52). *Oceana* calls not just the Protector but the whole nation to an adventure in reading and in creation.

The commonwealth thus established will indeed be balanced and harmonious, but it will be founded on a radical rereading of ancient prudence which will result in a new kind of *concordia discors*. Harrington believed that for all Machiavelli's genius his analysis had not been radical enough. He had made an opposition between two kinds of republic, the Roman, which had flourished because of its openness to popular participation but had been unstable for the same reason, and the Venetian, which had gained stability at the cost of diminishing the role of the people. Harrington believed that it was possible to square the circle, to secure the popular interest for all time by an ingenious political architecture that gained aristocratic stability without the danger of hereditary stagnation. Oceana's aristocracy is a wholly new creation, based on virtue and industry and imposing severe restrictions on hereditary wealth. Though based in land, the nation's wealth will be defended in arms: there will be no withdrawal into an Augustan peace, nor any slackening of national fibre by 'a nerve of war that is made of purs-strings' (197/332). Harrington's criticism of gold as the nerves of war is more emphatic than Waller's. The traditional English nobility has been laid waste by 'meer luxury and slothfullnesse; which killing the body,

(*Animasq; in vulnere ponunt.*)

kill the Soul also' (177/312). Here, in a neat twist, it is the bees of Virgil's monarchical *Georgics* (iv.237–8) who administer a republican sting. Like Marvell, Harrington refuses to idealize the ancient constitution, whose alleged balance was merely 'a wrestling match' between king, nobles and people (48/196).

One of the main responsibilities of this new aristocracy will be a recovery of ancient rhetorical skills. Harrington invokes Isocrates's *Areopagus* as a key text on public education, and echoes Isocrates's and Milton's praise of the art:

70 Scott, 'The Peace of Silence', p. 115 n. 86.
71 Noted by Holstun, *A Rational Millennium*, p. 258.

> *Elocution is of great use unto your Senators; for if they do not understand Rhetorick*
> *... the advantage will be subject to remain upon the merit of the Art, and not upon*
> *the merit of the Cause ... the treasures of the Politicks will by this means be so*
> *opened, rifled, and dispersed, that this Nation will as soon dote, like the Indians,*
> *upon glasse Beads, as disturb your Government with whimsies, and freaks of*
> *mother-wit; or suffer themselves to be stutter'd out of their Liberties.* (148–9/286)[72]

A nation educated in republican values will not repeat the mistake of the Romans who 'let-in the sink of *Luxury*, and forfeited the inestimable treasure of *Liberty*' (40/188). It is true that Harrington offers a more restricted place for rhetoric and the public sphere than other republicans.[73] Deliberative rhetoric is confined to the aristocracy, whose assembly, the Senate, is 'the *debate* of the *Common-wealth*' (24/173); debate in the popular assembly will be punishable by death. Nevertheless, an immensely elaborate system of voting will ensure that the (male) people as a whole have the final say on all decisions. Harrington can sound as emphatic as Hobbes and Davenant about the need to keep the people from meddling too much in public affairs, and the decisions they have to take are on resolutions that have been reduced to a kind of enlightened self-interest. Yet they will still need a considerable degree of education into political consciousness. There will be free state schools in every parish, for education is 'the Plastick art of government' and the 'education of a mans Children is not wholly to be committed or trusted unto himself' (162/299). Family education may encourage the preponderance of personal interests; public education enables children to share imaginatively in the public interest of the state.

Harrington's commonwealth offers a new and different kind of balance. Like Marvell, he consistently reworks traditional political imagery. The republic's leaders are

> the *Philosophers* which *Plato* would have to be *Princes* ... and their Steeds are those of *Authority* not *Empire*; or, if they be buckled to the Chariot of *Empire*, as that of the *Dictatorian power*, like the Chariot of the Sun it is glorious for terms and vacations or intervals. And as a *Common-wealth* is a *Government* of *Lawes* and not of *Men*; so is this the *Principality* of the *Virtue*, and not of the *Man*; if that fail or set in one, it riseth in another, which is created his immediate Successour.
> (*Uno avulso non deficit alter,*
> *Aureus, et simili frondescit virga metallo.*

---

72 Pocock tentatively suggests reading 'fluttered' for 'stuttered', but the association of absolutism with the erosion of confidence in public speech is typical of republican rhetorical theory, and is evoked by Harrington with characteristic alliterative vigour.

73 Gary Remer, 'James Harrington's New Deliberative Rhetoric: Reflection of an Anticlassical Republicanism', *History of Political Thought* 16 (1995), 532–57. Remer, however, contrasts Harrington's public sphere with ancient republics; by the standards of seventeenth-century England, popular participation in Oceana would still have been extensive.

And this taketh away that vanity from under the Sun, which is an errour proceeding more or lesse from all other Rulers under heaven but an equal *Common-wealth*. (34/182–3)

Here the solar imagery traditionally associated with monarchs is shown to be more appropriate for the perpetual renewal of republican power. The allusion to the golden bough that leads Aeneas into the underworld (*Aeneid* vi.143–4) harnesses the magical mystique of monarchy to a demystified republican order. The solar imagery is in turn given a Christian cast by the allusion to Ecclesiastes. When Archon withdraws from politics, the 'obscurity . . . into which my Lord *Archon* had now withdrawn himself, caused an universal sad-nesse and cloud in the minds of Men upon the glory of his rising Common-wealth' (209/343). Archon is associated with the sun in a conventionally monarchical way, but his people must learn that his withdrawal allows the republican sun to rise: the disruption of expectations here is parallel to the sunrise at the end of *The First Anniversary*, though in a more unequivocally republican direction.

Harrington reworks cosmic imagery in order to devalue organic stability and to bring his readers to prefer a movement and energy that offer sublimity. It is best not to base a commonwealth upon custom because 'manners that are rooted in men, bow the tendernesse of a *Common-wealth* coming up by twigs unto their bent' (59/207). Harrington does transfer to his republic Virgil's comparison of the resolute Aeneas to a tree (*Aeneid*, 4.445f):

For the depth of a Common-wealth is the just height of it.

Ipsa haeret Scopulis et tantum vertice ad auras
Aethereas, quantum Radice ad Tartara, tendit.
She raises up her head unto the Skies,
Near as her Root unto the center lies. (68/216)

But the 'root' here is a system of election. Waller had declared that the nation can 'lift her Head above the rest' only because Cromwell is 'rais'd above the rest'; Harrington uproots that kind of monarchical language. In another arboreal comparison, Archon declares that his state

must have earth for her root, and heaven for her branches.

Imperium Oceano famam quae terminet astris.(185/320)

At *Aeneid* i.287 Jove prophesies Rome's imperial destiny and the triumph of Caesar in the Augustan peace; but Archon goes on to show that the Augustan peace not only did not but could not work.

Again and again organic metaphors are deployed only to be revalued. A Parliament with perpetual rotation of members resembles 'an Orange-Tree: such as is at the same time an education or spring, and an harvest too' (125/264). The striking phrase 'an education or spring' brings together republican ideology with natural process, and also recalls the 'perpetuall spring, and harvest' of Spenser's Garden of Adonis (*The Faerie Queene*, III.vi.42). Where Harrington alludes to Eden, it is to focus on its ever-flowing rivers (124/264). His political earth is in exhilarating motion:

> But why should not this Government be much rather capable of duration and steddinesse by a motion? than which *God* hath ordained no other unto the universall Common-wealth of Mankind: seeing one Generation cometh, & another goeth, but the Earth remaineth firme for ever; that is in her proper Situation or Place, whether shee be moved or not moved upon her proper Center. (149–50/287)

Here the final clause pulls the ground momentarily from under the reader's feet, raising doubts about whether the Ptolemaic or Copernican system is correct, before relegating such doubts to insignificance beside wonder at the system's perpetual motion. (As will be seen, Milton was to aim at a comparable effect in *Paradise Lost*.) The voting process that secures representation at its most stable and transparent can also leap into the sublime because it is also ever-changing: '*The Bowl which is thrown from your hand, if there be no rub, no impediment, shall never cease: for which cause the glorious* Luminaries *that are the* Bowles *of* God, *were once thrown for ever; and next these, those of* Venice' (84/229). Like Marvell, Harrington associates the energy of a reformed commonwealth with circular movement: his commonwealth is a circle (206/339) and its 'Motions . . . are Spherical, and sphericall motions have their proper Center' (85/230). Unlike Marvell, however, he removes the consoling presence of an individual Protector from the centre; these motions are those of eternally valid laws rather than of individuals, and they thus resist easy imaginative embodiment.

Like Marvell, Harrington contrasts this political energy with the inert beauty of monarchical government. His fictitious names for monarchs evoke slothfulness: King James becomes 'Morpheus'. Any vitality that may still be shown by kingship is merely a death-spasm:

> Look you to it, where there is tumbling and tossing upon the bed of sickness, it must end in death, or recovery. Though the people of the world in the dregs of *Gothick* Empire, bee yet tumbling and tossing upon the bed of sickness, they cannot dye, nor is there any means of recovery for them, but by ancient prudence[.] (197/332)

Like Wither, Harrington uses biblical language to prophesy the end of empire:

> These Gothick Empires that are yet in the world, were at the first, though they had legs of their own, but an heavy and unweildy burden, but their foundations being now broken, the Iron of them entereth even into the souls of the oppressed, and hear the voice of their Comforters. *My father hath chastised you with whips, but I will chastise you with scorpions* (187/322, citing Rehoboam's absolutist counsellors, I Kings XII.11).

However, Harrington is readier than Wither to give secular explanations for biblical language. Like Marvell, he can view kings with mock-serious sympathy as a doomed species, blinded to their real interest by reason of state (22/171). Charles I never had a quieter elegy than the comment that 'the *dissolution* of the late *Monarchy was as natural as the death of a man*' (54–5/203). Cromwell will be censurable for limited thinking as much as for wickedness if he tries to take the crown: '*Aut viam inveniam aut faciam*, was an *Adage of Caesars*;[74] and there is no standing for a *Monarchy* unlesse she find this *Ballance* [the old, and no longer sustainable, balance] or make it' (50/199).

Not only will Cromwell be liable to the republican tradition's condemnation of Caesar if he takes the crown, he will make a fool of himself by trying to follow an impossible path. Harrington echoes the *Pharsalia* in describing the dissolution of the ancient constitution: 'the house of *Peers* . . . now sinking down between the *King* and the *Commons*, shewed that *Crassus* was dead, and *Isthmus* broken' (50/198, cf. *Pharsalia*, i.99–106). But if Virgil had been over-optimistic in his belief that Augustus could construct a benign political architecture, Lucan had in some ways been over-pessimistic, failing to see that remedies had been possible:

> *Rome* was said (*Mole sua ruere*) to bee broken by her own weight, but Poetically. For that weight by which she was pretended to bee ruined, was supported in her Emperors, by a farre slighter foundation. And in the Common experience of good Architecture, there is nothing more known, than that buildings, stand the firmer and the longer for their own weight[.] (185/320)

The problem with the Roman state was not its collapse but precisely the fact that it failed to collapse, that the emperors were able to patch up a corrupt structure and ensure that it endured for another millennium. Even where an individual like Augustus might make some good laws, the effect was only to shore up an ultimately repressive system (39/187). This Lucan quotation comes immediately after the reference to Jove's imperial prophecy: the effect is not so much to disparage poetry as to urge a more complex imaginative process which can synthesize and go beyond the achievements of the past. Those who refuse that process make themselves ridiculous. In *Oceana* the comic butt is the aristocratic fop Epimonus de Garrula, who laments that the new democratic order will be taken over by smiths and football-players (152–4/289–91). Archon's first retort is to cite a Virgilian reference to the forging of Aeneas' arms: even on traditional terms, smiths may have divine dignity, and these are 'Smiths of the fortune of the Common-wealth, not such as forg'd hobnails, but Thunderbolts' (154/291). As for the football-players,

---

74 This motto had been used on a royalist battle-flag: Alan R. Young and Beert Verstraete (eds.), *Emblematic Flag Devices of the English Civil Wars 1642–1660* (Toronto, Buffalo and London, 1995), p. 13.

they prompt a sudden shift from the ridiculous to the sublime: 'bright Armes were their Cudgels, and the World was the Ball that lay at their Feet' (154–5/291–2).

Much of *Oceana* sustains a cheerful confidence in Archon/Cromwell's ability to be won over by humanist republicanism and repudiate monarchical designs. The conception of this part of the work may date from the Commonwealth or from the earlier stages of the Protectorate, when Milton and more particularly Marvell were confident that Cromwell could be an agent of restored liberty. By the time the work appeared, however, such confidence was growing harder to sustain. *Oceana* was entered in the Stationers' Register on 19 September 1656, two days after the assembly of a Parliament for which republicans had mustered their forces and in which proposals for Cromwellian kingship were to be made. It was printed by John Streater and one edition was sold by the radical publisher Livewell Chapman; its publication lent its voice to the republican opposition. Harrington refrains for most of the treatise from the savage attacks of other republicans; like Milton and Marvell, Harrington presents Cromwell as the one man who alone can save the commonwealth, who will have 'reduced her unto her principles' (187/322), though Harrington offers a more complex model of reduction. Harrington likewise praises Cromwell for refusing the crown and suggests that republican virtue is more sublime than the superficial beauties of monarchy.

But the final section of *Oceana*, 'The Corollary', which addresses the kingship issue directly, strikes a different note. It is paginated separately and may be a late addition, addressing the Parliament's concerns.[75] 'The Corollary' is a fictionalized version of Marvell's subject, 'the first year of this Government' (218/352), re-imagined as the self-unkinging which Wither urged on the Protector; but the tone is far more stringent and ironic than in either of those works. 'Corollary' etymologically refers to a small crown; Harrington glances ironically at the debate over crowning Cromwell in placing his imagined abdication as a somewhat anticlimactic supplement, a consequence of his arguments which is so obvious that it scarcely needs spelling out.[76] The scene in which the senators, astonished at his sudden decision to abdicate, try to 'lay violent hands on him' to stop him leaving (208/342), is a brilliantly comic reversal of his dissolution of the Long Parliament. Harrington then offers an imagined version of his installation as Protector. The powers conferred on him resemble in some ways those of the Instrument of Government: he becomes 'the greatest Prince in the World' in 'the Pomp of his Court'

75 David Armitage, 'The Cromwellian Protectorate and the Languages of Empire', *Historical Journal* 35 (1992), 531–55 (548–9).

76 Holstun describes 'The Corollary' as 'a manual of state etiquette showing the people and their legislator how to behave when the former graciously show the latter to the door' (*A Rational Millennium*, p. 228).

(218/351), he is voted a substantial income and has command of the army and the reception of ambassadors. His powers, however, are far more radically limited than in the Instrument, for the army will be retained for three years only, and he has no other spheres of authority.

The speech in which the new regime is announced to the people gives a sharp republican twist to the oratory that actually accompanied his installation. The people should be especially grateful to God when they recall 'the Common wealth of *Rome* falling upon her owne victorious Sword' (211/345, cf. *Pharsalia* i.3). Alexander's kingly glory served only to 'infect the ayre with his heaps of carkases', and yet he might today be praised if he had 'restored the Liberty of *Greece*' (211/345). The commissioners recall Machiavelli's caveat: 'Let no man . . . be circumvented with the Glory of *Caesar*, from the false reflection of their pens, who through the longer continuance of his Empire in the name then in the family, changed their freedome for flattery' (212/345–6). Caesar was in fact more execrable than Catiline. It is difficult to thank Archon, because to be grateful is to imply that one owes something, and liberty should be a right rather than a gift from above. The conventions of demonstrative oratory receive a very sharp reduction to republican principles. The people's orator, Argus, praises Archon as 'he who is able to doe harm, and doth none' (215/348) – an echo of Shakespeare's sardonic praise of the coercive charm of the young man in sonnet 94.[77] Argus's speech is presented satirically, and yet we are also told with some irony that the tribunes 'are since become better Orators then were needfull' (216/350): the speech is an experiment in a new mode of democratic oratory. For all its ingenuousness, the speech does make the point that the people's gratitude is complex because the new constitution is a full expression of their own desires and interests, so that in effect they are merely thanking themselves. The Senate rather than the Protector are the fathers of the people (215/348–9). We are then told how, contrary to the arrogant expectations of 'men, addicted unto Monarchy', the commonwealth proceeds 'to cloath her self in Purple' (219/353): imperial attributes are transferred to the republic.

Even the account of the revival of drama is given a republican edge: in this state it is poets, not Protectors, who receive gold crowns. And their plays, we may assume, inculcate republican principles, as did the imaginary play before Julius Caesar with which Archon is uncomfortably regaled not long before his installation (204–5/338). The play contrasts murder and decadence under the Roman Empire with the republican virtue of the Genoese leader Andrea Doria, and leads Caesar to fall into a 'horrid distortion of limbs and countenance'. There is a parallel with the uncomfortable effect *Oceana* is calculated

---

77 Harrington expects readers to pick up an allusion to *1 Henry IV*, II.iv.265, in *The Prerogative of Popular Government* (*HPW*, p. 409).

to have on Cromwell: 'The aesthetic pleasure that both he and Lycurgus take in contemplating the motions of their republican orders is in part the pleasure of self-extinction'.[78]

The book ends when Archon 'had now seen fifty years measured with his own unerring Orbes' (224/357): his death – at the age of 116 years – blends into the natural cycles of the reformed commonwealth. Harrington draws a lengthy parallel with Timoleon, who hated tyrants so much that he killed his tyrannical brother, and was delighted when he was attacked by demagogues in the assembly because he had longed to 'live to see the *Syracusians* so free, that they might question whom they pleased' (225/358). Timoleon went blind but was treated with great reverence. Archon's life, we are told, was 'exactly the same again', 'save that he had his senses unto the last, and that his Character as not the Restorer, but the Founder of a Common-wealth, was greater' (225/358). Milton had cited Timoleon as a precedent for virtuous anti-tyrannical blindness in the *Second Defence* (*MPW*, IV:1, 585). Harrington's raising the possibility that Cromwell might go blind, and then withdrawing it, does not seem to have any political relevance unless it is meant both to link Cromwell with his most prestigious defender and to offer a vague threat.[79] Like Marvell, Harrington recounts the Protector's death in a work addressed to him.

By the time it appeared, *Oceana*'s political prophecies looked less and less likely to be fulfilled, with the Protectorate drifting towards monarchy. Harrington engaged in some controversial exchanges with his critics, but steered clear of further direct interventions in Protectoral politics. Instead, he turned to translating Virgil. He published his version of the first two books of the *Aeneid* along with the eclogues in 1658, and continued with the next four books in 1659. Harrington's preface wryly voiced his political disillusion: 'I have reason'd to as much purpose as if I had rimed, and now I think shall rime to as much purpose as if I had reason'd'.[80] He amplified this antithesis in a prefatory epigram:

> The man's unblest in time or season
> That neither thrives by rime nor reason.
> Reason hath been a sword of might.
> And rime hath been a forked dart.
> Reason could have subdu'd Sir Knight.
> And rime have reach'd a Ladies heart.
> In me alone a rime or reason
> Must either be a crime or treason. (sig. A3v)

78 Holstun, *A Rational Millennium*, p. 229.
79 Timoleon was, however, celebrated by Streater and Lilburne: Smith, 'Popular
   Republicanism in the 1650s', pp. 145–6.   80 Harrington, *An Essay . . .*, sig. A2r.

Yet Harrington does not remain content with this rather simple opposition between masculine rationality and feminine poetry. He also acclaims poetry as 'a sprightly liquor infused into the soule by God himself' (sig. A2v) and claims the precedent of 'the greatest masters of the gravest Arts, as *Moses*, *Lycurgus*, and *Machiavil*, all sufficiently known to have exercised and delighted themselves with Poetry' (sig. A3r). If founding a state resembled creating a building or writing a poem, writing a poem had its own concordant dignity.

In turning to Virgil, Harrington was resuming his contacts with royalist literary interests, and this may seem an unexpected development for a republican. On closer inspection, however, the translation can be seen to reflect his disillusion at the failure of his new synthesis of royalist and republican forms in *Oceana*. His irritation is vented in part on Virgil himself. The only extended commentary on the *Aeneid* translation has declared it a bizarre failure, belonging 'in the history of English eccentricity'.[81] Harrington's version is indeed unorthodox: he cuts extensively, and mingles high style with undignified colloquialisms. This can be put down to sheer incompetence, but given Harrington's interest in Virgilian politics, it is possible that ideological factors enter the equation.

Harrington does not undercut the poem's imperial ideology, perhaps considering it to be too central to be plausibly tampered with, but his general approach is iconoclastic. The 1659 preface was calculated at once to placate and to tease royalist admirers of Virgil. '*Virgil's* poetry,' he declared, 'is the best in Latine'. He added that 'he who can bring it to be the best in English, be his liberty for the rest what it will, shall be his truest translator: which granted, the English Reader may sufficiently judge of like translations, without referring himself unto the Originals'.[82] This claim to be able to equal the original brought Harrington on to more controversial ground. And in a poem addressed to Virgil, he took a briskly iconoclastic stance:

> *Virgil*, my Soveraign in Poetry,
> I never flatter'd Prince, nor will I thee[.] (A5r)

Not that he would be 'injurious to thy name', for it was a 'Crime' to 'hurt a princes fame'. But he proceeded to list seven slips and anomalies in the parts of the poem he was translating, and which he refused to retain:

> Leige Lord,
> In these I may not give thee word for word;
> Nor if my freedom be obtain'd in these,
> Shall I be nice to use it as I please. (sig. A5v)

---

81 L. Proudfoot, *Dryden's 'Aeneid' and its Seventeenth Century Predecessors* (Manchester, 1960), p. 146.

82 James Harrington, *Virgil's Aeneis: The Third, Fourth, Fifth and Sixth Books* (1659; v618), sig. A3v. For reference to first two books, see n. 53 above.

Here the elaborate feudal deference of the sentence's beginning has disappeared by the end. The poem makes it clear, a critic has commented, 'that the relationship of ruler and subject was one that engrossed Harrington's attention'.[83] To some extent Harrington seems to have been guided by a sense of literary decorum, making the protagonists live up to stricter ethical standards. He points out that despite conventional praise of Virgil's balance and harmony, he gives his characters extreme and excessive emotions:

> I will not yeild that the enamour'd Queen
> Should spare a tear that she to stay had no
> Little *Aeneas*, when the great would go.
> Like *Thyas* in the bouncing Bacchanal,
> Like *Pentheus*, mad *Orestes*, never shall
> I shew her overt passion. (1659, sig. A5v)

But Harrington was generally sympathetic towards human foibles, and he certainly did not have a narrow criterion of literary decorum, being ready to admit such 'low' words as 'pots and pans' (1658, p. 8), and to verge at times on mock-heroic effects that are 'anything but Augustan'.[84] Anyone who could speak of 'the Thunder-thumping way of Grandsire *Virgil*'[85] was liable to cause offence. Throughout his version Harrington ruthlessly cuts away moments of pathos and elevation, at times verging on the mock-heroic. The death of Priam, which had formed the end of Denham's 1656 published version, had clear resonances with the execution of Charles I; Harrington pares down the grandeur and pathos:

> His mighty trunk upon the shore is thrown
> A common carkass, and a corse unknown. (1658, p. 38)

He expands on Virgil to stress the laying low of courtly pride:

> Proud columns hatch'd with gold, with trophies hung,
> Are taught humility and laid along. (1658, p. 37)

And he goes a little further than Virgil in stressing Priam's senility:

> His *Troy* on flame, his pallace forc'd, the old
> King, feeble, and decrepid with his years,
> Yet full of courage and resolv'd appears
> In unaccustom'd arms to welcome death. (1658, p. 37)

Here the unclosed couplets and the extreme enjambement of 'old/King' are characteristic of Harrington's resistance to the metrical balance that Waller and Denham were aiming at. Proudfoot writes that Harrington's metre is

---

83 Proudfoot, *Dryden's 'Aeneid'*, p. 146.   84 Ibid., p. 151.
85 James Harrington, *Politicaster* (1659; E2112.2), p. 2; *HPW*, p. 707.

closer to that of 1759 than 1659: 'The decadence of the couplet is already pre-figured in its infancy.'[86] But Harrington may rather, like Milton, have absorbed an element of early humanism's dismissal of rhyme as a barbaric innovation. In 1651 his kinsman John Harington had declared that he had 'ever reckon'd the meer Feet, Rime onely but as the *Tincling part* of *Poetry*', and Milton was to make a similar claim in Harringtonian terms in a note to *Paradise Lost*.[87]

Yet Harrington's version of Virgil is not consistently iconoclastic: rather it invites a reading that places Virgil politically and historically, in the way he had recommended in his controversy with Hobbes. In a note to his version of the eclogues, he recalls Virgil's situation as a writer faced with the collapse of the republic and the offer of court patronage. In such a situation the mythology of monarchical balance might seem inviting and imaginatively powerful; but Harrington's historical notes remind us that the Augustan peace, based as it was on an unjust distribution of land, was ultimately unstable. It is on pre-cisely this point that he makes his one insertion as opposed to deletion in his translation, expanding a very brief reference to Ceres into

> Lawgiving Ceres *that inventing corn*
> *Is she, of whom bright Empire first was born,*
> *While men, for Acorns tasting bread, began*
> *To parcel fields by Laws Agrarian,*
> *And thence (as lots have chanc'd to rise or fall)*
> *Become the prize of One, or Few, or All[.]* (1659, p. 21)

The effect is to trouble the poem with a political unconscious, a reminder of problems that its own emergent monarchist myths cannot resolve – just as Harrington believed that figures like Plutarch, Ralegh and Bacon had gained insights which they were unable to acknowledge to themselves (607). Harrington is not uniformly scornful of those myths; his translation is far from being a burlesque, not least because he wishes to reclaim for his own cause those royalists who might too easily fall in with the idea that republicans were uncouth philistines. Indeed, in some cases where Harrington's version reads like an iconoclastic paring away of Virgil's courtly imagery, it proves to be the seventeenth-century royalist poets who are making Virgil more ornate: Harrington would have noted that Virgil was writing before the imperial system had reached its worst excesses. In later, more self-consciously deco-rous translations, including Dryden's magisterial version, 'Most of the virtues of Harrington perished along with the vices'.[88]

86 Proudfoot, *Dryden's 'Aeneid'*, p. 152.
87 John Harington, *The History of Polindor and Flostella* (1651; E1251.3), sig. A3r.
88 Proudfoot, *Dryden's 'Aeneid'*, p. 154.

Any claims that may be made for Harrington's Virgil must be limited. His version is an uneasy compromise between parody and tribute, and it would doubtless be paying him too great a compliment to suggest that all its clumsinesses are deliberate. It bears the signs of an impatient and ingenious writer marking time. The translation was never completed; by the time the second instalment appeared, another republican *occasione* had presented itself.

9

Culture and anarchy? The revival and eclipse of republicanism, 1658–1660

Oliver Cromwell died in September 1658. Less than two years later, Charles II was back on the throne. The intervening period is often described as 'the anarchy'. There was a bewilderingly swift succession of regimes, and after the Restoration it was easy to contrast republican anarchy with the restoration of literary culture under the Stuarts. That model of the relations between culture and anarchy, however, is too simple. Until well into 1660, the Restoration looked far from inevitable and the horizons in this period were unusually open – an experience that was indeed disturbing for many but was also exhilarating for some republicans. One form of monarchism collapsed, and the energies that had gone into trying to form a republican-Cromwellian synthesis could be released for a new republican settlement. The anarchy denounced by conservatives could be seen as part of a new restoration in a non-royalist sense, as a return to first principles; this chaos might be creative. The dizzily succeeding Harringtonian 'jumps' of this period deserve attention in their own right. They also throw light on the political complexion of *Paradise Lost*, on which Milton had already begun working. A closer look at the period without the benefit of hindsight opens up the very different kinds of context for his epic which would be offered had the republican cause prevailed.

The collapse of the Protectorate

One of the volumes which commemorated Oliver's rule was prefaced by an engraving of the Protector wearing a crown and holding a regal orb and sceptre (figure 15).[1] Innocent readers might have taken this to mean that Cromwell had been a king, but Cromwell had held back from being crowned

---

1 [Henry Dawbeny?], *The Pourtraiture of His Royal Highness, Oliver* (1659; D448A). The crown may have been made in the spring of 1657 when proposals for kingship were at their height: Roy Sherwood, *The Court of Oliver Cromwell* (1977), p. 165n.

to the end. The engraving in fact depicted the elaborate waxen effigy which had been displayed before his funeral, following the precedent of the funeral of James I. The crown that had hovered provocatively above his head for so long had settled there only on his death, and it was unaccompanied by any formal declaration of kingship. The funeral ceremony began with great pomp but petered out uncertainly, showing, a royalist observed, that the organizers were novices in regal ceremonial.[2] Poets commemorating the event were understandably hesitant.

> But soft, Must CROMWELL to an Abbey goe?
> The name of *Abbeys* is to *Cromwell*'s Foe:

asked Samuel Slater. But by invoking Thomas Cromwell's reforms under Henry VIII, Slater was able to root the Protectorate in royal tradition, and could imagine that the dust of Elizabeth and Edward VI would rise to greet him in 'Seventh *Henry*'s, or *Cromwell*'s Chappel, which you please'.[3]

The equivocations over the funeral capture the persistent ambiguity of Cromwell's own relationship with kingship. The Quaker Edward Burrough was moved by the funeral ceremonies to fiercely contradictory emotions that reveal how much of a strain the Protectorate had placed on radicals' allegiances. Returning to London without knowing the funeral was to be held that day, he was astonished to see Cromwell's effigy being carried along. He was so angry that he felt an urge to ride through the guards and urged the crowd to take revenge on 'this Image, and Image-makers, and Image'. He lamented that the great iconoclast should have ended up as an idol:

> Was it but a few years since that he, and his Army, and his Servants, and Children, and Officers were so zealous to overthrow Images, Pictures, and Idols, that they could not endure the sight and worshipping of them? and have they now made an Image of him, which his Officers, Children, and Kindred are carrying from place to place, and following it, and multitudes caused to wonder after it?

His response was not unusual: on the day of the funeral, printed papers attacking its expense and vanity and vindicating the Long Parliament were distributed.[4] But Burrough also shared with many citizens an ambivalence stemming from residual loyalty to Cromwell as the embodiment of the cause. Cromwell himself, he meditated, would never have approved of such idolatry; but then he reflected that he was not so sure, that he 'did too much forgett that good cause' of religious reformation, so that it was appropriate for

---

2 Moore to Hyde, 26 November 1658, *Calendar of the Clarendon State Papers, vol. IV: 1657–1660*, ed. F. J. Routledge and Sir Charles Firth (Oxford, 1932), 113.

3 Samuel Slater, *A Rhetorical Rapture* (1658; S3969).

4 François Guizot, *History of Richard Cromwell and the Restoration of Charles II*, trans. Andrew R. Scoble, 2 vols. (1856), I, 270; see also *The Clarke Papers*, ed. C. H. Firth, 4 vols. (1891–1901), III, 172.

15 Cromwell's funeral effigy: Title-page of [Henry Dawbeny?], *The Pourtraiture of His Royal Highness, Oliver*, 1659.

him to be commemorated in an idol. But then 'in the midest of my considerations, a pitty struck through me for once noble *Oliver*'.[5] Burrough was plunged into emotional turbulence by the difficulty of disentangling his hatred for the monarchical tendencies of the Protectorate from his personal feelings for Oliver.

Richard Cromwell had to make what he could of the monarchical trappings without the same kind of personal attachment. He was proclaimed Protector immediately on his father's death. The impression was then given that he had succeeded in monarchical manner by primogeniture – an impression all the stronger since Richard had shown far less ability for rule than his younger brother Henry. The 'Humble Petition and Advice' had never been more monarchical than in its giving the Protector *carte blanche* to declare any successor he pleased without consulting Parliament. To the present day, doubts have been raised as to whether Cromwell may not have nominated the army leader Charles Fleetwood; the circumstances of nomination and election were treated as mysteries of state which were and remain obscure to the public sphere. The funeral ritual had reinstated the idea that the state was indissolubly linked with the personal bodies of a dynasty. The effigy had been made by Thomas Simon, who had earlier crafted the Great Seal of the Commonwealth: now the imagery of an exchange between equals gave way to a frozen mask of personal rule.

At first the Cromwell dynasty seemed secure. Loyal addresses poured in, often stressing that celebrations for his acclamation outdid those of former monarchs. Faced with the Protectorate's appropriation of the royalist tradition, exiles despaired at the absence of signs of popular Stuart monarchism. Little by little, however, Cromwellian monarchism unravelled. Members of the 'prudentiall party' acclaimed Richard because 'itt would make our enemies stand amazed abroad to see such unity att home' but were biding their time for a possible change of government.[6]

The process by which the Cromwellian succession dissolved can be traced in the poems commemorating its foundation.[7] Some elegists for Cromwell adopted a straightforwardly Augustan language. A medal struck for his death set the tone by representing the realm as a pastoral world under the dynasty's protective olive-tree. The motto derived from Virgil's description of the golden bough; as has been seen, Harrington had revised these lines to refer to

---

5 E[dward]. B[urrough]., *A Testimony against a Great Idolatry* (1658; B6032), pp. 2–5.
6 *Clarke Papers*, III, 162.
7 The first stages in the formation of Cromwell's image are helpfully surveyed by John Morrill, 'Cromwell and his Contemporaries', in Morrill (ed.), *Oliver Cromwell and the English Revolution* (London and New York, 1990), pp. 259–81; though the present account offers a modest corrective to his assertion that pro-Cromwellian literature does not use classical parallels (p. 273).

the immortality of a commonwealth, but here they were adapted more conventionally to dynastic continuity.[8] One poet, turning the *Aeneid* to Richard's praise, told his wife:

> Though *Virgil* ben't much your acquaintance, yet
> You must confesse, you owe him no small debt ...[9]

Another equally baldly said to Richard: 'Your father *Julius* was; *Augustus* be'.[10] Cambridge University issued a commemorative volume, as it had regularly done for monarchs. One contributor, whether from tactlessness or subversiveness, drew attention to the very predictability of the process:

> Pardon, fam'd Sir, whil'st we thy praise reherse,
> That we confine thee to our scanty verse ...
> Thou art, what? stay —- the *Cesar* of our time,
> Pardon, we lisp, we must consult our Rhyme.

Another, inverting Lucan's opening, wrote that Oliver had banished war from the Emathian fields and closed the gates of Janus; another asked 'where is *Rome* if *Cesar* be not there'.[11] An Oxford elegist ran perilously close to recalling Lucan's tribute to the top-heavy Nero:

> His *Royall* burden would weigh down the Sphear,
> Had *He* not left his *Son* an Atlas here.[12]

Waller, the pre-eminent Cromwellian Augustan, issued a short poem which compared the Protector to Romulus, who had been worshipped as a deity on his death, and continued the *Panegyrick*'s emphasis on foreign conquests (*WP*, II, 34–5). The language was conventional to monarchist encomium: the elements had mourned in sympathy with his death. Waller's poem on the Santa Cruz victory, with its concluding prophecy of Cromwell's coronation, was republished in a memorial volume the following spring with praise of 'the English *Virgil* of our times, Mr. *Edmund Waller*'.[13] In his own celebration of Cromwell's 'Apotheosis', Payne Fisher praised the 'most incomparable ingenious Mr *Waller*' for this poem.[14]

But Waller's poetry once again found it impossible to rally the national

8 Annabel Patterson, *Pastoral and Ideology: Virgil to Valéry* (Berkeley and Los Angeles, 1987), fig. 2, p. 55.
9 Henry Dawbeny, *Historie & Policie Re-Viewed* (1659; E1799.2), p. 273.
10 Thomas Pecke, *Parnassi Puerperium* (1659; E1861.1), p. 170.
11 *Musarum Cantabrigiensium Luctus & Gratulatio* (Cambridge, 1658; C345), sigs. H3r, E1r, E4v, G4v.   12 T. M., *An Oxford Elegy* (broadside, n. pl., n. d.; M83A).
13 Samuel Carrington, *The History of the Life and Death of his most Serene Highness, Oliver* (1659; E1787.1), sig. A8v, pp. 195–8. Carrington misleadingly declared the poem to be 'never till now published'.
14 Payne Fisher, *Threnodia Triumphalis* (1659; F1040A), sigs. C1v, F1r.

consensus at which it aimed. Like the *Panegyrick*, the elegy provoked satires and parodies from both Stuart and republican directions.[15] This time Wither, who had long had the practice of sniping at Waller, joined the fray. As Wither unpicks the language of Waller's elegy, he is also discrediting the kind of guarded, politically critical Cromwellianism to which he himself had subscribed. *Salt upon Salt* is still in some sense a Cromwellian poem in that Wither declares himself ready to submit to Richard's rule.[16] He does so, however, in the most grudging terms possible, accepting his title 'by what way soe'er it was acquir'd' (p. 40) and repeatedly hoping that though his rule is an '*Expedient*' (p. 39), old liberties will eventually be 'restor'd' (pp. 40, 42). Wither undermines any complimentary status his current praise may have by calling in question his former writings:

> It is enough, that *Princes* whilst they live
> Are borne withal; and that whilst they survive
> We hide their failings . . . (p. 14)

Tyranny is better than anarchy. This Hobbesian view, however, is presented in terms that are even more demeaning for princes than for subjects: he will flatter rulers

>   so far
> As by our *Servants*, Children flatter'd are,
> To make them do their Duties . . . (p. 15)

And he laments Cromwell's fostering of monarchist tendencies with the familiar 'king-thing' rhyme:

> To *govern us*, we long'd for such a *Thing*
> As other Nations have; forsooth, a *King*,
> With all the former burthensome *Aray*
> Of *Kingship* . . .
> We gave him Attributes, which unto none
> Belongs, but to the *Deitie* alone;
> And towards him, our selves so oft behaved,
> As if by him alone, we could be saved . . . (pp. 30–1)

He hints that Cromwell's death may have been caused by continuing ambitions for kingship, and laments that he had been posthumously crowned, especially since the ceremonies were patterned on those for the idolatrous Philip II of Spain (p. 18): political idolatry was on the increase. And he extends his attack to the currently appearing elegies, which normally included praise

---

15 For royalist parodies, see [Richard Watson], *The Panegyrike and The Storme* (n. pl., 1659; W1092) sigs. D1vff, and two poems attributed to William Godolphin, one in *J. Cleaveland Revived* (1660; E2122.2), pp. 119–20, the other widely circulating in manuscript: see Beal, 567.   16 George Wither, *Salt upon Salt* (1659; E1827.2; *WMW*, IV).

of the current Protector.[17] Those who wished that Richard, like Elisha, should receive twice his predecessor's spirit were merely wishing more evil on him (p. 30).

Wither's main target was Waller's elegy, whose text he printed at the beginning of his own pamphlet (pp. 1–2) so that the reader could savour its systematic destruction. Wither begins by acknowledging the poem's virtues: it was the best of its kind. It soon becomes clear, however, that this is not much of a compliment, for it is the poetry of one who 'takes much more care then I,/What will best please' (p. 5). He attacks Waller's use of the pathetic fallacy as idolatrous: the storm on Cromwell's death may have been like the one which struck the Israelites when they asked Samuel for a king (pp. 34–5).

> *So,* Nature, *hath took Notice of His Death,*
> *And, sighing, swel'd the Ocean with her breath,*
> *The Death of her great* Ruler *to foreshew,*
> As 'twas presaged when my *Cat* did *Mew.* (p. 11)

Waller's

> On *Oeta's* top, thus *Hercules* lay dead,
> With ruin'd Oaks, and Vines about him spread

becomes

> *And, so, on* Oeta, Hercules *lay dead,*
> As *Chalk*'s like *Cheese,* and *Beer* is like to *Bread.*

Wither proceeds to attack Waller's secular grounds for praising Cromwell, the military victories which pave the way for empire:

> *So, from the Continent, He Towns hath torn,*
> As he, who tears a Hedge, and gets a Thorn . . . (p. 8)

Waller's vision is one of endless imperial expansion:

> The *Ocean,* which our Hopes had long confin'd,
> Could give no Limits to his Vaster Minde . . .
> Under the *Tropick,* is, our Language spoke,
> And Part of *Flanders* hath receiv'd our Yoke.

Wither deflates that vision in an early, and powerful, poetic protest against imperialism:

> What *Comfort* yields it, to impose a *Yoke*
> On others, if our *Fetters* be not broke? . . .
> What *Pleasure* brings it, if our *Confines* be

---

17 Wither singles out unfortunate phrases from John Rowland, *Upon the Much Lamented Departure of the High and Mighty Prince, OLIVER* (1658; 669f21.11); see *Salt upon Salt,* pp. 4, 29.

Inlarged, if in them, we are not free?
What *Profit* is it, unto us at *Home,*
That some in *Forraign Parts,* inrich'd become,
If, we mean while are *Beggars?* or else more
At least, impov'rish'd, then we were before?
What *Honour* is it, that, both *Tropics* hear
Our *Language,* if to speak *Truth,* few men dare? (p. 9)

Why, asks Wither, should we applaud

Those Deeds, for which, LAW, to their *Actors* gives
The stiles of *Pyrats, Murtherers* and *Thieves.* (p. 10)

These wars were waged without the full assent of Parliament.

Wither's language was now merging with that of the republican opposition
to Cromwell; and indeed his publisher, Livewell Chapman, was to be the
leading publisher of republican texts in 1659. In conclusion, he expressed the
somewhat unlikely hope that Waller might have 'so generous a minde' as to
thank Wither for putting him back on the right path – presumably by declaring his dissatisfaction with the regime (p. 49). Waller's political status was so
ambiguous that one royalist author of a reply to the *Panegyrick* had hoped he
might still somehow be redeemed for their cause. But the elegy destroyed that
hope; the attempt to placate the more conservative of both royalists and
Parliamentarians was very hard to sustain.[18]

The difficulty was clearly demonstrated in the most ambitious of the
elegies for Cromwell, that by Andrew Marvell. Marvell had moved closer and
closer to the regime in its last phase, having at last gained an official appointment in 1657. When two of Cromwell's daughters married into noble families later in the year, Marvell joined Waller and Davenant in composing
commemorative poems, celebrating Cromwell in courtly terms as '*Jove*'.[19]
Waller's elegy, hyperbolical as it may have been, conspicuously refrained
from mentioning Cromwell's son; and indeed the reference to Romulus was
not obviously favourable to Richard, since on that king's death the power of
appointing his successor had reverted to the people.[20] Marvell, more than
any other poet, treated Cromwell as a prince who had founded a dynasty;

18 [Watson], *The Panegyrike and The Storme,* sig. F2r. Waller's elegy was also parodied by
Mildmay Fane: 'Le Monde Renversé', Fulbeck Middle MS.
19 Hutchinson, p. 209; Marvell, 'Two Songs at the Marriage of the Lord *Fauconberg* and the
Lady *Mary Cromwell*', *MPL,* I, 125–9; *SR,* II, 157; Waller, 'On the Marriage of Mrs Frances
Cromwell', in Beverly Chew, *Essays and Verses about Books* (New York, 1926), pp. 29–32.
20 Thomas Scot cited in Parliament on 18 February the famous comment by Livy that the
Romans did not choose a republic on Romulus's death because they had not yet tasted
the sweets of liberty: *Diary of Thomas Burton,* ed. John Towill Rutt, 4 vols. (1828; rptd ed.
Ivan Roots, New York and London, 1974), III, 336, 18 February 1659; Harrington cited the
same passage in *Pour Enclouer le Canon* (1659; E980.6), p. 2; *HPW,* p. 728.

and he tried to establish a new ethos for his successor.[21] His elegy is normally, and not unreasonably, seen as inferior to his other Cromwell poems; but his political task made it essential to adopt a different tone. The Cromwell of *The First Anniversary* had been a unique agent of millennial and quasi-republican reform, and Marvell had already provided him with an anticipatory elegy lamenting the political chaos that would follow his fall. The abandonment of the Instrument of Government had already shifted the character of the Protectorate into a more traditional mould. Now that a dynasty had been established, he had to arouse loyalty for a very different kind of ruler. That this strategy was deliberate can be confirmed by comparing Marvell's elegy with verses by an Oxford poet which likewise claimed that it was easier to praise the Protector once one had the perspective provided by his death. In that poem, however, the emphasis is on Cromwell's sublime unrepresentability:

> Th' earth ne're was seen at once, nor can a minde
> Larger then that, & more unconfinde.[22]

In stressing that Cromwell was 'His owne originall & copy too' (p. 84), the poet leaves no space for celebrating his connections with a dynasty: Cromwell remains *sui generis*.

By contrast, Marvell is too concerned to establish common factors between father and son to retain this kind of sublimity. He sets the new note at the beginning by lamenting that the people

> blame the last Act like Spectators vaine
> Unlesse the Prince whom they applaud be slaine[.] (lines 9–10)

Cromwell's death is anti-climactic: where in the earlier Cromwell poems he is seen as bursting through generic boundaries, moulding traditional forms anew, here he seems unable to fill expected forms. As in the other poems, readers are invited to readjust their expectations, but this time they are brought from the sublime to the beautiful, and the pace is slowed down. In earlier poems Marvell had called on the poet to accelerate into Cromwell's orbit from his languishing shadows, but here Cromwell's death is both caused by and a mirror of his daughter's 'slow and languishing disease' (line 29). He is given the traditionally female attribute of the nurturing pelican, and the deep

---

21 Marvell, 'A Poem upon the Death of his late Highnesse the Lord Protector', Bodleian MS Eng.poet.d.49, pp. 151ff. The 1681 Folio text breaks off at line 184, but this copy contains a late seventeenth-century manuscript version of the whole poem. As Nigel Smith will argue in his forthcoming edition, this is preferable as copy-text to the composite version in *MPL*, 1, 129–37. See also Charles Larson, 'Marvell's Richard Cromwell: "He, Vertue Dead, Revives"', *Mosaic* 19:2 (1986), 57–67.

22 'On Oliver Ld Protector Occasiond by ye many coppies of verses made after his death', Bodleian MS Locke e 17, pp. 83, 85 (I owe this reference to Nigel Smith).

affinity between father and daughter is central to the poem. Though pathetic fallacy is mustered, as in Waller, to accompany Cromwell's end, we are told that the impact of Eliza's death was almost as great. The poem's central section does chronicle Cromwell's military achievements, linking him with English monarchical tradition in comparisons with Arthur and Edward the Confessor. But we then return to his 'tendernesse' (line 204), which extended from his family to the people as a whole. He is no longer the paradoxically anti-regal sun of *The First Anniversary* but a mild April sun (line 236). Marvell briefly attacks the radical opposition, but in keeping with his milder tone, he tempers his criticism; it is more in sorrow than in anger that he laments the failure of the present generation to represent him properly, being deluded by 'shadows' (line 273). And in a remarkable touch he compares Cromwell to a 'sacred Oake' which has been felled by lightning (line 261). Not only does Marvell draw back from the equation of Cromwell with lightning in the 'Horatian Ode' but he evokes Lucan's comparison of the doomed Pompey to an aged oak. The energetic Caesar has become his defeated antagonist.[23] Cromwell has lost his *virtù*; when we are told that Richard 'vertue dead/Revives' (line 306), it is as if the Machiavellian concept has modulated into a more predictably Christian one. As in *The First Anniversary*, Marvell uses the idea of foreshortening, but here the sublimity has been lost: space rather than time has been foreshortened, so that future generations alone will be able to praise him fully, and he will be celebrated 'As long as future time succeeds the past' (line 285) – a distinctly banal outcome for Marvell's earlier games with temporality.

If Marvell risks anticlimax, it is partly because it is difficult otherwise to position Richard as a logical and worthy successor. Since he lacks any significant political or civil experience, he can best be praised for sharing Cromwell's gentler qualities. Marvell holds back from describing Richard as a king: he is crowned only with the diadem of his tears. But it is only because Richard inherits his father's qualities, not because of his own achievements, that he has become ruler. Marvell claims that 'A Cromwell in an houre a Prince will grow' (line 312); but he has little evidence to offer. Richard did prove himself an unexpectedly eloquent, and attractively conciliatory, figure, and his attempt to unite opposing religious factions gained high praise from such influential ministers as Richard Baxter and may well have been a continuing point of reference for Marvell.[24] But he lacked the exceptional qualities and experience on which his father's rule had been based. *The First*

23 Annabel M. Patterson, *Marvell and the Civic Crown* (Princeton, 1978), pp. 91–3.
24 William Lamont, 'The Religion of Andrew Marvell: Locating the "Bloody Horse"', in Conal Condren and A. D. Cousins (eds.), *The Political Identity of Andrew Marvell* (Aldershot and Brookfield, 1990), pp. 135–56.

Anniversary had been all too accurate in its fears that the Protectorate, for all its institutional safeguards, was ultimately dependent on the charisma of one man. Marvell's plans to publish his elegy seem to have been wrecked by that problem.

On 20 January 1659, a volume to contain three poems on the memory of Cromwell, by Marvell, John Dryden, and Thomas Sprat, was entered in the Stationers' Register. This was a week before Marvell was due to sit for the Protectoral interest in the new Parliament, and the volume would have served as a common declaration of loyalty to the new regime. Marvell's experience, however, was to prove a gruelling one. Standing for his native city of Hull, he found amongst his opponents the redoubtable Sir Henry Vane. Like other committed republicans, Vane refused to admit the legitimacy of any other Parliament than the purged Long Parliament, for which he had been elected in 1640, and thus would have considered himself already to be a duly elected member for the city; but as they had done under Cromwell, the republicans had formed the tactic of exploiting whatever political advantage they could. In the event Marvell was chosen for Hull and Vane was not. 'Great endeavours,' wrote Ludlow, 'were used by the Court' to prevent his election, the government pressing for 'such men to be chosen as were their creatures, and had their dependencies on them'.[25] There is indeed some question as to the fairness of Marvell's election, and Vane protested against 'unjust practices'; in any event Ludlow and Vane would have included Marvell in the category of court-dependents.[26]

Republicans proceeded to exercise an influence on the Parliament far in excess of their number. This could perhaps have been foreseen. In the final session of Oliver's second Parliament, two veterans of the Commonwealth regime, Sir Arthur Haselrig and Thomas Scot, had gained admission to the Lower House and engaged in fiery republican polemics. Haselrig represented the more conservative side of the Commonwealth's leaders, his notoriously short temper betraying an oligarchical cast of mind which had made him an enemy of Lilburne. In the Protectoral Parliaments, however, he became a unifying focus of opposition, 'a personality of almost Texan exuberance and a phenomenal ability to dominate the House by means of bounce, verbosity and calculated eccentricity'. Haselrig was increasingly ready to use a more Harringtonian idiom.[27] A new Parliament had been scheduled for the

25 *The Memoirs of Edmund Ludlow*, ed. C. H. Firth, 2 vols. (Oxford, 1894), II, 51, 49.
26 Pierre Legouis, 'Andrew Marvell: Further Biographical Points', *Modern Language Review* 18 (1923), 416–26 (418–20); Violet A. Rowe, *Sir Henry Vane the Younger* (1970), p. 208; the evidence however is inconclusive.
27 *HPW*, pp. 101–2; J. G. A. Pocock, 'James Harrington and the Good Old Cause: A Study of the Ideological Context of his Writings', *Journal of British Studies* 10 (1970–71), 30–48 (43).

autumn of 1658, though it was delayed and then prevented by Cromwell's illness and death. Commonwealth and Harringtonian republicans had built up an alliance with godly opponents of monarchical rule, and had prepared to galvanize the new assembly by compiling a detailed counter-history of the previous meeting, giving lists of members who had supported kingship and the rewards with which they had allegedly been bribed.[28] Richard's advisers were over-confident that they could manage the new Parliament, and called on it to recognize Richard's succession in the expectation that it would be a pure formality. The republicans, however, seized the opportunity to undermine the regime's rhetoric. While proclaiming allegiance to the Protectorate, they consistently raised general political principles which called its legitimacy in doubt.

The Cromwellians based Richard's succession on the 'Humble Petition and Advice', but one member protested that this was as dead as the Protector himself.[29] Haselrig paid a warm personal tribute to the new Protector, but this is often quoted without recognizing the republican edge such tributes could be given. It was made explicit by another speaker, who declared that while he honoured him, he was not immortal, and that a good chief magistrate could be a disaster for the people.[30] Oliver's reign was held by republicans to have been a particularly strong support for their cause: if even a man of undoubted virtue and fortitude for liberty could be corrupted by high office, who could ever be immune? If Harrington had had some hopes at least in the early stages of *Oceana* that Oliver might be an instrument of republican reform, those hopes had been wholly confounded, and further reform now seemed possible only by undermining the Protectorate. Harrington was assaulting the theoretical basis of the Protectoral constitution in *The Art of Law-giving* at the same time as his friend Henry Neville was regaling MPs with historical arguments that the shifting balance of property made monarchy an unsustainable form of government in England.[31] The republicans apparently advocated the Harringtonian measure of secret ballots for this Parliament, suspecting that many potential supporters would be held back by the public pressure of their colleagues and patrons.[32]

---

28 *A Narrative of the Late Parliament, so called* (1658; E935.5) (on Downing as one of the 'Kinglings' see pp. 11, 22); for information that publication was planned under Oliver see *A Second Narrative of the Late Parliament (so called)* (1659; E977.3*), p. 37.

29 Burton, *Diary*, III, 226 (Thomas Tyrrell, 11 February 1659).

30 Burton, *Diary*, III, 104 (Haselrig, 7 February), 216–17 (Adam Baynes, 11 February).

31 James Harrington, *The Art of Law-giving* (1659; dated 20 February; H806), *HPW*, pp. 599–704; Burton, *Diary*, III, 132ff. Worden, 'Harrington's "Oceana": Origins and Aftermath, 1651–1660', *RLCS*, pp. 111–38 (126ff), stresses the difference in emphasis between the Harringtonians who wanted a radical change and the commonwealth's men who wanted the Long Parliament restored; but he also brings out Neville's tactical skill in uniting different groups.

32 John Thurloe to Henry Cromwell, December 1658, *TSP*, VII, 550.

The republicans' tactics in this Parliament are generally dismissed by historians as empty filibustering, and indeed their speeches were often long historical disquisitions. Yet Ludlow claimed that they had had a more than short-term rationale: 'time was gained to infuse good principles into divers young gentlemen, who before had never been in any public assembly, in hopes that tho for the present their previous engagements should carry them against us, yet upon more mature deliberation they might discover where their true interest lay'.[33] The passions that had motivated Ludlow's generation had lost their resonance for a younger generation who, it was claimed, were entirely Richard's.[34] But Parliament could be used to pass the torch on, and to remind political novices of a longer time-scale. Parallels from classical as well as English history were exceptionally abundant.[35] One member looked back to the time in 1643 when Marten was expelled from the house for declaring that one family could not be balanced with the interest of the people: republicans then had been in a small minority, yet their cause had been vindicated. The republican cause was consistently linked with openness and integrity of speech: truth was at last coming out of the corners into which it had been driven.[36] Again and again, speakers claimed that public language shrivelled into the nervous defence of private interest under the rule of a single person. William Packer, who had been punished by Oliver for oppositional activity, voiced deep cynicism about the panegyrics of the new Protector:

> if ye k. of Scots were landed at Douer, & had a force – to haue as many Addresses. Easily obtained people like a flock of sheepe horrid & abominable flatteryes[.][37]

Opposition sources widely claimed that the stock figures of praise of Richard, such as the comparisons with Joshua, had been orchestrated by Marvell's close associates, Nedham and Thurloe.[38]

These attacks hit at Marvell not only as a nascent politician but also as a poet. In a letter to Downing on the day of Packer's attack, he showed no sign of the impersonal coolness he was to gain in later Parliamentary correspondence:

---

33 Ludlow, *Memoirs*, II, 55–6.
34 John Cooper to Hyde, 4 March 1659, *Calendar of the Clarendon State Papers, vol. IV*, p. 158.
35 Worden, 'Harrington's "Oceana": Origins and Aftermath, 1651–1660', p. 130.
36 Burton, *Diary*, III, 212 (Robert Reynolds, 11 February 1659).
37 BL Additional MS 15, 862, fol. 103v, Burton, *Diary*, III, 161–3 (9 February 1659). I cite the speech in its disjointed note form for purposes of defamiliarization. Burton's diary is a fine compendium of republican rhetoric and was recognized as such by Rutt, its radical editor; but Rutt freely and silently expanded on Burton's telegraphic notes, and this is not evident from the form in which the speeches are normally quoted by historians.
38 See the exhaustive catalogue of addresses, with a commentary attacking their idolatry, published as *A True Catalogue* (1659; E999.12), especially pp. 3, 14, 47, 53, 73ff.

> Their Doctrine hath moved most upon their Maxime that all pow'r is in the
> people. That it is reuerted into this house by the death of his Highnesse, that M^r
> Speaker is Protector in possession and it will not be his wisdome to part with it
> easily, that this house is all England. Yet they pretend that they are for a single
> person and this single person but without negatiue voice without militia not
> upon the petition and advice but by adoption and donation of this House and
> that all the rights of the people should be specifyd and indorsed upon that
> Donation. But we know well enough what they mean . . . They haue much the
> odds in speaking but it is to be hoped that our justice our affection and our
> number which is at least two thirds will weare them out at the long runne.[39]

There is a distinct sense of helplessness in this highly articulate man's confession that his political opponents have so much more effective a command of
rhetoric, that numbers rather than arguments will have to carry the day. A
royalist correspondent writing the following day shared Marvell's belief that
the republicans seemed to have much the better of the argument despite
being outvoted.[40] While a royalist could admire the republicans' eloquence,
Marvell's comments sound more like Hobbes's suspicion of popular assemblies. The courtly tone which he had perfected during the Cromwellian era
was liable to ridicule in the more robust public sphere of the House. Like
Waller, but much more quickly, he was being subjected to a rough political
education in moving from courtly poetry to the tumults of Long Parliament
politics.

Scholars have debated whether this letter reflects Marvell's opinions or
those of his addressee: Downing was Marvell's superior as emissary to the
Netherlands and was celebrated for strongly anti-republican views. He feared
that constitutional wrangling would weaken England's international standing, and even that Richard might be thrown in the Tower.[41] Quite apart from
his patron's views, however, Marvell is likely to have been irritated by the
republicans' disingenuous use of a language of Protectoral praise which he had
explored so seriously in his elegy, and also by the risky tactical alliance that was
emerging between republicans and Stuart royalists. The following month he
protested against the republicans' backing of a petition to release some former
royalists who had been illegally transported.[42] Yet Marvell's support for the
regime put him in some difficult positions. For another political prisoner who

39 *MPL*, II, 307–8.
40 *TSP*, VII, 615–16 (John Barwick to Hyde, 16 February 1659). For the same analysis from a
   republican point of view, see *A True and Impartial Narrative of . . . the Late Parliament*
   (1659; E985.25), p. 6. Derek Hirst, 'Concord and Discord in Richard Cromwell's House
   of Commons', *English Historical Review* 103 (1988), 339–58, argues that the republicans
   were more co-operative than is often assumed.
41 Downing to Thurloe, 28 January 1659, *Clarke Papers*, III, 177, 183 n. 3; 'John Milton
   (1608–74) and Andrew Marvell (1621–78)', in Hill, *WR*, pp. 157–87 (p. 183 n. 30).
42 *MPL*, II, 308.

was released at this time under republican pressure was his old friend Robert Overton, who was weakened from long and unhealthy confinement. A supporter in Parliament had inaugurated the pressure for release by declaring that Overton had been charged merely with his inability to say that black was white.[43] He made a triumphal return to London: a huge crowd bearing laurel branches acclaimed him and diverted his coach from its planned path. The court, it was reported, was 'not at all pleased with his vanity'.[44] Some of Marvell's friends will have felt otherwise.

The three elegies eventually appeared later in the year, with Waller's elegy substituted for Marvell's. The exact reason for this change is unknown.[45] But the alarm he reported to Downing may have been a factor. Within Parliament, the legitimacy of the succession, on which his poem's unity depended, had been ruthlessly undermined; outside, the regime's panegyrists were open targets. In February, the most elaborate of all memorial tributes, Henry Dawbeny's *Historie & Policie Re-Viewed*, appeared with a massively defensive preface. Some readers, he complained, had attacked the book while it was still being printed, and the 'envenom'd Party' who shoot out bitter words against Cromwell 'are pleased to think too much of Panegyrick said of him, in the very Title-page'.[46] In his address to Richard Cromwell, Dawbeny twice claimed amongst other hyperboles that just like his father he could make the sun stand still (sig. A4r, p. 278). Marvell's *First Anniversary* had referred to that miracle (lines 191–2), but he did not risk transferring it to Richard. Dawbeny launched into a lengthy defence of Waller, perhaps in response to the attacks by Wither and others. Marvell may have been happy to see Waller rather than himself exposed to this critical fire at the head of the collection of elegies. Waller's poem was also more appropriate for the escalating crisis of the regime in that it made no mention of the succession. Sprat's poem did pay tribute to Richard, but Dryden, whose poem seems to have been written last,[47] likewise passed him over.

43 Burton, *Diary*, III, 212 (Reynolds, 11 February 1659).

44 Guizot, *History of Richard Cromwell*, I, 336.

45 It has been suggested that Marvell was slow in producing the poem and that the available Waller text was substituted for quick publication: Vinton A. Dearing *et al.*, 'Dryden's *Heroique Stanza's* on Cromwell: A New Critical Text', *Papers of the Bibliographical Society of America* 69 (1975), 502–26 (525); but Marvell's poem reads as if it was written soon after Cromwell's death.

46 Dawbeny, *Historie & Policie Re-Viewed*, sigs. a1v–2r. The book's publication was announced in the *Publick Intelligencer* no. 163, 7–14 February 1659; E761.11, p. 221.

47 Thomas Sprat, 'To the Happie Memorie of the most Renowned Prince, OLIVER', in *Three Poems upon the Death of . . . OLIVER Lord Protector* (1659; W526), pp. 29–30, ending with the stock comparison of Richard to Joshua; John Dryden, 'Heroique Stanza's, Consecrated to the Glorious Memory of OLIVER', ibid., pp. 1–9; *The Works of John Dryden, vol. 1: Poems 1649–1680*, ed. Edward Niles Hooker and H. T. Swedenberg, Jr (Berkeley and Los Angeles, 1956), p. 191.

Dryden was eventually to succeed Waller as the leading conservative public poet, and his elegy initiates the transition. It marks the weary end-point of Protectoral Augustanism, speaking for a generation for which the passions of the Civil War had little meaning. Though he had served the Protectorate in some kind of official function, his connections with the regime came through family associations rather than any ideological conviction. His cousin Sir Gilbert Pickering was a member of Cromwell's 'Other House' and Lord Chamberlain of his court, and hence had responsibility for the highly conservative funeral ritual. He came under attack for a flattering address to Richard.[48] The elegy reflects the climate of this late phase of the Protectorate when the regime was presenting itself mainly as a source of social stability. It draws heavily on Waller's *Panegyrick*, not only in stanza-form and verbal echoes but more generally in the repudiation of political or religious ideology in favour of a resigned acceptance of the *status quo*. In Dryden's poem, however, far more than in Waller's, any idealization of imperial glory is edged with a dourly pragmatic analysis of political interest undercut by recurrent uncertainties and hesitations.[49] There may also be echoes of *The First Anniversary*, but in a characteristically muted form. The opening stanza rebukes the 'Officious haste' of those who would perform Cromwell's funeral rites too quickly. Dryden thus both legitimizes the long-drawn-out, and much-criticized, funeral rituals and establishes a languid persona for the poet very different from the precipitancy of Marvell's earlier Cromwell poems; this poet will praise because it is not only his duty but his interest (stanza 4). Marvell's Cromwell cuts through the circles of normal monarchical time and 'shines the Jewel of the yearly Ring'; Dryden's Cromwell has a fame which is 'truly *Circular*' but is ultimately static, and rather than transcending crowns he merely adorns them, 'to our *Crown* he did fresh *Jewells* bring' (stanza 7). Cromwell is compared to an artist (stanza 24), but one who delegates the light and colours to others, being content only to plan the general design. His art thus becomes a mystery of state, beyond the reach of subjects:

> Thus poor *Mechanique Arts* in publique moove
>   Whilst the deep Secrets beyond practice goe. (stanza 32)

Dryden's only reference to the succession is that '*Faction* now by *Habit* does obey' (stanza 36): Richard is obeyed not because of his intrinsic qualities or his legitimacy but merely from force of habit. By the time the poem appeared, even this decidedly minimal statement of the regime's stability had been

---

48 James Anderson Winn, *John Dryden and his World* (New Haven and London, 1987), p. 80, states that there is no record of Dryden's receiving payment for any salaried post; *A True Catalogue*, p. 31.

49 For a subtle reading see Steven N. Zwicker, *Politics and Language in Dryden's Poetry: The Arts of Disguise* (Princeton, 1984), pp. 70–84.

proved false. Cromwellian Augustanism died in the Dryden–Waller–Sprat volume, though it was to return to haunt its authors after they shifted to celebrating Charles II as the new Augustus. If it was Marvell who decided to withdraw his Cromwell poem, he had judged the climate better than his self-consciously politic colleagues.

Marvell may also have been coming under pressure from Milton. It was probably shortly after Marvell wrote to Downing in defence of the transportation of political enemies that Milton received a letter from an old friend, Moses Wall, in praise of his *A Treatise of Civil Power in Ecclesiastical Causes.* Wall greeted this work as a return to the fold, a coded republican manifesto:

> I was uncerten whether yoʳ Relation to the Court, (though I think a Coṁonwealth was more friendly to you than a Court) had not clouded yoʳ former Light, but yoʳ last Book resolved that Doubt.[50]

Milton had been very cautiously distancing himself from the Protectorate. In 1658 he had prepared for publication two sharply contrasting works. *The Cabinet Council* was a collection of political maxims attributed to Sir Walter Ralegh. Its title associated the work with the crabbed, private intrigues of the kind of courtly reason of state which in republicans' view was becoming established under a single person's rule. As in *Areopagitica*, a classical tag on the title-page obliquely hinted at a political critique. In sharp contrast was a revised edition of his *First Defence*, to which Milton added some quotations from anti-tyrannical poets and a rousing conclusion declaring the work his immortal monument and insisting on its universal relevance. Magnanimous public speech was contrasted with the shrivelled wisdom of courts.[51] The work appeared after Oliver's death but its publication may have been planned to coincide with his next Parliament, where its praise of the republican spirit as opposed to Cromwell would certainly have offered inspiration to the opposition. At the end of the *Second Defence* Milton had called on Cromwell to separate civil and religious powers, but despite the Protector's personal dislike of excessive severity against heresy, the 'Humble Petition and Advice' had reflected conservatives' demands for stronger civil policing of ungodliness; Milton glances parodically at its language (*Treatise of Civil Power, MPW,* VII, 257). In his preface, addressed to Richard's Parliament, he recalled discussions he had heard when he served the republic's Council of State, '*so well joining religion with civil prudence, and yet so well distinguishing the different power of either*' (*MPW,* VII, 240). His language here echoes the sonnet to Vane.

---

50 *MPW,* VII, 510–11. On the possible dating to March rather than May 26 see *MPW,* VII, 83 n. 2.
51 *MPW,* IV:1.536–7; Martin Dzelzainis, 'Milton and the Protectorate in 1658', *MR,* pp. 181–205.

Though in Richard's Parliament Vane was mainly concerned with civil issues, he vigorously intervened to defend Henry Neville against charges of blasphemy. And one of the Parliamentary measures that eventually precipitated the army's intervention was a declaration against blasphemy. In undermining the growing religious conservatism that was becoming a major feature of the Ricardian regime, Milton had 'shaken hands again with the old Republican party'.[52] Its moment now came.

The republican revival

The closest Dryden's elegy had come to acknowledging the political crisis was his sardonic comment that the generals on opposing sides in the war 'The quarrell lov'd, but did the cause abhorre' (stanza 11). The phrase 'the good old cause' swept through political discourse in the spring of 1659 as the Protectorate gave way to a renewed republic. It has aroused the same kind of cynicism amongst later commentators as it did from Dryden, for it became used in a patently opportunistic way to paper over the huge divisions amongst republicans. In the spring of 1659, however, it had enough power to help bring down the government. On 21 April, under army pressure, Richard dissolved Parliament. Fleetwood, despite his shadowy claims as Oliver's true successor, eventually bowed to pressure from junior officers to bring back the Parliament that had been dissolved in 1653. On 7 May a reluctant and ageing Speaker led a small group of MPs back into the Commons chamber; later in the month Richard laid down his power.

The excitement that greeted the restored Parliament may seem puzzling, since many of those who acclaimed it had strongly supported its dissolution by the army back in 1653. Yet the occasion could for a time unite factions that had previously been bitterly divided. If history was being replayed, this time the army was acting with, rather than against, the Parliament. If some civilians such as John Hutchinson remained uneasy about owing their return to power to the army, there were many like John Streater for whom the end justified the means: 'Those that change Tyranny into Free States, do Justifie themselves by the Noble Ends of their proceedings'.[53] At least for the short term, there was a readiness to bury old differences and embark again on the political and religious experiments that had foundered under the Protectorate. For a veteran like Haselrig, the good old cause was a struggle for the supremacy of the House of Commons which could be traced back to time immemorial but

---

52 David Masson, *The Life of John Milton*, 7 vols. (1859–94; rptd New York, 1946), V, 600.
53 J[ohn]. S[treater]., *The Continuation of this Session of Parliament, Justified* (1659; E983.10), p. 16.

had achieved a basically satisfactory resolution in the single chamber of 1649. For Harringtonians, by contrast, the 'Old Cause' could only be realized by the full panoply of a wholly new system of Upper and Lower Houses. Both these groups were satisfied with some kind of broadly tolerant state church. Harrington feared that those who gave priority to freedom of conscience were dangerously liable to make too many concessions over civil liberty, as had happened under Cromwell.[54] For many religious radicals, however, 'the *Good Old Cause*, was (chiefly) *Liberty of Conscience*', and political forms were subordinate.[55] They opposed kingship not so much for reasons of civic prudence but because all earthly kings obstructed the rule of King Jesus. And if secular institutions proved resistant to tolerating the godly, the elect might have to take power into their own hands and rule as a spiritual elite.

To speak of 'the republicans' in this period, then, is to use a potentially very misleading shorthand.[56] And yet the pamphleteer who wrote of 'the Parliaments Cause in the greatest Turnings and Revolutions' was appealing to a sense that the cause had always been a process, discovering its further goals as it achieved initial ones.[57] Wrong turnings might be reached, necessitating a return to an earlier point, as many people believed to be the case of the army with the fall of the Protectorate; yet there might still have been a sense of shared goals. Religious and secular republicans were united in a belief that a sublime simplicity could be recovered from centuries of corrupt encrustation, but that the ultimate institutional form it would take was still in the process of being discovered. Godly rhetoric could be used to present insights derived from Machiavellian republicanism. One pamphleteer, offering detailed parallels between the struggles against ecclesiastical and regal tyranny, declared amidst a generally godly language that corrupt states tend to 'sinke under their own weight', a distant echo of Lucan, though probably mediated by Harrington.[58] Cromwellian rule was denounced above all because it had stifled the old 'lively active spirit'; the godly might urge 'Common-wealth's-men' that the spirit of Sion had to be added to a merely moral spirit, but they recognized a bond that was intangible and yet powerful.[59]

Republicans were ready to find an element of the sublime in the readiness

54 James Harrington, *A Discourse upon this Saying: The Spirit of the Nation is not yet to be trusted with Liberty* (1660; E983.12); *HPW*, pp. 735–45.

55 George Bishop, *Mene Tekel* (1659; E999.13), p. 4.

56 Elizabeth Skerpan, *The Rhetoric of Politics in the English Revolution 1642–1660* (Columbia and London, 1992), pp. 197–236, sees radical discourse in this period as irredeemably fissured.

57 *Some Reasons Humbly Proposed to the Officers of the Army* (1659; E979.8), p. 4.

58 R. Fitz-brian, *The Good Old Cause Dress'd in it's Primitive Lustre* (1659; E968.6), p. 2.

59 *A Narrative of the Late Parliament*, p. 32, *A Second Narrative of the Late Parliament (so called)*, p. 46.

of Richard and Fleetwood to return power to the people. A newsbook praised Richard for declaring 'the Vanity of all Earthly Power and Dignity, and that the Honours and Royalty, which adorned a Prince in his Throne of Majesty, might fitly be compared . . . to the various Bubbles, in mutable Waters'.[60] Streater acclaimed Fleetwood for nobly heeding counsels which Augustus had rejected.[61] The lead they had set could be taken up in a more thoroughgoing return to first principles. To restore the purged Parliament was in effect to restore a restoration, as Wither recalled when he wrote of 'this *Parliament*, which [Cromwell] violently interrupted, being now again by *GOD's* Mercy restored'.[62] Marten's seal for the Commonwealth had alluded to the Machiavellian *ridurre ai principii*, and some enthusiasts wished for a return to a reforming spirit that had become weakened under the Protectorate rather than to the particular stage which reform had reached by 1649 or 1653.[63] One celebratory pamphlet was entitled *Speculum Libertatis Angliae Re restitutae*, and hailed the restoration in Machiavellian terms as an opportunity to 'reduce and happily establish us in a just and equitable crasis [balance] and constitution of a reall Common-wealth', to 'reduce us to the full possession of our ancient birthrights as free-born English-men'. This was clearly not just a matter of going back to the past but of fully understanding and realizing for the first time the principles that had underlain earlier forms of political and spiritual liberty. The government must 'carry it on till it be fully accomplished, and we are made in very deed as now we are onely in name, a reall Common-wealth': going back to the republic of 1649 was a way of moving forward to the ideal republic of the future.[64] If historians have never termed the regime of 1659–60 the 'second republic', it is partly because of the widespread contemporary sense that there had never quite been a first republic. As more radical proposals emerged, there was a modest revival of Leveller literature, one pamphlet calling for weekly meetings to be held at Lilburne's tomb. For these radicals, the restoration of liberty had to go much further through society than a mere non-monarchical oligarchy: 'good people of *England* . . . have not you cut off *Charles*, and let the King live to this day?'[65]

The spring and summer of 1659 saw a flourishing of republican speculation. Parliament set up a constitutional committee, and London's coffee-houses as

60 *The Weekly Post* no. 3, 17–24 May 1659, E983.15, pp. 19–20.

61 J[ohn]. S[treater]., *A Shield Against the Parthian Dart* (1659; E988.11), pp. 20–1.

62 George Wither, *Epistolium-Vagum-Prosa-Metricum* (1659; E763.6; *WMW*, I), p. 2.

63 For the language of restoration see *The Armies Dutie* (1659; E980.12), p. 5; Streater, *The Continuation . . . Justified*, p. 14.

64 R. M., *Speculum Libertatis Angliae Re restitutae* (1659; E989.19), pp. 1–4.

65 H. N., *An Observation and Comparison between the Idolatrous Israelites, and Judges of England* (1659; E983.29), p. 9; *Lilburns Ghost* (1659; E988.9), p. 4.

well as its press formed part of a revived public sphere.[66] It was, commented one pamphlet, 'a time of great Liberty, where every one takes upon him, to speak a word for his Country'. So vigorous were republican voices that a belated defence of the Protectorate appeared under the plaintive title *Let me Speake Too?*[67] The number of tracts collected by Thomason rose from 282 in 1658, when he had resolved to abandon his collection because so little of interest was being published, to 652 in 1659, and new, militantly republican newsbooks began to appear.[68] It is symptomatic of the political climate that four editions of Livy appeared in 1659, while a translation of the British Livy, Buchanan's *History of Scotland*, was prepared for publication, though it was halted by the Restoration.[69] In June a translation of d'Aubigné's *Histoire Universelle* was announced, though this was likewise nipped in the bud by the Restoration.[70] The Fifth Monarchist John Canne displaced the discredited Nedham as editor of *Mercurius Politicus*. After a period of quiescence the Hartlibian radical Sir Cheney Culpeper re-entered public life.[71] The former Leveller John Wildman assembled a republican discussion group which paved the way for Harrington's celebrated Rota Club, on whose gatherings Aubrey was to look back with great fondness.[72] Intellectuals gained a heady taste of power, for 'to human foresight, there was no possibility of the Kings returne'.[73] Harrington was able to make a virtue of the long delay in restoring the republic. In the last phase of the Protectorate he had written:

> where seed is so well sowen and rooted, intervening possession and interests, are like such weather as holding back the Spring, but improves the Harvest; it may indeed be a chill season unto Commonwealths-men, but upon the Commonwealth must bestow fermentation.[74]

The republic's return seemed to bolster his case for the historical inevitability of the decline of monarchy under English conditions. He acknowledged that

66 Stephen B. Dobranski, '"Where Men of Differing Judgements Croud": Milton and the Culture of the Coffee Houses', *The Seventeenth Century* 9 (1994), 35–56.

67 *No Return to Monarchy; and Liberty of Conscience Secured* (1659; E985.16), p. 3; *Let me Speake too? Or, Eleven Queries Humbly Proposed to the Officers of the Army* (1659; L1329). Ronald Hutton, *The Restoration: A Political and Religious History of England and Wales 1658–1667* (Oxford, 1985), p. 47, writes that the world of this press is an 'important and unstudied feature of the period'.

68 Godfrey Davies, *The Restoration of Charles II 1658–1660* (San Marino, 1955), p. 118.

69 Derek Hirst, 'The Politics of Literature in the English Republic', *The Seventeenth Century* 5 (1990), 133–55 (153 n. 59) (these were reissues of Holland's Elizabethan translation, retaining the original dedication to Elizabeth); W. A. Gatherer (ed.), *The Tyrannous Reign of Mary Stuart: George Buchanan's Account* (Edinburgh, 1958), p. 206.

70 *SR*, II, 229. No English translation has ever been published.   71 *CL*, p. 149.

72 Maurice Ashley, *John Wildman: Plotter and Postmaster. A Study of the English Republican Movement in the Seventeenth Century* (1947), p. 142.

73 Bodleian MS Aubrey 6, fol. 98v; *ABL*, I, 290–91.

74 Harrington, *The Art of Law-Giving*, pp. 133–4; *HPW*, p. 701.

'the people of *England* may be twenty to one for monarchy', but insisted that there were at least 'fifty thousand of the more active and knowing' who would form an effective vanguard. A further ten years might be needed to establish a truly stable republic, but the time would come.[75]

The prospect of ten more years of civil disorder was hardly likely to appeal to a war-weary people. Yet Harrington was convinced that at least his active minority were excited enough at the prospect of a republic to sustain a further period of commotion. One Harringtonian treatise addressed the faint-hearted in its title, *Chaos*:

> It were happy if every day spoke not the same or worse language, so much resembling that of *Babel* or *Sodom*, as nothing ever appeared so like the Poets old Chaos as this present Age.

Yet Ovid's Chaos had been the prelude to the creation of the cosmos, and Ovidian mythology could easily be Christianized. In the same way, the political chaos of the present might prove to be the vigorous pre-history of a godly republic:

> As Light was the first thing in the Creation, and so properly called the work of the first day; so for her first days work she propounds for the Balancing of Interests, and reducing each piece to its proper place ... So as if any one piece seem to be wrested out of its place, the weight and frame of the whole prevents it.

The formation of the republic has a Longinian sublimity, linked here with a 'reducing' political architecture in the manner of Marvell's *The First Anniversary*. That the writer may have had some acquaintance with Marvell is suggested by his treatment of the *occasione* theme:

> But if, with *Miles* the Frier's man in the Fable, we flout and abuse this coy mistress TIME, and improve not the advantage and opportunity thereof, she will be gone, and then repentance may come too late.[76]

More often, the pamphlet strikes an epic note for the republican task:

> If *Aeneas* and his followers had the confidence (*Troy* being turned to ashes) to refuse the pleasures of the *Carthaginian* Court, and pass *Hercules* Pillars (where they met with nothing but dangers) in hopes of a new Kingdom afterwards to arise, what shall we do, who though in some want of present Money, have all things accommodable to furnish a well-being to our selves and our posterity, a rich and Potent People, more ready to obey, then the Magistrate to command, dis-obeying no Edict promulged by Authority, offering hands and estates to carry on the work beyond all difficulties, for an unbiassed [i.e. well-balanced] Republique?

---

75 Harrington, *Pour Enclouer le Canon*, pp. 2–3; *HPW*, p. 729.
76 Anon., *Chaos* (1659; second edition, E989.27), pp. 2–4. The reference is clearly in the first instance to a 'Fable' which I have not been able to identify.

A prefatory poem summoned up a vision of Britain commanding the waves as 'Queen/Of Islands'.[77]

Harrington had earlier argued that founding a republic, like writing the *Aeneid*, had to be the work of one man. By now, however, the idea of a reforming Machiavellian legislator had been completely compromised. In August Marchamont Nedham returned to the republican fray in a treatise that baldly acknowledged the collapse of his earlier hopes in Cromwell as a man who would bring new order out of chaos:

> he who created them [the Protectoral Parliaments] by his own Power, presently uncreated them to their first nothing, because as he was a man of high courage and great spirit, he could not endure to see the work of his own hands rise up and dispute (as he conceived) against him.

Nedham here continued his earlier audacious comparison of Cromwell to God the Creator, angry at those who would dispute with him (Romans IX.20–1 – a passage to be echoed by Milton, *Paradise Lost*, v.822). The dynamic activity of the Protectorate, however, had been rendered null by its failure to endure:

> the intervening space of time [must] be reputed as a great *Chasma*, a praeternatural vacuity or dead Interval, wherein all the Acts of supremacie, and matters relating thereto, that were used, became legally defunct as soon as they were done, coming into the world still-born[.][78]

If the foreshortened Cromwellian time that Marvell had celebrated had ended in stagnation, the most vital course was a return to an earlier affirmation of republican principles. In a startling shift of perspective, republicans in the spring of 1659 foreshortened time and addressed the Long Parliament as if it had continually existed:

> although for those many years your *Session* hath been *interrupted* by the late Protector, and your *visible being* withheld from this Nation; yet so long as a *Quorum* doth survive, (notwithstanding that or any other interruption) your *Authority* abideth, and you remain the onely *Legal Parliament of England*, until your *Legal Dissolution* . . . The several seeming Parliaments in this *deplorable interval* of your Authority, and the several Models of obtruded Government since, being no other, then as *one continued* Act of usurpation and innovation upon the Rights of the People, and their Power of Parliaments.[79]

Such arguments, of course, carried a strong degree of ingenious rationalization, especially where they came from people who had themselves served the Protectorate or sat in its Parliaments. When Nedham was rewarded for his

---

77 *Chaos*, sigs. A1v–2v.
78 Marchamont Nedham, *Interest Will Not Lie* (1659; E763.5), p. 40.
79 *A Declaration of the Well-Affected to the Good Old Cause* (1659; 669f21.27).

return to the republican fold by being restored to his editorships, there was a flurry of condemnation from the more godly republicans who recalled his leading role in propaganda for Richard's accession.[80] Wither, a much less adept political operator, was also unpopular because of his Protectoral links. Plunged into confusion by the events succeeding the dissolution of Richard's Parliament, Wither resolved to gain 'a *right understanding*, of that much *mistaken Cause*, which hath been lately carried on through many *Labyrinths*, *Turnings* and *Returnings*, until most men had quite lost the true *Notion*, of that, for which, they first contended'. In the process he went through again his writings of the Commonwealth period, convinced that in their own labyrinthine turnings he could find an underlying fidelity to the good old cause. As has been seen, there was some substance in the claim that he constantly pressured Cromwell towards some form of reduction of his powers. When the Long Parliament was restored he determined to publish not only the recent treatise but also his 'PROTECTORIA, (which is a collection of such *Addresses* and other *Writings*, as I had composed in relation to the *Protectors*, whilst they were in *being*' – including addresses which had remained in manuscript.[81] However, he decided to publish this work anonymously, 'lest it might have the less esteem'. Besides the ridicule his work generally attracted, he probably feared that his belated attacks on Cromwell in *Salt upon Salt* had not sufficed to clear his name from Protectoral associations. In the end he was unable to find a publisher. His petitions to the restored Parliament were blocked, and Wither became convinced that there were political motives. He was moved to publish again, comparing himself to Samson who was galvanized by private injuries into public action – a parallel which seemed to imply that he had badly compromised himself under the Protectorate. Elsewhere in the pamphlet he insisted that he had been absolutely consistent in his critical support of *de facto* power, and that he had warned Cromwell against taking the crown. What he could not deny was that he had defended what he now saw as the '*Interruption*' of 1653; it had looked at the time like a necessary reform of a dilatory institution. He now spoke of 'the time wherein *Oliver Cromwel*, by GODS permission usurped their *power*' as a single temporal unit, and acknowledged that the restored Parliament was straitened 'by reason of that condition, whereto their Obstructers and Interrupters have brought this *Republick*'.[82] Yet he could not overcome his indignation at the way in which his previous attempts to sway the Protectorate in the right direction were being written out of history.

Wither was not the only poet to find it difficult, in 1659, to give a completely

80 *A True Catalogue*, p. 15 and *passim*: the author of this treatise was strongly sympathetic to the religious radical John Canne, whom Nedham had displaced.
81 Wither, *Epistolium-Vagum-Prosa-Metricum*, pp. 29–30.
82 Wither, *Epistolium-Vagum-Prosa-Metricum*, pp. 15, 11.

coherent account of his relationship with the windings and turnings of the Cause over the last few years. In an address to the restored Long Parliament that has caused great scholarly controversy, Milton declared that the island's 'peace and safety, after a short but scandalous night of interruption, is now again by a new dawning of Gods miraculous providence among us, revolvd upon your shoulders'.[83] Commentators have been perplexed both by Milton's apparent dismissiveness towards the Protectorate he had served and by his description of those six years as 'short' immediately after his proud claim to have used Parliament's 'libertie of writing . . . these 18 years on all occasions to assert the just rights and freedoms both of church and state'. Milton's playing with temporality, however, was characteristic of the discourse of the revived republic. Like Wither, he wished to assert an underlying continuity to the cause of civil and religious freedom, and he did so by his emphasis on eighteen years' continuous service. More forcefully than Wither, and with something more like Nedham's love of metaphysical paradox – something, indeed, of his effrontery – he also asserted that the cause's time had been interrupted, that the Protectorate had been a twist of time that had ended up nowhere and 'revolvd' back to where it had started. The imagery of the Protectorate as night, found in several republican tracts, served to counter the regal imagery of Oliver and Richard as sun or star.[84]

As has been seen, like Wither, Milton had some grounds for claiming consistency in his complex relations with the Protectoral regime. Like Harrington, he turned in 1659 from epic poetry to prose, complementing the

---

83 *Considerations Touching the Likeliest Means to Remove Hirelings out of the Church*, *MPW*, VII, 274. Here I follow Austin Woolrych, 'Milton and Cromwell: "A Short but Scandalous Night of Interruption"?', in Michael Lieb and John T. Shawcross (eds.), *Achievements of the Left Hand: Essays on the Prose of John Milton* (Amherst, 1974), pp. 185–218, and Dzelzainis, 'Milton and the Protectorate in 1658', pp. 183–5. Christopher Hill, 'George Wither (1588–1667) and John Milton (1608–74)', *WR*, pp. 133–56 (pp. 141ff), points to parallels between the poets at this period.

84 See, for example, *A Publick Plea . . . Presented to the Parliament and Armies Consideration, in this morning of Freedom, after a short, but a sharp night of Tyranny and oppression* (1659; E983.18); the reference to 'the Night of our late Apostacy' in a letter published in *Mercurius Politicus* no. 568, 19–26 May 1659, E762.15, p. 459; William Sprigge's similar phrase, 'the late night of *Apostacy*', in *A Modest Plea, for an Equal Common-Wealth, Against Monarchy* (1659; E1802.1), p. 22; and *Panharmonia, or, the Agreement of the People Revived* (1659; P257), where the army is told that 'the night of trouble and opposition is somewhat over to you' (sig. A2r) and Milton's *Treatise of Civil Power* is invoked as outlining the agenda that should now be followed (p. 42). Some commentators have insisted that the 'short but scandalous night' must apply to the interval between the army's dissolution of Richard's Parliament and the Rump's return: see Robert Thomas Fallon, *Milton in Government* (University Park, 1993), pp. 178ff, and Corns, *UV*, p. 274. They are motivated by a desire for a common-sense reading, and for a complete consistency in Milton, that are inappropriate to the tortured convolutions of 1659.

Treatise of Civil Power in the summer with *The Likeliest Means to Remove Hirelings from the Church.* Unlike Harrington, however, he did not offer a detailed constitutional model, concentrating instead on the separation of church and state. Critics who are keen to construct a narrative for Milton's career of steady withdrawal from the public world into the inner conscience can find support here. And indeed he did not take up Wall's urging that he address social abuses, while Harrington crossed swords with him over his conception of religious freedom; from his point of view Milton's inward turn was a betrayal of the public emphasis of 'ancient prudence'.[85] But Milton's interventions could be held to have a tactical justification. Far from repudiating any of his earlier republican writings, he went out of his way to set his new pamphlets in the wider context of his career. In the *Treatise* he recalled that he had used the same proof-text 'heretofore against *Salmasius* and regal tyranie over the state; now against *Erastus* and state-tyranie over the church' (*MPW*, VII, 252). In the preface to the *Likeliest Means*, he recalled that he had defended the republican regime in political terms when the urgent need was to win over 'the uningag'd of other nations'. Now, however, many people were offering 'new modells of a commonwealth' (VII, 275), and Milton could afford to turn to an aspect of liberty that had not yet been pursued far enough. This was a remarkably over-optimistic view of the republic's stability in August 1659, the month of a royalist rising, but Milton argued that with civil liberty secured there was the more reason to press on with advances in religious liberty. He was doing so in the face of a growing social panic. The central demand of Milton's pamphlet, the abolition of tithes, alarmed many of the gentry because it would have struck at the basis of the traditional structures of power and patronage. The most militant campaigners against tithes were the Quakers, whose preference for the egalitarian 'thou' over the 'ye' of social deference epitomized their scorn for hierarchical traditions.[86] Parliament hesitated over the radicals' demands and never granted them, partly because they were likely to lead to a massive backlash.

Milton had no such doubts, insisting that 'no modell whatsoever of a commonwealth will prove successful or undisturbed' without setting religion free from 'the monopolie of hirelings' (VII, 276). In his attacks on the ossification of language and religious life under a state church, he often reverts to the language of *Areopagitica*, and here again there is an implicit link between religious and civil liberty. State churches go back to a historic wrong: the Roman emperors gave public lands to the church 'without suffrage of the people', and 'if without the peoples consent, unjustly' (VII, 307). Under a state clergy the

---

85 See the selections from Harrington's *Aphorisms Political* in *MPW*, VII, 518–21.
86 Barry Reay, 'Quaker Opposition to Tithes 1652–1660', *Past and Present* no. 86 (1980), 98–120.

people will remain infants, unable to assume 'thir spiritual priesthood, whereby they have all equally access to any ministerial function' (320). Milton does not flinch from the egalitarian nature of this Christian public sphere to which all have equal access. The practice of religion is shifted from the hierarchically controlled space of the visible church to a democratically governed sphere of common interaction and discussion: 'he who disdaind not to be laid in a manger, disdains not to be preachd in a barn' (304). Milton is aware that such a position was widely seen as subversive of civil as well as religious hierarchy. He turns such arguments back: it is the churchmen's greed that stirs up dissension, and it is in fact 'mechanique' (315) to take money for a religious obligation; the champions of tithes are 'levelling' (318). The fact remains that the independent, self-confident citizens of a democratic church would be unlikely to favour a mystical hierarchy in the state: that is the basis of Milton's claim that reform in the church is a prerequisite for political reform.

Milton, then, lent his public voice to the renewal of the good old cause, but he did not praise the new Parliament in verse. This was symptomatic of a wider absence that was noted by one 'W. H.':

> Can a true *English* heart now silent be,
> Being freed from Bondage and from Tyrannie?
> And will it not lowd *IO Paeans* sing?
> And shout forth praises to our Heavenly King?
> What makes our Muses silent now to be
> In this great change? Were all for Monarchie
> Inspir'd and tun'd? *Athens* I'me sure free State
> Brought forth great Captains, as well men of pate.
> Your Fountain's dry, or else your great *Pan*'s dead,
> Are all come life-lesse souls ha'ing lost your head?
> Or has the second birth of our Free-State
> Sent ye all packing hence, and wrought your fate?
> Some say that in a free-born Common-weal
> Wits will increase, and come more liberal.[87]

Contrary to this prediction, however, the Muses were largely silent on the current political upheavals – Wither's contribution being too disenchanted to qualify as a shout of praise.

'W. H.' himself indicates one possible factor when he points out how many mercenary writers had been ready to flatter Caesar/Cromwell. The republican campaign in the spring had ruthlessly attacked the conventional language of demonstrative rhetoric, and as has been seen, the crisis had affected Marvell.

---

87 W. H., *A Congratulation to our newly restored Parliament* (1659; 669f21.52).

The whole thrust of republican argument in 1659 was against any identification of the good of the state with a single person; this undermined traditional courtly modes of poetic address. The case was forcefully made by William Sprigge in an attack on the

> Poetical, if not prophane flourishes, wherewith Orators and Poets, the constant Parasites of Princes, use to guild ore Monarchy, pretending it the most natural and rational of all other forms of Government . . . paralleling it with Gods *Regimen* of the Universe, which is alledg'd as its prototype or first *Exemplar* . . . such trite, bald and slight reasonings, that they do not merit so much respect as to receive an answer . . . may we not, considering the pride, ambition, rapine, extortion, injury and oppression, that usually crowd into the *Courts* of the best *Princes*, with as much or more reason parallel absolute Monarchy, with that of the *Prince of Darkness*, in which there is no Trinity, as in the other, and therefore more exactly quadrate to the absoluteness, our proud Monarchs so much endeavour to obtain?

Sprigge reiterated humanist attacks on the regal plural:

> the very dialect of Princes . . . doth clearly speak the unnaturalness of such exorbitant monopolies of *power*, and that though they act in a *single capacity*, are *willing to speak* like a *Commonwealth*.[88]

Wither picked up this suspicion of previous literary forms in a work written the following month:

> I . . . took such special notice . . . both in the times of King *James* and King *Charles*, how the Peoples Liberties were encroached upon, and what farther Slaveries were likely to ensue, that I am well assured, the *Peace* and *Plenty*, which is by many magnified as effects of their good *Government*, was acquired by GOD's blessing upon the *Peoples Industry* in Queen *Elizabeths* raign, and during the time wherein those forenamed *Kings*, made use of those blessings to get settlement of power upon themselves, rather then by their just and prudent *Government*[.][89]

He had to concede that 'being educated under a *Tyranny*, which kept me ignorant of what I was born to', he had been guilty of 'many staggering and dubious *Expressions*, scattered here and there in my *Writings*, which I am content should remain upon Record, to testifie that I think not my self infallible'.[90] Wither was not merely looking backwards but attacking the current royalist cult of Charles I as martyr, which he dismissed as '*Fictions* and *Impostures*'.[91] And yet he himself was well known for having addressed Cromwell in hyperbolical terms.

The false turns of the Protectorate had indeed been perilous for poets. The

---

88 Sprigge, *A Modest Plea, for an Equal Common-Wealth*, pp. 17–20.
89 George Wither, *A Cordial Confection* (1659; E763.13), pp. 29–30.
90 Ibid., p. 8.		91 Ibid., p. 30.

revived republican culture of mid-1659 made heavy demands on poets, who had to celebrate creation and yet cultivate an intense suspicion towards traditional forms of poetic creativity. As will be seen in the next chapter, *Paradise Lost* can be seen as a long-term response to that challenge. But this second republican moment was granted a very short time before a new interruption.

From restoration to Restoration

> I have not forgot (though it was my perusal in my dayes of youth and jollity) a sober and prophetick Poem, intituled, *Britains Remembrancer*; where, in the Frontispiece is engraven a Map or Description of *England* in Epitome; save only that the Artificer hath confined his industry, by vailing the Remainder beyond the *Time*, under a dark and obscure Cloud: (the prophetical spirit of which Book hath not more reached the *English* than the *Scottish* Nation)[.][92]

The clouds on the title-page of Wither's *Britain's Remembrancer* seemed to one soldier in late 1659 the best emblem of the distracted state of the nation. He was a supporter of General George Monck, commander of the forces in Scotland, who was marching south to confront the army of John Lambert. Increasingly the darkness of the political landscape was changing from a potentially fertile chaos to a nightmare of anarchy.

The crisis began when the army, with Lambert's approval, dissolved the restored Long Parliament on 13 October 1659. This marked the end of the preceding year's precarious attempts at a coalition of differing political forces. Having regained power with the aid of the army, Parliament was making vigorous attempts to control it, and its grandees were unable to tolerate their reduction in status. As so often in the past, they claimed to speak especially for the cause of religious liberty. Though the restored Parliament had made enough concessions to religious radicals to provoke a social panic, it had failed to act on Milton's calls for thoroughgoing reforms. The army's action seemed to its opponents no more than a replaying of the dissolution of 1653: having tried to loop backwards in time to repeat the Commonwealth, they now had to repeat its collapse. The resultant split between Parliamentary and military forces left Milton and Wither virtually paralysed by the difficulty of taking sides. Civilian republicans attacked the army for cynically using religious language for secular motives: Milton's friend Bradshaw accused them of blasphemy. One republican theorist broke off a treatise that had suddenly been rendered irrelevant with a savage attack on the army's betrayal: 'Upon my word, these were fit to live *and reign with Christ a thousand years*, who cannot keep Faith an hundred dayes'. The language of chaos and creation that

---

92 *Mercurius Britanicus* no. 2, 8–15 December 1659, p. [13].

had briefly taken on optimistic overtones now lapsed into despair: '*you have made* England, Scotland, Ireland, *A Chaos, without form and void*, and I doubt your Omnipotency will never speak the word for such a creation, as any honest man shall say when he hath looked upon it, *that it is very good*'.[93] A more restrained commentator observed that even if the men in power were virtuous, rule by good men was incompatible with liberty if it were done 'of their meer grace, favour and courtesie'.[94] Milton censured the interruption of Parliament as 'barbarous, or rather scarce to be exampled among any Barbarians', reducing the nation to 'Anarchy' (*MPW*, VII, 327, 329, 336). Wither vividly portrayed the ruinous cynicism instilled by Lambert's coup:

> when by the Vollies of Shot, it was in *London* supposed that the Parliaments Guards, and the Armies Forces were engaged, the people who then flocked into the Temple, to look toward *Westminster*, where they hoped that *Engagement* was begun, did in my sight and hearing, express their barbarous joy, with so much disaffection to both Parties, and with such unchristian Language, and unmanly Gesticulations . . .

The republic's factions had been reduced 'to be torn and to tear each other to pieces' in 'the *Cirque* of a *Theater*'.[95]

And yet Milton and Wither did not align themselves unambiguously with the civilian defenders of Parliament, many of whom had come to view it as a bastion of political and religious discipline rather than a means of further reform. Vane, whose defence of religious liberty was so much admired by Milton, supported the new military regime. Ludlow wavered and tried to mediate. Overton accused Parliament of 'a persecuting tendency' and tried to hold his garrison at Hull independent of both factions.[96] The new Committee of Safety championed Milton's favoured cause of the abolition of tithes. Quite apart from religious anxieties, there were practical grounds for the argument that the republic could never survive without an agreement with the army, which in the absence of a Cromwellian single person was the only force capable of effecting a radical constitutional change. Harrington's dialogue *Valerius and Publicola*, published shortly after the coup, attacked the army for having 'overcast them with the mist of new affected phrases, and fallen on conjuring up spirits', but he also acknowledged that the army were the only force capable of setting up a thoroughgoing republic; and indeed Harringtonians were to gain some influence in a new constitutional committee established in the autumn.[97]

93 Anon., *The Grand Concernments of England Ensured* (1659; E1001.6), pp. 57, 55.

94 Lyon Freeman, *The Common-Wealths Catechism* (1659; E1870.2), p. 23. The author states that the tract was written three weeks after the interruption of Parliament.

95 Wither, *A Cordial Confection*, pp. 13–14.

96 *The Humble and Healing Advice of Collonel Robert Overton* (1659; O637), p. 3.

97 James Harrington, *Valerius and Publicola* (1659; E1005.13), p. 26; *HPW*, p. 800.

Wither likewise held back from total condemnation of the army, amongst whom so many of his readers were to be found. He sought some justification for their action in the criteria he had offered Oliver for his '*irregular Act*' in consolidating his power; and he expressed sympathy for the Quakers, whose activities had panicked many Parliamentarians.[98] Parliaments, after all, 'were originally ordained, for no other intent, but to preserve the Peace of other men so long and so far forth onely, as it might uphold their *Grandeur*, and make the people *Instruments* to enslave themselves thereunto' (p. 9). Even if Parliament ultimately prevailed against the soldiers, there was little to hope for: 'GOD, who raised up *Lazarus*, when he was dead, buried, & stunk, may (if he please) once again restore it' (p. 18). The 'Parliament Party . . . managed their Good Cause like—- like—- like—- (to tell you truly) like I know not what; for I can devise nothing under heaven, and above ground, whereto I may liken them' (p. 32). When Wither was at a loss for words, in a far from sublime context, things were indeed critical. Previous measures had been too piecemeal; the people's 'Liberties will never perfectly be recovered, until a Foundation be laid by the Power of the Peoples own Sword, in the hands of faithful *Trustees*, whereupon a just Government may be erected' (p. 9). Wither drafted this response to the coup but held back for some time from publishing it[99]; Milton drafted some proposals in the autumn but never published them, probably for similar reasons of political uncertainty. He was as scathing as Wither about the glories of the ancient constitution: the 'name of parlament,' he wrote, 'is a Norman or French word, a monument of our Ancient Servitude' (*MPW*, VII, 337). He would go no further in his praise of the Long Parliament than that 'they have deserved much more of these nations, then they have undeserved' (VII, 325).

For the soldiers marching southward with Monck, Wither and Milton had little to offer as a way out of the clouds. Monck's own motivations were themselves shrouded in obscurity. His public declarations were firmly republican, even Harringtonian, but he had embarked on a political odyssey that was to lead him to become the prime agent in the return of Charles II. The reverse temporality which had been put into effect at the fall of the Protectorate had started to work against the radicals; the word 'restoration' would gradually lose its connotation of radical reform and become associated first with the return of the MPs excluded in 1648 and ultimately with the return of the king. Monck triumphed in a civil war where neither side was willing to draw blood. The military regime began to crumble, and the republicans led by Haselrig were able in

---

98 Wither, *A Cordial Confection*, pp. 12–13.
99 *A Cordial Confection* eventually appeared in December, when a royalist neighbour was present at a public reading and reported Wither's comment, p. 17, that Charles had no more legal right to Britain than Wither had to France and Spain: Norman E. Carlson, 'George Wither and his Creditors', *Notes and Queries* 212 (1967), 333–6 (336).

late December to restore Parliament. They continued to place faith in the sincerity of Monck's declarations of commitment to a republic. But the General was playing a waiting game, sounding out different factions and pragmatically assessing their strength. Having arrived in London, on 11 February 1660 he issued a declaration that called on Parliament to fulfil immediately its promises to fill up the vacancies left by the purged members and to proclaim its own dissolution. The form of this declaration was as important as its content: Monck was by now sole possessor of military power in London, Parliament having agreed, against the republicans' protests, to withdraw its regiments, and he was effectively declaring that he could mould the political future. The news of Monck's ultimatum was greeted with joy. All over London fires were lit to roast rumps of beef, a powerful visual realization of the contemptuous nickname of the 'Rump'. The way was open for an outpouring of scatological satires against the Rump; the republicans were starting to lose control of the press.

They had not, however, entirely lost hope. Neville was working for a reconciliation between Presbyterians and Independents in the hope of salvaging as much as possible of a republican settlement, with a strong aristocratic element aiming to counter fears of military violence and sectarian anarchy.[100] When Parliament announced new elections on 17–18 February, it still imposed strict constraints on royalist participation. Wither and Milton both responded to this situation by renewing their allegiance to 'this *Republicks* Cause'; yet they also revealed their fears that the cause was lost.[101] In *Furor-Poeticus* (composed 19 February), Wither urged Monck that

> It is a much more honourable thing,
> To *save a People,* than to *make a King*[.] (p. 7)

He toyed with the possibility that Monck might take supreme power to make sure the Stuarts were kept out. But he undercut any great enthusiasm for such a move in the republican familiarity of his remark that his accession would

> more endear
> This Name of *George,* than *Dick,* or *Oliver*[.] (p. 5)

And he warned that siren-like '*gifts*' and 'flattering *Addresses*' might deflect him from his resolution. Wither recalled the scepticism about the previous year's addresses: Lucifer had fallen, and even

> he fell
> Whom some thought lately, more than parallel
> To *Moses, Josuah,* and many more ... (p. 10)

---

100 Nicholas von Maltzahn, 'Henry Neville and the Art of the Possible: A Republican *Letter Sent to General Monk* (1660)', *The Seventeenth Century* 7 (1992), 41–52, demonstrates Neville's authorship of *A Letter sent to General Monk* (1660; E1015.2), dated 29 January.
101 George Wither, *Furor-Poeticus (i.e.) Propheticus* (1660; E1818.2; *WMW,* v), p. 19.

So gloomy was Wither about the possibility of Monck's resisting corruption that the poem's conclusion virtually consigned the first part to anticipatory obsolescence by considering the political options if Charles should be restored – a possibility he had already floated in *A Cordial Confection* the previous year. Though he still harked back to his old prophecy of a king who would willingly unking himself, he did not sound very optimistic about the possibility.[102]

By contrast with Wither's contorted speech-act of affirming his support for the republic while simultaneously positioning himself for a possible Restoration, Milton's intervention was more clearcut. The first edition of *The Readie & Easie Way to Establish a Free Commonwealth* was probably composed over the same weekend as *Furor-Poeticus*; and Milton in this tract comes closer than before to Wither's favourite posture of the prophet denied honour in his own country, the beleaguered individual fighting for poetry and virtue. *The Readie & Easy Way* is sometimes seen as marking a further stage in Milton's disillusion with secular politics, a retreat from classical republicanism. This is an issue that needs addressing, for it has an important bearing on *Paradise Lost* as well as the immediate political context.

Has Milton by now come to find no more than meaningless anarchy in the chaos of republican politics? Support for that view can be found in his reworking of the characteristic republican imagery of architecture and creation as he warns that if their projects fail,

> what will they say of us, but scoffingly as of that foolish builder mentiond by our Saviour, who began to build a Tower, and was not able to finish it: where is this goodly tower of a Common-wealth which the *English* boasted they would build, to overshaddow kings and be another *Rome* in the west? The foundation indeed they laid gallantly, but fell into a worse confusion, not of tongues, but of factions, then those at the tower of *Babel*; and have left no memorial of thir worke behind them remaining, but in the common laughter of *Europ*. (*MPW*, VII, 357)

Here Milton conflates two different biblical towers. In the New Testament, Christ uses the analogy of the tower with incomplete foundations to urge the need for his followers to divest themselves of property: here the building is positive, though it requires great sacrifice for the common good. This tower, however, merges with the Tower of Babel, built by the arrogant tyrant Nimrod.[103] The

---

102 Wither, *Furor-Poeticus (i.e.) Propheticus*, p. 30. The relevant extract from *Prosopopoeia Britannica* had been reprinted in August 1659 as *An ancient and true PROPHESIE* (E993.23).

103 Wither had invoked Nimrod in *A Cordial Confection*, pp. 34, 40. William Kolbrener, *Milton's Warring Angels: A Study of Critical Engagements* (Cambridge, 1997), p. 47, uses the tower passage as evidence for Milton's withdrawal from secular politics in this tract, but also demonstrates continuities from *Areopagitica*. On differing uses of the Babel story see Sharon Achinstein, *Milton and the Revolutionary Reader* (Princeton, 1994), pp. 83ff.

confusion of factions of the collapsing republic is hard to distinguish from the confusion of tongues brought about by monarchical aspiration. Overton had used a similar analogy at the height of the army-Parliament split:

> Babel-like, our buildings are accompanied with nothing but confusion and con-
> tempt, which makes the Nations abroad to scoff and scorn, and our enemies at
> home to rejoyce in hopes of our ruine[.]

At this stage Overton was still ready to hope that discords could be overcome, that destruction could give way to creation:

> no foundation is laid that either bears any proportion with what we professe, or
> otherwise answers the ends of God, in that new Creation he is about to form
> throughout the whole Universe, by restoring of Judges as at the first, and
> Councellors as at the beginning[.][104]

Milton's image of the tower, however, brings creation and destruction uncomfortably close; and his treatise is full of anxiety about the dangers of a public sphere that is being captured by the royalists.

His solution to this problem is not a new constitution but a desperate combination of elements of the existing polity into a rigid oligarchy. Once new members had been elected, Parliament would be renamed a 'Grand Council' with members sitting for life, while vaguely conceived local assemblies would exercise power under the guidance of local magnates. Milton insists on the advantages of this system in keeping popular turbulence at bay. The people will 'sollicit and entreat' the Council 'not to throw off the great burden from thir shoulders which none are abler to bear' (VII, 373). Rather than something to be actively embraced, opinion-forming and the active life are burdens to be taken by the few – the kind of anti-political attitude which republicans often denounced as intrinsic to monarchy. As in *Areopagitica*, he cites as a pattern the Athenian Areopagus (VII, 370), but here he leaves no space for a counterbalancing, more democratic element.

Milton's concrete proposals do indeed make grim reading. And yet they did not constitute the tract's only interest. He was concerned to vindicate 'the language of the good old cause', and for all his anxieties about a lapse into Babel, Milton both practises and preaches a commitment to the power and value of republican language. The Babel analogy was widely used by republicans to denounce not democratic but royalist anarchy. Edmund Ludlow explained the republic's collapse as a divine punishment:

> that as there had bin a consenting (instead of building the howse, and doing the
> worke of God, when there was an opportunity) to build a Babell, and to prosecute

a personall interest before the publique, therefore are they given up to confusion of language, and to be divided one against another.[105]

Kingship, for him as for Milton, was the supreme example of placing a personal interest above a public one. The contrast between a common, republican language and divisive monarchical languages runs through *The Readie & Easie Way*. Milton echoes the repeated denunciations in the republican debates of 1659 of the language attracted by the rule of a single person, because it was both false, in confiscating the agency of the people as a whole, and demeaning. How 'unmanly must it needs be, to count such a one the breath of our nostrils, to hang all our felicitie on him, all our safety, our well-being' (VII, 362); whereas under a republic, governors 'may be spoken to freely, familiarly, friendly, without adoration' (VII, 360). During the Civil War, the king had responded to Parliament's protests against his tyranny with 'gratious condescensions and answers' (VII, 358); Milton treats this regal language with contempt, as assuming a right to supremacy for which there is no justification, and adds to the criticism in the second edition by making the condescensions 'divine' (VII, 423). By contrast, the 'expressions both of the Army and of the People, whether in thir publick declarations or several writings' had 'testifi'd a spirit in this nation no less noble and well fitted to the liberty of a Commonwealth, then in the ancient Greeks or Romans': this was 'a glorious rising Commonwealth' (VII, 356).

As in *Of Education*, Milton is concerned with the transmission of republican values and language. Schools teaching grammar and the liberal arts would diffuse 'knowledge and civilitie' throughout 'the whole nation' (VII, 384). In the second edition he explained that they would do so by 'communicating the natural heat of government and culture more distributively to all extreme parts, which now lie numm and neglected' (VII, 460). This is the passage cited by Raymond Williams as a significant transitional phase in the word 'culture', from a metaphor with strong agrarian associations to the more modern senses of aesthetic development or a whole way of life.[106] As Williams notes, the phrase has often had a defensive cast, with a 'culture' associated with a ruling elite threatened by anarchy from below. This is to some extent the case with Milton, with his fears of Babel. His usage, however, is rendered more complex by its context. He was after all defending a regime that was viewed by royalists as itself a lapse into anarchy, encouraging base-born upstarts to usurp power. In the second edition he specifically rejected the royalist charge of defending 'lawless anarchie' (VII, 427). This could in his view

105 Edmund Ludlow, *A Voyce from the Watch Tower Part Five: 1660–1662*, ed A. B. Worden (1978), p. 114.
106 Raymond Williams, *Culture and Society 1780–1950*, second edition (Harmondsworth, 1963), pp. 325–6.

be retorted against the royalists, who were undermining a language of common interest.

Milton was writing at a time of intense panic about the Babel-like prolife-ration of the sects; but like Wither, he refused to be panicked. He makes a characteristic republican link between ideas and institutions. Freedom of conscience is best safeguarded under a republic, which is 'most magnani-mous, most fearless and confident of its own fair proceedings', whereas king-ship, jealous of its private interests, is 'startl'd at everie umbrage' (VII, 382): this phrasing recalls *Areopagitica*, where religious toleration had been associated with republican magnanimity, intolerance with 'the shaking of every leaf' (*MPW*, II, 539). He also refers back to his tracts of the previous year, where he had argued that a republic could only be sustained if it encouraged the broadly democratic Christian public sphere that would help to nourish civic virtue; now his emphasis is on the need for republican institutions to safe-guard that sphere. Insofar as religion underpins *The Readie & Easie Way*, it is because Milton here goes further than ever before in suggesting that republi-can government is best not just in terms of secular prudence but by divine mandate: he cites Christ's own words to the sons of Zebedee (Matthew XX.25–7) to suggest that monarchy is inherently unchristian (*MPW*, VII, 359, cf. 364). Like Sprigge, Milton sees kingship as a form of blasphemy: it involves '*Gentilish* imitation', transferring language only appropriate to the heavenly kingdom to corrupt mortals (VII, 364). Christ had offered himself as a servant to man, and that, rather than lordship, was the true model for government (VII, 360, 362). Despite this appeal to transcendental truths, Milton also turned, for the first time since 1650, to the language of interest theory, which was mainly associated with secular republicans like Nedham; he warns against having 'king and bishop united inseparably in one interest' (VII, 357).[107]

The powerful peroration of *The Readie & Easy Way* may seem to abandon all such speculation about republican and Christian linguistic practice as idle. Milton imagines himself as the prophet Jeremiah with none to cry to but trees and stones (VII, 388). This passage, however, need not be read too literally.[108] The cry of Jeremiah with which the pamphlet ends (Jeremiah XX.24–29) was radically provocative, a curse on a corrupt dynasty, and in reiterating it against the Stuarts, Milton was making a powerful public commitment. One critic declares of *The Readie & Easie Way* that 'for Milton it has no real audi-ence'; but a tract that provoked both a satirical pamphlet and a full-length

---

107 See Joad Raymond, 'The Cracking of the Republican Spokes', *Prose Studies* 19 (1996), 255–74.

108 Corns, *UV*, pp. 283–4, corrects overemphasis on the text as Jeremiad (cf. James Holstun, *A Rational Millennium: Puritan Utopias of Seventeenth-Century England and America* (New York and Oxford, 1987), pp. 246–65).

defence of kingship had made at least as much of an impact as many academic books.[109] A royalist respondent picked up Milton's interest in republican rhetoric, claiming that he opposed kingship because

> such admirable eloquence as yours, would be thrown away under a Monarchy (as it would be) though of admirable use in a Popular Government, where Orators carry all the Rabble before them . . . all your Politiques are derived from the works of Declamers[.][110]

Another respondent saw Milton as one of a group of writers rather than a lonely Jeremiah:

> I am not ignorant of the *ability* of Mr. *Milton*, whom the *Rump* (which was well stored with men of *pregnant* although *pernicious* Wits) made choyce of, before others[.][111]

It is remarkable that a blind man should have familiarized himself so well with the current state of political argument – though he would have heard about discussions at the Rota through close friends like Cyriack Skinner even if he did not attend himself. Only in his pamphlet's symbolism was he a completely isolated voice. In fact this tract, like Wither's *Salt upon Salt*, Overton's *Humble and Healing Advice*, and Milton's own *Likeliest Means*, was published by Livewell Chapman, the publisher who was the leading focus for radical publishing throughout the republican revival. Milton's aim was 'perswasion' (VII, 388); his chosen method was to shame his readers by reminding them of their inconstancy and to alarm them by painting a vivid picture of the disastrous consequences of a Stuart restoration. If the multitude are 'misguided and abus'd' (VII, 388), the obligation is to provide better guides.

Milton's ideal of an aristocratic republic looks more unrealistic with hindsight than it did at the time. A fossilized Long Parliament might be an extremely unlikely vehicle of dynamic republican transformation, and Milton himself, as recently as the army coup the previous October, had been bitterly scathing about its imperfections. But in the political upheavals of that autumn, Parliament had emerged as the only body capable of establishing some form of republican consensus and common political language. One royalist feared in February that 'there is so insolent a spirit amongst some of the Nobility, that I really fear 'twill turn to an Aristocracy, Monk inclining that way too'. Edward Hyde, the king's Lord Chancellor, was so worried by this danger that on 18 February, around the time Milton was writing, he called for

---

109 Holstun, *A Rational Millennium*, p. 259. Davies, *The Restoration of Charles II*, p. 318, comments on the amount of response Milton's treatise aroused.

110 J. H., [Samuel Butler?] *The Censure of the Rota upon Mr. Miltons Book* (1660; E1019.5*), p. 8; on the authorship see Nicholas von Maltzahn, 'Samuel Butler's Milton', *Studies in Philology* 92 (1995), 482–95.

111 G[eorge]. S[tarkey]., *The Dignity of Kingship Asserted* (1660; E1915.2), p. 2.

pamphlets against the tyranny of republics to be published. Northumberland was rumoured to be planning to establish a Venetian-style republic.[112]

Milton was writing in great haste, and by the time he had finished, his pamphlet was already outdated. On Tuesday 21 February, after a series of negotiations in which Monck backed away from his earlier compromise with the republicans, the secluded members assembled at his quarters and were escorted by his troops to take their seats in Parliament. This was a potent reversal of the events of 1648: the army was now un-purging Parliament. That night the city was lit up with celebratory bonfires. Milton's easy way had been blocked, for members with royalist sympathies formed a large part of the House. Milton went ahead with the publication of *The Readie & Easie Way*, but he was forced to add a paragraph addressing the changed circumstances. He set a brave face on things, declaring that those now in power were still committed to 'a free Commonwealth' (*MPW*, VII, 354). The mostly Presbyterian members who had been readmitted had after all fought alongside the Independents against the king, and perhaps they could be persuaded of the dangers of monarchy. But things were moving so fast that by the time the pamphlet appeared, it had been resolved to hold elections for a new Parliament. Milton drafted a desperate appeal to Monck to prevent the election of royalists by force if necessary, but quickly abandoned the proposal, which was quite at variance with Monck's emergent intentions.[113] The readmission of the excluded members was the signal for a massive increase in satires against the republicans, creating a climate in which it would become very difficult to elect anyone but a staunch royalist.

The weeks leading up to this crucial election were a nightmarish time for republicans. Few of them had ever argued for thoroughgoing democracy, but they did claim that their rule was in some sense the people's, and the clamorous popular protests were a bitter irony. The night before the secluded members returned, a dispirited Harrington had presided over what may have been the last meeting of the Rota. The topic discussed, ironically enough, was 'whether learned or unlearned subjects are the best'.[114] Harrington was grappling with the same problems of democracy and republican culture as Milton. The intense politicization of the previous twenty years had transformed London apprentices into active political subjects, ready to submit petitions and debate constitutional questions. Now they were using this

---

112 Mordaunt to Nicholas, February 1660, Bodleian MS Clarendon 69, fol. 191r, *Calendar of the Clarendon State Papers*, vol. IV, 561; Hyde to Broderick, 18/28 February 1660, MS Clarendon 69, fol. 190r, *Calendar of the Clarendon State Papers*, vol. IV, 567.

113 'The Present Means, and Brief Delineation of a Free Commonwealth', *MPW*, VII, 392–5. Corns, *UV*, pp. 285–6, argues that Milton wàs urging a coup rather than merely applying pressure on elections.

114 *The Diary of Samuel Pepys*, ed. Robert Latham and William Matthews (1970–83), I, 61.

learning process to break down the impediments to a return of the monarch – though even now they retained the language of popular rule.[115] Harrington, relentlessly optimistic to the last, did try to find a new venue for his meetings in the Cockpit playhouse. As the setting for Davenant's political operas, this theatre was a reminder of Harrington's earlier hopes for a cultural alliance between republican oratory and the theatre.

But that alliance had been threatened by the continued distaste of many Puritans for the theatre; and there was an insurmountable distance from the assemblies of ancient Greece to the London crowds. Davenant had always been far more sceptical about the common herd than Harrington, and by the following month he was acclaiming Monck for saving culture from the anarchy of religious radicalism:

> As in destructive Warre, so you no lesse,
> Transcend them in the growing Arts of Peace.
> You can converse, and in a dialect
> Where no strange dresse makes us the truth suspect;
> Where plainnesse gracefull is...
> They write the style of spirits, you of men;
> Yet are their Swords lesse powerfull then your Pen.
>   Auspicious Leader! None shall equall thee,
> Who mak'st our Nation and our Language free.[116]

Davenant here echoed Waller's panegyric of Cromwell, but the clear implication, as in so much writing of this period, is that Monck should make way for Charles. Even now, however, monarchist language was kept slightly at bay. Though watching spectacles in which the king's return was prophesied, Monck continued to proclaim his disapproval of a restoration. The uncertainty about how far it was legitimate to go in proclaiming royalist sympathies is shown by the fact that several different speeches claiming to have been spoken at entertainments for Monck were often published, varying sometimes in the degree of their royalism. In one account of the entertainment at the Vintners' Hall, Bacchus declares with playful blasphemy that Monck must be divine because he had restored them as if water were turned to wine, and proclaims that

> he who slights
>   God *Bacchus* rites,
> – Turns Traitor to his Prince.

---

115 Brian Manning, *Aristocrats, Plebeians and Revolution in England 1640–1660* (1996), pp. 124ff, argues that popular politics in this period was anti-oligarchical rather than pro-monarchist.

116 Sir William Davenant, *A Panegyrick to his Excellency, the Lord Generall MONCK* (1660; 669f24.33).

Another speech ascribed to the same occasion, and repudiating alternative accounts, took a more cautious and sober tone. Monck was compared to such classical figures as Pericles and Demosthenes and urged to take a balanced course between restraining sects and allowing profane luxuries to flourish.[117] Another poem to Monck compared him to Caesar in the *Pharsalia*, urging the boatman to risk the storm – an analogy that seemed as likely to arouse as to quell political anxiety.[118] In this liminal period, monarchical and republican languages were held in suspension. Meeting a royalist acquaintance during the election campaign, Ludlow observed that

> It was twielight (as we call it) with us both: with me it was as that of the evening, when it darkens by reason of the departure of the sunne, but with him as that of the morning, when it vanisheth by reason of its rising[.][119]

Yet the direction of the twilight even now was not quite certain. One danger for the royalists was that they might overplay their hand. The dominant group in Parliament up to the dissolution was strongly Presbyterian, and thus hostile to the violently bawdy language and behaviour of some cavaliers. We should not too readily assume that the scatological satires against the Rump were the authentic voice of the whole people. Davenant might claim that the language was being purified of sectarian extravagances, but royalist extravagances might seem worse to some citizens. The Presbyterian and conservative Independent group which briefly gained political ascendancy included figures like Northumberland who had a long record of resistance to absolutism and who were not unequivocally enthusiastic about the king's return.[120] Even Ludlow had some hopes of the excluded members, for there had been validity in their 'doubting least the goverment of the army, being monarchycall, would therefore obstruct the interest of a Comonwealth, and reduce the civill goverment into the like constitution with itselfe'.[121] There remained then a glimmer of hope that the elections might return a group of MPs prepared to fight against a restoration.

It was in this spirit that an anonymous poet issued a versified election manifesto which studiedly resisted any mention of monarchy:

> Great God of Nations, and their Right,
>   By whose high Auspice *Brittain* stands

117 *Bacchus Festival* (1660; 669f24.63); Thomas Jordan, *A Speech made to his Excellency George Monck* (1660; 669f24.61).   118 *The Glory of the West* (broadside, 1660; G881).
119 Ludlow, *A Voyce from the Watch Tower*, p. 109.
120 Douglas R. Lacey, *Dissent and Parliamentary Politics in England, 1661–1689: A Study in the Perpetuation and Tempering of Parliamentarianism* (New Brunswick, 1969), pp. 2ff, gives the best account of this group.
121 Ludlow, *A Voyce from the Watch Tower*, p. 149.

So long, though first 'twas built on Sands;
  And oft had sunk but for thy might.

In her own Mainland-storms and Seas:
    Be present to her now as then,
    And let not proud and factious men
  Oppose thy Will with what they please . . .

They should reject those who might 'invade/The Commonwealth' and choose patriots:

Such the old *Bruti, Decii* were,
    The *Cippi, Curtii*, who did give
    Themselves for *Rome*: and would not live,
  As men, good only for a year.

Such were the great *Camilli* too,
    The *Fabii, Scipio*'s; that still thought
    No work at price enough was bought,
  That for their Country they could do:

And to her honour so did knit,
    As all their Acts were understood
    The Sinews of the Publick Good,
  And they themselves one Soul with it.[122]

The poet's description of the electorate as 'the *Tribes*', on a Roman model, suggests Harringtonian influence. The stanza-form distances the poem from the normal ballads or heroic couplets just as the references to classical heroes distance it from the emergent language of royal ceremonial. There is a striking contrast with another election poem which warned in jingling scatological stanzas against the election of Ludlow, John Hutchinson, Marten and others. Marvell, who was standing for Hull, was probably unsympathetic to Overton's attempts to hold the city for Jesus, but he may also have been uneasy about some of the electioneering company he kept in triumphing over the republican candidate Matthew Alured:

If *Alured* seeks your favour to gain,
Iones or *Millington* tell'um they labour in vain,
    Cause as swine do on Pearles
    They trampled on *Charles*,
      With the rest of their fellows the Bum.[123]

Milton made his own last attempt to rescue a higher republican tone from monarchist scurrility; in early April Milton issued a revised *Readie and Easie*

---

122 *Englands Vote for a Free Election of a Free Parliament* (1660; 669f24.50).
123 *Englands Directions for Members Elections* (1660; 669f24.29).

Way. The tone here is sometimes darker and more pessimistic than in the first edition.[124] The imagery links confusion of tongues with water: the people's Babel-like voice has become a threatening 'torrent', a 'deluge' which is so hard to keep in its 'due channell' that it will probably sweep the nation over a 'precipice of destruction' (*MPW*, VII, 463). Milton here seems to abandon Machiavelli's claim that the river of fortune can be contained by republican action, and to move closer to Denham's warning of popular immersion.[125] Ludlow, Hutchinson and Overton also compared the monarchist tumult to a flood.[126]

Yet selective quotation can exaggerate Milton's despair. The new edition showed a remarkable resilience in making the same text serve for progressively differing speech-acts. Milton was one of a small number of republicans, including Nedham, who had kept maintaining a presence in the press even though the government was now cracking down on their publications.[127] Chapman had gone into hiding after printing Nedham's inflammatory *Newes from Brussels*, but Milton struggled nonetheless to bring out a new edition. He still hoped that the elections might somehow yield his cherished republic: the writs, after all, had been sent out in the name not of the king but of the keepers of England's liberty (VII, 431). In adding to his attack on courtly ways a hit at 'grooms, even of the close-stool' (chamber-pot), Milton turned the royalists' scatological imagery against them (VII, 425). Like Nedham in *Newes from Brussels*, Milton compromised tactically by playing on issues central to Presbyterians.[128] He cut out a passage on the separation of church and state, while recalling traditional fears of the Stuarts' leaning to Catholicism, and expanding his account of the vain luxury of Stuart courts (VII, 425). In a direct appeal to the 'new royaliz'd presbyterians' (VII, 451) he recalled the anti-cavalier satire of the early years of the Civil War (VII, 452).[129] Their necks might be 'yok'd with these tigers of Bacchus', a reference that would have acquired a particular topical twist for readers of the Bacchus entertainment for Monck.

Milton's desire to contrast republican order with royalist disorder may account for his insertion of a lengthy critique of Harrington. Harrington was himself obsessively concerned to avoid the tumults of popular debating assemblies, but Milton now contrives to imply that even this cautious degree

---

124 The Yale edition prints the two texts separately; comparison is much easier in the conflated version in *The Ready and Easy Way to Establish a Free Commonwealth*, ed. Evert Mordecai Clark (New Haven and London, 1915).

125 Cf. Holstun, *A Rational Millennium*, p. 259.

126 Overton, *The Humble and Healing Advice*, p. 3; Hutchinson, p. 223; Ludlow, *A Voyce from the Watch Tower*, pp. 101, 105, 122, 149. Worden points out, p. 37, that Ludlow's memoirs, written after the event, draw on Milton's pamphlets, so an echo may be in question.   127 See Raymond, 'The Cracking of the Republican Spokes'.

128 Corns, *UV*, pp. 287ff.   129 Corns, *UV*, p. 288.

of democracy would be a danger. In his last published work Harrington had responded to Henry Stubbe, a defender of Vane's godly oligarchy, by insisting on the democratic character of Spartan and Athenian republicanism, and had cited Isocrates's Areopagitic oration.[130] In his second edition Milton considers the objection to his lifelong assemblies that the Areopagus had had the counterweight of 'popular remedies'; but he sweeps aside any such 'licentious and unbridl'd democratie' (VII, 438). As for Harrington's agrarian laws, they are 'the cause . . . of sedition' (VII, 446). Rotation of office is too much like 'the wheel of fortune' (VII, 435), and the English have been tempted by it only because of 'the fluxible fault . . . of our watry situation' (VII, 437). Milton's sarcasm dries up Harrington's oceanic sublime; his suspicion of the 'watry' here links with his anxiety about the streams of royalist discourse. Harrington's system had already been characterized by a certain rigidity, and Milton's strategic adaptation was more rigid still. The second edition of *The Readie and Easie Way* offers a republic less as a sublime opportunity than as a means of containing instability. Yet Milton also adds further nervous admonitions about the possibility that the people may find the regime tyrannical, an objection that Harrington would undoubtedly have made, and admits the possibility of a Harringtonian rotation of offices. Milton implies that his proposals are merely a short-term expedient while the crisis defers other possibilities; 'it may be referrd to time, so we be still going on by degrees to perfection' (VII, 444).

Had Milton entirely lost hope at this point, *The Readie and Easie Way* would have served as his swan song.[131] Critics' desire to fit his career into a neat pattern of withdrawal from politics seems to be in part responsible for a certain irritation that has been shown towards his last pamphlet of 1660. In early April he clutched at a straw of hope: a former royal chaplain, Matthew Griffith, was imprisoned for publishing a militantly royalist sermon. Its dedication to Monck was profoundly embarrassing because it openly linked him with the royal cause at a time when the general was still trying to sustain a broadly-based coalition. Griffith's vengeful tone, and his hostility to all Puritans whether Presbyterians or Independents, was not far removed from the parody of cavalier attitudes with which Nedham had tried to frighten those inclining towards a restoration in *Newes from Brussels*. Griffith's imprisonment was a sign that the press was not yet entirely lost to republican discourse.

---

130 James Harrington, *A Letter unto Mr. Stubs* (1660; E1017.13), pp. 6–7; *HPW*, pp. 829–31.
131 Austin Woolrych, 'Dating Milton's *History of Britain*', *Historical Journal* 36 (1993), 929–43 (943), suggests that Milton composed the 'Digression' between the two editions of *The Readie and Easie Way*. This accords with a pattern of steadily increasing pessimism, but is hard to square with Milton's attempts, however grudging and uneasy, to form a last common front with the Presbyterians. The evidence, discussed in chapter 4 above, remains inconclusive.

In attacking Griffith, Milton again tries to unite the old Puritan coalition against monarchy: 'The Presbyterians therefor it concerns to be well fore-warnd of you betimes' (*Brief Notes upon a Late Sermon*, MPW, VII, 485). Near the end, Milton returned very briefly to the idea he and Wither had enter-tained a little earlier, that if there really had to be a king, Monck would be a better choice than Charles; but this was hardly a serious proposal, for Milton undermined it by declaring it at best tolerable (VII, 482). The pamphlet is indeed lacking in concrete proposals, and its nit-picking critique of his adver-sary's language is often viewed as oddly frivolous given the republicans' dire situation.[132] But Milton wants to show that the return of monarchy will bring a Babelian corruption of language that will undermine political and religious virtue. He therefore mercilessly assaults Griffith's flattering analogy between Charles and the Deity, which 'degrades God to a Cherub, and raises your King to be his collateral in place' (VII, 472–3). Milton reverts to the humanist mode of his attacks on Salmasius for his insensitivity to classical language, and to the debates of the 1650s over the status of Virgil, when he quibbles with Griffith for a misreading of storm-rebellion analogy in the *Aeneid*, i.250–51 (VII, 478). Pedantic though his correction is, Milton cannot bear to see classi-cal poetry and rhetoric invoked against his cause. His conclusion leaves Griffith's pamphlet to 'the just censure already pass'd upon you by the Councel of State' (VII, 486). In the light of Milton's career, it was not as anom-alous as it may seem that the author of *Areopagitica* should have bidden fare-well to the republican era by praising the imprisonment of an author. He was also praising the last republican institution to survive.

Brief Notes may seem to deprive Milton of lofty Olympian dignity, but con-temporary responses to it and other tracts of the spring of 1660 show that he was not perceived in that way: he was closely linked with Nedham and other republicans who were still feared as dangerous adversaries. Roger L'Estrange published a point-by-point reply to one late tract published by Chapman, *Plain English*, on the grounds that it had been diffused too widely to be sup-pressed, but he showed some unease at publicizing the kind of language he wanted to obliterate. *Plain English*, like *The Readie and Easie Way*, did show signs of an internalization of republican politics. It alluded to the obliteration in mid-March of the inscription at the exchange, 'Exit Tyrannus Regum Ultimus', and countered: 'yet it is written with the Pen of a Diamond in the hearts of many thousands, and will be so hereafter in the adamantine Rolls of Fame and History'.[133] Yet the tract insisted that however prudent it might be

132 Corns, *UV*, pp. 292–3.
133 *Plain English* (1660; P2359), p. 1; [Roger L'Estrange], *Treason Arraigned* (1660; E1019.14), p. 4. Worden, 'Milton and Marchamont Nedham', *MR*, pp. 156–80 (179 n. 113), inclines to accept the attribution to Nedham.

to be silent, it was essential to speak out against Charles, 'that the world may see we yet own our Cause' (p. 5). If Davenant claimed that Monck would make plainness graceful, the pamphlet's title insisted that republican plainness was the most honest form of language. Because there were 'too many in the City who wait the good time to re-erect his Statue, we desire in the first place to present you his Picture, as it was drawn by a good hand, the Parliament, in the year 1647' (p. 2). The republic's sublime iconoclasm was being inverted, but written texts would maintain political memory against obfuscatory images.

Monck in fact had no intention of following this tract's conception of 'the Common Cause', but Milton seems to have had brief hopes that he would use his troops against a Restoration, and Ludlow meditated some kind of coup. Resources, however, were limited. Overton, one of the last military commanders who seemed likely to move against the royalists, had now surrendered Hull, his millennial dreams becoming the butt of exultantly blasphemous rhyming:

> But *Overton* most with wonder doth seize us,
> By securing of *Hull* for no less than Christ Jesus,
> Hoping (as it by the story appears)
> To be there his Lieutenant for one thousand years.[134]

But one last military stand was made. In early April Lambert escaped from captivity. He tried to rally forces at Edgehill, the site of the first major Parliamentarian victory. Chapman was implicated in the rising, his *Plain English* being allegedly used as its manifesto.[135] Lambert's final throw, however, collapsed ignominiously. He prepared different manifestos to be issued according to where his strongest support was to be found, but a rising with so little conviction was not likely to inspire. In the end he declared for Richard Cromwell, who had been remaining hopefully in the wings, believing that he offered 'a Golden Mediocrity between A Topping Head & a Filthy Tayle'. This was indeed 'a Dialect peculiar to Himself'; Richard had been unable to create a convincing political language.[136] Given the chaotic ambiguity of his cause, the numbers who came out for Lambert were not negligible[137]; but he needed the support of figures like Ludlow, who feared that he was advancing 'a personall instead of [a?] publique interest'[138], and Streater,

---

134 *Arsy Versy: Or, The Second Martyrdom of the Rump* (1660; 669f24.31).

135 Leona Rostenberg, 'Sectarianism and Revolt: Livewell Chapman, Publisher to the Fifth Monarchy', in *Literary, Political, Scientific, Religious and Legal Publishing, Printing and Bookselling in England, 1551–1700: Twelve Studies*, 2 vols. (New York, 1965), I, 203–36 (227–8).

136 Sir Alan Broderick to Hyde, Bodleian MS Clarendon 58, fol. 119r, cited in Brendan O Hehir, *Harmony From Discords: A Life of Sir John Denham* (Berkeley and Los Angeles, 1968), p. 135 n. 41; its source makes this quotation rather suspect.

137 Hutton, *The Restoration*, p. 115.   138 Ludlow, *A Voyce from the Watch Tower*, p. 112.

who was instead amongst the troops sent to arrest him. Streater had no stomach for a republic retained by military repression.

Lambert's defeat left Parliament as the only republican hope. The new Convention assembled on 25 April. Ludlow and Hutchinson took their seats, persuading themselves that even now it was just possible that the day might be saved. Ludlow was shocked by the sudden shift in Parliamentary discourse: former restraints against royalist language were cast off. One member attacked Marten as one

> whose name would be infamous to posterity; which discourse, together with the flattering of Charles Steward (wherein none exceeded Mr. William Pryn), made my eares to tingle, and my heart to ake, all thinges running counter to what the providencyes of the Lord had lead to for twenty yeares past.

But there was a possibility that, like Griffith's sermon, high-flying language might alienate some of the more cautious Presbyterians. One of their number, Sir Arthur Annesley, had asked him to take his seat as a counterbalance to the 'young heady party in the Howse who upon all occasions flew high': it was necessary to 'keepe them in order'. One young MP expressed the wish that Vane, who had failed to be elected, were in the House 'to ballance the royall interest', and Ludlow still had hopes that 'the Lord might yet make him and others serviceable for the releeving us from the tyranny and oppression that was coming like a flood upon us'.[139] Even the return of the House of Lords, the old republican bugbear, offered some hopes, for some of the leading Presbyterian peers were very anxious not to concede what they had fought for in the war. But they had not been able to exclude monarchist peers from the Lords, and they lacked leadership in the Commons, where there were too few republican voices for Ludlow to repeat the experience of Richard's Parliament and establish a republican redoubt on hostile territory.[140] It was soon clear that the most that could be hoped for was a restoration of the king on tight terms that might include lenience for republicans. Even this did not happen, however; instead, Parliament accepted the king's Declaration of Breda, which was reassuringly moderate in tone, and left detailed negotiations for later.

139 Ibid., pp. 120–3. It is tempting to wonder whether he might have included Marvell in this category. Though as in 1659 he had won his seat ahead of a committed republican, some of his former associates, including Thurloe and St John, were very late converts to a Stuart restoration. Marvell does not seem to have joined the chorus of poets who greeted Charles's return, though he played a reasonably prominent part in Parliament: Pierre Legouis, *André Marvell: poète, puritain, patriote 1621–1678* (Paris and London, 1928), pp. 221ff.

140 Davies, *The Restoration of Charles II*, p. 333, suggests that at least ninety per cent of MPs wanted the king's return – which would correlate roughly with Harrington's estimate the previous year that about 5 per cent of the population was republican.

The king was summoned back, to immense popular rejoicing. Yet exactly what was meant by his restoration remained ambiguous. He was being summoned by a representative body which had not been elected in his name: in effect, he returned as an elected king. It was unclear what exactly was being restored: was it the status quo in 1640 or 1641 or 1648? There was still a lot to play for. Such considerations made it easier for a wide political spectrum to join in the celebrations; though they were not quite universal.[141] The woman of the house where Ludlow was hiding lit a bonfire merely to avoid suspicion.[142] Ludlow maintained thereafter a kind of Platonic faith in the Long Parliament as 'still the *lawfull* authority of the nation, being never dissolved by its owne consent'. But he came to the conclusion that the new regime had some legitimacy as the best present means of securing the people's welfare. He viewed the Restoration as an interruption like that of 1653, which might still allow some scope for republican activity. The nation might be happy in the king 'should he looke only forward'.[143]

It soon became clear, however, that Parliament was determined to look backwards. The Declaration of Breda had offered an amnesty to those who declared their loyalty to the king within a certain time; and the vengeful bloodbath of which Milton and other republicans had warned did not take place. But there was an ominous clause giving the right to make exceptions. Republicans were thus kept on a knife-edge: if they gave themselves up they might gain a pardon but they ran the risk of being one of the exceptions. The exceptions were to receive a traitor's punishment: they were hanged and then cut down while still alive, their genitals were cut off and their entrails cut out and burned, and their dismembered quarters were put on public show. It became quite impossible to guess who might be spared and who might not, and this unpredictability was in some ways harder to bear than a clear-cut policy. Ludlow hesitated for a long time before deciding that he would not be spared and going into exile. After much agonizing John Hutchinson sought and gained pardon, but his wife came to blame herself for having denied him the chance of showing solidarity with other republicans.[144] Milton went into hiding and awaited events.

While republicans debated on their best course of action, the royalist muses turned from hurling excrement at the Parliamentarians to scattering spring flowers over the king.[145] Charles entered London on 29 May. Mildmay

141 For an excellent account of literary contexts see Nicholas Jose, *Ideas of the Restoration in English Literature 1660–71* (1984), ch. 1.

142 Ludlow, *A Voyce from the Watch Tower*, p. 158.   143 Ibid., pp. 162, 173.

144 Hutchinson, pp. 229ff.

145 Masson, *Life of Milton*, VI, 12–17, gives a memorably acerbic account of changed allegiances in this period; Gerald MacLean is preparing an edition of poems greeting Charles's restoration.

Fane entered this date at the centre of his manuscript of Horatian imitations: the return for which he had waited so long was a reality.[146] The following day, Waller's *To the King, upon his Majesties Happy Return* was entered in the Stationers' Register.[147] Waller was one of the first poets to contribute to the growing volume of poems in praise of the king's return. Only a month before, Monck rather than Charles had been the object of panegyrists' praise. Robert Wild's *Iter Boreale*, published on 23 April, had opened the floodgates by modulating from praise of Monck to a detailed prophecy of the scene as the king returned. He situated his poem in the long tradition of poems on royal returns going back to Charles's return from Spain: this time there was a popular Monck rather than a wretched Buckingham to greet him.[148] Wild's style, however, was rugged and satirical. Waller – whose poetic career had begun with a poem on Charles's Spanish journey – hastened to set the tone for this new reign with a restored Augustanism. Charles is presented as an Aeneas-like figure of heroic fortitude, and the poem ends by celebrating the revival of the Muses. Republican rhetoric was to give way to adroit compliment.

For all the stress on the king's clemency, however, there is an undertone of menace. Charles has 'power unbounded, and a will confin'd' (line 104): if he is merciful to his rebellious people, it will be as a grace, a concession. Waller brings in a biblical parallel which likewise stresses Charles's absolute power: the nation is like Queen Esther, who pleaded with King Ahasuerus to waive his proclamation to exterminate the Jews (lines 15–17). Since Esther had persuaded the king instead to hang an unpopular minister, the bid for clemency was not without reference to revenge. At the start of the poem Waller emphasizes the nation's universal guilt:

> if your Grace incline that we should live,
> You must not (SIR) too hastily forgive . . .
> All are obnoxious[.] (lines 11–12, 15)

To Milton and Ludlow, anxiously waiting in hiding, the injunction that the king should not forgive too hastily must have seemed distinctly menacing. And indeed Waller seems to hit at Milton directly:

> Great *Britain*, like blind *Polipheme*, of late
> In a wild rage became the scorne and hate
> Of her proud Neighbours . . .

146 Harvard University Library fMS Eng 645, p. 95.
147 1660; E1080.3, dated by Thomason 9 June. A revised edition appeared in the same year.
148 George Wild, *Iter Boreale* (1660; E1021.10); *Poems on Affairs of State: Augustan Satirical Verse, 1660–1714*, ed. George de F. Lord *et al.*, 6 vols. (New Haven and London, 1963–75), I, 17. Wild's poem has sometimes been held to echo Marvell's 'Horatian Ode', though the resemblances do not seem to me very great.

But You are come, and all their hopes are vain,
This Gyant-Islle hath got her Eye again[.] (lines 19–24)

During the regicidal controversy Milton had been compared to Cyclops. The
reviving royalist literature of 1660 had renewed the charge that Milton's
blindness was a punishment for his support of regicide. One pamphlet had
suggested that Milton should be given the one eye of Colonel Hewson, an
officer who had been responsible for killing several royalist demonstrators in
a riot;[149] L'Estrange issued a pamphlet entitled *No Blind Guides*. Milton had
tried to counter such attacks by presenting his blindness as the sign of a higher
sublimity. Waller, however, reinterprets this republican sublimity as
uncouthness and incivility. Instead, the poem greets a new Augustan beauty
by reworking Denham's classic simile of royal concord. The people are
returning to their natural loyalty:

> So the injur'd Sea, which from her wonted course,
> To gain some acres, avarice did force,
> If the new Banks, neglected once, decay,
> No longer will from her old Channel stay,
> Raging, the late-got Land she overflowes,
> And all that's built upon't to ruine goes. (lines 67–72)

Here republican architecture is seen as a futile meddling with the monarchical course of nature. Waller will now return poetry to its due royalist bounds
just as the king will set the people their bounds (line 44).

Waller faced a problem that confronted many poets at this time, however. It
was difficult to restore a Stuart Augustanism without reviving memories of
Cromwellian Augustanism. Only the previous year, he had been linked with
Nedham and Milton as a republican who would be hanged when the king
returned. As recently as the end of March, an attack on Milton's *Readie and Easie
Way* had described Waller as 'a modern Protector-Poet' and alluded to lines on
Lucretius in which he had playfully compared the whole cosmos to a republic.[150] With this well-established reputation, Waller does not even try very hard
to conceal his reworkings of his *Panegyrick to my Lord Protector*. Like Cromwell,
Charles is greeted by neighbouring princes like ears of corn (line 88); both men
are compared to Alexander (lines 77–82). Waller even seems to rework Marvell's
simile of the returning sun in *The First Anniversary* (lines 47–50). Readers might
also have recalled the much-satirized conclusion to his elegy for Cromwell, with
Nature's sighs swelling the sea, when they were told that

---

149 *The Out-Cry of the London Prentices for Justice* (1660; E1013.12).
150 [Butler], *The Censure of the Rota upon Mr. Miltons Book*, p. 8, alluding to Waller's commendatory verses to John Evelyn, *An Essay on the First Booke of T. Lucretius Carus*
(1656; L3446), pp. 3–4.

the revolted Sea
Trembles to think she did Your Foes obey. (lines 17–18)

Waller had amply borne out Packer's comment in Richard's Parliament that if Charles landed in Dover the panegyrists' hyperboles would be transferred to him. Within a few weeks Waller was joined by his fellow-elegist for Cromwell, Dryden, whose *Astraea Redux* likewise cast the Restoration as a return to a better kind of beauty, and recast Milton's republican sublimity as barbarism:

Blind as the *Cyclops*, and as wild as he,
They own'd a lawless salvage Libertie,
Like that our painted Ancestours so priz'd
Ere Empires Arts their Breasts had Civiliz'd.[151]

Waller had been directly linked with Milton in Watson's parodies of his Cromwell poems; by attacking the Miltonic ethos, and assuming a penitential tone, he and Dryden were ritually disengaging themselves from their political pasts – though at the cost of seeming to offer up Milton as a sacrifice. Another of Cromwell's elegists, Payne Fisher, was at work on his celebration of Charles's return by July.[152] A week after Waller's poem appeared, the Commons ordered the *First Defence* and *Eikonoklastes* to be burned and proceedings to be opened against Milton.

The very blatancy of Waller's tactics seems to have appealed to the new ruler's travel-weary cynicism. Legend has it that Charles teased him with having written a better poem for Cromwell than for him, and that Waller replied, 'Sir, we poets never succeed so well in writing truth as in fiction' (*WP*, I, lxii). Confronting the thousands of acclamations that greeted him, Charles wryly declared that if he had known his subjects had missed him so much, he would not have stayed away so long. In a nation that had passed through so many upheavals, the fiction of a unanimous and uncomplicated longing for a deified king was welcome; but it was more apparent at the time than it has become in retrospect just how much of a fiction it was.

By June, the new Augustanism was well-established. With Milton and so many other republicans going underground, it was left to the indefatigable Wither to register a public protest against this development. Two days after Waller's poem was registered, Wither composed his response to the Restoration, *Speculum Speculativum*. As at the time of Cromwell's fall, Wither contrasted his own rhapsodic, inspired, godly poetry with the flattery of courtly poets. Though he did preface the poem with an address to the king, it was only in case it '*comes accidentally to his View*', a prospect made immediately unlikely by the frank declaration that it 'hath not to your *praise*/One *single Page*'.[153] Indeed, he

151 John Dryden, *Astraea Redux* (1660; E1080.6), p. 6.   152 Pepys, *Diary*, I, 209.
153 George Wither, *Speculum Speculativum* (1660; E1814.1; *WMW*, v), sig. A2v.

ventured to suggest that Charles might have committed secret crimes that were known only to God (p. 27). His poem, he claims with a hit at Waller,

> By *not commending*... much more *commends*,
> Than all their *Panegyricks* who bestrow
> Those men with *praises* whom they do not know;
> And, magnifie, when they ascend the *Throne*,
> All *Kings* alike; which *praise* is less than *none*[.] (sig. A2v)

He attacks the bonfires and other festivities for the king's return, which he regarded as idolatrous vanities, and recalls the addresses to the Cromwells:

> As much they magnifide them in their *Lyricks*.
> Heroick *Poems*, *Odes*, and *Panegyricks*,
> As they extoll the *King*. (p. 71)

He claims that Charles

> probably, in *Flanders* had remain'd
> If, otherways, their ends they could have gain'd,
> And *Dick*, perhaps, GEORGE, *Jack*, or any thing,
> With *popular applauses* had been *King*. (p. 72)

One contemptuous line lumps together Richard Cromwell, George Monck, and, effectively, any Tom, Dick, or Harry – or Charlie. Wither thus demystifies Restoration poetry before much of it has appeared: the king is merely a blank sheet on which subjects write their political desires.

Wither evokes Augustanism only in a distinctly negative way: if the king does not read the book, he may, like Caesar, regret it. And indeed the poem, while urging submission to Charles's *de facto* power, does also contain warnings that if he neglects his subjects he may be cast down. Where Waller had stressed the nation's guilt, Wither urges the king to be careful in his punishment of regicides, and expresses his fear of a terrible time ahead not only for the leading champions of the republic but also for those like himself who merely supported *de facto* power. Rather than ushering in the panegyrists' paradise, the king's return might re-enact the Fall, unleashing the infernal powers of Sin and Death (p. 14). Wither speaks of the regicide without the horror that was becoming obligatory:

> And, once when sick to death the *Body* lay,
> 'Twas cur'd by taking of the Head away. (p. 17)

He bitterly attacks the bishops' attempts to revive their power, and warns Charles that he does not know how tyrannical they were before the war: it was they who were to blame for its outbreak (p. 106). Wither had an interest to declare here, for he had bought lands confiscated from the bishops during the war; but he insisted that he would not try to hold on to them by flattering the new order (sig. A5r).

Speculum Speculativum is far more outspoken than any other of the poems addressing the king; it reads like a voice from an era that is already past. Wither stops short of open sedition. He accepts the king's authority and indeed argues that since he came in by conquest he did not need to limit his power to the ancient constitution (p. 60). He responds to the Restoration much as he had done to the Protectorate: hoping that great powers placed in the hands of one man may be used to good reforming ends, but fearful that the power may corrupt. The godly people are urged to be submissive: the era when they played an active part in political change is over, for the time being at least: they will

> overcome
> By being vanquisht, and prevail much more
> By *loosing*, than by *winning* heretofore.

He urges passive obedience:

> We, lately, active were ev'n unto blood;
> But, now such *activenesse* will do no good,
> And, we must *passive* be, till GOD shall please
> Our sins to pardon and to give us ease[.] (p. 56)

Yet the passivity is qualified: God may one day change the situation:

> For, his way, to the highest exaltations.
> Is by Debasings, and by Degradations. (p. 50)

Wither declares that the year 1666 as prophesied in Revelation is going to usher in the last days which will bring in the reign of Christ (pp. 129ff). The fate of Charles's dynasty remains open.

The very act of publishing *Speculum Speculativum* was far from simply passive. Though the main part of the poem is dated to mid-June, Wither hesitated before publishing it, acknowledging that some people would say he deserved hanging (sig. A4v). When it appeared some months later it was from the press of John Hayes, publisher of many oppositional books including martyrological accounts of the trials of the regicides. When his shop was raided by the authorities in 1662, *Speculum Speculativum* was one of the books seized.[154] By this time Wither was in prison for further indiscreet writings. If Milton had moved closer to Wither in *The Readie and Easie Way*, Wither perhaps returned the compliment, taking up Milton's reference to Jeremiah and his imagery of reviving stones. His epigraph read:

> *When thou comest to* Babylon, *thou shalt read these words; and when thou hast made an end of reading this Book, thou shalt binde a stone to it, and cast it into the midst of* Euphrates, *and say, Thus shall* Babylon *sink.* (Jeremiah LI.63)

154 Richard L. Greaves, *Deliver us from Evil: The Radical Underground in Britain, 1660–1663* (New York and Oxford, 1986), pp. 216–7.

Wither, like Milton, thus presents himself as a lone and futile voice; but also like Milton, he insists that he will not be ignored for ever.

> Yea, though into the *Thames* it should be thrown,
> Like that which being tide unto a *Stone*
> Was sunk in *Euphrates* (and no more seen
> After in *Babel* it once read had been)

yet God will before long use the book for His glory (p. 126). This pattern of sinking and elevation mirrors the strategy of passivity and ultimate vindication which he has urged on the godly. Virtuous discourse has had to go underground – or rather underwater – but it will one day be vindicated. Wither was indeed to be vindicated after 1688 when there was a renewed posthumous vogue for his prophecies. And in publishing *Speculum Speculativum* at all, Wither was insisting on remaining in the public view; and indeed it seems to have been a success with the public, going through three editions. The Restoration might seem to be a new '*Act*' in the drama of history, but it would turn out to have been only an '*Anti-mask*'; the world would be turned upside down once again (p. 129).

The Restoration did not silence voices like Wither's and Milton's. But its more militant apologists did work very hard, and with considerable long-term success, to obliterate the traces of a republican literary culture. The obliteration was carried out under the banner of Augustanism. The change was heralded by a Kent royalist, John Boys, who had been threatened with imprisonment by the republic after submitting a royalist petition in January 1660. Boys went into hiding and devoted part of his time to translating Virgil's sixth book. Boys saw himself as continuing the sequence of Virgil translations that had been appearing in the 1650s. He pointed out that Virgil's second, fourth and sixth books had had the special distinction of being revised for reading to Augustus. Denham having translated the second book, and Godolphin and Waller the fourth, it devolved on Boys to translate the sixth. When he published his translation the following year, Boys included a lengthy note which recorded his horror on hearing some contemporaries praising Brutus's tyrannicide, and declared that such an act was not justified even if Tarquin was a tyrant. Though he did not name Harrington, he also attacked Gracchus's agrarian laws. Boys also composed a poem for Charles's restoration in which he presented himself as Virgil to Charles's Aeneas. He published translation, panegyric and royalist petition together, insisting on their common elements as royalist speech-acts.[155] He followed this volume up with a version of Book III in which he praised Charles for taking revenge.[156] On his accession to power Augustus had erected a temple of Mars the revenger, and

---

155 John Boys, *Aeneas his Descent into Hell* (1661; E1054.3), sigs. A1r–v, pp. 157–60, 186, 218ff.
156 John Boys, *Aeneas his Errours, or his Voyage from Troy into Italy* (1661; v621), pp. 57–68.

this was alluded to in the triumphal arches for Charles's entry to his coronation in May 1661. Appropriately, one of the devisers was the Virgil translator John Ogilby, who was to embark on a twelve-book epic on King Charles II.[157]

The more vengeful royalists did not have everything their way. The Bodleian Library, honouring its connections with Milton, did not burn his political works but discreetly hid them.[158] He was released after a brief imprisonment; Marvell, Davenant and Annesley are amongst those likely to have pleaded for him.[159] Marten was exempted from pardon but was able to call in the favours he had shown to many royalists and lived on in prison for many years. But more republicans were executed than had been originally envisaged; and royalist revenge extended to the dead. In December 1660 it was decided to exhume Cromwell's body from Westminster Abbey and subject it to a grisly posthumous execution along with Ireton, Bradshaw and Pride. Slater's prophecy two years earlier that the dust of deceased monarchs would rise to greet Cromwell had been grotesquely reversed. Marvell had prophesied that the dust would rise against Thomas May, but he is unlikely to have imagined such a literal fulfilment. May was included in a further wave of exhumations, which included several people Marvell had celebrated in verse: Cromwell's mother and Admirals Blake and Deane. Isaac Dorislaus, who had first experienced censorship of his republican views back in 1627, and then been assassinated by royalists in 1649, was now subjected to posthumous suppression. Lucan had warned that monarchies tried to erase the memory of republicanism; his name had been invoked on the tombs of Thomas May and possibly of Ireton. Now Lucan's translator was amongst those expelled from the Abbey. English literary culture has never entirely undone those expulsions.

---

157 John Ogilby, *The Entertainment of His Most Excellent Majestie Charles II*, ed. Ronald Knowles (Binghamton, 1988), pp. 25–6; Katherine S. Van Eerde, *John Ogilby and the Taste of his Times* (Folkestone, 1976), p. 87.

158 Nicholas von Maltzahn, 'Wood, Allam, and the Oxford Milton', *Milton Studies* 31 (1994), 155–77 (159, 172).

159 Annesley had been one of the first readers of *Areopagitica* (copy at the University of Michigan, Ann Arbor; purchased 28 November 1644) and after the Restoration was active in trying to keep the press open for Milton and other dissenting voices.

CHAPTER 10

Paradise Lost and English republicanism

The poem's speech-acts

During the twists and turns of the Cause in the later 1650s – the glorification of the Protector as the God-like Creator of a new republic, the collapse of Protectoral politics and the revived imagery of collective creation and restoration, the final collapse in 1660 – Milton was planning, and beginning to write, *Paradise Lost*.

That simple, and well-attested, fact runs counter to some influential interpretations of the epic which reached their height during the Cold War period and are still very much with us. Blair Worden speaks for innumerable critics when he argues that Milton 'withdraws from politics into faith', into 'eternal verities'.[1] Youthful idealism gives way to serene maturity, political anarchy to timeless culture. Milton's praise of God's kingship over Satan's rebellion, it is often assumed, was a return to a monarchist imagination. And yet Worden, in his role as political historian, also brings into sharp focus Milton's prominent role in the republican crisis of 1659–60. Milton, it would seem, was ready to stake his life on behalf of republicanism at exactly the same time as he was rejecting its values in favour of serene resignation.

The closer we bring *Paradise Lost* to its original context, the more we try to imagine our way beyond post-Restoration hindsight, the harder it becomes to square a blandly apolitical or defeatist reading of the epic with its author's values. Milton may have laid claim to prophetic status, but this does not mean that he foresaw the Restoration. Indeed, the very word 'restoration' had in the 1650s political connotations radically different from those imposed by the post-1660 order. His first sketches for a drama on the Fall go back to the early 1640s, at a time when he was losing faith in early plans for an epic set in the days of King Arthur. His nephew Edward Phillips told Aubrey that he heard Milton recite Satan's first soliloquy on arriving on Earth during the early 1650s, and that Milton began work in earnest on the

---

1 Blair Worden, 'Milton's Republicanism and the Tyranny of Heaven', in Gisela Bock, Quentin Skinner and Maurizio Viroli (eds.), *Machiavelli and Republicanism* (Cambridge, 1990), pp. 225–45 (p. 244).

epic about two years before the Restoration and finished three years after it. His close friend Cyriack Skinner stated that he began work on *Paradise Lost*, along with *Christian Doctrine* and a Latin dictionary, after the onset of blindness but when he was still acting as a government official. The evidence points, then, to a beginning of composition in the mid to late 1650s; Milton's major biographers settle on 1658.[2] At the end of the revised *First Defence* he announced that he hoped to testify to still greater achievements, a possible reference to his epic (*MPW*, IV:1, 537). As has been seen, the new edition amounted to a revival of republican rhetoric, a harbinger of the renewal in 1659. To read a poem with such origins as a document of post-Restoration disillusion flies in the face of this evidence. On Aubrey's reckoning, at least two-fifths of the epic may have been written by the time the king came in. As one 'long choosing, and beginning late' (ix.26), Milton would surely have planned the overall structure of his poem carefully in advance. It is normally presumed, reasonably enough, that he proceeded book by book, but we do not know.[3] The darker tone of the last two books may reflect his disillusion after the Restoration; but the end of the drama which he had sketched much earlier was not exactly cheerful, concluding with 'a mask of all the evils of this life & world' (*MPW*, VIII, 560). We can hardly imagine that when Milton embarked on the story of the Fall he expected to give it an easy happy ending. If the poem has a dark side, then, it cannot be ascribed simply to the restored monarchy. The centre of gravity of the poem, its major creative impulse, belongs in the revolutionary period.

It is true that some or most of the poem would have been composed after 1660, and may have been subjected to later revision. The last two books seem to reflect the outlook of 1660s Dissent more than 1650s Puritanism.[4] Yet Dissent in the 1660s was not always as subdued as has sometimes been thought; and the evidence suggests that far from retiring into political resignation, Milton made every effort to intervene in the now-diminished public sphere as far as he possibly could. After the publication of *Paradise*

2 David Masson, *The Life of John Milton*, 7 vols. (1881; reprint, New York, 1946), V, 405–8; William Riley Parker, *Milton: A Biography*, second edition, 2 vols., ed. Gordon Campbell (Oxford, 1996), I, 509.

3 Hugh Trevor-Roper, 'Milton in Politics', in *Catholics, Anglicans and Puritans: Seventeenth-Century Essays* (1987), pp. 277ff, writes of 'the end of ideology'. For earlier attempts to establish the chronology, neither of which places much emphasis on a post-Restoration date, see Grant McColley, *'Paradise Lost': An Account of its Growth and Major Origins* (Chicago, 1940), ch. 12, and Allan H. Gilbert, *On the Composition of 'Paradise Lost': A Study of the Ordering and Insertion of Material* (Chapel Hill, 1947). E. M. W. Tillyard, *Milton* (1930; revised edition, 1966), p. 164, writes that the *Second Defence* is 'the one prose work that sprang directly from the mood which first conceived *Paradise Lost'*.

4 Thomas N. Corns, *Regaining 'Paradise Lost'* (London and New York, 1994), p. 133.

Lost he brought out at least one work in verse or prose each year, as if testifying to his refusal to remain silent. His first post-Restoration appearance in print came in 1662, when the sonnet to Vane was printed in George Sikes's adulatory biography. Vane had become a republican martyr when he was tried and executed in breach of the Act of Indemnity. Sikes gave a very prominent place to the sonnet, as a transition between a religious meditation and a detailed account of Vane as '*A Common-Wealths-Man* . . . a dangerous Name to the Peace and Interest of Tyranny'. Sikes used the sonnet's three parts as the basis for his division of his material over the following ten pages, including a provocative discussion of the Romans' rightful abolition of monarchy; he offered what was in effect the first detailed commentary on one of Milton's poems.[5] The speech-act of this publication was strongly oppositional, and the normal assumption that the disillusioned Milton cannot possibly have been involved perhaps needs rethinking. The fate of regicides like Vane may also have been pointed to in *Samson Agonistes*.[6] *Paradise Lost*, on Phillips's testimony, may have been largely complete by the year after the Vane volume appeared, though it did not appear until 1667. Milton seems to have delayed publication until a moment when he would be least threatened by censorship, at a time when the government was in disarray after the Great Plague, the Great Fire, and a mismanaged war with the Dutch which contrasted strikingly with the republic's successes.[7] The literary battles of the 1650s were being replayed. Once again Waller had put himself forward as a panegyrist of the court, this time a Stuart one, exaggeratedly praising a naval encounter in his *Instructions to a Painter*. Once more Wither, who had been undeterred by periods of imprisonment under the Restoration and still had millennial hopes, satirized Waller's flattery in a poem that the authorities tried to suppress.[8] A series of manuscript retorts to Waller was crowned by Marvell's ferocious *Last Instructions to a Painter*, which functioned as a Lucan to Waller's Virgil.[9] Overton, though consigned to prison, continued with such writing as was possible. He worked on a political testament and after his wife's death in 1665, which he blamed on the authorities, he embarked on a

5 [George Sikes], *The Life and Death of Sir Henry Vane* (1662; S6323C), pp. 93–102.
6 Blair Worden, 'Milton, *Samson Agonistes*, and the Restoration', in Gerald MacLean (ed.), *Culture and Society in the Stuart Restoration: Literature, Drama, History* (Cambridge, 1995), pp. 111–36; Annabel Patterson, *Early Modern Liberalism* (Cambridge, 1997), pp. 83–6.
7 Nicholas von Maltzahn, 'The First Reception of *Paradise Lost* (1667)', *Review of English Studies* 47 (1996), 479–99.
8 George Wither, *Sigh[s] for the Pitchers* (1666; WMW, 3; W3190), p. 22, responding to Waller's *Instructions to a Painter*, lines 319–20.
9 On Lucan and Marvell see A. B. Chambers, *Andrew Marvell and Edmund Waller: Seventeenth-Century Praise and Restoration Satire* (University Park and London, 1991), pp. 117ff.

long memorial manuscript for her, adapting Donne's poetry for bitter attacks on Monck.[10]

At the time *Paradise Lost* appeared, then, oppositional voices were by no means silenced, and Milton gives not the slightest sign of cowed recantation in his speech-acts after the Restoration. The speech-act of *Paradise Lost* when ultimately published would have inevitably differed from the one he had originally envisaged; but it had its own pointedness.[11] Tactical considerations would indeed have encouraged a toning down of explicit republican enthusiasm, so that he could evade the censorship and mobilize a broader religious coalition than he had been ready to work with before the Restoration. I would argue, however, that the poem's pessimistic elements have been put down too simply to the loss of his earlier political ideals. Milton certainly regarded the Restoration as a shaming disaster; but to equate it with the Fall would be to give it a metaphysical dignity it did not deserve. If his mind had turned in the 1650s to the Fall, it was partly because he was always aware of the precariousness of the republican experiment, and was taking out an imaginative insurance policy against its failure. Against the larger background of the primal human failure, even a transitory recovery of liberty was something. Milton chose a very general narrative to distance himself from his immediate milieu in order to place its local events in a cosmic perspective. This does not mean that he was abandoning politics for timeless concerns. Milton was not to know that the monarchy was back for such a lengthy stay, and he continued to the end of his life to work with those who were determined to give it a hard time.

Paradise Lost, of course, belongs to a different genre of discourse from republican pamphlets. The epic's declared topic of justifying God's ways to men is far more general than the concerns of the republican tracts. The poem spans a bewildering variety of political registers from the absolutist to the republican. These registers are used metaphorically to describe realms in which the *polis* is either irrelevant, as in heaven, or not yet in being, as in Eden. I shall try to bring out just how problematic the poem's treatment of kingship and rebellion would have been for a contemporary republican; and Milton foregrounds the problems rather than trying to pass them over. But it is a little misleading to go on to say, with one critic, that his purpose is to delineate 'universal spiritual values, not partisan ideologies'.[12] Had that been so, he could

---

10 David Norbrook, ' "This Blushing Tribute of a Borrowed Muse": Robert Overton's Overturning of the Seventeenth-Century Poetic Canon', *English Manuscript Studies 1100–1700* 4 (1993), 220–66.

11 On the Restoration resonances see Laura Lunger Knoppers, *Historicizing Milton: Spectacle, Power, and Poetry in Restoration England* (Athens and London, 1994), pp. 87–91.

12 Robert Thomas Fallon, *Divided Empire: Milton's Political Imagery* (University Park, 1995), p. ix.

have omitted much explicitly partisan matter from his poem. And to declare that poetry deals with universal qualities independent of specific political forms, in terms of the debates of the 1650s, is not to advance a neutral position but to side with Hobbes's method of reading as opposed to Harrington's; on this particular issue, Milton is likely to have aligned himself with the latter. The difficulties readers have had with his political imagery stem from the specificity of his political language, which runs at odds with any attempt at a detached timelessness. For his Protestantism and his humanism, the struggle to justify God's ways was a time-bound and a *polis*-bound activity. The 1650s had been a decade of startling shifts of temporality, with the 'foreshortened time' of the Protectorate itself being retrospectively redefined out of existence as an 'interruption': the relations between the time-bound and the timeless had become infinitely complex. Milton's heretical *Christian Doctrine* opens by drawing attention to the changes in understanding God over the preceding century (*MPW*, VI:117–24), and for Milton those changes had been intimately bound up with changes in the structures of religious and political communication.

Milton's monism, his rejection of a sharp split between spirit and matter, worked also against a comparable split between theology and politics. His prose justification of God's ways was considered so partisan and so blasphemous that the Restoration regime took active steps to suppress it.[13] Depoliticized theological readings of the poem often miss that polemical edge. Stanley Fish's powerful and influential reading, while alert to the poem's radical 'surprises', places them within a quietist framework. 'Humility,' he maintains, 'is what [Milton] seeks to instil in his readers by exploding the promise of a terrestrial Paradise': Milton harasses them into abandoning worldly hopes. The effect is to transform him into something very like the orthodox Presbyterians he detested.[14] I shall try instead to construct something of what the poem might have meant to less submissively-minded republican readers, those willing to read in the critical, iconoclastic spirit that he had advocated in *Areopagitica*.

Paradise Lost, I believe, reflects its republican milieu less in specific allusions than in its overall intellectual and generic structures. I shall concentrate on three main areas. I shall demonstrate that the poem's anti-Augustanism,

---

13 Milton's authorship of *Christian Doctrine* has recently come into question. Gordon Campbell *et al.*, 'The Provenance of *De Doctrina Christiana*', *MQ* 31 (1997), 67–121 suggest that the manuscript represents a partial Miltonic revision of a different treatise, so that some sections probably reflect his personal views much more than others.

14 Stanley Fish, *Surprised by Sin: The Reader in 'Paradise Lost'* (1967; Berkeley, Los Angeles and London, 1971), p. 128; John P. Rumrich, *Milton Unbound: Controversy and Reinterpretation* (Cambridge, 1996), p. 32; cf. William Kolbrener, *Milton's Warring Angels: A Study of Critical Engagements* (Cambridge, 1997), pp. 126ff.

which has embarrassed many critics trying to link Milton with the epic tradition, belongs to the republican reassessment of classical literary culture in the mid-century, and shall emphasize the continuing stream of allusions to the *Pharsalia* that has been missed by those in search of Virgilian references. I shall argue that the poem's themes of creation and reduction link the poem at a more profound level with republican ideology than the much-discussed problem of a republican's describing a heavenly king. Finally, in discussing the problems of speech and freedom in Eden, I shall show the poem's links with the difficult intersections between political and domestic spheres that had been explored in the prose tracts of the 1640s.

A tragic epic: *Paradise Lost* and the *Pharsalia*

The very qualities in the poem that have led to its being linked with a post-1660 reaction against republicanism make sense in republican terms. Milton's political development was not a straight curve from optimism to pessimism: moments of sharp pessimism of the intellect alternated or even coincided with urgent enactments of an optimism of the will. Commentators who see the dark and tragic elements of Milton's epic as a political retreat seem to imagine that the appropriate epic for a republic would be an optimistic celebration of a great hero. As has been seen, however, the difficulty of adapting heroic poetry to a republican order was a major preoccupation of the republic's defenders. Payne Fisher had shown one possible course. Under the Commonwealth he had turned Lucan's sharply ironic epic mode into a vehicle for straightforward panegyric, like the crudely flattering canvases that provoked foreign ambassadors' laughter. Under the Protectorate it had become ever easier for Fisher and other poets simply to place Cromwell in the role previously assigned to Augustus. The *Second Defence* shows Milton's unease with that kind of strategy. Though Milton was ready to defend the regime for immediate polemical purposes, he did not believe that the foundations of a true republic had yet been laid. Virgil may have been able to celebrate the Empire as the realization – however imperfect – of his political goals, but the shifting regimes of the 1650s offered Milton no such realized ideal.

Milton's unease with Augustan mythology, and epideictic narrative, had emerged in the *History of Britain*. As the major work which he wrote in parallel with *Paradise Lost*, it deserves more attention than it has received as a context for the poem. As was seen in chapter 4 above, the 'Digression' took a starkly unoptimistic view of the possibilities for a republican culture, largely because England excelled in the virtues of military heroism – the primary classical epic virtues – but lacked civil prudence. The sections of the *History* dealing with the Roman conquest make for peculiarly difficult reading because they are equally critical of the Britons for failing to seize political opportunities and of the Augustan bias of the available histories: 'For . . . *Caesar*, whose Autority we are now first to follow, wanted not who tax'd him of mis-reporting in his Commentaries, yea in his Civil Warrs against *Pompey*, much more, may wee think, in the *British affairs*, of whose little skill in writing he did not easily hope to be contradicted' (*MPW* v:1, 37).[15] The reference to Caesar's *De Bello Civili* is a reminder that Milton at this point is in the same rhetorical position as Lucan in his epic, drawing heavily on Caesar's writings but also signalling a republican distance. He takes a sharply sardonic view of Caesar's and other emperors' triumphs, and his preference for what he terms 'the *Roman* Free State' (v, 41) is evident. We are reminded that even well into imperial history, a governor could be dismissed for making 'an Oration against Monarchie' (v, 100). One of Lucan's cast of characters, the redoubtable Scaeva, makes an appearance in Milton's narrative, allegedly the first to jump out of his landing-craft to assault the British enemy. Milton recounts an alternative version that has Caesar jumping out of the boat first, only to add that 'this were to make *Caesar* less understand what became him then *Scaeva*' (v:1, 46). Since Milton goes on to cast considerable doubt on Caesar's sense of what became him, we are left with a picture of Caesar hovering between rash bravery and lying vainglory. Despite the acclaim with which his return to Rome was greeted, 'other antient writers have spok'n more doubtfully of *Caesars* Victories heer; and that in plaine termes hee fled from hence; for which the common verse in *Lucan* with divers passages heer and there in *Tacitus* is alleg'd' (v:1, 56). Milton here alludes to the *Pharsalia* (ii.572).[16] The Roman legacy is highly ambivalent: Caesar's landing brings at the very same time republican civility and the monarchical tendencies that will undermine it.

This was not the kind of history to cheer and inspire. Milton clearly believed, however, that an unflinching awareness of the difficulties to be overcome was more important than confident action without such an awareness. This was a tragic history, some of its subject-matter echoing his early plans for tragedies. As an admirer of Euripides, Milton was well aware that the most democratic culture of classical antiquity had not produced a cheerfully accepting literature, had on the contrary prided itself on its refusal to shy away from difficult questions. If the republicans' favourite epic was the *Pharsalia*, it was not just despite, but because of, its darkness of tone. Lucan presents the tragic defeat of the cause of liberty as a gigantic, cosmic disaster;

15 Cf. Nicholas von Maltzahn, *Milton's 'History of Britain': Republican Historiography in the English Revolution* (Oxford, 1991), pp. 111ff.
16 This passage was also cited by Hutchinson, p. 279.

he thus galvanized republicans with a sense of the urgency of their task. *Paradise Lost* originated as a tragedy, and it shares the tragic spirit of the *Pharsalia* – which did not preclude a sharp, sceptical wit.

That wit has often been missed by scholars seeking to turn Milton into a votary of the classical tradition. A good example is the proem to Book IX:

> Sad task, yet argument
> Not less but more Heroic then the wrauth
> Of stern *Achilles on his Foe pursu'd*
> *Thrice Fugitive about Troy Wall; or rage*
> *Of Turnus for Lavinia disespous'd,*
> *Or Neptun's ire or Juno's, that so long*
> *Perplex'd the Greek and Cytherea's Son . . .*
> Not sedulous by Nature to indite
> Warrs, hitherto the onely Argument
> Heroic deem'd, chief maistrie to dissect
> With long and tedious havoc fabl'd Knights
> In Battels feign'd; the better fortitude
> Of Patience and Heroic Martyrdom
> Unsung . . . (ix.13–19, 27–33)[17]

'Let's try, if we can find *Milton* among all this Rubbish.' The choleric eighteenth-century scholar Richard Bentley was baffled by Milton's wayward treatment of classical tradition, which confused the different themes and actions of both Homer and Virgil. The reference to Turnus he found 'Silly, as if the *Aeneid* was wrote for *Turnus*'s Sake and Fame, and not for *Aeneas*'s, whose name it bears'. Bentley was worried that Milton made it look as if Aeneas' mission to Latium were an unjust conquest rather than an imperial destiny.[18] So confident was Bentley that Milton could never have written such things that he invented the hypothesis of a foolish amanuensis or printer and duly emended or cut (for example the lines italicized above) according to Milton's assumed intentions. More recent critics have been less officious but they have sometimes adopted a different strategy for defusing the force of Milton's attack on the glories of epic. He was of course being ironic, expecting the knowing classicist to read between the lines to find the author's true admiration for Virgil and Homer.[19] Milton the fierce critic of tradition thus

---

17 Citations from *Paradise Lost* are from the 'eclectic old-spelling' edition of the 1674 text by Roy Flannagan (New York, 1993). The 1667 text would presumably be closer to the poem's originally conceived speech-act, but all critical discussions are tied to the 1674 version, and the variations, other than structural ones discussed below, are not significant to my argument. Lucan is cited from J. D. Duff's Loeb edition (Cambridge, Mass. and London, 1928).

18 Richard Bentley (ed.), *Milton's 'Paradise Lost': A New Edition* (1732), p. 267.

19 William M. Porter, *Reading the Classics and 'Paradise Lost'* (Lincoln and London, 1993), pp. 88–9.

becomes aligned with an unproblematic 'epic tradition', and the adventurous iconoclasm of the republican era is sanitized.

The best critics of Milton's language have, however, been prepared to give Bentley his due: the extreme rigidity of his model of epic decorum at least drew attention to the areas where Milton wilfully transgresses decorum. Keen to 'dissociate [*Paradise Lost*] from any stain of radical politics or metaphysics'[20], Bentley provided a kind of linguistic filter that expertly caught any impropriety. There was plenty to catch. Far from being the continuous organ-voice of an old critical stereotype, *Paradise Lost* has a strong vein of the iconoclastic wit of mid-century republicanism. As has been seen, Harrington had been quite ready to omit passages from Virgil of which he disapproved. Milton's reference to Hector as 'Thrice fugitive' parallels, whether or not it directly echoes, Harrington's declaration that he will not recount 'How *Hector* round his *Troy* should be dragg'd th[r]ice'.[21] Harrington had begun his translation of the *Aeneid* in a mood of impatience at the failure of his *Oceana* to persuade Cromwell to institute a republicanized Augustanism. At around the same time Milton, also to some extent disaffected with the Protectorate, was turning to his epic. (He was also working on his massive Latin thesaurus, for which he would surely have run through his lexical memory of the Roman poets.) For all the immense differences between the projects, Harrington and Milton shared both a genuine admiration for Virgil and a political disaffection with the cult of Augustus; both men were willing to rethink and correct the texts of the past. Harrington had insisted that such texts should be read not merely to identify with heroes but to think about the political contexts that formed them. Milton had less confidence in the effect of political structures than Harrington, but he shared an intensely political interest in classical literature.

The provocative tone of the Book IX proem would not have looked so odd to readers familiar with Lucan's aggressively assertive narrator. One author of commendatory verses to Gorges's translation had declared that

> HOMER and MARO, that did Poetize,
> As much in manner, as in kinde of stile,
> Did thereby dimme the glorious deeds the while
> Of them, whose acts they meant to memorize.

Lucan, by contrast, disdained to interweave his heroes' achievements with 'idle vanities'. Another poet praised Lucan for showing that 'flatteries and fictions' might 'please a tyrant', and contrasted his truth-telling poetry with

> the *Trojan* Theamers, fit for schooles,
> Fabling of this and that in Heauen, Earth, Hell[.][22]

20 Kolbrener, *Milton's Warring Angels*, p. 115.
21 James Harrington, *Virgil's Aeneis* (1659; v618), sig. A5r.
22 *Lucans Pharsalia*, trans. Sir Arthur Gorges (1614; 16884), sigs. A5r, A6r.

Lucan had described Caesar's claim of Trojan descent as a mere fable (iii.212); and throughout the *Pharsalia* he undermines imperial mythology. May had contrasted martial glory with the more inward virtue shown by Lucan's Cato:

> see here
> Good *Cato's* strength orecome what taske so ere
> His Cruell Mistresse *Vertue* could command;
> And marching ore scorch'd Affricks desert sand
> Winne (as our Author thought) more honour far
> Then any Laurell'd Roman Conquerer
> By Lands subdu'd, or blood of Nations shedd,
> When captiu'd Monarchs their proud Chariotts ledd.[23]

Cato anticipates Milton's 'paradise within thee, happier farr' (xii.587). Payne Fisher's Lucanian epic of the English Civil War had been contrasted by one admirer with the fictions of the tale of Troy.[24] One of the commendatory poems to the 1674 *Paradise Lost* claimed that Milton had made the *Iliad* and *Aeneid* look like mock-epics, and concentrated on the war in heaven; since the probable author, Samuel Barrow, had served with Monck's army in Scotland[25], he is very likely to have encountered Fisher.

During those campaigns of the 1650s, Cromwell was being both praised in an Augustan mode and denigrated in the spirit of Lucan. Milton had tried to steer a course between these extremes, but by the end of the decade he had given up that possibility. He would have begun *Paradise Lost* in earnest at that period of disillusion. His Satan has very pronounced associations with Lucan's Caesar, and had the poem appeared in a period of republican revival, it is likely that readers would have looked back to Cromwell as the last instantiation of the general principle of the corruptions inherent in rule by a single person. This is not to say that the poem is a topical allegory. Milton is concerned with the general issue of the subordination of the common interest to a private will. Early in the Protectorate he would still have thought of Charles I as embodying that principle and Cromwell as skilfully sidestepping it; by 1667 the Stuarts were again the main objects of concern. In giving a semi-republican rhetoric to Satan, however, Milton was linking him more closely with Cromwell than with either Charles. Like Lucan, he demonstrates how republican ideals can become corrupted by personal ambition.

Lucan was a continuing point of reference in tracing such corruption; and Milton had associated Satan with Lucan's Caesar as far back as his youthful

---

23 May, *Lucan's Pharsalia* (1627; 16887), sig. Q2r: dedication to Warwick.
24 Pierre de Cardonnel, commendatory verse to Payne Fisher, *Marston-Moor, sive de Obsidione proelioque Eboracensi Carmen* (1650; E535), sig. a1v.
25 Nicholas von Maltzahn, '"I admird Thee": Samuel Barrow, Doctor and Poet', *MQ* 19 (1995), 25–8.

poem on the Gunpowder Plot.[26] Traditions of interpretation of *Paradise Lost*, however, have largely lost that context.[27] The ten-book structure of the 1667 edition, which aligned the poem with Lucan, is now seen as a puzzling deviation from the Virgilian norm, duly corrected in 1674.[28] Patrick Hume, author of the first full commentary on the poem, which appeared in 1695, offered more references to the *Pharsalia* than any later commentator.[29] In the following analysis, I shall pay close attention to these parallels. They do not, of course, exclude the chains of reference to Homer and Virgil that have attracted more critical attention: Milton's admiration for both poets was immense, whatever ideological quarrels he might have had with the latter. The Lucan allusions, however, offer a way of reading the poem in a more critical and iconoclastic spirit than has sometimes been allowed. Allusion is a difficult and slippery topic. One critic proposes an upward gradation from appropriation, where a poet may take over a phrase without expecting this to be recognized, through reference, where varying degrees of similarity will be recognized, to allusion, which involves a 'miniature hermeneutic dialogue' where difference as well as similarity may be foregrounded.[30] The examples cited below, I believe, fall in the second and third categories. I shall follow Satan's trajectory through the poem not in the poem's narrative order with its extensive flashbacks, but according to the underlying chronology.

Both in the *Pharsalia* and in *Paradise Lost*, the question of the epic hero is notoriously problematic. Caesar and Satan dominate the forward action of both poems, to the extent of suggesting to some critics a degree of

26 'In Quintum Novembris', l. 48, echoing Lucan i.183: *John Milton: Complete Shorter Poems*, second edition, ed. John Carey (London and New York, 1997), p. 40.

27 For an exception see Charles Martindale, *John Milton and the Transformation of Ancient Epic* (1986), ch. 5.

28 For a recent discussion see John K. Hale, '*Paradise Lost*: A Poem in Twelve Books, or Ten?', *Philological Quarterly* 74 (1995), 131–49. Numerological critics have claimed that Milton structured the 1667 edition symmetrically around the Son's descent in his chariot (vi.761–2). This structural balance would be more Virgilian than Lucanian in spirit (as is observed by David Quint, *Epic and Empire: Politics and Generic Form from Virgil to Milton* (Princeton, 1993), pp. 41–2); but Hale points out some difficulties in the argument. Notably, it assumes that the blind Milton had counted the number of lines exactly even though the printer misnumbered them. For a numerological reading of the ten-book version see Maren-Sofie Røstvig, *Configurations: A Topomorphic Approach to Renaissance Poetry* (Oslo, Copenhagen and Stockholm, 1994), pp. 461–534.

29 P[atrick]. H[ume]., *Annotations on Milton's 'Paradise Lost'* (1695); contrast the later commentary by Jonathan Richardson, father and son, *Explanatory Notes and Remarks on Milton's Paradise Lost* (1734). Admittedly Hume tended to accumulate correspondences without much selection; but it is still noteworthy that it is the Lucan allusions that have tended to be dropped in later editions, far more than those to Virgil. On Hume's later influence see Patrick Daly, Jr, 'Patrick Hume and the Making of Addison's *Paradise Lost* Papers', *Milton Studies* 31 (1994), 179–95.

30 Porter, *Reading the Classics and 'Paradise Lost'*, pp. 21ff.

identification between writer and villain.[31] Of Lucan's chief defenders of the republic, Pompey is weak and fallible, Cato inhumanly virtuous; Milton's Satan has been regarded as the exception to a general want of human interest. The analogy with Caesar helps to throw light on the theory that Milton's unconscious sympathies were with Satan. In Book IX of the *Pharsalia*, the poet addresses Caesar as he tramples over the ruins of Troy – and of an older epic tradition rendered obsolete by his ruthlessness – and declares that our Pharsalia, 'Pharsalia nostra', will live: on a certain level, Lucan depends on Caesar for the success of his epic even though Caesar has also destroyed the liberty whose loss he laments. On that basic narrative level, Satan is likewise the poem's real hero; and in rhetorical terms he is the poem's most eloquent performer; he is an 'Author' and 'Architect' (ii.381, 864, vi. 262, ix.771, x.236, 356).

The analogy may point us further than it often does. Discussion of Milton's Satan has often centred on the way he unbalances the poem: readers looking for a Virgilian balance and harmony will be disconcerted by a violent asymmetry. Explanation for these structural faults in both epics is then sought in the poets' unconscious minds. As was seen in chapter 1, however, an ideological reason can be given for Lucan's refusal to offer a clear-cut hero. Augustan architecture which placed the monarch at the centre was in fact repressive and top-heavy. Suspicious of concord that was too easily concordant, Lucan aimed at a diffusion of interests, and made his readers suspect their own tendency to centre their imaginations on Caesar. With extraordinary audacity, Milton pushes this strategy much further. He gives us a Janus-faced Caesar, one who embodies all of the vicious ambition of Lucan's anti-hero, but who is also the poem's most powerful republican rhetorician. Lucan offered a germ of this process in Caesar's first address to his troops – from whose introduction Milton borrows at x.456–8. Caesar adopts a rhetoric of constitutional propriety: Pompey is a tyrant, a usurper, his troops have invaded the courtrooms, and Caesar's goal is simply to dislodge him: 'detrahimus dominos urbi servare paratae' (i. 351), 'Nor spoile those armes doe seeke, nor Soveraignty:/But to free Rome, though bent to slauery' (May, sig. A6v). However, he has already declared that he has no more respect for law (i.225–7); and his constitutionalist rhetoric leaves his troops cold, while it is the fiery Laelius who rallies their support by appealing to self-interest and cruelty.

In Lucan it is clear that Caesar's adoption of republican rhetoric is merely cynical, and the typically sardonic point of this episode is that it is too cynical to work. His troops are not susceptible to this persuasion. What distinguishes the fallen angels from Caesar's troops is that they are susceptible to the ideals

---

31 Jamie Masters, *Poetry and Civil War in Lucan's 'Bellum Civile'* (Cambridge, 1992) develops the parallels at length.

of liberty. Milton's first republican readers must have been endlessly perplexed as to how to read Satan's speeches. Later criticism has been equally perplexed. Pro-Satanists, from Shelley to William Empson, point to the analogies between Satan's language and Milton's republican prose, and find him to have been sympathetic to Satan's rebellion against the heavenly king.[32] Anti-Satanists retort that Satan's republicanism is merely specious, a mask for tyrannical ambition.[33] A further possibility is that Milton is seeking to discredit his earlier republican ideals by placing them in Satan's mouth. None of these explanations can account for the vertiginous experience of reading Satan's great speeches, where a reader attuned to mid-century radical discourse is swept in a moment from enthusiasm to dismay. As in the *History of Britain*, Milton refuses his readers any easy position of identification, his iconoclasm extending even to potential republican heroes.

Milton politicized the story of the fall of the angels further than any predecessor. God's elevation of his Son is cast in terms of a monarch's nomination of a 'Vice-gerent'; his imperative speech-act demands that knees should be bowed without offering any reasons for his choice (v.600–15). This immediately gives Satan the opportunity to cast his rebellion in terms with which Milton himself would have sympathized; in a sense he functions as Pompey as well as Caesar. His first speech to his troops (v.772–802) is a palimpsest of republican and oppositional themes. He finds the Sonship offensive because proclaimed 'by Decree'; the speech-act is a private rather than a common one. Like the monopolists Milton had attacked in the 1640s, God has 'ingross't/All Power'. This includes a monopoly of language: the 'meerly titular' angels have become 'eclipst under the name/Of King anointed'. And indeed we have already been told that Heaven, like the Caesars, has 'blotted out and ras'd' its adversaries' names (i.362). Satan raises the kinds of complaint that had been made against Charles I at the time of the ship-money controversy, that he would not allow subjects safe possession of their property: God will oppress those 'possest before/By none'. Again and again in the poem he associates himself with the public against the private (cf. ii. 448, iv.389).

As Empson says, the first readers 'would not be at all sure how far the author meant the devil's remarks to be wrong. After all, none of the scandal-mongers accused him of ratting here, and said: "We were astonished that his life was

---

32 This is, of course, a simplification, Shelley being far from an unqualified admirer of Satan. William Empson, *Milton's God* (1961; revised edition, 1981), forcefully restated the case for Satan; much later criticism – including Fowler's annotations to *Paradise Lost* – has amounted to a defence not so much of Milton as of God.

33 Stevie Davies, *Images of Kingship in 'Paradise Lost': Milton's Politics and Christian Liberty* (Columbia, 1983), and Joan S. Bennett, *Reviving Liberty: Radical Christian Humanism in Milton's Great Poems* (Cambridge, Mass., and London, 1989), ch. 2, give excellent statements of this point of view, and I take much of their analysis for granted.

spared, until we found him meekly ascribing to Satan his own political opinions".[34] Commentators have often worked to diminish the provocation of this
speech.[35] It appeals to a high-flown republican idiom which is indeed alien to
post-Restoration political culture; it was one of the speeches attacked by Eliot
the monarchist for the emptiness of its rhetoric. More recent commentators
have deflected criticism from Milton to Satan. It is pointed out that Satan calls
not for total equality but for equality in freedom; but it is hard to see why Satan
should be condemned for views which Milton regularly expressed.
Harrington would have agreed with him that 'Orders' are essential for liberty:
the bulk of *Oceana* is taken up with outlining its thirty orders of government.
The rousing finale, where Satan declares the angels 'ordain'd to govern, not to
serve', clashes with the claim in *The Readie and Easie Way* that kings wrongly
aspire to be not the people's servant but their lord (*MPW*, VII, 362). On the
other hand, Milton had written in *The Tenure of Kings and Magistrates* that
man before the Fall was 'born to command and not to obey' (*MPW*, III,
198–99); and Adam's face declared 'Absolute rule' (iv.301).[36] It is the emphasis
on 'Imperial Titles' in the closing phrase that gives the speech's rhetoric of
liberty a more uneasily monarchical air. There is, however, enough language
with which a republican reader could sympathize to cause some unease.

In a certain sense, then, Milton is indeed, not necessarily of the devil's
party, but certainly of its language. The unfallen angels are shown to be naturally susceptible to republican language. Satan's language becomes more
monarchist the further he falls from heaven. From the very beginning, he is
compromised by the fact that a language of liberty is being exploited by him
in speech-acts that magnify his personal power; but that does not in itself
invalidate the language, any more than Monck's declarations of republican
principle were rendered invalid in themselves by his engineering of the king's
return. The massive tension between language and speech-act, however, is a
warning of the difficulty of translating theory into practice. Only for immediate rhetorical purposes did Milton claim that it was easy to build a republic.
The 1650s showed that the republic's most insidious enemies might be those
who borrowed its language.

Satan's republican moment is a brief one. His Pompeian aspects quickly
fade into a Caesarian persona. In the *Pharsalia*, the republicans must learn
that to fight for Pompey in person, rather than for liberty in general, is to fight
for tyranny; Pompey had found true greatness only when his sobriquet,
'Magnus', became ironically unfitting to his military career. The fallen angels,

---

34 Empson, *Milton's God*, p. 82.
35 The notes by Flannagan, and by Fowler in *The Poems of John Milton*, ed. John Carey and
    Alastair Fowler (1968), make instructive reading.
36 Roger Lejosne, 'Milton, Satan, Salmasius and Abdiel', *MR*, pp. 106–17 (109).

with their quest for glory, never learn that lesson; fallen man, too, believes that war is 'the highest pitch/Of human Glorie', leaving 'what most merits fame in silence hid' (xi.693–9). These tensions mark Milton's most problematic episode, the war in heaven.

It was this part of the poem that most offended Bentley's neoclassical sense of decorum. Bentley edited Lucan as well as Milton, and condemned both poets for similar vices. In coming to Milton's heavenly battle he warns: 'Now our Author is come to that Part of his Poem, where he is most to exert what Faculty he has of *Hypsos*, Magniloquence of Stile, and Sublimity of Thought'. However, 'the danger is, of being hurried away by his unbridled Steed; and of deserting Propriety, while he's hunting after Sound and Tumour' (p. 189). One such example, for Bentley, was the first encounter between Satan and Michael:

> such commotion, such as to set forth
> Great things by small, If Natures concord broke,
> Among the Constellations warr were sprung,
> Two Planets rushing from aspect maligne
> Of fiercest opposition in mid Skie,
> Should combat, and thir jarring Sphears confound. (vi.310–15)

Hume noted an allusion here to the celebrated passage early in the *Pharsalia* where the dissolution of the republic is compared to the future dissolution of the cosmos:

> Sic, cum conpage solutus
> Saecula tot mundi suprema coegerit hora,
> Antiquum repetens iterum chaos, *omnia mixtis*
> *Sidera sideribus concurrent* . . . totaque discors
> Machina divolsi turbabit foedera mundi.
> In se magna ruunt . . .(i.71–4, 79–81)
> So when the knot of Nature is dissolu'de,
> And the worlds Ages in one houre inuolu'd
> In their old Chaos, Seas with Skyes shall ioyne,
> And Starres with Starres confounded loose their shine: . . .
> The falling worlds now iarring frame no peace,
> No league shal hold; great things themselues oppresse[.]
> (May, sig. A2v)

This is one of many passages in Lucan to which Bentley objected. Lucan characteristically draws attention to his destruction of a simple verbal order – in 'omnia mixtis/Sidera sideribus' the first word agrees with the third, the second with the fourth, enacting the mingling process in a way that Bentley found illogical.[37] He found a comparable disorder in the way Milton had got

37 *M. Annaei Lucani Pharsalia cum notis Hugonis Grotii et Ricardi Bentleii* (Strawberry Hill, 1760), p. 9.

carried away and mixed up his tenses. In fact sense can be made of the passage[38], but like Lucan, Milton is enacting in his language a breakdown of concord, emulating Longinus's prescriptions for a mode of writing that gains sublimity by verging on disorder. His simile is a massive out-troping of Lucan's. Lucan is using cosmic discord as a metaphor for the Roman civil war; Milton suggests that even the end of the universe will be small beside his subject-matter. This war is taking place in heaven, before the creation of the earth and the stars, which are relatively small by comparison with the divine universe. Lucan's Roman civil war has the same proportion to the end of the universe as the end of the universe has to Milton's heavenly civil war. The allusion does, however, make the point that it is a civil war that Milton is narrating. And this is the first of all wars. In that sense, the *Pharsalia* is more of the primal, originary epic than the Virgilian text it parodies.

Critics have found it very hard to place the tone of the war in heaven, with its moments of punning word-play and the grotesque physicality of angelic combat. To see it wholly as comic is to miss the crucial weight it bears in the poem's action, yet to play down the comedy is to exaggerate this epic's orthodoxy.[39] Seventeenth-century readers would have been somewhat less perplexed, given their familiarity with the *Pharsalia*'s seriocomic presentation of Caesarean heroism. There are many levels of allusion in the war in heaven, with Hesiod and Virgil also in play; but Milton gives a distinctive emphasis on civil war. The war is twice described as 'intestine' (ii.1001, vi.259), reminding us of Lucan's third line, 'In sua victrici conversum viscera dextra'.[40] Milton enacts Lucan's 'concordia discors'[41] not only with direct allusion, as we saw earlier, but with the harsh abrasiveness of his style: within fifteen lines of his opening description of battle he makes the same verbal echo:

> Arms on Armour clashing bray'd
> Horrible discord (vi.209–10)
>   of Power
> Armie against Armie numberless to raise
> Dreadful combustion warring. (vi.223–5)[42]

38 I have not followed Flannagan in substituting a period for the 1667 comma after 'small'.
39 The first critic to emphasize the comic elements as a deliberate effect, Arnold Stein, *Answerable Style: Essays on 'Paradise Lost'* (Minneapolis, 1953), p. 24, misses the Lucanian analogies because of an over-solemn reading of Lucan: we should not read it 'as if it were the sort of humorless exaggeration that Statius and Lucan can assault the reader with'.
40 At ii.1001, some editors emend 'our' to 'your'. On the connotations of 'viscera' – a word that occurs forty-two times in the *Pharsalia* – see Philip Hardie, *The Epic Successors of Virgil: A Study in the Dynamics of a Tradition* (Cambridge, 1993), p. 55.
41 Milton quoted the phrase in his Latin grammar (*MPW*, VIII, 121).
42 This passage was quoted as illustration by William Smith in his translation, *Dionysius Longinus on the Sublime* (1739; third edition, 1752), p. 36; see Annabel Patterson, *Reading Between the Lines* (Madison, 1993), p. 269.

The repetitions may evoke memories of Virgil's famous preamble 'Arma virumque cano', and undermine its dignity by a reductive repetition; the episode ends when Christ, a greater man, brushes both parties aside. Just before that climactic anticlimax, the narrator has declared that 'Warr seem'd a civil Game/To this uproar' (vi.667–8). The phrase directs us to the comparable ironies of Lucan's opening, 'Bella plus quam ciuilia', and to the Roman poet's witty treatment of violence. Milton aims at a similar unevenness of tone in a very distinctive mode of the sublime. Through Raphael he aspires to

> lift
> Human imagination to such highth
> Of Godlike Power (vi.299–301)

yet he also allows the sublime to hover on the verge of the ridiculous, reminding us that such swelling terms have been appropriated for very dubious secular causes. In a phrase like

> all Heav'n
> Resounded, and had Earth bin then, all Earth
> Had to her Center shook (vi.217–9)

hyperbole is risked, almost thrown away, and reclaimed with disorienting speed.[43]

Though Milton's heavenly war is necessarily different from Lucan's very secular conflict, there are structural parallels. There were several neo-Latin epic treatments of the war in heaven, but Milton is unique in making the fight so evenly matched, in making it so much more of a civil war than a mere rout.[44] Lucan declares that the republicans suffered civil war whereas the Caesarians waged it (vii.500–1); similarly it is Milton's fallen angels who take

---

43 Milton's hyperbole is not so very far from Fisher's Lucanian narrative of Marston Moor – which incidentally has in common with Milton the unusual feature of blank verse:

> And now that Showre soone turnd into a Storme,
> And such a storme: as rockt y^e Cradle of
> The clouds and cast Dame Nature in a Trance.
> The discompacted Fabrick neere recoyld
> To hir first Chaos; and strook the staggering earth
> In such a Palsie: as thoe the grand Assize,
> Or Generall *Dooms-Day* of y^e World drew on . . .
> The Shock=soare=Center groand agen; and sanck
> Beneathe hir ladeing:

'Fancies occasionly written of seuerall Occurrances', BL Additional MS 19,863, fols. 28r–v.

44 Stella Purce Revard, *The War in Heaven: 'Paradise Lost' and the Tradition of Satan's Rebellion* (Ithaca and London, 1980), p. 190. I do not believe that Milton follows Cowley in directly allegorizing the events of the English Civil War, though Christopher Hill, *Milton and the English Revolution* (London and Boston, 1977), pp. 371–4, makes some suggestions along these lines.

the initiative. The first phase of the battle brings the revelation that angels can be wounded but their wounds will heal themselves. The fallen angels' endless self-reconstitution recalls the cartoon-like indestructibility of Caesar's manic centurion Scaeva (*Pharsalia* vi.144ff) – who had been mentioned in Milton's *History*. In a grotesque parody of Caesar's narrative of the civil war, he defies an apparently lethal wound in the eye by pulling out spear and eye together. He did not know 'in armis Quam magnum virtus crimen civilibus esset' (vi.147–8), 'in a civill war/How great a crime the souldiers valours are' (May, sig. K1v). Milton's narrator similarly declares that the fallen angels' deed should remain in oblivion,

> For strength from Truth divided and from Just,
> Illaudable, naught merits but dispraise
> And ignominie[.] (vi.381–3)

Satan's next move when faced with military stalemate is to invent the cannon. This decidedly unclassical innovation runs parallel to the endless technological resourcefulness of Lucan's Caesar, who refuses to be defeated by physical objects. At Massilia he builds a huge rampart to link two hills and besiege the city; to do so he cuts down the trees of a sacred grove, and there are overtones of rape and sacrilege as he hacks at a sacred oak with his axe (iii.434–5). There are similar overtones in Satan's raiding of the bowels of Heaven to find gunpowder for his cannon, whose barrels are compared to 'hollow'd bodies made of Oak or Firr/With branches lopt' (vi.574–5). The language with which Satan describes the new weapon concretizes the idea of 'viscera sua', of intestine war:

> those deep-throated Engins belcht, whose roar
> Emboweld with outragious noise the Air,
> And all her entrails tore, disgorging foule
> Thir devilish glut ... (vi.586–9)

The combat becomes grisly black comedy as the unfallen angels are made to dance while Satan and Belial, in breach of traditional epic decorum, pun vigorously. The eventual counter-attack, which involves uprooting mountains and trying to bury the cannon under them, likewise verges perilously on the comic, and again the style becomes harshly repetitive: 'Thir armour help'd thir harm' (vi.656).[45]

The defeated angels are swept down to Hell, against whose dramatic backlighting readers first encounter Satan. We know that Lucan was in

---

45 Milton's 'So Hills amid the air encounterd Hills' (vi.664) parallels Lucan's hyperbole in
    describing the omens before Pharsalia, 'multis concurrere visus Olympo/Pindus'
    (vii.173–4, 'They saw Olympus meete with Pindus hill', May, sig. M1r). Quint, *Epic and
    Empire*, p. 41, draws a parallel with the *Aeneid*, viii.692, 'montis concurrere montibus';
    since Lucan may be echoing Virgil both references are possible.

Milton's mind as he composed this episode, for he borrowed his
'Adamantine Chains' (i.48) from May's translation of Lucan, vi.801 (May,
sig. L4r).[46] Lucan's Hell is a characteristic inversion of Virgil's reverentially
presented underworld, where Aeneas's father gives him a vision of the
future glories of the Caesarian line. Lucan's vision of the afterlife is mediated by the corpse animated by the witch Erictho, who declares that civil war
has spread to the underworld. While the ghosts of noble republicans
lament, demagogues like the Gracchi are applauding as far as their chains
allow. There is a characteristic reflexive irony here: in a sense it is Lucan's
own poem that its villains applaud. But Brutus, the expeller of the Tarquins,
is applauding too, for he knows that his descendant will succeed in killing
Caesar. Lucan is aware that his poem will arouse divided responses from
differing political factions. Though the demagogues enjoy the gore, they
will soon be joined by Caesar and his allies, for whom Pluto is preparing his
chains, while Pompey will be welcomed to the Elysian Fields. Lucan thus
reverses and caricatures the political priorities of Virgil's underworld.
Satan's chains have become a critical crux: in a celebrated essay T. S. Eliot
argued that Milton lacked a visual imagination because Satan is then seen
moving across the burning lake without any reference to his escaping the
chains.[47] An easy reply is that the narrator tells us that God permitted his
release. It is also worth noting that in Lucan's Tartarus the chains are not all-
constraining, for Catiline has escaped from his (i.793).

Many critics have objected that Milton diminishes Satan between Books I
and VI, stripping him of the heroic grandeur he at first displays, and have
linked the change with his growing political disillusion.[48] It seems unlikely,
however, that some such change of mode was not planned from the first. The
fallen angels are at first seen in part through a more conventionally idealizing
epic lens, before they are subjected to Lucanian iconoclasm. On rereading the
poem, however, the continuities become more apparent. The narratorial
voice can be as iconoclastic in Book I as in the proem to Book IX: there is a
direct parallel to the later dismissal first of epic and then of romance in the
epic simile as Satan reviews the angels – which Bentley likewise dismissed,
deeming it 'Romantic Trash' (i.573–87).[49] This is succeeded by the celebrated
comparison of his eclipsed glory to a solar eclipse which

---

46 Noted by Martindale, *John Milton and the Transformation of Ancient Epic*, p. 199. Porter,
   Reading the Classics and 'Paradise Lost', pp. 98ff, offers elaborate parallels between
   Virgil's underworld episode and *Paradise Lost*, but Lucan's revision of Virgil has been
   neglected.   47 T. S. Eliot, 'Milton II', in *On Poetry and Poets* (1957), pp. 146–61 (156).
48 Worden, 'Milton's Republicanism and the Tyranny of Heaven', p. 253.
49 For a possible topical allusion see *The Poems of John Milton*, ed. Carey and Fowler, p.
   496: during Booth's Rising in 1659 Charles II met French and Spanish envoys at
   Fuentarrabia, Milton's '*Fontarabbia*' of i.187.

with fear of change
Perplexes Monarchs. (i.598–9)

Toland reported that this passage was questioned as subversive by the licenser in 1667, and the official in question was indeed very concerned about the use of eclipses as political prophecies.[50]

Like Lucan's Hell, Milton's is a disconcerting mixture of political discourses, so that it is hard for the republican reader to know when to applaud. The complexities are especially great when the fallen angels assemble in their 'infernal States' (ii.387), a body which claims to be governed by 'popular vote' (ii.313) and decides 'with full assent' (ii.388). They use the republican language of 'occasion' (ii.341). Critics often describe the meeting as a Parliament, and the structure of the episode certainly draws on a mainly royalist tradition of 'Parliament of Hell' satires.[51] Milton's assembly, however, is not a Parliament but a 'Councel' (i.755), the word favoured by Milton and other republicans in the 1650s. The assembly of this body can be seen as a parody of Harrington's electoral schemes, where the nation was organized into quasi-military divisions, analogous to the Hebrew division into hundreds and thousands, and attended public meetings with elaborate ceremonial. Here 'the worthiest' are called 'with awful Ceremony/And Trumpets sound', 'with hunderds and with thousands' from every 'Band and squared Regiment' (i.753–4, 758–60). In a remarkable *tour de force* they are reduced in size so that their huge number can fit into the Council chamber, and the poet compares them to bees and to fairies. In *The Readie and Easie Way* Milton had attacked the 'unweildie . . . bulk' of Harrington's popular assembly as far too large to be manageable. In a somewhat gratuitous image he says that voting would become a 'forrest of fingers' (VII, 441); the assembled angels raise 'a Forrest huge of Spears' (i.547, for further forest references see 613, 782). There is a curious analogue to Milton's imagery in a newsbook at the time of the restored Long Parliament, which mocks the attempts under the Protectorate to restore an Upper House:

> such Instruments are out of tune, and a period put to those Organs, being built upon Fairy ground, which had several supporters, viz. The House of Lords, or House of Peers; the upper House, the other House, the under House, some House, or no House.[52]

---

50 Von Maltzahn, 'The First Reception of *Paradise Lost* (1667)', 481. The astrologer William Lilly had used eclipses to prophesy Charles I's overthrow: Ann Geneva, *Astrology and the Seventeenth Century Mind: William Lilly and the Language of the Stars* (Manchester and New York, 1995), pp. 202ff.

51 Sharon Achinstein, *Milton and the Revolutionary Reader* (Princeton, 1994), pp. 199–210. On this episode see also Michael Wilding, *Dragons Teeth: Literature in the English Revolution* (Oxford, 1987), pp. 211ff.

52 *The Weekly Post* no. 7, 14–21 June 1659, E986.14, p. 52.

This passage shares musico-political punning – Pandemonium had risen up to organ-music (i.708). The resemblances are probably best explained by a common source in a tradition of political satire which belittled courtiers as fairies – an example would be William Browne's *Britannia's Pastorals*.[53] More specifically, Milton's wording – 'Reduc'd thir shapes immense' (i.790) – may also glance at the Harringtonian *ridurre ai principii*.[54] Milton's accompanying simile is wittily appropriate. Virgil's *Georgics* (iv.149–227) had long given bees an association with monarchical order; here we see a process of quasi-republican reduction, made grotesquely literal. Though the constitutional position is unclear, the smaller assembly in which the senior devils then meet (i.795) would seem to be the kind of second chamber Harrington recommended, though its thousand members make it about the size of Harrington's popular assembly. These members retain their own size, so that once again there is an effect of crowding and claustrophobia.

It is possible, then, that Milton's polemics against Harrington found their way into the early books of his poem, which were probably composed in the late 1650s. While republican readers would thus have found themselves disoriented, however, the force of these episodes is not ultimately anti-republican. In Hell, the 'result', that Harringtonian key-word, is not left to the people after the process of debate but is merely announced by the debaters with 'Trumpets regal' (ii.515). The fallen angels are surrounded with the imagery of absolute monarchy. Pandemonium is linked with Egyptian monuments, recalling Lucan's long description of Cleopatra's palace (x.111ff), which is proleptic of Rome's decadence under the Empire. It is also compared to the Tower of Babel (i.694), that central image of monarchical monopolies of power and language. The inner council is a 'secret conclave', a word with Papal associations (i.795), and Satan presides from a 'Throne of Royal State' (ii.1), claims 'Imperial Sov'ranty' (ii.446) and is described as a 'Monarch' (ii.467). Like the Caesar of Lucan's first book, he lacks confidence in his followers' response and he prudently prevents anyone from replying to his final speech: the council has been rigged. This assembly is radically different from the only other representative body in a major epic, the meeting of the exiled Senate at Epirus. Lucan insists that the symbols of civil authority, the rods and fasces, prevented this body from being merely an expression of military power (v.12–14). It becomes clear that Satan's council is little else. And his stratagem is a military adventure that will consolidate his personal authority by conquering a new world. This plan has more affinity with Cromwell's Western Design than with any Stuart project.[55] Mammon and Belial

---

53 Norbrook, *PP*, p. 209.

54 *OED* ('reduce', 26a) quotes this passage in a sense parallel to the discussion of reduction in the church in *The Reason of Church-Government* (*MPW*, I, 853).

55 Fallon, *Divided Empire*, p. 63, points out the parallels between the Satanic Council and the Cromwellian Council of State in its arguments over the Western Design.

call for a commonwealth for preservation, a 'nether Empire' (ii.296), Beelzebub and Satan for a commonwealth for increase. In each case, the arguments are fatally flawed by their spokesmen. Mammon echoes Sallust in his stern call for a 'Hard liberty' which can create 'great things of small' (ii.256–8); but he goes on to endorse 'Magnificence' (273).[56] Satan justifies his incursion into Eden by 'public reason just'; the narrator retorts that this is 'necessitie,/The Tyrants plea' (iv.389, 393–4).[57]

Though the narratorial comments are often described as crudely didactic and deflationary, they build up to offer a complex way of reading the Satanic assembly:

> Towards him they bend
> With awful reverence prone; and as a God
> Extoll him equal to the highest in Heav'n:
> Nor fail'd they to express how much they prais'd,
> That for the general safety he despis'd
> His own: for neither do the Spirits damn'd
> Loose all thir vertue;[58] least bad men should boast
> Thir specious deeds on earth, which glory excites,
> Or close ambition varnisht o're with zeal. (ii.477–85)

The deification is an extreme form of the monarchical exaltation of private over public interest, yet Satan is being praised in this monarchical way for a pre-eminently republican virtue; the speech-act is in extreme tension with the content. A cynical reaction would be to dismiss the republican rhetoric as a mere mask for tyranny – a stock royalist response. The narrator, however, argues that such a response becomes precisely the kind of duplicity it decries: it allows a superior contempt for any form of political virtue to legitimize open hypocrisy. The particular form this hypocrisy takes is interesting: 'close ambition varnisht o're with zeal'. This passage would seem to predate the Restoration, when zeal of an ostentatiously godly kind was no longer an avenue for ambition; professions of piety had become discredited. In the Cromwellian era, however, things worked differently, and the satire seems to fit a 1650s context. The extreme oscillations in the Satan episodes between republican and monarchical discourse form a meditation on Milton's difficulties in responding to the Protectorate – and, more generally, on Roman discussions of the deterioration of language under the Empire.[59]

The most important point being made in this passage is that diabolic – or Cromwellian – language of public interest should not discredit the language itself, merely the context in which it becomes the vehicle for tyrannical

56 Martin Dzelzainis, 'Milton's Classical Republicanism', *MR*, pp. 3–24 (23–4).
57 On these points see David Armitage, 'John Milton: Poet against Empire', *MR*, pp. 206–25.
58 Here I follow the 1667 'thir' against 1674's 'her' at ii.483.
59 Davies, *Images of Kingship in 'Paradise Lost'*, pp. 99ff.

speech-acts. The fallen angels' ability to muster superb quasi-republican eloquence is a sign of their heavenly origins. The more time passes from his initial rebellion, the more monarchical Satan's language becomes. By the temptation scene, there is a complete disjunction between his posture as a great orator of '*Athens* or free *Rome*, where Eloquence/Flourishd, since mute' (ix.671–2) and his readiness to court Eve as a deity. Milton opens the poem at a point where the balance between different languages is radically unstable, putting readers immediately on guard. They are thus prepared for – though perhaps still surprised by – the even more powerful defences of liberty in Satan's war of words before the war in heaven.

As Satan plans and executes his expedition to earth, a chain of allusions links him with Lucan's Caesar and creates a parallel between the loss of republican liberty at Pharsalia and the loss of Eden.[60] They would have been far more widely recognized by seventeenth-century readers than they are today; they come from key moments in each poem. When Satan has outlined his plot against mankind, the narrator asks

> whence,
> But from the Author of all ill could Spring
> So deep a malice, to confound the race
> Of mankind in one root, and Earth with Hell
> To mingle and involve, done all to spite
> The great Creatour? (ii.380–85)

Through tempting Adam and Eve Satan is able to damage the Universe; Eden becomes a synecdoche for the universe in *Paradise Lost* just as does Pharsalia in Lucan's epic. Caesar was favoured by Fortune to win all at a single cast, and Pharsalia gave him the whole world to conquer at once, 'Pharsalia praestitit orbem' (iii.296–7); Lucan may have been recalling Caligula's comment that he wished Rome had one neck so that he could kill it.

The buffeting Satan receives as he journeys through Chaos has long been recognized as recalling Caesar's rash sea-voyage in Lucan's fifth book, an episode that laid bare the chaos underlying the monarchical will to power:[61]

> earth then added was
> To Neptunes kingdome, when the sea confounded,
> All lands, and *Tethys* by no shore was bounded,
> Contented with no limit but the skyes . . .
> The heavens then trembled; the high pole for feare
> Resounded, when his hindges mooved were.
> Nature then fear'd the old confusion:

---

60 It is far harder to find an equivalent for Satan in the *Aeneid*, though strained attempts have been made to link him with Juno or Turnus.

61 William Blissett, 'Caesar and Satan', *Journal of the History of Ideas* 18 (1957), 221–32 (229–31); the connection was made by Hume.

> The elementall concord seem'd vndone;
> And night, that mixt th'aetheriall deityes
> With the infernall, seem'd againe to rise; . . .(May, sigs. 12r-v)
>> if this frame
> Of Heav'n were falling, and these Elements
> In mutinie had from her Axle torn
> The stedfast Earth. At last his Sail-broad Vannes
> He spreads for flight, and in the surging smoak
> Uplifted spurns the ground, thence many a League
> As in a cloudy Chair ascending rides
> Audacious, but that seat soon failing, meets
> A vast vacuitie[.] (ii.924–32)

(Bentley objected that a chair was 'too mean a Carriage'; that was surely Milton's intention – even if the chair is thought of as descending in masque scenery.)

Milton clinches the Lucanian atmosphere by drawing on a different part of the poem, the vertiginously unstable terrain of the Syrtes (ix.303ff):

> These Syrts, when all the worlds first structure was,
> Nature as doubtfull left twixt sea, and land;
> (For neither sinke they quite like seas to stand,
> Nor yet like land with shores repell the maine,
> But doubtfull, and vnpassable remaine,
> A shelfe-spoil'd sea, a water cover'd land,
> Where sounding waues let in by sands command . . .(May, sig. Q2r)

Hume declares Milton's lines 'exactly agreeing with *Lucan*'[62]:

>   that furie stay'd,
> Quencht in a Boggie *Syrtis*, neither Sea,
> Nor good dry Land: nigh founderd on he fares,
> Treading the crude consistence, half on foot,
> Half flying; behoves him now both Oare and Saile. (ii.938–42)

Amongst the figures surrounding Chaos's pavilion is Demogorgon (ii.965). Hume traced him back to Lucan, where Erictho invokes a deity whose name made the earth quake (vi.744–6). Lucan did not give the name himself, and Bentley wanted to delete 'Demogorgon'; but the figure was to have a powerful afterlife as an image of popular resistance in Shelley's *Prometheus Unbound*.

Satan continues his journey and is at last rewarded with a view of the world:

---

62 Hume also notes Milton's immediately succeeding reference to the Arimaspians (ii.945), who appear in Lucan, iii.280–1, vii.755–6; this should perhaps be seen as a borrowing rather than an allusion.

> As when a Scout
> Through dark and desart wayes with peril gone
> All night; at last by break of chearful dawne
> Obtains the brow of some high-climbing Hill,
> Which to his eye discovers unaware
> The goodly prospect of some forein land
> First-seen, or some renown'd Metropolis
> With glistering Spires and Pinnacles adornd,
> Which now the Rising Sun guilds with his beams.
> Such wonder seis'd, though after Heaven seen,
> The Spirit maligne, but much more envy seis'd
> At sight of all this World beheld so faire. (iii.543–54)

This recalls the episode in the *Pharsalia* when Caesar, after a long campaign, first wonders at the sight of Rome; both are associated with the north:

> Now Anxurs steepest hills he had orepast,
> Where a moist path ore Pontine fennes is plac'd;
> Where the high wood does Scythian *Dian'* show:
> Where to long *Albas* feasts the Consuls goe.
> From an high rocke he viewes the towne afar
> Not seene before in all the Northren war.
> Then thus (admiring his Romes walls) he spake,
> Could men not forc'd by any fight forsake
> Thee the gods seate? (iii.84–92; May, sig. D5v)

(For Henry Marten's application of this passage to Cromwell, see above, p. 319.) In each case the effect is disturbing because the reader sees the prey through the predator's eyes; and the fact that he can wonder at it, can gain a kind of aesthetic pleasure from what he is about to destroy, is one of the many troubling links in each poem between the villain's evil and certain kinds of art.[63] Caesar has passed through a sacred and elevated, '*sublime*', wood; Satan has glimpsed heaven before finding the earth. Readers' patriotism is stirred by the way the lowlier scene is what attracts them most, and vexed by the fact that the preference is threatening.

The parallels between Caesar's campaigns and Satan's continue at the climactic episode of the Fall:

> So saying, her rash hand in evil hour
> Forth reaching to the Fruit, she pluck'd, she eat:
> Earth felt the wound, and Nature from her seat
> Sighing through all her Works gave signs of woe,
> That all was lost. (ix.780–84)

---

63 Milton seems also to echo this passage in introducing his own account of the Roman conquest of Britain (*MPW*, v:1, 37).

Critics have associated Eve here and elsewhere in the poem with Virgil's Dido, and this passage with the storm that marks the adultery of Dido and Aeneas (*Aeneid*, iv.165–70).[64] But there is a closer parallel with Lucan's description of the aftermath of the battle of Pharsalia, where the Earth likewise is involved:

> Ingemuisse putem campos, terramque nocentem
> Inspirasse animas, infectumque aera totum
> Manibus et superam Stygia formidine noctem. (vii.768–70)
>   you would haue thought the feild
> Had groan'd, and that the guilty earth did yeild
> Exhaled spirits, that in the aire did moue,
> And Stygian feares possest the night aboue. (May, sig. N2v)[65]

Satan has brought the heavenly civil war to earth, and the cosmic disruption that ensues renders the Earth more like the fissured, tragic landscape of Pharsalia that Lucan had evoked so powerfully in the passage leading up to the battle. Thessaly had been raised from the sea; better, the narrator laments, that it had remained drowned forever (vi.350). A similar pathos attaches to the moment when Eden sinks below the waves (xi.829–35). Lucan laments that the sun could look on the loss of liberty even though it had withheld its eyes from Thyestes's cannibalism:

> He at *Thyestes* feast could shut vp day,
> Involving *Argos* in a suddaine night;
> And can he lend Thessalia his light,
> Where brothers fight, and sonnes 'gainst fathers are? (vii.451–4; May, sigs. M5r–v)

Milton echoes this passage when describing the cosmic convulsions after the Fall:

>   At that tasted Fruit
> The Sun, as from *Thyestean* Banquet, turn'd
> His course intended; else how had the World
> Inhabited, though sinless, more then now,
> Avoided pinching cold and scorching heate? (x.687–91)[66]

Milton, out-troping Lucan, tells us that the sun not only withheld its eyes but changed its course. God's newly created cosmos in all its ingenious balance and concord, with all the advantages lacking to Lucan's discordant Roman polity, proves to have been just as precarious, easily tipped over into cataclysm by Satan's Caesarian ingenuity.

---

64 Porter, *Reading the Classics and 'Paradise Lost'*, pp. 112–13.
65 Porter, *Reading the Classics and 'Paradise Lost'*, p. 195 n. 46, notes that Hume brought in Ovid, *Metamorphoses* i.200–3, which is a reference to the assassination of Caesar. The anti-Augustan Lucan may have been adapting this passage to render a very different view of republicanism.
66 Hume makes the connection, also citing Horace and Seneca.

The perverse creativity that has been seen in the invention of the cannon continues in the transformation of the postlapsarian cosmos. Sin and Death build a causeway to link hell with earth, and Milton recalls the gigantic fence built by Caesar to wall in Pompey's forces:

Then with a bridge of fastned ships the Land
He joynes; each Galley doe foure anchors stay:
Once ore the Sea proud *Xerxes* such a way
Made by report: when ioyn'd by bridge he saw
Sestos t' *Abydos*, *Europe* t' *Asia*;
And fearing not th'Eastwinde, nor Wests affront
Walk'd ore the curled backe of Hellespont,
When ships their sayles round about Athos spread;
So now this Haven's mouth Ships straightened,
On which their Bulwarkes vp apace they raise,
And lofty towers stand trembling on the seas.
    (ii.672–9; May, sigs. C8r-v)

    broad as the Gate,
Deep to the Roots of Hell the gather'd beach
They fasten'd, and the Mole immense wraught on
Over the foaming deep high Archt, a Bridge
Of length prodigious joyning to the Wall
Immovable of this now fenceless world
Forfeit to Death; from hence a passage broad,
Smooth, easie, inoffensive down to Hell.
So, if great things to small may be compar'd,
Xerxes, the Libertie of *Greece* to yoke,
From *Susa* his *Memnonian* Palace high
Came to the Sea, and over *Hellespont*
Bridging his way, *Europe* with *Asia* joyn'd,
And scourg'd with many a stroak th' indignant waves. (x.298–311; Bentley finds line 309 'very low and creeping'.)

Like Lucan, Milton draws a parallel with Xerxes's bridge of boats; he sharpens the political rhetoric with his stress on 'Libertie'.[67]

Sin greets Satan on his arrival at the world of which he will now 'Monarch reign' (x.375); Satan in turn sends Sin and Death down to act as his 'Substitutes ... Plenipotent' (x.403–4). The links between anarchy (x.283) and monarchy, between monarchy and death, in the postlapsarian order are strongly emphasized. We recall Satan's first encounter with Death, with the celebrated description:

    what seem'd his head
The likeness of a Kingly Crown had on. (ii.672–3)

---

67 Hume noted this allusion; Bentley complained that Milton made too much of this causeway, which was anticipated at ii.1024ff.

16 Kingship as death: from *The Woefull Mirrour of Monarchy*, 1652.

For Burke the menacing obscurity of 'what seem'd his head' was a quintessentially sublime line; and its sublimity has regicidal overtones. One republican tract had presented King Death, a crowned skeleton, as triumphing over all the Stuart dynasty (figure 16):

> Whereas the Crown and Scepter of *England*, *Scotland*, and *Ireland* have so often been taken from me, notwithstanding all my Re-inthronizations, and I have been still laid by, yet now my Victorious Sword hath placed me in Tryumph, where I sit clothed with the Royall Robes, and weare the Crown without disturbance, where Wormes are my Companions, and the Bones of all the dead my Subjects . . . now I have begun to set such good footing on this part of the Earthen Globe, that I shal attempt to Conquer all the Emperours, Kings and Monarches in the World.[68]

In Milton's allegory of Sin and Death, kingship is seen 'as a deadly, allegorical projection and alienation of the subject's true freedom'.[69]

As Death prepares his devolved monarchy over the Earth, Satan returns to Hell. Appropriately, his last appearance in the poem is marked by the most

68 Edmund Burke, *A Philosophical Enquiry into the Origin of our Ideas of the Sublime and the Beautiful*, ed. James T. Boulton (Oxford, 1987), p. 61 (II:[iv]); *The Woefull Mirrour of Monarchy* (1652; 669f16.29).

69 Victoria Kahn, *Machiavellian Rhetoric: From the Counter-Reformation to Milton* (Princeton, 1994), p. 223. The association between death and monarchy thus predated the restoration, with which Quint, *Epic and Empire*, p. 271, specifically links Milton's Sin and Death; but Wither did associate the return of the monarchy with the reign of Sin and Death in *Speculum Speculativum* (see above, p. 429).

explicit of all the allusions to Lucan. In a piece of grisly comedy, God transforms the fallen angels into snakes. The introduction to Satan's speech glances
at Caesar's very first speech to his troops:

> Straight to the Standard all his Souldiers
> *Caesar* assembling, 'middst their murmuring noise
> Commands a silence with his hand and voice[.] (i.296–8; May, sig. A5v)

> Forth rush'd in haste the great consulting Peers,
> Rais'd from thir Dark *Divan*, and with like joy
> Congratulant approach'd him, who with hand
> Silence, and with these words attention won. (x.456–59)

Caesar presents himself as a new Aeneas looking for land for his followers[70],
and calls on them to rise and take possession: 'Tollite iampridem victricia,
tollite, signa' (i.347), 'March on victorious colours, march away' (May, sig.
A6v). Satan similarly concludes:

> What remains, ye Gods,
> But up and enter now into full bliss. (x.502–3)

Caesar's speech is at first undercut by the soldiers' failure to respond; Milton
turns this silence into the hissing of snakes:

> he would have spoke,
> But hiss for hiss returnd with forked tongue
> To forked tongue, for now were all transform'd
> Alike, to Serpents all, as accessories
> To his bold Riot: dreadful was the din
> Of hissing through the Hall, thick swarming now
> With complicated monsters head and taile,
> Scorpion and Asp, and *Amphisbaena* dire,
> *Cerastes* hornd, *Hydrus*, and *Ellops* drear,
> And *Dipsas* (not so thick swarm'd once the Soil
> Bedropt with blood of *Gorgon*, or the Isle
> *Ophiusa*) but still greatest hee the midst,
> Now Dragon grown, larger then whom the Sun
> Ingenderd in the *Pythian* Vale on slime,
> Huge *Python*, and his Power no less he seem'd
> Above the rest still to retain . . . (x.517–32)

This is another of the lapses from epic decorum that perplexed Bentley, who
dismissed it as 'trifling'.[71] It closely follows a celebrated episode in Book IX of
the *Pharsalia* where Cato's forces, crossing the North African desert, are
attacked by snakes. They become the new vehicles of Caesar's malign power:

---

70 Frederick M. Ahl, *Lucan: An Introduction* (Ithaca and London, 1976), p. 202.
71 Bentley (ed.), *Paradise Lost*, p. 325; Hume noted the parallel.

the vipers fight in his place and the adders win the civil war (ix.850–51). Milton borrows many details from Lucan's snake catalogue at ix.700–29. As in the war in heaven, the comedy is too grotesque to destroy our sense of the devils' menace, but their slithering motion deflates their aspiration to the 'Sublime' (x.536).

In the last part of Lucan's epic, there is a process of sublimation as the cause broadens out from a particular time and place. In a celebrated speech, Cato declares that God is not to be found in particular shrines:

> Is there a seate of god, saue earth, and sea,
> Aire, heaven, and vertue? why for god should we
> Seeke further? what ere moues, what ere is seene
> Is *Ioue*. (ix.578–80; May, sig. Q6v)

Michael echoes these words as he tells Adam that even after his expulsion from Paradise he will still be able to find God's traces:

> *Adam*, thou know'st Heav'n his, and all the Earth,
> Not this Rock onely; his Omnipresence fills
> Land, Sea, and Aire, and every kinde that lives,
> Fomented by his virtual power and warmd[.] (xi.335–8)

Michael tells Eve not to be bound to one place (xi.292) and by the last speech of the poem she is ready to leave Paradise:

> In mee is no delay; with thee to goe,
> Is to stay here; without thee here to stay,
> Is to go hence unwilling; thou to mee
> Art all things under Heav'n, all places thou,
> Who for my wilful crime art banisht hence. (xii.615–9)

Eve is transforming her earlier word-play: '*Eden* were no *Eden* thus expos'd' (ix.341). Milton may be reworking here Pompey's speech on leaving Lesbos after being reunited with his wife:

>   this land (quoth he)
> That I of all the world most deare esteem'd
> By this great pledge I left with you it seem'd
> She was the hostage that my loue was here,
> That here my houshold gods, and countrey were;
> Heere was my Rome[.] (viii.129–33; May, sigs. N7r-v)

Pompey continues the process of internalization that had been signalled when the exiled senators declared that it was the royalists who remained in Rome who were the real exiles, and recalled that when Camillus was at Veii, Veii was Rome (v.27–9).

In a certain limited sense, liberty in the *Pharsalia* is not lost but regained. It is realized above all in the self-mastery of Cato, who reigns as a king over himself and needs nothing to do with earthly kingship. But this does not diminish the tragedy of loss. In the *Aeneid*, the loss of Troy leads to the foundation of Rome; the *Pharsalia* offers no such consolation. In *Paradise Lost*, the prospects for freedom are almost as bleak. There is no evidence that Milton had lost his preference for a republic: given the conditions under which the poem was published, it is surprising how explicit he manages to be. The emphasis, however, is on the recurrent tendency for kingship to triumph. The catalogue of fallen angels in the first book becomes a long chronicle of idolatrous and tyrannical kings: the 'horrid King' (i.392), the 'uxorious King' (444), the 'sottish Conquerour' (472), the 'Rebel King' (484), with the rare exception of the iconoclastic Josiah (418). Amongst the classical deities, we are reminded that Jove was a usurper (514). In the history of human society as it is shown to Adam in Books XI–XII, we see a gradual development from simpler forms of organization to an urban society in which there is a 'Council'. It is 'factious' (xi.664) and an omen of the growing corruption that will lead to God's punishment in the Flood; but kingship has not yet been born.

The following book opens after the Flood with a long period of peace and prosperity in 'faire equalitie, fraternal state' (xii.26); but this is undermined by Nimrod's bid for 'Dominion undeserv'd' (xii.27), epitomized by the Tower of Babel. Adam, it emerges, is naturally, instinctually republican, and he attacks inequality in terms similar to Satan's in Book V: the title of 'Lord' should be reserved for God alone (xii.70). In a witty stroke, Milton describes his indignation at Nimrod as 'fatherly' (xii.63). Absolutist theorists conflated familial and political rule, justifying monarchy by analogy with the role of the father – a process that was to culminate in Sir Robert Filmer's *Patriarcha* (printed 1680, written several decades earlier), where Nimrod became a precedent for absolutism. To describe Adam's republican attack on Nimrod as fatherly was teasingly provocative – and as will be seen below, it did provoke.[72]

Immediately afterwards, however, Milton offers a certain counterweight to the provocation: Raphael insists that 'Tyrannie must be' (xii.95). When nations allow passion to overcome reason, God justly subjects them to conquest by violent lords; if they sink very low, 'Justice, and some fatal curse annext' will deprive them of their outward liberties (xii.99). The 'must' of this passage seems to introduce a discourse of divine necessity, of external imposition, at odds with Milton's emphasis on freedom and responsibility, and can be seen as reflecting post-Restoration pessimism and quietism.[73] It can certainly

---

72 See Patterson, *Reading Between the Lines*, p. 253; cf. Howard Erskine-Hill, *Poetry and the Realm of Politics: Shakespeare to Dryden* (Oxford, 1996), p. 192.

73 John Rogers, *The Matter of Revolution: Science, Poetry, and Politics in the Age of Milton* (Ithaca and London, 1996), pp. 158ff, emphasizes the contrast between differing models of divine agency in Book XII.

be seen as a concession to the licenser. Yet Milton maintains a certain edge in his language. He insists that divine necessity does not absolve tyrants from moral culpability. The 'must' here registers a particular disquiet. In the long proleptic narrative of Book XII, everything Michael narrates 'must be' in the sense that it can already be foreseen, 'shall' and 'will' being the normal verbs of futurity. The 'must' here combines the senses of futurity and necessity with particular force, creating a political tension that is to some extent released a few verse paragraphs later, where 'must' is the main verb describing 'the Signes and Judgements dire' visited on the 'lawless Tyrant' Pharaoh (xii.173ff). In the years immediately before the poem's publication, such signs were being accumulated by republicans and alarmed the government.[74] The passage's locutionary submission is thus in some tension with an illocutionary resistance.

Insofar as Milton does play down the role of human agency, moreover, this cannot be attributed solely to a post-Restoration pessimism. The long view he is here offering throws into relief the tendency of government, especially monarchical government, towards tyranny that he had already noted in the regicidal tracts. He had there said that what from one point of view was human agency was God's will from another (for example *Tenure of Kings and Magistrates*, *MPW*, III, 211); this is one aspect of the contrast between foreseeing and willing that is central to the theodicy of *Paradise Lost*. As has been seen, Milton's optimism about political agency had always been sharply qualified. In the Commonwealth period he had written of the Irish as an irredeemable race, and the 'Digression' indicates how desperately he feared that the English might undergo such a fate. He had ended the *First Defence* with a warning that if they failed to rise to the republican occasion, God would turn against them (*MPW*, IV:1, 536).

This general lapse into tyranny is used as a backdrop for the emergence of the Israelites, who do at first love liberty, and escape their Egyptian bondage:

> the Race elect
> Safe towards *Canaan* from the shoar advance
> Through the wilde Desert, not the readiest way,
> Least entring on the *Canaanite* allarmd
> Warr terrifie them inexpert, and feare
> Return them back to *Egypt*, choosing rather
> Inglorious life with servitude; for life
> To noble and ignoble is more sweet
> Untraind in Armes, where rashness leads not on.
> This also shall they gain by thir delay
> In the wide Wilderness, there they shall found
> Thir government, and thir great Senate choose
> Through the twelve Tribes, to rule by Laws ordaind[.] (xii.214–26)

---

74 Knoppers, *Historicizing Milton*, pp. 143ff.

Whether this passage was written before or after *The Readie and Easie Way*, the collocation points to the desperate urgency of Milton's tactics in 1660, his willingness to persuade himself that avoiding the path back to Egypt was easy. Here a long preparatory stay in the wilderness is necessary; and it is succeeded by Moses's foundation of a republican constitution. The narrative of Hebrew kingship is condensed, but not without glancing polemical overtones. There is a note of menacing relish in Michael's refusal to tell 'How many Kings destroyd' (xii.262). He proceeds to tell the entire history of Hebrew kingship in one sentence, moving at breakneck speed from its origins to its transcendence in the Son, 'of Kings/The last' (xii.329–30) – which echoes Marten's inscription on the site of Charles I's statue, 'Exit Tyrannus Regum Ultimus' (for similar wording cf. *Tenure of Kings and Magistrates*, *MPW*, III, 256). Milton's chronicle of the Hebrew kings is the crisply weighted: 'Part good, part bad, of bad the longer scrowle' – though he concedes also the 'popular summe' of vices (xii.336–8). From the time of the Babylonian captivity onward, Milton shifts his attention from secular to religious issues: the priests are condemned for usurping secular power and denying Christ his right[75], and this leads into a long attack on the usurpers of religious liberty. As has been seen, this concern had become increasingly urgent with Milton during the 1650s; the sudden intrusion of an attack on 'lewd Hirelings' when Satan enters Eden (iv.193) may indicate composition at that time.

Milton's presentation of human history in *Paradise Lost* is much closer to Lucan's tragic vision – or to d'Aubigné's *Les Tragiques*[76] – than to any form of republican triumphalism: this is certainly not a republican *Aeneid*. There may be a final Lucan allusion towards the end of the chronicle:

> so shall the World goe on,
> To good malignant, to bad men benigne,
> Under her own waight groaning[.] (xii.537–9)

Here we are brought back to Lucan's top-heavy Rome, 'sub pondere lapsus' (i.71) – as well as to the stock anti-royalist term 'malignant'. There is none of

---

75 Corns, *Regaining 'Paradise Lost'*, p. 141, points out that this passage seems close to Milton's attacks on the Presbyterians at the time of the regicide.

76 Milton never mentions d'Aubigné, so any suggestion of influence needs caution. However, Judith Sproxton, 'D'Aubigné, Milton and the Scourge of Sin', *Journal of European Studies* 11 (1981), 262–78, offers some general comparisons and contrasts, which could perhaps be supplemented by biographical connections. One of the revised manuscripts of *Les Tragiques* was sent to London in 1630 to his widow's brother, Philippe Burlamacchi, a relative and friend of the Diodati family with which the young Milton was intimately associated; in 1638 Milton himself visited Geneva and probably met Théodore Tronchin, d'Aubigné's literary heir: Donald Clayton Dorian, *The English Diodatis* (New Brunswick, 1950), pp. 53–4, 176, 307–8. The proposed translation of the *Histoire Universelle* in 1659 indicates significant interest in d'Aubigné in the republican period.

the hope expressed in *The Readie and Easie Way* for a republic that would last until the Second Coming. The vision of history in the last book is bleak; most readers have also found it dull. These judgements can be accepted, without moving to the conclusion that it manifests a pessimistic political withdrawal.

A basic factor to be borne in mind here is the constraint of censorship. If he wished to enter the public sphere, Milton could not possibly have enlivened the narrative in some ways he might have found congenial: for example, chronicling the fate of the regicidal martyrs as Ludlow did in his *Memoirs*, which would at least have made the writing more concrete if not more consoling. There are, however, also structural reasons for the lack of concreteness. There is a reflexive element in the last two books: Adam is presented with visions and narratives and is taught by Michael how to respond to them. He has a tendency to premature optimism: he wishes to read history as an epic of the triumph of virtue and freedom, and is constantly confounded. At the climax of Michael's prophecy of Christ's reign (xii.369–71), his wording seems to glance both at Jupiter's prophecy of Augustus (*Aeneid*, i.287) and at Anchises's prophecy to Aeneas in the underworld (vi.781–82).[77] When Adam expresses rapture at this redemption of history, however, he is checked by Michael, who proceeds to narrate the crucifixion. It is as if Adam expected to be offered a *First* and *Second Defence* and was instead subjected to readings from the *History of Britain*. Michael wants to guard him against the disillusion that will follow from unrealistic expectations and a lack of historical perspective; the ultimate aim of Michael's darkness of tone is to console Adam, to enable him to face the fallen world unflinchingly.

In this part of the poem Milton is giving a long view of secular history: literally so. He is playing with temporal perspectives; we have leapt back to the first man and are looking forward with him to the end of history, and there is a vanishing effect towards the horizon. Michael has switched from vision to narration, as even with magical enhancement his sight can reach no further. Readers' powers of vision are of course being taxed in a similar way as they struggle to look back to the origins of their own history. They are asked to set contemporary struggles in a massively larger time-scale. To set forth great things by small, there is a parallel with Milton's and Nedham's games with temporality in 1659, when the entire Protectorate could be reduced to a brief 'interruption' – Satan's mission against mankind is several times associated with interruption (ii.371, iii.68, 84, ix. 512). In the poem's perspective, the overall pattern, like Lucan's, is closer to tragedy than to epic; the forces of monarchy and idolatry prevail again and

77 K. W. Gransden, 'The *Aeneid* and *Paradise Lost*', in Charles Martindale (ed.), *Virgil and his Influence: Bimillennial Studies* (Bristol, 1984), pp. 95–116 (95–6).

again. But the speech-act of narrating a tragic story is not necessarily one of dissuading from action: tragedy can galvanize – in its Lucanian mode, with wit as well as pain.

We are fortunate to have a response to the conclusion of *Paradise Lost* from one of its first royalist readers, John Beale, who had been a member of the Hartlib circle. Lamenting the failure of censorship to crack down on dissident writings, he noted that Milton 'holds to his old Principle', and gave line-references to the Nimrod episode. Milton's 'Plea for our Original right', he reaffirmed the following year, was one of the 'great faults in his *Paradyse Lost*'. Beale complained that 'he mistakes the maine of Poesy, to put such long & horrible Blasphemyes in the Mouth of Satan, as no man that feares God can endure to Read it, or without a poysonous Impression': Beale found Milton's strategy of giving the devil his due blasphemous and subversive. A year after that he complained that Nedham '& Milton, with all their Junto, are able to doe us more mischiefe, than millions of S[tubbe] & C[asaubon?]'. Beale was assimilating Milton the poet with Nedham the pamphleteer. And he had a good sense of where to locate *Paradise Lost* generically within the epic tradition. For Milton and his like:

> I have no other fondness, y^n I should have had for Ovid, Martiall, Petronius, & Lucan, wch were all four, either lascivious, obscaene, dissolute, or traiterous; for so I construe Lucans Divinity – Victrix causa deis placuit, sed victa Catoni. Yet (to my tast) he hath more of a raving Jarr, & of a boysterous strentgh [sic] of wit y^n of true Poetry, & solemne Harmony.[78]

For Beale, the publication of *Paradise Lost* was a forceful, and deeply unwelcome, act.

Creation and reduction: the heavenly legislator

Barrow's commendatory poem to *Paradise Lost* concentrates on the moment where Milton overgoes not only Homer and Virgil but also Lucan, where a wholly new form of warfare is unleashed against military glory as the Son interrupts the battle and drives the fallen angels down to Hell. His chariot is a revision of imperial triumphal cars:

>   forth rush'd with whirlwind sound
> The Chariot of Paternal Deitie,
> Flashing thick flames, Wheele within Wheele undrawn,

---

[78] British Library, Evelyn Collection, MS Letters, John Beale to John Evelyn, 18 November 1667, 18 December 1669, 24 December 1670, 4 February 1671; the relevant passages are published by Nicholas von Maltzahn, 'Laureate, Republican, Calvinist: An Early Response to Milton and *Paradise Lost* (1667)', *Milton Studies* 29 (1992), 181–98.

It self instinct with Spirit, but convoyd
By four Cherubic shapes, four Faces each
Had wondrous, as with Starrs thir bodies all
And Wings were set with Eyes, with Eyes the Wheels
Of Beril, and careering Fires between;
Over thir heads a chrystal Firmament,
Whereon a Saphir Throne, inlaid with pure
Amber, and colours of the showrie Arch . . .
Attended with ten thousand thousand Saints,
He onward came, farr off his coming shon,
And twentie thousand (I thir number heard)
Chariots of God, half on each hand were seen:
Hee on the wings of Cherub rode sublime
On the Crystallin Skie, in Saphir Thron'd. (vi.749–59, 767–72)

The vision of wheels within wheels draws on Ezekiel I; but it can also be seen as a reply to royalist iconography which placed the sun-king at the centre of the cosmos – and perhaps also to the Protectoral imagery of Cromwell as chariot-eer. The chariot is linked to the whole cosmos which is the Son's vehicle; this Son as the true sun-king eclipses secular suns. The imagery of accelerated cycles recalls, but goes further than, Marvell's revision of monarchical solar imagery in *The First Anniversary*. If this is an image of the *machina mundi*, it is not Lucan's 'discors machina', but neither is it a conventional image of concord. As the penultimate line of the huge sentence that describes the chariot emphasizes, it is 'sublime'.[79] Rather than offering its beauty to the spectator for contempla-tion, the chariot is itself wheeled along by eyes whose gaze terrifies the rebel-lious angels, who fling themselves off the edge of Heaven without any need of force. Eternal wrath 'Burnt after them to the bottomless pit' (vi.866): the extreme irregularity of this famous line – which Bentley, alarmed about 'strange Monsters in verse', duly rewrote – reminds us that infinite divine energy can dispense with easy symmetry. In a sense what defeats the rebel angels is the sublimity of Milton's own art. The episode can be read as dis-placing pagan warfare with Christian inward virtue, but though the Son says that he is putting on the Father's mightiness, having declared his readiness for sacrifice (vi.734–5), he is still surrounded with martial panoply. Milton does not spell out just how his victory might be translated into secular terms, but it does not bode well for kings. The proem had linked 'better fortitude' with martyrdom; but in *The Tenure of Kings and Magistrates*, 'better fortitude' was 'to dare to execute highest Justice on them that shall by force of Armes endeav-our the oppressing and bereaving of Religion and thir liberty at home' (III, 238).

The Son's ascent marks the high point of the poem's iconoclasm, its exultant destruction of corrupt forms. But *Paradise Lost* is a poem not only of

79 Likewise cited by Smith in his Longinus translation, p. 40.

iconoclasm but also of sublime creation. Republicanism's critics always portrayed it as a carping, negative ideology, ungratefully spurning the benefits of kingship, and also the beauty of court culture. The *Pharsalia* is indeed open to the objection that it depends upon the Virgilian conventions it parodies. In the 1650s, however, republicans were exploring a different model, in which the central figure was the Machiavellian legislator whose political architecture resembled both poetic creation and God's creation of the cosmos. That figure combined some of the properties of a monarch with a sublime willingness to lay down monarchical power, to trust his creation to its own development. Milton and most republicans tended to phrase all objections to rule by a single person with a qualification: a single person of exceptional virtue just might benefit a nation, but the strength of character needed would be all but supernatural, and the succession would carry with it all kinds of problems. Who, Milton asked in the *First Defence*, 'is worthy of holding on earth power like that of God but some person who far surpasses all others and even resembles God in goodness and wisdom?' The answer was clear: 'The only such person . . . is the son of God whose coming we look for' (*MPW*, IV:1,428). The basic datum the poem asks republican readers to accept is that God and his son represent, and alone can fully understand, the general interest of the entire cosmos. Milton's Father and Son have all the qualities that Milton, Harrington, Marvell, Nedham and Wither demanded of Cromwell without the human failings. Here was an author capable both of writing an epic and of founding just polities. Obedience to such an entity was fully compatible with the positive liberty demanded of the republican citizen.

The process of creation, however, was always fraught with difficulty. Republicans urged subjects against timid return to the old ways: the frightened architects of Marvell's 'Horatian Ode' needed to learn the benefits of new construction. As was seen in the pamphlet *Chaos*, the imagery of divine creation was especially useful in confounding the alarm of the faint-hearted for whom the process of political change was a lapse into Babel-like chaos and anarchy. The republican retort from Ludlow and from Milton was that it was monarchy – including Protectoral monarchy – that was Babel-like, replacing a common language of public interests with the clashing, atomized languages of contending private interests. A return to first principles would build a more lasting order out of a period of tumult. The process would have a poetic as well as political aspect. William Sprigge had complained that in destroying the king and court without a thoroughgoing refoundation, 'Have we not deprived our selves of all the conveniences of Monarchy, of whatever of excellency or beauty was in it, and retained only the flaws and evils of it?'[80] It was

---

80 William Sprigge, *A Modest Plea, for an Equal Common-Wealth, Against Monarchy* (1659; E1802.1), sig. A4v.

futile to hold on to the old building, the external forms of the ancient constitution, but Sprigge, like Harrington, was sensitive to the claim that courtly culture did offer a beauty not to be found in republican austerity. The answer was to be more, not less, radical in the process of reduction, to discover the sublimity of a new creation.

During the political tumult of 1659–60, Milton was at work on that project. His opening invokes the Muse who

> didst inspire
> That Shepherd, who first taught the chosen Seed,
> In the Beginning how the Heav'ns and Earth
> Rose out of *Chaos*[.] (i.7–10)

Moses was still believed to have been the author of Genesis, whose account of the creation of light had been assimilated by Longinus to the classical sublime, and was regarded by many commentators as the source of Ovid's myth of creation from Chaos. Salmasius had taken the republicans to task for saying that kingdoms existed before the king, which, he alleged, was like saying that there was light before the sun. Milton had eagerly pointed out that according to the Bible that had indeed been the case; Salmasius's monarchist imagination had not grasped the full sublimity of the passage that had attracted Longinus (IV:1, 506). This slip, he argued, was utterly characteristic of the way in which his monarchist blinkers distorted truth and beauty. Milton resumed the argument in *Paradise Lost*, complementing his menacing reference to eclipses by the narratorial emphasis: 'before the Sun, / Before the Heavens thou wert' (iii.8–9). Harrington had invoked Moses both as a legislator and also as a poet, presumably in the same sense, as author of a sublime account of the creation. In his last book Milton moves from Moses the writer to Moses the man of action, though he stresses Moses's religious rather than legislative role, reflecting an important point of difference between the two republicans (xii.227ff). In the passage quoted above, the slippery positioning of 'in the beginning' blurs Moses's priority as religious and poetic creator with the story of divine creation that he tells. According to some commentators, the ensuing reference to '*Siloa's* Brook' (i.11) is associated with the pool from which Christ healed the blind man – the legend to which Marten alluded in his defence of the republic's use of the word 'restored'.

From the very beginning of the poem, creation is associated with Chaos; Milton's political imagery, here as so often, is double-edged. As Satan journeys from Hell towards the newly-created universe, we see Chaos through his eyes as a Babel-like hubbub, an 'Eternal *Anarchie*' (ii.896); particular emphasis is placed on the noise. We can readily see this passage as reflecting some of Milton's own discomfort at the negative aspects of the revolutionary period: Chaos is a nightmare version of the radical public sphere, especially in the turbulence of 1659–60. His representation of Chaos has been seen as a retreat from his earlier openness to political change: in Raphael's narrative 'cold Infernal dregs' are expelled to Chaos (vii.238), an unassimilable residue that has to be purged away, and it is easy to link this recalcitrance with Milton's fears of anarchy, of the masses.[81] As has been seen, however, his stance even at that dark time was a little more complex than a simple vindication of order against anarchy. He was objecting not to building the republican tower but to the failure to complete it, while the cacophonous voices he was attacking were those calling for a return to monarchy. There is a similar complex of associations in the description of the Tower of Babel in Book XII, where the 'hubbub' and 'Confusion' that refer back to the Chaos description (xii.60, 62) are caused by monarchical aspiration. Milton saw monarchy as anarchic in that it gave free rein to private interests over the public good, and attacked the conservatives who confused 'a frugal and self-governing democratie' with 'lawlesse anarchie' (*The Ready and Easie Way*, *MPW*, VII, 427). If we are attuned to republican culture, we can start to read the outpourings of panegyrics, first to Richard Cromwell in 1658–9 and then to Charles II, not as a return to beauty and harmony but as a cacophony, based on a massive imbalance between language and equity. In *Paradise Lost*, Chaos is seated on a throne, and in a brilliant coinage Milton describes him as an Anarch, a back-formation from 'monarch' (ii.988). Milton had earlier marvelled how

> he whose office is to execute Law and Justice upon all others, should sit himselfe like a demigod in lawlesse and unbounded *anarchy* . . . (*Observations upon the Articles of Peace*, III, 307)

Throughout the poem, a similar link is made between monarchy and anarchy – a link that was implicit in Lucan, and that Shelley was to develop in his *Masque of Anarchy*. As has been seen, Chaos is partly patterned on Lucan's description of the republican forces' confrontation with adversity. In a

---

81 Rogers, *The Matter of Revolution*, pp. 103–43. Rogers suggestively parallels Milton's political retreats with his withdrawal from a vitalistic monism, a belief in the interconnectedness of matter and spirit; but as Rogers acknowledges (p. 138) the changes may not have followed a steady path. The parallel to the 'Infernal dregs' passage in Lucretius, *De rerum natura*, v.497, speaks of *faex*, dregs, a term which Milton had earlier refused to have applied to the English people (*Second Defence*, *MPW*, IV:1, 339). Yet every seventeenth-century statesman was familiar with Cicero's comment that Cato was unrealistic in trying to live 'tamquam in Platonis Politeia, non tamquam in Romuli faece', as if in Plato's ideal republic instead of the imperfect materials with which the state had to be built; the imperfection was to be accepted (*Ad Atticum*, II.i.8, in Cicero, *Letters to Atticus*, trans. E. O. Winstedt, 3 vols. (London and Cambridge, Mass., 1944–5), I, 108–9). Lucretius associated *faeces* with the corruptions of kingly government at v.1141, in a part of the poem that may have caught Milton's eye for its contrast between tyranny and the simplicity of living on a little – 'ut satius multo iam sit parere quietum' (v.1127) is virtually translated by 'to obey is best' (xii.561).

parody of Machiavellian terminology, Satan offers to reduce the cosmos to its first principles by reclaiming it from the usurper, God, when

> I that Region lost,
> All usurpation thence expell'd, reduce
> To her original darkness and your sway
> (Which is my present journey) and once more
> Erect the Standard there of *ancient Night*[.] (ii.982–86)

His first principles, however, involve not the subordination of private interests to a common public interest but an internecine war of private interests, of factions and 'Clanns' (ii.901 – Milton's use of this word presumably hits at the Scots-sympathizing Presbyterians, and would have been more topical in the 1650s than thereafter).

Insofar as Milton associates Chaos with political disorder, then, it is to make an anti-monarchist rather than the stock anti-republican point. And Milton's Chaos is not inherently evil. As with his presentation of Satan, Milton arouses expectations of a baldly anti-republican reading only to frustrate them. Chaos appears differently when viewed through eyes other than Satan's – and we are reminded that the viewpoint in Book II is Satan's by the long suspension of the 'looked' that at last completes the repeated 'Into this wilde Abyss' (ii.910–18). Milton departs from nearly every theological and poetic precedent, and even risks charges of materialist heterodoxy, to insist that Chaos is essential to creation, that creation was not out of nothing but out of prime matter. Milton echoes the passage from the opening of Ovid's *Metamorphoses* that the author of *Chaos* took as his epigraph; giving so much attention to Chaos highlights a basic radicalism in the poem, a desire to go back to the simplest components and start again. Milton's God is not frightened by the risk of apparent imbalance; he knows that this can be turned into a more complicated and vital kind of balance. Chaos is as it were the cosmos's default mode, transformable into concord only by a continued process of careful intervention.[82] Raphael notes how 'late' God has elected to 'build/In *Chaos*' (vii.92–3). The new building is a response to 'intestine broiles' (ii.1001), a cosmic civil war in which there is as yet no complete resolution. At the edge of Heaven Chaos retires 'As from her outmost works a brok'n foe' (ii.1039), but the defeat is not total; 'vast infinitude' was 'confin'd' (iii.711) only in a relatively tiny area.

The omnipresence of Chaos perhaps explains God's apparent preference

---

82 For a detailed argument to this effect see Rumrich, *Milton Unbound*, pp. 118–46. Regina M. Schwartz, *Remembering and Repeating: On Milton's Theology and Poetics* (Chicago and London, 1993), ch. 1, argues forcefully for the evil of Chaos; but her reading makes the poem's politics a little more orthodox than seems plausible. See also Kolbrener, *Milton's Warring Angels*, pp. 97ff.

for asymmetrical forms. Adam and Eve are both troubled by 'disproportions' between different parts of the cosmos (viii.27) which arouse fears of a return to chaos (iv.665–7). Raphael responds with a *tour de force* of diversionary rhetoric (viii.67–178), playing with different models of the cosmos in such a way as to discredit any simple analogy between human and cosmic orders. The disproportions display

> The Makers high magnificence, who built
> So spacious, and his Line stretcht out so farr;
> That Man may know he dwells not in his own;
> An Edifice too large for him to fill . . . (viii.101–4)

This is not a predictable courtly symmetry but a sublime *concordia discors*, straining the boundaries of representation (and perhaps echoed in Milton's proud description of his bound-breaking metre, 'the sense variously drawn out from one Verse into another'). This cosmology is republican in the sense that it plays down any sense of monarchy as a natural order and strongly emphasizes the element of artifice in any polity.[83] The poem once again devalues the stock monarchist associations between the king and the sun. Far more than Marvell's Cromwell, Milton's God dizzyingly perplexes conventional models of the universe. Even in Eden there is a sense that order can be maintained only at the cost of a constant process of active lopping and cutting back, of reforming (iv.625) and redressing (ix.219). Like Harrington with his politicized ideal landscape, Milton emphasizes the perpetual flow of Eden's rivers. The more attention is paid to the underlying motion of Chaos, the more we are aware of God as the true 'Author and end of all things' (vii.591), the 'sov'ran Architect' (v.256). If Lucan's Caesar was in a certain sense his Muse, Milton could look beyond Satan for the main author of his narrative. Lucan could iconoclastically demolish the Virgilian idealization of the epic hero; but Milton was able to offer a 'greater Man' who really could 'Restore us'.

That prominent placing of 'Restore' is often taken as a hit at Charles II. In the poem's later speech-acts of 1667 and 1674, that would indeed have been the case. As has been seen, however, the idea of restoration had a central and positive place in republican politics. Sir Cheney Culpeper – whose interest in Milton's writings has been seen (see above, chapter 3) – had republicanized the cosmic order:

> & thus haue I proued the People (in all politicall creations) to be (with reuerence may I speake it) like God in the creation of the worlde; in whom (as the creatures in God) all our politicall creatures (be they as proude as Lucifer)

---

83 I differ here from Quint, *Epic and Empire*, pp. 43–4, who sees Milton as translating an Augustan ideology into the divine sphere. Quint makes a sharp antithesis between linearity, coherence and political conformity on the one hand and chaotic disorder and political liberty on the other; Milton, I would argue, refuses those alternatives.

muste acknowledge themselues to liue & moue & haue their continuall beinge, excepte (like Lucifer) they will deserue to be caste out of the politicall heauen; a thing which is shortly (I beleeue) to come to passe, when the Fowles of the Ayre shall be called to the Supper of the greate God, & shall feede on noe lesse daintyes, then the Fleshe of [K*ings*] et caet, & that the time comes, when there shall be a newe politicall heauen & a newe earthe[.][84]

Culpeper continued this imagery a few years later:

the stone is rollinge, & (I am confidente) will not ly still any where but in the peoples true Intereste of an equall, frequente, & powerfull Parliamente . . . For a politicall creature to receiue its beinge, & yet (Luciferianlike) to holde it from itselfe without any future acknowledgement of its creater, was that which firste made that thinge wee call the Deuill, & caste him out of heauen without possibility of returne; & this woord heauen hathe a politicall sence in the reuelation[.][85]

Culpeper believed that the 'sonnes of Adam' should regain their 'naturall inherente liberty'.[86] His label for monarchism was 'Nimrodisme'.[87]

The language of a return to pristine beginnings was crucially important for English republicanism; as has been seen, it became all-pervasive in its final phase of 1658–60. Opponents of the House of Lords had seen its abolition as a reduction of illegitimate power to the people; when the Cromwellian Upper House was introduced, comparable calls were made for reduction. In January 1658 Thomas Scot had used the Genesis myth to justify the sovereignty of the people. God had given his power to the people just as he had left it to Adam to name the creatures. Those who would claim that power for themselves were going against God's first principles. Scot went on provocatively to compare the House of Commons to Adam and the Lords to Eve, a rib out of its side; the power of naming had remained with Adam. Rather than contrasting divine with earthly government, Scot was arguing that the English state needed to be brought closer to heavenly principles.[88]

The plot of *Paradise Lost* can be seen as a series of restorations or reductions. In political terms, God's role is that of a dynamic, Machiavellian legislator. He is open to conflict and discord and does not aim to achieve concord by enforcing sterility. While he enjoys the panoply of kingship, he is ready to undergo sacrifice for the general good. God's creation of the Son epitomizes the principle of divine reduction.[89] In the carefully paralleled debate scenes in

84 Culpeper to Hartlib, 22 September 1647, *CL*, p. 307.
85 Culpeper to Hartlib, 5 April 1648, *CL*, p. 331.
86 Culpeper to Hartlib, 15 September 1647, *CL*, p. 305.
87 Culpeper to Hartlib, 15 August 1649, p. 356.
88 *Diary of Thomas Burton*, ed. John Towill Rutt, 4 vols. (1828; rptd ed. Ivan Roots, New York and London, 1974), II, 391–2.
89 On the elevation as one of many examples of divided sovereignty in the poem, see Fallon, *Divided Empire*, p. 5 and *passim*.

Books II and III, Satan's volunteering to set off to found his new empire is contrasted with the Son's readiness to lower himself by becoming mortal: he will 'Freely put off' his glory (iii.240). It is through this act of descent from being 'Equal to God' (iii.305) that mankind will be 'restor'd' (iii.288):

> Therefore thy Humiliation shall exalt
> With thee thy Manhood also to this Throne;
> Here shalt thou sit incarnate, here shalt Reign
> Both God and Man, Son both of God and Man,
> Anointed universal King; all Power
> I give thee, reign for ever, and assume
> Thy Merits; under thee as Head Supream
> Thrones, Princedoms, Powers, Dominions I reduce[.] (iii.312–19)

This episode is closely parallel to a king's abdicating and showing solidarity with his people. The word 'reduce' here means 'subordinate'; but the poem's whole movement tends to undermine absolute distinctions between putting down and raising up. It is in the context of this divine reduction that the poem first refers to the Son as king: he is crowned from merit, not mere hereditary right. And within a few lines we are looking forward to his final apocalyptic triumph and then his abdication:

> Mean while
> The World shall burn, and from her ashes spring
> New Heav'n and Earth, wherein the just shall dwell
> And after all thir tribulations long
> See golden days, fruitful of golden deeds,
> With Joy and Love triumphing, and fair Truth.
> Then thou thy regal Scepter shalt lay by,
> For regal Scepter then no more shall need,
> God shall be All in All. (iii.333–41)

The Son's kingship, however longlasting from a human point of view, is a temporary expedient.

Readers of the poem encounter this episode before they come to the Son's elevation, the incident that provokes Satan's rebellion. They are thus able to see more clearly than Satan how God differs from a magnate trying to consolidate his personal power. His speech proclaiming his Son (v.600–615) is a palimpsest of quotations from Psalm II, which contains a prophetic warning that unjust kings will be punished – a warning Abdiel goes on to make, and which Beelzebub remembers in Hell (v.886–8, ii.326–8). The psalm was often cited by the king's enemies during the Civil War.[90] And the elevation is the moment when Milton comes closest to revealing his own theological heterodoxy, his

90 Michael Lieb, *Poetics of the Holy: A Reading of 'Paradise Lost'* (Chapel Hill, 1981), pp. 278ff.

insistence that the Trinity did not exist from all eternity but that God created the Son at a particular historical moment.[91] The elevation is not the same as the Creation, but it emphasizes the break in the continuity of the heavenly kingdom which God has chosen. Satan's resistance to innovation, his reification of titles of honour into unassailable idols, then aligns him with conservative opponents of Christ's reanimating spirit, defenders of a traditional constitution who fail to see the need for periodic change. He sees the Son's supporters as sectaries, 'singular and rash' (v.851), their tongues 'Inspir'd with contradiction' (vi.155) – the terms used by Presbyterians and Anglicans to attack religious subversives. But such people are drawn to God's cause and open to the Son's innovatory rule. The elevation is fully in accordance with divine first principles, because central to the poem's deity is the need to diffuse himself, to communicate his own energies as far as possible.

Abdiel's reply to Satan is inflected by the language of reduction: the Son is

> how farr from thought
> To make us less, bent rather to exalt
> Our happie state under one Head more neer
> United . . .

> he the Head
> One of our number thus reduc't becomes,
> His Laws our Laws, all honour to him done
> Returns our own. (v.828–31, 842–5)

Syntactic ambiguity here poises 'reduc't' between the sense of bringing under control and a more participatory, Machiavellian sense of the word. The angelic host are to a certain extent reduced, in the sense of subordination, by acknowledging the Son's lordship. On that reading, 'our number' hovers between the sense of discrete individuals, in which case a reduction of the number through the addition of one would become paradoxical, and that of a political collectivity in which there is strength in increased numbers. Reduction would then still carry the sense of discipline and control, rather as Michael

> soon reduc'd
> His Armie, circumfus'd on either Wing,
> Under thir Head imbodied all in one. (vi.777–9)

Yet that 'imbodied' stresses also the Son's active sharing and participation in the heavenly host, and in Abdiel's speech the primary sense is of self-diminution. In the three words 'exalt', 'under', and 'united' we glimpse a tensely interactive process of divine reduction. Precisely because the Son is on such a vastly different level of creation, his kingship is for him analogous to a

---

91 Cf. *Christian Doctrine*, I, v; *MPW*, VI, 205–10.

Machiavellian reduction, a self-lowering that is in a sense a return to first principles even if it is also an innovation. Abdiel speaks of God's 'unsucceeded power' (v.821): the problem of succession, which was so difficult in the 1650s when the Machiavellian legislator moved towards founding a dynasty instead of laying down his power, does not arise when the son can 'succeed' the father only to be succeeded by him.

Milton's God, then, is a king with distinct overtones of a republican founding legislator. He is a king nevertheless. It has become a cliché of Milton criticism to point to the tensions between Milton's republicanism and divine kingship. A reply to *The Readie and Easie Way* jested that

> You must prove that [Christ] erected a Republique of his Apostles, and that notwithstanding the Scripture, every where calls his Government the Kingdome of Heaven, it ought to be Corrected, and Rendred the Common-wealth of Heaven, or rather the Common-wealth of this World[.][92]

This question has nevertheless come to loom much larger than it did when the poem was being conceived. Butler was mounting his attack at a time when the monarchy's return was near-certain, and a harmony between secular and heavenly systems was ideologically important to establish. During the 1650s, the differences rather than the resemblances between earthly and heavenly government were emphasized. The period saw the height of the Fifth Monarchy movement, which again and again invoked the kingship of Christ not to glorify secular monarchy but to vilify it. The language of divine kingship was marshalled against Cromwellian monarchism. Milton was not a Fifth Monarchist and was more ready to give Cromwell the benefit of the doubt, but *The Readie and Easie Way* attacked '*Gentilish* imitation' of the heavenly king (*MPW*, VII, 364), just as *Paradise Lost* satirizes Satan's 'God-like imitated State' (ii.511). Abdiel emphasizes that Satan's rebellion is using an inappropriate language. Subjection to Father and Son cannot be tyrannical because the angels are in no sense their equals; they are their creation (v.822ff). It is simply invalid to make analogies between heavenly rule and earthly government. In 1659 William Sprigge had playfully suggested that if one were to draw analogies between heavenly and earthly government, one might as well compare the Trinity to the Roman triumvirate.[93]

And yet the problem of divine kingship is not quite so simply resolved. It is impossible to talk about the divine world at all without some approximation to human concepts; and Milton seems to go out of his way to blur the distinctions. His monism, his rejection of a sharp split between spirit and matter, implied a comparable rejection of a sharp split between theology and politics. Raphael muddies the waters when he tells Adam that he is accommodating

92 J. H., [Samuel Butler?] *The Censure of the Rota upon Mr. Miltons Book* (1660; E1019.5*), p. 10.   93 Sprigge, *A Modest Plea, for an Equal Common-Wealth*, p. 18.

heavenly events to his limited human understanding, and then goes on to ask whether Earth may not be

> but the shaddow of Heav'n, and things therein
> Each to other like, more then on earth is thought? (v.575–6)

At this stage in history, of course, there has not been much time for thinking on Earth about the question. The comment is really addressed to Milton's readers more than to Adam; but it is hard entirely to forget that Adam has no political experience whatever, and from his responses in Book XII his mentality seems naturally republican, so that using monarchical imagery to explain heavenly events is merely to explain one unfamiliar world by analogy with another. Up to a point, Milton had no choice; his presentation of Heaven is based on Scriptural texts, where kingship is an unvarying point of reference. But he also amplifies the political terms of the original. Once the Satanic assembly in Hell has been mediated by republican terminology, comparable political expectations may be brought to bear on the carefully paralleled colloquy in Heaven in Book III. However clear the distinction between earthly and heavenly kingship may be in the abstract, in reading the exchanges between Satan and Abdiel we are constantly denied a stable point of reference. Abdiel may draw on Machiavellian ideas of reduction, but at times his vindications of God's absolute authority seem to echo Salmasius. If the distinction between earthly and heavenly forms of kingship is absolutely unambiguous, Satan and Abdiel are simply not having a dialogue, they are speaking past each other; and there is a comic sense in which that is the case. Satan is using a republican language for a speech-act designed to consolidate his personal power; Abdiel is using monarchist language for a speech-act aimed at affirming public over private interests. Yet they both come from the same milieu: where then did the confusion arise? God has already mocked Satan's politicizing:

> Neerly it now concernes us to be sure
> Of our Omnipotence, and with what Arms
> We mean to hold what anciently we claim
> Of Deitie or Empire, such a foe
> Is rising, who intends to erect his Throne
> Equal to ours, throughout the spacious North . . . (v.721–6)

God, it would seem, has no problems: it is self-evidently ludicrous for Satan to use a political language, and the Son praises him for his secure laughter. But God's security is not the reader's; his smile is disturbing. If such language was inappropriate, why did God himself use it in proclaiming his Son? The prospect that all the characters in the poem may be talking at cross-purposes is dizzying.

One kind of answer would hold, following Stanley Fish, that here and elsewhere Milton is testing his readers, holding out the bait of idolatry and then chastening them with awareness of their own tendency to fall. There is an element of truth in this analysis; but it makes the poem sound more complacent and conservative than it is. Once readers become accustomed to such an approach, they can always pre-empt it, moving beyond the dubious image to the certain truth. But Milton, whose own theological position was far from orthodox, does not seem to be aiming to produce such readers; rather, he encourages a vigilant, self-reliant process of questioning. He pushes the psalm's laughter into a querulous sarcasm that is more profoundly alienating. The imagery of heavenly kingship helped to pose the question of heavenly justice in the sharpest and most provocative way to a republican reader. The poem's wager is that God's ways can be justified, but they must first be held up to difficult scrutiny. His cause is justified only if it is the cause not only of God but of Truth (vi.31–2). It would appear that Milton worked on the *Christian Doctrine*, with its eloquent call to freedom of inquiry even into questions normally thought heretical, in the 1650s and abandoned it at the Restoration: the spirit of free religious inquiry was associated for him with civil liberty. There is a sense in which his basic questions are rather like Lucan's. Why did the gods allow a cataclysmic triumph of tyranny? Why did they approve Caesar rather than Cato? Republicans like Chaloner and May seem to have gone a long way to sharing Lucan's deistic or atheistic answers to these questions. Less drastic interpretations of Lucan's theology were possible, however. Grotius combined great admiration for Lucan with an Arminian theological position, condemning Calvinist predestination to damnation because it made God tyrannical. Milton shared Grotius's critique of Calvinism, and incorporates it in his poem with his constant insistence on free will. God is justified because of his refusal to treat his subjects as mere puppets or instruments.

It remains true that there are limits to the apparent open-mindedness of Milton's deity. These are to some extent the limits imposed by Milton's own republicanism and by his Bible-centred Protestantism. The comparison between Satanic and divine assemblies might lead us to expect something like a heavenly public sphere to counter Satan's manipulations. Milton does indeed place great emphasis on the fact that 'all' the angels are present to hear God's colloquy with his son (iii.217, 272, 344, v.617). To an extent, communication is central to Milton's God; his Son is the Word whose role is to create, to extend and communicate the divine substance. But this is a very special form of communication in which there can be no equality, in which all speech-acts are ultimately echoes of the divine speech-act. They can either return that echo appropriately or be censured for dishonesty, for failing to recognize the terms of their existence. Abdiel rejects Satan's

Words which no eare ever to hear in Heav'n
Expected (v.810–11)

as a wholly inappropriate speech-act for one

> by whom
> As by his Word the mighty Father made
> All things, ev'n thee, and all the Spirits of Heav'n[.] (v.835–7)

There is no room in Heaven for deliberative rhetoric, for the arguments of the forum. The angels are engaged in a continual act of praise, expressed by kneeling – a posture Milton would have found idolatrous in earthly religion – as well as in speech. God reveals his purposes to the angels; there is no question of their being offered for discussion. This unanimity is shattered when Satan proposes a move to the deliberative mode:

> new Counsels, to debate
> What doubtful may ensue[.] (v.681–2)

In response to his exchanges with Abdiel

> as the sound of waters deep
> Hoarce murmur echo'd to his words applause (v.872–3)

– the hubbub conjures up Milton's negative views of the chaos of the public sphere. And though there are very special conditions for supramundane communication, the unease about debate expressed here is not totally separate from the reservations implicit in the conservative side of his republicanism. For all his championing of an open religious public sphere, Milton saw it as a means to an end. It gave an opportunity for escaping from the distorted communication imposed by secular hierarchies, but in the end it would lead to the revelation of a single, absolute truth. In heaven the dividing-lines between truth and error are absolute; the fallen angels reveal themselves as unworthy of participation in the heavenly regime as soon as they disagree with God, and the reader is made to savour the pleasure of driving out from the community all who are lacking in the appropriate virtue. This action is more likely to seem tyrannical to the modern reader than to the early modern republican who was used to limiting political participation to the virtuous or godly. For all the differences between heavenly and earthly orders, Milton feels able to blend in his own poem with the angelic speech-act of praise, sharing in 'the copious matter of my Song' (iii.413). His God is not a tyrant, but he is certainly not a modern democrat. Nonetheless, republican unease about traditional hierarchies deeply informs Milton's presentation of the heavenly kingdom, and will emerge still more clearly in his presentation of the human world.

'Social communication': language and politics in Eden

One of the poem's key points of sublimity is the moment when Satan first catches sight of Adam and Eve (iv.288ff). For the first three books, in the company of supernatural beings, we have been transported from the lowest to the highest reaches of the universe and back down again. Now we can encompass the experience of looking at humanity from the outside, as a species just created, and sharing the wonder. The tableau of Adam and Eve can be seen as a republican icon. The narrator lays great emphasis on their nudity – so much so that Eliot found this spectacle more shocking than Milton's Hell. Empson chided Eliot's prudishness[94], but his response so many centuries later is a reminder of how deliberately provocative Milton was being in glorifying his characters' sexuality. He would have known how Michelangelo's David had embodied the spirit of the young Florentine republic; in their different way the newly-created Adam and Eve speak for a republican delight in returning to the beginning, in stripping away false customs. Like so many republicans, Marten had appealed to another anti-Augustan text, Ovid's description of the Creation, in a similar spirit:

> The Roman Poet that fetchd ye world from its cradle like Moses & (as some think) by reading Moses, could observe that man was a holyer creature, & more capable of high thoughts than ye rest & therefore fitt dominari in caetera not in seipsum. over his own kinde, euery one of whom is by nature (if vn-interrupted) equally holy, & high-minded[.]

In interpreting Ovid's myth as a gloss on Genesis, Marten was following a long humanist tradition.[95] Ovid's first humans, he insists, are worthy of domination over other creatures (*Metamorphoses* i.77), but not over each other. Marten was here responding to a treatise that called for a Hobbesian obedience to the Protectorate; he invokes biblical and classical creation myths against monarchism. The first humans' primal simplicity has a heaven-oriented high-mindedness ('os . . . sublime', *Metamorphoses*, i.85, echoed in Milton's 'Eye sublime', iv.300) quite different from the desire for elaborate titles shown by Cromwell and his panegyrists.[96] The republican poet R. Fletcher invoked Adam in a similar spirit:

> *Adam* knew no Star-chamber, (as we see)
> Unlesse you mean the heavn'ly Canopie:
> And there few Bishops sate . . .
> See Man in *Adam*, and you'le find that we
> Are but a lineall fraternity.[97]

94 Empson, *Milton's God*, p. 30.
95 Don Cameron Allen, *Mysteriously Meant: The Rediscovery of Pagan Symbolism and Allegorical Interpretation in the Renaissance* (Baltimore and London, 1970), pp. 163–4, 175, 177, 188, 192.   96 BL Additional MS 71,532, fol. 9v (reply to Thomas White).
97 R. Fletcher, *Radius Heliconicus: Or, The Resolution of a Free State* (1651; 669f15.83), lines 77–9; R. F[letcher]., *Mercurius Heliconicus. Or, the Result of a Safe Conscience* no. 1 (1651; E622.14), p. 3.

Satan is discomfited by the sight of Adam and Eve. He marvels at their beauty, yet he is also perplexed by the fact that they are 'Into our room of bliss thus high advanc't' (iv.359): they disrupt his sense of hierarchy and decorum. He will conquer this new world, and to rule it Hell will 'send forth all her Kings' (iv.383). Kingship will enter Eden with the Fall. Satan is looking with eyes that have become increasingly monarchical, increasingly obsessed with maintaining status. He cannot properly understand the process of divine 'reduction' that is manifested most fully in the creation of humanity. Like the Son's elevation, it baffles him: man has

> O indignitie!
> Subjected to his service Angel wings[.] (ix.154–5)

But this lowering of divine matter, which to Satan is a 'foul descent', is also an elevation. On God's original plan, the emanation of divine being into the created world will gradually return to its source as man rises up the scale of creation, 'And Earth be chang'd to Heavn, & Heav'n to Earth' (vii.160). Satan's language of public affairs rings hollow in Eden, where there is a household but no state and certainly no court. One of Milton's radical departures from classical epic is the elevation of a familial narrative to the dignity of more conventionally public affairs: a form of generic 'reduction'. Bentley, ever-insistent on conventional propriety, found the term 'domestick *Adam*' (ix.318) 'absurd and ridiculous'; but it is central to the poem's values.

This polemical, and to some extent egalitarian, element in the presentation of Adam and Eve, however, needs to be set against the poem's insistence on the hierarchy within the couple. They seem formed, we are told, 'Hee for God only, shee for God in him' (iv.299). Disquiet at these lines is not merely a modern phenomenon. Even the redoubtable Bentley believed this line could not have been Milton's – 'A shameful Error to have pass'd through all the Editions' (he preferred 'God and him'). In 1700 the pioneering feminist Mary Astell attacked Milton for crying up liberty but denying it to females.[98] Astell was one of a number of women writers who considered monarchical rule to be more sympathetic to their sex's cause. For Astell, and for some later feminist critics, Milton was hostile to female equality not despite but because of his republicanism.

One way of defusing the provocation of 'Hee for God only' is to point out that we first see Adam and Eve through the eyes of Satan: the apparently natural hierarchy, it has been argued, seems so only to Satan, who is importing his corrupt monarchical values into his reading of the scene.[99] There

---

98 Ruth Perry, *The Celebrated Mary Astell: An Early English Feminist* (Chicago and London, 1986), p. 165.

99 Michael Lieb, '"Two of Far Nobler Shape": Reading the Paradisal Text', in Diana Treviño Benet and Michael Lieb (eds.), *Literary Milton: Text, Pretext, Context* (Pittsburgh, 1994), pp. 114–32, offers an especially complex reading of this passage.

would be a parallel here with the way Chaos is presented through Satan's eyes. This argument works only up to a point: it would be difficult to treat all parts of this description as Satanic, and after the Fall the Son himself punningly declares that her gifts 'Were such as under Government well seem'd,/ Unseemly to beare rule' (x.154–5). The poem seems to hesitate between treating Eve as an agent and as an ornament. We are told that Adam is fit for absolute rule, Eve for subjection (iv.301, 308). This pairing of terms is problematic, for absolute rule or lordship is what mankind as a whole has been assigned over the beasts (iv.290, viii.344, and cf. the Ovidian passage recalled by Marten), but its counterpart, subjection, is what Eve is expected to show to Adam. In secular political terms, subjection is associated with postlapsarian tyranny (xii.93).[100] There then seems room for the claim that Milton the republican permitted tyranny within the household. The content of the 'God only' line is made all the more disquieting by its metrical form. The neatly balanced pentameter (imitating Tasso's baroque rhetoric) seems at odds with the blank verse's normal aspirations to an experimental, sublime openness.

It is hard to believe that Milton did not intend an acerbic moment in that 'subjection', a rebuke to women like the duchess of Newcastle who were ready on some occasions to claim equality for the sexes. It will not do to present Milton as simply echoing an unproblematic consensus: the use of the Fall narrative to restrict women's education and status was being challenged long before *Paradise Lost*.[101] The fact that many women writers did have royalist leanings may have coloured Milton's presentation of his primal husband and wife. Eve's loveliest role, says her husband, is to 'studie houshold good' (ix.233): in this prelapsarian world we find a characteristically republican delineation between the public sphere and the household. Satan's initial advances to Eve adopt a characteristic language of courtly flattery (ix.532ff), and after eating the apple she wishes to be 'more equal', for 'inferior who is free?' (ix.823–5). The 'wedded Love' of the secluded bower is contrasted polemically with 'Court Amours' (iv.750, 767).

Did Milton's republicanism, then, make him more tyrannical than royalists towards women? Certainly it did not make him a feminist. But it did render more traditional forms of female subordination problematic. For a conservative royalist like Filmer, Adam's role as both father and king was a buttress for all subsequent societies based on traditions of subordination and mystery of state. Milton needs ideologically to distinguish Adam's role in the household from the monarch's role in the state. This was indeed the course of much later liberal theory, which separated women off from the social contract

---

100 'Subjection' is of course the term used by Paul when he justifies woman's silence in church on analogy with Eve's inferiority to Adam (1 Timothy II.11, cf. 1 Peter III.1).
101 See, for example, *The Poems of Aemilia Lanyer: Salve Deus Rex Judaeorum*, ed. Susanne Woods (New York and Oxford, 1993), pp. 84–7.

and therefore left the household as a naturalized unit not open to political negotiation.[102] Milton and many mid-century Puritans, however, also strongly believed in the 'companionate marriage' as a realm for inquiring into the truth with a common political purpose. So it was that Lucy Hutchinson could describe herself as an 'image' in terms very similar to Milton's in Book IV, but also devote herself to writing on the most controversial religious and political topics: knowing that her husband too was no more than an image, she could unite with him in overturning idolatry.[103] If Virgil's royalist epic gave a significant role to Queen Dido, Lucan had countered with a sympathetic portrayal of Pompey's wife Cornelia, who shares responsibility and political agency with her husband, and marshals opposition to Caesar after his death. Having set up a sharp dividing-line between male and female abilities, Milton then has to negotiate a view of the good life which privileges common interest and shared communication.[104] In his version of the Fall story, the emphasis passes from mysterious taboos to a drama of moral choice with a strong humanist inflection, where faith in God is complemented by a practical prudence and an effective understanding of language. Adam and Eve, whatever their inequalities, are both considered by God to be equal to these standards.

Eve, it is true, fails her test. But her failure cannot be put down crudely to an inferior female power of rationality, or to royalist passion overcoming republican reason. Though when the poem lingers on her body Eve may appear to embody the beautiful as opposed to Adam's masculine sublimity, she has her own sublime potential. She easily dismisses Satan's courtly flattery; what gives her particular pause is to find 'Language of Man pronounc't/By Tongue of Brute' (ix.553–4). Satan tells her that eating the fruit improved his reason and gave him speech. If mankind can speak with angels,

---

102 Carole Pateman, *The Sexual Contract* (Oxford, 1988), ch. 4; for a response, see Margaret R. Sommerville, *Sex and Subjection: Attitudes to Women in Early-Modern Society* (London and New York, 1995) pp. 222ff (Sommerville finds no significant difference between theorists of different political views on the status of women).

103 David Norbrook, 'Lucy Hutchinson's "Elegies" and the Situation of the Republican Woman Writer', *English Literary Renaissance* 27 (1997), 468–521; Hutchinson, pp. 2, 32–3. Hutchinson narrated the Fall story without demurring from the incorporation of Eve in Adam's identity: *On the Principles of the Christian Religion* (1817), pp. 26, 32–6.

104 Michael C. Schoenfeldt, 'Gender and Conduct in *Paradise Lost*', in James Grantham Turner (ed.), *Sexuality and Gender in Early Modern Europe: Institutions, Texts, Images* (Cambridge, 1993), pp. 310–38, argues that Eve's linguistic independence derives from the idiom of courtly conduct-books; though his detailed readings are perceptive, he fails to demonstrate why courtly rather than republican sources should have been so important to Milton. James Grantham Turner, *One Flesh: Paradisal Marriage and Sexual Relations in the Age of Milton* (Oxford, 1987), pp. 281–7, gives a good account of the ways in which the poem seems to go against some of its more simple statements of hierarchy; I am trying to suggest political reasons why this may be so.

why not beasts with mankind? Where do the possibilities of free conversation end? Satan's language parodies the republican idiom of restoration and opening the eyes:

Why then was this forbid? Why but to awe,
Why but to keep ye low and ignorant,
His worshippers; he knows that in the day
Ye Eate thereof, your Eyes that seem so cleere,
Yet are but dim, shall perfetly be then
Op'nd and cleerd, and ye shall be as Gods . . . (ix.703–08)

As in his temptation of the angels, Satan appeals to an anti-monarchical idiom. Just as there, of course, he blends it with a temptation to personal power and domination: what he really offers them is a diminution, not an enhancement, of vision, a narrow perspective that loses sight of the cosmic common interest. Nevertheless, Eve is responsive to the language of renewed sight. We are reminded of the links between republicanism and rhetoric at this point: in a lengthy simile Milton compares this climactic speech to the oratory of '*Athens* or free *Rome*, where Eloquence/Flourishd, since mute' (ix.671–2). The irony here is complex. Like many of Milton's similes, this one works by unlikeness; and the comparison is undercut – 'part', 'Motion', 'act', are rhetorical terms with double meanings of hypocrisy. At this high point of his drama, however, he is also dividing the sympathies of readers with republican leanings. Satan's eloquence, his ability to seize the 'Occasion' (ix.480), is something he retains from his unfallen state. The more emphasis is placed on Satan's rhetorical powers, the more Eve's capitulation becomes understandable – though of course never in the poem's terms excusable.

What makes Satan's temptation so powerful is that it centres on an area, the pragmatics of communication, in which the prelapsarian universe already seems problematic. In many ways, this is an extraordinarily open universe, in which the huge vertical distances between different levels are bridged by free horizontal communication. This point is emphasized in the central books, where Raphael eats with Adam and Eve. Raphael's wings may constitute 'regal Ornament' (v.280), but Adam goes to meet him

without more train
Accompani'd then with his own compleat
Perfections, in himself was all his state,
More solemn then the tedious pomp that waits
On Princes, when thir rich Retinue long
Of Horses led, and Grooms besmeard with Gold
Dazles the croud, and sets them all agape. (v.351–7)

This kind of polemical narratorial intrusion aligns Milton with Lucan's outspokenness rather than Virgilian discretion. The striking phrase 'besmeard with Gold' brings home the point that external distinctions are mere accretions to the essence of humanity. The angel uses the fact that he can share a meal with them to draw attention to the many common factors between angels and men, the easy continuity between the spiritual and the corporeal (v.404ff). As messengers of the divine word, the angels are part of a general process of the diffusion of the divine image; angels, man and woman are all images of God and all, at the same time, infinitely removed from his absolute goodness. The point of the famous 'No fear lest Dinner coole' joke (v.396) is that they thus have more time for 'discourse'; their conversation is open and spontaneous. Raphael later declares that angels think of mankind as 'our fellow servant', the object of God's 'Equal Love' (viii.225–8).

The problem with this emphasis on equality is that it draws attention all the more sharply to inequalities. Behind Adam's and Eve's questions about cosmic disproportions there seems to lie an anxiety not only about the work-ings of the planets but also about the cosmic structures of power and communication, with their vertiginous leaps from level to level. Such anxiety risks missing the sublimity of divine reduction, seeing it instead as a baffling lapse from a narrower conception of beauty and hierarchy. In mocking rival cosmologies (viii.67–178), Raphael tries to keep Adam and Eve focused on their immediate concerns, but only at the cost of devaluing human potential for fitting naturally into the cosmic scheme.

In one sense, it is true, the progress of the dialogue between Adam and Raphael shows angelic and human levels coming closer together. After the epic of the war in heaven, Adam asks him to 'descend now lower' and tell of the creation of his own part of the universe (vii.84). The 'descend' here echoes Milton's own invocation to the Muse at the book's opening, regis-tering the process of generic 'reduction' that will be further signalled after the creation narrative, when Adam suggests that the conversation should 'descend' (viii.198) to tell his own story. Now that he is on his own ground, Adam is able to establish his own claims to discursive authority. First of all, Raphael happens not to know the story, so that their natural imbalance of knowledge is rectified, and Adam can gain Raphael's praise for his skill in the arts of speech (viii.218–23). By the end of their exchange, Adam is ready to tease the angel, responding to his warnings about being blinded by passion by asking him about angelic sex, and bringing a blush to his cheek (viii.617–9). In his narrative of his own creation, Adam's speech-act itself privileges mutuality of communication. Adam tells of a God who is ready to speak without any intermediaries to the beings he has created. He is not like the Cromwell denounced by Nedham in 1659, who could not endure the beings he had created to dispute with him. He is rather more like Harrington's God, so committed to popular government that he was willing to be deposed by his people when they voted for a king against his wishes.[105]

But there are unpredictable limits to such openness; Adam feels that the 'Colloquie sublime' is 'streind to the highth' (viii.454–5). The strain derives in part from the immense difficulty of a finite creature's maintaining a sense of the infinite. Adam relates that he found the 'fealtie' and 'subjection' of the beasts inadequate (viii.344–5), asking:

> Among unequals what societie
> Can sort, what harmonie or true delight? (viii.383–4)

After the Fall he will emerge as a natural republican; it is a similar impulse that makes him ask for an equal before the Fall. God teases Adam for some time, declaring that he himself has no one to 'hold converse' with; Adam replies that man needs 'Collateral love' and 'Social communication' (viii.426, 429) – terms insisting on mutuality. Finally God says that he will bring Adam 'thy hearts desire'. He brings him Eve. This transaction can be seen as giving Adam's subjective desire a divine validity, but there is an uncomfortable residue of manipulation. If Adam is an author, he has a ghost-writer. And though Adam has asked for an equal, God brings him a being who proves unequal. Adam knows that she expresses less

> The character of that Dominion giv'n
> O're other Creatures (viii.545–6)

but he cannot reconcile that inferiority with the fact that to him she seems 'absolute'. It is not altogether surprising that the outcome of God's teasing should confuse him. Though Adam praises her creation as an exciting revolution, 'This turn' (viii.491), he also shows unease at the fact that she was made 'Occasionally' (viii.556). Still going by God's manipulation, he thinks of Eve as an afterthought who was not part of God's original plan. He thus fails to see her creation as an *occasione* in a more positive sense, a further process of reduction in which God reveals yet further aspects of himself. After the Fall he is to denounce God for creating this 'noveltie', woman (x.888ff). Adam's unease about Eve runs parallel to the unease he had earlier expressed about the cosmos: in each case he is troubled by a sense of disproportion, by the difficulty of holding together likeness and unlikeness.

In the middle books, angel and humans succeed, however precariously, in maintaining a dialogue, a conversation. In humanist discourse, the dialogue was quintessentially a masculine form. In this case, however, a woman is present, at least for a time. But establishing equality of communication

---

105 Mark Goldie, 'The Civil Religion of James Harrington', in Anthony Pagden (ed.), *The Languages of Political Theory in Early-Modern Europe* (Cambridge, 1987), pp. 197–222; *HPW*, p. 175.

between man and woman would appear within the poem's schema to raise at least as many difficulties as the colloquies of humans and angels, and to be liable to directly comparable tensions. When Raphael approaches the bower, Eve is 'within', while Adam is sitting 'in the dore' (v.299). This seems to confirm a strict division between a public sphere accessible to males and a domestic space reserved for females: Eve is to mediate with the public through her husband. In fact she is present for the first part of the conversation; but she is silent, confining herself to ministering – we are rather gratuitously told – 'naked' (v.444), so that she seems to participate more in the physical than the intellectual natures of Adam and Raphael. The narrative seems uncertain about what to do with her. After relating the war in heaven, Raphael tells Adam to 'warne/Thy weaker' (vi.908–9), even though we learn that he has been listening 'with his consorted *Eve*' (vii.50), and Adam says that he has warned 'us' (vii.74). During the creation narrative she sits 'retir'd in sight,/With lowliness Majestic' (viii.41–2), the paradoxical formulations indicating a certain difficulty in accounting for her. Her absence causes at least as much difficulty as her presence for the narrator, who feels obliged to explain that she did not leave because she was incapable of 'studious thoughts abstruse' but because she wanted to hear the story from Adam, intermingled with kisses. Had Eve simply set the food on the table and retreated, these narratorial interventions would be unnecessary; they arise because Milton wishes both to include and to exclude her. They have confused Milton's editors, who cannot agree when Eve was present and when she was not.[106] The same ambiguity occurs in her relationship to Raphael's final warning. We subsequently learn that she was returning at this point and was just close enough to overhear the warning: once again, she is present and not present (ix.276–8). *Paradise Lost* thus replicates the tensions in Milton's tracts of the 1640s, with the wife's contradictory roles as a 'fit conversing soul' but with conversations confined to 'delightfull intermissions' for her husband (*MPW*, II, 251, 597).[107] Immediately before her lyrical 'With thee conversing I forget all time,' she has declared: 'Unargu'd I obey' (iv.635ff).

The dialogue in these middle books is exploratory in ways that all the protagonists to some extent find exciting: they are discovering some of the rules of this new universe as they go along, and the lines of communicative demarcation are not clear-cut. It is not at all surprising that there are some tensions. In *Paradise Lost*, the concord which God has drawn out of Chaos is always perilously close to collapse. That instability can be a source of excitement as well

---

106 See Flannagan (ed.), *Paradise Lost*, pp. 478–9.

107 On the problems of the private sphere in *Paradise Lost*, see Mary Nyquist, 'The Genesis of Gendered Subjectivity in the Divorce Tracts and in *Paradise Lost*', in Mary Nyquist and Margaret W. Ferguson (eds.), *Re-Membering Milton: Essays on the Texts and Traditions* (New York and London, 1987), pp. 99–127.

as of fear: in the sublimity of the unfallen universe there is an exhilarating openness and variety, which is matched in the spontaneous, unpremeditated prayers of Adam and Eve. But the structures of communication are not entirely open; as in the more oligarchical forms of republicanism, there is emphasis both on common interests and language and on the strong need for hierarchical distinctions. These may not make the Fall inevitable, but they certainly offer points that Satan can exploit.

Eve occupies a particularly problematic position in this universe. She seems to think of herself as a not fully welcome latecomer, an anxiety manifested in her worries about the practical utility of the stars, while her sense of not belonging makes it harder for Adam to assert the authority he has been told to exercise.[108] Satan will play on her unease about the apparent lack of 'proportion' (ix.711), and remind her that she can eat the same food as the angels, a point Raphael has strongly made in playing down hierarchical differences. On the day of the Fall, when Eve proposes her plan for going off to work alone, Adam thinks that she must be satiate with 'much converse' (ix.247). In view of the foregoing analysis, that comment is a little ironic: in terms of a genuine conversational exchange, Eve has hardly been satiated. She insists to Adam on the need for self-sufficiency, for virtue to be tried. As has often been pointed out, her arguments echo *Areopagitica*. If Adam stops her going out on her own, he will be like the licenser stifling thought by stifling utterance. In turning from the divorce tracts to *Areopagitica*, Milton had been able to make a clear-cut move from the domestic sphere to the public sphere; but in the prelapsarian world those lines are harder to draw.[109]

Once the Fall has taken place, the limits between masculine and feminine spheres become firmer. The Son's judgement firmly reinstates the degree which Eve and Adam have in turn challenged (ix.883, 934); but even after the Fall there are ambiguities. He tells Adam that Eve should be 'under Government' (x.154), restating the terms of the description in Book IV. But he goes on, as if this is a new command, to order Eve:

> to thy Husbands will
> Thine shall submit, hee over thee shall rule. (x.195–6)

Adam's lordship over her is thus presented as an unwelcome effect of the Fall, a retreat from rather than a reduction to first principles.[110] It is uncomfortably parallel with the growth of kingly distance between mankind and supernatural beings. On descending to usher Adam and Eve out of Paradise,

---

108 For an interesting analysis of the relationship in theological terms, see Quint, *Epic and Empire*, pp. 281–308.

109 On the political implications see Bennett, *Reviving Liberty*, p. 117.

110 In *Christian Doctrine* Milton wrote that the husband's power increased after the Fall, which was why the Hebrew word for 'husband' also signified 'Lord' (*MPW*, VI, 355).

Michael takes care to make his presence more distant, more 'sublime' (xi.236), than Raphael's. Even though he appears 'as Man/Clad to meet Man' (xi.239–40), he is 'Kingly' enough not to return Adam's low bow. The growth in kingliness is matched by a more rigid hierarchy of communication. He addresses Adam alone, and Eve is left to overhear his words. When she does break in with an 'audible lament' (xi.266), Michael interrupts her, albeit mildly (xi.286). While Adam is instructed in the history of the future, Eve is given her own separate communication in a dream: the unstable situation earlier in the poem has been resolved into a sharp communicative hierarchy.

The image of God that shone so brightly in our first view of the couple has been dimmed; but in mourning its loss so powerfully, the poem also raises the possibility of its recovery, albeit in a different form of 'restoration'. Adam in his anguish asks God to 'reduce me to my dust' (x.748), giving up any hope in a form of reduction that could redeem the situation. But they gradually compose themselves to ask forgiveness; and in this posture they are compared to Deucalion and Pyrrha, who 'restore' the world after the flood in Ovid's *Metamorphoses* (xi.12). It is Eve who is given the last word spoken in the poem. Her 'restore' (xii.623) refers us back to the 'greater Man' of the poem's opening who will 'Restore us'. By the time the poem was published, the word could be taken as a direct, polemical contrast with Charles's Restoration. In the context of the poem's origins, however, it would have retained a more radical, republican meaning, one that looked back to a pristine liberty and revived a longing for its return.

However strongly the last two books insist on the extent of the loss, they also reveal in history a process of recovery after loss. Even the Flood is not irredeemable, a point Milton emphasizes in the 1674 edition by having Michael pause between Books XI and XII, 'Betwixt the world destroy'd and world restor'd' (xii.3). This long-term approach makes it possible to see the Restoration in perspective, as a humiliation but not the end of all hope. The poem's central narrative, with its rapid sequence of vast reversals and reductions, takes place within an extraordinarily short compass – thirty-three days, on Fowler's computation.[111] It is in the very speed and volatility of these reversals, rather than in any specific allusions, that the poem is most profoundly related to its historical context. Like the English republicans, the poem's God undertakes a series of experiments in freedom and finds them confounded to the point of arousing his enemies' derisive laughter. Yet nothing deters him from further experiment. When Milton began the poem, the course of future political events in England was uncertain. The chances of a republican *occasione* were still there, but there was a good possibility that it would fail. Nonetheless, Milton flung himself into the political process with

---

111 *Poems*, ed. Carey and Fowler, p. 444.

something of the energy he had tried to portray in creating his Creator. Though he is unlikely to have said so explicitly, one of the consolations the poem offers is that even if the new order created by the English republicans was unstable and short-lived, at least it lasted longer than God's. As eventually published, *Paradise Lost* had no occasion to seize; but it could still transmit to future generations the republican principles that were waiting in their Chaos.

Epilogue: the survival of republican literary culture

In 1674 Milton published a new edition of his epic, with some minor revisions and a new division into twelve books. Two sets of commendatory verses were included, and Marvell's contribution formed a further dimension in the poem's coded political interventions.[112] Marvell's poem (*MPL*, I, 137–9) arguably remains the most perceptive reading of the epic. It is also a commentary on what has happened to literary culture since the Restoration. Marvell presents himself as a voice of religious and social orthodoxy. He begins by expressing the fear that the poem will be blasphemous, will 'ruine . . . the Sacred Truths'. Here he raised a sensitive issue, for Milton's *Christian Doctrine* was indeed to be suppressed when posthumous publication was attempted two years later. Marvell then compares Milton to Samson groping the temple's pillars. This was a stock image for post-Restoration dissenters, but of course it was especially appropriate for Milton, whose blindness was seen by royalists as a punishment for his political views, and who had retorted with the defiant *Samson Agonistes*. Marvell presents himself as made uneasy by the aggressive, iconoclastic aims of Milton's epic, which run counter to the patriotic harmony the conservative reader might ask for. As he reads on, however, he sees that the poem's impulses are ultimately more creative than destructive. Like the bird of paradise, the poet has plumes that are strong, equal and soft. The strength and softness direct us to the unusual combination of epic grandeur and domestic simplicity. The equality perhaps refers in the first instance to the poem's decorum, but reminds us also of its urgent concern with justice. Marvell indeed has not lost his interest in poetic justice, for in saying that 'At once delight and horrour on us seize' (line 35), he is echoing Lucretius's praise of the atheist Epicurus (*De rerum natura*, iii.29). Marvell was picking up the strong echoes of Lucretius in the Proem to Milton's third book, and discreetly signalling the poem's bold engagement with the most

---

112 Discussions include Henry F. Lippincott Jr, 'Marvell's *On "Paradise Lost"*', *English Language Notes* 9 (1971–72), 265–72; Patterson, *Reading Between the Lines*, pp. 256ff; Sharon Achinstein, 'Milton's Spectre in the Restoration: Marvell, Dryden, and Literary Enthusiasm', *Huntington Library Quarterly*, 59 (1997), 1–28.

outspoken critiques of orthodoxy.[113] As Marvell moves to his climax, the
initial objections return as praise: Milton's blindness is as prophetic as
Tiresias's, and

> Thy Verse created like thy *Theme* sublime,
> In Number, Weight, and Measure, needs not *Rhime*.

Having begun by suspecting Milton of blasphemy, Marvell ends by risking the
accusation himself in comparing Milton's creation to God's.

A third party is involved in this poem: Dryden, who had asked permission
to turn the story into a rhyming play. Since their period as Cromwellians the
two men had drifted far apart politically, and Milton and Marvell were championing the dissenters against his royalist literary culture. Dryden had
become the successor to Waller as the most effective defender of monarchy in
verse. More attuned than Waller to the extreme religious reaction after 1660,
he recurrently equated religious dissent of all kinds with republican sedition.
Dryden was to continue the tradition of royalist translations of Virgil. His
Aeneid, and *Absalom and Achitophel,* were to some extent responses to
Paradise Lost.[114] As Marvell's poem reminds us, he had responded more
directly soon after the poem's first appearance by adapting the epic into a
rhymed heroic play. Marvell had satirized that genre and linked it with the
regime's religious policies in *The Rehearsal Transpros'd.* A reply to that satire
had linked him with Milton: 'the odds betwixt a *Transproser* and a *Blank Verse
Poet,* is not great'; Milton was 'nonconformable in point of Rhyme'.[115] The
allusion takes up Milton's own politicization of metre in his note on 'The
Verse'. In reply, Marvell makes the vogue for closed couplets epitomize the
general triumph of a conservative royalist culture, a concern for easy beauty
as against the strenuous and challenging sublimity of *Paradise Lost.* But
Milton's literary claims carry with them wider cultural implications. Marvell
self-mockingly presents himself as 'transported by the *Mode*': political and
literary fashions have moved on, the language of the Good Old Cause is outmoded. By that 'transported', however, he places himself in the position of
Satan: God derisively points out the rage that 'Transports our adversarie'
(iii.81). The current 'mode' is aligned with the Satanic.

Marvell's poem, then, engages the new edition of *Paradise Lost* in the controversies of the 1670s. It has been less often noticed, however, that there are

---

113 Philip Hardie, 'The Presence of Lucretius in *Paradise Lost*', *MQ* 29 (1995), 13–24 (13, 21
    n. 7).
114 On the politics of Virgil translation after the Restoration see Erskine-Hill, *Poetry and
    the Realm of Politics,* pp. 201ff.
115 John T. Shawcross (ed.), *Milton: The Critical Heritage* (1970), pp. 77–8; for attribution
    of *The Transproser Rehears'd* (Oxford, 1673; L1020) to Samuel Butler, see Nicholas von
    Maltzahn, 'Samuel Butler's Milton', *Studies in Philology* 92 (1995), 482–95 (483–5).

also links back to the mid-century. Marvell's opening, 'When I beheld the Poet blind, yet bold', would have had a personal resonance for Milton with the letter Marvell had addressed to him twenty years earlier in praise of the *Second Defence*, a prose work with epic aspirations: 'When I consider how equally it turnes and rises with so many figures . . .'. As has been seen (above, chapter 8), that letter had linked the *Second Defence* with the sublime, as well as with tyrannicidal aggression: Milton's pillars were raised by shaking those of monarchy. Milton's friend Thomas Ellwood directly recalled his epic struggles against Salmasius in a manuscript elegy probably written the following year.[116] Addressing the public, and following the mode, Marvell is more circumspect.

Despite the caution, there is yet another level of allusion to republican literary culture. Marvell echoes Ben Jonson's commendatory poem to May's Lucan, which likewise begins with doubt and ends with high praise, and having feared that the carefully-built structure might be destroyed, celebrates the poem's 'Number . . . and Measure'.[117] The original ten-book structure of *Paradise Lost* formed a parallel with the *Pharsalia*; the Lucanian echo served as a kind of counterpoint to the reworking into a more Virgilian twelve-book form. Milton's purpose in making the change remains obscure, but Marvell's commendatory poem would have been one way of making clear that he was not trying to make his poem more courtly and Virgilian. His quotation of May can also be seen as a kind of oblique reparation. He had already echoed Jonson's poem to May in 'Tom May's Death'. Cromwellians and republicans had both suffered from the post-1660 purges, and Marvell was moving in the 1670s towards a more radical position, paying posthumous tribute to Harrington, who had lost his sanity after a period of imprisonment.[118] Now that May had been expelled from the Abbey, his republicanism looked a much less significant target than courtly absolutism and religious repression. And Marvell had his own republican skeletons in the cupboard. Dryden's poems occasionally quoted from the 'Horatian Ode', so indirectly that he may have been noticed by Marvell alone[119]; but it was a way of reminding him that he had a compromised history. The republican poetry of the mid-century had indeed been displaced by the post-Restoration 'mode'; but it maintained a powerful hidden presence. In glancing back, however indirectly, to the mid-century political culture from which it emerged, Marvell made the publication of *Paradise Lost* much more than a gesture of political resignation. Seven years later, at the height of the controversy over the succession to Charles II, a

116 Thomas Ellwood, 'Upon the excellently-learned John Milton, An Epitaph', in
   Shawcross (ed.), *Milton: The Critical Heritage*, pp. 85–7.
117 Andrew Shifflett, '"By Lucan Driv'n About: A Jonsonian Marvell's Lucanic Milton',
   Renaissance Quarterly 49 (1996), 802–23.   118 *ABL*, I, 293.
119 I owe this point to an unpublished paper by Paul Hammond.

bold attempt was made to include the 'Horatian Ode' in his posthumous collected poems. The publisher, Robert Boulter, allegedly 'did not question to
see the monarchy reduced into a commonwealth and very speedily'.[120] Two
years earlier, May's Lucan had appeared for the first time since 1659.

The Restoration had been far from stilling the political questions raised by
the mid-century revolutions. Harrington had been over-sanguine in his
belief that even if the monarchy were restored in 1660, the underlying social
tendencies would soon restore a republic. But his analysis of the polity as
subject to uneven 'jumps' between republicanizing and absolutist tendencies
was borne out by events. Literary and political history have still much to do in
exploring the persistent oppositional currents. If textbooks still present the
period after 1660 as the triumph of Augustanism, they are leaving a great deal
out of the picture.

Things are starting to change with a renewed interest in republican theory
and practice in Britain. Perhaps one day even Thomas May will be reinstated
in Westminster Abbey. As has been seen, however, mid-century republicans
tended to be suspicious of monumentality even in a good cause, and the substitution of a republican for a monarchist heritage industry would not really
be appropriate. The last word can best be left to Henry Marten, who outlived
most of his republican contemporaries to die in 1680 – anticlimactically, and
peculiarly like his old friend May, of choking. He left no political testament
beyond this acrostic self-epitaph:

> H ere or elsewhere (all's one, to you, to me,)
> E arth, air, or water, gripes my ghostless dust
> N one knows how soon to be by fire sett free
> R eader if you an oft tryed rule will trust,
> Y ou'll gladly do and suffer what you must.
>
> M y life was spent with serving you, and you,
> A nd death's my pay (it seems) and welcome too;
> R evenge destroying but itself, while I
> T o birds of prey leave my old cage, and fly.
> E xamples preach to th'eye, care then (mine says)
> N ot how you end, but how you spend your dayes.[121]

Plainness here aims at a kind of sublimity. As in Lucan's description of the
defeated republicans of Pharsalia, or the anonymous elegy for Felton, Marten
abjures the need for a local place of burial. Though he did, unlike less fortunate regicides, achieve burial within a church, the inscription has been badly

---

120 *MPL*, I, 241.
121 William Coxe, *An Historical Tour in Monmouthshire*, 2 vols. (1801), II, 390: the tombstone has suffered damage and Coxe, 391, reprints a facsimile on which he bases his
   own reconstruction. See Ivor Waters, *Henry Marten and the Long Parliament*
   (Chepstow, 1976), p. 73.

damaged – legend has it because his body was moved out of fears that it profaned the sanctity of church and king. Marten pushes his Roman note to the point of a defiant agnosticism about the afterlife – perhaps recalling conversations with May and other members of his 'gang'. He maintains his distinctive wit: in reminding his readers that he has spent his life in their service, he reproaches them for turning to the false gods of the Restoration regime. The last line seems to be a pointed rejoinder to the cult of the martyred Charles I. For the iconoclastic Marten, however beautiful Charles's death on the scaffold might have been, what counted was the wrongs he had done during his lifetime. Conversely, what counted in his own life was not the uncertain purchase he might or might not make on the nation's memory, but whatever practical good he had managed to do.

Marten did not exactly welcome the oblivion or ridicule that was to encompass himself and so much of mid-century republican culture, but he shared that culture's alertness to the fickleness of political memory. He may have remembered that in the *Pharsalia*, Cordus snatches the embers for Pompey's fire from the still-burning cremation of a corpse whose unloving kin had long ago departed. His epitaph serves as a reminder of the need to scrutinize the monuments of the past with an eye to what they leave out, as well as what they preserve.

Appendix: Henry Marten's poem to Cromwell
(BL Additional MS 71,532, fol. 16r.)

I am much indebted to Ingrid de Smet and Ben Tipping for help. As will be seen from the reproduction (figure 14), the poem is a draft which was never properly completed, and the version below cannot be more than an approximation.

Yield place (so the English Fates have bounteously willed it), you old or modern heroes, whether from Greece or from Rome which was emulous of Greece, its empire spread over the world. This is the man who was hoped for so long in the northern world, and is worthy also of the southern scene, to be celebrated from the rising to the setting sun. This famous Cromwell fills the throne to the acclamation of the British people. For he owes this honour not to ancient descent; he is more famous than his ancestors, famous though they were; he did not court the votes of the fickle people, nor did one victory alone give the palm to this man, but a series of merits and also hidden deeds, a hand invincible in war, and greater in response to dangers, the force of his spirit enduring the struggles of summer and winter campaigns, and experienced in advancing on enemies or repressing citizens. The great deeds of our hero flutter through many men's mouths – the dynast of whom the neighbourhood whispers: Where do his achievements come from? What a great man! where will he go in the end? where is it right for him to stop? Does he gain his power from deliberation, or from his fierce ardour, or has Fortune kissed his cheeks and held out her hand to his boldness? Be that as it may, it is God who has blessed us with victorious arms, with this Protector. The cry is Io Paean; cry Io Paean three times.

Index